INTRODUCTION TO
Clinical Psychology
An Evidence-Based Approach

INTRODUCTION TO
Clinical Psychology
An Evidence-Based Approach

JOHN HUNSLEY | CATHERINE M. LEE

JOHN WILEY & SONS, INC.

Acquisition Editor:	Christopher Johnson
Publisher:	Jay O'Callaghan
Designer:	Jeof Vita
Senior Photo Editor:	Lisa Gee
New Media Editor:	Lynn Pearlman
Marketing Manager:	Danielle Torio
Production Manager:	Janis Soo
Senior Production Editor:	Joyce Poh

Cover photo credits:
Picture frames: Pavel Losevsky/iStockphoto
Little girl: iStockphoto
Woman: Media Bakery
Man: iStockphoto
Guy with glasses: Media Bakery
Woman with yellow/green shirt: Media Bakery
Family: Aldo Murillo/iStockphoto

This book was set in 10/12 Times Roman by Thomson Digital and printed and bound by R.R. Donnelley. The cover was printed by R.R. Donnelley.

This book is printed on acid free paper.

Evaluation copies are provided to qualified academics and professionals for review purposes only, for use in their courses during the next academic year. These copies are licensed and may not be sold or transferred to a third party. Upon completion of the review period, please return the evaluation copy to Wiley. Return instructions and a free of charge return shipping label are available at www.wiley.com/go/returnlabel. Outside of the United States, please contact your local representative.

Library of Congress Cataloging-in-Publication Data

Hunsley, John, 1959-
    Introduction to clinical psychology : an evidence-based approach/John Hunsley, Catherine M. Lee.
        p.; cm.
    Includes bibliographical references and index.
    ISBN 978-0-470-43751-3 (cloth: alk. paper) 1. Clinical psychology–Textbooks. I. Lee,
Catherine M. (Catherine Mary), 1955- II. Title.
    [DNLM: 1. Psychology, Clinical–methods.   2. Mental Disorders–diagnosis.   3. Mental
Disorders–prevention & control.   4. Psychological Tests. WM 105 H938i 2010]
    RC467.H77 2010
    616.89–dc22

                                                                                    2009026528

Printed in the United States of America
10 9 8 7 6 5 4 3 2 1

Preface

Between us, we have over half a century of experience in clinical psychology. We share a passion for a profession that has the potential to make an important contribution to the understanding of human nature and to the alleviation of human suffering. We have written this book to introduce to students the theories and practices of clinical psychology and convey the important work done by clinical psychologists. The book is designed to be helpful not only to those who will go on to careers in clinical psychology, but also to those who will choose other career paths.

KEY FEATURES

Clinical psychology has evolved greatly in recent decades. In order to convey the nature of contemporary practice of clinical psychology, we have incorporated three distinct features through all of the chapters.

Evidence-Based Approach

Concerns about health care costs, together with growing demands from well-informed health care consumers, have highlighted the need for clinical psychology to adopt evidence-based assessment and interventions. Unfortunately, many popular theories that have guided clinical practice for decades do not have supporting evidence. Throughout the text, we present theories and practices and examine the extent to which they are supported by research. If a technique or strategy is used frequently in practice but has not been supported empirically, we say so. We believe that our approach reflects the new realities in clinical psychology and the ongoing commitment of psychologists to deliver services that are the best science has to offer.

Diversity

Clinical psychology must address the needs of a diverse population. We highlight the need for sensitivity to gender, age, culture, ethnicity, sexual orientation, socioeconomic status, family type, and geographic location. Throughout the text we include relevant assessment and treatment examples to illustrate the importance and the challenges of professional sensitivity to diversity issues in research and practice.

Life-span Perspective

We have adopted a life-span perspective throughout the text. We include examples illustrating issues with respect to children, adolescents, adults, and older adults. As many undergraduate students taking an introductory course in clinical psychology are unlikely to have decided on the age of clients with which they eventually wish to work, it will be appealing to learn about clinical psychology across the life span. It is important for the student to appreciate that assessment and treatment plans can vary depending upon the age of the individual.

TEXT ORGANIZATION

The text can be divided into three sections. The first section provides an overview of issues that set the stage for the second section on assessment, which in turn is the foundation for the third section on intervention in clinical psychology. In Chapter 1 we provide a definition of clinical psychology, describing its history and explaining similarities and differences between clinical psychology and other mental health professions. Chapter 2 addresses the diverse roles of clinical psychologists, all of which are based on the pillars of science and ethics. The importance of attention to ethical issues is highlighted not just in this chapter but throughout the text. The third chapter is an overview of issues related to classification and diagnosis. In this chapter, we introduce two individuals, an adult (Teresa) and an adolescent (Carl), whose psychological services we describe in subsequent chapters. Chapter 4 presents key issues on research methods, underlining the ways they are employed to address clinically meaningful questions.

In the second section, Chapters 5–9 address assessment issues in clinical psychology, highlighting ethical issues that must guide psychological practice. Chapter 5 provides an overview of the purposes of psychological assessment, a review of key concepts in psychological testing, and an examination of the distinction between testing and assessment. Chapter 6 presents information on clinical interviews and clinical observation, emphasizing developmental considerations relevant to these commonly used assessment methods. We discuss intellectual and cognitive assessments in Chapter 7. Chapter 8 covers self-report and projective assessment, with in-depth examination of the usefulness of different assessment strategies. The challenges of integrating assessment data and making clinical decisions are illustrated in Chapter 9, with reference to services for Teresa (who was introduced in Chapter 3).

The third section on intervention covers both prevention and treatment. Chapter 10 highlights issues in prevention, describing programs designed for at-risk youth. In Chapter 11 we provide a brief overview of approaches to psychological intervention, describing the theoretical foundations of current evidence-based approaches and presenting data on the nature and course of psychotherapy. Chapters 12 and 13 present an overview of current evidence-based treatments for adults (Chapter 12) and for children and adolescents (Chapter 13). The case of Carl (whom we introduced in Chapter 3) is used to illustrate issues in developing treatment plans. Chapter 14 provides information on evidence-based treatment elements derived from therapy process and therapy process-outcome research. Finally, in Chapter 15, we examine issues in the practice of clinical psychology in the areas of clinical health psychology, clinical neuropsychology, and forensic psychology.

The book includes two appendices. The first lists journals in clinical psychology and should help students as they research topics in greater depth. The second appendix, entitled Applications to Graduate School, is designed to help students in decision making about graduate school applications as well as in planning an application.

FEATURES OF INTEREST TO THE STUDENT

Within each chapter many features have been incorporated to aid student learning. This text is designed to introduce clinical psychology in a reader-friendly and accessible manner, highlighting the varied and dynamic areas of the discipline. To enhance student learning, there is extensive cross-referencing of material across chapters. There are also many features to help students better understand and integrate text material, including (a) helpful hints about clinical psychology services, (b) scenarios that ask readers to imagine their own reactions in situations, and (c) directly examining the application of issues to common aspects of the reader's life.

Chapter Outline

Each chapter begins with an outline that prepares the student for the material to be covered.

Case Studies

In courses in clinical psychology, case examples are the tool through which abstract material is brought to life. In addition to the extended case presentations in Chapters 9, and 13, case material is embedded throughout the text to illustrate issues in different developmental periods and with a diverse clientele. Reflecting the terminology in current practice, we alternate our use of the terms "patient" and "client." All the case examples we describe are based on our clinical experience. We have blended details about different people into composites to illustrate clinical issues. The case examples do not, therefore, represent specific individuals, and all the names are fictitious.

Viewpoint Boxes

In each chapter controversial issues and new directions in the field are highlighted in Viewpoint Boxes. In addition to addressing historically important themes, such as "Dealing with Anger: Does Venting Help or Harm?" these boxes explore new directions in clinical psychology, such as "Psychological Resilience in the Face of Potential Trauma," the controversies over "Why Do Questionable Psychological Tests Remain Popular with Some Psychologists?" and "Psychological Testing on the Internet." The inclusion of Viewpoint Boxes on "Developmental Considerations in ADHD" and "Assessing

Cognitive Functioning in Older Adults" reflect a life-span perspective. Debates around evidence-based assessment are discussed in Viewpoint Boxes examining "Child Custody Evaluations," "Risk Assessment," and "Are Projective Drawings Welcome in the Courtroom?" The expansion of the practice of clinical psychology to health is illustrated in Viewpoint Boxes "Health Promotion and Prevention in Older Adults" and "Insomnia: No Need to Lose Sleep Over It!" Current issues in treatment research are explored in Viewpoint Boxes including "Developing Treatments for Borderline Personality Disorder" and "Sudden Gains in Therapy."

Profile Boxes

In order to bring to life the reality of being a clinical psychologist, we have used Profile Boxes to introduce clinical psychologists. We invited 18 clinical psychologists to answer questions about their careers. Furthermore, to give students a sense of the varied activities in which psychologists engage, we asked six psychologists who work in different types of settings to describe a typical work week. We invited colleagues whom we consider fine examples of clinical psychologists, and we chose people whom we hope the readers will find inspiring. As students read the Profile Boxes, we know they will be struck by the wide range of activities in which clinical psychologists engage, the challenges they address in their work, and the creativity with which psychological principles are applied to reduce human suffering and improve psychosocial functioning.

Think About It!

Throughout each chapter, we have also included questions that encourage the student to consider specific text material more deeply and more personally. These questions usually ask the reader to consider the impact that a certain professional or empirical issue could have on someone's life. There are also questions that encourage students to consider how the manner in which clinical psychologists make decisions about professional services is similar to and different from the manner in which people make routine decisions.

Summary and Conclusions

At the end of each chapter, a section draws together the material discussed in the chapter.

Critical Thinking Questions

To help in identifying themes for discussion, key questions have been designed to provoke debate on both traditional and emerging issues in clinical psychology.

Key Terms and Key Names

Throughout each chapter, important terms and names are highlighted in bold. These are an important study aid to highlight the most salient points of each chapter.

Additional Resources

To help provide some guidance for students who wish to explore an issue in greater depth, additional resources have been cited for various journals and books. The Check It Out! feature provides Web site links that allow readers to find out more about important issues raised in the chapter.

Acknowledgements

We have appreciated the support and guidance of many people during the preparation of the second edition of this book. Thanks are due to Chris Johnson, the Acquisitions Editor who promoted the idea of a text on contemporary clinical psychology. Lisa Gee, Janis Soo, and Joyce Poh were exemplary in their attention to the myriad details involved in the production of the book. Hélène Dore-Lavigne offered useful comments on the Appendix on *Applications to Graduate School*. The book is enriched by the contributions of the psychologists who agreed to be profiled. We appreciate their cooperation and willingness to talk about their careers, and special thanks go to them. They are: Drs. Patricia Alexander, Martin Antony, Howard Garb, Robert Glueckauf, Stephen Lally, James Maddux, Jeanne Miranda, Charles Morin, John C. Norcross, Jacqueline Persons, Aurelio Prifitera, Alexandra Quittner, Wendy Silverman, Tony Strickland, Carolyn Webster-Stratton, John Weisz, Stephanie Woo, and Eric Youngstrom. Thoughtful and informative reviews helped us to clarify the text. Thanks are due to Wiley Editorial Assistant Carrie Tupa.

Last, but not least, we are grateful for the ongoing support of friends and family. Their questions, words of encouragement and willingness to provide their views on diverse aspects of textbook production were greatly appreciated. Our sons Rob and Nick sustained remarkable patience, allowing us the opportunity to focus on the book for well over a year. Thank you both for your tolerance and your interest in our work.

About the Authors

John Hunsley received a PhD from the University of Waterloo in 1985. He is a professor in the clinical psychology program at the University of Ottawa and is the director of the program. Dr. Hunsley teaches graduate courses in Clinical Research Methods and Psychological Assessment. Dr. Hunsley's research interests focus on the delivery of psychological services and the scientific basis of psychological assessment. He has authored over 90 articles, chapters, and books on these topics. Dr. Hunsley is a Fellow of the Canadian Psychological Association (CPA) and the Clinical Psychology Section of CPA. He has received the CPA Award for Distinguished Contributions to Education and Training in Psychology. From 2007–2010 he served as the editor of *Canadian Psychology*; he has also served on the editorial board of *Assessment, Journal of Personality Assessment, Professional Psychology: Research and Practice, and Scientific Review of Mental Health Practice.*

Catherine M. Lee earned a PhD from the University of Western Ontario in 1988. She is Vice Dean of the Faculty of Social Sciences and Professor of Psychology at the University of Ottawa. Dr. Lee teaches graduate courses in Psychology of the Family, Evidence-Based Services for Children and Families, and Psychological Assessment. Her research interests focus on the promotion effective parenting and co-parenting, as well as on the implementation of evidence-based services for children and youth. She has authored over 50 articles, chapters, and books on these topics. Dr. Lee is a Fellow of the Canadian Psychological Association (CPA). Dr. Lee is an *ad hoc* reviewer for many granting agencies and scholarly journals and she serves on the editorial boards of *Canadian Psychology and* of *Cognitive and Behavioral Practice*. She is the former Chair of the Clinical Section of the CPA and was President of the CPA in 2008–2009.

Brief Table of Contents

Table of Contents

CHAPTER 1

The Evolution of Clinical Psychology

INTRODUCTION

Mental health is a state of well-being in which the individual realizes his or her own abilities, can cope with the normal stresses of life, and is able to make a contribution to his or her community.

World Health Organization (2007)

- About half of mental disorders begin before age 14.
- Worldwide, 800,000 people commit suicide every year.
- In emergencies, the number of people with mental disorders is estimated to increase by 6–11%.
- Mental disorders increase the risk for physical disorders.
- Many health conditions increase the risk of mental disorders.
- Stigma prevents many people from seeking mental health care.
- There are great inequities in the availability of mental health professionals across the world.

World Health Organization (2007)

In these early years of the twenty-first century, the potential for clinical psychology to make important contributions to the health of individuals, families, and society is abundantly clear. In this opening chapter we introduce you to the profession of clinical psychology, its scope, and its remarkable history. Throughout this text we will illustrate with compelling evidence that clinical psychologists have developed assessments that are helpful in understanding problems and interventions that are effective in preventing, treating, and even eliminating a broad range of health problems and disorders. To fully appreciate the importance of such health services, it is necessary to understand the scope of the public health problem facing health care systems in the United States and other parts of the world.

Compiling data from national epidemiological studies, the National Institute of Mental Health (NIMH) estimated that 26.2% of Americans age 18 and older suffer from a diagnosable mental disorder in a given year (NIMH, n.d.). **Table 1.1** shows the percentages of American adults diagnosed with mood disorders, anxiety disorders, or schizophrenia in a given year, the numbers of American adults affected, and the average age of onset of the disorder.

It is striking that 1 in 4 adult Americans suffers from a mental disorder in any given year. You may be very surprised to learn that the National Comorbidity Replication Study (NCMRS) conducted

TABLE 1.1   Mental Disorders in America

Disorder	Percent of adults	Number of Americans affected	Median age of onset	Comment
MOOD DISORDERS	9.5%	20.9 million	30	Often co-occur with anxiety disorders
Major depressive disorder	6.7%	14.8 million	32	More common in women
Dysthymic disorder	1.5%	3.3 million	31	
Bipolar disorder	2.6%	5.7 million	25	
ANXIETY DISORDERS	18.1%	40 million	75% have first episode by age 21.5	
Panic disorder	2.7%	6 million	24	One in three with panic disorder also develops agoraphobia
Obsessive-compulsive disorder	1.0%	2.2 million	19	
PTSD (post-traumatic stress disorder)	3.5%	7.7 million	23	19% of Vietnam veterans experienced PTSD
Generalized anxiety disorder	3.1%	6.8 million	31	
Social phobia	6.8%	15 million	13	
Specific phobia	8.7%	19.2 million	7	
Agoraphobia	0.8%	1.8 million	20	
SCHIZOPHRENIA	1.1%	2.4 million	Men: late teens or early 20s; Women: 20s or early 30s	

Adapted from NIMH: The Numbers Count: Mental Disorders in America (http://www.nimh.nih.gov/health/publications/the-numbers-count-mental-disorders-in-america.shtml)

in 2002 also revealed that the first signs of these disorders appear at a young age. Half the cases of mental disorder begin by age 14, and three quarters have begun by age 24 (Kessler, Berglund, Demler, Jin, & Walters, 2005). The onset of anxiety disorders often occurs in late childhood, mood disorders in late adolescence, and substance abuse in the early 20s (Kessler, Berglund, et al., 2005). However, most people do not receive services for these problems for many years; some never receive services. For example, a survey of 539 patients with anxiety disorders seen in primary care settings revealed that almost half received no treatment whatsoever (Weisberg, Dyck, Culpepper, & Keller, 2007). The situation with respect to children is even more troubling: The Surgeon General's Report on Mental Health revealed that although 1 in 10 children and adolescents has a mental disorder severe enough to impair functioning, in a given year, fewer than 1 in 5 of those in need receive services (U.S. Department of Health and Human Services, 1999). Given the early age of onset of mental disorders compared to physical disorders, the disability associated with mental disorders occurs in what would otherwise be the prime of life. In addition to the suffering associated with mental disorders, the financial burden is staggering. Over a one-year period, 1.3 billion disability days resulted from mental conditions (Merikangas et al., 2007). Data from the 2002 NCMRS indicated that the major mental disorders cost the American economy $193 billion a year in lost earnings alone (Kessler et al., 2008).

Similar findings in other countries have led to politicians taking action. *The Depression Report* released in 2006 by the London School of Economics found that despite the estimate that one family in three is affected by depression or anxiety, only 2% of the expenditures of the National Health Service (NHS) in the United Kingdom (UK) are allocated to the treatment of these disorders. Lost work productivity due to depression and anxiety is estimated to cost the UK economy £12 billion a year, which represents 1% of total national income. A million people in the UK receive disability benefits because of mental disorders, at a cost of £750 a month (about US$1500) per person. The UK National Institute for Clinical Health and Excellence (NICE) is an independent interdisciplinary organization mandated to provide national guidance on promoting good health and preventing and treating ill health. Systematic literature reviews by NICE concluded that evidence-based psychological therapies, which cost approximately £750 per person, are effective for at least half the people with anxiety and depression and are at least as effective as medication in tackling these mental health problems. The UK government therefore set a target by 2010–2011 to spend £170 million a year on improving access to psychological therapies by training mental health professionals, including, but not limited to, psychologists. In addition to the enormous potential human benefits in reduced suffering and increased well-being, policy-makers predict that this investment will yield economic benefits in terms of both reduced claims for disability and increased productivity.

Data from the World Health Organization (presented in **Table 1.2**) illustrate the scope of mental health problems in different countries. Worldwide, there are hundreds of millions of people suffering from mental disorders. However, most mental disorders are overlooked or misdiagnosed, and only a small percentage of those who suffer from a mental disorder ever receive treatment. Even if these people receive treatment for other health concerns, in most cases—regardless of the wealth or level of development of the country in which they live—mental health problems are neglected. This is particularly troubling because there are relatively inexpensive treatments (psychological and/or pharmacological) that are effective for most of these conditions.

TABLE 1.2 Mental Health: The Bare Facts

- At any given time, there are 450 million people worldwide suffering from mental, neurological, and behavioral problems.
- It is predicted that the number of people suffering from these problems will increase in the future.
- Mental health problems are found in all countries.
- Mental health problems cause suffering, social exclusion, disability, and poor quality of life.
- Mental health problems increase mortality.
- Mental health problems have staggering economic costs.
- One in every four people seeking other health services has a diagnosable mental, neurological, or behavioral problem that is unlikely to be diagnosed or treated.
- Mental health problems are associated with poor compliance with medical regimens for other disorders.
- Cost-effective treatments exist for most disorders; if they were applied properly, people could function better in their communities.
- There is greater stigma associated with mental health problems than with physical health problems.
- Most countries do not allocate sufficient funds to address mental, neurological, and behavioral problems.

Adapted from World Health Organization (2004a)

Perhaps due to the stressfulness of living and/or working conditions, the rate of mental health problems is even higher among certain groups than in the general population. In a longitudinal study of 50,184 American troops, Smith et al. (2008) found evidence of new onset of post-traumatic stress disorder (PTSD) in 4.3% of troops deployed in Iraq and Afghanistan and in 2.3% of nondeployed troops. Deployment itself did not appear to be the critical risk factor: only 1.4% of those who were deployed but did not experience combat had new onset of PTSD, whereas for those exposed to combat, the figure was 7.6%. Combat exposure increased threefold the risk of developing PTSD. Similar results were found in a health survey of members of 8,441 active Canadian military personnel that examined all types of mental disorder. Sareen et al. (2007) found that 15% reported some type of mental disorder in the previous year, and 23% were considering whether they required mental health services. Being deployed to combat operations and witnessing atrocities were associated with increased risk of disorder and need for services.

In addition to the pressing problems posed by mental disorders, there is mounting evidence that lifestyle and psychosocial factors are related to many of the causes of death in Western countries. As you will learn in Chapters 10 and 15, there is evidence that psychological services can dramatically reduce the negative health impact of these lifestyle and psychosocial risk factors. A large-scale study of the causes of mortality in the United States reached startling conclusions (Mokdad, Marks, Stroup, & Gerberding, 2004). Although dramatic causes such as motor vehicle accidents accounted for 2% of deaths and shooting fatalities accounted for 1% of deaths, the leading causes of death were related to tobacco smoking (18.1%), poor diet and physical inactivity (16.6%), and alcohol consumption (3.5%). Adding the numbers together, these data demonstrate that at least 40% of fatalities were attributable to entirely preventable—or treatable—factors.

DEFINING THE NATURE AND SCOPE OF CLINICAL PSYCHOLOGY

As we consider the pain and suffering experienced by people with mental and physical health problems, the interpersonal effects of their distress on their family, friends, and coworkers, and the tragedy of untimely death, the need for effective services to identify and address these problems is evident. It is inevitable that at many points in our lives each of us will be affected, either directly or indirectly, by the emotional distress of psychological disorders. The first experience may be helping a friend through confusion and anger stemming from a loved one's suicide. As a university student you may be faced with the challenges of helping a roommate with an eating disorder who binges and purges. Young parents may provide support to another young parent who is desperate to find appropriate services for a child with autistic disorder. In midlife, you may be faced with the burden of caring for an elderly parent suffering from dementia, or you may be attempting to support a partner who is chronically anxious and avoids social gatherings. As you age, you may face the death of your partner and friends, and you may have to cope with your own increasing infirmity and pain. Clinical psychology is the branch of psychology that focuses on developing assessment strategies and interventions to deal with these painful experiences that touch everyone's life.

 Think about the challenges and stressors that you have faced and those faced by the people you care about. Can you identify the things that made your distress worse? On the other hand, what helped you in dealing with difficulties?

Let's consider some definitions of clinical psychology. **Table 1.3** provides examples of definitions and descriptions of clinical psychology from different countries. Despite some differences in emphasis, a common theme running through these definitions from the United States, Britain, Canada, and New Zealand is that clinical psychology is based firmly on scientifically supported psychological theories and principles. Clinical psychology is a science-based profession. Furthermore, the development of effective assessment, prevention, and intervention services relies on basic research into the nature of emotional distress and well-being. The practice of clinical psychology uses scientifically based methods to reliably and validly assess both normal and abnormal human functioning. Clinical psychology involves gathering evidence regarding optimal strategies for delivering health care services.

Over the decades the nature and definition of clinical psychology has shifted, expanded, and evolved. From an initial primary focus on assessment, evaluation, and diagnosis, the scope of clinical psychology has grown. Clinical psychology now also includes numerous approaches to intervention and prevention services that are provided to individuals, couples, and families. The practice of clinical psychology also covers indirect services that do not involve contact with those who have a mental disorder, such as consultation activities, research, program development, program evaluation, supervision of other mental health professionals, and administration of health care services. Given the ever-changing nature of the field, the only certainty about clinical psychology is that it will continue to evolve. Only time will tell whether this evolution ultimately leads to a decreasing focus on traditional activities of assessment and treatment (as predicted by some experts), to an increasing focus on the use of psychopharmacological agents to treat mental illness and mental health problems (as promoted by some psychologists and some psychological associations), or to the adoption of universal prevention programs designed to enhance our protection from risk. The changing nature of clinical psychology

TABLE 1.3   Definitions of Clinical Psychology

American Psychological Association, Society of Clinical Psychology

"The field of Clinical Psychology integrates science, theory, and practice to understand, predict, and alleviate maladjustment, disability, and discomfort as well as to promote human adaptation, adjustment, and personal development. Clinical Psychology focuses on the intellectual, emotional, biological, psychological, social, and behavioral aspects of human functioning across the life span, in varying cultures, and at all socioeconomic levels."

British Psychological Society, Division of Clinical Psychology

"Clinical psychology aims to reduce psychological distress and to enhance and promote psychological well-being by the systematic application of knowledge derived from psychological theory and data."

Canadian Psychological Association

"Clinical psychology is a broad field of practice and research within the discipline of psychology, which applies psychological principles to the assessment, prevention, amelioration, and rehabilitation of psychological distress, disability, dysfunctional behaviour, and health-risk behaviour, and to the enhancement of psychological and physical well-being."

New Zealand College of Clinical Psychologists

"Psychology is the science of behaviour. Psychologists seek to understand emotion, thinking, personality, skill, learning, motivation, perception, and sensation through the study of individuals, families, groups and culture. Clinical Psychology seeks to apply psychological understandings with individuals and families who may wish to change or develop, often for the alleviation of suffering and the achievement of their personal goals."

does, however, require that any definition of the field be treated as temporary, to be maintained for as long as it accurately reflects the field. The definition of clinical psychology must be altered and updated as innovations and new directions emerge.

EVIDENCE-BASED PRACTICE IN PSYCHOLOGY

Despite the apparent overlap in the various definitions of clinical psychology that we presented in Table 1.3, there is still very active debate about the extent to which clinical psychology can or should be based solely on the science of psychology. Some psychologists doubt that clinical psychology can ever be effectively guided by scientific knowledge. Critics of a science-based approach to clinical psychology express concerns that:

a. Group-based data cannot be used in working with an individual; critics argue that because a great deal of psychological research is based on research designs that involve the study of groups of individuals, it is difficult to determine the relevance of research results to any specific individual.

b. Clients have problems now and we cannot afford to wait for the research; developing, conducting, and replicating research findings takes substantial time and thus the information provided by researchers inevitably lags behind the needs of clinicians to provide services to people in distress.

    c. Each individual's unique constellation of life experience, culture, and societal context makes it unlikely that general psychological principles can ever provide much useful guidance in alleviating emotional distress or interpersonal conflict.

    d. There is simply no research evidence on how to understand or treat many of the human problems confronted by clinical psychologists on a daily basis.

Although these kinds of concerns sound reasonable enough, they lead to the suggestion of basing clinical practice on the individual psychologist's gut feelings, intuition, or experience. The idea that clinical psychology is primarily a healing art, rather than primarily a science-based practice, is extremely problematic. As we discuss in subsequent chapters, there is ample evidence that people are prone to a host of decision-making errors and biases. Because clinicians are not immune from these errors and biases, they risk making serious mistakes in evaluating and treating clients. Thus, over-reliance on the clinician's professional experience and general orientation toward understanding human functioning can be risky if it is not balanced with the application of scientifically based knowledge.

At the other end of the spectrum there are clinical psychologists for whom the current definitions of clinical psychology do not go far enough in ensuring that science is at the heart of all clinical services offered to the public. A passionate proponent of this position is Richard McFall, who in his 1991 presidential address to the Society for a Science of Clinical Psychology (a section of the American Psychological Association's Society of Clinical Psychology), challenged the field to provide only psychological services that had been established through research to be effective and safe (McFall, 1991). The key elements of his *Manifesto for a Science of Clinical Psychology* are presented in **Table 1.4**.

McFall's manifesto adopted a position on the role of science in clinical psychology that many clinical psychologists initially found too extreme. McFall's demand that only scientifically supported

---

TABLE 1.4   McFall's Manifesto for a Science of Clinical Psychology

Cardinal Principle

Scientific clinical psychology is the only legitimate and acceptable form of clinical psychology.

First Corollary

Psychological services should not be administered to the public (except under strict experimental conditions) until they have met the following four minimal criteria:

Criterion 1: The exact nature of the service must be described clearly.

Criterion 2: The claimed benefits of the service must be stated explicitly.

Criterion 3: These claimed benefits must be validated scientifically.

Criterion 4: Possible negative side effects that might outweigh any benefits must be ruled out empirically.

Second Corollary

The primary and overriding objective of doctoral programs in clinical psychology must be to produce the most competent clinical scientists possible.

Adapted from McFall (1991)

treatments should be offered to the public met with strong opposition from many clinical psychologists. The manifesto sparked a lively debate about the appropriateness and the ethics of routine psychological service (or any health service for that matter) that does not have documented, scientifically sound evidence demonstrating its effectiveness. There is no doubt that the vast majority of people who seek psychological services are in significant distress and hope to receive treatments that will reduce their distress and improve their overall functioning.

Do you think it is responsible to offer services that have no evidence of effectiveness? When effective treatments exist, is it reasonable to continue to offer services of undocumented effectiveness? If you were advising a friend to seek services, wouldn't you suggest looking for services that have been shown to be helpful for similar problems? If not, then why not?

In recent years, questions surrounding the appropriateness of adopting a science-based approach to the practice of clinical psychology have taken center stage in discussions about the nature of clinical psychology. Originally developed within medicine, the **evidence-based practice** (EBP) model: (a) requires the clinician to synthesize information drawn from research and systematically collected data on the patient in question, the clinician's professional experience, and the patient's preferences when considering health care options (Institute of Medicine, 2001; Sackett, Rosenberg, Gray, Haynes, & Richardson, 1996) and (b) emphasizes the importance of informing patients, based on the best available research evidence, about viable options for assessment, prevention, or intervention services. The EBP model is now being integrated into many health and human service systems, including mental and behavioral health care, social work, education, and criminal justice (Barlow, 2004; Mullen & Streiner, 2004). In order to practice in an evidence-based manner, a health care professional must be familiar with the current scientific literature and must use both the research evidence and scientifically informed decision-making skills to determine the ways in which research evidence can inform service planning for a patient.

As you will learn in the next chapter, current training models in clinical psychology all emphasize the need for psychologists to be competent in the use and interpretation of scientific methods. Indeed, the EBP model has been endorsed by the American Psychological Association as the basis for the professional practice of psychology (APA Presidential Task Force on Evidence-Based Practice, 2006). Importantly though, the manner in which APA policy operationalizes the EBP is not entirely consistent with the stance taken in other health care professions, a point that we will discuss further in Chapter 12. Nevertheless, it is fascinating to note that the movement for evidence-based practice in health care services places demands on all health services that are remarkably similar to those expressed by McFall's first corollary. Within two decades, a position that was originally considered extreme has become mainstream in many health care systems and a goal espoused by several health care professions.

MENTAL HEALTH PROFESSIONS

The definitions of clinical psychology provide an important perspective on the nature and function of modern clinical psychology. However, it is also useful to describe other health care professions whose services and client populations overlap with those of clinical psychology. In the following pages, we describe several other health professions, including different types of psychology, as well as psychiatry, social work, psychiatric nursing, and other professions such as counseling and psychotherapy.

Within the field of psychology, what is unique about clinical psychology? The definitions we presented emphasized that clinical psychology is primarily concerned with the *application* of psychological knowledge in assessment, prevention, and/or intervention in problems in thoughts, behaviors, and feelings. Of course, in addition to providing psychological services many clinical psychologists also conduct psychological research and contribute important information to the science of psychology. Nevertheless, the objective of research in clinical psychology is to produce knowledge that can be used to guide the development and *application* of psychological services.

Clinical psychology shares many of the research methods, approaches to statistical analysis, and measurement strategies found in other areas of psychology. Many areas of psychology—such as cognitive, developmental, learning, personality, physiological, and social—generate research that has direct or indirect applicability to clinical psychology activities. However, the key purpose of research in these other areas of psychology is to generate basic knowledge about human functioning and to enhance, in general terms, our understanding of people. The fact that some of this knowledge can be used to assess and treat dysfunction and thereby improve human functioning is of secondary importance.

There are many psychologists who apply their knowledge in diverse applied fields. In Chapter 15, you will learn about health psychologists, forensic psychologists, and neuropsychologists—typically these professionals are trained in clinical psychology and also have specialized training for their specific areas of research and practice. Two other areas of applied psychology, counseling psychology and school psychology, also provide important mental health services to the public. Although there is some similarity to clinical psychologists in their training and practices, these psychologists do bring unique skills to the assessment, prevention, and treatment of mental health problems.

Counseling Psychology

It is important to distinguish between counseling psychology and counseling. Counseling is a generic term used to describe a range of mental health professions with various training and licensure requirements (Robiner, 2006). Estimates indicate that there are 49.4 counselors per 100,000 people in the United States; the comparable figure for psychologists is 31.1 per 100,000 (Robiner, 2006). Counseling psychology has a great deal in common with clinical psychology. The roots of counseling psychology can be traced to the vocational guidance movement, in which knowledge of personality traits, aptitudes, and interests that affect job performance and satisfaction were applied to help match employees to the most suitable jobs. After World War II the Veterans Administration contracted with universities and colleges for services advising on vocational and educational matters. Historically, the distinction between clinical and counseling psychology was in terms of the severity of problems treated. Traditionally, the focus of clinical psychology was on the assessment and treatment of psychopathology: that is, manifestations of anxiety, depression, and other symptoms that were of sufficient severity to warrant a clinical diagnosis. On the other hand, counseling psychologists provided services to individuals who were dealing with normal challenges in life—those predictable developmental transitions such as leaving home to work or to attend college, changes in work or interpersonal roles, and handling the stress associated with academic or work demands. Simply put, counseling psychologists dealt with people who were, by and large, well-adjusted, whereas clinical psychologists dealt with people who were experiencing significant problems in their lives and who were unable to manage the resulting emotional and behavioral symptoms.

Another distinction between the two professions was the type of setting in which the practitioners worked. Counseling psychologists were most commonly employed in educational settings (such as university counseling clinics) or general community clinics in which various social and psychological services are available. Clinical psychologists, in contrast, were most likely to be employed in hospital settings—both in general hospitals and in psychiatric facilities. These traditional distinctions between clinical and counseling psychologists are fading due to changes within both professions. Nowadays, counseling psychologists provide services to individuals who are having difficulty functioning: for example, treatments for university students suffering from disorders such as major depressive disorder, panic disorder, social phobia, or eating disorders (Benton, Robertson, Tseng, Newton, & Benton, 2003; Kettman et al., 2007). Both clinical and counseling psychologists are now employed in a wide range of work settings, including both public institutions and private practices.

Over time, clinical psychologists have expanded their practice to address human problems outside the usual realm of mental health services by providing services such as couple therapy, consultation, and treatment for people dealing with chronic illness and stress-related disorders. Thus, clinical psychologists developed services for individuals who would not meet criteria for any psychopathological condition. They have also begun to develop programs that are designed to prevent the development of problems. At one level, it is a rather tenuous decision to mark professional boundaries between counseling and clinical psychology on the basis of the possible differences between what constitutes "normal" range distress and abnormal levels of distress. Depending on the point in time in which someone seeks help, the same person might present with symptoms severe enough to meet diagnostic criteria for a mental disorder or with less severe, subclinical symptoms. A fascinating example of this point comes from the Collaborative Longitudinal Personality Disorders Study (Gunderson et al., 2003). Researchers found that 14% of the people diagnosed with borderline personality disorder at the outset of the study no longer evidenced symptoms consistent with diagnostic criteria six months later. Initial errors in diagnosis could not explain these results, especially as a diagnosis of a personality disorder requires evidence of a lifelong pattern of problems beginning in late adolescence or early adulthood. Instead, it appeared that the temporary abatement of symptoms could be traced to the resolution of significant stressors in people's lives. These data indicate that both counseling and clinical psychologists need to be able to understand, assess, and treat symptoms that may fall on either side of a diagnostic boundary.

Just like clinical psychology, counseling psychology promotes the use of scientifically based interventions. This drive to provide evidence-based services is likely to have substantial implications for both training and practice in counseling psychology (Waehler, Kalodner, Wampold, & Lichtenberg, 2000). Clinical and counseling psychologists are usually trained in different academic settings and in different academic traditions. Counseling psychology programs are found, for the most part, in faculties of education and/or departments of educational psychology. Counseling psychologists are trained at the doctoral level in Ph.D. or Ed.D. programs. Clinical psychology programs, on the other hand, are based in psychology departments in Ph.D. or Psy.D. programs.

Data from surveys by Norcross and his colleagues indicate that clinical psychology programs attract far more applicants than do counseling psychology programs (Norcross, Kohout, & Wicherski, 2005; Norcross, Sayette, Mayne, Karg, & Turkson, 1998) and that counseling programs have a greater representation of ethnic minority students (Norcross et al., 1998). Research on clinical disorders is more commonly conducted in clinical psychology programs, and research on minority adjustment and academic/vocational issues is more frequently conducted in counseling psychology programs.

School Psychology

School psychologists have specialized training in both psychology and education. School psychologists are employed in diverse organizations such as schools, clinics, and hospitals, and in private practice. Given the focus on children's functioning, there is a natural overlap between school psychology and child clinical psychology. Historically, school psychology emphasized services related specifically to the learning of children and adolescents, including the assessment of intellectual functioning, the evaluation of learning difficulties, and consultation to teachers, students, and parents about strategies for optimizing students' learning potential. Clinical child psychology focused on the treatment of diagnosable mental disorder.

Over time, the scope of school psychology has expanded in response to the demands of parents, school systems, and governments. Because of growing awareness of the deleterious effects on learning of child and adolescent psychopathology, parental psychopathology, and stressful family circumstances, the work of school psychologists now addresses students' mental health and life circumstances more broadly. The role of school psychologists now includes attention to social, emotional, and medical factors in a context of learning and development. These changes, combined with legal obligations that schools provide the most appropriate education for all children, have resulted in school psychologists diagnosing a range of disorders of childhood and adolescence as well as developing school and/or family-based programs to assist students in learning to the best of their abilities. School psychologists have also taken a leadership role in the development of school-based prevention programs designed to promote social skills, to reduce bullying, to facilitate conflict resolution, and to prevent violence (Kratochwill, 2007). These programs are described in detail in Chapter 10.

In the United States, there are estimated to be 11.4 school psychologists per 100, 000 population (Robiner, 2006). Despite the increasingly close connections between school and child clinical psychology, it is likely that the two disciplines will remain distinct, at least in the near future. A survey of school and child clinical psychologists clearly illustrates this point. Tryon (2000) found that, in a sample of 363 psychologists, whereas three quarters of school psychologists endorsed the position that training programs in school and clinical psychology should merge in order to provide improved services for school-based and school-linked mental health services, fewer than half of the child clinical psychologists endorsed a merger. It therefore appears likely that distinctions in training will continue.

Psychiatry

Although we have focused on psychology-based professions thus far, it is important to note that primary care physicians provide more mental health services than any other health care profession

(Robiner, 2006). As medical generalists, these physicians are usually the first health care professionals consulted for any health condition, be it physical or mental. Psychiatrists are physicians who specialize in the diagnosis, treatment, and prevention of mental illnesses. Like all physicians, in four years of medical school training they learn about the functioning of the human body and the health services that physicians provide. As with other medical specialties, training as a psychiatrist requires five years of residency training after the successful completion of basic medical training. A range of residency options are possible, including both broad training in psychiatric services as well as specific training in subspecialties such as child psychiatry or geropsychiatry. Once they have completed specialization in psychiatry, psychiatrists rarely examine or treat the basic health problems that were covered in their medical training.

Psychiatric training differs in important ways from applied psychology training. First, psychiatric training deals extensively with physiological and biochemical systems and emphasizes biological functioning and abnormalities. Psychiatrists are well qualified to determine whether mental disorders are the result of medical problems and to unravel the possible interactions between physical illnesses and emotional disturbances. Psychiatric training provides the skills to evaluate the extent to which psychological symptoms result from or are exacerbated by medications used to treat physical ailments and chronic illnesses. On the other hand, compared with psychologists, psychiatrists receive relatively little training in human psychological development, cognition, learning, or psychological functioning in general. Standard psychiatric training provides only limited training in research skills such as research design and statistical analysis. Many psychiatrists have become active researchers and have contributed in important ways to the knowledge base of the neurosciences and human sciences. Nevertheless, the average psychiatry resident receives far less training in research than does the average graduate student in clinical psychology. An expert panel warned that, unless research training in psychiatric residency programs was dramatically strengthened, research by American psychiatrists risked dwindling to the point of "extinction" (McLellan, 2003).

Another fundamental difference between training in clinical psychology and psychiatry is that psychiatric training generally emphasizes psychopharmacological treatment over psychological treatment. Accordingly, compared with psychologists, psychiatrists tend to receive less training in the use of scientifically based psychological assessment and psychotherapy. Historically, psychiatrists were trained in forms of psychoanalytic and psychodynamic treatments such as those developed by Sigmund Freud, Carl Jung, and Alfred Adler. Due in part to the proliferation of effective psychopharmacological treatments in recent decades and the growing emphasis on evidence-based practice in psychiatry, there has been a waning of emphasis on training in psychoanalytic and long-term psychodynamic psychotherapy. There is growing attention paid to training psychiatrists in evidence-based treatments, which may include cognitive-behavioral and interpersonal therapies (cf. Hoge, Tondora, & Stuart, 2003; Martin, Saperson, & Maddigan, 2003). Despite the tendency for many psychiatrists to favor psychopharmacological approaches to treatment, psychiatrists were among the pioneers in the development of evidence-based psychological treatments: **Aaron Beck** was the primary developer of cognitive therapy for depression (and subsequently other disorders), Gerald Weissman was the primary developer of the interpersonal treatment of depression, and Isaac Marks has played a prominent role in the development of cognitive-behavioral treatments for anxiety disorders. Thus, although the relative emphasis of psychotherapy within the profession differs from that in clinical psychology, the provision of psychotherapeutic services remains, for many psychiatrists, a central aspect of psychiatric services. Attesting to this, in 1998, the American Academy of Child and Adolescent Psychiatry took the position that psychotherapy must remain a core skill in the practice of child and adolescent psychiatry.

Until recently, an important distinction between clinical psychologists and psychiatrists was that only psychiatrists could prescribe medication. However, in some jurisdictions, this is no longer the case. Programs through the federal Department of Defence and the Indian Health Service as well as some state legislatures have made provisions for psychologists to receive training to prescribe psychoactive medication.

Dr. Aaron Beck. (*Source:* Clem Murray/Philadelphia Inquirer/MCT/NewsCom)

In the United States there are estimated to be 13.7 psychiatrists per 100,000 people (Robiner, 2006). The profession of psychiatry is facing a worldwide problem in recruiting new professionals. In many countries, even those as socially and economically different as Britain and India, the number of graduating medical students who wish to specialize in psychiatry has been insufficient to meet the demand for psychiatrists (Brockington & Mumford, 2002; Tharyan, John, Tharyan, & Braganza, 2001). In the United States, the number of medical students seeking psychiatric residencies has fallen by over 40% since the 1980s—only 3% of American medical students now seek psychiatric training (Tamaskar & McGinnis, 2002). Several surveys of medical students have found that psychiatry is considered less professionally satisfying than other medical specialties. Feifel, Moutier, and Swerdlow (1999), for example, found that internal medicine, pediatrics, and surgery were all seen as more desirable career choices than psychiatry.

Social Work

Social workers focus on ways to assist individuals, families, groups, and communities to restore or enhance their social functioning. Social workers emphasize the importance of social conditions that facilitate optimal development. Social work practice includes activities such as policy development, program planning, program management, research consultation, case management, discharge planning, counseling, therapy, and advocacy (National Association of Social Workers [NASW], 2008). Social workers are employed in diverse settings including hospitals, community mental health centers, mental health clinics, schools, advocacy organizations, government departments, social service agencies, child welfare settings, family service agencies, correctional facilities, social housing organizations, family courts, employee assistance programs, school boards, and private counseling and consultation agencies (NASW, 2008).

Across states, there is considerable variability in licensure requirements. Most states require a degree in social work, BSW in some states and MSW in others, followed by supervised experience. Doctoral-level social workers tend to be employed in academic or research settings (Robiner, 2006).

The number of registered social workers has been growing steadily. In the United States there are 463 accredited baccalaureate social work programs and 191 accredited master's social work programs (Council on Social Work Education, 2008).

Many social workers function as part of a mental health team in the role of caseworkers who, in collaboration with the patient, coordinate services with a range of social and community agencies, medical services, and other services (such as vocational or sheltered employment activities). In their role as case managers, social workers assist patients to navigate what is often experienced as a maze of service providers and a series of conflicting demands presented by various agencies. Case management is especially important in assisting people who suffer from severe and debilitating mental disorders such as schizophrenia and bipolar disorder.

As is the case in applied psychology and psychiatry, social work faces increasing demands to provide evidence-based services (e.g., Myers & Thyer, 1997). Given the move across so many mental health professions toward evidence-based services, evidence-based therapy, such as interpersonal therapy or cognitive therapy for the treatment of adult depression, could be provided by psychologists, psychiatrists, or clinical social workers.

Other Mental Health Professions

Psychiatric nurses are professionals who offer services to individuals whose primary care needs relate to mental and developmental health (Robiner, 2006). Psychiatric nurses are responsible for managing administrative matters in inpatient settings, providing psychoeducation and counseling, and supervising ancillary services provided by others (such as nurses' aides and volunteers). Psychiatric nurses are employed in diverse settings including acute psychiatry, long-term geriatric care and home care, residential and community programs for the developmentally handicapped, forensic psychiatry, institutional and community-based corrections facilities, community mental health programs, special education programs for children, employee assistance programs, child guidance and family therapy clinics, chemical dependency programs, hospitals and special care homes, women's shelters and clinics, residential and community programs for adolescents, psychiatric nursing education, sheltered workshops, rehabilitation programs, vocational programs, and self-help groups, as well as private practice. In all these settings, psychiatric nurses are on the front lines providing direct services, as well as training and consultation. Robiner (2006) estimated that there are 6.5 psychiatric nurses per 100,000 people in the United States. Practitioners of this specialty typically receive their training as part of a two- or three-year diploma program or a baccalaureate degree. In addition to the regular training in general nursing, psychiatric nurses receive training in the management and treatment of those with mental disorders warranting admission to a hospital or other similar institution. Nurse practitioners with graduate training have prescriptive authority in 49 states and the District of Columbia (Robiner, 2006).

In the residential care of children and adolescents with emotional and behavioral problems, frontline services may also be offered by child and youth care workers. Child and youth care workers usually have two-year college training in child development and behavior management. In an attempt to meet the demand for mental health services while minimizing costs of services, outpatient services are often provided by mental health counselors. In most cases these counselors have a college diploma or certificate based on a structured program of training (often less than two years in duration) focused on the assessment and treatment of specific mental health problems such as addictions or trauma. There are also a growing number of counselors trained in applied behavioral analysis, a systematic form of assessment and intervention that is the treatment of choice for pervasive developmental disorders such as autistic disorder. Of all the professionals presented in this chapter, child and youth care workers and counselors have the least training and are the least likely to be members of a regulated profession.

As you can see, mental health services are offered by diverse professionals with varied backgrounds and training. There is concern across all mental health professions to adopt evidence-based practice, which clearly requires an appreciation of the research foundations of our assessment tools and interventions. Psychologists are well-placed to conduct and interpret the research foundations of effective practice. The composition of the mental health workforce is constantly shifting as professions seek more cost-effective strategies to ensure that their services can be accessed by a broad range of people who require care. As it becomes clear that evidence-based services can be provided effectively by trained professionals with different backgrounds, the roles of clinical psychologists will inevitably alter.

AVAILABILITY OF MENTAL HEALTH SERVICE PROVIDERS

There is wide variability in access to major mental health professions in different countries. Data from the World Health Organization indicate that the mental health needs of approximately half the world's nations are woefully underserved by trained professionals, with less than psychologist, psychiatrist, or social worker for each 100,000 people (World Health Organization, 2004a). Recall the data on the prevalence of mental health problems, in which even conservative estimates indicate that 1 in 10 people has a mental disorder. Thus, in half the world, there is only one mental health professional for each 10,000 people with a mental disorder.

Table 1.5 provides details on the relative numbers of psychologists and psychiatrists in different countries. You may have noticed that the values presented for the United States are lower than those

TABLE 1.5   World Health Organization Data on Psychologists and Psychiatrists in Selected Countries

	Psychologists (per 100,000 people)	Psychiatrists (per 100,000 people)
United States	26.4	10.5
Australia	5.0	14.0
Canada	35.0	12.0
Ireland	9.7	5.2
New Zealand	27.0	6.6
United Kingdom	9.0	11.0

Adapted from World Health Organization (2004b)

reported by Robiner (2006). It is important to note that there is always some imprecision in calculating workforce estimates, as different organizations and researchers may refer to different sources to generate their estimates.

In the United States, Canada, and New Zealand, there are substantially more psychologists providing mental health services than there are psychiatrists. This pattern does not apply in all countries, however, as evidenced by the data from the United Kingdom, where there are comparable numbers of psychologists and psychiatrists, and Australia, where there are substantially more psychiatrists than psychologists. Although the sheer numbers of professionals providing mental health services in a country provide some indication of the adequacy of the health care system, they can mask regional disparities that affect the population. Key among such regional disparities is the difference between services available in urban and rural areas. By and large, those living in rural areas have access to fewer mental health professionals than do those living in urban areas.

A BRIEF HISTORY OF CLINICAL PSYCHOLOGY

In considering the history of clinical psychology, it is useful to think in terms of interwoven threads that include the history of assessment and intervention within clinical psychology, the history of clinical psychology becoming a profession, the history of the treatment of mental illness, the history of prevention, and the history of psychology itself. In the remainder of the chapter, we will provide an overview of key aspects of clinical psychology's history. Because clinical psychology has developed in differing ways and rates in various countries, we cannot do justice to the multitude of important events that have shaped, and continue to shape, the discipline worldwide. In this section we highlight events that have contributed significantly to the current form of clinical psychology evident in most English-speaking countries. Due to space constraints, we have not included all critical occurrences that were instrumental in the development and application of clinical psychology in non-English-speaking countries. Nevertheless, in reading the following pages you should get a general sense of the influences that contributed to the growth of clinical psychology in North America and elsewhere. Given the key role of American clinical psychology in shaping the face of clinical psychology worldwide (Benjamin, 2005), much of what follows highlights key events within the United States. You will notice that not all the key figures who were influential in the development of clinical psychology were psychologists; the key figures also include philosophers and psychiatrists and members of related professions.

The Roots of Clinical Psychology

Numerous scholarly texts on the history of psychopathology and its treatment describe early proponents of the view that mental disturbances arose from natural causes, rather than from demonic possession. Among the early Greek scholars in the period of 500–300 B.C., Hippocrates (often called the father of medicine) emphasized what is now known as a **biopsychosocial approach** to understanding both physical and psychological disorders (i.e., biological, psychological, and social influences on health and illness must be considered). From textbooks on abnormal psychology and personality, you will have learned about Hippocrates' "bodily fluid" theory that imbalances in the levels of blood, black bile, yellow bile, and phlegm are responsible for emotional disturbance. The philosophers Plato and Aristotle are both credited with promoting some of Hippocrates' ideas, even though they did so in different ways. Plato emphasized the role of societal forces and psychological needs in the development and alleviation of mental disorders, whereas Aristotle emphasized the biological determinants of mental disorders.

In the late 1500s, St. Vincent de Paul proposed that mental and physical illnesses were caused by natural forces and that the extreme manifestations of mental disturbances such as psychotic behavior were not caused by witchcraft or by satanic possession. Unfortunately, the dominant approach to the treatment of mental illness in Europe and North America in the subsequent centuries was anything but humane. Those suffering from severe mental illness were isolated in asylums, most of which were far from conducive to the promotion of mental health. Numerous accounts of these institutions paint a picture of pain, despair, and desolation. Living conditions were often squalid, and the more aggressive patients were chained to walls. Treatments consisted of *time-honored* approaches to calming extreme behavior such as bleeding with knives or leeches (this was believed to reduce excitation due to an excess of blood) or immersion in frigid water.

During the period of the Enlightenment in Europe and North America that began in the latter half of the 1700s, a new worldview emerged in which problems could be analyzed, understood, and solved and the methods of science could be applied to all natural phenomena, including the human experience. The impact of this philosophical movement on the treatment of the mentally ill was astounding. Reformer Philippe Pinel, the director of a major asylum in Paris in the late 1700s, ordered that the chains be removed from all mental patients and that patients be treated humanely. Around the same time in England, William Tuke advocated the development of hospitals based on modern ideas of appropriate care and established a country retreat in which patients lived and worked. In the United States, Benjamin Rush promoted the use of moral therapy with the mentally ill (a treatment philosophy that encouraged the use of compassion and patience rather than physical punishment or restraints).

About this time, within European medicine the specialty of neurology was growing rapidly. The increased attention to mental disorders led to the recognition that a number of conditions, such as hysteria (i.e., extreme, dramatic, and often odd behavior including limb paralysis), could not easily be accounted for with purely biological explanations. Jean Martin Charcot, in France, is credited with being the primary developer of clinical neurology. As his fame grew, so did his emphasis on the role of psychological factors in hysteria. Charcot's use of suggestion and hypnosis to treat this condition initially attracted the attention of many physicians and medical students. Notable members of this group include Pierre Janet and Sigmund Freud, who initially embraced Charcot's theories and his use of hypnosis but later went on to develop their own theories to account for hysteria.

The History of Assessment in Clinical Psychology

The early history of clinical psychology is largely the history of clinical assessment, as clinical psychology developed from psychology's focus on measuring, describing, and understanding human behavior. Indeed, with some exceptions that we discuss in the next section, clinical psychology was almost entirely an assessment-based discipline until the middle part of the twentieth century. Milestones in the history of assessment in clinical psychology are noted in **Table 1.6**.

By the latter part of the 1800s, the influence of the Enlightenment worldview was also evident in the burgeoning application of scientific principles to understanding both normal and abnormal

TABLE 1.6 Timeline for the History of Assessment in Clinical Psychology

1879	Germany: *Measurement.* Wundt opens the first psychology laboratory measuring sensory processes.
1899	Germany: *Diagnosis.* Kraepelin develops the first diagnostic system.
1905	France: *Intelligence testing.* Binet and Simon develop a test to assess intellectual abilities in school children.
1917	United States: *Intelligence testing.* Army Alpha and Army Beta tests developed to select soldiers.
1920s	Switzerland: *Projective testing of personality.* Rorschach publishes a book on the interpretation of inkblots.
1939	United States: *Intelligence testing.* Wechsler develops the Wechsler-Bellevue test of adult intelligence.
1940s	United States: *Projective testing of personality.* Murray and Morgan publish the Thematic Apperception Test.
1943	United States: *Actuarial assessment of personality.* Hathaway publishes the Minnesota Multiphasic Personality Inventory.
1946	United States: *Development of psychological services.* The Veterans Administration begins providing practicum and internship training for psychologists, initially in assessment and then in treatment.
1952	United States: *Diagnosis.* American Psychiatric Association publishes *Diagnostic and Statistical Manual of Mental Disorders.*
1954	United States: *Challenge to clinical decision-making.* Meehl distinguishes between statistical and clinical decision-making.
1968	United States: *Challenge to personality assessment.* Mischel proposes an alternative behavioral approach to assessment.
	United States: *Diagnosis.* American Psychiatric Association publishes the second edition of *Diagnostic and Statistical Manual of Mental Disorders.*
1970s	United States: *Dimensional approach to child problems.* Quay, Achenbach, and Conners publish empirically based rating scales of child problems.
1980	United States: *Diagnosis.* American Psychiatric Association publishes third edition of *Diagnostic and Statistical Manual of Mental Disorders.*
1990s	Worldwide: Increasing incorporation of behavioral assessment techniques into typical assessment practices.
1990s	Worldwide: Widespread use of computers for scoring and interpreting psychological test results.
1994	United States: *Diagnosis.* American Psychiatric Association publishes the fourth edition of *Diagnostic and Statistical Manual of Mental Disorders.*
2000s	Worldwide: Increased attention to the development of country-specific norms for commonly used measures of intelligence.
2000s	United States & Canada: Increased attention to the principles of evidence-based assessment in the selection and use of assessment instruments.

human behavior. In England, Francis Galton studied individual differences among people, especially differences in motor skills and reaction times, which he believed were related to differences in intelligence. In Germany, Wilhelm Wundt, who studied sensation and perception, established the first psychology laboratory and was a central figure in advocating for psychology as the study of human experience. The American James McKeen Cattell, who at one time worked with Wundt, focused scientific attention on the connection between reaction time and intelligence. He is credited with coining the term *mental tests* to describe the battery of tests and tasks he developed to evaluate people's cognitive functioning.

Without a doubt, the pre-eminent individuals who influenced the early work on assessment in clinical psychology are the German psychiatrist **Emil Kraepelin** and the French psychologist **Alfred Binet**. Kraepelin was convinced that all mental disorders were due to biological factors and that the biological causes of the disorders could not be effectively treated by the rather primitive methods available in the late 1800s and early 1900s. Accordingly, he devoted his career to the study and classification of mental disorders in the hope that his work would result in a scientifically based classification system that would have treatment implications. Consistent with scientific approaches of the time, a key component of Kraepelin's approach to classification was to examine the way in which various symptoms covaried. Kraepelin assumed that by examining the symptomatic behavior of a large number of patients, it would be possible to discern the kinds of disturbances of affect, thought, and behavior that typically co-occurred. In Kraepelin's view this would provide insights into the nature of mental disorders. Kraepelin called these groups of symptoms that frequently co-occurred **syndromes**, and his classification system was built around identifying the ways in which these syndromes related to and differed from each other. Thus, the presence of a single symptom was considered of little value in determining the nature of the disorder suffered by the patient. However, Kraepelin assumed that by considering the entire range of symptoms exhibited by the patient, it should be possible to identify the precise disorder the patient had. As his study of symptoms and syndromes deepened, he realized that there were consistent differences between disorders in terms of when the symptoms first occurred (i.e., onset of the disorder) and the manner in which the disorder progressed subsequently (i.e., the course of the disorder). Kraepelin's classification system was unparalleled, and his classification of what is now known as schizophrenia was one of his major accomplishments. Even though some clinical psychologists have reservations about the value or validity of psychiatric diagnosis, Kraepelin's influence on modern psychiatry and clinical psychology is substantial. The nature and structure of current mental disorder classification systems, such as the American Psychiatric Association's *Diagnostic and Statistical Manual* and the World Health Organization's *International Classification of Diseases* (which are discussed in Chapter 3), have their origins in Kraepelin's work. Reference to these classification systems is an integral part of routine professional activities ranging from conducting psychopathology research to billing for psychological services.

Alfred Binet's contribution to clinical psychology is quite different from Kraepelin's although no less substantial. In the early years of the twentieth century, the French government wanted all children to receive schooling to maximize their potential to learn and develop. In particular there was concern to provide an education to those children with limited cognitive abilities who were unlikely to benefit from typical teaching methods. Before any special educational programs could be implemented, it was necessary to reliably identify children in need of such programs. Binet and his colleague Theodore Simon were invited to develop a strategy to measure mental skills that could yield information relevant

Alfred Binet (1857-1911). (© Albert Harlingue/
Roger-Violet/The Image Works).

Emil Kraepelin (1856-1926). (*Source:* Hulton Archive/
Getty Images, Inc.)

to the identification of children with limited intelligence. By 1908 the two colleagues had developed the Binet-Simon scale of intelligence, which consisted of more than 50 tests of mental skills that could be administered to children between the ages of 3 and 13 years. Binet and Simon gathered extensive data on a large number of children: that is, they established norms. As we describe in more detail in Chapter 5, norms allow for the comparison of test scores obtained by an individual to the range of scores within the general population or within specific subgroups of the general population. Thus, by comparing the intelligence test score obtained by a particular child with norms for children of the same age, the child's level of intelligence could be determined. In 1916, Lewis Terman published a modification of this scale for use in the United States—the Stanford-Binet Intelligence Test—that was the first widely available, scientifically based test of human intelligence. Binet's work established the importance of standardization in the development of psychological tests and the importance of references to normative data in interpreting test results.

Building on Binet's pioneering work and Terman's adaptation of the Binet-Simon test, the field of psychological assessment grew rapidly. With the entry of the United States into World War I, the American government needed procedures to quickly determine the fitness of many thousands of recruits to serve in the military. Physicians were employed to evaluate the physical fitness of the recruits for various military activities. In addition, it was necessary to find a way to evaluate mental fitness and mental abilities. Therefore, a committee of the relatively newly established American Psychological Association (APA, established in 1892) was struck to develop a system for classifying the men in terms of their mental functioning. This committee was chaired by Robert Yerkes, APA president. Within a short time the committee developed a measure of verbal mental abilities, called the Army Alpha test, that could be administered in a group format (thus minimizing the cost and time of administration). The committee also developed a test of nonverbal mental abilities, the Army Beta test, for assessing recruits who were unable to read or who had limited English language skills. This involvement of psychologists in a key American government initiative set the stage for psychologists to be recognized in North America for their expertise in test construction and in the measurement of individual differences. A second legacy of this process was the establishment of the first standards for the development of scientifically sound psychological tests. A third legacy was that, as a result of the value placed on these testing-related skills, the discipline of clinical psychology was officially recognized within the APA by the creation of the Section on Clinical Psychology in 1919.

During the next two decades, several approaches to clinical assessment flourished. Measurement of abilities continued to be a central focus for clinical psychologists. A milestone in the development of intelligence tests for adults was reached in 1939 with the release of the Wechsler-Bellevue test. Its developer, David Wechsler, subsequently developed intelligence tests for the entire age range (Wechsler Preschool and Primary Scale of Intelligence, Wechsler Intelligence Scale for Children, Wechsler Adult Intelligence Scale) and the most commonly used general measure of memory (Wechsler Memory Scale). Although other intelligence scales have since been developed for children and adults, the Wechsler scales are considered the *gold standard* in the assessment of intellectual abilities. The Wechsler scales will be discussed at length in Chapter 7. This period also saw the development of interest tests, with measures such as the Strong Vocational Interest Blank and the Kuder Preference Record, which were developed for training and personnel hiring purposes. Early self-report measures of temperament and personality became available with the release of Woodworth's Personal Data Sheet and the Allport-Vernon Study of Values.

Group testing of US army recruits. (*Source:* Time Life Pictures/US Signal Corps/Getty Images, Inc.)

The 1930s also witnessed the emergence of projective tests to evaluate personality and psychological functioning. Whereas intelligence tests measure performance on a task, and paper and pencil personality tests are based on self-description, projective tests are predicated on the notion that an individual's interpretation of a situation is determined by his or her personality characteristics. Thus, a person's response to an ambiguous stimulus is presumed to tell us something about the person's mental functioning. One of the most influential and widely used projective tests, the Rorschach inkblot test, was published by Swiss psychiatrist Hermann Rorschach in 1921. Although the test received a decidedly cool reception among psychiatric and psychological circles in Europe, it received a new lease on life when German psychologist Bruno Klopfer, who emigrated to the United States in 1934, began instructing psychology students at Columbia University in the use of the inkblots. The Rorschach inkblot test was also used in assessing children. Another projective technique that was considered suitable for both adults and children was the House-Tree-Person test, which involved interpretation of the psychological meaning of qualities of the person's drawing. Around the same time, American psychologists Henry Murray and Christina Morgan, working at the Harvard Psychological Clinic, published the Thematic Apperception Test (TAT) that was comprised of 20 pictures. Strongly opposed to the growing tendency to study psychological phenomena with experimental methods, Murray distanced himself from the mainstream of academic psychology but was greatly influenced in his thinking by the psychoanalytic writings of Sigmund Freud and Carl Jung. The development of projective tests proceeded without attention to the basic test construction objectives of standardization, reliability, validity, and norms, which has led to long-standing concerns about the quality and utility of many projective tests. These issues will be discussed at greater length in Chapter 8.

With the advent of World War II, psychologists once again became actively involved in the development and use of selection tests for the armed forces. At the close of the war, training opportunities provided by the Veterans Administration were largely responsible for the growth of clinical psychology. The assessment milestone of the 1940s was unquestionably the publication of the Minnesota Multiphasic Personality Inventory (MMPI) by psychologist Starke Hathaway in 1943. The MMPI was, for many years to come, the epitome of the criterion-oriented approach to psychological test construction. The MMPI was designed to be an easily administered test that could effectively screen for psychological disturbances among adults. To this end, Hathaway generated hundreds of test items that were administered to psychiatric patients; items that were strongly associated with specific diagnoses were retained and then combined to make scales within the test. The ability of these scales to distinguish between those with and without psychiatric diagnoses was examined, and modifications to the scales were made based on these data. Evidence for the final scales' reliability and validity was gathered and normative data (although rather poor) were obtained. Thus, in contrast to the projective tests, the development and interpretation of the MMPI relied extensively on attention to statistical procedures and test development criteria. Research on the MMPI is discussed in Chapter 8.

The fundamental differences between projective tests that rely heavily on clinical judgment and the MMPI that relies on statistical analysis set the stage for a critical evaluation of the value and accuracy of assessment in clinical psychology in the 1950s and 1960s. The 1954 review by **Paul Meehl** of the relative strengths of clinically and statistically based assessment highlighted a number of problems that plagued the assessment enterprise in clinical psychology. In essence, Meehl's review of the literature found that a purely clinical approach to assessment was typically inferior to a more statistically oriented approach to accurately describing or diagnosing adults. By clinical, Meehl referred to the typical collection of interview and other information that was then used, sometimes with standardized test data, to generate descriptions and predictions of behavior. The statistical approach, in contrast, involved the use of basic demographic information (such as age, gender, and health information) and data from standardized tests that were entered into statistical equations to yield descriptions and/or predictions. This latter approach was similar to risk estimates calculated by insurance companies to assign differential insurance policy costs based on estimated risk. A point often lost in the ensuing debate about the value of clinical judgment was that Meehl advocated strongly for the use of clinical experience in generating hypotheses about human functioning or about particular client characteristics. He maintained, however, that once these hypotheses were formulated, whether for research or clinical purposes, scientific methods (including, whenever possible, standardized psychological measures) must be used to test the viability of the hypotheses.

The publication in 1968, a little over a decade after Meehl's critique of clinical assessment practices, of Walter Mischel's compelling analysis of the shortcomings of personality traits for understanding human behavior further eroded many clinical psychologists' confidence in the validity of their assessment work. Up to then, much of the research on personality had focused on the measurement and study of traits—that is, co-occurring characteristics that not only defined the personality of an individual but also were the primary influences in determining how an individual would react in a given situation. Mischel's work illustrated that these personality traits had more to do with how a person was viewed by others than with what a person actually did. Moreover, research on the predictive validity of personality traits typically yielded results of only moderate strength—in other words, knowing someone's personality traits provided very little useful information if you wished to know what someone would actually feel, think, or do in a particular situation. Much more accurate predictions of psychological experience could be obtained by considering both the person's past experiences in similar situations and the environmental influences on the person's behavior in the situation.

Although many personality researchers and clinical psychologists believed that Mischel had underestimated the influence of personality factors and overestimated the power of social situations in determining behavior, Mischel's analysis bolstered the rising influence of behavioral assessment approaches on clinical assessment. Initial behavioral approaches to assessment involved the identification of specific behaviors deemed to be central to the person's distress, either by virtue of being a key symptom that should be changed in therapy or by being a central factor responsible for causing and/or maintaining the person's distress. Based on learning principles encompassed under operant, classical, and observational learning paradigms, behavioral assessment focused on easily defined and observable events, current behaviors, and situational/environment determinants of behavior. For much of the 1960s and 1970s, behavioral assessment largely involved obtaining frequency, rate, and duration measures describing the behaviors of interest. Compared with the self-report and projective personality assessment approaches, behavioral assessment was much more focused on the gathering of clinical data that had immediate and obvious value in the planning and evaluation of treatment strategies. As behavioral strategies often require observation by a third party, they were most commonly applied in treating problems of children and of patients in hospitals or residential institutions. Observation strategies are described in Chapter 6.

Although sound tools for the assessment of children's intellectual functioning were developed early in the twentieth century, empirically based assessment of children's emotional and behavioral problems did not begin in earnest until the 1970s, with the publication of the first rating scales of children's behavior. Different scales pioneered by Thomas Achenbach, Herbert Quay, and Keith Conners shared the same reliance on description of behaviors and on empirically derived scales to assess children's functioning. These scales required parents to rate the extent to which a particular behavior was typical of their child. Like the MMPI, the items on these scales were subjected to factor analysis, so that scale scores were derived empirically. Such rating scales provide information on children's functioning on a number of dimensions rather than yielding a categorical diagnosis.

In the 1980s, the publication of the third edition of the American Psychiatric Association's *Diagnostic and Statistical Manual of Mental Disorders (DSM)* led to increased attention on the value of structured interview approaches to gathering diagnostic information. For many years, research had consistently demonstrated that clinicians (including clinical psychologists and psychiatrists) were very inconsistent in how they interviewed patients; such inconsistencies were evident from clinician to clinician and even within the same clinician over time. The result of these inconsistencies often led to the same individual being assigned very different diagnoses from clinicians. Such diagnostic inconsistency has the potential to dramatically affect the types of treatments recommended to the patient. The DSM-III was an explicit attempt to improve the reliability of psychiatric diagnoses by providing as much clear guidance as possible on specific criteria that must be met to render a diagnosis. Based on the common measurement strategy in psychopathology research of using a standardized, structured interview to generate diagnostic information, clinicians were strongly encouraged to either use scientifically established structured interviews to diagnose DSM-III disorders or, at a minimum, to ensure that the necessary diagnostic criteria were met before a diagnosis was assigned. In the development of structured diagnostic interviews for children, there has been particular attention to ensure that questions are formulated in a manner that is developmentally appropriate. So, for example, it is not suitable to ask complex questions about the duration of a problem to a child who has not yet developed a concept of time. Issues related to interviewing are addressed in Chapter 6.

Finally, there have been a number of striking changes in psychological assessment over the past three decades. One important change has been the kind of rapprochement among different perspectives on how best to conduct psychological assessments. For most assessment purposes, it is generally accepted that assessment data should be obtained from (a) multiple methods, such as interviews, observations, and self-reports and, increasingly, (b) from multiple informants (i.e., not just from the client alone). A second important change has been the recognition that best practices in assessment should be based on assessment methods and measures that have solid scientific support. Issues of the psychometric properties of measures and the representativeness of norms used to interpret test scores are now commonly considered by psychologists. We will comment more on these issues in the chapters on assessment.

Another important change in psychological assessment has been the increased attention to the relevance of assessment data for treatment planning and treatment evaluation. Decades of research amply demonstrate that psychologists can create assessment tools for myriad constructs. Many thousands of studies have been published on the reliability and validity of a huge range of psychological measures. However, it has become increasingly clear that to justify the time and expense involved in clinical assessment, this vast knowledge must be applied in ways that are directly pertinent to improving the lives of people suffering psychological distress. Combined with concerns about costs and accountability of health care systems worldwide, this has highlighted two issues that clinical psychologists involved in assessment are beginning to address. The first issue is one of **clinical utility**: that is, does having assessment data on a patient actually provide information that leads to a clinical outcome that is better (or faster, or less expensive) than would be the case if the psychologist did not have the assessment data? This issue reflects the problem that all too often research on clinical psychology is disconnected from research on interventions in clinical psychology and vice versa. As concerns about health care costs mount, clinical psychologists must justify to those who pay for their services the relevance of their assessment activities. The second, and related, current issue is one of **service evaluation**. Put bluntly, individual clinical psychologists are under increasing pressure to demonstrate that their services work. This has resulted in renewed attention to the role of clinical assessment in documenting progress and outcome in treatment. However, this need to demonstrate treatment effectiveness leads to a different type of clinical assessment than has often been used in the past. Whereas many clinical psychology measures were developed to give a broadly based psychological picture of the whole person, current assessment practices require that measures focus on specific problems (or strengths), that they are brief, and that they are amenable to repeated use. The measurement tools that are useful for generating an individual's psychological profile are not necessarily the ones that are relevant to the repeated assessment of someone receiving treatment. Accordingly, a minor revolution in the nature of clinical assessment is currently under way, with some traditional measures falling from favor and some longstanding, but with underused assessment strategies coming to the fore. These issues are discussed in greater detail in Chapters 6, 7, and 8.

The History of Intervention in Clinical Psychology

Milestones in the evolution of intervention in clinical psychology are noted in **Table 1.7**. The modern history of psychotherapy is typically seen as beginning with the work of Sigmund Freud and the development of psychoanalysis. As indicated earlier in this chapter, a number of European psychiatrists such as Charcot and Janet were actively involved in using verbal rather than physical approaches to the treatment of mental disorders in the late 1800s. Freud is credited with developing the first elaborated approach to the psychotherapeutic treatment of common psychological difficulties, even though subsequent historical analysis of his work suggests that it may not have been as original or revolutionary as he often suggested (Ellenberger, 1970). The 1900 publication of his book *The Interpretation of Dreams* marked an important milestone for the psychoanalytic movement and attracted both supporters and detractors. In subsequent years, psychiatrists such as Carl Jung and Alfred Adler

TABLE 1.7   Timeline for History of Intervention in Clinical Psychology

1896	United States: Witmer opens the first psychology clinic.
1900–1930s	Europe, United States, United Kingdom: Development of psychoanalytic approaches.
1920s	United States: First behavioral treatment of anxiety by Cover Jones.
1940s	United States & Europe: Increased demand for services to deal with war-related distress.
1942	United States: Rogers publishes *Counseling and Psychotherapy*, introducing a client-centered approach.
1952	England: Eysenck publishes a review questioning the usefulness of psychotherapy with adults.
1957	United States: Levitt publishes a review questioning the usefulness of psychotherapy with children.
1958	South Africa: Wolpe publishes an article on the behavioral treatment of phobias.
1977	Canada & United States: Meichenbaum publishes *Cognitive-Behavior Modification: An Integrative Approach.*
1979	United States: Beck, Rush, Shaw, and Emery publish *Cognitive Therapy for Depression.*
1980	United States: Smith, Glass, and Miller publish *Effects of Psychotherapy*, providing results of a meta-analytic review of treatment for adults.
1987	United States: Weisz, Weiss, Alicke, and Klotz publish a meta-analytic review of treatment for children and adolescents.
1995	United States: American Psychological Association, Division of Clinical Psychology defines criteria to evaluate degree of empirical support for treatments.
1995	United States: American Psychological Association adopts a model psychotropic medication prescription bill and a training curriculum in psychopharmacology for psychologists.
1996	United Kingdom: Roth and Fonagy publish *What Works for Whom? A Critical Review of Psychotherapy Research.*
1998	United States: Nathan and Gorman publish *A Guide to Treatments that Work.*
2005	United States: American Psychological Association adopts a policy on evidence-based practice in psychology.

joined Freud to develop and promote a psychoanalytic approach to the understanding and treatment of mental disorders. Ultimately, they and other followers split from Freud to develop their own theories and interventions.

The early decades of the 1900s were marked by the growth of numerous psychodynamic treatment approaches in Europe, which then spread to North America. These approaches differed widely in their core principles and techniques, but all were based on the assumption that most psychopathology stemmed from unconscious processes. For Freud, the unconscious was the source of all psychic energy as well as the repository of all our disappointments, hurts, and unfulfilled sexual and aggressive desires. He hypothesized that to protect ourselves from the pain of continually re-experiencing these negative emotions and memories we use a number of strategies called defense mechanisms such as denial, repression, and intellectualization. The goal of treatment is for the patient to gain insight into the origin of his or her problems (i.e., the painful contents of the unconscious) and the ways in which the defense mechanisms inadvertently block the person's full psychological development. Jung's model involved an aspect of the unconscious similar to Freud's (called the personal unconscious) but also included a much more positive form (called the collective unconscious) that could promote the individual's psychological growth. Jungian treatment emphasized, therefore, not only the importance of developing an awareness of the personal unconscious but also an appreciation and harnessing of the power of the collective unconscious.

Later psychodynamic models tended to de-emphasize the importance of unconscious determinants of behavior. Alfred Adler's approach, for example, focused on the role of societal forces and socialization pressures in the development of personality and the treatment of disorders. His theory emphasized the impact of birth order on personality and the impact of social comparison processes in which we may underestimate or overestimate our personal strengths and weaknesses. Anna Freud, a daughter of Sigmund Freud, who had received analysis from her father when she was a child, developed ego psychology that encourages the person to develop skills that can help address current problems. Although her approach still considered the unconscious a force to be reckoned with, she highlighted the role of conscious efforts to adjust to past difficulties and current life obstacles. Anna Freud took a leading role in modifying psychoanalytic approaches in treatment with children.

Even though they were undoubtedly influential in the development of clinical psychology treatments, these psychodynamic approaches were not the only contributors to our current forms of psychotherapy. Two other distinct approaches to the treatment of psychological distress emerged during the first decades of the twentieth century. Lightner Witmer, an American student of Wundt's credited with being the first to use the term "clinical psychology," developed a clinic offering psychological services in 1896 and university training in clinical psychology in 1904. Witmer was a university professor whose interests lay primarily in the application of research on learning and memory processes. He consulted with teachers and others in school settings to apply the new science of psychology to the assessment and remediation of learning difficulties, intellectual and developmental delays, and, to some extent, behavior problems. In retrospect it is ironic that the psychologist often described as the father of clinical psychology was really setting the stage for what would now be seen as school psychology. A second example of the application of scientific psychology to the understanding and treatment of psychological disorders can be found in conditioning research in the 1920s. John Watson demonstrated that it was possible to use conditioning principles to explain the development of phobias with his famous experiment with little Albert and furry white animals and objects. The next significant step that had important implications for treatment purposes was when Mary Cover Jones showed that the principles of conditioning could be used to extinguish a phobic reaction in a child. This initial work utilizing animal and human learning concepts and procedures set the stage for what would later become behavior therapy.

In the 1940s and 1950s the demand for psychotherapy grew dramatically, due largely to the need to provide mental health services for both members of the military and to members of the public who were affected by the horror and losses of the war. In the United States, for example, the need for mental health professionals to provide counseling and therapy to returning soldiers could not be met by the relatively small number of psychiatrists practicing in the country. As a result, the Veterans Administration agency turned to the profession of clinical psychology, hiring many psychologists and providing a substantial infusion of funds to aid in the formation of new training programs in clinical psychology. This led to an enormous increase in the number of clinical psychologists in the United States and to the eventual establishment in later decades of clinical psychologists' reputation as among the best trained practitioners of psychotherapy.

Dr. Carl Rogers. (*Source:* Photo by Michael Rougler/ Time & Life Pictures/Getty Images, Inc.)

The 1940s and 1950s also saw a proliferation in the forms of psychotherapy available to the public. A major new movement in psychotherapy was initiated with the publication in 1942 of **Carl Rogers**' book *Counseling and Psychotherapy*. In contrast to the then-dominant psychoanalytic approach, Rogers' approach was rooted in an assumption that people were inherently capable of developing in a positive, healthy manner. The primary goal of therapy, therefore, was to provide a supportive environment in which clients could reconnect with their emotions, their losses, and their aspirations and thereby discover their true potential for growth. Rogers' work was crucial in the development of humanistic approaches to the understanding and treatment of human problems, an approach that has been termed the third force in psychotherapy (with psychodynamic and behavioral approaches being the first two). Of equal, if not greater importance, Rogers was an early and firm advocate of the need to conduct systematic research on the process and outcome of psychotherapy. His position was markedly different from the typical view of the time, as what frequently passed as psychotherapy research was little more than case studies. You will learn more about the limitations of the case study approach to the study of human functioning in Chapter 4.

Changes were occurring in the psychodynamic approach to treatment as well, with Alexander and French publishing their book *Psychoanalytic Therapy* in 1946 in which they made a compelling case for briefer forms of psychoanalytic treatment. In the mid-1950s Harry Stack Sullivan provided details on interpersonally focused strategies for intervening with patients. Outside the psychodynamic realm, new approaches within a humanistic/existential/experiential tradition were introduced, including Fritz Perls' concepts and procedures of gestalt therapy and Viktor Frankl's logotherapy. Finally,

Joseph Wolpe published his work on systematic desensitization in 1958, thus setting the stage for the dramatic growth of the behavioral (and cognitive) therapies.

Hans Eysenck's (1952) critique of the effectiveness of psychotherapy was a turning point for psychotherapy research and training. Eysenck argued that the rates of improvement among clients receiving either psychodynamic or eclectic (i.e., an unspecified mix of theories and techniques) therapy were comparable to rates of remission of symptoms among clients receiving no therapy at all. He contended, therefore, that there was no evidence that the most commonly used forms of psychotherapy had any demonstrable effect. Although later proponents of these treatments pointed out substantial flaws in his arguments, Eysenck's review had two dramatic effects on the field. First, it crystallized

Hans Juergen Eysenck. (*Source:* AFP Photo EPA-Pressenbild Files/NewsCom)

dissatisfaction among many psychologists who did not agree with a psychodynamic approach to treatment and led to efforts to establish treatments that were directly connected to psychology's empirically derived knowledge. Second, it resulted in a flurry of research activity in the coming decades focused on evaluating both new and traditional forms of psychotherapy. As we will see throughout this book, advances in psychological services for children and families often follow the same trends as are seen in services for adults; however, there is usually a time lag of a few years. Reviews of the child psychotherapy research (Levitt, 1957) reached conclusions similar to Eysenck's with respect to adult psychotherapy.

The 1960s and 1970s, consequently, were decades marked by an increase in both the numbers of psychotherapies available to the public and the amount of research devoted to understanding whether psychotherapy was effective (and, if it was, what made it effective). In the early 1960s Albert Ellis developed Rational Emotive Therapy, and Eric Berne introduced Transactional Analysis (an early forerunner of therapies aimed at enhancing personal growth and development as much as treating psychopathology). Using learning principles such as contingencies, shaping, and reinforcement, behavior modification and behavior therapy became widely used during this time to address problems as diverse as self-injurious behavior, phobic avoidance, hyperactive behavior, and sexual dysfunction. In tune with the growing attention to cognitive phenomena in psychology in general, behavior therapy began to address cognitive elements in treatment. The publication in the late 1970s of two influential books laid the foundation of what is now known as cognitive-behavior therapy. These now classic texts were Don Meichenbaum's *Cognitive-Behavior Modification: An Integrated Approach,* which was published in 1977, and the first comprehensive treatment manual, *Cognitive Therapy of Depression: A Treatment Manual* by Aaron Beck and his colleagues John Rush, Brian Shaw, and Gary Emery, which appeared in 1979. Cognitive-behavioral approaches are equally applicable to address adults' and children's problems and gained popularity in the 1970s.

Another milestone was reached in 1980 when Smith, Glass, and Miller used a statistical technique called **meta-analysis** to review 475 controlled studies of psychotherapy. This technique (described in detail in Chapter 4) provides a means by which groups of studies can be statistically combined and compared. Their primary finding was that psychotherapy, in general, was clearly very effective, with the average person receiving therapy being better off after therapy than 80% of people with similar problems who did not receive therapy. The researchers also examined the efficacy of various types of treatment. Using different analytic techniques, they found that although there was general equivalence across divergent forms of psychotherapy, some therapies were superior to others for specific disorders and clinical problems. As we will see in Chapters 12 and 14, these results fueled debates about the relative merits of psychotherapies that persist to the present. Seven years later, a meta-analysis reported similar results for psychotherapy for children and adolescents, with 79% of treated children being better off after treatment than children and adolescents with similar problems who did not receive psychotherapy (Weisz, Weiss, Alicke, & Klotz, 1987). We address the impact of research such as this in Chapter 13.

The 1980s and 1990s saw several key developments in the history of psychotherapy. During this time, there was a dramatic increase in the amount of research on psychotherapy. Furthermore, there was a profound improvement in the methodological sophistication of those studies, with an increasing use of treatment manuals to guide interventions and standardized diagnostic criteria for assessing those receiving treatment. Numerous societal and health care pressures fueled the demand for the development and dissemination of effective short-term treatments (i.e., fewer than 20 to 25 sessions). This demand for short-term treatments was welcomed by proponents of disorder-specific cognitive-behavioral treatments. In addition, psychodynamic and humanistic/existential/experiential approaches were adapted to provide services over a shorter period of time. Numerous forms of interpersonally focused psychodynamic treatments emerged in Britain, Canada, and the United States, including Time-Limited Dynamic Psychotherapy developed by Hans Strupp and his colleagues. Within the experiential orientation the emphasis was on more structured and directive interventions that melded traditional principles and values with contemporary knowledge of emotional functioning. Key among the proponents of this process-experiential treatment approach were Les Greenberg in Canada and Robert Elliott in the United States. During this same time period, prescription privileges for psychologists became a reality, initially in the Department of Defense and then in several states. APA passed resolutions on prescription privilege that remain very contentious within the profession. Nevertheless, the push for psychopharmacology training and prescription privileges has continued with remarkable vigor.

It should be clear from this overview that the practice of clinical psychology has been greatly influenced by research on the impact of psychotherapy. Another landmark event occurred in 1995 with the release of the report by the American Psychological Association Division of Clinical Psychology's Task Force on Promotion and Dissemination of Psychological Procedures. The impetus for this task force came from increasing pressure in the United States for health care practices to be both demonstrably effective and cost-effective. Legislation and state case law were being used to shape the nature of both federal and state health care policy, and there appeared to be a very real danger that access to mental health and behavioral health care services might be diminished because of perceptions that such services were both expensive and relatively ineffective. Clearly a response from organized psychology was needed to underscore the efficacy of psychological interventions for certain disorders and conditions. The task force developed empirical criteria to aid in the determination of whether an intervention was efficacious in the treatment of a given disorder or clinical problem. Using these criteria, the task force then produced an initial list of efficacious treatments. The term efficacy is used to denote evidence that a treatment was shown to work under research conditions that emphasized internal validity, with the term effectiveness being reserved to describe evidence that the treatment was shown to work in real-world conditions. Predictably, this initiative was embraced by some clinical psychologists and treated with scorn by others.

Regardless of the strengths or limitations of this and related initiatives (which we discuss in Chapters 12 and 13), it has forever changed how clinical psychologists view the connection between empirical evidence and their therapeutic services. In the 1990s, several books were published that reviewed the research base of psychological treatments for a range of disorders; key among them were books by Nathan and Gorman and by Roth and Fonagy. These influential texts have been updated to include recent research findings, and we will discuss them more in the chapters on psychological treatments. The emphasis on grounding psychological services firmly in science culminated in the adoption by APA of the policy on evidence-based practice, which we described earlier in this chapter. Although the policy touches on all aspects of psychological services, it is likely that it will have the most impact on the treatment services provided by psychologists both within and outside of the United States.

The History of Prevention in Clinical Psychology

Unfortunately, the history of prevention efforts in clinical psychology is much shorter than the history of assessment or intervention. This is because, as outlined above, the profession of clinical psychology started with an assessment focus and then added the dimension of intervention. As clinical psychologists were incorporated into national health care systems in both public and private sectors, they adopted the priorities of these systems, which, until very recently, did not include much in the way of prevention efforts. Due to growing concerns about the dire health consequences of smoking and the need to promote safer sex practices to reduce the incidence of AIDS and sexually transmitted diseases, clinical psychologists now frequently play an important role in public health initiatives to change lifestyle-related illnesses. Concerns about the apparent increase in depression in the United States have led a number of clinical psychologists to develop prevention programs aimed at educating adolescents and young adults about depression and the types of psychological coping skills that can be used to maintain good mental health.

THE FUTURE

Predicting future events is always an uncertain business. Nevertheless, some brave psychologists have ventured to give their prognostications for future developments in clinical psychology. Groth-Marnat (2000), an authority on psychological assessment issues, recently offered some predictions about what is likely to transpire in the realm of clinical assessment in the next 50 years. Some of his predictions are almost sure bets, such as revisions to the DSM, the Wechsler intelligence tests, and the MMPI.

For others, he went out on a limb, predicting that advances in virtual reality technology will allow ability testing based on the simulation of life and work situations by 2020. The most dramatic prediction was that by 2035 measures based on the results of human genome research will be incorporated into clinical assessments.

Of course only time will tell which, if any, of these predictions will come to pass. Given the history of clinical psychology, perhaps the only certainty for the future is that exciting changes are in store for the profession and for those whose practice it. That being said, trends commencing in the past decade or two can give us some idea about the ways in which clinical psychology will develop and grow. Accordingly, it is almost certain that clinical psychology will be influenced by, among other factors, the following: application of psychological services to an array of health problems, not just mental health problems; developing services that respond to the health care needs of an ageing population; ensuring that psychological assessments, prevention programs, and treatments are both evidence-based and appropriate for the diverse range of people who receive these services; and enhancing the impact of concurrent use of psychological and pharmacological interventions.

SUMMARY AND CONCLUSIONS

Worldwide, mental health problems have staggering emotional and financial costs. Compared with physical health problems, mental health problems are woefully underserved. There is a trend across all mental health professions to develop and disseminate evidence-based services so that these serious problems can be effectively and economically addressed.

Clinical psychology shares with other mental health professions a concern to assess and intervene in the prevention and treatment of emotional, behavioral, and neurological problems. In contrast to psychiatry and psychiatric nursing, which have their roots in the treatment of pathology, psychology is grounded in the science of human behavior. Among the mental health professions, psychology is unique in its long-standing research tradition. From the beginning of their academic training, students in psychology learn to understand, interpret, and conduct methodologically sound research.

In tracing the history of psychological assessment, intervention, and prevention, it is clear that systematic observation and evaluation is a hallmark of clinical psychology. Drawing on a wealth of knowledge about human functioning and development, clinical psychologists have earned recognition of their expertise in assessment, treatment, and prevention of serious problems. The field of clinical psychology is in a process of constant evolution.

Critical Thinking Questions

Are mental health problems as serious as physical health problems?

In what ways is clinical psychology similar to other mental health professions?

In what ways is clinical psychology distinct from other mental health professions?

How has scientific thinking shaped the evolution of clinical psychology?

Key Terms

biopsychosocial approach: a theoretical framework that takes into account biological, psychological, and social influences on health and illness

clinical utility: usefulness of assessment data to provide information leading to a clinical outcome that is better (or faster, or less expensive) than would be the case if the psychologist did not have the assessment data

effectiveness: evidence that a treatment has been shown to work in real-world conditions

efficacy: evidence that a treatment has been shown to work under research conditions that emphasized internal validity

evidence-based practice: practice model that involves the synthesis of information drawn from research and systematically collected data on the patient in question, the clinician's professional experience, and the patient's preferences when considering health care options

meta-analysis: review technique by which groups of studies can be statistically combined and compared

service evaluation: activities designed to examine whether or not services work

syndrome: groups of symptoms that frequently co-occur

Key Names

Alfred Binet

Hans Eysenck

Emil Kraepelin

Richard McFall

Paul Meehl

Carl Rogers

ADDITIONAL RESOURCES
Books

Barlow, D. H. (Ed.). (in press). Oxford handbook of clinical psychology. New York: Oxford University Press.

Routh, D. K. (1994). Clinical psychology since 1917: Science, practice, and organization. New York: Plenum Press.

Journals

Clinical Psychology: Science and Practice

Clinical Psychology Review

Professional Psychology: Research and Practice

Check It Out!

The website of the American Psychological Association includes material related to the sciences and practice of psychology: www.apa.org

Psychologist Kenneth Pope's website provides resources on ethics, intervention, and critical thinking: www.kspope.com

The website for the National Institute of Mental Health provides information on diagnosis and treatment of mental disorders: www.nimh.nih.gov

The website of the UK National Institute for Health and Clinical Excellence provides clinical guidance on health issues: www.nice.org.uk

CHAPTER 2

Contemporary Clinical Psychology

INTRODUCTION

Clinical psychology is a fascinating profession. Few university graduate programs prepare students for such varied and challenging careers. Depending on personal preferences and job requirements, a clinical psychologist may devote professional time to (a) providing psychological services, (b) conducting research and providing clinical training, (c) consulting with other professionals and agencies, or (d) all of the above. Moreover, it is common for the relative balance of activities to shift over the span of a career, so that a clinical psychologist may have phases in which she or he devotes the greatest emphasis to research and other times that are mainly devoted to administration or teaching. In this way, the psychologist has a multitude of different interests within a single career in psychology. Clinical psychologists work with individuals (at any stage in the lifespan), couples, families, groups, and organizations. Many clinical psychologists work in the domain of mental health (e.g., treating anxiety disorders, disruptive behavior disorders, mood disorders, schizophrenia, or substance abuse disorders). A large number of clinical psychologists conduct research and provide health services outside the traditional practice domain (e.g., stress, coping with pain, promoting adherence to medical treatment regimens) and/or provide services related to relationship functioning (e.g., couples therapy, parent training, family therapy).

In 2004, *Psychology Today* and *PacifiCare Behavioral Health* commissioned a survey of adults' experience with and attitudes toward mental health treatment entitled *Therapy in America 2004*. Five hundred adults took part in telephone interviews and 1,730 adults completed the survey online. One question asked "which mental health profession is most helpful in resolving personal, emotional, or mental health problems?" Of those who had an opinion on this, psychologists were seen as the most helpful by 29% of respondents, whereas psychiatrists were seen as the most helpful by 19%. It is heartening to know that the public views psychologists as helpful mental health care providers. However, there are enormous international disparities in the extent to which people have access to mental heath services from psychologists. The United States, Canada, New Zealand, and the Scandinavian countries are, relatively speaking, well served by psychologists. Unfortunately, the same cannot be said of many other countries, especially those in Africa and Asia.

In this chapter we will describe the range of activities in which clinical psychologists engage and some of the settings in which they work. To bring these activities to life, we have asked three clinical psychologists who work in different settings to describe their usual professional activities over the course of a week. In reading these descriptions of professional activities in the three profile boxes, you will probably be struck by the busy and varied nature of their professional time.

You may recall that in Chapter 1 we talked about what we consider a touchstone of clinical psychology: science-based practice. In this chapter, we introduce a second touchstone of clinical psychology: professional ethics. Because clinical psychologists, as health care providers, must meet training and licensing requirements in order to practice, we provide a perspective on licensing requirements. In the final sections of the chapter we will describe the nature of clinical psychology and the nature of training in clinical psychology.

ACTIVITIES OF CLINICAL PSYCHOLOGISTS

Over the years, a number of surveys have documented the nature of the activities undertaken by clinical psychologists. Some activities, such as assessment and research, have stayed relatively constant in terms of the numbers of psychologists who frequently engage in them. As we explained in Chapter 1, following the Second World War there was a steady rise in the numbers of clinical psychologists providing psychotherapy. **Table 2.1** shows data from a survey of psychologists (Norcross, Karpiak, &

TABLE 2.1 Professional Activities of Clinical Psychologists—Percentage of Psychologists Who Engage in Each Activity

Activity	Percent
Assessment	64
Psychotherapy	80
Consultation	47
Research	51
Teaching	49
Supervision	50
Administration	53

Adapted from Norcross, Karpiak, and Santoro (2005)

Santoro, 2005) indicating the percentages of clinical psychologists who engage in different professional activities. As you can see, the majority of psychologists engage in many different professional activities. In interpreting these data, we must remember that survey information can provide a useful overview of general trends among clinical psychologists but does not indicate the variability in professional activities among individual clinical psychologists.

Profile Boxes 2.1, 2.2, and 2.3 introduce three clinical psychologists. Dr. Jim Maddux is a professor in the clinical psychology program at George Mason University in Washington, D.C. (Box 2.1); Dr. Jackie Persons (Box 2.2) is a psychologist in private practice in California; and Dr. Pat Alexander is chief psychologist in a state hospital in Mississippi (Box 2.3). You will notice that these psychologists have full and varied schedules.

PROFILE BOX 2.1

DR. JAMES E. MADDUX

I received my Ph.D. in Clinical Psychology in 1982 from the University of Alabama (Tuscaloosa) after completing a clinical psychology internship at what is now the Oregon Health Sciences University in Portland. My first academic position was as an Assistant Professor in the clinical psychology Ph.D. program at Texas Tech University in Lubbock, where I remained for four years. I then became an Assistant Professor in what was then a clinical psychology Psy.D. program (now an APA-accredited Ph.D. program) at George Mason University in the fall of 1985. I have remained at George Mason University, becoming an Associate Professor in 1987 and a Professor in 1994. Over the past 12 years I have held three different administrative positions in the Department of Psychology, including Associate Chair for Graduate Studies, Acting Department Chairperson, and Director of Clinical Training, and I also

Dr. James E. Maddux

spent a year as a Visiting Professor in the Department of Health Psychology at the Free University in Berlin, Germany. Additionally, for six years I was the Editor of the *Journal of Social and Clinical Psychology*. My major research interest is the interface of social and clinical psychology, and I am interested very broadly in ways we can use theories from social psychology to shed light on questions and problems about psychological adjustment and well-being. Most of my research has been concerned with applications of self-efficacy theory and related models of self-regulation and goal attainment.

A Typical Week

One of the best aspects of an academic position, especially in a Ph.D. clinical psychology program, is the variety of the activities you can work on and the variety of people you work with. Because no two days and no two semesters are exactly alike, it is difficult to describe a typical day, a typical week, or even a typical semester. That being said, the following is a composite description of a typical week when my main major responsibilities were teaching graduate courses, providing clinical supervision to four clinical students who were working with clients at our training clinic, serving as a journal editor, serving on the university committees, and serving as Director of the clinical Ph.D. program.

On Monday I worked from home dealing with a variety of emails related to the clinical program. Students and faculty frequently have questions about program policies, and problems and concerns often arise due to the complex and intense nature of clinical doctoral training. For example, several students had questions about their selection of elective courses, and several newer faculty members had questions about dissertation requirements. Then I spent some time in planning for the site visit of our program by the evaluators from the American Psychological Association Committee on Accreditation. All accredited clinical programs are re-evaluated on a regular basis. I worked to coordinate the schedule for the site visitors who must meet with a large number of people (including the dean and the provost) during the brief two-day visit. In the afternoon I had a series of meetings on campus with students. First I met a student for clinical supervision of the services she was providing to a client dealing with a fear of riding in elevators. Next I met one of my research advisees to discuss progress on his dissertation dealing with forgiveness in romantic relationships. After that, I met with a student for whom I was serving as a dissertation committee member. At the end of the afternoon I met with the department chairperson to talk about the plans for the upcoming site visit and some issues regarding our training clinic.

Tuesday morning began with responding to more program-related emails. The rest of the morning was devoted to reviewing my notes for the graduate psychopathology class I was teaching later in the day. Although I had worked in the summer to update readings and prepare my PowerPoint slides, I always like to schedule time the same day to re-read the assigned journal articles and look over my notes. In the afternoon I taught the psychopathology class, which was on generalized anxiety disorder and panic disorder. At the end of the afternoon, I attended the weekly professional seminar featuring a speaker from outside the university who addressed issues regarding working with Latino clients.

Wednesday morning consisted mainly of journal editing work. I received new submissions, which I will either send to one of the Associate Editors or send out for review myself, and exchanged emails with my Associate Editors about editorial decisions. I responded to emails from authors with questions about their submissions, reviewed evaluations received on a manuscript, and prepared a letter to the author explaining my decision. The afternoon was spent in a university committee meeting. This week it was a three-hour meeting of the Human Subjects Review Board, which is responsible for ensuring that all research involving human subjects conducted by university faculty and students is in compliance with federal and state laws and professional ethical standards.

PROFILE BOX 2.2

DR. JACQUELINE PERSONS

I completed my Ph.D. in clinical psychology at the University of Pennsylvania and a postdoctoral internship at the Behavior Therapy Unit at Eastern Pennsylvania Psychiatric Institute, which was then headed by Dr. Joseph Wolpe. Just as I finished my postdoctoral internship, my husband was offered a faculty position at the University of California at Berkeley, a job he very much wanted to take, in part because his family lived in northern California. Although I had been trained to be a researcher, I was not driven to pursue a full-time research career, and so we went to California with a plan for me to work in a clinical setting. I am licensed as a psychologist in California, where I have forged a career that combines clinical work, research, teaching and training, and writing. Since 1995 I've been Director of the San Francisco Bay Area Center for Cognitive Therapy in Oakland, California, a group private practice. At the Center we most often provide treatment

Dr. Jacqueline Persons

for individuals who have mood and anxiety disorders and related difficulties. I see 15 to 20 patients a week and conduct small-scale studies, usually without any grant funding, on questions related to my clinical work. I also hold a non-tenure-track position at University of California at Berkeley in the Psychology Department, where my most common role is to provide clinical supervision for a graduate student in clinical psychology, although I occasionally teach a graduate course. The accomplishments of which I am most proud include my writings on case formulation, especially my first book (*Cognitive Therapy in Practice: A Case Formulation Approach*, published by Norton in 1989) and my most recent one (*The Case Formulation Approach to Cognitive-Behavior Therapy*, published by Guilford in 2008), my success in conducting research as a clinician, and my service as president of the Association for Behavioral and Cognitive Therapies.

A Typical Week

On Monday I often spend the first couple of hours of the day handling email and getting ready for the week. At 11:30 I meet with colleagues in a conference call meeting; we are working to develop an online tool that psychotherapists can use to monitor their patients' progress. In the afternoon I see three or four patients. I also meet with my postdoctoral fellow and volunteer research assistant to work on a database we are creating of information collected in the course of our routine clinical work to monitor our patients' progress in treatment. We are investigating the process and outcome of cognitive-behavior therapy in routine clinical practice and recently submitted a manuscript based on our findings to a journal. In the evening at home I read a manuscript that I have been asked to review for a journal.

Tuesday starts with a session with a patient who is making nice progress in overcoming his obsession that he has contracted AIDS. Then I get ready for the research meeting I lead every other Tuesday. The research meeting is attended by my postdoctoral fellow, the research assistant, and another clinician in the community who, like me, is pursuing research goals in a clinical setting. We discuss the paper based on our archival database. In the afternoon I see three or four patients. I end my workday with a telephone session with a consultant who helps me apply the dialectical behavior therapy skills I'm learning to some of my patients who suffer from borderline personality disorder and similar problems.

On Wednesday I spend the morning working on tasks related to the online monitoring tool and my research. Then I meet with one of my partners to work on solving some problems our group has encountered with our voicemail system. Throughout the day (and all days!), I handle telephone calls and email about clinical services, research, and training. In the afternoon I see three or four patients.

On Thursday I spend the morning working on a chapter on case formulation that I'm writing with a UC-Berkeley graduate student on the topic of case formulation for an edited book. Then I take my lunch to the weekly meeting I hold with my partners for consultation on clinical cases. Afterward I meet with the UC-Berkeley graduate student in clinical psychology whose clinical work I am supervising as she treats a middle-aged man who has bipolar disorder and other problems. I end the day with sessions with two patients.

Friday I meet with a small group of clinicians to whom I provide clinical consultation, and spend some time writing an initial consultation report for one of my new cases. Then I meet with my postdoctoral fellow for clinical supervision and end the day with one or two therapy sessions with patients who come to see me at the end of their workday. Over the weekend I don't usually attend meetings or do any clinical work, but I typically spend several hours in my office on Saturday working on research and writing projects.

PROFILE BOX 2.3

DR. PAT ALEXANDER

I obtained my doctoral degree in clinical psychology from the University of Mississippi, after having careers as a high school teacher and in state government counseling management. I began working as a psychology supervisor in the 1,000-bed state hospital of my state. About nine years ago, I became the chief psychologist of the hospital. Although demanding, this position allows me to use all of the clinical and organizational skills I have developed over the years. My duties involve oversight of our APA accredited predoctoral internship program, assessment team, behavior management programs, and supervision of unit psychologists. I have served on several task forces involving redefining and expanding our psychology career ladder and development of curriculum for

Dr. Pat Alexander

mental health therapist licensure for our state Department of Mental Health. I serve on a variety of hospital committees, including planning, discharge advisory, bed utilization review, and health records.

I am a member of our state psychological association, where I have served as the newsletter editor and the Public Education Coordinator. As a member of the American Psychological Association, I have served as chair of the Public Service Division state and community hospitals section and I am currently serving on the Commission on Accreditation. In my private practice I engage in three different types of activities: evaluating candidates to determine whether they are psychologically suitable for ministry, consulting with lawyers on cases involving damage settlements involving mental issues (mental stability/health or cognitive functioning), and consulting for a state disability agency that determines whether or not a person is disabled from mental impairments (e.g., cognitive functioning, traumatic brain injury, serious mental illness, substance abuse). Although I am busy most of the time, I thoroughly enjoy my work. I like to "fix things," that is, try to improve both processes and people. Although I am not always successful in accomplishing all of my goals, the challenges in attempting to complete my goals are very exciting.

A Typical Week

On Monday I begin checking emails and returning phone calls (including contacting the travel office at APA to make travel arrangements for an upcoming meeting). At 9:00 I interview a job applicant and refer him to the units with appropriate openings. In the afternoon I first meet with the Internship Training Director to offer my assistance and to get an update on a report due next week. I then meet with psychology staff in our satellite crisis centers for weekly clinical supervision. After that, I contact administrative supervisors to develop action plans to correct health records documentation deficiencies I have discovered. The deficiencies can cover a wide range of items, including patients' treatment plans, clinical progress notes, and assessments that are not timely or lack sufficient clinical observations. Following this, I meet an employee who requests advice on the educational requirements associated with some possible career paths. Finally, I begin working on the materials the training director asked me to compile earlier in the afternoon, and I finish the day by checking emails and making some phone calls.

After dealing with my emails on Tuesday morning, the Social Services Director and I conduct a teleconference in-service training session with two of the crisis centers on a new psychosocial assessment we developed. During lunch I make a few phone calls. In the afternoon I attend a hospital committee meeting and then speak with the Nurse Executive to coordinate upcoming training on behavior management principles she has requested for nursing staff that will be provided by one of our psychology interns. Next, I meet with my supervisor at the hospital to discuss the best course of action to take with an employee who is having difficulty in accepting guidance provided in clinical supervision. After checking emails and attending the weekly utilization review for cases above the average length of stay, I leave to attend to my disability private practice.

On Wednesday, after emails and phone calls, I spend the morning wrestling with draft revisions of our credentialing, assessment, and biofeedback policies and send them out to psychology supervisors for feedback. I have clinical supervision with nursing home psychology staff in the afternoon, after which I meet with a doctoral staff member to discuss his concerns about how things are progressing with the new practicum student he is supervising. At the end of the afternoon, after reviewing emails, I realize I will need to work on an evaluation survey for the Commission on Accreditation after work.

Thursday begins with a meeting with one of our psychologists to discuss the ways in which she can meet licensure requirements and some programming issues she has to deal with. Following this meeting, I conduct the last teleconference in-service training presentation with the crisis center. After lunch with my co-workers to discuss hospital issues, I provide some basic orientation for a new staff member. I begin preparing for a meeting with psychology supervisors, where we discuss issues involving professional boundaries and the need for documentation of supervision. After the meeting, two psychology supervisors want to discuss practicum student issues and the supervision role of a former psychology intern who has been hired on our staff.

Friday, after responding to and sending emails, I plan a schedule of recruitment for the next week, meet with a psychology staff member who is interested in a social work field placement, and then talk with her supervisor and the Social Services director. Later, I field phone calls from various staff members dealing with wide ranges of concerns, such as instructions on conducting competency ratings for their supervisees, decreasing the time to respond to requests for psychological evaluations from psychiatrists, and how to best refuse a request from other disciplines to sit in on an individual therapy session. Although I am scheduled to leave at 1:00 p.m. for my private practice, I am delayed another hour after making sure the hospital crisis pager is covered for the weekend and giving the operator my personal cell phone number again as a backup. The rest of the afternoon is devoted to my private practice.

Assessment and Diagnosis

It is virtually impossible to be a clinical psychologist and not do some form of psychological assessment. You may recall from Table 2.1 that Norcross, Karpiak, and Santoro (2005) found that almost two thirds of the respondents to their survey engaged in assessment and diagnosis. As you can see in the profile boxes, all three psychologists spend part of their time in activities that involve psychological assessments and diagnoses. Most commonly, assessment activities involve evaluating the psychological functioning of an individual or a relationship (such as a couple, a parent–child relationship, or a family). Some assessments focus on the way a social unit functions (such as interactions within and between departments of an agency or between an agency and the recipients of the agency's services). The precise nature of the assessment activities depends, to a large part, on the purpose of the assessment. Let's take an example of a psychologist who wants to be able to judge with confidence whether 7-year-old Joshua has behavior problems that are serious enough to justify placement in a special service. The psychologist may focus on whether Joshua's behavior meets criteria for a diagnosis of oppositional defiant disorder. If, however, the psychologist is conducting an assessment prior to beginning parent training, the focus of the assessment will be to gain a precise understanding of the behaviors that the parents wish to change (such as the intensity, frequency, and duration of defiant behavior) and contextual variables that affect Joshua's behavior (such as parental consistency, marital conflict, or the presence of a replacement teacher in the classroom). Thus, if the goal of the assessment is to determine eligibility for a service, assessment may be the sole function of the psychologist's service. On the other hand, even when the primary service is psychotherapy, assessment plays an important role in the planning, monitoring, and evaluation of the intervention.

In the later chapters on assessment you will see the ingenuity with which psychologists have developed scientifically sound assessment tools to assess a host of psychological phenomena in infants, children, adults, and the elderly. Generally speaking, these tools fall into one of several categories that will be discussed in Chapter 6 (interviews and observational systems), Chapter 7 (intellectual and cognitive measures), and Chapter 8 (self-report measures and projective measures). Moreover, as you will learn in Chapter 9, in reaching a clinical formulation most clinical psychologists combine data obtained from a number of assessment methods such as interviewing, self-report measures, observations, performance (or skill) tasks, and reports from informants other than the patient. Dr. Jackie Persons has played a key role in the development of case formulation procedures.

As you will see in Chapter 5, regardless of the precise form and purpose of the assessment activity, all assessments share a primary goal of aiding the understanding of the person's current level of psychosocial functioning. Without a sense of how the person is doing now, in terms of such important human variables as emotions, behaviors, symptoms, and relationships, it is simply not possible to provide meaningful psychological services. However, as you will learn in Chapter 9, psychological assessment is much more than just testing: it involves the collection of multiple types of data that are then integrated into a coherent formulation of the problem experienced by the person or groups being assessed.

In many instances, formulating a diagnosis is part of the assessment process. As we describe in more detail in Chapter 3, diagnoses provide a concise statement about the nature of a person's disorder or dysfunction. Having established a diagnosis, the psychologist can efficiently search the scientific literature to update his or her knowledge of the disorder's etiology, course, prognosis, and beneficial treatments. In the United States the diagnostic system used by clinical psychologists is the *Diagnostic and Statistical Manual of Mental Disorders* (DSM) published by the American Psychiatric Association, of which the most recent version is the DSM-IV-TR. Other countries have adopted the World Health Organization's (WHO) *International Classification of Diseases* (ICD), now in its tenth edition (ICD-10).

 To what extent do you think you would enjoy the challenge of conducting psychological assessments? What would you find most interesting about assessment activities? Are you the kind of person who enjoys addressing questions by gathering and integrating diverse data?

Intervention

Survey data from Norcross, Karpiak, and Santoro (2005) indicated that the majority of clinical psychologists offer psychotherapy. As we describe in Chapters 12 and 13, there is a wealth of evidence to suggest that psychological treatments can be effective in treating a wide range of health problems. In Chapter 14, we provide information about a range of client and clinician factors, including the quality of the therapeutic alliance, that influence the outcome of treatment. As illustrated in the profile boxes, the proportion of time devoted to psychotherapy varies across the different employment settings. However, as we discussed in Chapter 1, psychologists are not the only health care professionals who offer psychotherapeutic services. Many of the services provided by medical practitioners involved the provision of psychoactive medications, a form of treatment that psychologists are permitted to provide in a few jurisdictions, including the Department of Defense and in the states of New Mexico and Louisiana. (See Viewpoint Box 2.1: The Prescription Privileges Debate).

VIEWPOINT BOX 2.1

THE PRESCRIPTION PRIVILEGES DEBATE

The Psychopharmacology Demonstration Project (PDP), conducted by the U.S. Department of Defense in 1991–1997, provided training to clinical psychologists in the military in prescribing psychoactive medications to treat mental disorders in patients age 18–65. This ignited an intense debate around the issue of whether other psychologists ought to have the authority to prescribe medication. Advocates of prescription privileges for psychologists (e.g., Ax et al., 2008) argue that given strong evidence of brain–behavior links, a biological approach to the treatment of psychological disorders is not incompatible with psychological training; they also note that psychologists can be at least as competent as other health care professionals in prescribing medication for psychological disorders. They highlight the fact that most psychoactive medications are prescribed by general practitioners whose training in mental health issues is limited to a few weeks of placement with a psychiatrist. These advocates suggest that underserved segments of the population such as those in rural areas and the elderly could benefit from the extension of prescription privileges to psychologists.

Physicians have strongly opposed the extension of prescription privileges to psychologists, citing the importance of full medical training to prepare the practitioner to understand the impact of psychoactive medication on other physical systems (Rae, Jensen-Doss, Bowden, Mendoza, & Banda, 2008). Within psychology, critics argue that psychologists' distinctive expertise is in the development and application of evidence-based assessment and psychological interventions. They express concern that the inclusion of adequate training in psychopharmacology would inevitably come at the expense of training in psychological issues (e.g., Stuart & Heiby, 2007).

The American Psychological Association has played a key role in providing resources to state associations proposing prescriptive authority. Bills have been introduced and rejected in over a dozen states. To date, two states, New Mexico and Louisiana, and the territory of Guam have legislation granting prescriptive authority to psychologists who have received appropriate training (Munsey, 2008). In New Mexico, psychologists seeking prescriptive authority must complete 450 hours of instruction, followed by a 400-hour supervised practicum serving a minimum of 100 patients, and must pass the Psychopharmacology Exam for Psychologists (PEP) before they can apply for a two-year conditional certificate. As of December 2007, 10 psychologists were prescribing under the two-year conditional certificate, and three had graduated to unrestricted certification. All psychologists with prescriptive authority are required to maintain a collaborative relationship with the patient's primary care physician. In Louisiana, psychologists seeking prescriptive authority are required to complete a postdoctoral master's degree in clinical psychopharmacology and to pass the PEP. As of December 2007, there were 42 medical psychologists in Louisiana with authority to prescribe psychoactive medication in consultation with the patient's physician (Munsey, 2008).

In popular movies and television series, psychotherapy is often presented as a lifelong commitment to frequent treatment sessions with a psychologist or psychiatrist. In reality, the majority of people who receive psychotherapy attend fewer than 10 sessions. A large minority of clients attends only one or two sessions, and the median number of therapy sessions is in the range of 5 to 13. This is true internationally, across clients presenting dramatically different problems (Phillips, 1991).

As the expression "talk therapy" implies, psychotherapy uses verbal means for the therapist to promote change. But what actually happens in psychotherapy? An innovative survey examined this question. In a Web-based questionnaire, the Practice Directorate of the American Psychological Association (APA Practice Directorate, 2003) asked 241 clinical psychologists questions just after they completed a psychotherapy session. Across theoretical orientations, virtually all psychologists reported discussing current stressors related to the client's problems and interpersonal relationships or relationship patterns. The most commonly reported techniques (reported by more than 75% of respondents) were to identify or challenge thoughts, relate thoughts to feelings, focus on affect by validating or labeling emotions, gather information, and guide or direct the client.

 Do you find the idea of offering psychological interventions appealing? Are you surprised to learn that most clients attend very few sessions? Does the idea of helping clients to learn ways to change how they think, feel, and behave interest you?

As we indicated in Chapter 1, different theoretical approaches to psychotherapy emphasize different aspects of human experience in understanding and treating psychological distress and disorder. The dominant approaches include psychodynamic, cognitive-behavioral, experiential, and interpersonal (which, in some forms, is closely related to psychodynamic). Additionally, a number of clinicians describe their orientation as eclectic or integrative, meaning that they blend concepts and strategies from two or more approaches. **Table 2.2** presents data from surveys on the theoretical orientation of clinical psychologists and graduate students in clinical psychology. The general picture suggests that, in North America, a cognitive-behavioral approach is the most popular single orientation among clinical psychologists. This is likely to continue as graduate students also endorse this orientation more commonly than any other. Although cognitive-behavioral approaches are popular, substantial numbers of clinical psychologists describe their practice as eclectic.

TABLE 2.2   Theoretical Orientations of Clinical Psychologists and Clinical Graduate Students

Orientation	Psychologists[a]	Graduate Students[b]
Cognitive-Behavioral	38%	68.9%
Experiential	2%	27.1%
Interpersonal	4%	27.1%
Psychodynamic	15%	27.4%
Integrative/Eclectic	29%	34.3%

Note: In the second column, the total reported exceeds 100% because respondents were permitted to indicate more than one orientation in the survey.
[a] Norcross, Karpiak, and Santoro (2005); [b] Cassin, Singer, Dobson, and Altmaier (2007)

Does the theoretical orientation actually make a difference in what therapists do in sessions? Although the evidence from the APA (2003) online survey revealed a number of commonalities in therapy sessions across clinical psychologists, clear orientation-related differences were also apparent. For example, compared with psychodynamic clinicians, cognitive-behavioral clinicians were significantly more likely to spend time providing psychoeducation by informing the client about the nature of the presenting problem; they were also more likely to encourage the client to ask questions, to collaboratively set an agenda for the session with the client, to encourage the client to engage in specific activities (including homework assignments to be done between therapy sessions), and to teach coping skills. In contrast, compared with cognitive-behavioral clinicians, those espousing a psychodynamic approach were significantly more likely to explore the client's childhood experiences, to relate the client's reactions to the therapist to patterns in the client's family of origin, and to explore dysfunctional patterns of behavior and relationship expectations.

Prevention

You may remember from Chapter 1 that prevention activities are a relatively new addition to the skill set of clinical psychologists. Accordingly, only a small percentage of clinical psychologists devote professional time to this activity. Prevention services are categorized according to the stage in the course of a disorder at which they are introduced. Primary prevention involves the prevention of a disease or disorder before it actually occurs. Secondary prevention is designed to reduce the recurrence of a disease or disorder that has already developed and been diagnosed. Tertiary prevention refers to efforts to reduce the overall disability that results from the disease or disorder.

You will learn more about prevention in Chapter 10. Generally speaking, prevention activities tend to focus on either reducing risk factors or enhancing protective factors. Risk factors are characteristics of an individual or of an individual's life circumstances that increase the likelihood of the development of a disorder. You are probably quite familiar with physical factors such as smoking, being overweight, having high cholesterol levels, and having a family history of heart disease, which are all risk factors for the development of heart disease. Protective factors, on the other hand, are individual or environmental characteristics that lessen the likelihood of eventually developing a disease or disorder. Regular exercise and a diet low in saturated fats are considered protective factors that reduce the risk of developing heart disease. As we describe in more detail in Chapter 10, risk factors for the development of many psychological disorders in children and adolescents include inconsistent discipline, conflict in the family, and parental psychopathology.

Prevention efforts are usually based in community settings, as opposed to institutional settings such as hospitals or private clinical psychology practices. Prevention programs can be offered to large groups of people at a time, such as educating children about ways to resist pressures to abuse alcohol or educating parents about issues around bullying in the schoolyard. Alternatively, prevention programs may be offered in a one-on-one format, as is often done in teaching life skills to individuals already diagnosed with severe mental illness. Most commonly, the role of the clinical psychologist is to develop, implement, and evaluate the prevention programs. The prevention program is often delivered by mental health professionals such as nurses, counselors, or social workers.

Can you recall any prevention programs that were offered when you were in school? What features of the prevention programs did you like and what features do you think might make the programs effective?

Consultation

Clinical psychologists often act in the role of consultant, as Dr. Alexander described in her profile box. Providing information, advice, and recommendations about how best to assess, understand, or treat a client is called **clinical consultation**. When the focus of the consultation is related to developing a prevention or intervention program, evaluating how well an organization is doing in providing a health care or related service, or providing an opinion on policies on health care services set by an organization, the terms **organizational consultation** or "community consultation" are typically used.

Throughout the history of the profession, clinical psychologists have offered clinical consultation. As a member of a multidisciplinary team, a clinical psychologist receives requests to provide guidance about a patient who is under the care of another professional. For example, one of us was asked to suggest how hospital staff could best handle an elderly, demented patient's confusion and growing anger over his inability to understand what was being served to him in his meals. Another request came from a child day care center that wanted help in dealing with a disruptive 2-year-old. It is a common (and highly ethical) practice for a clinical psychologist to request an opinion from a fellow clinical psychologist on how to handle a particularly difficult or challenging assessment or treatment issue that has arisen.

Consultation to agencies often falls into one of several categories: needs assessment, program development, program evaluation, and policy consultation. Needs assessments are required to determine the extent of an unmet health care need in an identified population. A clinical psychologist might be asked, for example, to conduct a needs assessment to determine whether there are mechanisms to ensure that new immigrants are aware of health care services available in their community. Once a needs assessment has established the scope of the need, a psychologist might be hired to develop a program to educate the target population about the available services. The final step involves determining whether or not the program was successful in achieving its goal, by conducting a program evaluation. The program evaluation assesses the extent to which the program was carried out as intended and the extent to which the program objectives were met. Another type of consultation, policy consultation, focuses on determining whether an agency's policy is congruent with its mission or is consistent with professional standards or scientific evidence. For example, a clinical psychologist might be engaged to provide an opinion on the suitability of a health care company's policy regarding reimbursement of psychotherapy services to health care providers.

 How interested are you in consultation services? In what ways do you think consultation skills may be similar to and different from the skills required in providing direct services like psychotherapy?

Research

All clinical psychologists are trained to conduct and evaluate research. University coursework provides initial training in research methods that is put into practice by conducting a doctoral dissertation.

According to APA's ethical code, psychologists must demonstrate a commitment to increasing scientific and professional knowledge as well as a commitment to use that knowledge to improve the conditions of individuals, organizations, and society (APA, 2002a). Whereas all clinical psychologists should be informed research consumers, only a minority of clinical psychologists regularly engage in producing research. Drs. Maddux and Persons both described devoting time to keeping up with the latest research and disseminating this knowledge to other professionals and to the public. In the past, much of the research in clinical psychology came from university settings and was conducted or supervised by clinical psychology faculty members

Some clinical psychologists devote considerable time to conducting research. (*Source:* Media Bakery)

in departments of psychology or in medical schools. University faculty members are typically expected to devote their professional time to research and teaching. With the growing recognition of the need for science-based health care in many parts of the world, it is now increasingly common for clinical psychologists in publicly funded institutions such as hospitals to devote part of their workload to research. Because of psychologists' extensive training in research methodology and statistics, in some instances hospital-based clinical psychologists are employed primarily as researchers, with psychological service delivery as a secondary component of their work. Such psychologists may actually have a greater proportion of their workload devoted to research than most academics have. A survey of university clinical psychology faculty members (Himelein & Putnam, 2001) found that conducting and supervising research accounted for only 17% of professors' work time. Because of the central role that empirical evidence plays in guiding the provision of psychological services, some private practitioners, such as Dr. Persons, have also made it a priority to be regularly involved in research activities.

Clinical psychologists conduct research on an impressive range of topics, including normal human functioning, psychopathology, assessment, intervention, and/or prevention. Let's consider examples of the types of research conducted by clinical psychologists. In studying normal human functioning, clinical psychologists conduct research on personality, memory processes, intimate relationships, parenting, child development, and aging. Clinical psychologists carry out research aimed at improving our understanding of the nature and causes of conditions as varied as sexual pain disorders, depression in the elderly, disruptive behavior disorders, pathological gambling, and insomnia. Measures of perfectionism, anxiety sensitivity, infant pain, trauma, and scores of other phenomena have been developed in recent years. With respect to prevention and intervention, clinical psychologists study resilience in the face of adversity, treatments for marital conflict, early intervention strategies for childhood anxiety disorders, factors that predict premature termination from therapy, and patterns of mental health service use in various countries. To help you locate clinical psychology research, **Appendix 1** provides an overview of the major journals in the field.

Think of your research experiences thus far in your psychology training. Which parts of the research process were most challenging? Which were most rewarding? Are you a person who enjoys formulating testable questions and gathering the data to answer them?

Teaching and Supervision

Full-time professors in clinical psychology engage in different types of teaching activities. They typically teach both undergraduate and graduate courses in psychology, and in some programs they also supervise graduate students in the provision of psychological services. Himelein and Putnam (2001) found that these different teaching activities accounted for 26%, 11%, and 4%, respectively, of the average clinical psychology professor's work time.

Courses

The type of courses taught depends on the professor's areas of specialization and expertise. Undergraduate courses commonly taught by clinical psychology professors include psychopathology, personality theories, human adjustment, interpersonal processes, psychology of women, family psychology, geropsychology, and, of course, introduction to clinical psychology. In addition, these professors teach advanced courses to small groups of graduate students on topics such as professional ethics and issues, psychological assessment, psychotherapy, multicultural counseling, psychopathology, clinical research methods, program evaluation, and health psychology. Dr. Maddux devotes a significant part of his workload to graduate teaching.

University courses are taught by both full-time and part-time professors. In most universities some clinical psychologists who work in the community are employed as part-time instructors and teach one or two undergraduate courses each year. Clinical psychology programs also hire these professionals to teach specialized graduate courses in areas not covered by full-time faculty (e.g., neuropsychology, rehabilitation psychology). Psychologists employed in hospital settings often contribute to the training of both psychology and medical students by offering seminars or workshops on select aspects of clinical psychology.

 What are the qualities that make an excellent teacher? What do you think would be the rewards of teaching others about clinical psychology?

Clinical Supervision

A central part of the training of clinical psychologists involves conducting psychological assessment and intervention. After taking advanced courses in these topics, graduate students provide services to the public under the close supervision of licensed clinical psychologists. Clinical supervision is offered in either a group or an individual format. This first clinical experience under the supervision of a licensed psychologist is called a **practicum**. Some clinical psychology programs operate an in-house psychology training clinic in which faculty members supervise students in the provision of services such as intellectual assessment, diagnostic evaluation, individual therapy, group therapy, and family therapy. All training programs, including those that offer in-house training, rely on the active participation of clinical psychologists in the community in providing training opportunities for graduate students. Within the clinical psychology community, there are strong links between university-based training programs and community-based training in diverse settings. Thus clinical psychologists in general medical hospitals, residential treatment settings for adolescents, rehabilitation centers, and psychiatric hospitals may all contribute to the supervision and training of future clinical psychologists. As an example, all three psychologists profiled earlier in this chapter are engaged in the supervision of practicum students, interns, postdoctoral fellows, or newly graduated psychologists.

Students applying for internships through the Association of Psychology Postdoctoral and Internship Centers (APPIC) between 2005 and 2008 had completed, on average, 1,920 hours of practicum training during their graduate training (APPIC, 2008) Following the completion of all other aspects of their training (with the possible exception of the defense of a doctoral thesis), students then complete a full-time, year-long **internship** in which they are supervised in the provision of psychological services in settings such hospitals, workers' compensation agencies, or community agencies.

Research Supervision

The guidance provided by the research supervisor (who may be a psychologist working outside the university) is evident at many stages of the student's program. Initially, supervision involves assisting graduate students in understanding the research literature in a chosen area and then conceptualizing the research that the student will conduct as part of his or her degree. Before the research is conducted, the supervisor ensures that it will be done in an ethical manner and is approved by an institutional review board. The supervisor typically provides input on study design, sampling considerations, measurement selection, statistical analysis, and, finally, the interpretation and presentation of the research. Dr. Maddux devotes many hours a week to research supervision.

 In considering professors who may supervise your undergraduate research in psychology, have you thought of asking their current students to describe the professors' research supervision skills?

Administration

Of necessity, most clinical psychologists are involved in administrative activities. In a private practice this includes the activities necessary to maintain an efficient and professional business, such as bookkeeping and supervision of personnel. Dr. Persons and Dr. Alexander noted that many hours are devoted to these responsibilities. In institutional settings such as hospitals and universities, psychologists are expected to contribute to the overall running of the institution by involvement in committees and by assuming management positions. For example, clinical psychologists often serve on institutional research ethics boards. In hospital settings, they may sit on committees dealing with research, quality assurance, and community relations. Dr. Alexander is engaged in various multidisciplinary committees within the hospital and at a national level. Within universities, clinical psychologists often serve on committees for the hiring of new professors, the running of the undergraduate psychology program, and the selection of new graduate students. Management positions in universities are likely to include director of the clinical psychology program, director of the training clinic, chair of the psychology department, and possibly dean of the faculty. Clinical psychologists in hospital or related medical settings may be found in a range of management positions including professional practice leader within a mental health team, chief psychologist in a department of psychology, or director of an entire service (e.g., rehabilitation services, child mental health services). The opportunity to assume administrative responsibilities begins in graduate school.

EMPLOYMENT SETTINGS

So far, we have mentioned a range of work settings in which clinical psychologists might be employed. Surveys examining the employment settings of clinical psychologists indicate that the number of clinical psychologists like Dr. Persons working in independent practice has grown considerably in the past three decades (Norcross, Karpiak, and Santoro, 2005). Moreover, even those psychologists employed in an institutional setting like Dr. Alexander frequently have part-time private practices. A large number of clinical psychologists are employed in hospitals or outpatient clinics. Historically, these settings were linked to departments of psychiatry, rehabilitation services for war veterans, or pediatric services. Currently within hospitals, traditional organizational structures based on departments have been replaced by program models in which health professionals, including psychologists, are appointed to a specific program or service and by matrix models in which psychologists have responsibility to both a specific program and general psychological services.

In addition, clinical psychologists are often employed in residential treatment clinics, correctional and forensic settings, government agencies focused on personnel selection and training, and private research and consulting firms. Some clinical psychologists with expertise in public policy are employed in government ministries and departments, public health organizations, and research granting agencies.

THE TWO PILLARS OF CLINICAL PSYCHOLOGY: SCIENCE AND ETHICS

As we emphasized in Chapter 1, the profession of clinical psychology is founded on the application of the results of empirical research to address emotional, behavioral, and neurological problems. In all their activities, whether providing psychological services to the public, planning new research projects, teaching undergraduate courses, or providing input on health care policy matters, it is crucial that clinical psychologists maintain their knowledge of research relevant to their activities (APA, 2002a). All three psychologists profiled in this chapter devote regular time to keeping up to date with research in their field. This is not simply a reflection of the theoretical model in which they are trained—as you will learn in this section, ethical codes of conduct require that all psychologists maintain their knowledge of the scientific foundation of their professional activities. The American Psychological Association developed a code of ethics for psychologists shortly after the Second World War and has revised it several times, most recently in 2002. The code underlines the central role of science in psychology.

> "Psychologists are committed to increasing scientific and professional knowledge of behavior and people's understanding of themselves and others and to the use of such knowledge to improve the condition of individuals, organizations, and society."
>
> APA Ethics Code (2002a, p. 3).

In all their professional activities, clinical psychologists must always remain aware of the importance of questioning one's services. Questions such as "What is the evidence for what I am planning to do?" and "What are the relative risks and benefits to my patients (or students, or research participants) of the course of action I am considering?" must always be foremost in the mind of a clinical psychologist. **Table 2.3** describes the five general principles identified in the APA Ethics Code (2002a) as a guide to professional practice.

Most clinical psychologists agree that professional services should be informed by research evidence. Disagreement starts to creep in when the discussion turns to just "how" the research should inform (or determine) practice and just "what" constitutes research evidence. You may recall that in Chapter 1 we described McFall's manifesto for a science of clinical psychology, which urged that no service should be provided unless there is empirical evidence that it is valid and effective. At the other extreme, some psychologists take a position that they should simply be mindful of general, basic research findings on human functioning. The "what" issue ranges from the position that all personal and clinical experience should be considered research evidence to the position that only the results of experimental studies should constitute the knowledge base of clinical psychology. Of course, very few psychologists hold opinions represented by these extremes; nevertheless, there is considerable

---

TABLE 2.3   The Five General Principles of the APA Ethics Code

- *Beneficence and nonmalficence.* Psychologists are expected to attempt to benefit those with whom they work and avoid doing harm.

- *Fidelity and responsibility.* Psychologists are expected to develop relationships of trust with those with whom they work; they are expected to demonstrate awareness of their professional and scientific responsibilities.

- *Integrity in professional relationships.* Psychologists are expected to promote honesty and truthfulness in the science, teaching, and practice of psychology.

- *Justice.* Psychologists are expected to recognize that all people should have access to benefit from the contribution of psychology; psychologists are expected to avoid bias and to not condone unjust practices.

- *Respect for people's rights and dignity.* Psychologists are expected to respect people's right to privacy, confidentiality, and self-determination.

Source: Adapted from APA, 2002a

variability in how the role of science is interpreted. For example, Peterson (2004) suggested that we should accept that some of the problems facing clinicians cannot be studied by scientific methods. Accordingly, he argued that we must rely on intuition and experience in such cases. In response to this, Nathan (2004) suggested that one must be aware of the potential harm that may occur to patients when there is no science to guide practice. Rather than relying on intuition in such situations, he countered that the best practice in such a scenario would be to offer no service rather than risk providing the wrong or harmful treatment.

Despite the large body of evidence available to clinical psychologists, science cannot provide a research-based solution for each situation confronted by a clinician. From our perspective, an evidence-based approach to clinical services involves the use of the research evidence whenever it is available—however, when no research evidence is available to guide services, the clinical psychologist can optimize services by maintaining a scientific frame of mind. This involves using a systematic, questioning, and self-critical approach to determining the relevance of a service and then monitoring its effects to determine whether the outcome is primarily beneficial or harmful. Lilienfeld, Lynn, and Lohr (2003) suggested this requires the clinician to strike a balance between excessive open-mindedness (i.e., "anything goes") and excessive skepticism (i.e., "only proven services are acceptable"). Science is an evolving compilation of ideas, theories, and facts. Science is also a method of formulating and testing hypotheses. As you will find in Chapter 4, the same type of scientific thinking that influences methodological designs behind multi-million-dollar treatment studies can also be employed by each individual clinical psychologist to ensure that clients receive the most effective services.

So what, exactly, is the problem with the call from Peterson (and many other clinical psychologists) for clinicians to use their intuition and experience to guide their work? Intuition is often described as a felt-sense about something that cannot be entirely described, put into words, or accounted for. From a scientific perspective, the problem with using intuition to guide service delivery is that, by definition, a systematic, questioning, and self-critical approach is the polar opposite of intuition. From a health care system perspective, there is another issue: how would you feel about a dentist, surgeon, or gynecologist using intuition in providing services to you or to someone you care about? Imagine your reaction to a dentist who told you that she *felt* that fluoride treatments were not useful, a surgeon who said he had a *sense* of the tissue that needed to be removed and so did not rely on laboratory analysis, or a gynecologist who said she knew that some women find Pap tests difficult and *guessed* you looked healthy enough so would not bother with the test? Similarly, how would you feel on learning that a psychologist failed to provide a treatment that was known to be effective for a problem such as agoraphobia, explaining that he had a strong intuition that you would be better served by another approach?

So what about relying on clinical experience? After all, it only seems reasonable to assume that experienced clinicians are better than novice clinicians, doesn't it? Unfortunately, this assumption is contradicted by most research on clinical psychologists and other health service providers. Numerous studies have shown that when given identical information, experienced clinicians are no better than clinicians-in-training at making accurate, valid decisions (Garb, 1998). The main reason that experience does not necessarily guarantee the highest quality service is that it is exceedingly difficult to learn from clinical experience. Clinical psychologists must frequently deal with complex and ambiguous situations in which they must make decisions and, in almost all instances, they receive no feedback about the accuracy of these decisions (Garb & Boyle, 2003). Without the possibility of corrective feedback, it is extremely unlikely that those poor practices can be detected and stopped or that good practices can be identified and enhanced. Therefore, a scientifically oriented clinical psychologist must be constantly aware of the need to check his or her assumptions and activities.

We often rely on the basic assumptions of a theoretical orientation to guide our clinical practice. That is, of course, the whole point of a theoretical orientation: it directs the clinician's attention to phenomena and to possible explanations that are deemed most relevant, and it diverts attention from aspects of the client's experience that are deemed irrelevant. It is important to remember, however, that theories of human functioning are essentially maps and that, to truly know whether the map is accurate, it must be put to the test. Sometimes, theories are wrong, and the failure to test a theory can have serious consequences. You may recall from previous psychology courses how Freud became puzzled at the number of young female patients who reported sexual abuse. It seemed inconceivable to him that so many women had been abused as children, so he developed an alternative explanation or theory that these women were expressing sexual fantasies. Freud's theories carried great conviction and were accepted as correct without scientific testing. Surveys conducted many years later revealed that alarming numbers of children of both genders are, indeed, sexually abused. Reliance on the credibility and authority of the proponent of a theory, rather than on data stemming from appropriate tests of the theory, can lead to very serious consequences.

Fortunately, most theorists have permitted their theories to be scientifically tested. The best illustration of this is the work of Carl Rogers. As you learned in Chapter 1, Carl Rogers proposed that therapy must provide a supportive environment in which clients reconnect with aspects of themselves and thereby discover their potential for growth. Rogers balanced his own strong convictions with powerful advocacy of the need for research into psychotherapy. He masked the identity of his clients, then provided researchers with transcripts of his therapy sessions. Truax (1966) analyzed sessions of a successful long-term therapy case to determine whether client-centered therapy's key therapeutic condition of *unconditional positive regard* occurred and, if it did, whether it was linked to positive client outcomes. Contradicting Rogers' own model, Truax found that Rogers did not provide positive regard unconditionally. Instead, (consciously or unconsciously) he employed empathy, acceptance, and directiveness as reinforcers of selective client behavior. In other words, consistent with basic learning models, Rogers *shaped* client behavior over the course of the therapy and used the reinforcers of empathy and acceptance to bring about client change. So, for example, he paid more attention when the client talked about emotions than he did when the client talked about other issues. This is, of course, important information about how a therapist can help a client change, but it also illustrates that the client-centered condition of *unconditional* positive regard is not likely to be a key aspect of successful treatment. We owe a debt of gratitude to Carl Rogers for being more concerned to learn about the process of change than he was about promoting his own views. Adopting a scientific position involves putting our ideas to the test and risking the discovery that some ideas that make a lot of sense to us, may, in fact, be wrong. The best scientists are driven by curiosity that is combined with openness to input and a willingness to be proved wrong.

How willing are you to put your cherished beliefs to the test? What do you think it requires to submit for evaluation an intervention that you have spent years developing? As a psychologist, would you be willing to gather the data that may show that you were wrong? As a consumer of psychological services, would you prefer to see a psychologist who was 100% convinced that his or her approach is the best or a psychologist who was willing to examine the evidence?

Basing clinical psychology services on research is crucially important, but so is the need to provide services ethically. According to Sinclair (1993), the modern interest in developing ethical codes for research and professional services can be traced to the Nuremberg war crime trials that occurred after the Second World War. After the horrific discovery of atrocities conducted by the Nazis under the guise of medical science, a code of ethics in medical research was developed. This code was the first to incorporate the idea that the person who is being experimented on must understand what is being done and must agree to participate. This concept of **informed consent** now applies both to patients and to research participants and is the cornerstone of professional and research ethical codes. Psychologists also have an ethical obligation to ensure that their services are not affected by their own distress, an issue discussed in **Viewpoint Box 2.2.**

VIEWPOINT BOX 2.2

DISTRESS IN CLINICAL PSYCHOLOGISTS AND HOW THEY DEAL WITH IT

The APA ethical code requires psychologists to be self-aware and to ensure that they do not offer psychological services when their functioning is impaired. Just as any health professional should not offer services when laid low with incapacitating allergies or a vicious flu virus, psychologists should not offer psychological services when their own emotional health gets in the way of doing their job effectively.

Are psychologists psychologically healthy?

Psychologists are not immune from the life events that affect everyone. Like everyone else, psychologists experience painful events such as the death of a loved one, serious illness, or accident. Psychologists are human—they sometimes doubt their professional competence, they have children who get into trouble, they argue with their partners, worry about their elderly parents, and feel lonely when they are away from their friends and loved ones for an extended time. Not surprisingly, in a survey of 522 practicing psychologists, Sherman and Thelen (1998) found that the more life events psychologists experienced, the more impairment in professional roles they reported.

What kinds of work stress do psychologists face?

Like many health care professionals, psychologists face challenges in effectively managing their time, making sure that they find a balance between offering services, writing notes and reports, answering phone calls, supervising training activities, providing service to the profession, and engaging in continuing education to keep up to date with research advances in the field. Furthermore, the nature of their work may expose psychologists to particular stressors. People often wonder how psychologists cope with a professional life spent working with troubled clients who have experienced trauma or abuse, who are angry, sad, afraid, confused, or difficult to get along with. Sherman and Thelen reported that almost three quarters of the psychologists who responded to their survey worked with difficult clients who had serious emotional problems or who were suicidal.

Are psychologists traumatized by their work?

It has been suggested that working with people who have experienced trauma can cause psychologists to experience symptoms such as intrusive thoughts, extreme distress, and changes in beliefs and attitudes. This phenomenon has been referred to as vicarious traumatization, burnout, compassion fatigue, and secondary traumatic stress. Although there has been a great deal of clinical attention to this phenomenon, there has been relatively little systematic research on the topic. A review by Sabin-Farrell and Turpin (2003) found evidence that mental health professionals have emotional responses to hearing traumatic material, but noted that these responses are a natural and short-term reaction. Some studies have found more intense psychological distress to be associated with the percentage of trauma survivors in the caseload and to being newer to that type of work. Research has not demonstrated evidence that working with trauma survivors is associated with changes in beliefs and attitudes.

How do psychologists cope?

Research has found that psychologists engage in a number of health-promoting activities. Work-related strategies include taking breaks during the workday, consulting with colleagues on difficult issues, practicing good time management including scheduling time for paperwork and phone calls, and limiting the caseload in terms of both volume and in the types of clients seen. Other health-promoting activities included devoting time to hobbies, taking vacations, engaging in regular exercise, and taking part in church and spiritual activities. A survey of 595 psychologists conducted by Rupert and Kent (2007) underlined the importance of a sense of humor, maintaining a balance between work and personal life, and spending time with friends and family. In dealing with personal and professional challenges, psychologists engage in constructive problem-solving. Psychologists also seek psychological services to address serious difficulties. So, just as a dentist needs to practice oral hygiene and have regular checkups, psychologists need to adopt healthy lifestyles and seek professional help when they encounter difficulties.

 How easy is it for you to maintain a healthy balance in your life? Are there coping strategies that you use now that would help you if you were to become a clinical psychologist?

TRAINING IN CLINICAL PSYCHOLOGY

Psychology programs are extremely popular in all universities and colleges. For many years, clinical psychology has been the most popular field within graduate programs in psychology. Clinical psychology programs attract far more applications than do other graduate programs in psychology, and they also graduate more students than do other psychology programs. The 2006 data for American universities show that 34% of Ph.D.s in psychology was in clinical psychology. In comparison, 13% of Ph.D.s awarded that year was in counseling psychology and 4% were in school psychology (National Opinion Research Center, 2007). The primary employment activities of those receiving a psychology Ph.D. in 2006 were providing professional services (38%), teaching (30%), research and development (24%), and administration (8%); secondary activities were research and development (31%), teaching (19%), administration (14%), and providing professional services (9%) (National Opinion Research Center, 2007). Data compiled by the American Psychological Association Center for Workforce Studies illustrate that if all types of doctorates are considered (Ph.D., Psy.D., and Ed.D.), the proportion receiving a clinical degree represents almost half of the psychology doctorates (47%), with 8% receiving a doctorate in counseling psychology and 6% a doctorate in school psychology (APA Center for Workforce Studies, 2007).

Models of Training in Clinical Psychology

Three models guide the training of clinical psychologists: the scientist-practitioner model, the clinical scientist model, and the practitioner-scholar model (McFall, 2006). Most doctoral programs awarding the Ph.D. in clinical psychology endorse the scientist-practitioner model. This training model was first endorsed by the APA at a training conference held in Boulder, Colorado (Raimy, 1950) and is known as the *Boulder model*. In the **scientist-practitioner model**, graduate students must develop and demonstrate competencies in research and psychological service provision. As in any other Ph.D. program, students demonstrate competency in research by undertaking original research, which they write up in a dissertation and successfully defend in an oral examination. Clinical skills, such as interviewing, test administration, assessment report writing, psychotherapy, and clinical consultation, are learned in practicum training throughout the program. These skills are enhanced and refined during the internship year, a period in which the student is employed full-time to deliver psychological services under the supervision of licensed psychologists in an organized health care setting. The guiding philosophy underlying the scientist-practitioner model is that clinical psychologists should be capable of producing research and utilizing empirical evidence to guide their clinical services. There is substantial variability among scientist-practitioner–oriented programs regarding the relative balance of science and practice in training and, more importantly, regarding the manner in which students are trained in the integration of science and practice. Some programs that strongly promote the development of research skills now identify themselves as espousing a **clinical scientist model**, a model in which the primary goal is to have graduates be equipped to contribute to the knowledge base of psychology and related disciplines.

In the 1950s and 1960s, most graduates from Boulder model programs were employed in practice settings with primary responsibility for clinical service. These psychologists very rarely conducted any research after completing the doctoral dissertation. At a training conference in Vail, Colorado, participants expressed their dissatisfaction with the manner in which the scientist-practitioner model was applied in many training programs and developed a new model, the **practitioner-scholar model**, which was refined at subsequent conferences (Peterson et al., 1991). The practitioner-scholar model was designed to emphasize training in the clinical skills that most clinical psychologists would need in a service setting and to place less emphasis on research skills taught in Ph.D. programs. Programs training students in the practitioner-scholar model offered a different degree, the Psy.D. Many Psy.D. programs have developed research requirements that include considerable research training and the completion of a research project. Compared with Ph.D. Programs, Psy.D. programs place less emphasis on experimental designs and large sample analyses and greater emphasis on naturalistic designs and the evaluation of individual cases or service-oriented programs. Psy.D. programs are designed to train research consumers who are informed by science in their service activities but who do not need the skills to conduct research.

Ph.D. programs in professional psychology are offered by universities; Psy.D. programs are found both at universities and in free-standing professional schools. Many in the profession have expressed concerns about the proliferation of the free-standing schools. Critics note factors that negatively affect the quality of students' training, including larger class sizes, lower financial support, and an over-reliance on part-time instructors with little experience in research or teaching (McFall, 2006).

The main distinction between Ph.D. and Psy.D. models of training is the weight given to science and practice. Using survey data from APA accredited scientist-practitioner and practitioner-scholar programs, Cherry, Messenger, and Jacoby (2000) found distinct profiles consistent with the nature of each model. Students in both types of program had comparable amounts of clinical service delivery during their training, but students in scientist-practitioner programs were more involved in research than were students in practitioner-scholar programs. Similarly, graduates of both programs spent the majority of their professional time providing clinical services (around 60%), whereas graduates from scientist-practitioner programs spent more time than did graduates from practitioner-scholar programs in research activities (10% versus 2%). There are other important factors to consider, however, in selecting a training program. Norcross, Castle, Sayette, and Mayne (2004) compared the characteristics of APA-accredited clinical psychology programs offering Ph.D. and Psy.D. degrees. Clinical-scientist Ph.D. programs accepted, on average, 11% of applicants, scientist-practitioner Ph.D. programs accepted 17% of candidates, and Psy. D. programs accepted an average of 41% of applicants. Acceptance rates were higher in the free-standing professional schools (50%) than they were in university-based Psy.D. programs (34%). Financial support is higher and tuition costs lower in Ph.D. programs than in Psy.D. programs, with 84% of students entering clinical-scientist Ph.D. programs receiving full financial support in terms of fee waivers and assistantships; the comparable figures for scientist-practitioner Ph.D. programs was 57%, for university-based Psy.D. programs 38%, and for students in a free-standing professional school only 9%. In terms of theoretical orientation, there are some clear differences in programs as well. Although behavioral and cognitive-behavioral orientations are the dominant orientation in all clinical psychology programs, the highest number of faculty endorsing cognitive-behavioral orientations is in Ph.D. programs (44.2% versus 28% in Psy.D. programs); humanistic/phenomenological approaches are more commonly endorsed by faculty in free-standing professional schools (16%) than they are by faculty in university-based Ph.D. (8%) or Psy.D. programs (9%). In general, the class size in Psy.D. programs is much larger than in Ph.D. programs.

Which training model appeals most to you? How do you weigh the benefits of higher acceptance rates against the disadvantages of lower funding in free-standing professional programs? If you were seeking services, would it matter to you whether the psychologist was trained in a university-based program or in a free-standing professional school?

Accreditation of Clinical Psychology Programs

The American Psychological Association (APA) was the first to develop an **accreditation** process designed to ensure that training programs maintain standards that meet the profession's expectations for the education of clinical psychologists. The APA Committee on Accreditation evaluates the quality of clinical psychology training in both clinical training models. A program that receives accreditation from APA has met, therefore, the high standards of training set by the profession, and graduates from the program are likely to receive some of the best training available in clinical psychology. Students are strongly advised, therefore, to seek training in an accredited clinical psychology program. A list of accredited programs can be found at http://www.apa.org/ed/accreditation/doctoral.html

A major challenge facing all training programs is to ensure that students are prepared to provide psychological services to an increasingly diverse population. Data from the 2000 U.S. census indicate that 1 of 4 Americans was of a race other than White (U.S. Census Bureau, 2002). Hispanics represent the largest minority group, accounting for 15% of the population; Blacks are the second largest minority group (13.5%), followed by Asians (9.5%), American Indians and Alaska Natives (1.5%), and Native Hawaiians and other Pacific Islanders (.33%) (U.S. Census Bureau, 2008). Because the issue of diversity is influenced by geographical, historical, and sociological factors, there is no single way for clinical psychology training to address diversity training. As an example, think of the challenges for a training program in developing a curriculum and a set of training experiences to educate students in working with indigenous peoples. Such programs in the United States, Canada, and New Zealand would look very different for several reasons. One reason for these differences would be the degree of cultural heterogeneity within the indigenous population (greater in North America than in New Zealand). Another reason for the differences would stem from the history of relations between the indigenous communities and the dominant culture in each country. The history of open conflict and of treaty agreements is starkly different when comparing, for example, the Native Americans in the United States, the First Nations and Inuit in Canada, and the Maori in New Zealand.

Diversity is more than culture and language, however. Clinical psychologists must be aware that diversity encompasses age, income, sexual orientation, disability, family structure, and geographical location. Those wishing to provide services in a rural setting, for example, need to be aware of the distinct nature of stressors people face in rural areas (e.g., higher levels of unemployment and accidents) and of the fact that rural areas tend to have higher levels of indigenous people and a lower overall level of education compared with urban settings (Helbok, Marinelli, & Walls, 2006). Because of the myriad ways in which diversity is expressed, it is highly unlikely that all clinical psychologists could develop special knowledge of all the types of diversity they may encounter. What is more important (and more respectful of the ways in which diversity might be expressed among a psychologist's clients), therefore, is for a psychologist to (a) be aware of diversity issues, (b) be open to discussing these issues with clients (when appropriate), (c) have the interpersonal skills to effectively communicate about these issues, and (d) have the research skills to interpret and design research that is sensitive to diversity factors (cf. Whaley & Davis, 2007). Attention to diversity issues requires a balancing act in which universal human norms, specific group norms, and individual characteristics are considered in tandem with the continuum of normal–abnormal behavior.

LICENSURE IN CLINICAL PSYCHOLOGY

Health care professionals are licensed to provide their services in the jurisdiction in which they practice. Licensed health care professionals, such as clinical psychologists, must meet minimal requirements for their academic and clinical training and are required by law to provide ethical and competent services. They are also regulated by a professional organization (e.g., state licensing boards) that holds them accountable for their professional activities. State licensing boards help citizens to identify qualified practitioners and have the power to suspend or remove the license of a person whose professional practice has been incompetent or unethical. Without some form of licensing there is no regulatory body to ensure that the public is protected when receiving health care services. To be licensed as a psychologist, the person must meet requirements including education, examination, and supervised experience.

Licensure requirements in clinical psychology vary from country to country. In the United States, doctoral training is required to become a clinical psychologist. In most European countries, a master's degree is required, whereas in other countries, such as Canada, Australia, New Zealand, and Britain, doctoral-level training is preferred, although it may be possible for someone with master's-level training to become licensed as a clinical psychologist. In some countries, such as New Zealand, registration is compulsory for psychologists working in the public sector but is optional (although strongly recommended) for psychologists in private practice.

Licensure usually requires that the candidate has successfully completed a period of supervised practice. To become a psychologist, it is necessary not only to have the knowledge, but also to have demonstrated that you have the skills to put the knowledge into practice effectively before you can use the title "psychologist." In some states, training in an accredited program (or training comparable to that received in an accredited program) is required for licensure. In some jurisdictions, the supervised practice included in doctoral training is sufficient for licensure, but in others, the candidate must also have successfully completed a period of postdoctoral supervision.

To assist students who may be considering a career in clinical psychology, **Appendix 2** describes procedures for applying to graduate school in clinical psychology. The appendix begins with the important question of how to decide whether pursuing training in clinical psychology is the right choice for you. Subsequent sections address whether you would be eligible for admission to a doctoral program in clinical psychology, the application process itself, and, finally, strategies to strengthen your application.

Doctoral-level training in clinical psychology is broad based and prepares the student to eventually work in a variety of settings. As the practice of psychology in the United States has become more complex, there has been an increasing trend toward specialization. Psychologists who wish to develop advanced skills in a specialized area can seek additional training and experience. This training and experience can be evaluated by peers, and specialty certification can be received from a variety of specialty boards listed in **Table 2.4.**

TABLE 2.4   American Board of Professional Psychology: Specialty Boards

- The American Board of Behavioral Psychology

- The American Board of Clinical Psychology

- The American Board of Clinical Health Psychology

- The American Board of Clinical Neuropsychology

- The American Board of Counseling Psychology

- The American Board of Family Psychology

- The American Board of Forensic Psychology

(Continued)

- The American Board of Group Psychology
- The American Board of Psychoanalysis in Psychology
- The American Board of Rehabilitation Psychology
- The American Board of School Psychology
- The American Board of Clinical Child and Adolescent Psychology
- The American Board of Organizational and Business Consulting Psychology

SUMMARY AND CONCLUSIONS

Clinical psychologists engage in diverse activities and are employed in many different settings. Graduate training in clinical psychology involves coursework, supervised practicum training, a doctoral dissertation, and a full-time internship. There is debate within the field about the relative weight that should be given to research in both training and the practice of clinical psychology. An increasing number of accredited programs have well-developed training models that vary in research emphasis. That being said, both science and ethics are important in the practice of psychology. Anyone considering a career in clinical psychology should carefully consider the licensing requirements before undertaking a course of graduate study in psychology.

Critical Thinking Questions

What role should intuition play in the practice of clinical psychology?

What is the usefulness of theories in the practice of clinical psychology?

How can a psychologist prepare for all the diversity he or she will encounter in a professional career?

How does training in the different models of clinical psychology (scientist-practitioner, practitioner-scholar, and clinical scientist) prepare students for different types of positions in clinical psychology?

What are the advantages and disadvantages of psychologists having the privilege of prescribing psychoactive medication?

Key Terms

accreditation: process designed to ensure that training programs maintain standards that meet the profession's expectations for the education of clinical psychologists

clinical consultation: provision of information, advice, and recommendations about how best to assess, understand, or treat a client

clinical scientist model: training model that strongly promotes the development of research skills

informed consent: ethical principle to ensure that the person who is offered services or who participates in research understands what is being done and agrees to participate

internship: period of supervised training in the provision of psychological services that is a requirement of the doctoral degree; sometimes referred to as residency; usually a one-year, full-time period

licensure: regulation to ensure that minimal requirements for academic and clinical training are met and that practitioners provide ethical and competent services; regulation of the profession helps in protecting the public when receiving services

organizational consultation: services to an organization focused on developing a prevention or intervention program, evaluating how well an organization is doing in providing a health care or related service, or providing an opinion on policies on health care services set by an organization

practicum: initial supervised training in the provision of psychological services that is a requirement of the doctoral degree; usually part-time

practitioner-scholar model: training model designed to emphasize clinical skills and competencies as a research consumer

scientist-practitioner model: training model designed to emphasize competencies in research and psychological service provision

ADDITIONAL RESOURCES
Books

Barnett, J. E., & Johnson, W. B. (2008). *Ethics desk reference for psychologists.* Washington, DC: American Psychological Association.

Hersen, M., & Gross, A. M. (Eds.). (2007). *Handbook of clinical psychology. Volume 1: Adults.* New York: John Wiley and Sons.

Hersen, M., & Gross, A. M. (Eds.). (2007). *Handbook of clinical psychology. Volume 2: Children and adolescents.* New York: John Wiley and Sons.

Check It Out!

American Board of Professional Psychology http://www.abpp.org provides information on a variety of postdoctoral specialty designations.

American Psychological Association http://www.apa.org provides information on accreditation and lists accredited programs, and also gives links to licensing organizations in the United States.

Association of State and Provincial Psychology Boards http://www.asppb.org is the association of Canadian and U.S. licensing boards in psychology.

Australian Psychological Society http://www.psychologicalsociety.com.au provides information on licensure in Australia, including an assessment of psychology qualifications for candidates from overseas who wish to be registered as a psychologist in Australia.

British Psychological Society http://www.bps.org.uk includes an excellent publication, *So you want to be a psychologist,* that is packed with information about training and careers in psychology in the United Kingdom.

Canadian Psychological Association http://www.cpa.ca provides information on accreditation as well as listing accredited programs. The site also gives links to licensing organizations in Canada.

New Zealand Psychological Society http://www.psychology.org.nz contains links to the regulatory body, the New Zealand Psychologists Board.

CHAPTER 3

Classification and Diagnosis

INTRODUCTION

Every person is unique: each of us has his or her own aspirations, goals, challenges, vulnerabilities, and problems. Everyone is influenced by genetics, physiology, life experiences, and current life circumstances. Yet as we all know from daily experience, in order to describe, understand, and predict the responses of others, we must search for common elements of human behavior in this ocean of uniqueness. To manage the complexities of life we tend to categorize, classify, and search for patterns. Without a way to conceptualize and categorize the reactions of friends, family members, and coworkers, it would be impossible for us to navigate through life.

Classification is also a central element of all branches of science and social science. A classification system allows scientists to organize, describe, and relate the subject matter of their discipline, whether it includes subatomic particles, microscopic forms of life, social systems, or celestial bodies. A range of features can be used to classify objects or concepts, including form, function, and purpose. Moreover, any object can be classified in a number of ways: a stone can be classified based on its composition, its shape, its value, its site of origin, or the geological period in which it was formed. As we will see in this chapter, two key aspects of the adequacy of classification systems are validity and utility (Kendell & Kablensky, 2003). **Validity** refers to the extent to which the principles used in classifying an object are effective in capturing the nature of reality. **Utility** refers to the usefulness of the resulting classification scheme. Another critically important issue we will discuss in the chapter is the underlying structure of the classification system.

Classification can be based on a **categorical approach**, in which an object is determined to either be a member of a category or not. The assumption underlying categorical classification is that there is an important qualitative difference between objects that are members of a category and those that are not. An extreme example of a categorical approach is to classify objects as either living or nonliving. A categorical approach to psychopathology involves assigning a diagnosis such as major depressive disorder: the person is judged to have the disorder or not to have the disorder. In a categorical classification, system categories may or may not be overlapping, but members of a category should be very similar to one another.

In contrast, a **dimensional approach** to classification is based on the assumption that objects differ in the extent to which they possess certain characteristics or properties. This approach focuses on quantitative differences among objects and reflects the assumption that all objects can be arranged on a continuum to indicate the degree of membership in a category. Weight and height are prime examples of ways that dimensional approaches are used to classify objects or people. Within a dimensional classification system the different dimensions may or may not be related, but it is essential that the dimensions reflect significant higher-order constructs rather than simple descriptive features (e.g., a construct such as neuroticism, rather than specific psychological phenomena such as sadness, nervousness, loneliness, poor self-esteem, or poor self-confidence). In the field of child psychopathology, researcher **Thomas Achenbach** has gathered information about children's difficulties from multiple informants and then used factor analysis to identify the symptoms that tend to co-occur. Achenbach's work has yielded two broad-band dimensions of problems: externalizing problems and internalizing problems. Externalizing problems are acting-out problems such as yelling, destroying things, stealing, and showing aggression. Internalizing problems refer to feelings of sadness, worry, and withdrawn behavior. Using a dimensional approach, a child's functioning could be described according to

How do you categorize people? (*Source:* Stockphhotopro/Stock4b)

the intensity of externalizing and internalizing problems. Later in the chapter we will examine ways in which these two dimensions may underlie psychopathology across the age range.

Take a moment and think about how you classify people, including your friends, family members, classmates, and even strangers you see on a bus or in a coffee shop. What qualities do you tend to use in classifying them? Do you look at physical characteristics? Style of dress? Interpersonal style? Do you tend to think in terms of categories (e.g., friendly or not friendly) or dimensions (e.g., friendliness) when you compare people you know?

TABLE 3.1   The Uses of a Diagnostic System

- Provide a concise description of essential aspects of the patient's condition

- Reflect best current scientific knowledge of psychopathology

- Provide a common language for clinicians, researchers, and, increasingly, patients to use in discussing mental health conditions

- Indicate possible causes of the current condition (i.e., etiology)

- Indicate possible future developments in the condition (i.e., prognosis)

- Provide guidance on possible co-existing problems or conditions that should be evaluated

- Provide guidance on treatment options to be considered

- Provide a key term that can be used by clinicians to search the scientific literature for most current information on the condition

- Provide a framework for determining reimbursement of health services and eligibility for special programs or services

---

Whether based on a categorical or a dimensional approach, a **diagnostic system** is a classification based on rules used to organize and understand diseases and disorders. When these decision-making rules are applied to the symptoms of a specific individual, the classification system yields a **diagnosis** that concisely describes the symptoms that comprise the person's condition. **Table 3.1** lists some of the purposes of diagnostic systems used by psychologists and psychiatrists. Most health care practitioners are generally in favor of using diagnostic systems, for all the reasons listed in the table. Despite the advantages of diagnosis, there are also possible drawbacks, such as stigmatization of the person receiving the diagnosis and the potential for an inaccurate diagnosis to result in harmful or inappropriate treatment. A reality faced by most health care providers (whether practicing in an institutional setting such as a hospital or in a private practice setting), is that it is necessary to diagnose a patient to determine whether the patient is eligible for certain services (e.g., extra academic support for students with learning disabilities). Furthermore, many managed health care companies require a diagnosis before they will agree to reimburse the clinician for services.

As we discussed in Chapter 1, modern attempts to classify and diagnose abnormal human behavior can be traced to **Emil Kraepelin**, whose initial work on dementia praecox (now called schizophrenia) and manic-depressive insanity (now called bipolar mood disorder) set the stage for current psychiatric diagnostic systems. The so-called neo-Kraepelinian approach to classification has several specific characteristics. These include viewing each diagnosis as a medical disease, using specific criteria to define a category, and emphasizing the importance of diagnostic reliability (Blashfield, 1991). In the past few decades, this approach to psychiatric classification has been augmented with elements of a **prototype model**. The defining feature of the prototype model approach is that members of a diagnostic category may differ in the degree to which they represent the concepts underlying the category. As an example, dogs are more prototypic of the category "mammals" than are platypuses. Applying the prototype model to psychiatric diagnosis implies that not all people receiving the same diagnosis have exactly the same set of symptoms. Accordingly, in contrast to strict neo-Kraepelinian assumptions, two people with the same diagnosis may not have exactly the same disorder and therefore may require somewhat different treatment.

In this chapter we will present the classification and diagnostic systems most commonly used by clinical psychologists. The main example we will examine is the *Diagnostic and Statistical Manual of*

Mental Disorders of the American Psychiatric Association. We will concentrate much of our discussion in this chapter on determining the validity and utility of a diagnostic system. We begin by examining what constitutes abnormal human behavior and how scientists try to understand the ways such behaviors develop into full-blown clinical disorders.

DEFINING ABNORMAL BEHAVIOR AND MENTAL DISORDERS

As we mentioned in Chapter 1, clinical psychologists now provide a range of psychological services to people with and without diagnosable conditions. Therefore you may wonder who cares about determining what constitutes abnormal behavior. The quick answer is that most of us care about whether our experiences and behaviors are normal or abnormal. In fact, many people consult psychologists to find out whether the problems and symptoms they (or their loved ones) are experiencing are normal or abnormal. For example, Ryan may be very concerned that he and his partner are having occasional disagreements, Rebecca may be concerned that she sometimes feels sad about the recent death of her father, Amanda may be worried about her son Tony, who counts backward from 100 and says a prayer every time he begins to feel nervous, and Courtenay may be worried by the frequent thoughts of hurting herself that seem to be put into her mind by other people. In all likelihood the first two clients are experiencing normal, predictable events that occur to almost everyone in a similar situation. A responsible psychologist should convey this information to the clients and determine whether any treatment is truly warranted. In some cases, brief psychoeducation and reassurance may be the only services that are required. In contrast, the child of the third client may be developing a clinical disorder (depending on how much the activities interfere with his daily functioning) and the fourth client is clearly having an experience that is abnormal. In these latter two cases, the psychologist is likely to recommend further assessment and treatment.

Individuals may seek psychological services to find out whether what they are experiencing is normal. (Source: Media Bakery)

Abnormal behavior is not just rare, unusual, or bizarre behavior. Determination of whether a behavior is abnormal requires knowledge of the context in which the behavior occurs. Consider the following behaviors: Lizzie throws herself on the floor when asked to do anything such as take a bath, tidy up her things, or stop an enjoyable activity; Paul cannot be left alone with the family pets as he treats them roughly; Justin says he and his stuffed turtle are going on a magic adventure; Heather often rubs her genital area in public; Danielle cries uncontrollably for extended periods and is disinterested in food. Are these behaviors abnormal? Without more information, we cannot say. One important issue is the person's age. We will interpret Lizzie's temper tantrums and oppositional behavior differently according to whether she is 2, 22, or 82. If she is two-years-old there is likely no cause for alarm. Although the behavior would be grossly abnormal for both a 22-year-old and an 82-year-old, it is likely that the underlying cause would be different at different ages. Similarly, rough treatment of animals is not unusual in a preschool-age child but is often associated with serious psychopathology when it occurs in older children. We cannot judge the behavior of Justin or Heather without knowing their ages: what would be age-appropriate in a very young child would be very troublesome in an adolescent or adult. Danielle's sad behavior cannot be understood without knowing the context; if she has just learned of the death of a loved one, her behavior is likely part of a normal reaction to grief. Her cultural heritage will also contribute to the way in which her grief is expressed: in some cultures a grieving person is expected to appear outwardly unmoved by a loss, whereas in other cultures it may be common for the person to wail and rip her clothing. Diagnostic criteria for many childhood disorders specify that the symptom must be developmentally inappropriate. Therefore the clinician must have a good sense of the range of normal behavior in a particular developmental period in order to be able to judge what is abnormal.

Cultural heritage influence the way grief is expressed. (Source: Media Bakery)

Developmental Psychopathology

A **developmental psychopathology** approach examines problem behavior in relation to the milestones that are specific to each stage of development. This approach recognizes biological and behavioral systems as constantly changing. It also emphasizes the importance of major developmental transitions (such as starting day care, learning to speak, going to school, or puberty) as well as disruptions to normal patterns of development (such as loss of a parent, the effects of poverty, or exposure to trauma). Central to this approach is a reliance on empirical knowledge of normal development. So, for example, in understanding problems in very young children, it is essential to be informed by research on a wide range of issues, including interpersonal attachment, cognitive development, and sleep patterns. Understanding difficulties that are evident in preschool-age children requires, in particular, knowledge of language development and of ways that adults promote children's self-esteem and self-control. Problems in school-age children can be considered in the context of what we know about academic functioning, peer relationships, and harmonious families.

The developmental psychopathology approach has been particularly useful in understanding problems of infancy and childhood, but it can also be applied to help us understand the challenges of later phases in development such as retirement. A developmental psychopathology approach involves not only a snapshot of the client's current difficulties, but also consideration of the course of the problem if left untreated. The adoption of this approach has allowed clinical psychologists to draw on a vast literature about parenting, child neglect and abuse, and the effects of conflict on family members when considering diagnostic issues.

Diagnosis

No diagnosis is based on a single symptom. Diagnostic criteria always include a cluster of symptoms that co-occur. Medical students often report that in learning about different disorders they recognize symptoms that they have experienced and worry that they may suffer from the serious disorder they are studying. Parents, too, hear about symptoms that are associated with childhood disorders and may be

Children and adults express happiness in different ways. (*Source:* Media Bakery)

tempted to assign an amateur diagnosis of attentiondeficit/hyperactivity disorder to the child at the next table in a restaurant who is whooping with delight and flicking food at a friend.

Much has been written about the degree to which personal, cultural, or professional values influence the determination of what is abnormal or disordered. In defining abnormality it is extremely important to rely on scientific evidence, not just value judgments. For example, beliefs based on theoretical models of human functioning may, at times, interfere with an ability to see forms of psychological distress and suffering. One of the clearest examples is the diagnosis of depression in youth. Although the problem of depression in adults has been recognized for centuries, it is only since the 1980s that mental health professionals have turned their attention to childhood depression. The major reason for this stunning oversight is that, based on tenets of the dominant theoretical model, childhood depression was impossible. According to psychoanalytic models, depression is a disorder of the superego. It is therefore impossible to develop depression until the stage of development at which the superego emerges. Prior to this stage, a child's psyche is not sufficiently developed to use the types of defenses that result in the experience of depression. Simple application of behavioral models developed on adults also made it impossible to detect depression in children. A primary symptom of adult depression is sadness. However, children express both happiness and sadness in different ways from adults. A very young child may laugh aloud expressing spontaneous pleasure, she may sing, or skip exuberantly. Such overt expressions of pleasure are unusual in adults. Adults may express sadness verbally, whereas children are more likely to express disinterest or boredom. Another example of age-related similarities and differences in a diagnosis is discussed in **Viewpoint Box 3.1.**

VIEWPOINT BOX 3.1

DEVELOPMENTAL CONSIDERATIONS IN ATTENTION-DEFICIT/ HYPERACTIVITY DISORDER

Attention-deficit/hyperactivity disorder (ADHD) is one of the most common disorders of childhood, affecting one or two children in every school classroom. It is a disorder that is found far more commonly in boys than in girls. Parents usually recall that the first signs of ADHD occurred when their children were toddlers. Diagnostic criteria require the appearance of problems before the age of 7. The most common time for a child to be diagnosed is in elementary school, but some children with the disorder may never receive a formal diagnosis. The diagnosis of ADHD requires evidence of difficulties in multiple settings, not just in the classroom or in the home. Children with ADHD often have other mental disorders, including disruptive behavior disorders, mood disorders, and anxiety disorders.

Children diagnosed with ADHD show persistent and maladaptive symptoms of inattention and/or hyperactivity-impulsivity that are *inconsistent with their developmental level*. This means that the child's behavior is outside the range of behavior that is commonly seen in children of that age. ADHD presents a diagnostic challenge, as there is great variability in very young children's ability to sustain attention, to engage in quiet activities, and to think before acting. There is also considerable instability in children's behavior, so that not all 3-year-olds with extreme inattention, hyperactivity, or impulsiveness go on to develop ADHD.

When children begin school they face increased demands to sustain attention, to work quietly, and to control their impulses. This often sets the stage for teachers to identify those children whose behavior is outside the range of normal behavior. For example, although parents of an only child may feel at a loss in determining whether their son's high-energy, demanding style is just part of being a boy, teachers have the advantage of being able to compare their son to the hundreds of other boys with whom they have worked.

Over the decades, various definitions of the disorder have emphasized different features. Each version of the DSM reflected contemporary efforts to make meaningful distinctions between different subtypes. An important shift occurred in DSM-III when the core difficulties of the disorder were seen as cognitive difficulties with attention rather than as a problem of overactivity. As we have noted before, the way we think about a disorder can lead clinicians to have some blind spots. Because the extremely disruptive physical signs of hyperactivity tend to decrease with age, it was originally thought that this was a chronic disorder of childhood that diminished during adolescence. It was only once the disorder was viewed as based on attention difficulties that it was possible to recognize continuity of symptoms into adulthood. Indeed, adults with ADHD are at risk for disruptions in their work, education, and relationships. Some parents with ADHD will have children who develop ADHD. Accordingly, researchers have recently recognized that, in these circumstances, it may be useful to address parental ADHD symptoms before attempting to train parents in techniques to help children manage their symptoms.

In the search to understand the etiology and course of ADHD, researchers rely on knowledge derived from developmental psychology, cognitive psychology, and psychology of the family. Even though this disorder is biologically based, psychological factors affect its course as well as the development of comorbid disorders often associated with ADHD.

Defining Disorder

The *Diagnostic and Statistical Manual of Mental Disorders, fourth edition-text revision* (DSM-IV-TR; American Psychiatric Association, 2000) defines a mental disorder in the following manner:

"... each of the mental disorders is conceptualized as a clinically significant behavioral or psychological syndrome or pattern that occurs in an individual and that is associated with present distress (e.g., a painful symptom) or disability (i.e., impairment in one or more important areas of functioning) or with a significantly increased risk of suffering death, pain, disability, or an important loss of freedom. In addition, this syndrome or pattern must not be merely an expectable or culturally sanctioned response to a particular event, for example, the death of a loved one. Whatever its original cause, it must currently be considered a manifestation of a behavioral, psychological, or biological dysfunction in the individual. Neither deviant behavior (e.g., political, religious, or sexual) nor conflicts that are primarily between the individual and society are mental disorders unless the deviance or conflict is a symptom of a dysfunction in the individual, as described above."(American Psychiatric Association, 2000 p. xxxi)

This widely accepted definition is somewhat cumbersome. It would be valuable to have a clear, concise definition of mental disorder that could be applied to any behavior or pattern of behaviors to determine whether a disorder is evident. Fortunately there is just such a definition. Wakefield (1992) proposed simply that mental disorder be defined as a **harmful dysfunction**. This widely endorsed definition implies that a classification of abnormality or disorder necessarily involves some value judgment. Thus, the diagnosis of a disorder does not just require the co-occurrence of a set of statistically rare symptoms or behaviors; it also requires that there is something wrong or dysfunctional and that this dysfunction causes harm to the individual or to those around him or her. In other words, some form of pathology is evident and this pathology causes impairment. The requirement that both conditions be satisfied is critical, as it is relatively common to have some form of pathology without it necessarily resulting in impairment. A biological example of this is that a person who has mild hypertension might not be aware of any impairment in functioning. A psychological example is that a fear of heights that does not restrict a person's usual daily activities would not constitute a harmful dysfunction.

Terms such as "dysfunctional" and "harmful" are, of course, somewhat value-laden, but as we presented in the section on developmental psychopathology, research evidence can be used, at least partially, to operationalize these concepts. Widiger (Widiger, 2004; Widiger & Sankis, 2000) has suggested that a third concept—**dyscontrol**—be added to this definition of mental disorder. That is, the resulting impairment must be involuntary or, at least, not readily controlled. This addition is important, especially in legal contexts, because it means that someone who intentionally and wilfully engages in unacceptable behavior such as sexually abusing a child would not be considered to have a mental disorder. Dyscontrol, however, is also a value-laden term that is difficult to operationalize. After all, how can you accurately determine whether or not another person is unable to control a behavior or is simply choosing not to control the behavior? Profile box 3.1 introduces Dr. Eric Youngstrom who research examines bipolar disorder.

PROFILE BOX 3.1

DR. ERIC YOUNGSTROM

As an undergraduate, I was a double major in Psychology and a string of other subjects, starting with Chemistry, then Philosophy, then Liberal Studies and finally Religion. I met my wife as an undergraduate, and we worked together in the same laboratory in graduate school; she too is now a clinical psychologist. We attended the University of Delaware, where we worked closely with Drs. Carroll Izard, Brian Ackerman, and Joseph

Glutting. We moved to Baltimore for her internship, and then to Pittsburgh for my internship and her postdoctoral fellowship, before moving to Cleveland for our first "real" jobs. I am now an Associate Professor of Psychology and Psychiatry at the University of North Carolina at Chapel Hill, licensed in the states of Ohio and North Carolina, and doing research on assessment and bipolar disorder.

Dr. Eric Youngstrom

How did you choose to become a clinical psychologist?

I have always been curious, and my family and friends nurtured and amplified that trait. My mother is a nurse who returned to university to get a Ph.D. in nursing education, and my father is a research chemist. What appealed to me about clinical psychology was that it offered the opportunity to think scientifically about problems (like my father does!) but do things that directly connect with and help people (like my mother does!).

What is the most rewarding part of your job as a clinical psychologist?

The combination of intellectual stimulation and helping people is extremely rewarding. Working with people, one should never be bored. I remember an excellent clinical supervisor telling me that family therapy is often an "edge of the seat" experience, and that once you find that your back is resting against the chair, it is probably an indication that therapy goals have been accomplished and therapy is winding down for that family. I find a similar sense of excitement in trying to understand why some people seem to shake off challenges, and others develop severe problems—and how to help them to regain control of their lives. As a graduate student, I wanted to look at the role of emotions in psychotherapy. I designed research to develop a better understanding of the role of mood in the assessment process. Over the course of my career, I have found this a fascinating issue that, as it turned out, I have continued to explore for many years.

What is the greatest challenge you face as a clinical psychologist?

I think that the great challenge for the field remains how to integrate science and practice. There is no single right answer, but there are many wrong ones. As researchers, psychologists can lose sight of the goal of helping people and, as clinicians, psychologists can stop reading research, and make professional choices based on intuition or conventional wisdom that often will do little to benefit their clients. Although I am licensed to practice psychology in two states, I decided that the way I could help the greatest number of people was to concentrate on teaching and research. A full case load for me as a private practitioner would probably be over 30 patients at a time. I hoped that if I could teach five graduate students a year to be better clinicians, or if I could write articles that affected the care of a large number of people, then I would be helping even more people. Keeping this goal in mind has definitely changed the way that I write articles, as I to try to emphasize the clinical value of my research.

Some people suggest that bipolar disorder in children and adolescents is not a valid diagnosis or that it is overdiagnosed. As a psychologist who has researched bipolar disorder, what is your reaction?

My opinion is that it is a valid diagnosis, but it is overdiagnosed in many clinics; it is also underdiagnosed in other settings. How is this all possible at the same time? First, the validity of a diagnosis (whether or not it is "real") is a separate issue from how often people diagnose it. We have learned that bipolar disorder can be a valid diagnosis and that it has one of the strongest genetic contributions of any major mental illness.

Is bipolar disorder being overdiagnosed? Yes, almost definitely in some settings. Misdiagnosis is most likely when people base diagnosis solely on unstructured clinical interviews. But bipolar disorder is also often missed by clinicians who were taught that it is an "adults only" diagnosis. As scientifically informed practitioners, we cannot ignore the fact that many youths are at biological risk for developing bipolar disorder and that early onset depression may also be a risk factor. If unwarranted skepticism about the validity of the diagnosis causes us to discount the possibility of the diagnosis before we consider the evidence for a particular patient, then we are no longer acting like ideal scientists or clinicians.

How do you integrate science and practice in your work?

Integrating science and practice is a work in progress. The most exciting model that I have found is the Canadian version of Evidence-Based Medicine (EBM)—it advocates burning our textbooks (but not this one, of course!) and going online to do up-to-the-minute searches to find the best ways of caring for our patients. Basically, it means keeping up with the science, which is evolving very rapidly. In working with clients or supervising students I apply these tenets of EBM in order to provide the best services to the clients and to learn about the challenges of basing clinical practice on scientific evidence. The EBM movement also provides guidelines for improving research and making it more useful for clinicians. I am trying to weave these ideas into my writing and my teaching.

What do you see as the most exciting changes in the field of clinical psychology?

Medicine and the popular press are enraptured by genetics and by the brain, and clinical psychology is poised to make exciting contributions to these areas. In recent years we have learned that "heart disease" involves a combination of genetic risk, diet, exercise, personality, and stress; likewise, we are beginning to learn that "brain disorders" are complex and are influenced by both early life experiences and current lifestyle factors. Accordingly, major contributions from psychology will be required to understand these disorders and to develop optimal rehabilitation or treatment services. Another important change has to do with technology, as advances in this field are going to change the ways that we conduct assessment and therapy.

Prevalence of Mental Disorders

So just how common are mental disorders? Using the DSM-IV definition of mental disorder and its criteria for anxiety disorders, mood disorders, impulse control disorders (such as bulimia and

TABLE 3.2   Prevalence of Selected Mental Disorders

Country	Anxiety	Mood	Impulse-Control	Substance Abuse	Any Disorder
Colombia	10.0%	6.8%	3.9%	2.8%	17.8%
Mexico	6.8%	4.8%	1.3%	2.5%	12.2%
United States	18.2%	9.6%	6.8%	3.8%	26.4%
Belgium	6.9%	6.2%	1.0%	1.2%	12.0%
France	12.0%	8.5%	1.4%	0.7%	18.4%
Germany	6.2%	3.6%	0.3%	1.1%	9.1%
Italy	5.8%	3.8%	0.3%	0.1%	8.2%
Netherlands	8.8%	6.9%	1.3%	3.0%	14.9%
Spain	5.9%	4.9%	0.5%	0.3%	9.2%
Ukraine	7.1%	9.1%	3.2%	6.4%	20.5%
Lebanon	11.2%	0.8%	1.7%	1.3%	16.9%
Nigeria	3.3%	0.8%	—	0.8%	4.7%
Japan	5.3%	3.1%	1.0%	1.7%	8.8%
China-Beijing	3.2%	2.5%	2.6%	2.6%	9.1%
China-Shanghai	2.4%	1.7%	0.7%	0.5%	4.3%

Adapted from World Health Organization Mental Health Survey Consortium (2004)

attention-deficit/hyperactivity disorder), and substance abuse disorders, the World Health Organization (WHO) Mental Health Survey Consortium (2004) carried out surveys of people 18 years of age and older in 14 countries: the United States, Colombia, and Mexico (the Americas); Belgium, France, Germany, Italy, the Netherlands, Spain, and Ukraine (Europe); Lebanon (the Middle East); Nigeria (Africa); and Japan and China (Asia). All survey interviews were conducted in person by trained interviewers. To ensure the comparability of data obtained from all countries, the WHO Consortium used standardized interviewer training procedures, WHO translation protocols, and numerous quality control procedures. Sample sizes ranged from approximately 1,700 participants in Japan to almost 9,300 participants in the United States. Twelve-month prevalence data (i.e., the percentage of people meeting diagnostic criteria during the period of a year) from this massive survey are presented in **Table 3.2.**

As you can see in the table, overall prevalence rates varied greatly from country to country, ranging from 4.3% in Shanghai to 26.4% in the United States. In all but one country (Ukraine), anxiety disorders were the most common mental disorder, with mood disorders being the next most common set of mental disorders. It is interesting to note that the six countries included in the surveys that are classified by the World Bank as having lower per capita income (China, Colombia, Lebanon, Mexico, Nigeria, and Ukraine) had some of the lowest and highest total prevalence rates. The authors of the report recognized that the failure to include schizophrenia in the surveys was problematic. They argued, however, that previous research has shown that many people diagnosed with schizophrenia would also receive a diagnosis that was included in the surveys. Therefore, the authors believed that the overall picture of the worldwide prevalence of people meeting criteria for at least one mental disorder is accurate.

In addition to collecting prevalence data, the World Mental Health survey also collected data on the disability and treatment of mental and physical disorders (Ormel et al., 2008). The results from the survey may surprise you. Across countries, mental disorders were viewed as being more disabling than physical disorders such as chronic pain, heart disease, cancer, and diabetes. The disabilities associated with mental disorders were seen as especially elevated in the spheres of social and personal relationships. At the time of the interview, survey participants with mental disorders were much less likely to be receiving treatment for the disorders than were those with physical disorders, and this was especially true for lower-income countries. Specifically, in higher-income countries, 65% of all physical disorders were treated, compared to 24% of mental disorders. For lower-income countries, treatment rates were 53% of all physical disorders and 8% of mental disorders.

Knowing that millions of people worldwide suffer from mental disorders and that these disorders cause substantial disability is important, but it is also necessary to be able to imagine what life is like for an individual who suffers from a mental disorder. To provide you with a fuller appreciation of what mental disorders are like, we have included cases describing two people—Carl, an adolescent, and Teresa, an adult—who were referred to us for the treatment of anxiety symptoms. The cases we present in the book are based on our clinical practice. Whenever we present an example of a person suffering from a mental disorder, we have taken care to conceal the person's identity by changing some parts of the background information. You will learn more about the services Carl and Teresa received in later chapters, when we focus on assessment and intervention.

 case example CARL

Carl is a 12-year-old boy whose family left his country of origin when he was 10. He was referred for psychological services to address symptoms of anxiety, hypervigilance, and sleep disturbance. According to his mother, Carl was a normal child whose birth and early childhood were unremarkable. However, when Carl was three-years-old, his country suffered extreme strife and conflict that culminated in ethnic cleansing. Carl, his mother, and twin sister were separated from his father and learned only months later that the father had been brutally killed. Following the loss of his father, repeated exposure to mob violence, and months of sheltering from continued threat of death, Carl displayed behavior that is found in some very young children's response to trauma—he withdrew from the world and became mute. Although he has made remarkable progress and in many ways has a normal life, to this day, Carl continues to re-experience images of the scene in which the family was fleeing for their lives, the small children clinging to their parents. In addition, he re-experiences images of corpses, blood, and body parts, drawn not only from direct experience, but also from personal accounts he has heard and media images he has seen.

As his mother attempted to rebuild the family life following such horrific loss and exposure to violence, Carl sought reassurance by clinging to two attachment figures: his mother and his twin sister. The availability of these two people to provide comfort and reassurance enabled him to gradually venture into the world by attending school. During this time, as safety was slowly reestablished, Carl was surrounded by evidence of the genocide. All the adults in his life had experienced terror and loss. The fragile equilibrium that had been achieved by the time he was nine years old was shattered when the family was exposed to renewed threats of death unless they dropped charges against those accused of killing Carl's father. In contrast to the experience at the age of three, when he was too young to cognitively understand what was happening and could respond only on an emotional level, at the age of nine Carl was intellectually mature enough to understand that his family could be harmed. He was terrified at the possibility of unprovoked attacks and at the risk of dying or losing yet another family member.

Since leaving his country of origin, Carl has begun the process of rebuilding his life. He attends school and has friends with whom he enjoys spending time. He is a keen soccer player. Although he and his twin no longer cling to one another, they are very important to one another. Nevertheless, Carl continues to be haunted by his experiences. Images of the violence disturb his sleep. He is fearful at night, unwilling to sleep alone and troubled that noises are of intruders coming to murder the family. Battle scenes in movies evoke memories and a panic response. Carl is troubled by talk about the genocide experiences, covering his ears and yelling at his mother to stop talking about it. Carl experiences somatic symptoms of anxiety including pounding heart and dizziness. This symptom profile is consistent with a diagnosis of posttraumatic stress disorder (PTSD). In addition to experiencing unusual symptoms, there is clear evidence of harmful dysfunction: the symptoms get in the way of Carl enjoying all the regular experiences of a teenager, they interfere with his sleep, and they are distressing to him. Despite his best efforts and those of his family, Carl is unable to control these symptoms.

Carl's current adjustment is a testament to his mother's resolute determination to create security for her children. He has benefited from the secure life he experienced prior to the genocide, by his mother's steadfast efforts to create a normal life, and by the availability of a twin sister. However, he was exposed, not to a single life-threatening experience, but to sustained life-threatening experiences over a prolonged period. Nothing will erase the memories and psychological scars of his early childhood trauma. Toward the end of the book we will discuss evidence-based psychological services that could reduce symptom severity, so that Carl would be able to function without daily, debilitating anxiety.

 c a s e e x a m p l e **TERESA**

Teresa is a married 27-year-old mother with a six-month-old baby Evan. Teresa was referred for psychological services by her family physician due to intrusive worries and repeated checking behaviors. Teresa had a regular childhood in a loving family. She describes herself as always having been a worried person, but as never previously having had to seek psychological services. Her husband Jeff is a successful executive in an information technology company. The couple lives in a pleasant suburb and enjoys an above-average income. They attend social activities associated with Jeff's work. In addition, Teresa attends a mother and baby group with other young mothers whom she met in prenatal classes. Teresa reports that over recent years she has been increasingly preoccupied with worries about making mistakes that might harm other people. She first became aware of these worries in her role as a nurse. Having been proud of her profession for several years, Teresa became preoccupied with worries that she might make an error in dispensing medication and that one of the people in her care would be harmed by her actions. As her worries increased, she became progressively more distressed at the potential harm she might cause and devoted more and more time to checking that she was not making errors. She finally dealt with her stress by quitting her job when she became pregnant with her first child.

Even though Teresa eliminated her work stress she continued to feel worried. She is particularly troubled by fears when driving that she has inadvertently knocked over a pedestrian or a cyclist. These thoughts are triggered whenever she hits a bump in the road or if she has momentarily lost concentration during her driving. When Teresa has such thoughts she imagines the victim lying injured in the road, so she circles back looking for him or her. She has a tendency to stop the car and examine the pavement for signs of blood. She may ask passers-by whether they witnessed an accident or whether they have seen an injured person limping away. Only when she has circled the block many times without discovering evidence of an accident is she able to continue. Episodes of checking delay most journeys, including grocery shopping, trips out with the baby, and picking Jeff up from work. Even after she has searched for evidence, Teresa is vigilant in listening to the radio and watching television to check for reports of a hit and run accident. She also quizzes people she knows about whether they have heard of an accident.

Teresa also worries that she may accidentally harm her baby. Cleaning the house poses a special challenge, as she becomes distressed at thoughts that she may have spilled a household cleaning product near the baby. She responds to these worries by changing the baby's clothes and washing the area in which the baby is located. The cleaning routines required to reassure her that the baby has not been contaminated with a toxic product can take several hours.

Teresa recognizes that these worries are unusual. She believes that her thoughts are excessive and that her checking is out of proportion to the likelihood she has actually caused any harm. She is embarrassed by her symptoms and worries that other people will think that she is crazy. She is grateful to Jeff for tolerating her extreme thoughts and behaviors. Teresa's symptom profile is consistent with a diagnosis of obsessive-compulsive disorder.

Even though Teresa recognizes that these thoughts and behaviors are out of proportion to the likelihood that she has harmed anyone, she is unable to control them. Her husband's attempts at reassurance and reasoning have also met with failure. Despite his desire to be loyal and supportive, Jeff is frustrated at Teresa's odd behaviors. Her need for reassurance is emotionally draining, and he is embarrassed to think that his wife may be crazy. In the assessment chapters we will present tools that can be used to assess the extent of Teresa's problems and will describe the process of assessing her difficulties.

Understanding the Development of Mental Disorders

Modern theories of the etiology of mental disorders are all based on a biopsychosocial model. Although theories vary in the emphasis they give to different factors within the general biopsychosocial model (e. g., some biological theories emphasize genetic elements, whereas most psychological theories tend to emphasize cognitive, developmental, and interpersonal elements), there is a consensus among psychopathology researchers that the presence of a mental disorder is determined by a blend of biological, psychological, and social factors (e.g., Kendler, 2008). Of course, the precise contribution of each of the three factors is likely to vary from disorder to disorder. The contribution of these factors may also change over the life course: for example, in a longitudinal study of common fears, the impact of genetic factors that influenced fear intensity during childhood tended to diminish over time, whereas the impact of life experiences increased over time (Kendler et al., 2008).

In keeping with our emphasis on the need for empirical evidence in evaluating theories and services, we move on now to consider some of the research on the development of abnormal behavior. This is a huge body of scientific literature, and we have space to highlight only a few of the most important issues in the emergence of psychological disorders. One such issue is the role that the buildup of life stress plays in placing people at risk for developing a disorder. A good example of this line of research is a study by Turner and Lloyd (2004). These researchers interviewed more than 1,800 young adults (age 18–23 years). Researchers asked questions about a wide range of major stressful experiences, such as parental unemployment, being abandoned by one or both parents, life-threatening illness, forced sexual intercourse, being shot at with a gun, witnessing someone being seriously injured or killed, being in a serious car crash, and experiencing physical abuse from a dating partner. Some, but not all, of the experiences they asked about are potentially traumatic. In addition they asked questions about both current psychological symptoms and lifetime experience of diagnosable disorder. The researchers' goal was to examine the links between stress and first episodes (i.e., the first occurrence of a diagnosable condition) of anxiety and depressive disorders. Of the 33 stressors they examined, 26 were associated with significantly increased risk of subsequently developing an anxiety or mood disorder. Across gender and ethnicity (Hispanic American, African American, and non-Hispanic White American), the odds of developing a disorder increased with the number of stressors experienced. A second example, using an interpersonal stress model, comes from a study by Hammen, Shih, and Brennan (2004) that examined the complex intergenerational transmission of depression among approximately 800 Australian adolescents and their mothers. The researchers found that depression in maternal grandmothers predicted maternal depression and interpersonal stress. The maternal depression, in turn, influenced the mothers' interpersonal stress and the development of their children's social competence. The interpersonal stress experienced by the mothers also contributed to the children's interpersonal stress and to their children's depression. The final piece of the stress/disorder chain was that the poor social competence and high interpersonal stress in the children predicted their own development of depressive symptoms.

Although life stress is clearly implicated in the development of many disorders, not all people exposed to major stressors develop a disorder and, if disorders do develop, they do not do so at the same time or rate for all people. As you saw in Viewpoint Box 3.2, the majority of tsunami and hurricane victims did not meet criteria for diagnosis of a mental disorder, despite having experienced tremendous loss and devastation. It is relatively easy to understand how a natural disaster can provoke debilitating psychological symptoms—most of us can imagine that we would feel distraught if we were to witness the sudden death of many loved ones and the loss of our homes. It is equally important to try to understand the variables that enable some people to survive trauma without developing a psychological disorder.

An emerging area of etiological research explores individual differences in the development of psychological disorders. This research requires the longitudinal study of large numbers of people and the use of very sophisticated statistical analyses. A fascinating example of such research is a study by Cole et al. (2002) in which 12 waves of data were collected (grades 4 to 11) from 1,570 children/adolescents and their parents. The main goal of the study was to investigate normative developmental shifts in the rate at which depressive symptoms emerge. The researchers found that

VIEWPOINT BOX 3.2

PSYCHOLOGICAL RESPONSES TO NATURAL DISASTERS

Natural disasters such as tornados, floods, hurricanes, and earthquakes strike with little warning and can result in enormous devastation and loss of life. In the following paragraphs, we examine the psychological effects that can accompany these tragic events. Whether they occur in less developed countries or in highly developed countries, disasters have the potential to adversely affect the well-being of numerous individuals, often for many months and years after the disaster. Long after homes have been rebuilt and life has returned to some semblance of normality, the psychological scars will remain for some people.

Natural disasters are associated with increases in anxiety disorders.
(*Source:* Lannis Waters/Zuma Press)

In December 2004, a massive tsunami devastated parts of East Africa and South Asia. The island country of Sri Lanka was particularly affected, with more than 31,000 deaths, more than 23,000 people injured, and more than half a million people displaced by the devastation. The scope of the disaster in southern Sri Lanka was almost unimaginable: people lost family members and friends, whole villages and towns were destroyed, many people's livelihoods were swept away by the disaster, and much of the infrastructure supporting daily life activities, including transportation and communication systems, was wiped out in the region. Initial studies of the disaster's psychological impact indicated that approximately 40% of youth and 20% of their parents experienced PTSD four months after the tsunami (Wickrama & Kaspar, 2007). Studies from other countries in the affected regions also found high rates of PTSD as a result of the disaster.

A little over a year and a half after the tsunami, researchers conducted a thorough survey of one severely affected region in Sri Lanka to determine the prevalence of psychological symptoms and disorders. Using questionnaires adapted for use in the region, Hollifield and colleagues (2008) interviewed 89 adults by approaching one third of the 223 inhabited homes in one town. Among their sample, 51% lost family members in the tsunami, 80% lost friends, and 75% had extensive damage to their property and belongings. One quarter of respondents had moderate to severe PTSD symptoms, 16% had clinically elevated depression symptoms, and 30% had clinically elevated anxiety symptoms. Taken together, the researchers estimated that 40% of those interviewed were experiencing mental disorders many months after the tsunami.

In August 2005, Hurricane Katrina formed in the Atlantic Ocean. After striking the Bahamas and Florida, it crossed over the Gulf of Mexico, gaining strength as it progressed. The Category 5 hurricane ripped into several states, with its strongest effects felt in Alabama, Louisiana, and Mississippi. As a result of the hurricane and the associated storm surge, more than 1,800 people died, more than half a million people were displaced, and more than $100 billion in damages occurred. It was the worst natural disaster in the United States for many decades. Galea and colleagues (2007) surveyed more than 1,000 adults living in the affected areas in Alabama, Louisiana, and Mississippi. Several months after the hurricane passed, over a quarter met criteria for an anxiety or mood disorder and 12.5% met criteria for PTSD. Among the residents of New Orleans, a city devastated by the hurricane and the breaching of the levees, the rates of DSM-IV disorders were much higher. Almost 50% met criteria for an anxiety or mood disorder and 30% met criteria for PTSD. The researchers speculated that the slow government response to the disaster served to exacerbate the stress experienced by respondents and thus negatively affected the mental health of the people who lived through Hurricane Katrina.

Another survey of adults who survived Katrina adds an important element to our understanding of the effects of natural disasters. Wang et al. (2008) interviewed more than 1,000 adults about mental health needs and mental health treatments in the aftermath of Katrina. Because of disruptions caused by the hurricane, almost one quarter of individuals who had been receiving mental health services prior to Katrina experienced a reduction in, or termination of, services following the hurricane. Among adults who developed a mental disorder as a result of the disaster, fewer than 20% received any type of mental health treatment, and almost two thirds of those who did receive treatment received medication without any form of psychological treatment. As a result of their findings, the researchers recommended that disaster management plans should be designed to address both the widespread failure to initiate needed mental health treatment and the disruptions that occur to existing mental health services.

the rate at which depressive symptoms occurred in children and adolescents was not consistent over the course of their development. Data from both parents and children indicated that there was a significant increase in the rate of depressive symptoms between the sixth and seventh grade. The average rate of change before this period and after this period was relatively stable, suggesting that there are destabilizing factors influencing child development and the subsequent experience of depressive symptoms in late childhood/early adolescence. Also worth noting was the observation that symptoms of depression increased much more rapidly for girls than for boys, starting at the period between the fifth and seventh grades. Based on these data, researchers interested in examining the initial development and maintenance of depression can now focus on the critical time period identified by Cole and colleagues to more closely investigate factors implicated in the emergence (and nonemergence) of depression.

Normative data help us to determine the need for service. *(Source:* Stockphoto/ Imagebroker)

Longitudinal studies can also inform us about what happens to people following the development of a psychological disorder. Eaton and colleagues (2008) collected data on almost 3,500 adults in 1981 and then obtained follow-up data 23 years later. Of most interest were the 92 people who had their first episode of diagnosable depression during the course of the follow-up. Fully 15% of these 92 adults did not have a single year free of depressive episodes following their initial episode. In contrast, approximately 50% of people who experienced a first episode of depression recovered and had no subsequent episodes of depression. These findings are like the proverbial glass of water that is half full: the good news is that half of people who experience depression are unlikely to have a recurrence; the bad news is that half of people who experience depression will have recurrent depression, with some of these individuals experiencing depression that is virtually unremitting. The challenge for researchers, of course, is to try to determine the factors that discriminate between the individuals who comprise the "good news" and "bad news" groups.

A final line of etiological research we would like to illustrate deals with the importance of having solid normative data on what constitutes typical distress and problem behaviors. All children, adolescents, and adults have occasional psychological challenges and difficulties, but just how many of these problems is it normal to have? Bongers, Koot, van der Ende, and Verhulst (2003) examined this question using parent-reported data from the Child Behavior Checklist (a measure we discuss more in the final section of the chapter) for a representative sample of more than 2,000 Dutch children. The sample was recruited through municipal registers and data were collected over a 10-year period at two-year intervals. The researchers examined normal levels of such problems as anxiety, somatic complaints, aggressive behavior, attention problems, and social problems. Results from this study provide clinicians with valuable normative data for each year between the ages of 4 and 18 (for girls and boys separately). For example, a clinical psychologist providing services to a family can determine whether the level of a child's aggressive behavior reported by a parent is comparable to, or much greater than, what is normally expected for a child of that age and gender. This information, in turn, is likely to influence the nature of the information and services offered to the family.

THE DSM APPROACH TO DIAGNOSIS

In the following sections we describe the historical context for the development of the current diagnostic system used in much of the world: the DSM-IV and the DSM-IV-Text Revision (DSM-IV-TR). We then describe the main features of the DSM-IV before moving on to consider the shortcomings of the approach to diagnosis that underlies the DSM.

The Evolution of the DSM

Each edition of the DSM reflects the status of diagnosis at the time of its publication. The first edition of the DSM published by the American Psychiatric Association in 1952 was rather vague and heavily emphasized psychodynamic etiological factors for the majority of the disorders. According to Shea (1991), the limitations of the original DSM were relatively unimportant, as diagnosis was not seen as an important or pressing issue and only one form of treatment— psychoanalysis—was available. At the time of the publication of the second edition in 1968, new treatment options were becoming available (including drug treatments) and psychiatric researchers were increasingly examining biological and neurological aspects of mental disorders. As a result, in the second edition the psychodynamic orientation was less prominent and there was greater precision in terminology (Shea, 1991).

The third edition of the DSM, published in 1980, marked a dramatic departure from the first two editions. Under the guidance of the task force chair, Robert Spitzer, enormous effort was devoted to improving the organization and classification of mental disorders. This was evident in many different ways. First, the manual was explicitly atheoretical—this allowed for the possibility of greater acceptance within the mental health field and for the introduction of concrete behavioral descriptions of most disorders. Second, the diagnostic criteria were much more explicit than was the case previously, with lists of symptoms provided for each diagnosis. Third, as a significant part of the effort to improve upon the reliability of psychiatric diagnoses, thousands of patients and hundreds of clinicians were involved in field trials of the diagnostic system. Fourth, a multiaxial diagnostic system was introduced, which encouraged clinicians to consider more than just symptoms in diagnosing a person. These were ambitious changes that required much more attention to the scientific literature and to scientific classification principles than did the previous two editions. In order to reflect advances occurring in the burgeoning psychopathology literature, a revision of the DSM-III with updated information and some alterations in diagnostic criteria was published in 1987.

Given the widespread acceptance of DSM-III and DSM-III-R in the clinical and research communities, the use of the manuals by many different mental health professionals, and their use for teaching and reimbursement purposes, great efforts were made in the preparation of the DSM-IV. Work groups composed of research experts and clinicians in the field were established for each major class of mental disorders. Exhaustive literature reviews were written, and proposals were developed for diagnostic criteria. Liaisons were established with scores of mental health and professional organizations, both within the United States and internationally. The resulting manual, although far from perfect as we will see in a subsequent section, was developed in a far more collaborative and scientifically informed manner than were any of the preceding editions of the DSM.

The DSM-IV was published in 1994. The DSM-IV-Text Revision, published in 2000, corrected errors identified in the DSM-IV text, updated the scientific information provided about disorders, and made some alterations to enhance the educational value of the DSM-IV. These changes in the text are particularly important because DSM-IV information was based on reviews of the scientific literature that were completed in 1992. As much had been learned since then, and the next new edition of the DSM was not slated for publication for several years, the text revision provided an important bridge between the DSM-IV and the future DSM-V. The text revision did not include changes in the criteria used to diagnose a disorder or changes in the listing of disorders. For ease of reading, we will refer to the

DSM-IV when discussing the structure and criteria, as these are identical in both fourth edition versions of the diagnostic system.

Plans are currently under way for the next version of the DSM. The groundwork for this began in 1999, when an initial planning conference was held to set research priorities for developing the DSM-V. In subsequent years, research plans were formalized, position papers on issues related to psychiatric classification were commissioned, and international consultations were held with the WHO and the World Psychiatric Association. In the past few years, a number of conferences were held that focused on specific diagnostic categories or issues. In 2008, the final membership of the working groups for each diagnostic category was announced. A number of prominent clinical psychologists are involved in these working groups. Future steps include the finalizing of the information and criteria for each diagnostic category, field testing the diagnostic criteria, and obtaining feedback from multiple stakeholders. The American Psychiatric Association expects that the DSM-V will be released in 2012.

The DSM-IV

The DSM-IV is an example of a categorical approach to classification. As we described earlier in the chapter, this means that mental disorders are classified on the basis of specific defining criteria. In reviewing the organization of the DSM-IV, Clark, Watson, and Reynolds (1995) expressed concern about the lack of a unified scientific system underlying the structure of the classification system. As shown in **Table 3.3**, there are 17 diagnostic classes within the DSM-IV. Clark et al. pointed out that, although the majority of diagnostic classes are based on shared characteristics of their constituent

---

TABLE 3.3   DSM-IV and DSM-IV-TR Diagnostic Classes

Disorders Usually First Diagnosed in Infancy, Childhood, or Adolescence

Examples: mental retardation, pervasive developmental disorders, attention-deficit and disruptive behavior disorders

Delirium, Dementia, and Amnestic and Other Cognitive Disorders

Examples: substance intoxication delirium, dementia of the Alzheimer's type, substance-induced persisting amnesic disorder

Mental Disorders Due to a General Medical Condition

Examples: catatonic disorder due to general medical condition, personality change due to general medical condition

Substance-Related Disorders

Examples: alcohol-related disorders, inhalant-related disorders, nicotine-related disorders

Schizophrenia and Other Psychotic Disorders

Examples: schizophrenia, schizoaffective disorder, delusional disorder

Mood Disorders

Examples: depressive disorders, bipolar disorders

Anxiety Disorders

Examples: social phobia, obsessive-compulsive disorder, generalized anxiety disorder

(Continued)

TABLE 3.3 (*Continued*)

Somatoform Disorders

Examples: conversion disorder, pain disorder, body dysmorphic disorder

Factitious Disorders

Examples: factitious disorder with predominantly psychological signs and symptoms, factitious disorder with predominantly physical signs and symptoms

Dissociative Disorders

Examples: dissociative amnesia, dissociative fugue, dissociative identity disorder

Sexual and Gender Identity Disorders

Examples: sexual dysfunctions, paraphilias, gender identity disorders

Eating Disorders

Examples: anorexia nervosa, bulimia nervosa

Sleep Disorders

Examples: primary sleep disorders, sleep disorders related to another mental disorder, other sleep disorders

Impulse-Control Disorders Not Elsewhere Classified

Examples: kleptomania, pyromania, pathological gambling

Adjustment Disorders

Examples: adjustment disorder with depressed mood, adjustment disorder with disturbance of conduct

Personality Disorders

Examples: paranoid personality disorder, borderline personality disorder, avoidant personality disorder

Other Conditions That May Be a Focus of Clinical Attention

Examples: medication-induced movement disorders, relational problems, problems related to abuse or neglect

Adapted from the *Diagnostic and Statistical Manual of Mental Disorders, Text Revision* (2000)

symptoms such as anxiety disorders or sleep disorders, about a third of the classes are organized on what can only be described as rather eclectic and pragmatic grounds. For example, the only common feature among the disorders listed in the class "Disorders Usually First Diagnosed in Infancy, Childhood, or Adolescence" is the likely age at which the disorder is diagnosed. Moreover, many mood and anxiety disorders are first diagnosed in childhood and persist into adulthood, yet they are not included in this diagnostic class (Widiger & Sankis, 2000). As we will see when we later discuss limitations to the DSM-IV, this approach can be misleading and may have, at times, little clinical value (or utility).

The DSM-IV uses a multiaxial classification approach. Aspects of a person's symptoms and general functioning are rated on five different axes. As illustrated in **Table 3.4**, the first two axes provide specific details about the nature of the mental disorder(s) experienced by the person. The remaining three axes provide information on the medical and psychosocial context in which the symptoms and disorders are occurring.

For each mental disorder listed in the DSM-IV, a wealth of information is provided on diagnostic features, subtypes (if applicable), associated features and disorders, prevalence, course, familial

---

TABLE 3.4   The Multiaxial Classification System of the DSM-IV

Axis I: Clinical Disorders and Other Conditions That May Be a Focus of Clinical Attention

This axis includes all the mental disorders in the DSM-IV except for personality disorders and mental retardation. If more than one Axis I disorder is present, all disorders are diagnosed and reported on this axis.

Axis II: Personality Disorder and Mental Retardation

This axis includes all diagnoses related to personality disorders and mental retardation. The listing of these disorders on a separate axis was done to ensure that these conditions are not overlooked when attention is directed to the Axis I disorders. This is important, as it is often the Axis I disorders for which people seek treatment.

Axis III: General Medical Conditions

This axis is for providing information on the person's current medical conditions that is potentially relevant to the understanding and/or treatment of the person's Axis I and Axis II disorders.

Axis IV: Psychosocial and Environmental Problems

This axis is for reporting psychosocial and environmental information that may influence the diagnosis, treatment, and prognosis of the mental disorders diagnosed on Axis I and Axis II. The elements to be considered include the following:

- problems with the primary support group
- problems related to the social environment
- educational problems
- occupational problems
- housing problems
- economic problems
- problems with access to health care services
- problems related to interaction with the legal system/crime
- other psychosocial and environmental problems

Axis V: Global Assessment of Functioning

On this axis the clinician provides an overall rating of the person's level of functioning. The Global Assessment of Functioning (GAF) Scale is included for this purpose. The GAF Scale ranges from 1 to 100 based on consideration of psychological, social, and occupational functioning. For example, someone who is rated in the 1–10 range is in persistent danger of hurting himself, herself, or others; someone who is rated in the 41–50 range has serious symptoms or has serious impairment in social, occupational, or school functioning; and someone who is rated in the 81–90 range has no or minimal symptoms, with good functioning in all areas of life.

Adapted from the *Diagnostic and Statistical Manual of Mental Disorders, Text Revision* (2000)

---

pattern, differential diagnosis, and specific culture, age, and gender features. These details provide a context for a fuller appreciation of what is known about the mental disorder and alert the clinician to important aspects that should be considered during the evaluation of the person. Following this information, the necessary diagnostic criteria are presented. For some disorders, such as bulimia nervosa, the same diagnostic criteria must be met by everyone who is assigned the diagnosis, although some variability in subtypes of the disorder is possible (see **Table 3.5**).

TABLE 3.5   DSM-IV Diagnostic Criteria for Bulimia Nervosa

A. Recurrent episodes of binge eating. An episode of binge eating is characterized by both of the following:
   (1) eating, in a discrete period of time (e.g., within any 2-hour period), an amount of food that is definitely larger than most people would eat during a similar period of time and under similar circumstances
   (2) a sense of lack of control over eating during the episode (e.g., a feeling that one cannot stop eating or control what or how much one is eating)

B. Recurrent inappropriate compensatory behavior in order to prevent weight gain, such as self-induced vomiting; misuse of laxatives, diuretics, enemas, or other medications; fasting; or excessive exercise.

C. The binge eating and inappropriate compensatory behaviors both occur, on average, at least twice a week for 3 months.

D. Self-evaluation is unduly influenced by body shape and weight. F. The disturbance does not occur exclusively during episodes of Anorexia Nervosa.

Specify type:

Purging type: During the current episode of bulimia nervosa, the person has regularly engaged in self-induced vomiting or the misuse of laxatives, diuretics, or enemas.

Nonpurging type: During the current episode of bulimia nervosa, the person has used other inappropriate compensatory behaviors, such as fasting or excessive exercise, but has not regularly engaged in self-induced vomiting or the misuse of laxatives, diuretics, or enemas.

Reprinted with permission from the *Diagnostic and Statistical Manual of Mental Disorders, Text Revision.* Copyright 2000. American Psychiatric Association

For many disorders, unlike the case with bulimia nervosa, there is enormous variability permitted in the constellation of symptoms required for the diagnosis. A clear example of this is posttraumatic stress disorder (PTSD; see **Table 3.6**). For this diagnosis, both elements of criterion A must be met, but criterion B can be met in five different ways, and criteria C (at least three of any of seven symptoms) and D (at least two of any of five symptoms) can be met in dozens of different ways. Bulimia nervosa is an example of a diagnosis that is defined *monothetically* (i.e., all criteria are met in the same manner for people with the diagnosis), whereas PTSD is an example of a diagnosis that is defined *polythetically* (i.e., people diagnosed with this disorder may exhibit markedly different patterns of symptoms).

In the development of the DSM-IV, attention was focused on ethnic and cultural considerations. This is extremely important for the system to be relevant and valid for international use (such as the World Health Organization Mental Health Survey described previously) and use in culturally diverse populations within a country. The DSM-IV and DSM-IV-TR include several types of information that enhance the cultural relevance of the diagnostic system. First, when the scientific evidence exists for cultural/ethnic variations in the clinical presentations of a mental disorder, this information is provided in the text accompanying the diagnostic criteria. Second, a number of culture-specific disorders (often called culture-bound syndromes) are described in an appendix. Examples include *boufée delirante* (a syndrome observed in West Africa and Haiti involving a sudden outburst of agitated and aggressive behavior, along with considerable confusion and excitement), *mal de ojo* (a concept of the "evil eye" found in many Mediterranean cultures; children are at heightened risk for this syndrome, which may include symptoms of fitful sleep, crying with no apparent cause, vomiting, and fever), and *pibloktoq* (a syndrome found primarily in Inuit communities involving a dissociative episode accompanied by extreme excitement and followed by convulsive seizures and coma lasting up to 12 hours). Finally,

TABLE 3.6   DSM-IV Diagnostic Criteria for Posttraumatic Stress Disorder

A. The person has been exposed to a traumatic event in which both of the following were present:
   (1) the person experienced, witnessed, or was confronted with an event or events that involved actual or threatened death or serious injury, or a threat to the physical integrity of self or others.
   (2) the person's response involved intense fear, helplessness, or horror. **Note:** In children, this may be expressed instead by disorganized or agitated behavior.

B. The traumatic event is persistently re-experienced in one (or more) of the following ways:
   (1) recurrent and intrusive distressing recollections of the event, including images, thoughts, or perceptions. **Note:** In young children, repetitive play may occur in which themes or aspects of the trauma are expressed.
   (2) recurrent distressing dreams of the event. **Note:** In children, there may be frightening dreams without recognizable content.
   (3) acting or feeling as if the traumatic event were recurring (includes a sense of reliving the experience, illusions, hallucinations, and dissociative flashback episodes, including those that occur on awakening or when intoxicated). **Note:** In young children, trauma-specific re-enactment may occur.
   (4) intense psychological distress at exposure to internal or external cues that symbolize or resemble an aspect of the traumatic event
   (5) physiological reactivity on exposure to internal or external cues that symbolize or resemble an aspect of the traumatic event

C. Persistent avoidance of stimuli associated with the trauma and numbing of general responsiveness (not present before the trauma), as indicated by three (or more) of the following:
   (1) efforts to avoid thoughts, feelings, or conversations associated with the trauma
   (2) efforts to avoid activities, places, or people that arouse recollections of the trauma
   (3) inability to recall an important aspect of the trauma
   (4) markedly diminished interest or participation in significant activities
   (5) feeling of detachment or estrangement from others
   (6) restricted range of affect (e.g., unable to have loving feelings)
   (7) sense of a foreshortened future (e.g., does not expect to have a career, marriage, or children, or a normal life span)

D. Persistent symptoms of increased arousal (not present before the trauma), as indicated by two (or more) of the following:
   (1) difficulty falling or staying asleep
   (2) irritability or outbursts of anger
   (3) difficulty concentrating
   (4) hypervigilance
   (5) exaggerated startle response

E. Duration of the disturbance (symptoms in Criteria B, C, and D) is more than 1 month.

F. The disturbance causes clinically significant distress or impairment in social, occupational, or other important areas of functioning.

Specify if:
Acute: if duration of symptoms is less than 3 months **Chronic:** if duration of symptoms is 3 months or more

Specify if:
With Delayed Onset: if onset of symptoms is at least 6 months after the stressor

Reprinted with permission from the *Diagnostic and Statistical Manual of Mental Disorders, Text Revision.* Copyright 2000. American Psychiatric Association

Review the information we presented about Carl, and consider in Table 3.6 the criteria he would meet. Do you have sufficient information to determine whether Carl's symptoms fit the criteria? Based on what you know about him so far, do you think that PTSD might be a possible diagnosis for him?

information is provided to assist the clinician in making a culturally sensitive and appropriate diagnosis and overall clinical formulation. This information includes directing attention to the cultural identity of the person being evaluated, cultural explanations for the individual's disorder, cultural factors related to the psychosocial environment and the person's functioning, and cultural aspects of the relationship between the person and the clinician.

Comorbidity occurs when a person receives diagnoses for two or more disorders at a specific point in time. Hierarchical exclusionary rules were used in DSM-III to deal with the challenge of people presenting with comorbid disorders. In essence these rules meant, for the majority of diagnoses, that it was possible to meet criteria for only one diagnosis at a given point in time. If a person met criteria for two or more disorders, a diagnosis was given only for the disorder that was highest in the disorder hierarchy developed for DSM-III. For example, if a person met criteria for major depressive disorder and for an anxiety disorder, only the mood disorder diagnosis could be given. No theoretical rationale or empirical evidence was provided to support these rules. The decision to handle the challenge of comorbidity by defining it out of existence had little positive effect on research or practice. As a result of considerable professional protest, most of these rules were dropped for the DSM-III-R.

The extent of comorbidity in clinical populations is substantial. Brown, Campbell, Lehman, Grisham, and Mancill (2001) assessed the comorbidity of current and lifetime DSM-IV anxiety and mood disorders in more than 1,100 adults seeking services for stress and anxiety disorders. Among individuals currently meeting diagnostic criteria for an anxiety or mood disorder, 57% also met criteria for another Axis I disorder. For example, among those diagnosed with panic disorder, 36% met criteria for another anxiety disorder and 17% met criteria for a mood disorder. Among those diagnosed with major depressive disorder, 64% met criteria for an anxiety disorder. Comorbidity is also evident in youth: a review of the clinical records of almost 1,300 youth receiving outpatient psychiatry services in New York State revealed that comorbidity was evident in almost half of the cases (Staller, 2006).

Overall, whether based on clinical samples (i.e., those seeking services) or on community samples, most epidemiological surveys find, in country after country, comorbidity rates that exceed 40% (Clark et al., 1995). When individuals with a single disorder are compared with those with comorbid disorders, a very clear pattern emerges: those with comorbid conditions are more severely impaired in daily life functioning, more likely to have a chronic history of mental health problems, have more physical health problems, and use more health care services than those with a single disorder (Newman, Moffitt, Caspi, & Silva, 1998). These characteristics have clear consequences for both research and clinical services. On the research side, accurately representing the extent of comorbidity in research samples is necessary to accurately estimate the relation between a disorder and its correlates. On the clinical service side, people with comorbid disorders are likely to present with psychosocial characteristics that make the planning and delivery of services more complex (Newman et al., 1998). Moreover, if these services are based on treatment research that used patients without comorbid disorders or if these services are focused on only one of the disorders, the services may be suboptimal and may underestimate the scope or duration of treatment necessary for satisfactory outcomes. Because of these concerns, as we will see in the chapters on psychotherapy, psychotherapy researchers are increasingly attuned to the importance of not excluding individuals with coexisting disorders from their studies.

Taking this a step further, anxiety disorder expert **David Barlow** has recently developed and tested a unified treatment for emotional disorders that incorporates aspects of efficacious treatments for mood and anxiety disorders (Barlow, Allen, & Choate, 2004). Barlow's efforts are consistent with an emerging consensus that the DSM categories of mood and anxiety disorders do not adequately reflect what is known from decades of psychopathology research. Instead of forming separate categories, researchers argue that these disorders are better conceptualized as representing a broad class of related internalizing disorders that incorporate symptoms of both distress and fear (Clark & Watson, 2006). As we discuss near the end of this chapter, this is just one example of the growing trend to view psychopathology from a dimensional, rather than a categorical, perspective.

There is no question that the later editions of the DSM have revolutionized psychiatric diagnosis. As a result of the improvements that started with the DSM-III, the system has become the gold standard for establishing diagnoses in most areas of psychopathology research. Kendell and Jablensky (2003) defined the utility of a diagnostic system as the extent to which the system provides nontrivial information about prognosis or treatment outcome and/or provides testable propositions about variables associated with the diagnosis. On the basis of this definition, they argued that the DSM-IV has utility, as it provides clinicians with information on likelihood of recovery, relapse, deterioration, and social functioning. The presentation of clear descriptive information has also facilitated the diagnostic training of mental health professionals. This clarity of presentation, combined with unprecedented access to information via the Internet, also allows the public to access comprehensible information on mental disorders that they can use in understanding their symptoms and in seeking mental health services. Indeed, the concept of clinical utility is becoming so important in health care services that a number of prominent experts on psychiatric diagnosis have strongly argued for the consideration of utility to be explicitly considered in planning the DSM-V (First et al., 2004).

Limitations of the DSM-IV

Early versions of the DSM have often been described as highly politicized, with science sometimes taking a backseat to prevailing professional views. The current process of requiring systematic research reviews for established diagnoses and for diagnoses proposed for inclusion in the manual has reduced, but not eliminated, such concerns (see our later discussion in this chapter of acute stress disorder). The DSM-IV is not, however, without problems. In this section we will highlight questions that have been raised about the system in the following realms: the definition of abnormality, diagnostic reliability, the heterogeneity of symptom profiles within a disorder, the validity of diagnoses, and the continuing use of a categorical approach to classification.

Defining Abnormality (Revisited)

Earlier in the chapter we presented the DSM-IV and DSM-IV-TR definition of mental disorder. Although this definition should apply to all conditions described in the diagnostic system, Wakefield (1997) has shown that this is not the case. One of the examples he provided was that a depressive reaction, if it is due to uncomplicated bereavement, is not seen as a mood disorder. This is presumably due to the assumption that depressive symptoms are a normal part of grieving. However, even though research has established that depressive symptoms are a common reaction to other significant life stressors, such as divorce or terminal illness, no such exclusions apply to these stressors. Indeed, among individuals meeting the main criteria for major depressive disorder, there are very few differences in the symptoms experienced by those whose depression is related to bereavement and those whose depression is related to the break-up of a marriage or the loss of a job (Wakefield, Schmitz, First, & Horwitz, 2007). It is clear that the requirement that the disorder must not be "merely an expectable or culturally sanctioned response to a particular event" is not applied consistently. As researchers learn more about usual responses to stressful events, this raises the very significant question about the relevance of excluding "expectable" reactions from diagnostic consideration even if these reactions clearly meet the criteria of clinically significant distress or disability.

What is a normal response to loss?
(*Source:* Flirt/Superstock)

A second concern that has been raised repeatedly since the introduction of the DSM-III is that, in an effort to ensure coverage of all forms of clinical distress, the diagnostic system may overdiagnose mental disorders. The statistic we cited earlier in the chapter about one quarter of all American adults having a mental disorder is not an isolated finding, with other estimates suggesting that at least 30% of American adults meet diagnostic criteria for a mental disorder (e.g., Regier et al., 1998). Such epidemiological data have led to calls for more stringent definitions of mental disorder, as many experts doubt that the prevalence of mental disorders can be this high. In response to these concerns, Kessler et al. (2003) used epidemiological data to examine the extent to which diagnostic data predicted psychosocial functioning a decade later. They began by categorizing the diagnostic data based on the severity of the condition: 3.2% of survey respondents met criteria for severe disorders, 3.2% met criteria for serious disorders, 8.7% were classified as having a moderate severity disorder, and 16.0% were classified as mild cases of disorders. Next, they related this classification information to data gathered for the decade following the diagnosis; these data included information on hospitalization for mental health problems, work disability due to a mental disorder, suicide attempts, and whether the survey participants met the criteria for serious (or severe) mental disorder. Kessler and colleagues found a linear relation between disorder severity and subsequent problems in psychosocial functioning. The elevated risk for subsequent psychosocial problems was evident even among those classified as having mild disorders. In fact, compared with people with no diagnosable condition, those with a mild disorder were 2.4 times more likely to develop significant psychosocial problems. Accordingly, the researchers argued that, like physical disorders, mental disorders vary in severity, but even mild mental disorders are associated with substantial subsequent risk for impaired functioning and should be represented within a diagnostic system.

Diagnostic Reliability

Since the third edition, the DSM has been designed to enhance the reliability of clinical judgment—that is, to enhance the extent to which professionals agree on the presence of a diagnosable condition and on the nature of the condition. Each new version of the system has undergone field testing to determine the extent to which the goal of improved reliability has been attained. Without question, in comparison to DSM-II, there have been substantial improvements in diagnostic reliability. However, evidence from these field trials and other research indicates that the level of interrater reliability on the assigning of diagnoses falls below ideal levels.

Kirk (2004) summarized reliability data for several child and adolescent disorders. In evaluating diagnostic reliability, it is important to consider two types of reliability. First, reliability studies have examined the ability of independent evaluators to provide diagnoses that fall within the same general category (e.g., within the category of attention-deficit and disruptive behavior disorders). Most studies examining this form of reliability have found that reliability values can sometimes, but not always, attain an acceptable level (i.e., a value of at least .70 on a measure of interrater reliability known as the kappa statistic). Second, reliability studies have also examined the extent to which independent evaluators agree on the same specific diagnosis (e.g., separation anxiety disorder, conduct disorder). Kirk reported that, in such studies, reliability levels often fail to attain an acceptable level. He also noted that there is often extreme variability in reliability values noted from different sites in DSM field trials, with reliability (kappa) values ranging from extremely low (e.g., .18) to extremely high (e.g., 1.0). Because the presence or absence of a diagnosis often determines whether a child is eligible for special health and/or educational services, much more needs to be done to improve the reliability of the DSM system. As we describe a bit later, part of the problem here may be the continuing reliance on a diagnostic system that is based on categories rather than dimensions. Simply put, the coding of a symptom as a dichotomous variable (i.e., present or absent) can negatively affect the reliability of symptom coding compared to rating the same symptom as a continuous variable.

Heterogeneity of Symptom Profiles

Another aspect of the DSM that could contribute to problems with reliability is the polythetic nature of most of the disorders. Although it would be unrealistic to have a rigid set of criteria that must be met by everyone who has the same disorder, the fact that such extensive symptom variability is permitted in the DSM-IV negatively affects interrater reliability. There may also be another critical drawback to the polythetic approach to diagnosis. Variability in response to treatment, whether psychological or pharmacological, could be related to variability in symptom profiles among treated patients. Yet, because the level of analysis is typically on the relation between diagnosis and outcome, the connection between different symptom profiles and treatment responsiveness could be overlooked. For example, simply knowing that the symptoms of 55% of depressed patients improve when using a certain medication tells us nothing about why the medication helps many, but not all, patients. On the other hand, knowing that 85% of those with elevated physical symptoms of depression responded well to the medication, in contrast to only 25% of those with elevated cognitive symptoms, yields important information for subsequent research and has implications for prescription practices.

Individuals who purge are likely to have more severe psychopathology than are those who don't. (*Source:* Media Bakery)

Limitations of a polythetic approach have been recognized for decades, and attempts to address these limitations have often focused on establishing clinically relevant subtypes within a diagnosis. As Clark et al. (1995) noted, few of these efforts have been successful, and many of the subtypes described in DSM-IV have only limited empirical support. The distinction between purging and nonpurging types of bulimia (see Table 3.5) is one of the few with a firm empirical basis: individuals who purge are likely to have more severe psychopathology than are those who don't purge. There are many disorders for which no viable or useful subtypes have been established. As Clark et al. (1995) pointed out, an incredible range of specifiers is available for major depressive disorder, including severity, chronicity, and the nature of some symptoms (e.g., catatonic or melancholic features). The resulting range of symptoms and features covered under this diagnosis is so diverse that it seems verging on impossible—or meaningless—for a single diagnosis to be applied to all the possible patient profiles.

Diagnostic Validity

As we discussed earlier in the chapter, validity is a central criterion that must be considered in evaluating a classification system. Kendell and Jablensky (2003) viewed diagnostic validity as an indication that a disorder is a discrete entity that has clear boundaries with other disorders. Kendell and Jablensky suggested that very few mental disorders have demonstrated diagnostic validity. It is noteworthy that all the examples of valid diagnoses that they listed were conditions with clear biological causes, including Down's syndrome and Huntington's disease.

A prime example of a diagnosis with questionable validity is acute stress disorder (ASD). This diagnosis involves the development of anxiety, dissociative features, and other symptoms within a month following exposure to a traumatic stressor. As Harvey and Bryant (2002) noted, ASD was introduced into DSM-IV to fill a vacuum that existed around the diagnosis of PTSD. A diagnosis of PTSD cannot be applied to such symptoms if they occur within a month of the traumatic event (see Table 3.6). ASD was defined, therefore, as a disorder in which PTSD-like disorders occurred shortly after the trauma. If symptoms of ASD persist for more than a month after the event, then a diagnosis of PTSD may be appropriate and the ASD diagnosis would be superseded. This opens the possibility that researchers might be able to establish the nature of connections between initial distress following trauma (i.e., ASD) and more chronic distress (i.e., PTSD).

There have been a number of criticisms raised about ASD, all of which raise major questions about its diagnostic validity. The criticisms, as summarized by Harvey and Bryant (2002), include the following: the requirement for dissociative symptoms is not consistent with research on trauma reactions; it is inappropriate to introduce a diagnosis into DSM-IV in order to predict another diagnosis;

it is inappropriate to introduce a diagnosis that has almost no supporting empirical evidence; it is not justifiable to distinguish between two diagnoses with comparable symptoms simply on the basis of symptom duration; and there is a great likelihood that the diagnosis could pathologize transient stress reactions that do not require the attention of mental health professionals. Importantly, many studies have found that there is only a weak association between meeting criteria for ASD and, after more time has passed, meeting criteria for PTSD (e.g., Creamer, O'Donnell, & Pattison, 2004; Kangas, Henry, & Bryant, 2005). The introduction of ASD has certainly served to promote research into acute stress reactions. Nevertheless, it seems clear that the questions raised by the inclusion of this diagnosis outweigh any value it has had in serving as an impetus for research.

Categorical Versus Dimensional Classification

Comorbidity is a clinical fact. When a categorical classification system is used, the presence of comorbidity contradicts the assumption that diagnostic categories are discrete and nonoverlapping. The DSM-IV explicitly acknowledges that each category of mental disorder need not be a discrete entity—yet doing so opens up the possibility that a dimensional system may better represent the nature of mental disorders. As noted in the DSM-IV, there are no commonly agreed upon dimensional systems that could replace the DSM-IV categorical approach. However, that may be changing, as steps are being taken now to conceptualize many Axis I (e.g., Krueger, Watson, & Barlow, 2005) and Axis II (e.g., Widiger & Trull, 2007) disorders within dimensional models.

The question of dimensionality can be considered within a specific disorder. There has been a great deal of controversy in the area of depression research about whether depression is a discrete diagnostic category or whether it should be viewed as existing on a continuum that includes both clinical symptoms and subclinical distress. The most sophisticated research now suggests that depression may encompass both a specific condition and a continuum. Santor and Coyne (2001), for example, obtained clinician ratings of symptoms on samples of clinically depressed adults and nonclinically depressed—but distressed—adults. When depressed and nondepressed individuals with comparable levels of clinician-rated depressive symptoms were compared, group differences on specific symptoms were apparent. Depressed mood, anhedonia (lack of pleasure), and suicidality were more likely to be evident in the depressed group, whereas hypochondriasis and insomnia were more evident in the nondepressed group. Thus, although the severity of depressive symptoms can be expressed on a continuum, Santor and Coyne argued that the use of a continuum (or dimensional) model might mask important and diagnostically relevant group differences. Using self-report measures of depressive symptoms, research on both clinical (Ruscio & Ruscio, 2000) and nonclinical (Beach & Amir, 2006; Hankin, Fraley, Lahey, & Waldman, 2005) samples have found evidence for both categorical and dimensional features. Generally speaking, analyses of self-report items expressing distress (e.g., discouragement, loss of interest in others) appear to yield a dimensional perspective on the continuum of subclinical to clinical depression. In contrast, analyses of self-report items of somatic symptoms (e.g., sleep disturbance, weight loss) appear to provide strong evidence that some depressive symptoms are best understood as constituting a discrete disorder.

In conducting research on the underlying dimensions of mental disorders, we can also step back from examining a specific disorder and explore patterns that may exist across disorders. Based on epidemiological data, it is increasingly clear that comorbidity cannot be explained as being simply due to either symptom overlap among diagnostic categories or to methodological problems in research.

VIEWPOINT BOX 3.3

PSYCHOLOGICAL RESILIENCE IN THE FACE OF POTENTIAL TRAUMA

In describing the case of Carl and the extent to which natural disasters can cause extreme psychological distress in Viewpoint Box 3.2, you might have the impression that psychological disorders such as depression and PTSD are the invariable result of experiencing life-threatening situations. Actually, the contrary is more accurate: people are amazingly resilient, and most are able to recover their psychological equilibrium after experiencing potentially traumatic events. For example, in population surveys, researchers have found that, although two thirds of children report experiencing at least one traumatic event by the age of 16 years, less than 15% develop posttraumatic stress symptoms, and less than 1% will meet criteria for PTSD (Copeland, Keeler, Angold, & Costello, 2007).

In a series of studies and reviews, Bonanno (e.g., Bonanno, 2004; Bonanno, 2005; Mancini & Bonnano, 2006), has underscored the fact that most people are surprisingly resilient when faced with extreme circumstances. One of the most important findings in his research is that, regardless of the nature of the potentially traumatic events that people must confront, approximately one third to one half demonstrate psychological resilience. In other words, such individuals experience only a passing period of mild distress and/or disruption in daily activities. After the normal initial distress that almost everyone feels when dealing with life-threatening situations or the death of loved one, resilient individuals quickly regain their previous level of well-being and mental health, often within days or weeks. A second important finding is that recovery is not the most common response to potential trauma—resilience is! Recovery is defined as the experience of moderate to severe distress in the face of trauma, followed by a gradual return to normal functioning over a period of many months. Across all types of trauma, Bonanno and colleagues have estimated that 15% to 35% of people recover within 2 years.

What are the factors that characterize resilient individuals? They include the presence of supportive relationships and the ability to flexibly adapt to change when required. You will learn more about this in Chapter 10 when we describe how educational and treatment programs build on these "protective factors" in an effort to prevent the development of clinically significant distress. Bonanno and colleagues have also found that expressing more positive emotions than negative emotions is characteristic of many resilient people. Moreover, consistent with a great deal of research on the mental health benefits of overly positive views of oneself (e.g., Taylor & Brown, 1988), they also reported that the tendency to overestimate one's own abilities and positive qualities is frequently associated with resilience. Given the fact that loss and trauma are invariably part of the human condition, research on resilience holds great promise for helping countless individuals better cope with both predictable and unpredictable severe stressors.

Instead, it seems that there are a number of core pathological processes that underlie the overt expression of a seemingly diverse range of symptoms (Krueger & Markon, 2006). As an example, the internalizing and externalizing dimensions that were first identified with respect to American children's problems have been found to be applicable across countries as diverse as Ethiopia, Iceland, Korea, Israel, and Jamaica (Ivanova et al., 2007). These dimensions are also helpful in understanding adult problems. A major cross-cultural study examining the structure of psychiatric comorbidity in 14 countries (Netherlands, Germany, United Kingdom, France, Italy, Greece, Turkey, Japan, China, India, Nigeria, Brazil, Chile, and the United States) tested for the presence of these factors. Krueger, Chentsova-Dutton, Markon, Goldberg, and Ormel (2003) found that depression, somatic disorders, and anxiety consistently formed a single factor, whereas symptoms of alcohol abuse consistently formed a second factor. The inclusion of data from a variety of Western and non-Western countries strengthens the conclusion that there may be internalizing and externalizing psychopathological characteristics that underlie many mental disorders. We will return to this perspective in the final section of this chapter.

OTHER CLASSIFICATION SYSTEMS

The *International Statistical Classification of Diseases and Related Health Problems* (ICD-10) is the statistical classification of all health conditions developed by the World Health Organization and is now in its tenth edition (WHO, 1992). The way in which the ICD-10 is used varies from country to country. Most countries use it, at a minimum, to classify causes of death. In the United States and some other countries, a clinical modification of the ICD has often been used to classify diagnoses for all conditions and reasons for visits for health care services. The clinical modification provides more precision about each diagnosis and the person's condition than does the comparable ICD; this is important because more detail is required if the information is to be used for service provision purposes than if it is to be used for statistical purposes (such as reporting population-based trends in illness). The Mental and Behavioral Disorders section found in the ICD-10 is compatible with the DSM-IV, although there are some differences in the way in which diagnoses are described or conceptualized. For example, acute stress reaction is defined differently than is the DSM-IV acute stress disorder—it is not seen as a potential precursor to PTSD—and a broader, more diffuse set of anxiety and depressive symptoms is presented, with the timeframe for symptom expression being the first two days following a traumatic event (Harvey & Bryant, 2002).

The World Health Organization has also developed a companion classification system for the ICD that is called the *International Classification of Functioning, Disability and Health* (ICF). Moving beyond the classification of disease and illnesses, the ICF provides a system for describing health and health-related conditions. With respect to functioning and disability (i.e., impairments in functioning, activity limitations, or participation restrictions), information is coded for both the person's body (functions of body systems and body structures) and the person's societal involvement (activities and participation). It is also possible to use the ICF to code environmental factors that affect a person's health functioning. The focus on overall functioning and disability, as opposed to just a clinical diagnosis, is particularly important for psychologists working in rehabilitation and pain management services.

A fundamentally different approach to the classification of mental disorders is found in the *Achenbach System of Empirically Based Assessment* (ASEBA; Achenbach, 2002). With the recent development of scales for adults, ASEBA is a family of empirically derived assessment tools to measure competence and problems across the lifespan. The ASEBA broad-band dimensions of internalizing and externalizing problems have been shown to be useful in understanding both child and adult problems. Measures are available to be completed by parents of very young children (Child Behavior Checklist/1.5–5) and school-age children (CBCL/6–18). Parallel measures can be completed by adolescents (Youth Self Report: YSR) and by young adults (Young Adult Self-Report: YASR). In addition, measures have been developed for teachers and caregivers of very young children (Caregiver-Teacher Report Form/2–5) and for teachers of school-age children (Teacher Report Form, TRF 5–18). Finally, measures are available to evaluate the functioning of adults (Adult Self-Report/18–59, Adult Behavior Checklist/18–59, Older Adult Self-Report/60–90+, Older Adult Behavior Checklist/60–90+).

The ASEBA was designed to provide a standardized, normative framework for rating behavior competence and problems and for integrating information from different raters. As mentioned earlier in the chapter, behavior problem scales were derived empirically through factor analysis. The scales yield broad-band measures of internalizing (withdrawn, somatic complaints, and anxious/depressed) and externalizing (delinquent and aggressive) problems, as well as measures of finer-grained syndromes. Some syndromes are found only for certain age and sex groupings, and some are evident only on one measure. Clinical cut-off scores allow both a dimensional and categorical approach to be taken. In addition, some of the measures allow an assessment of DSM symptoms. Research with the ASEBA has confirmed that it is common for there to be only modest correlations between different raters of a child's problems. One very helpful feature of the ASEBA is a Cross-Informant Comparison that provides information on the correlation between different raters of the same problem, as well as a comparison to normative data. So, for example, 14-year-old Will's responses to the YSR might show that he sees himself as having only a few externalizing problems, whereas his mother sees him as having clinically significant externalizing problems, but the degree of agreement between them is average for 14-year-olds and their mothers.

SUMMARY AND CONCLUSIONS

Classification is a fundamental human activity. The classification of mental disorders draws on both a neo-Kraepelinian tradition as well as on a more recent developmental psychopathology approach that takes into account contextual variables such as developmental stage. The definition of a mental disorder requires not only that behaviors are abnormal, but also that they cause harm to the individual and that they are outside the individual's control. In North America, the most commonly used system is the *Diagnostic and Statistical Manual of Mental Disorders*. Over time this manual has moved toward placing a greater reliance on evidence-based diagnosis. In turn, the development of clear decision-making rules has enabled advances to be made in the study of psychopathology. Cross-cultural studies using the DSM system have revealed great variability across countries in the incidence of disorders. The most common types of disorders found in all countries are anxiety disorders and mood disorders. An alternative approach to categorical diagnosis is to assess individuals on important dimensions of functioning. In particular, the dimensions of internalizing and externalizing problems that were originally identified from studies of child psychopathology are also proving to be useful in understanding adult psychopathology.

Critical Thinking Questions

What are the benefits of classification?

Why should we care about whether a behavior is abnormal or not?

How does culture influence definitions of normality and abnormality?

What is the role of basic research in psychology in informing the diagnosis of mental disorders? How can we make sense out of differing prevalence rates of mental disorders across countries?

What are the advantages and disadvantages for a young person such as Carl of receiving a diagnosis of PTSD?

Key Terms

categorical approach to classification: an object is determined to either be a member of a category or not

classification validity: the extent to which the principles used in classifying an object are effective in capturing the nature of reality

classification utility: the usefulness of the resulting classification scheme

comorbidity: the situation of a person receiving diagnoses for two or more disorders at the same point in time

developmental psychopathology: a framework for understanding problem behavior in relation to the milestones that are specific to each stage of a person's development

diagnosis: the result of applying the decision-making rules of a diagnostic system to the symptoms of a specific individual

diagnostic system: a classification based on rules used to organize and understand diseases and disorders

dimensional approach: classification based on the assumption that objects differ in the extent to which they possess certain characteristics or properties

dyscontrol: the impairment resulting from a disorder must be involuntary or not readily controlled

harmful dysfunction: behaviors associated with a disorder are dysfunctional and cause harm to the individual or to those around him or her.

prototype model of diagnosis: model in which members of a diagnostic category may differ in the degree to which they represent the concepts underlying the category

Key Names

Thomas Achenbach

David Barlow

Emil Kraepelin

Robert Spitzer

ADDITIONAL RESOURCES
Books

American Psychiatric Association. (2000). *Diagnostic and statistical manual of mental disorders* (4th ed., text revision). Washington, DC: Author.

First, M. B., & Tasman, A. (Eds.). (2004). *DSM-IV mental disorders: Diagnosis, etiology, and treatment.* Hoboken, NJ: John Wiley & Sons.

Journals

Journal of Abnormal Psychology

Journal of Abnormal Child Psychology

Archives of General Psychiatry

American Journal of Psychiatry

Check It Out!

Information on the DSM-IV, including its history and use, can be found at this American Psychiatric Association site: http://www.psych.org/MainMenu/Research/DSMIV.aspx

More on the development of the DSM-V can be found on this American Psychiatric Association site: http://www.psych.org/MainMenu/Research/DSMIV/DSMV.aspx

For information on the World Health Organization's International Classification of Diseases, go to: http://www.who.int/classifications/icd/en/

The National Institute of Mental Health provides a wealth of data on the prevalence of mental disorders: http://www.nimh.nih.gov/health/publications/the-numbers-count-mental-disorders-in-america.shtml

CHAPTER 4

Research Methods in Clinical Psychology

INTRODUCTION

"Will I be able to stop binge eating if I follow this therapy?"
"I have a bipolar disorder, so how likely is it that my children will have this disorder too?"
"Is there anything that can be done to help my son who has autism?"
"How much time is my mother likely to have before her dementia makes it impossible for her to safely live on her own?"
"What effect will my divorce have on my young daughter?"

Psychologists who provide services to the public face questions like these on a daily basis. Clinical psychologists are constantly confronted with questions that require answers based on solid research data. The people asking these and myriad similar questions deserve far more than a response based simply on a hunch—they deserve the best information that science can provide. That is why a review of clinical research methods is essential in understanding clinical psychology. You may recall learning in Chapter 1 that among the health professions, clinical psychology provides the strongest research training. In this chapter, you will learn about the ways that research methods inform and guide the delivery of psychological services.

This chapter provides a brief introduction to the kinds of issues that must be considered in designing and interpreting research in clinical psychology. The majority of issues that we touch on apply to research in other areas of psychology, but we will highlight their relevance to the practice of clinical psychology and discuss some challenges that only clinical researchers face in testing their research hypotheses. Our intent is to provide an overview of the issues and methods that are central to conducting research in clinical psychology. Although important for clinical practice, we will not touch on various applied research/evaluation strategies, such as program evaluation. Likewise, we will not address qualitative research approaches (such as focus groups, participant observations, and document analysis) used in some areas of clinical psychology research. The quantitative research designs we discuss in this chapter focus on testing hypotheses generated by the researcher, whereas, in general, qualitative research tends to be more exploratory in nature (interested readers can learn more about qualitative research methods in psychology from helpful publications such as Elliott, Fischer, and Rennie, 2003, and Silverman and Marvasti, 2008).

To give you a sense of the whole research endeavor, we begin by discussing why we need research and the ways that research hypotheses can be generated. Then we emphasize ethical issues in the planning, conduct, and reporting of research. Next, we describe a number of clinically relevant research designs, and highlight aspects of sampling, measurement, and statistical analyses. We conclude this chapter by attending to factors that influence the reporting and utilization of research results. It is important to be aware that the type of disciplined thinking required to design a good study is also necessary to design and evaluate psychological services.

According to our professional standards and our ethical codes, people have a right to expect psychological services that are firmly based on psychological science. As described in Chapter 1, this is known as evidence-based practice—basing clinical services and health care policy, whenever feasible, on replicated evidence gathered from scientific studies (Institute of Medicine, 2002; Sackett, Rosenberg, Gray, Haynes, & Richardson, 1996). Evidence-based practice requires psychologists to be not only sensitive and empathic, but also well-informed about current research relevant to the services they provide. The effective scientist-practitioner thinks in a scientific manner and applies knowledge derived from research with care and compassion. The antithesis of evidence-based practice is practice based on tradition and authority, which some have facetiously called *eminence-based practice,* in which recommendations are accepted because the person delivering them is seen as an expert. The public should be skeptical about accepting opinions simply because they come from a supposed expert on a television talk show. As Mullen and Streiner (2004) rightly stated, the opinions of even recognized experts are just that—opinions—unless their views are supported by the best available empirical evidence. Moreover, as illustrated in **Table 4.1**, we cannot simply rely on common sense as a guide to appropriate decision-making, as there are often logical inconsistencies in the way people process information and make decisions. Although such inconsistencies may be of little consequence when facing a decision about what brand of breakfast cereal to buy, they can have enormous effects on decisions related to seeking and following through on health care services.

The evolution of the treatment of obsessive-compulsive disorder (OCD) is a good example of the way that research can inform practice (Thomas & Rosqvist, 2003). You may recall that in Chapter 3 we described Teresa, who has OCD. Literature dating back centuries describes people who had what we now call obsessions and compulsions. The clinical focus on OCD started in the 1800s, when these obsessions and compulsions were seen as a mental problem. Until the 1960s, OCD was considered an untreatable disorder, so someone like Teresa might have received a diagnosis but would not have received services that were likely to help. However, the prognosis for individuals with OCD changed dramatically with the development of behavioral treatments that included the

TABLE 4.1 Some Common Errors in Thinking

Faulty Reasoning: A form of argument that is inaccurate or misleading in some way. *Example: "Psychologists have provided effective services for decades without having research available on what makes treatment effective. Therefore there is no reason for me to bother reading this research in order to be effective."* One of the ways in which this is inaccurate is that the argument does not provide any proof that the services of these unspecified psychologists were effective.

False Dilemma: This fallacy takes the form of reducing the range of options available to just two (usually extreme) options. *Example: "Either I accept the treatment that the psychologist is suggesting or I just give up trying to change."* Clearly other options are available, including asking the psychologist what treatment options might be available or consulting another psychologist (or other health care provider) to obtain a second opinion.

Golden Mean Fallacy: This logical error involves assuming that the most valid conclusion to reach is a compromise of two competing positions. *Example:"I have heard that both cognitive and psychodynamic treatments can be helpful for the type of problems I have, so I really should look for a treatment that combines both cognitive and psychodynamic elements."* Assuming that the original statement about effective treatments is correct, there is no reason to assume that a synthesis of the two treatments would be more effective than either treatment on its own.

The Straw Person Argument: This involves mischaracterizing a position in order to make it look absurd or unpalatable. *Example: "Anyone who would prescribe a drug to treat my son's symptoms just wants to turn active kids into zombies."* It is highly unlikely that the health care professional recommending medication has this goal in mind, but it provides a simplistic rationale for rejecting the possibility of taking the medication.

Affirming the Consequent: This logical error takes the following form: first, assume that *x* is a cause of *y*, then, when *y* is observed, conclude that *x* must have caused it. *Example: "People who have schizophrenia always act in a bizarre manner. This person is acting bizarrely. So obviously, this person has schizophrenia."* There are problems with this, including the fact that people with schizophrenia do not always act in a bizarre manner and that there can be many explanations for bizarre behavior other than the presence of a psychotic disorder.

Appeal to Ignorance: This mistake takes the form of arguing that, because there is no evidence to prove a position is wrong, the position must be correct. *Example: "There is no scientific evidence that having my patients sing and dance while they remember the trauma that they experienced harms them or is ineffective. So, of course, this new form of therapy has to be helpful."* The lack of evidence to demonstrate harm or ineffectiveness is not, of course, equivalent to the presence of evidence for the beneficial effects of the treatment.

Adapted from K. S. Pope, 2003

key treatment components of exposure and response prevention. Exposure involves generating anxiety for the individual by deliberate exposure to the anxiety-provoking thoughts or external stimuli. Response prevention involves stopping the person from engaging in the rituals that are typically used to inappropriately manage the anxiety. Research has shown that when this form of treatment is used, most people with OCD experience substantial improvements in functioning (Kobak, Greist, Jefferson, Katzelnick, & Henk, 2004). However, the road to the development of effective behavioral therapy for OCD was not a direct one, and there were many dead

Imagine the response from these students if you were working at the next table and suddenly yelled "Stop" as part of your thought-stopping treatment. (*Source:* Media Bakery)

ends and wrong turns along the way. For example, it was common in the 1970s and 1980s for a thought-stopping component to be included in OCD treatments. This required the person to yell "Stop" or to make a loud noise whenever unwanted, intrusive thoughts occurred. Although this strategy fit with a behavioral theory about obsessions and compulsions, it was not very practical. Even more problematic, later research showed that trying not to think about something often has a paradoxical effect: it results in the increased persistence of intrusive thoughts! This is a good example of how clinical psychology practice must change when evidence shows that a theoretically sound intervention does not work.

Imagine the response you might get from others in the library or the bus if you were to yell "Stop" or make a loud noise every now and again. If we ask you not to think of taking a break from studying and having a delicious snack, you may notice that images of appetizing snacks keep popping into your head.

Profile Box 4.1 introduces Dr. Charles Morin who has conducted ground-breaking work on insomnia.

PROFILE BOX 4.1

DR. CHARLES MORIN

I earned a Ph.D. in clinical psychology from Nova South-eastern University in Florida. I then completed a pre-doctoral clinical internship at the University of Missis-sippi Medical Center and a postdoctoral fellowship at Virginia Commonwealth University, where I remained on the faculty as professor of psychiatry from 1987 to 1994. Since 1994 I have served as a professor of psychology and director of the Sleep Research Centre at Laval University in Quebec City. I am a licensed psychologist in Virginia and in Quebec. I have developed a clinical

Dr. Charles Morin

research program on sleep disorders and established an international reputation for my work on psychological and behavioral approaches to treating insomnia. My research is funded by the National Institute of Mental Health and the Canadian Institutes for Health Research. I have published 175 articles and chapters and 5 books. I am an associate editor for the journals *Sleep* and *Behavioral Sleep Medicine*. My contributions to psychology have been recognized with several awards, including a Distinguished Scientific Award for an early career contribution to psychology by the American Psychological Association and two Canadian awards for an exceptional career contribution to psychology as a science and a profession.

How did you choose to become a clinical psychologist?

My initial curiosity about the mind–body connection gradually evolved to an interest for themes related to psychology and health. As a pragmatic person, I have also been interested by the utilitarian and practical aspects of psychology and intrigued by how psychological interventions could improve health and quality of life. My professional interests became more focused on subspecialties such as behavioral medicine and clinical health psychology and, over the years, behavioral sleep medicine has been my primary area of specialization.

What is the most rewarding part of your job as a clinical psychologist?

To make meaningful changes in how people sleep at night. A great source of satisfaction is derived from feedback from clinicians or the lay person that a particular book or article I have written has been helpful to improve their sleep or their clinical practice. Also, as a psychology professor, I derive great satisfaction from working with and supervising very bright students who bring energy and new ideas and guiding them in making the right career choices.

What is the greatest challenge you face as a clinical psychologist?

The diversity of my work as a clinical psychologist and university professor is very appealing—teaching, research, consulting, clinical practice, supervision, and administration. With this diversity, however, comes the challenge of keeping an adequate balance and, at times, it is essential to make choices to become more focused on some of these activities.

Tell us about your research on insomnia

My research program is concerned with sleep disorders, with a primary focus on the development, validation, and dissemination of psychological interventions (mostly cognitive-behavioral therapies, CBT) for treating insomnia. Current research protocols examine the active therapeutic ingredients of CBT and evaluate whether CBT works best when used as a single therapy or in combination with medication. We have also designed effective methods to assist chronic users of medications to promote sleep to reduce or discontinue medication usage. To promote broader dissemination of these interventions to the general public, we have also validated different cost-effective delivery methods (group therapy and self-help approaches). A more recent addition to our research program is concerned with the epidemiology of insomnia, particularly the natural history of insomnia, its risk factors, and comorbidity with psychological disorders such as depression and anxiety.

How do you integrate science and practice in your work?

I am a strong advocate of the scientist-practitioner model. As much of my work is devoted to clinical research, I keep reminding myself that what we do as investigators must be applicable and generalize to the real clinical world. For example, it has become clear that insomnia presents more often with comorbid psychological (anxiety, depression) and medical conditions (pain) than as a primary problem. As such, most of our recent studies have focused on the treatment of comorbid insomnia. Also, as a clinician, if I need to plan an intervention for a problem I am not familiar with, I will go back to the recent literature and check what treatment has been shown effective in recent controlled trials.

What do you see as the most exciting changes in the field of clinical psychology?

The increasing acceptance that psychological therapies must be evidenced-based is both exciting and refreshing. With this change, however, comes the challenge to integrate empirically supported psychological therapies into the mainstream of health care delivery. As such, an important challenge for the future will be to develop more effective methods to disseminate validated psychological therapies to both clinicians and the general public.

GENERATING RESEARCH HYPOTHESES

How does a researcher decide what to study? **Table 4.2** shows some of the many possible sources of research ideas, including personal experience, professional experience, and knowledge of the scientific literature. As Dr. Morin noted, clinical work can be a rich source of research hypotheses. You will see that many of the psychologists profiled in this book also emphasize the extent to which their clinical work leads them to generate hypotheses that they then test in their research. Whatever the source or inspiration for our research ideas, our thinking is always influenced by the type of theory we hold about human behavior. In some instances the researcher uses a formal theory to generate a research idea; this is known as following a deductive process. In other instances the researcher follows an inductive

---

TABLE 4.2   Possible Sources of Research Ideas

Everyday Experience and Observation

Example: Noticing that your children's friends are troubled by their parents' divorce.
Professional Experience and Observation

Example: Noticing a pattern among one's patients that suggests a connection between feelings of social rejection and specific early childhood experiences.
Addressing Applied Problems and Needs

Example: Testing whether a successful psychoeducational treatment package for helping police officers better manage work stress can be adapted to alleviate the distress of victims of serious motor vehicle accidents.

Previous Research

Example: Attempting to reconcile contradictory findings in previous research by comparing the phenomenon in clinic and community samples, as variations in sampling may be responsible for these inconsistent findings.

Theory

Example: Directly comparing the ability of two different theories of motivation to predict which distressed couples will stay in couples therapy and which couples will terminate services prematurely.

process—for example, deriving an idea from repeated observations of everyday events. Even though the inductive process is not explicitly guided by theory, it is influenced by the researcher's informal theories, including his or her theoretical orientation and general worldview. Thus with a strong behavioral background, Dr. Morin is likely to pay attention to aspects of learning that may explain problematic sleep patterns. Theories not only influence the types of research ideas the researcher generates, they also influence the way the researcher interprets the data he or she obtains from the completed research study. In other words, researchers are not immune from the potential biasing effects of their own beliefs and values. Despite the potential for theories to mislead researchers in their interpretation of research data, science could not progress without theories, for theories serve to organize and give meaning to the results of research endeavors and to generate new ideas to be tested in future research. Theories are not a problem, unless the researcher treats them as facts—as long as the researcher is willing to formulate and test hypotheses, theories are extremely useful.

After developing a general research idea, scientists follow a number of steps to ensure that the hypothesis is properly formulated and tested. First, the researcher consults the published research on the phenomenon of interest. Second, assuming that there is no research that has directly tested the idea, the researcher begins to formalize ideas so they can be tested in a scientific manner. This requires translating abstract ideas into something that can be measured. For example, a researcher interested in violence may decide to measure the frequency and intensity of violent acts in the previous year. Part of this task of *operationalizing* an abstract concept requires that the researcher consider the precise nature of the relations among the concepts that form the research idea (see **Table 4.3**). A major challenge in operationalizing an idea is ensuring that the resulting operational definition fully captures the key

---

TABLE 4.3   Conceptualizing the Relations Among Concepts/Variables

1. **What are the relations among the variables of interest?**
   Correlation: The variables are associated with each other.
   Example: Mothers' ratings of children's behavior problems are correlated with fathers' scores of children's behavior problems.
   Cause: One variable directly or indirectly influences the level of a second variable.
   Example: A child's hyperactive symptoms result in parental stress.

2. **What are the factors that influence the relations among variables?**
   Moderation: One variable influences the direction or size of the relation between two other variables.
   Example: The negative effects of marital conflict on children are lower in families with a strong parental alliance than they are in families with a poor parental alliance.

3. **How does one variable influence a second variable?**
   Mediation: The influence of one variable on a second variable is due, in whole or in part, to the influence of a third variable.
   Example: The link between maternal HIV status and children's depressive symptoms is partially explained by maternal depressive symptoms.

4. **Is it possible to alter an outcome of interest?**
   Prevention: An attempt to decrease the likelihood that an undesirable outcome occurs.
   Example: School-based programs to decrease bullying.
   Intervention: An attempt to decrease or eliminate an undesirable outcome that has already occurred.
   Example: Treatment to reduce bingeing and purging.

Adapted from Kazdin (1999)

aspects of the original idea. Third, the researcher must carefully consider the extent to which the research idea may be based on cultural assumptions that may limit the applicability or relevance of the planned research (American Psychological Association, 2003a). The value of the research is enhanced by ensuring the cultural relevance of the planned research and the use of appropriate samples of participants. Fourth, the researcher must consider ethical issues in testing the idea. For example, ethical considerations might make some research designs unsuitable, such as using random assignment in an experiment to determine the effects of violence. Finally, the researcher must draw together all the results of the previous steps to sketch out the study procedures. Along the way, some aspects of the planned study may need to be dropped or modified due to practical constraints (e.g., insufficient funds available, lack of appropriate measures).

Choices about the ethical conduct, type of research design, sample of participants, and measures used all influence the research hypothesis that will be tested. For example, a simple statement such as "Increased anxiety is associated with more errors in social interactions" could be translated into a number of very different research hypotheses, each dependent on choices made about methodological features of the study. To determine whether increased anxiety was associated with more errors in social interaction across people with different levels of trait anxiety, the design would include research participants of varying anxiety levels. If the researcher wished to determine whether the statement was true within individuals as they became more or less anxious, then the design would require that participants be tested repeatedly as they experienced different levels of anxiety. This might also involve the researcher attempting to manipulate the participants' anxiety levels, in which case the hypothesis would be recast as "An increase in anxiety causes more errors in social interactions." If the researcher wished to determine whether the statement was true for all ages, this would require participants of different ages. The bottom line is that researchers must ensure that the research methods match the hypothesis to be tested.

 If you wanted to test out the idea that mental disorders are associated with stigma, what kind of hypotheses might you generate?

ETHICS IN RESEARCH

We cannot overemphasize the importance of close attention to ethical factors in the design, conduct, and reporting of research. This is true for all science, but it is especially important in clinical psychology research in which research participants may be vulnerable due to their psychological distress and/or to the fact that they may be receiving treatment services as part of the research. The quest for knowledge must never compromise the welfare of research participants. Many psychological organizations, such as the American Psychological Association (see Chapter 2), the Australian Psychological Society, and the British Psychological Society include in their ethical codes sections that specifically address the application of ethical principles in a research context (Rae & Sullivan, 2003).

Illustrating the range of ethical issues that must be considered throughout the research process, **Table 4.4** provides a summary of research-relevant ethical principles found in the APA code of conduct

TABLE 4.4   American Psychological Association Ethical Principles for Research and Publication

1. **Institutional Approval**
   When required, institutional approval for research must be obtained and the research must be conducted in accordance with the approved research protocol.

2. **Informed Consent for Research**
   When obtaining informed consent, potential participants must be informed of the purpose of the research, their rights to decline or withdraw participation, the possible consequences of declining or withdrawing, the possible consequences of being involved in the research, any benefits stemming from research involvement, limits of confidentiality, incentives for research participation, and whom to contact for questions about the research and participants' rights.

3. **Informed Consent for Recording**
   Informed consent for recording voices or images must be obtained prior to the recording unless the research consists solely of observations in public places or the research design involves some form of deception that requires that informed consent be sought after the recording has been completed.

4. **Client/Patient, Student, and Subordinate Research Participants**
   When research is conducted with clients/patients, students, or subordinates, steps must be taken to protect the potential participants from adverse consequences of declining or withdrawing participation.

5. **Dispensing With Informed Consent**
   It may be possible to dispense with informed consent only where the research would not be expected to cause harm or distress or where permitted by law or government regulation.

6. **Offering Inducements for Research Participation**
   Excessive or inappropriate monetary or other inducements for research are to be avoided if such inducements are likely to coerce participation in the research.

7. **Deception in Research**
   Deception is not used in research unless it is justified by the study's likely value and the use of nondeceptive procedures is not feasible. Deception cannot be used if the research is likely to cause physical pain or severe emotional distress. When deception is used, participants must be informed about the nature of deception as early as is feasible.

8. **Debriefing**
   Participants must have an opportunity to promptly obtain information about the nature, results, and conclusions of the research and steps must be taken to attempt to correct any misconceptions about the research.

9. **Humane Care and Use of Animals in Research**
   Animals used in research must be acquired, cared for, used, and disposed of in compliance with laws, government regulations, and professional standards. All those involved in the use of animals in research must be instructed in the care, maintenance, and handling of the animals. Reasonable efforts are made to minimize the discomfort and pain of animal subjects and, if an animal's life is to be terminated, the act must proceed rapidly and with an effort to minimize pain.

10. **Reporting Research Results**
    Fabrication of data is not permitted and reasonable steps must be taken to correct any significant errors found in published research reports.

11. **Plagiarism**
    The work or data of others is not presented by a researcher as his/her own.

12. **Publication Credit**
    Authorship of a publication must accurately reflect the contributions of the author(s); minor contributions to the research or the writing of the publication do not merit authorship.

13. **Duplicate Publication of Data**
    Data that have been previously published are not published subsequently as original data.

(Continued)

TABLE 4.4 *(Continued)*

14. **Sharing Research Data for Verification**
    After results are published, researchers must ensure that their data are available for verification or re-analysis by other competent professionals.

15. **Obligations on Reviewers**
    Those who review material submitted for publication or for grant support respect the confidentiality of the material.

Adapted from APA (2002a).

(2002a). These principles underline that attention to the welfare of research participants (and animal subjects) and honesty in the presentation of research findings are overarching themes to which psychologists must attend.

As indicated in Table 4.4, researchers have an ethical obligation to those involved in their studies. The issue of informed consent from research participants is particularly important, as this provides an assurance that a research participant is fully aware of the benefits or risks of research involvement. An example of a consent form for a clinical psychology research study is presented in **Table 4.5**. Once researchers have published the results of their studies, they also have an ethical obligation to share their data with other researchers (see Table 4.4). This ensures that other qualified scientists can access the data and verify the results of the research. However, such sharing may occur much less frequently than is desirable. For example, after many months and repeated efforts to obtain data from the authors of studies published in some of the best journals in psychology, Wicherts, Borsboom, Kats, and Molenaar (2006) reported that almost three quarters of the authors refused to provide their data for re-analysis.

Prior to data collection, the researcher must obtain approval for conducting the research from the institution in which he or she works. In universities and health care facilities, institutional review boards (IRBs) are charged with ensuring that the proposed research conforms to the policy statements on the ethical conduct of research formulated by the Department of Health and Human Services and funding agencies such as the National Institutes of Health. This means that the researcher must provide extensive details about the proposed study to the institution's IRB. The details include both general information about the nature of the study and the procedures involved, as well as information specific to ethical considerations in the recruitment and research involvement of participants. **Table 4.6** lists the types of information that a researcher must provide when seeking IRB approval to conduct a study.

RESEARCH DESIGNS

As we describe in the following sections, numerous research designs are used in clinical psychology research. These designs vary in the degree of experimental manipulation (from naturalistic observation of behavior to true experimental designs) and in the number of participants involved (from single-participant designs to epidemiological designs using tens of thousands of participants). Although it is tempting to view certain designs as better, or stronger than others, this is an oversimplification of research in a given domain. All designs have advantages and disadvantages. As we describe below, some designs are better than others in their capacity to control certain threats to research validity. We cannot

TABLE 4.5 Sample Consent Form

Dr. Chris Brown

Department of Psychology, Central University

Telephone number: (123) 456-7890

Email address: chrisbrown@centralu.edu

We are conducting a study to better understand the factors that are involved in decisions to seek and receive psychological services. This study is being conducted by Dr. Chris Brown, a professor at the Department of Psychology at Central University. We would like to interview you about the factors that played a role in your decision to request psychological services at the Department of Psychology's Psychological Service Center and about the expectations you have for therapy or counseling. The interview will take place either prior to or following an appointment you have at the Psychological Service Center. Participation in the interview will take approximately 30 minutes. You will receive an honorarium of $15 for your participation in this study. This will be given to you following the completion of the interview.

I consent to participate in this study. I understand that I am agreeing to be interviewed and that the interview will involve approximately 30 minutes of my time. I understand that as the questions deal with personal decisions about seeking psychological treatment, I may experience some slight distress in answering the questions. I have received assurances from the researcher that every effort will be made to minimize the likelihood of any distress. Nevertheless, I have the right to refuse to answer any question. I also understand that I am free to withdraw from this study at any time. Any decision to withdraw from the study will not affect the status of the services I am receiving at the Psychological Service Center.

I understand that all my answers will be kept strictly confidential; not even my therapist will have access to any information related to this study. My information will be kept in a locked filing cabinet, and members of the research team will have access to the information. I also understand that the Central University Institutional Review Board may inspect research study records as part of its auditing process, although these reviews focus on the researchers and the study, not on my participation in the study.

I understand that my anonymity will be assured by never using my name or identifying information in the analysis and reporting of this study. Only a code number will be used to identify my information, and all reports of this study will involve combined information from all participants.

I understand that if I have any questions or concerns about the study I can contact Dr. Brown at (123) 456-7890 or at chrisbrown@centralu.edu. If I wish, I can also contact the university officer for ethics in research at (1 23) 456-0000 or at centralethics@centralu.edu to obtain information or to make a complaint about the ethical conduct of this study.

Finally, I understand that I can receive a summary of findings at the completion of the study.

There are two copies of this consent form, one of which I may keep.

Participant's Signature: _____

Date: _____

Researcher's Signature: _____

Date: _____

I wish to receive a summary of the findings of this study upon its completion.

YES ❑   NO ❑

TABLE 4.6   Sample Form for Requesting Ethics Evaluation of a Research Project

This application form must be completed and submitted by all researchers planning to use human participants in their research study. All questions must be answered fully.

1. **Type of Research**
   Example: Honors' student thesis project, doctoral dissertation, professor's research

2. **Researchers**
   Please provide names, addresses, and institutional affiliations.

3. **Research Project**
   Please provide title, anticipated starting and completion dates, and funding source. Please provide a summary (i.e., no more than six pages) of the proposed research that includes full details of the proposed methodology.

4. **Research Participants**
   Please provide details about the number of participants required, their ages and other demographic characteristics, and any special characteristics they must possess. Please explain why you are focusing on this specific population of participants.

5. **Participant Recruitment**
   Please provide details on how and where participants will be recruited. If an organization has consented to provide support for participant recruitment, please provide evidence of this consent. Who will be responsible for contacting potential participants? Please provide copies of all forms or scripts used to recruit participants. If children are to be recruited, what steps have been taken to ensure that they and their legal guardians are provided with developmentally appropriate descriptions of the research and the nature of participation in the research?

6. **Screening of Participants**
   Will any steps be taken to select or exclude individuals from research participation? If yes, please include copies of the materials used for this screening.

7. **Research Participation**
   What, exactly, are the participants asked to do in the research? Please provide copies of all measures or interviews that will be completed and a full description of all tasks that participations will be asked to complete.

8. **Informed Consent**
   Please provide a copy of the consent to research form. What steps have been taken to ensure that there is no coercion to participate in the research? What steps have been taken to ensure that all requests for participants and descriptions of the research are done in a respectful and culturally appropriate manner?

9. **Potential Harms and Benefits**
   Please describe the potential harms to research participants, including physical harm, psychological harm, legal harms or inconveniences, or economic inconveniences. What steps are to been taken to minimize these harms? Please describe the potential benefits of the research and why the potential benefits of the study outweigh its potential harms. Please indicate how participants will be debriefed at the end of their participation in the study.

10. **Anonymity**
    What steps will be taken to ensure the anonymity of participants during the research and in any presentation of the research results?

11. **Confidentiality**
    Please describe who will collect the data, who will have access to the data, and how the data will be stored. How long will the data be maintained?

---

determine the value of a design without knowing the state of knowledge in a research domain. For example, once a research area is well developed, correlational designs are unlikely to add anything new to the scientific literature. On the other hand, in a relatively new research area, even a relatively simple case study may make a meaningful contribution to the literature.

No single study can answer all of the important questions in a research area. Often a good study generates far more questions than answers. Research must be seen as cumulative, with each study contributing to the knowledge base of an area. Clinical psychology, as broadly defined in Chapter 1, involves the application of scientific knowledge to the understanding, assessment, prevention, and treatment of psychological disorders and distress. Many different research areas are relevant to the practice of clinical psychology. It is obvious that clinical practice should be informed by research on assessment, prevention, and intervention. In addition, clinical practice can be enriched by knowledge of research on psychopathology, stress and coping, normal development, normal family processes, and many other areas.

Some psychology students may find the rationale behind a number of research design features obscure or hard to comprehend. A useful way to think of these design features is as strategies that address potential shortcomings of psychological research. For example, some studies use control (or comparison) groups to examine similarities and differences between groups. This is done to address the criticism that a pattern seen in the research group of interest—such as the tendency for depressed adolescents to report conflictual relationships with their parents—may also be true for adolescents who are not depressed. In experimental designs, participants are randomly assigned to the experimental groups. This strategy is also used to increase the likelihood that all groups are comparable prior to an experimental manipulation occurring (such as receiving treatment or being on a waiting list prior to receiving treatment). After all, if groups are not equivalent prior to the manipulation it is much more difficult to argue that any group difference evident after the manipulation is indeed due to the manipulation. For example, in examining the efficacy of a computer-based treatment for depressed adolescents, it would be necessary to ensure that adolescents were randomly assigned to treatment or waiting-list groups; otherwise, positive changes in the computer-based treatment group might be attributed to preexisting differences between the groups, rather than to the effects of the specific treatment. Researchers usually remain cautious about study results until the study is replicated, preferably by a different group of researchers. No matter how important the results of a study appear to be, they are of limited value unless similar results are independently obtained by others working in the field. Imagine that a car manufacturer advertises a new car with incredible fuel efficiency. These claims are not very convincing unless they are obtained by others who, independently of the manufacturer, evaluate the same model of car and obtain comparable results.

You have probably noticed that published research studies include extensive detail about how the study was conducted, what statistical analyses were used, and what the results were. You may find these details boring and tend to skip over them. Now imagine that you are reading a study in order to attempt replicate it for your honors thesis—in this case, you will be eager to know the precise details so that you can conduct your study in the same way.

Over the years, psychologists have identified a relatively large number of design problems that can undermine the validity of a research study. Of course, if steps are taken to overcome these problems prior to conducting a study, the validity of a study is protected or strengthened. Therefore, researchers have gone to great lengths to develop and promote the use of a classification system that covers the majority of potential problems. As originally conceptualized by **Donald Campbell** (e.g., Cook &

TABLE 4.7   Some Common Threats to the Internal Validity of a Study

History: This threat involves the influence of events that occur outside the context of the study that influence or account for the results of the study.

Maturation: Changes in the participants due to their psychological or physical development that cannot be disentangled from the experimental manipulation can pose a threat to internal validity.

Testing: Repeated testing may influence the results of a study due to the participants' familiarity with a test and their memory of how they responded previously on a test or measure.

Instrumentation: In longitudinal studies, changes in the definition of constructs and in their measurement can make the interpretation of changes in participants' responses much more difficult, if not impossible.

Statistical Regression: Extreme scores on measures, both high and low, tend to be less extreme upon retesting. This may mean that changes in scores in a study may be due to regression, rather than to an experimental manipulation.

Selection Biases: This threat involves the effect that systematic differences in recruiting participants or assigning participants to experimental conditions may have on the outcome of the study.

Attrition: The loss of participants in a study over time may bias the results if there are systematic differences between those who remain in the study and those who withdraw from the study.

Adapted from Cook and Campbell (1979)

Campbell, 1979), these potential design problems are classified as representing threats to the *internal validity, external validity,* or *statistical conclusion validity* of a study. We will deal with the first two categories of threats to validity now and will discuss threats to statistical conclusion validity later in the chapter.

Internal validity refers to the extent to which the interpretations drawn from the results of a study can be justified and alternative interpretations can be reasonably ruled out. **Table 4.7** describes the types of threats to internal validity that psychologists must attend to in designing their research. External validity refers to the extent to which the interpretations drawn from the results of a study can be generalized beyond the narrow boundaries of the specific study in question. **Table 4.8** describes the types of threats to external validity that psychologists must address when designing their research.

A close reading of these two tables shows that there is no perfect study, and researchers must balance internal and external validity. Generally speaking, the more a researcher attempts to deal with threats to internal validity, the more he or she opens up the study to threats to external validity, and vice versa. By reducing threats to internal validity, the researcher opts to have as "clean" a study as possible. Typically, scientists initially give priority to concerns about internal validity, as this allows a relatively straightforward interpretation of the study's findings. Once again, though, the need to give priority to addressing internal or external validity threats depends on the state of the research field. Take, for example, the field of psychotherapy research. Research from the 1970s to the 1990s emphasized the need to control threats to internal validity. Treatment manuals were used to operationalize the nature of treatments, and numerous methodological and statistical strategies were developed to minimize effects due to selection biases and to attrition. Careful attention to threats to internal validity enabled scientists to gather relatively unambiguous

---

TABLE 4.8 Some Common Threats to the External Validity of a Study

Sample Characteristics: External validity can be limited because of the degree to which the characteristics of the research participants, such as their sociodemographic and psychological characteristics, map on to other samples and populations of interest.

Stimulus Characteristics and Settings: Aside from the participants, features of the study such as the institutional setting and the characteristics of those involved in the conduct of the study (e.g., therapists in a treatment study) may constrain the generalizability of obtained results.

Reactivity of Research Arrangements: By virtue of being in a study, participants may respond differently than they would in other contexts. This can severely limit the extent to which the results of the study provide information about how people behave outside of the research context.

Reactivity of Assessment: Participants' awareness that their behaviors, moods, attitudes, etc. are being monitored may influence how they respond in the study, and these alterations in response may not be consistent with their responses once the study is completed.

Timing of Measurement: The decision about when to measure variables may result in conclusions that are not true for all time points (e.g., observed effects that appear stable over time may in fact not be stable between measurement periods).

Adapted from Cook and Campbell (1979)

---

evidence of the clinical efficacy of many treatments. As you learned in Chapter 1, "efficacy" is the term used to describe treatment effects in tightly controlled experimental designs. Once psychotherapy researchers know that these treatments are helpful under tightly controlled conditions, they can move on to loosen some experimental controls on internal validity in order to enhance the external validity of subsequent treatment studies. Thus, in the next stage of treatment research, participation selection criteria may be relaxed, close monitoring of therapist interventions may be eliminated, and timelines for the delivery of services may be made more flexible, permitting an assessment of clinical effectiveness. In Chapter 1 you learned that effectiveness refers to treatment effects in real-world treatment settings and contexts, with typical patients and typical therapists.

Case Studies

As in medicine, case studies have a long and important history in clinical psychology. Descriptions of unusual presenting problems or of novel treatments have enriched the professional literature. A typical case study involves a detailed presentation of an individual patient, couple, or family illustrating some new or rare observation or treatment innovation. Case studies are a valuable format for making preliminary connections between events, behaviors, and symptoms that have not been addressed in extant research. Case studies can be a rich source of research hypotheses regarding the etiology or maintenance of disorders. They can also be the initial testing ground for innovative assessment or intervention strategies. Case studies have heuristic value—they draw the attention of other professionals to a phenomenon.

Changes in Joe's difficulties around homework might occur for many different reasons. (*Source:* Media Bakery)

The scientific value of case studies is in their potential to generate hypotheses; however, they do not allow for the rigorous testing of hypotheses. The major weakness of the case study method is that most threats to internal validity cannot be adequately addressed (Kazdin, 1981). Take, for example, a case study on the treatment of Joe's temper tantrums around homework. Usually, the author of a case study reports the client's symptoms or presenting problems prior to and following treatment (such as the number of tantrums and their intensity). Although the author would probably like to claim that any improvement was due to treatment effects, alternative explanations cannot be ruled out in this simple research design. The observed changes could be due to a number of other factors unrelated to therapy, including normal developmental changes (i.e., maturation—the simple effects of Joe growing older or having no homework during the holidays), the abating of symptoms that typically occurs over time (i.e., regression to the mean), or life events outside of therapy (i.e., history effects, such as getting a new teacher).

Single-Case Designs

The limitations of the case study can be at least partially addressed in a number of ways, even when the focus of the study remains on an individual patient (or couple or family) or on a very small number of patients (Hayes, Barlow, & Nelson-Gray, 1999; Morgan & Morgan, 2001). Threats such as maturation and regression to the mean can be easily handled by the simple strategy of extending the period of time that the person is assessed and the frequency with which the assessments occur. To address the threat of changing criteria or definitions of the problems/symptoms (i.e., instrumentation), the same measures can be used at each assessment point, rather than, for example, relying on one parent's ratings for pretest and the other parent's ratings for posttest. Also, the measures should be standardized and, if at all possible, well established, rather than potentially unstable and biased clinician observations. The possibility that observed changes are due to extra-treatment events can be partially addressed by clearly defining the nature of the therapeutic intervention and precisely noting when it occurred. Thus, *if* the problems were relatively consistent and stable prior to the target intervention *and* the change occurs very shortly after the intervention, *then* a case can be made for the change being due to the intervention. **Figure 4.1** illustrates a number of these features in what is commonly known as an A-B single-case design, with the A period representing the level of symptoms prior to the intervention (also known as the baseline) and the B period representing the level of symptoms following the intervention. Although intervention effects are typically determined by visual inspection of graphed data (such as represented in Figure 4.1), a number of statistical tests can be used to determine whether statistically significant changes occurred (e.g., Morley & Adams, 1989). Such tests can be especially valuable if the baseline assessment of symptoms shows a very variable pattern.

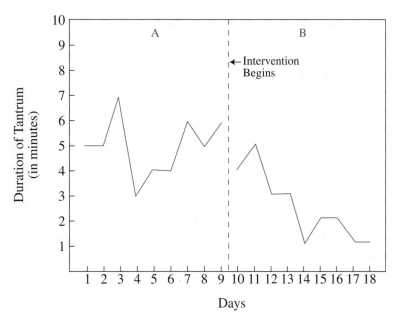

FIGURE 4.1 A-B Design

Two design strategies improve on the straightforward A-B design by ruling out the threat of history to the validity of the study. The first option is to conduct a small series of A-B designs using the same intervention with a number of individuals presenting with similar problems. If the data for three or four cases are collected sequentially (i.e., the people receiving the intervention do not all receive the intervention at the same point in time) and the symptom levels consistently appear to change following the intervention, then support for the contention that the intervention was responsible for the change is very strong. A second option is to use what is known as an A-B-A single-case design. This is similar to the A-B design except that the treatment is withdrawn after a few weeks and data continue to be collected for a second A period (i.e., a period in which no treatment occurs). For example, Joe's parents could be asked to ignore tantrums and reward homework completion during period B, and to return to their regular reaction of reminders and threats during the second A period. If Joe's tantrums return to pretreatment levels, then a strong case can be made for the effectiveness of the intervention. The major drawbacks to this design are that (a) it may not be possible to have the person refrain from using the treatment strategies during the second A period, especially if the strategies have been effective in reducing symptom levels for a few weeks and (b) ethical considerations may make clinicians unwilling to remove, however briefly, a treatment strategy that appears to be working well.

Correlational Designs

Correlational designs are probably the most commonly used research designs in clinical psychology. The focus of these designs, no matter how complex they are, is on the examination of association among variables. Although researchers may be tempted to make causal statements about associations in the data, they are inappropriate, because correlational designs can never determine causality. Even when one variable temporally precedes another variable, a causal connection cannot be established, because the apparent effect of the first variable on the second could be due to the influence of an unmeasured third variable. The hallmarks of the scientific study of causality in human functioning are the use of experimental manipulation and random assignment to conditions. Both of these design features are absent in correlational designs.

It is a mistake to equate correlational *analyses* with correlational *designs*. Correlational designs can be analyzed with all types of statistics, including correlations, partial correlations, multiple regression, *t*-tests, or analysis of variance (ANOVA). For example, many studies compare the performance on a laboratory task (e.g., a simulated social interaction) of people diagnosed with a DSM-IV disorder with the performance of people with no diagnosis. Even though there are discrete groups and an ANOVA is conducted to analyze group performance on the lab task, the design of the study is correlational in nature. No manipulation occurs (i.e., all participants experience the same conditions in the study) and participants are not randomly assigned to conditions. Sometimes researchers using a correlational design decide to artificially create groups from the data they collected by using median splits or some type of cut-off score to categorize participants as high or low on a dimension. Again, the use of group comparisons in the data analysis should not be confused with an experimental design. It is also worth noting that the common strategy of dichotomizing continuous variables is rarely appropriate and can frequently yield misleading results (MacCallum, Zhang, Preacher, & Rucker, 2002; Streiner, 2002). One of the main drawbacks of this strategy is that median splits are often used to form the two groups (i.e., half of the participants are assigned to each group) and whether a participant is assigned to the "high" group or the "low" group on the basis of his or her score depends on the median score for the set of participants. Therefore, as median scores are likely to differ across studies, the same participant score may be assigned to the "high" group in one study and the "low" group in another. This makes it extremely difficult to summarize findings across studies, as the precise nature of a "high" score varies from study to study.

Correlational designs come in many forms. Some are purely descriptive, such as the bulk of epidemiological research on the study of the incidence (the rate of new cases of a disorder in a specific time period), prevalence (the overall rate of cases of a disorder in a specific time period) and distribution (rates of disorders across geographic areas and/or sociodemographic characteristics) of disorders in a population. A good example of this type of study is the WHO World Mental Health Survey Consortium (2004) study of the prevalence of mental disorders that you learned about in Chapter 3.

Correlational designs can be used to examine the underlying structure of a measure or a set of measures using a procedure, known as **factor analysis**. Factor analysis is often used in the development of a measure to determine which items contribute meaningfully to the test. Despite the test developer's best efforts, some items may simply not work as well as others in assessing the construct the test was designed to evaluate—factor analysis can reveal which items "work" and which don't. Factor analysis can also be used to determine the conceptual dimensions that underlie a set of tests. For example, a researcher may have data from participants who completed measures on a range of variables such as anger, anxiety, loneliness, shyness, and dysphoria. Through the use of factor analytic techniques, the researcher can determine whether these measures all assess distinct constructs or whether they are better understood as tapping into a single, broad construct often labeled general distress or negative affectivity. Although factor analysis comprises a large range of statistical techniques, there are two basic

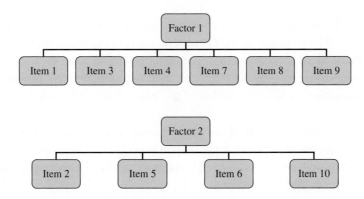

FIGURE 4.2   An Illustration of How Items in a Test Form Different Factors

forms of factor analysis. Exploratory factor analysis is used when the researcher has no prior hypotheses about the structure of the data. In this situation, the pattern of correlations among variables or test items provides the evidence for the underlying factor structure in the data. In contrast, a more demanding form of factor analysis, known as confirmatory factor analysis, is used to test a specific hypothesis regarding the nature of the factor structure. With confirmatory factor analysis, the researcher specifies, a priori, what the factor structure should be and how each variable or test item contributes to this structure. The statistical analysis then provides information on how well the structure observed in the data fits with the hypothesized factor structure. **Figure 4.2** illustrates the way test items from different factors.

Most frequently, correlational designs are employed to examine the relations among discrete variables in an effort to develop or test a conceptual model. One such design involves the testing of a **moderator** variable (see Table 4.3). A moderator variable is one that influences the strength of the relation between a predictor variable and a criterion variable (Holmbeck, 1997). For example, the relation between the experience of stressful life events and psychological distress may be moderated by the type of coping strategies used. Given comparable levels of life stress, the greater use of coping strategies designed to actively engage and resolve problems may result in lower levels of distress. In general, moderator analyses are used to enhance the researcher's ability to predict as much variance as possible in a criterion variable by exploring the ways in which other variables can be combined to predict the criterion. Another common design involves the testing of **mediator** variables. A mediator variable explains the mechanism by which a predictor variable influences a criterion variable (Holmbeck, 1997). For example, the relation between parental psychopathology and child adjustment may be due, partially or entirely, to the quality of the relationship between parent and child. In general, mediator analyses are used to explicate the conceptual link among variables. As an aside, moderator and mediator analyses can be used with both correlational and experimental designs (Kraemer, Wilson, Fairburn, & Agras, 2002).

A final correlational design that is increasingly used in clinical psychology research is known as **structural equation modeling** (SEM; e.g., Ullman, 2006). SEM is a comprehensive approach to testing an entire theoretical model. This design combines elements of confirmatory factor analysis and mediator analyses. First, the researcher lays out a structural model that shows how all the variables in the model are related to each other; this is akin to mediator analyses. For example, the model may be one in which both client beliefs about the benefits about treatment and the severity of client problems are hypothesized to predict the extent to which treatment is successful. The effect of beliefs about treatment on treatment outcome is hypothesized to be mediated by motivation to engage in the various aspects of treatment, whereas the effect of problem severity on treatment outcome is hypothesized to be direct, with no mediating variables. In SEM, the ability of the whole model to predict treatment outcome is assessed.

In a second step, the researcher considers how best to measure each variable in the model (in our example, this includes treatment expectations, problem severity, treatment motivation, and treatment outcome) and selects multiple measures for each variable in the model; the specification and testing of this measurement model is akin to confirmatory factor analysis. There are several strengths to this design. The analysis of the measurement model allows the researcher to obtain relatively pure measures of a construct that are derived from multiple measures used for each variable. These measures are then used to test a comprehensive structural model, rather than testing isolated aspects of the model one at a time as is typically done in mediator analyses. However, despite the complexity and strength of this design, SEM can only determine the extent to which a hypothesized causal model fits the study's data; it cannot unequivocally demonstrate that the hypothesized causal model is true. Nevertheless, it is possible to apply SEM to data gathered from experimental designs to make stronger statements about causal relations among some variables (MacCallum & Austin, 2000). One challenge in conducting SEM is that it requires a relatively large sample (i.e., more than 200 participants), which may be difficult to obtain in some research areas.

Quasi-Experimental Designs

Quasi-experimental designs involve some form of manipulation by the researcher, such as variations in the nature of the information provided prior to undertaking some task, exposure to different levels of noise while completing a task, or different types of treatment conditions. Quasi-experimental designs do not, however, involve random assignment to experimental conditions. A weakness of this design is that, because participants are not randomly assigned to the different conditions or levels of the independent variable, the effect of the independent variable on the dependent variable may be confounded with extraneous influences.

Of course, this raises the question of why anyone would choose not to use an experimental design. The answer is very simple: in many situations it is simply not ethical or feasible to randomly assign participants to conditions. A study of health care systems by Bickman (1996) illustrates the usefulness of quasi-experimental designs when experimental designs are not suitable. The study was designed to determine whether the provision of enhanced mental health care services, in addition to usual care, resulted in improvements in participants' psychological and social functioning. The enhanced care condition was extensive, with cost and training considerations limiting the availability of the condition to a single site. Because all participants in the area knew that the enhanced care was available, it would have been impossible to randomly assign participants to enhanced and usual care conditions. Instead, the researchers selected a site elsewhere that was comparable in terms of the population of potential participants and in terms of the usual mental health services available. Data were collected from participants at both sites to determine the effect of the enhanced care intervention.

The most frequently used quasi-experimental designs involve the comparison of two previously established groups of participants. In the simplest design, one group receives the intervention, the other doesn't. Data are collected after the intervention and then analyzed. This design is cost-effective and relatively straightforward because only one wave of data collection is required, but this must be balanced against the obvious weakness of this design: that the two groups may differ substantially prior to the intervention, thereby confounding the results. Data collection prior to the intervention strengthens the design, as preintervention differences can be controlled for statistically.

Experimental Designs

Experimental designs involve both random assignment to condition and experimental manipulation. These features allow the researcher to draw relatively unambiguous conclusions about the effects of the independent variable on the dependent variable. We say "relatively" unambiguous because results may be confounded by unplanned variability in the manner in which the manipulation occurred (e.g., therapists who are supposed to be providing the same treatment may differ in how closely they follow the treatment manual) or by the random assignment of participants failing to yield groups equivalent on all dimensions prior to the intervention (this is often due to using too small a sample).

Compared with all other research designs, experimental designs provide the best protection against threats to internal validity. As with quasi-experimental designs, the strongest design is one in which both preintervention and postintervention data are collected. Sometimes, however, concerns about reactivity to testing may lead a researcher to dispense with obtaining preintervention data, which weakens the ability to determine initial equivalence of groups. By skimming the pages of scientific journals in clinical psychology you will find many examples of experimental designs, often called true experiments. In the realm of psychotherapy research, these types of designs are typically known as **randomized controlled trials.** Randomized controlled trials involve the random assignment of participants into one of two or more treatment conditions. In many instances, a no-treatment condition (often called a wait-list condition) is included in which research participants do not immediately receive any form of intervention. Then, in order to meet ethical standards, once a period of time has passed that is comparable to the duration of the treatment(s) being investigated, those in the no-treatment condition are offered treatment.

Meta-Analysis

Until the 1980s, reviews summarizing research findings in a specific research realm were based on qualitative (that is, nonnumerical) methods. Somewhat like a sophisticated term paper, reviews provided a narrative account of the various studies, their strengths, weaknesses, and findings, and then drew conclusions about the state of knowledge in the research area. This traditional form of review is still used for summarizing conceptual and methodological approaches used in researching a topic. However, a quantitative form of research review known as **meta-analysis** is now the standard for making a general statement about the findings in a research field (Harris, 2003). Meta-analysis brings scientific rigor to the process of reviewing the results of research, which allows investigators to use explicit decision rules and computations in reporting findings. Consequently, meta-analytic studies are more frequently cited in the work of researchers than are studies using the other research designs we have described (Patsopoulos, Analatos, & Ioannidis, 2005). Meta-analysis involves a complex set of statistical procedures to quantitatively review research in an area. An analogy to a typical research study may be helpful to explain what meta-analysis is. A typical study involves the collection of data from multiple research participants; the data are then summed, and overall trends in the group of participants are examined using statistical procedures. The same general process occurs in meta-analysis, but the "participants" in a meta-analysis are research studies rather than individuals.

In a single research study, similar data are collected from all participants. Obviously this is not possible in a meta-analysis, for the original research studies are likely to have employed different measures for assessing outcome. Meta-analysis combines the results of prior research using a common metric called an **effect size** (Rosenthal & DiMatteo, 2001). Effect sizes can be calculated for almost all types of research designs and statistical analyses. For correlational analyses, the correlation coefficient is typically used as the effect size. For analyses involving differences among groups, the effect size is obtained by calculating the difference between the means of two groups (e.g., the treatment and no-treatment groups) and then dividing by the standard deviation of either one of the groups or the pooled sample of both groups. Although it may seem that these are relatively simple calculations, researchers have found that great care must be taken in quantitatively summarizing a research area, as it is very easy for errors to creep into the calculations of effect sizes (Gøtzsche, Hróbjartsson, Marić, & Tendal, 2007).

Meta-analysis offers numerous advantages over traditional research reviews or single empirical studies. For example, statistical analyses, rather than the author's impressions, guide the conclusions drawn about a research topic. Moreover, by including data from many studies, the number of research participants on whom conclusions are based is dramatically increased. This greatly enhances the researcher's power to detect an effect and improves the generalizability of the conclusions drawn on the basis of the literature. Given its methodological and statistical strengths, meta-analysis is increasingly used to determine the current state of knowledge about many areas of research and to assist in the development of health care policies regarding the provision of medical and psychological services. In Chapters 12 and 13 we describe several meta-analyses that have been influential in shaping views of the efficacy of psychological treatments for patients of all ages.

Researchers need to be aware of how differences in the characteristics of research participants may affect the generalizability of their results. (*Source:* Jasper White/Image Source Limited)

SELECTING RESEARCH PARTICIPANTS AND MEASURES

We cannot emphasize enough that no single study can answer all the questions in a research field. At best, a study adds a small amount of knowledge to a field. To be certain that this knowledge is meaningful, researchers must be cognizant of the strengths and limitations of their studies and must strive to reduce threats to the validity of the research. As we described in Tables 4.7 and 4.8, many of the threats to the internal and external validity of a study can be addressed by considering a number of participant sample and measurement parameters. In the following sections we highlight some issues that researchers must consider in order to maximize the validity of a study.

Selecting the Sample

Biases in sample characteristics and selection can have an enormous impact on the researcher's ability to accurately interpret study results. For example, a study based on data obtained from Caucasian male university students is likely to have rather limited generalizability, and the researcher must ensure that his or her conclusions accurately reflect the fact that the findings may not apply across age, gender, ethnicity, educational level, and socioeconomic status. Likewise, a study of parenting values based on data from two biological-parent European American families residing in the same home may provide very valuable information, but the results may not generalize to other ethnic groups or to other family constellations, such as step-families, single-parent families, or families with same-sex parents. As a starting point, therefore, the researcher needs to consider how best to optimize the fit between (a) the characteristics of the population to which the results will be generalized and (b) the type of sample that should be recruited for the study. It is also important that the researcher fully describe the characteristics of the participants involved in the research and the manner in which participants were recruited for the study—surprisingly, this is not always done in published research (Lee, et al., 2007). Without such information, it is not possible to determine whether the results may be biased by the sample composition.

Selecting the Sampling Strategy

It is rarely possible to obtain data from all members of a population, regardless of whether the population is defined as all citizens of a country, all those who experienced a specific stressor (such as surviving a hurricane), or all people with a specific mental disorder (such as schizophrenia). Accordingly, researchers must make decisions about how to obtain data from a subset of the population of interest—this is known as the research sample. Decisions about the strategies used to recruit participants can affect the validity and generalizability of a study. Two examples illustrate the potential research limitations of sampling strategies. A number of studies have examined the extent to which victims of childhood sexual abuse exhibit psychological symptoms and disorders as adults. Contradictory findings have been reported with respect to dissociative symptoms, with some studies finding little evidence of dissociative symptoms and others finding substantial evidence of the link between childhood victimization and later dissociative symptoms. Much of the apparent discrepancy between such findings appears to be due to variations in sampling strategies. The studies finding little or no connection tend to use community samples, whereas those reporting strong connections tend to use samples from psychological or psychiatric clinics. Thus, evidence for dissociative symptoms depends on the extent to which participants are experiencing clinical distress and/or seeking services for their distress (Rumstein-McKean & Hunsley, 2001). A second example comes from research on marital functioning. Karney and colleagues (1995) conducted two studies: in the first, couples were recruited through newspaper advertisements and, in the second, research participants were solicited from public records of marriage licenses. The two samples of participants differed on many sociodemographic, psychological, personality, and marital quality variables. Because of these differences, many of the significant associations found among these variables in one study were not found in the second. These two examples demonstrate the need for researchers to attend to sampling strategies, both in the design of a study and in interpretation of findings.

There are two basic forms of sampling: probability sampling and non-probability sampling (Henry, 1990). Probability sampling focuses on the use of numerous strategies to ensure that the research sample is representative of the population (e.g., obtaining data from every tenth household in a neighborhood, using census information to determine how many participants with different levels of income need to be recruited in a study, contacting a randomly selected 20% of all psychologists licensed in a jurisdiction and requesting their involvement in a study). The term "probability" sampling comes from the fact that, with these types of sampling strategies, the researcher knows the probability of selecting participants from the population of interest. This is the type of sampling is used in surveys that are frequently reported in the media on topics such as preferences for political parties or candidates, views on government priorities, and attitudes on issues such as immigration, health care, and the environment. Probability samples are required when the researcher is interested in obtaining an accurate and precise estimate of the strength, level, or frequency of some construct in the population. For this reason, probability sampling is typically used in epidemiological studies of the prevalence of mental disorders or the utilization of mental health services.

Although some psychological research uses probability sampling strategies, psychologists more commonly rely on non-probability sampling approaches. These sampling strategies may include advertising for research participants in a newspaper, on an electronic listserve, or in a mental health treatment setting. As you probably know from experience, many psychological studies rely on university students as research participants. Because the researcher does not know how many people read an ad for participation in the study, it is not possible to determine the probability of obtaining participants from the pool of potential participants. Furthermore, because the researcher is not specifically recruiting in order to ensure the representativeness of the sample, data from non-probability samples are unlikely to be as generalizable as data obtained from probability samples. However, in much psychological research, this is assumed not to be a major problem.

Setting the Sample Size

The final consideration is the number of participants required for the study. Without a sufficient number of participants, a study will not have the statistical power needed to detect the very effect it was designed to examine. Psychotherapy outcome research illustrates this challenge. Most experimental studies in which a treatment condition is compared with a no-treatment control condition have sufficient sample sizes and power to detect an effect due to treatment. However, a review of experiments in which two treatments were compared with each other found that only half of published studies had sufficient sample sizes and power to detect a difference between treatments (Kazdin & Bass, 1989). Although the conclusions of this review have been available for many years, there are still frequent problems with studies having low power to detect treatment effects. As we will discuss in Chapter 14, this means that a common interpretation that all psychotherapies have comparable effects may be based, at least partially, on research design weaknesses. Based on the statistical work of **Jacob Cohen**, many tools are available to assist in determining the optimal number of participants to recruit for a study based on the phenomenon under investigation, the research design, and the type of planned data analysis (e.g., Cohen, 1992).

Measurement Options and the Importance of Psychometric Properties

The idea that catharsis is helpful is a myth; in contrast, there is strong evidence that relaxation techniques are helpful. (*Source:* Media Bakery)

A multitude of measurement options are available to clinical psychologists conducting research. No option is necessarily the best for all types of studies. Instead, as we have repeatedly emphasized, the strengths and limitations of a measurement option (or a research design or a sampling strategy) must be carefully considered, along with the degree to which the measurement option fits the research hypothesis and other aspects of the planned study. **Table 4.9** provides a summary of the range of general measurement modalities that may be appropriate for a study. In many studies, multiple measures of each variable are selected, which enhances the likelihood that the variable of interest has been fully or adequately measured in the study. However, as the time required for study participation increases, it may have an effect on the study by selectively influencing the type of person who is able and willing to take part, thereby affecting the study's external validity.

The psychometric properties of a measurement strategy have a dramatic effect on the outcome of a study. Reliability—the degree of consistency in the measurement—and validity—the degree to which the construct of interest is accurately measured—both affect the quality of a study and the likelihood that a hypothesis is tested appropriately. **Table 4.10** provides a summary of the psychometric properties that a researcher should consider in selecting a measurement tool. Although there are literally thousands of established measures and assessment procedures available, in some instances researchers may choose to develop a measurement tool specifically for the study. In such cases the researcher must be sure to use a measure that is both reliable and valid.

VIEWPOINT BOX 4.1

DEALING WITH ANGER: DOES VENTING HELP OR HARM?

There are many expressions that give the sense that anger is something that accumulates and must be vented: people say they are "bottling up" their anger, but are concerned that once they reach a "boiling point" they will simply "explode," blow a fuse," "blow off steam," or "hit the ceiling." Using the metaphor of a pressure cooker, people are often encouraged to reduce their anger "pressure" by letting it off in a controlled manner. For example, numerous self-help books recommend so-called "safe" strategies for venting anger, such as throwing things onto a couch, hitting a pillow, breaking old dishes, or simply yelling and screaming. Although this makes intuitive sense, is there evidence that strategies to "let out" anger do any good?

The psychological theory that underlies the venting notion is known as catharsis, and it suggests that, by expressing anger, aggressive feeling, thoughts, and impulses will subsequently be reduced and a person will be less likely to behave in an angry fashion. Over the course of several decades, psychologists have designed many ingenious studies to test the catharsis hypothesis as it applies to anger. As summarized by Lohr, Olatunji, Baumeister, and Bushman (2007), in study after study, researchers have discovered that expressing anger does little to reduce aggressive tendencies and, frequently, may actually increase angry feelings and aggressive tendencies. Whether one's anger is directed at inanimate objects (e.g., hitting a punching bag, pounding nails, ripping papers, breaking glasses) or people (e.g., making negative statements about the target of the anger, responding with anger to people who were not the original source of the anger), anger seems to beget anger. In some instances people do report temporary relief after physically venting their anger, but usually this is little different from what occurs when people are encouraged to relax or simply let go of the anger. Forcefully expressing other negative emotions, such as sadness and fear, also seems to have little benefit, unless a person works at understanding and handling these emotions (e.g., Kennedy-Moore & Watson, 2001).

If expressing anger does not help, then what does? Several meta-analyses have found that the most efficacious treatments are those that include components of (a) teaching people to recognize the early signs of anger, (b) encouraging the use of relaxation strategies and other strategies aimed at reducing physical tension and arousal, and (c) helping individuals to analyze and respond to anger-provoking situations in a problem-solving manner rather than an emotional charged manner (e.g., Del Vecchio & O'Leary, 2004). Importantly, these treatments appear to work well for all ages, although children seem to benefit less than do adolescents and adults. As Lohr and colleagues (2007) remarked, psychologists have an ethical obligation to strive to ensure that their services do not harm clients and, as a result, they should provide services that are based on scientific evidence about what can help and what can harm.

TABLE 4.9 Measurement Options

Self-Report Measures: The research participant completes a questionnaire describing some aspect of himself or herself. This may range from global self-ratings, such as overall happiness or psychological adjustment, to very specific self-ratings, such as anxiety while completing a research task.

Informant-Report Measures: Information about a target research participant is gathered from other individuals. In clinical psychology research, this is typically someone who is well acquainted with the participant, such as a partner, a parent, or a teacher. Data may also be obtained from individuals with only limited experience with the participants: in studies of social interaction, for example, informant-report measures may be gathered from all the participants who interacted with a given participant.

Rater Evaluations: Data may be obtained from someone knowledgeable about a participant's involvement in a study, such as a rater who viewed videotapes of the participant performing a task or a therapist who provided treatment to the participant. Such rating can range from evaluations of very specific to very global features.

Performance Measures: Participants may be asked to complete tasks in a study, such as a visuo-motor task, a response time task, an identification task, or a task related to specific intellectual or social skills. The quality of the participant's performance on the task is used as data in the study.

Projective Measures: A technique such as a storytelling task may be used to assess the underlying needs or motives of a research participant. The assumption in using such measures is that they provide data that are different from those obtained through self-report.

Observation of Behavior: Coding systems or general ratings may be used to summarize elements of a participant's actual behavior. This may occur in either naturalistic settings such as the family home or in laboratory settings.

Psychophysiological Measures: A range of measurement options is available to evaluate a participant's biological characteristics. These include measures of autonomic arousal, cardiovascular activity, and neurological functioning.

Archival Data: Research data are often obtained from information sources that exist apart from the actual research study. Such sources may include police records, health care utilization records, and academic records.

ANALYZING THE DATA

Once data are collected, the researcher must conduct data analyses to determine the extent to which the research hypotheses have been supported. Appropriate data analysis is an integral part of a valid study, so researchers must carefully choose from a multitude of options for data analysis when designing the study. Guidelines on statistical methods are available to assist a researcher in making these important decisions (Wilkinson & the Task Force on Statistical Inference, 1999). Just as there are a number of threats to the internal and external validity of a study, so too are there many threats to the **statistical conclusion validity** of a study. Statistical conclusion validity refers to aspects of the data analysis that influence the validity of the conclusions drawn about the results of the research study. Common threats to statistical conclusion validity are outlined in **Table 4.11** As with other threats to validity, careful attention to these threats during the design of a study can increase the likelihood of accurately detecting an effect in the study.

Statistical and Clinical Significance

Researchers in psychology commonly rely on statistical tests to determine the outcome of a study and the degree to which a research hypothesis was supported. However, it is important to remember that,

TABLE 4.10   Psychometric Properties of Measures

RELIABILITY

Internal Consistency: The degree to which elements of the measure (such as items on a test) are homogeneous.

Test-Retest Reliability: The stability over time of scores on a measure.

Interrater Reliability: The consistency of scores on a measure across different raters or observers.

VALIDITY

Content Validity: The extent to which the measure fully and accurately represents all elements of the domain of the construct being assessed.

Face Validity: The extent to which the measure overtly appears to be measuring the construct of interest.

Criterion Validity: The association of a measure with some criterion of central relevance to the construct, such as differentiating between groups of research participants.

Concurrent Validity: The association of a measure with other relevant data measured at the same point in time.

Predictive Validity: The association of a measure with other relevant data measured at some future point in time.

Convergent Validity: The association between a measure and either other measures of the same construct or conceptually related constructs.

Discriminant Validity: The association between measures that, conceptually, should not be related.

Incremental Validity: The extent to which a measure adds to the prediction of a criterion beyond what can be predicted with other measurement data.

TABLE 4.11   Some Common Threats to the Statistical Conclusion Validity of a Study

Low Statistical Power: Statistical power refers to the ability to detect group differences when such differences truly exist. If a study has low statistical power, often caused by the use of samples that are too small, the researcher may not be able to accurately conclude that group differences were found in the study.

Multiple Comparisons and Their Effects on Error Rates: Most studies involve the testing of multiple research hypotheses, with multiple measures used to operationalize key constructs. The researcher needs to consider the number of analyses to conduct and the error rate to use for analyses in order to have a reasonable balance between the desire to avoid *Type I errors* (i.e., concluding there is an effect when no true effect exists) and *Type II errors* (i.e., concluding there is no effect when a true effect exists).

Procedural Variability: Even with clear instructions and procedures to follow, those conducting the research (such as interviewers, observational raters, and therapists) may differ in how they interpret or use the instructions and procedures. Increases in variability in a study decrease the ability to detect a phenomenon or experimental effect.

Participant Heterogeneity: Variability in participant characteristics may result in differential results within the sample. Again, by increasing variability within a study, it is more difficult to detect a true effect.

Measurement Unreliability: The less reliable a measure, the more that measurement error influences the data obtained from participants. This increases within-study variability and negatively affects the ability to detect an effect.

for many psychological measures, there is no direct correspondence between the scores on a measure and a person's experience in the world. For example, what does it mean to receive a score of 11 on a measure of anxiety: how is a score of 11 manifested in the person's day-to-day life? Because many psychological measures have an arbitrary metric with limited or no real-world correspondence, it is important that researchers learn more about what the score on a measure actually means in the life of a person and just how meaningful, in real-life terms, differences in scores really are (Blanton & Jaccard, 2006; Kazdin, 2006). Knowing that two groups differ in a statistically significant manner on their scores on a particular measure is important, but it does not provide information about whether the difference is a meaningful one.

Therefore, in many types of clinical psychology research, statistical significance is necessary but not sufficient to fully evaluate the results of a study. Because the field of clinical psychology focuses on the application of psychological knowledge to improve human functioning, researchers must also address whether the results have any practical significance. In treatment research, this is known as **clinical significance**. Clinical significance has been defined in a number of ways, but all definitions share an emphasis on evaluating the degree to which the intervention has had a meaningful impact on the functioning of the treated participants. Just as there are different definitions, so too are there several distinct methods for calculating clinical significance; some of these use group data and others focus on the data from individual participants in a treatment study (Kraemer et al., 2003; Wise, 2004). One commonly used approach is to evaluate, for each participant, whether the participant could be said to be in the normal range of functioning. This may involve the use of norms, cut-off scores on scales, or predetermined criteria (such as being employed or being able to function without assistance when performing self-care tasks) to operationalize normal range functioning. A second commonly used method, developed by **Neil Jacobson** and colleagues, called the *reliable change index,* determines whether a participant's pretreatment to posttreatment change on a scale is statistically greater than what would be expected due to measurement error. If it is, and if the score on the scale has moved to within two standard deviations of the mean score for a nondistressed sample, then a clinically significant change is said to have occurred (Jacobson & Truax, 1991). It is important to note that different methods for calculating clinical significance may yield different conclusions (Bauer, Lambert, & Nielsen, 2004) so, as with traditional data analyses, the researcher must make sure that appropriate clinical significance methods are used in a study.

SUMMARY AND CONCLUSIONS

Throughout this book, we emphasize the importance of a solid research foundation for the practice of clinical psychology. In this chapter we have given a brief overview of the research process, highlighting the decisions that the researcher must make at all stages of the process in order to conduct ethical research and to balance the needs of internal and external validity. Perhaps the most important message is that there is no perfect study and that the different methodological features all have advantages and disadvantages. Just as the researcher must weigh different choices carefully, so too must the informed research consumer be aware of the effects of different methodological features in interpreting results in

---

TABLE 4.12   How to Critically Evaluate a Research Study

The fact that a study is published does not mean that it is perfect. In fact, there is no such thing as a perfect study. Instead, studies vary in the degree to which the researchers have successfully addressed important issues and have successfully dealt with threats to internal, external, and statistical conclusion validity. Below are some questions you should ask yourself when reading a published study in order to develop a critical eye for research.

Title: Does the title accurately reflect the content of the article?

Introduction: Is the background information on the research area presented clearly and logically? Is there unnecessary detail that is confusing or misleading? Is there a clear statement of the purpose of the study and/or of the research hypotheses?

Participants: Are the chosen participants appropriate for the study topic? To what extent can results be generalized from the study's sample to other populations of interest? Are recruitment methods described? Were any analyses conducted to determine whether there were effects due to differing methods? Was there attrition in the study and, if so, how was it handled statistically and interpretatively? If control/comparison groups were used, were they appropriate for the hypotheses being tested? In an experiment, was assignment to condition truly random?

Measures: Are the psychometric properties (i.e., reliability and validity) reported, and are they adequate? If interviewers or coders were used, are interrater reliability values reported? Are the chosen measures developmentally and culturally appropriate for the participants? How well do the measures evaluate the variables included in the research hypotheses?

Procedures: In general, are the procedures appropriate for testing the research hypotheses? For example, was the training of raters/interviewers/therapists reported, and does it seem adequate? Overall, are the procedures described in sufficient detail that the study could be replicated?

Results: Are the statistical analyses appropriate for the research hypotheses and the research design? Are the assumptions for the analyses met or were they violated? Was there any attention to whether the sample size was sufficient to detect a true effect in the study? Was there an appropriate balance between avoiding Type I and Type II errors? Do the tables provide enough detail (or too much) to aid in understanding the obtained results? Were post hoc analyses conducted and, if they were, did the researchers exercise caution in interpreting the findings? If the study was a randomized clinical trial, were clinical significance methods used?

Discussion: Are the results fully discussed? Are there clear statements about the extent to which the research hypotheses were supported? Does the researcher inappropriately interpret nonsignificant results? Is there a reasonable discussion of the limitations of the study? How well does the researcher integrate his or her findings with previous work in the area? Are viable alternative explanations of the obtained results considered in a meaningful manner?

---

a reasonable manner. **Table 4.12** summarizes a number of issues that, as novice research consumers, you should consider when reading the clinical psychology research literature.

Critical Thinking Questions

What are the differences between evidence-based practice and eminence-based practice? How can science help if the treatment is unhelpful?

How is the science of clinical psychology different from the science of other types of psychology? What ethical issues are particularly important in the science of clinical psychology?

How do theories affect the research process?

How can different research designs be suitable at different stages of the development of knowledge in a field? How does a psychologist decide whether to maximize internal validity or external validity? Should greater weight be given to the findings of experimental studies than to other types of designs?

If a psychologist wants to study people diagnosed with a specific disorder, why does it matter how they are recruited into the study?

Key Terms

clinical significance: in addition to the results of a study attaining statistical significance, this requires that the results are of a magnitude that results in changes in some aspects of daily functioning of participants

effect size: a standardized metric, typically expressed in standard deviation units or correlations, that allows the results of research studies to be combined and analyzed

external validity: the extent to which the interpretations drawn from the results of a study can be generalized beyond the narrow boundaries of the specific study

factor analysis: a statistical procedure used to determine the conceptual dimensions or factors that underlie a set of variables, test items, or tests.

internal validity: the extent to which the interpretations drawn from the results of a study can be justified and alternative interpretations can be reasonably ruled out

mediator: a variable that explains the mechanism by which a predictor variable influences a criterion variable

meta-analysis: a set of statistical procedures for quantitatively summarizing the results of a research domain

moderator: a variable that influences the strength of the relation between a predictor variable and a criterion variable

randomized controlled trial: an experiment in which research participants are randomly assigned to one of two or more treatment conditions

statistical conclusion validity: the extent to which the results of a study are accurate and valid based on the type of statistical procedures used in the research

structural equation modeling: a comprehensive statistical procedure that involves testing all components of a theoretical mode

Key Names

Donald Campbell   Jacob Cohen   Neil Jacobson

ADDITIONAL RESOURCES
Books

Hayes, S. C., Barlow, D. H., & Nelson-Gray, R. O. (1999). *The scientist practitioner: Research and accountability in the age of managed care* (2nd ed.). Needham Heights, MA: Allyn & Bacon.

Kazdin, A. E. (2003). *Research design in clinical psychology* (4th ed.). Needham Heights, MA: Allyn & Bacon.

Kazdin, A. E. (Ed.). (2003). *Methodological issues and strategies in clinical research* (3rd ed.). Washington, DC: American Psychological Association.

Roberts, M. C., & Ilardi, S. S. (2003). *Handbook of research methods in clinical psychology*. Oxford: Blackwell Publishing Ltd.

Thomas, J. C., & Hersen, M. (Eds.). (2003). *Understanding research in clinical and counseling psychology*. Mahwah, NJ: Lawrence Erlbaum Associates.

Check It Out!

APA has a number of sources of information and links to resources for students interested in conducting research: http://www.apa.org/apags/members/resres.html

Although the focus is on social psychology, this is a wonderful website that contains numerous links to resources on research methodology, research ethics, and statistics. http://www.socialpsychology.org/methods.htm

This site has extensive resources for understanding statistical procedures commonly used in psychology, along with online calculators that provide you with the option of conducting statistical analyses. http://faculty.vassar.edu/lowry/VassarStats.html

A collection of short, easy-to-read articles on statistics from the *British Medical Journal* is available at: http://www.bmj.com/cgi/search?&titleabstract=%22statistics+notes%22&&journalcode=bmj&&hits=20

If you are interested in learning more about meta-analysis, free meta-analysis software is available at several sites, including http://ericae.net/meta/metastat.htm and http://userpage.fu-berlin.de/~health/meta_e.htm

CHAPTER 5

Assessment: Overview

INTRODUCTION

Ishmael is having difficulty concentrating in school. He is having a hard time learning to read. Is he entitled to receive special education services?

Cara has been cranky and unwilling to do her homework. She seems to get upset at the slightest provocation. Is this just regular teenager moodiness, or does she have a serious problem?

Since he received a potentially lethal electric shock at work, Boris has had difficulty managing his temper. He is moody and unpredictable. What are the prospects for him returning to work?

As we outlined in Chapter 3, the classification of phenomena is a central feature of all sciences and social sciences. Classification requires the collection of data in a process known as assessment. People are routinely assessed and classified for a variety of purposes. In the educational system, students are assessed virtually every day from the time they begin school at the age of four or five until they complete their education some 12 to 25 years later. Assessments of knowledge and skill through examinations, projects, homework assignments, and class presentations are used to assign grades and to determine whether the person has met criteria to graduate. Based on these grades and other assessment data (such as personal interviews and entrance examinations), students gain admission to (or are rejected from) private schools, colleges, universities, or graduate programs. In the work realm, most people undergo some form of assessment to determine whether they should be offered a job. In many cases such assessments are highly subjective and thus are potentially biased and unfair. Once hired, employees are subject to constant informal assessment of their job performance by their supervisors. More and more, salary increases and advancement in the organization are related to results of performance evaluations. Even when you apply

Is Cara a regular teen or does she have a serious disorder? (*Source:* Charles Gullung/Image Source Limited)

Psychological assessments may be initiated to diagnose learning disorders. (*Source:* Corbis Digital Stock)

for a credit card, loan, or mortgage, you (or more precisely your credit history and credit risk) are assessed.

Psychological assessment strategies and tools are used increasingly for a number of educational and employment purposes. In this chapter and in the following four chapters, you will learn about the use of psychological assessment for clinical purposes. Along the way we introduce you to the domains and methods of assessment most commonly found in clinical psychology. In these chapters we will show you the potential value of clinical assessment and make you aware of the challenges that clinical psychologists face in gathering and integrating assessment information.

PSYCHOLOGICAL ASSESSMENT

As we just highlighted, we are all assessed on a regular basis. Moreover, as human beings, we all constantly engage in informal assessment activities related to our day-to-day lives. We use information (i.e., assessment data) to help us make both small decisions (such as whether to ask a professor to explain a concept that is unclear, whether to agree to an invitation to have a meal with a friend) and more important decisions (such as whether to accept an offer for graduate school or to move in with an intimate partner). Data such as facial expressions, tone of voice, previous experiences with a person, and our own emotional reactions all influence our decisions. In most cases these assessment processes occur automatically. As you will learn in Chapter 9, automatic decision making can be vulnerable to many types of errors.

What makes psychological assessment, or more specifically clinical assessment, different from other types of assessment? Psychological assessment is an iterative decision-making process in which data are systematically collected on the person (or persons), the person's history, and the person's physical, social, and cultural environments. Based on an initial understanding of the problem to be assessed, preliminary information is gathered that, in most cases, leads to a refinement of the understanding of the problem and to an alteration in assessment activities. This cycle then repeats itself until the psychologist decides enough information has been collected to adequately respond to the assessment question. Psychological assessment involves the gathering and integration of multiple types of data from multiple sources and perspectives; at a minimum, this involves information provided by the client and information based on the psychologist's observation of the client during a clinical interview.

All psychological assessments are undertaken to address specific goals such as (a) evaluating a child's cognitive abilities to determine whether the child is eligible for remedial services, (b) identifying the characteristics and behaviors associated with an adolescent's repeated social rejection, so that a treatment plan can be devised, or (c) determining the extent of emotional impairment experienced by an adult who was in a car accident.

Guided by assessment goals, the psychologist clearly and precisely formulates the questions to be addressed during the assessment. In turn, these questions inform the selection of the most appropriate assessment methods. Throughout the process of data collection, the psychologist generates hypotheses about the client and, therefore, may alter or refine the initial assessment questions to examine these hypotheses. This typically leads to the use of additional assessment procedures and the review of other data. Once all the assessment data have been collected, the psychologist then must make sense of the information and meaningfully address the inevitable inconsistencies and contradictions that occur in all assessment situations. As part of this integration and interpretation process, the psychologist generates more hypotheses and strives to evaluate the extent of the evidence for and against these hypotheses. In most instances, before generating a final set of conclusions designed to answer the assessment questions, the psychologist consults with the client (and possibly others) about the accuracy of these conclusions. Of course, as with all psychological services, psychological assessment must be conducted in a manner that is informed by an awareness of human diversity and is sensitive to client characteristics including, but not limited to, age, gender, ethnicity, culture, sexual orientation, and religious beliefs.

All clinical psychologists should be competent in conducting assessments. The 1999 presidential task force of the American Psychological Association's Division 12 (Clinical Psychology) established a model training curriculum in clinical assessment. You can see in **Table 5.1** the

---

TABLE 5.1   A Model Curriculum for Clinical Psychology Assessment: Recommendations From the American Psychological Association, Division 12 Presidential Task Force (1999)

Conceptual Areas

    Normality, norms, and standardization

    Reliability

    Validity

    Threats to validity (bias, deception, malingering)

    Clinical decision making (sources of error, optimal strategies)

Applied Topics

    Intellectual assessment

    Self-report personality assessment

    Neuropsychological assessment

    Diagnostic assessment (meaning of diagnoses, reliability, sources of data)

    Structured interviews and behavioral observation with children and adolescents

    Parent rating scales for child/adolescent assessment

    Specific skills relevant to focus of graduate program (e.g., test construction, assessment of disabled individuals, risk assessments)

    Assessment data integration and report writing

    Ethics and legal issues in assessment

TABLE 5.2   Core Competencies in Psychological Assessment

- Knowledge of:
  - Psychometric theory
  - The scientific, theoretical, empirical, and contextual bases of psychological assessment
- Knowledge, skills, and techniques to assess cognitive, affective, behavioral, and personality dimensions of human experience
- Ability to:
  - Assess intervention outcomes
  - Evaluate critically the multiple roles, contexts, and relationships in which clients and psychologists function and the reciprocal impact of these on the assessment activity
  - Establish, maintain, and understand the collaborative professional relationship involved in the assessment activity
- Understanding of the relation between assessment and intervention, assessment as an intervention, and intervention planning
- Technical assessment skills, including problem/goal identification and case conceptualization, understanding and selection of appropriate assessment methods, effective use of the assessment methods, systematic data gathering, integration and analysis of information, understandable, useful, and responsive communication of findings, and development of recommendations

Adapted from Krishnamurthy et al. (2004)

---

knowledge and skills that graduate students in clinical psychology must master in order to be competent in conducting psychological assessment. You will notice that the applied skills build on the foundational knowledge of psychometric theory covered in undergraduate programs. Information provided in this chapter and in the next four chapters will help you become better acquainted with these topics.

Subsequently as part of a 2002 conference on defining and evaluating competencies in professional psychology, a psychological assessment working group identified core competencies for professional psychologists. As you can see from **Table 5.2**, achieving and maintaining competence in psychological assessment is no easy feat. Consistent with the recommendations for training in Table 5.1, competence in assessment requires both conceptual knowledge and practical assessment skills. Although not explicitly recognized in the competency listings, another significant challenge is for clinical psychologists to ensure that their knowledge and skills are up to date. As we will see in Chapters 7 and 8, new measures continue to be developed, and many of the major psychological tests are regularly updated every few years.

The Purposes of Psychological Assessment

As you may remember learning in Chapters 1 and 2, psychological assessment has always been an important professional activity for clinical psychologists. Even though the roles of clinical psychologists have expanded over the decades, assessment activities remain a central part of the role of a clinical psychologist. Psychological assessments are conducted for many reasons. The first important distinction is between situations in which psychological assessment is the primary clinical service provided and situations in which the psychological assessment is an element of the clinical service.

Assessment-Focused Services Versus Intervention-Focused Services

Some psychological assessments are stand-alone services. Examples include child custody evaluation to determine the best parenting arrangements for children whose parents are separating or divorcing, psychoeducational assessments to diagnose learning disorders and to identify cognitive strengths and weaknesses, neuropsychological assessments to evaluate the extent of cognitive and memory impairment following a serious concussion, and psychosocial functioning/diagnostic assessment to evaluate the psychological aftermath of a motor vehicle accident. In these cases an assessment is initiated to answer basic questions about the person's current functioning or eligibility for services and to provide recommendations for remediation of problems, whether by a psychologist or by another health care or education specialist. In some instances the clinical psychologist may also be asked to provide an opinion on whether the person's current level of functioning is substantially different from a prior level of functioning (e.g., before a car accident or a work-related injury).

These **assessment-focused services** are conducted primarily to provide information that can be used to address a person's current or anticipated psychosocial deficits. Thus the conclusions and recommendations provided by the psychologist may have an enormous impact on the person's life circumstances, such as whether a child has primary residence with one parent or whether an injured worker will receive a disability pension. Given the importance of the decisions that are based on assessment results, psychologists must use evidence-based assessment tools and must follow all ethical standards in providing these services (a point we address more fully later in the chapter).

An individual may request a psychological assessment; at other times the request for an assessment is made by another person or an organization (e.g., a court-mandated child custody evaluation). In conducting the assessment the psychologist must be cognizant of these referral factors, because they may influence the extent to which the person wishes to cooperate with the assessment, as well as motivation to emphasize psychological strengths or psychological impairments (see Table 5.2 regarding the importance of awareness of the context of assessment). It is also important that psychologists have thorough knowledge of the legal context in which their assessments will be used. It is possible, for example, that their assessments may be challenged by the person being assessed or by an institution or agency that initially requested the assessment (e.g., an insurance company or health management organization).

Psychological assessment must take context into account. (*Source:* Media Bakery)

VIEWPOINT BOX 5.1

CHILD CUSTODY EVALUATIONS

The majority of divorcing parents reach an agreement about the arrangements for parenting their children on their own or with the help of legal and mental health professionals. A small minority of parents who are unable to reach an agreement turn to the legal system to resolve the dilemma of parenting arrangements after divorce. Judges in turn seek advice from mental health professionals by ordering child custody evaluation by a mental health professional.

With training in child development and expertise in psychological assessment, clinical psychologists should be well placed to offer informed opinions about optimal parenting plans for these conflicted families. However, the provision of child custody evaluations is a professional minefield, yielding large numbers of complaints about professional misconduct. In response to these problems, guidelines have been drawn up by various organizations including the American Psychological Association (APA, 1994) and the Association of Family and Conciliation Courts (AFCC, 2006). The guidelines lay out in detail the many types of assessment data that must be gathered to perform a competent assessment. It is easy to see how the process of conducting interviews with parents, children, and new partners, carrying out observations of various family members, administering psychological tests to adults and children, and synthesizing reports from collateral sources such as teachers and therapists is likely to be a lengthy and costly procedure. A survey of psychologists indicated that the evaluation process took on average 21.1 hours (Ackerman & Ackerman, 1997). Given the hourly rates charged by psychologists, it is clear that the cost of the average child custody evaluation runs into thousands of dollars. Ackerman and Ackerman also presented some very troubling data on the tests most commonly used by psychologists in child custody evaluation. In assessing children, psychologists reported commonly using a range of projective tests such as the Children's Apperception Test, the Sentence Completion Test, the Rorschach test, and projective drawings. These projective tests for children fall far short of the scientific standards of demonstrating reliability and validity and having norms (Hunsley, Lee, & Wood, 2003). In assessing adults, the most commonly used test was the MMPI-2, followed by the Rorschach. No validity studies have supported the usefulness of these tests in predicting the best parenting arrangement for divorced families. Of particular concern is that there are several Web sites describing the subscales of the MMPI-2 and advising parents on the most appropriate responses to provide in order to appear well functioning.

To more directly assess what it is evaluators do, Horvath, Logan, and Walker (2002) conducted content analyses of 135 reports included in official court documents. In contrast to the self-report methodology used by Ackerman and Ackerman (1997), this strategy allowed the investigators to directly examine what evaluators did, rather than what they said they do. Horvath and colleagues found great variability in the extent to which APA guidelines were followed. Interviews sometimes failed to address critical issues such as domestic violence and child abuse. Results of this study underline the need for practitioners to use multiple methods to evaluate family functioning and to rely only on well-validated assessment strategies in making recommendations that are of such importance to children and their families.

Although it is preferable for parents to reach their own agreement on post-divorce parenting arrangements, this is not always possible.

Parents seeking a child custody evaluation should consult professional guidelines, which are easily accessed on Web sites, so they can ensure that the professional who is offering to conduct a child custody evaluation will complete a comprehensive and valid assessment that will yield helpful recommendations.

As clinical psychologists have become more involved in providing intervention services to patients, there has also been a shift in the type of assessments they conduct. Psychological assessments are most commonly conducted in the context of intervention services. In these **intervention-focused assessment services**, the psychological assessment is not a stand-alone service, but is conducted as a first step in providing an effective intervention. All intervention should involve some assessment. For example, an initial evaluation of the client's life circumstances and psychosocial functioning is necessary to determine whether psychological treatment is warranted or whether some other form of intervention should be recommended. Pretreatment assessment findings are used to determine appropriate psychological interventions. These data also provide a useful point of comparison for interpreting subsequent assessment findings during or after treatment.

Thus far we have categorized assessment activities as roughly falling into one of two domains: stand-alone assessment, in which the main intent is to present conclusions and recommendations about the person's functioning, and assessments in which the main intent is to intervene to improve the person's functioning, with the assessment data being used in support of this service. Although this dichotomy is useful in thinking about psychological assessment, it is rather simplistic and does not fairly represent the variety of purposes for which assessment is conducted. Therefore, to deepen your knowledge of why psychologists conduct assessments, we will focus on the following range of interrelated assessment purposes: screening, diagnosis/case formulation, prognosis, treatment design and planning, treatment monitoring, and treatment evaluation. We will return to several of these topics in Chapter 9 when we examine the decision-making processes associated with the clinical use of assessment data.

Screening

Given their expertise in measurement and psychometrics, psychologists are often called on to assist in the development or implementation of **screening** measures. Depending on the nature of the screening and the screening site, psychologists may or may not be directly involved in conducting screening assessments. The purpose of screening for a disorder, condition, or characteristic is to identify, as accurately as possible, individuals who may have problems of a clinical magnitude or who may be at risk for developing such problems. Individuals who are screened may not have sought out assessment services; rather, they may be receiving the assessment as part of the routine operations of a clinic, school, hospital, or employment setting. For example, there are now a number of instruments that are routinely used in schools to identify youth with mental health problems; then psychological services are offered to those who have been identified as having problems (Levitt, Saka, Romanelli, & Hoagwood, 2007).

People may also actively seek out a screening assessment. There are national screening days for a number of psychological disorders, including the National Alcohol Screening Day and the National Depression Screening Day. These screening days have many sponsors, including the American Psychiatric Association, the American Psychological Association, and American Medical Association. The screening can be done online or in person at many community-based health care settings such as general hospitals, mental health clinics, and specialty health care providers' offices. Hundreds of thousands of Americans each year are screened for mental health problems in this manner. Information on the Web sites for these screening services is included at the end of this chapter.

Although screening is useful in identifying those at risk, it is important to remember that screening tools are not the same as tools used in diagnosis. So for example, if you score high on a depression-screening instrument that does not mean that you would necessarily meet diagnostic criteria for depression.

Diagnosis/Case Formulation

As you learned in Chapter 3, assessment data are used to formulate a clinical diagnosis such as those listed in the DSM-IV-TR. Interview data, psychological test data, and reports from significant others provide information on the symptoms the person is experiencing. Information on symptoms is compared with diagnostic criteria to determine whether the symptom profile matches criteria for Axis I or II diagnoses. As we described in Chapter 3, knowing the diagnosis for a person helps clinicians communicate with other health professionals and search the scientific literature for information on associated features such as etiology and prognosis. Diagnostic information can also provide key information on the types of treatment options that have been found to be effective in clinical trials (Nelson-Gray, 2003). Thus, diagnosis can provide an initial framework for a treatment plan that can be modified to fully address the client's concerns and life circumstances.

Historically, the term "diagnosis" was used to describe the entire process of conducting a psychological assessment and formulating a clinical picture of the client. The term originated when diagnostic criteria for psychological and psychiatric disorders were ambiguous and relatively uninformative for clinical purposes (i.e., during the era of DSM-I and DSM-II). Thus, in the past, "diagnosis," or "psychodiagnosis," referred to the process in which the psychologist used interview and testing data to render a comprehensive representation of the patient's psychological makeup (cf. Rapaport, Gill, & Schafer, 1968). Although the term "psychodiagnosis" is still used by some clinicians (primarily those with a psychodynamic orientation), the term **case formulation** is now more commonly used to describe the use of assessment data to develop a comprehensive and clinically relevant conceptualization of a patient's psychological functioning.

Prognosis/Prediction

Whether or not it is stated explicitly, psychological assessment always implies some form of prediction about the patient's future. For example, recommendations that the person seek psychotherapy to address bulimic symptoms or that special academic tutoring is needed to compensate for a learning disability imply that, without some form of intervention, the present problems will either continue or worsen. A dentist would not recommend implants to deal with a lack of teeth in a patient age 6 months—it would be assumed that, in time, the teeth would grow. Similarly, if the psychologist believed that eating unusually large amounts of food was simply related to an adolescent growth spurt, or that a child's reading difficulties were an inevitable part of the learning process, then it would be unnecessary to recommend intervention—the passage of time would be sufficient to correct the problem. **Prognosis** refers to the use of assessment data, in combination with relevant empirical literature, to make predictions about the future course of a patient's psychological functioning. Although the psychopathology literature provides information for this task, it must always be remembered that these studies deal with future outcomes at the group level. The clinician's task is to use this probabilistic information (e.g., "60% of patients with this diagnosis experience a recurrence of their symptoms within two years") in a manner that takes into account the unique circumstances of the patient being assessed.

One of the biggest challenges for clinicians is to predict as accurately as possible. In considering ways to enhance the accuracy of predictions, the psychologist must weigh a number of factors such as time and cost, the consequences of inaccurate decisions, and the base rate of the predicted outcome. Although it is always possible to collect more and more assessment data, this comes with certain consequences. Time spent on assessment may mean less time is available to provide an intervention for the patient. The cost of an assessment should not be underestimated: more time spent on assessment means that someone (e.g., the client) or some organization (e.g., the client's health maintenance organization) must cover these costs. The clinician must therefore strike a balance between the desire to obtain more information and the need to be conscious of the very real constraints that influence the scope of the assessment.

Prediction errors are inevitable—no one can predict with 100% accuracy. However, not all errors have the same psychological or financial cost. Psychologists should be aware of these issues, and their selection of assessment strategies and instruments should be based on conscious choices about the types of errors they wish to minimize. A failure to detect attention-deficit/hyperactivity disorder may result in several years of frustration and academic and social failures for a child and his or her family, whereas failure to detect a mild specific phobia is unlikely to have the same generalized impact. In older adults, symptoms of impaired memory, difficulties in thinking, and problems in concentration may occur as features of both major depressive disorder and dementia. A misdiagnosis has the potential not only to result in ineffective treatment but also to add to the burden experienced by the individual. Errors can also occur in which a person is diagnosed when, in fact, no diagnosis is warranted. For example, if a person showing signs of uncomplicated bereavement was mistakenly diagnosed with major depressive disorder, it could lead to both unnecessary treatment and stigmatization. All of these types of errors are influenced by the **base rate** of a problem or diagnosis—that is, the frequency with which the problem/diagnosis occurs in the population. In a nutshell, the less frequently a problem occurs, the more likely a prediction error will occur. Because many of the predictions that clinical psychologists make are about

TABLE 5.3   Accuracy and Errors in Clinical Prediction

Prediction	True Event	True Non-Event
Event	True Positives (A)	False Positives (B)
Non-Event	False Negatives (C)	True Negatives (D)
Sensitivity: A/(A + C)		
Specificity: D/(D + B)		

rare conditions or *low base rate events*—such as the presence of an eating disorder, the likelihood that the person will be violent in the future, or the likelihood of a future suicide attempt—the consequences of error must be seriously considered.

Errors in clinical prediction can occur in many assessment activities, including screening efforts, diagnosis, and case formulation. To better understand how clinical psychologists attempt to address the issue of error, it is necessary to understand some of the basic concepts of decision theory. To begin, there is, of course, the situation in which the prediction is accurate. As presented in **Table 5.3**, this can mean either that the prediction that an event will occur was accurate (*true positive*) or that the prediction of a non-event was accurate (e.g., that no diagnosis was warranted or that a specific event such as a suicide attempt would not occur—*true negative*). However, just as a prediction can be correct in two distinct ways, there are two types of incorrect predictions. A *false positive* occurs when the psychologist predicts that an event will occur but, in fact, it does not occur (e.g., the psychologist diagnoses ADHD in a child who does not have the disorder). Conversely, a *false negative* occurs when an event occurs that was not predicted by the psychologist (e.g., the psychologist fails to diagnose someone who has a personality disorder).

In referring to accuracy in clinical predictions, psychologists employ two additional concepts: sensitivity and specificity. **Sensitivity** refers to the number of times an event is predicted, across cases, compared with the total number of times that the event actually occurs. More simply, sensitivity (or selectivity; Hogan, 2007) is the proportion of true positives identified by the assessment (Groth-Marnat, 2003). Sensitivity is determined arithmetically by dividing the number of true positives by the sum of true positives and false negatives. In contrast, **specificity** deals with the prediction of non-events. It refers to the number of times a non-event is predicted across cases compared with the total number of times that no event occurred; alternatively, it can be considered as the relative proportion of true negatives (Groth-Marnat, 2003). Specificity is determined arithmetically by dividing the number of true negatives by the sum of true negatives and the false positives.

Let's assume that a psychologist conducted assessments on hospital inpatients in a patient care unit in order to predict who was at risk for future suicide attempts. In our example, sensitivity provides information on how well the assessment procedures were able to detect future suicide attempts, and specificity provides information on how well the assessment procedures were able to identify individuals who would not attempt suicide. There are serious consequences associated with failing to detect a person who went on to make a suicide attempt, but there are also costs and consequences for each nonsuicidal person who is erroneously categorized as potentially suicidal—the person's freedom and privacy will have been restricted, and considerable personnel resources will have been directed into monitoring the person. Of course it would be ideal if an assessment had both high sensitivity and high specificity but, in reality, this is rarely the case. Therefore, a decision about which assessment procedures to select should be informed by a thorough consideration of the procedure's sensitivity and specificity and the psychological and financial costs stemming from inaccurate clinical predictions.

Treatment Planning

As we discussed earlier in the chapter, a great deal of psychological assessment is designed to inform treatment-related decisions. Once the psychologist and client have reached a decision that some treatment is required, the next question is what exactly the treatment should be. Treatment planning is the process by which information about the client (including sociodemographic and psychological characteris-

It is always necessary to tailor the treatment to suit the client's unique circumstances. (*Source:* Media Bakery)

tics, diagnoses, and life context) is used in combination with the scientific literature on psychotherapy to develop a proposed course of action that addresses the client's needs and circumstances. Treatment planning provides a clear focus for treatment and gives the client realistic expectations about the process and likely outcome of treatment. The plan also establishes a standard against which treatment progress can be measured. Within the context of health service provision, a treatment plan is a valuable tool that facilitates communication among professionals working with the client, provides a clear statement about the nature of the planned services to agencies that may need to authorize and/or pay for the services, and provides a document that can be reviewed as part of an agency's quality assurance activities to ensure that appropriate services are being provided. The collaborative effort between psychologist and client to develop and implement a treatment plan should also establish a good foundation for the subsequent challenges of psychotherapy. Rather than simply agreeing to a vague statement about therapy, a formal treatment plan ensures that a client can provide truly informed consent for the procedures he or she is about to undertake.

The first step in developing a treatment plan is to determine whether there are treatment options with established effectiveness for the types of problems the client presents. The psychologist must consider the extent to which the characteristics of the client match those of research participants in relevant clinical trials. The better the fit, the greater the psychologist's confidence in choosing one form of treatment. However, even if the fit is relatively poor—as may be the case in dealing with clients with a minority ethnic/cultural background—treatment outcome studies can still provide a useful starting point for developing a treatment plan. Regardless of the fit, it is always necessary to tailor the treatment to the client's unique circumstances.

A useful treatment plan must address three general areas: problem identification, treatment goals, and treatment strategies and tactics (Mariush, 2002). A clear statement of the problems to be addressed provides the necessary starting point for understanding the proposed treatment and for, eventually, determining the treatment's success. For treatment to be efficient and focused, goals must be specified. Goals can include both ultimate goals for treatment and intermediate goals that must be attained in order to reach the ultimate treatment goals. For example, in helping Morgan overcome bulimic symptoms, the ultimate treatment goal may be the development of appropriate body image and effective emotion-regulation skills. The short-term goal, on the other hand, may be the reduction of bingeing behavior by establishing a routine of eating three healthy meals a day. For Cynthia, who has been cutting her arms, the short-term goal may be a reduction in self-harming behavior, with a longer-term goal of establishing good study habits, enlarging her social network, and dealing with conflict in her family. Finally, a description of treatment *strategies* provides information on the general approach to addressing the clinical problems, whereas a description of treatment *tactics* provides details of specific tasks, procedures, or techniques that will be used in treatment. To address Simon's symptoms of depression and relationship conflict, for example, the treatment strategy may be to use individual interpersonal therapy or to use emotionally focused couples therapy (EFT) with both Simon and his partner Chris. The treatment tactics, however, would deal with the specific elements of treatment, such as, within EFT, having the couple work on emotionally reconnecting with each other and developing renewed trust in each other's emotional availability. Only with a thorough and accurate assessment is it possible to specify the type of strategies and tactics that are best suited to deal with a client's presenting problems.

Treatment Monitoring

Once a clear treatment plan is in place, the psychologist closely monitors the impact of treatment. Treatment monitoring is a crucial element of effective treatment, as it enables the psychologist to change the treatment plan based upon the patient's response to treatment. If a patient is progressing extremely well, it may be possible to shorten treatment or to focus subsequent phases of treatment on other issues of concern to the patient. Alternatively, if the treatment is less than optimally effective, close monitoring of treatment progress provides an opportunity to alter the treatment. **Figure 5.1** shows an example of treatment monitoring data for Cynthia, who received services to deal with self-harming behavior. All clinicians have an implicit sense of how the patient is progressing, but we are referring to explicitly monitoring progress through the use of specific questions or psychological measures. By providing data on problems in the process of treatment (such as difficulties in the therapeutic relationship) and obstacles the patient is encountering in following through on therapeutic activities (such as not doing assigned tasks outside the therapy session), treatment monitoring can provide an opportunity to reorient treatment efforts to avoid potential treatment failure (Mash & Hunsley, 1993).

   To repeatedly evaluate elements of the treatment process (such as the therapeutic relationship and compliance with tasks) and alterations in psychological functioning (including changes in symptom

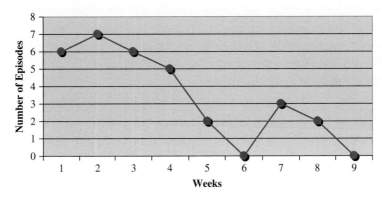

FIGURE 5.1   Frequency of Cynthia's Self-Harm Episodes During the Past Week

frequency, intensity, and duration), psychologists use interviews, brief psychological tests, and/or tests specifically tailored to the client's problems and goals (Kazdin, 1993). Research by psychologist **Michael Lambert**, a major contributor to the research on assessing changes due to treatment, demonstrated compellingly that routine treatment monitoring can substantially affect treatment outcome. In a meta-analysis of three large-scale studies, Lambert et al. (2003) found that by using monitoring data to alert clinicians to treatment progress, the likelihood of client deterioration was reduced and the positive effects of psychotherapy were enhanced. In these studies, treatment monitoring data were routinely collected on more than 2,500 patients in a range of treatment settings such as university counseling centers and outpatient treatment clinics. Services were provided by qualified professionals who espoused the full range of theoretical orientations typically found in practice settings. The same very simple experimental manipulation was used in all studies: patient and clinician dyads were randomly assigned either to a "no feedback condition" in which the treatment monitoring data were not provided to the clinician or to a "feedback condition" in which the clinician was given the data. Across studies in the "no feedback condition," Lambert and colleagues found that 21% of patients deteriorated and 21% experienced clinically important improvements in functioning. However, in the "feedback condition," the number of clients who experienced deterioration was reduced by a third (to 13%) and the proportion of successful treatment cases increased by two thirds (to 35%). These results present a convincing argument that clinical psychologists have an ethical responsibility to routinely gather treatment monitoring data in order to enhance the likelihood of successful treatment outcome.

Treatment Evaluation

In most clinical psychology settings, treatment outcome data have typically been collected to document the extent to which psychological services such as psychotherapy are effective in achieving stated goals. A comparison of outcome data with intake data provides an indication of how much change, if any, has occurred during treatment of a particular individual. You might wonder why such data are necessary—surely health care providers know how much their patients have improved. Research evidence indicates that this is not usually the case. For example, in a study of services provided by a group of 23 mental health professionals (including psychologists) who routinely provided therapy to children, no significant correlations were found between the professionals' perceptions of client improvement and data from self-report measures completed by both parents and children (Love, Koob, & Hill, 2007).

Outcome data can also be used as indicators of how well an entire system of care is functioning. Whereas data gathered for treatment monitoring can affect treatment services provided to an individual client, data gathered for treatment outcome purposes can yield information relevant to an entire psychological practice or service (Ogles, Lambert, & Fields, 2002). At the level of individual psychologists working in an agency, aggregating data across patients can provide useful information about a psychologist's success in working with patients. When compared with data obtained from other psychologists in the agency, these data also have the potential to yield information about psychologists who are performing at above or below average levels. Those psychologists whose treatment services are less successful could receive feedback and given additional supervision or training to rectify the situation. On the other hand, a practice analysis of the relatively successful clinicians' activities could provide indications of certain clinical skills or knowledge that set these individuals apart from their colleagues. Training sessions for all clinicians could then focus on the dissemination of these identified areas of strength in order to improve the overall effectiveness of those working in the service setting. Of course, whether providing feedback to an individual psychologist or making group comparisons among practitioners, it is essential to take into account the service context. For example, if one psychologist in an agency provides services to clients with chronic mental health problems and a history of unsuccessful treatment, it would be unfair to compare that clinician's outcome data with the data obtained by psychologists working with less distressed clients.

Treatment outcome data can also be used to document the typical range of outcomes clients experience and the nature and duration of treatment required to obtain successful outcomes. With these data in hand, clinicians can then provide accurate estimates to clients and any third-party payers about the likely benefits, duration, and costs of treatment. Comparing these data across agencies providing similar services may reveal particular strengths and weaknesses in an agency. Consultation with other agencies could then yield avenues for improved outcomes through changes in administrative and/or clinical procedures (e.g., adopting more effective treatment strategies for dealing with clients diagnosed with cocaine dependence and cocaine abuse). Based on data available from published clinical trials of psychotherapy or from treatment centers acknowledged to be leaders in the field, individual practitioners and agencies can set benchmarks against which their own treatment outcome data can be compared. Such comparisons can lead to quality assurance strategies for improvements in areas of suboptimal service delivery.

Data on typical treatment responses can be used to enhance the outcome of a course of treatment for a client. Several groups of psychotherapy researchers have used large data sets based on repeated measures of client progress to establish profiles of symptom reduction and improvements in functioning over the course of treatment. When this information is used by clinicians in the context of treatment monitoring, it becomes possible to identify when the client's progress is less than what is typically found for those with similar problems. Ogles et al. (2002) described a data-monitoring system in which a graph depicting typical client progress is used as a comparison against which the progress of a specific client can be charted. On a session-by-session basis, if the client's assessment score is found to be significantly less than the score obtained by the typical client, the clinician is alerted to the fact that progress is suboptimal and that, eventually, treatment failure is a possibility. Based on this, the psychologist can then engage the client in discussions about problems in the process of treatment, thus potentially resulting in changes in the treatment plan.

PSYCHOLOGICAL TESTING

You will have learned in psychology courses that psychologists have expertise in the development and use of tests in the study and treatment of human functioning. Although you may find magazines filled with quick tests of various concepts, developing a scientifically sound psychological test requires more than simply writing a few questions and finding a good name for the test. The *Standards for Educational and Psychological Testing* (American Educational Research Association, American Psychological Association, & National Council on Measurement in Education, 1999) set out principles that psychologists must follow in developing and using tests and assessment procedures. As we will see in the following sections, a number of criteria must be met if a psychological test is to have any value in research or clinical practice.

First, let's consider what exactly a psychological test is. Although it might seem to be a relatively simple task to define a test, it turns out to be a rather difficult thing to do. In the *Standards* (American Educational Research Association et al., 1999) a test is defined in the following manner: "An evaluative device or procedure in which a sample of an examinee's behavior in a specified domain is obtained and subsequently evaluated and scored using a standardized process" (p. 183). This definition, although general enough to encompass various methods of testing (including interviewing, observation, and self-report), is rather awkward and may not be immediately understood by nonpsychologists. Hunsley, Lee, and Wood (2003) defined a test according to its intended use. *If* (a) the clinician's intent is to collect a sample of behavior that will be used to generate statements about a person, a person's experiences, or a person's psychological functioning *and* (b) a claim is made or implied by the clinician that the accuracy or validity of these statements come from the way in which the sample of behavior was collected and interpreted, and not just from the clinician's expertise, authority, or special qualifications, *then* the process used to collect and interpret the behavioral sample is a psychological test and must meet the standards established for psychological tests. So, for example, although you may be able to quickly develop a questionnaire designed to measure some aspect of human functioning, it is not a test until it has been demonstrated to have met the standards of reliability, validity, and norms.

Psychological assessment typically involves gathering information from interviews, psychological tests, and other data sources. (*Source:* Media Bakery)

Why does it matter how a psychological test is defined? Although there are numerous technical reasons why it is important, there is a practical reason that has very important real-world consequences. Psychological tests are frequently used in legal and quasi-legal contexts, such as when a judge must decide on child custody or when a panel is convened to evaluate an injured worker's claim for an employer-funded disability pension. Without safeguards to ensure that psychological tests meet scientific standards, it would be possible for the results of any set of questions to be called a "test" and to be assumed to provide scientifically accurate and valid information.

If you are considering psychological testing on the Internet, you need to be just as careful as if you were seeking psychological testing in a traditional format. You need to consider the credentials of the organization that is offering services and the scientific basis of the tools. No score should ever be interpreted in isolation. To be useful, it must be considered part of the information gathered in the process of psychological assessment.

VIEWPOINT BOX 5.2

PSYCHOLOGICAL TESTING ON THE INTERNET

With the exponential growth in access to the Internet and its increasing use in diverse activities, it is inevitable that mounting numbers of people may use the Internet to find information about mental health issues. One survey found that 23% of Internet users have searched for information about mental health issues online (Pew Internet, 2003). As you surf the Internet you have probably come across sites that offer psychological testing. Some of these sites are offered as a public service by health organizations. Others are more like commercials for pharmaceutical companies—once you have agreed that you suffer from a number of symptoms of a disorder, you may receive a recommendation to talk to your physician about the usefulness of a particular medication in treating those symptoms. Some sites offer psychological testing as a form of entertainment, and others are commercial enterprises requiring you to pay for psychological testing. It is important to know that these online services are psychological *testing* rather than psychological *assessment.* Online testing is not the same as having a psychological assessment. Online testing may be part of a psychological assessment, but it can never be considered a substitute for a psychological assessment (Buchanan, 2002).

Many paper-and-pencil psychological tests in questionnaire format can easily be adapted for online administration. Currently, many well-respected psychological tests may be completed online through secure sites. Online completion of tests allows for accurate scoring and rapid feedback. Tests can be updated quickly and new versions introduced at very low cost. Test administration can be adapted to clients with special needs, and versions can be made available in many different languages. The potential to offer psychological testing services cheaply to large numbers of people, some of whom may live in remote areas and who may have only limited access to face-to-face services with a mental health professional, is a very appealing one. However, before we accept unconditionally the potential benefits of psychological testing via the Internet, we must consider psychometric, ethical, legal, and practical issues (Naglieri et al., 2004).

The use of psychological tests on the Internet should be guided by the same principles that guide the use of any psychological tests. However, as you are aware, the Internet is unregulated. Ethical practices dictate that the test developer must demonstrate that the test has been found to be reliable and valid when used for specific purposes with specified populations. In most instances, it is also critical that the test developer provide appropriate norms for the test. The issue of the availability of appropriate norms is particularly important because Internet access may make a test that was normed on a homogeneous sample available to a much broader sample of the population. One of the most important professional issues is whether Internet testing is conducted as part of a psychological assessment in which the psychologist also gathers other data about the client and in which the client is provided face-to-face feedback about the assessment results.

Research shows that Internet samples are diverse and that results found through Internet responses are similar to those obtained by traditional methods (Gosling, Vazire, Srivastava, & John, 2004). This suggests that the use of the Internet for psychological research and testing can be done appropriately and, therefore, will likely increase in the coming years.

Assessment Versus Testing

Not all information gathered by a psychologist involves psychological testing. This underscores a more general point that psychological assessment and psychological testing are not synonymous. Consistent with the definitions of psychological tests, testing occurs when a particular device is used to gather a sample of behavior from a client, a score is assigned to the resulting sample, and comparisons with the scores of other people are made in order to interpret the client's score. Assessment is more complex and multifaceted than testing and may or may not involve the use of psychological tests. Assessment requires the integration of life history information and clinical observation of the client with, in most cases, the results obtained from psychological tests and information on the client provided by significant others in the client's life (Groth-Marnat, 2003). The result from a test is a score that can be interpreted based on comparisons with the scores of others; the result from an assessment is a coherent, unified description of the client or selected aspects of the client's experience.

All mental health professionals conduct assessments, but, compared with other mental health professionals, psychologists receive far more training in issues related to testing and are far more likely to use tests. The data in **Table 5.4** illustrate this point. Palmiter (2004) surveyed a sample of professionals providing mental health services to children and adolescents. As shown in the table, according to the survey, all professionals are likely to interview the child/adolescent and the family. However, compared with other mental health professionals, psychologists are much more likely to use tests to obtain information about their young clients. These differences were evident for all forms of

TABLE 5.4   Assessing Children and Adolescents: What Do Clinicians Do?

Assessment Method	% Clinicians[a]	% Psychologists[b]
Family interview	89.1	90.9
Individual child/adolescent interview	83.0	83.3
Review previous treatment records	70.7	63.6
Review previous educational testing	50.9	62.1
Naturalistic observation	44.3	33.3
Review recent report cards	37.4	54.5[*]
Parent behavior rating scales	34.8	60.6[*]
Teacher behavior rating scales	33.5	50.0[*]
Child/adolescent self-report rating scales	25.7	40.9[*]
Intelligence testing	26.1	40.9[*]
Achievement testing	17.8	33.3[*]
Personality testing	16.5	33.3[*]

[a]Data are from a sample of 230 clinicians (psychiatric social workers, psychiatric nurses, counselors) who work with children and adolescents (Palmiter, 2004).

[b]Data are from a sample of 66 doctoral-level psychologists who work with children and adolescents (Palmiter, 2004).

[*]Percentages using this method are significantly different at $p < .05$.

tests, including measures completed by parents and teachers, measures completed by the child/ adolescent, and measures of intelligence and academic achievement. The accurate psychological assessment of children and youth poses a considerable challenge. Unlike adults, children and adolescents are in a process of rapid cognitive, physical, and emotional development. Furthermore, children and adolescents rarely refer themselves for psychological services—they are referred by adults such as parents and teachers. The lives of children and adolescents are best understood with reference to the contexts in which they are embedded—in families, schools, and peer groups. Therefore, assessment of children and adolescents requires that a much larger number and variety of tests and measures be used than is typically the case for adults (Mash & Hunsley, 2007). Adding to this challenge is that child and adolescent assessment, by its very nature, involves the integration of information obtained from multiple methods (e.g., interviews, ratings, direct observations), informants (e.g., child, parent, teacher), and settings (e.g., home, classroom).

PROFILE BOX 5.1

DR. MARTIN M. ANTONY

I received my Ph.D. in clinical psychology from the University at Albany, State University of New York. I am a Professor and Director of Graduate Training in the Department of Psychology at Ryerson University in Toronto. I am the 2009–2010 President of the Canadian Psychological Association and Director of Research at the Anxiety Treatment and Research Centre, St. Joseph's Healthcare, Hamilton. I am licensed as a psychologist in the province of Ontario and am board certified in Clinical Psychology with the American Board of Professional Psychology.

Dr. Martin M. Antony

What is the most rewarding part of your job as a clinical psychologist?

I love doing many different things, and my career in clinical psychology has allowed me to do just that. I am actively involved in training psychologists and other professionals, conducting research, writing books, providing clinical service, developing new programs offering training and clinical service, and administration of our clinical program. My career has also allowed me to feed my entrepreneurial spirit. A portion of my income comes from providing continuing education to mental health professionals, consulting, and private practice. My work in anxiety disorders is particularly rewarding because (1) anxiety disorders are among the most prevalent of psychological problems and lead to significant impairment), and (2) because people with anxiety disorders can usually experience significant improvements in a relatively brief time when they receive evidence-based psychological treatment.

What is the greatest challenge facing you as a clinical psychologist?

Perhaps the biggest challenge to me personally is trying to find the time to do all the things I want to do. In recent years, I have started to turn down some opportunities, with the long-term goal of achieving a better balance between work and other pursuits. So far, the plan is proving a challenge. Exciting opportunities keep coming up, and it is difficult to say no.

Tell us about the role of assessment tools in treatment planning

In my practice, patients receive an evidence-based diagnostic interview to establish a diagnostic description that best captures their problems. Treatment decisions are based on the results of the interview (for example, a person with a principal diagnosis of social anxiety disorder would likely be offered a treatment including strategies that have been shown to be useful for this problem, including psychoeducation, cognitive restructuring, exposure, and perhaps social skills training). In addition, specific symptom severity measures are used to plan particular components of the treatment. For example, I often use data from the *Mobility Inventory for Agoraphobia* (Chambless, Caputo, Jasin, Gracely, & Williams, 1985) to help generate items for the exposure hierarchy, which in turn guides the behavioral component of treatment for people with panic disorder and agoraphobia.

How do you integrate science and practice in your work?

First, staying actively involved in research and writing allows me to be up to date with respect to scientific advances in the treatment of anxiety disorders and other problems. Over time, the tools I use for assessment and treatment are updated in response to recent scientific findings. Second, I often work within a team that is offering treatment in the context of scientific research. For example, we recently completed a study comparing a home-based treatment for obsessive-compulsive disorder to a standard office-based treatment. So as part of the study, many individuals received services for obsessive-compulsive disorder. Finally, we take an empirical approach to delivering clinical services. For example, we collect outcome data routinely, using standard, evidence-based assessment methods.

What do you see as the most exciting changes in the profession of clinical psychology?

One of the most exciting changes in the profession of clinical psychology is the move toward greater accountability. Increasingly, treatment facilities, funding agencies, and the public are demanding that assessment and treatment procedures be based on solid evidence. We still have a long way to go, but the situation has improved considerably compared to when I started my training. The publication of evidence-based treatment guidelines by various groups have been important steps along the way. For example, in response to guidelines published by the National Institute for Health and Clinical Excellence (NICE), the government in the United Kingdom recently announced that it will spend over 600 million U.S. dollars to train 3,600 new therapists to provide evidence-based psychological treatments, such as cognitive behavioral therapy. This is a momentous step toward improving care for people suffering from mental health problems.

The collection of diverse forms of information and the subsequent integration of this information are defining aspects of psychological assessment. As previously outlined in Table 5.2, many distinct competencies are required for psychologists to conduct meaningful assessments. Gary Groth-Marnat (2003), who has authored some of the most commonly used resources for teaching psychological assessment, nicely captured what is required of a clinical psychologist when conducting an assessment:

> "The central role of the clinician performing psychological assessment is that of an expert in human behavior who must deal with complex processes and understand test scores in the context of a person's life. The clinician must have knowledge concerning problem areas and, on the basis of this knowledge, form a general idea regarding behaviors to observe and areas in which to collect relevant data. This involves an awareness and appreciation of multiple causation, interactional influences, and multiple relationships" (p. 4).

Psychometric Considerations

The entire range of issues involved in test construction and validation are covered in courses on test construction and psychometric theory. As many of you have probably already completed such a course, we restrict our discussion here to reviewing the basic requirements for a test to be both scientifically sound and clinically useful. These psychometric elements, which hold for all types of psychological tests, are standardization (of stimuli, administration, and scoring), reliability, validity, and norms.

Most students find that psychometric considerations are not as interesting as case material. However, before you skip over them, it may be useful to imagine that you are in the emergency room, having broken your hand in a fall. Would you wish to have your X-ray read by a person who has aced the anatomy course, or by someone who had skipped the anatomy class that covered the bones in the hand, because it was simply too boring? To conduct competent, evidence-based assessments, psychologists must have a sound understanding of psychometrics.

Standardization

Standardization is an essential aspect of a psychological test, and it implies consistency across clinicians and testing occasions in the procedure used to administer and score the test (Anastasi & Urbina, 1997). Without standardization it is virtually impossible for the clinician to replicate the information gathered in an assessment or for any other clinician to do so. Furthermore, without standardization, test results are likely to be highly specific to the unique aspects of the testing situation and are unlikely to provide data that can be generalized to testing by another psychologist, let alone to other situations in the person's life. To reduce variability in the testing situation, test developers provide detailed instructions regarding the nature of the stimuli, administrative procedures, time limits, and the types of verbal probes and permissible responses to the client's questions. Instructions are provided for scoring the test. For many tests only simple addition of responses is required, but for many tests there are complex scoring rules that may require extensive training to achieve proficiency. It is essential that psychologists are trained in scoring the test and that they adhere to established scoring criteria. Unfortunately, it is relatively common for some psychologists to disregard the use of such scoring criteria in favor of nonstandardized, personally developed approaches to scoring. For example, in a survey of 293 school psychologists, Kennedy, Faust, Willis, and Piotrowski (1994) found that approximately 50% of survey respondents used personalized scoring for projective tests, and more than 10% used personalized scoring for self-report measures of depressive symptoms.

 How would you feel if a psychologist made decisions about your psychological adjustment based on an untested and unstandardized scoring system?

Reliability

We briefly touched on the psychometric properties of reliability and validity in Chapter 4 (see Table 4.10). You may remember that reliability refers to the consistency of the test, including whether all aspects of the test contribute in a meaningful way to the data obtained (**internal consistency**), whether similar results would be obtained if the person was retested at some point after the initial test (**test-retest reliability**), and whether similar results would be obtained if the test was conducted and/or scored by another evaluator (**interrater** or **interscorer reliability**). Reliable results are necessary if we wish to generalize the test results and their psychological implications beyond the immediate assessment situation. Standardization of stimuli, administration, and scoring are preconditions for good reliability, but do not ensure adequate test reliability. A test may consist of too many components that are influenced by irrelevant client characteristics, the testing situation (such as the demand characteristics associated with the purpose of the testing), or the behavior of the assessing psychologist. Also, the scoring criteria for the test may be too complicated or lacking in detail to permit reliable scoring.

   A question that typically arises in both clinical and research situations is just how reliable a test must be. As with many questions in psychology, the answer to this is not entirely straightforward. First, strictly speaking, the test itself does not have reliability—reliability must be considered in a broader context that takes into account both the purpose for which the test is being used and the population it is being used with. Simply because high levels of reliability have been found for an instrument when used with young adults, it should not be assumed that comparable levels of reliability will be found when used with older adults. Second, there are numerous psychological tests for which one would not expect internal consistency or test-retest reliability to be very high (Streiner, 2003). Take the example of a measure of stressful life events. You have probably seen such tests in other psychology courses or in popular magazines. They involve the listing of various possible life events that an individual may experience (e.g., death of a significant other, loss of employment, marriage, birth of a child) and usually ask the respondent to indicate which events occurred in the last year. Internal consistency of such tests is irrelevant, as the items are not necessarily related to each other. Likewise, if such a test was taken at the age of 18 and then again at the age of 25, one would not necessarily expect high test-retest reliability—such a test is not intended to measure a characteristic that is stable over time.

Let's return to the question of how much reliability is necessary. As Hogan (2007) suggested, this is a similar question to how high a ladder should be—the answer in both cases is that it depends on the purpose you have in mind. Nevertheless, there is a clear consensus that the level of acceptable reliability for tests used for clinical purposes must be greater than it is for tests used for research purposes. In considering internal consistency reliability, a number of authors have suggested that a value of .90 is the minimum required for a clinical test (e.g., Nunnally & Bernstein, 1994). For research purposes, values greater than .70 are typically seen as sufficient, with lower values being unacceptable (e.g., Kaplan & Saccuzzo, 2001). The main reason that high reliability is so important for clinical purposes is that reliability influences how much error there is in a test score. This can be extremely important in clinical work where precise test cut-off scores are used, such as in determining whether a child's measured intelligence is high enough to warrant access to a gifted school program.

Validity

When we consider test validity we are evaluating the degree to which the test truly measures what it purports to measure. A standardized and reliable test does not necessarily yield valid data, because a test purported to measure one construct may in fact be measuring a different construct. Test validity is a matter of ensuring that the test actually includes items that are representative of all aspects of the underlying psychological construct the test is designed to measure (**content validity**), that it provides data consistent with theoretical postulates associated with the phenomenon being assessed (**concurrent validity** and **predictive validity**), and that it provides a relatively pure measure of the construct that is minimally contaminated by other psychological constructs (**discriminant validity**). In applied contexts, such as in clinical assessment, an additional form of validity should be considered, namely **incremental validity**: the extent to which a measure adds to the prediction of a criterion above what can be predicted by other sources of data (Hunsley & Meyer, 2003; Sechrest, 1963). It is not necessarily a case of "the more data, the better" in clinical assessment. As described previously, there are costs associated with the collection of assessment data. The collection of excessive amounts of data can lead to both unnecessary costs and the introduction of unnecessary error creeping into the assessment. Despite the clear importance of incremental validity in conducting clinical assessments, there is currently very little research available to guide clinical psychologists in their selection and use of tests.

Although it is common to talk about a test being either valid or invalid, validity is not a dichotomous variable. Many psychological tests consist of subscales designed to measure specific aspects of a more general construct. For such tests it is inappropriate to refer to the validity of the test per se, because the validity of each subscale must be established. Moreover, validity is always conditional and must be established within certain parameters. Simply because a test is valid for specific purposes within specific groups of people, it does not follow that it is valid for other purposes or groups. For example, knowing that an intelligence test is a valid predictor of academic functioning does not also automatically support its use as a test for determining child custody arrangements.

We should not automatically assume that a test that has been shown to be valid for members of one ethnic group will be valid for members of a different ethnic group. When deciding whether it is appropriate to use a test with a client, the psychologist should determine whether there is validity evidence based on research with members of the same ethnic group as the client. Fernandez, Boccaccini, and Noland (2007) outlined a four-step process psychologists can use in identifying and selecting translated tests for Spanish-speaking clients (and that is applicable to translated tests in other languages). First, the range of translated tests should be identified by reviewing the catalogues and Web sites of test publishing companies. Next, research evidence for each relevant translated test, not just the original English language versions, must be examined. Third, the nature of the Spanish-speaking client samples used in the studies should be examined to determine whether the results are likely to be relevant to the client (e.g., research conducted in Spain may not be generalizable to a client who recently emigrated from Ecuador). Finally, the strength of the validity evidence must be weighed in determining whether the test is likely to be appropriate and useful in assessing the client.

Norms

To meaningfully interpret the results obtained from a client, it is essential to use either norms or specific criterion-related cut-off scores (American Educational Research Association et al., 1999). Without such reference information, it is impossible to determine the precise meaning of any test results. So if you were told you had a score of 44 on a test of emotional maturity, it would provide no meaningful information unless you knew the range of possible scores and how most other people score. In psychological assessment, comparisons must be made either to criteria that have been set for the test (e.g., a certain degree of accuracy as demonstrated in the test is necessary for the satisfactory performance of a job) or to some form of norms.

For most purposes in clinical psychology, test developers establish norms. Most importantly, decisions must be made about the populations to which the test is to be applied. It is possible to establish norms for comparing a specific score to those that might be obtained within the general population or within specific subgroups of the general population (e.g., gender-specific norms). So if your score of 44 for emotional maturity turned out to be significantly higher than the average in the general population, you might be very pleased. It is also possible to establish norms for determining the likelihood of membership in specific theoretical or concrete categories (e.g., nondistressed versus psychologically disordered groups). As with validity considerations, it may be necessary to develop multiple norms for a test based on the group being assessed (i.e., norms relevant for different ages and ethnic groups) and the testing purpose. A critical aspect of test norms is the quality of the normative sample. It is very common to find tests that have norms based on samples of convenience—in other words, data were obtained from a group of research participants in a specific location and may not be representative of scores that would be obtained by others. Common convenience samples include undergraduate students, hospital inpatients, or patients in a single psychology clinic. Such norms should be treated very skeptically, as no effort was taken to ensure that the members of the normative group were comparable in age, gender, ethnicity, or educational level (for example) to those who are likely to take the test as part of a clinical assessment. There are some commonly used psychological tests, such as the Wechsler scales of intelligence (see Chapter 7), that have nationally representative norms. With these types of norms, great care has been taken to ensure that test scores were obtained from a group of research participants selected to be representative of the national population for whom the test will be used. Accordingly, one can have much more confidence in the value and relevance of such norms.

As you may know from having taken a course in psychometrics and test construction, there are three main categories of test norms: percentile ranks, standard scores, and developmental norms (Hogan, 2007). A *percentile rank* indicates the percentage of those in the normative group whose scores fell below a given test score. If a test score of 25 is associated with a percentile rank of 81, this indicates that 81% of those in the normative group scored at or below a test score of 25. As you may have seen in Appendix 2, most students applying to graduate programs in clinical psychology are required to take the *Graduate Record Examination (GRE)*. Typically, the results from this test are reported as percentile ranks. The use of *standard scores* is very common with psychological tests. To develop a standard score, a z-score is calculated. As you may recall from other psychology courses, this involves subtracting the mean of the test scores from a specific test score and dividing the resulting number by the standard deviation of the test scores. Many psychological tests, such as the Minnesota Multiphasic Personality Inventory-2 (MMPI-2; described in detail in Chapter 8), convert a calculated z-score to a distribution in which the mean score is 50 and the standard deviation is 10 (i.e., a T-score). The GRE uses a different distribution in which the mean score is set at 500 and the standard deviation is 100.

Figure 5.2 presents the distribution of scores under a normal curve and allows you to interpret the normative meaning of a percentile rank or a standard score. Using this figure, you can see that a T-score of 71 on the MMPI-2 means that the score is greater than the score obtained by more than 98% of the normative sample.

Finally, *development norms* are used when the psychological construct being assessed develops systematically over time. The intelligence test developed by Alfred Binet used mental age equivalents to quantify the intellectual status of children (i.e., a child's score was comparable to the average child of a given age). The Woodcock-Johnson III Tests of Cognitive Abilities use both age equivalents (i.e., the age level in the normative sample at which the mean score is the same as the test score under consideration) and grade equivalents (i.e., the grade level in the normative sample at which the mean score is the same as the test score under consideration) to quantify achievement performance.

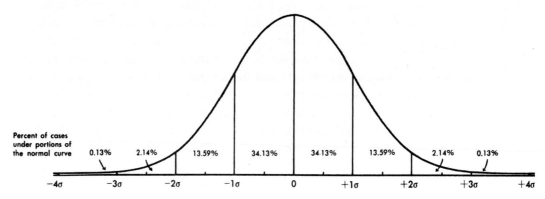

FIGURE 5.2   Equivalence of Several Types of Norms in the Normal Curve
Reprinted with permission from Harcourt Assessment Inc.

Testing Practices in Clinical Psychology

In Chapter 2 we described testing and assessment as central activities for most clinical psychologists. In Chapters 7 and 8 we describe in detail a number of commonly used psychological tests, with a particular emphasis on those that have substantial evidence of reliability and validity. Our intent in this section is to briefly present to you the tests that clinical psychologists typically use. As you read the following paragraphs, keep in mind the unfortunate fact that, as Groth-Marnat (2003) noted, many clinical psychologists fail to take into account the psychometric qualities of tests or the strength of the empirical literature regarding the tests. In other words, although some commonly used tests have outstanding psychometric properties, others fall woefully short of professional standards. We will have much more to say about this lamentable state of affairs in subsequent chapters.

There is a long history of surveys of clinical psychologists' practice activities and use of different types of tests. **Table 5.5** presents information from such surveys. Data from Cashel's (2002) survey of 162 clinical psychologists working with children and adolescents suggested that intelligence tests, behavior rating scales completed by parents and teachers (and, in some cases, the youths themselves), and brief projective tests are commonly used. In their survey of 137 clinical psychologists, Piotrowski, Belter, and Keller (1998) asked respondents about the most important tests used in clinical practice. Although the specific tests differed from those reported in the Cashel (2002) study, a similar pattern emerged, with intelligence, self-report personality inventories, and projective measures seen as most important. Of concern in both these surveys is the frequent reliance on projective tests. Compared with intelligence tests, personality inventories, and behavior rating scales, projective tests are far less likely to be standardized, to have norms, or to possess

---

TABLE 5.5   Test Usage Among Clinical Psychologists

Five Tests Most Commonly Used in Child and Adolescent Assessment[a]

Wechsler Intelligence Scale for Children

Achenbach System of Empirically Based Assessment

Sentence Completion Tests

Conners' Parent and Teacher Rating Scales

Draw-A-Person Test

Five Tests Rated as Most Important in Assessment Practices[b]

Minnesota Multiphasic Personality Inventory (both adult and adolescent versions)

Wechsler Intelligence Scales (both adult and child versions)

Rorschach Inkblot Test

Millon Inventories

Thematic Apperception Test

[a]from Cashel (2002); [b]from Piotrowski, Belter, and Keller (1998)

acceptable levels of reliability and validity (Hunsley et al., 2003). For example, although the Rorschach Inkblot Test can be administered, scored, and interpreted in a standardized manner, this is not the case for the clinical use of sentence completion tasks, the Draw-A-Person Test, or the Thematic Apperception Test.

Both country of practice and nature of doctoral assessment training appear to influence psychologists' test usage. Bekhit, Thomas, Lalonde, and Jolley (2002) found that British psychologists were much less likely than North American psychologists to use psychological tests. In a survey of 158 British clinical psychologists, the tests seen as most important for clinical practice were the Wechsler intelligence scales (adult and child versions), the Wechsler Memory Scale, the Beck Depression Inventory, the National Adult Reading Test, and the Millon Personality Inventories. Extremely few respondents rated the Thematic Apperception Test and the Rorschach as important for clinical use. Childs and Eyde (2002) surveyed approximately half the APA-accredited clinical psychology programs in the United States and Canada. They found that more than two thirds of surveyed programs taught doctoral students to use the Wechsler intelligence scales, the MMPI scales, the Rorschach Inkblot Test, and the Thematic Apperception Test. These findings definitely help explain the Piotrowski et al. (1998) data: psychologists are simply using the tests that they were trained to use. If we consider the model curriculum recommendations found in Table 5.1 and the competency requirements found in Table 5.2, the Childs and Eyde (2002) data suggest that there are some very significant weaknesses in the way in which most programs approach assessment training. For example, although almost every surveyed program provided training in the interpretation and reporting of test results, less than two thirds provided instruction on the topics of reliability and validity, and only 20% had a course that covered issues related to norms.

Evidence-Based Assessment

Recent years have witnessed a renewed emphasis on the scientific evidence underlying psychological tests and assessment. This emphasis is attributable to the increased focus on the use of scientific evidence guiding the provision of health care services as well as greater awareness of shortcomings in the ways in which some clinical psychologists assess their clients. **Evidence-based assessment** (EBA) is an approach to psychological evaluation that uses research and theory to guide (a) the selection of variables to be assessed for a specific assessment purpose, (b) the methods and measures to be used in the assessment, and (c) the manner in which the assessment process unfolds. It involves the recognition that the assessment process is a decision-making task in which the clinician must repeatedly formulate and test hypotheses by integrating data obtained throughout the assessment (Hunsley & Mash, 2007).

At this point in the development of EBA, the primary focus has been on identifying a range of psychological instruments (including interviews, self-report measures, observational coding systems, and self-monitoring measures) that have been demonstrated to possess solid psychometric properties. Hunsley and Mash (2008) developed a rating system for instruments used for specific assessment purposes (e.g., diagnosis, treatment monitoring, treatment evaluation) within specific conditions (e.g., depression, self-injurious behaviors, couple conflict). The rating system requires the attainment of predetermined psychometric levels in the areas of reliability, validity, and norms across published studies (e.g., repeated evidence of internal consistency values of .90 and above is designated as "excellent").

Psychological Testing and Assessment: Ethical Considerations

As we described in Chapter 2, the profession of clinical psychology is founded on two main pillars: science and ethics. Thus far in the chapter we have focused almost exclusively on the scientific side of psychological assessment. It is now time to consider the main ethical issues psychologists encounter in conducting assessments. Both the American Psychological Association (APA, 2002a) and the Association of State and Provincial Psychology Boards (ASPPB, 2005) have codes of conduct that contain elements specific to assessment activities. In order to avoid differences in codes and legal requirements across jurisdictions, we focus our presentation of ethical issues on generic issues in assessment rather than on a specific code of conduct.

If you are considering seeking a psychological assessment, you should ensure that you obtain sufficient details about the assessment to be able to make an informed decision about participation. This includes information about the nature and purpose of the assessment, the fees, the involvement of other parties in the assessment, and any limits to confidentiality.

When considering ethical issues in assessment, the first and foremost issue is that of informed consent. In some instances it may not be possible to obtain freely given informed consent because the person is, in some fashion, being compelled to undergo the assessment. Common examples include situations in which a court has mandated an assessment or an assessment is being undertaken to determine an individual's competence or capacity to make decisions. For example, Toni, a seriously depressed mother who is engaged in a battle for the custody of her child with her formerly abusive partner, may feel that she has little choice about whether to participate in a child custody evaluation if she wishes to retain her parenting arrangement with her child. Similarly, Trent, who was charged with manslaughter following a motor vehicle accident, may feel he has little choice about participating in a psychological assessment that will address whether symptoms of attention-deficit/hyperactivity disorder contributed to the accident. In these situations, psychologists should still strive to provide as much information about the assessment as is appropriate in these cases. Most codes of conduct indicate that psychologists have a responsibility to adequately communicate the results of the assessment to the client. Not only must the psychologist provide the information, but he or she must also take reasonable steps to ensure that the client understands the results.

All information collected as part of a psychological assessment must be treated as confidential. This means that no information gathered in the assessment can be released to others without the client's consent. Although this seems rather straightforward, there are exceptions to this. For example, if the psychologist learns that the client is intent on committing suicide, has a clear plan for this, and has the means to carry out the plan, the psychologist has an obligation to break confidentiality in order to secure the client's safety. When a child volunteers in the course of intelligence testing that he or she is upset because a parent punished him or her with a belt, then the psychologist has a legal obligation to inform the child protection authorities. Limits to confidentiality thus must be explained to the client as part of the informed consent procedures.

In many jurisdictions, legislation allows people to access their health records. In other words, whatever is in a client file, with very few exceptions, can be seen by the client, and clients can authorize the release of file information to others such as teachers, lawyers, or other health care providers. This poses a potential challenge for psychologists, as they are also required to protect the security and copyrights of test materials. As a result, it is becoming standard practice among psychologists to distinguish between test data and test material per se. Test data, like other parts of a client file, may be released to clients and appropriate others upon the request of the client (or the client's guardian or legal representative). Test material, including actual test questions and manuals, are not part of the file and must not be released. The distinction between test data and test material has caused publishers of psychological tests to alter the format of some tests. It was common practice for self-report measures, for example, to have both the test questions and a space for scoring the test on the same sheet. This made it impossible to physically separate the test data (i.e., the client's score or circled responses to questions) from the test itself. Accordingly, the format of many of these tests has been altered to provide a separate sheet on which the client provides a response and the test is scored.

In conducting assessments, psychologists have an ethical responsibility to be knowledgeable about test properties such as standardization, reliability, validity, and norms. They must also be familiar with the proper use and interpretation of the tests they use. It is particularly important that psychologists be aware of the tests' strengths and limitations with respect to psychological characteristics such as age, gender, ethnicity, and cultural background. When providing feedback about the assessment to the client or to others designated by the client, psychologists have a responsibility to clearly indicate the limits to the certainty of their findings. This pertains to all aspects of assessment results, including diagnoses, clinical judgments, and clinical predictions. They also have an obligation to indicate the basis for their results and must clearly indicate the sources of data used in an assessment. It is becoming increasingly common for psychologists to use computer-generated interpretive reports when using personality, intelligence, or achievement tests. Psychologists who use the interpretive statements contained in the computer-generated report should acknowledge the sources of the statements in the assessment report. This ensures that the basis for the conclusions obtained from the interpretive report is clearly presented.

SUMMARY AND CONCLUSIONS

In this chapter we have reviewed some of the many purposes of psychological assessment. We have highlighted that in addition to stand-alone assessment services, psychological assessment can be used in screening, diagnosis and case formulation, prediction, treatment planning, and monitoring the effectiveness of interventions. An important distinction was drawn between psychological assessment, which refers to an entire process of inquiry, and psychological testing, which may be used as part of that process. We have argued that psychologists have special expertise in the use of tests, and that for a tool to be considered a psychological test it must meet strict criteria in terms of standardization, reliability, validity, and norms. The development of criteria for evidence-based assessment holds the promise of enhancing the scientific quality of instruments used by clinical psychologists. Finally, we reviewed ethical issues related to client consent to assessment services.

C r i t i c a l   T h i n k i n g   Q u e s t i o n s

How is psychological assessment different from other types of assessment?

Why is it important for clinical psychologists to understand psychometric considerations?

Why do psychologists collect multiple types of information in their assessments?

What are the essential ingredients of a useful psychological test?

Is there a problem with basing decisions on unstandardized tests?

K e y   T e r m s

assessment-focused services: services conducted primarily to provide information on a person's psychosocial functioning

base rate: frequency with which the problem/diagnosis occurs in the population

case formulation: comprehensive and clinically relevant conceptualization of psychological functioning developed by using assessment data

concurrent validity: extent to which scores on the test are correlated with scores on measures of similar constructs

content validity: extent to which the test samples the type of behavior that is relevant to the underlying psychological construct

discriminant validity: extent to which a test provides a pure measure of the construct that is minimally contaminated by other psychological constructs

evidence-based assessment: use of research and theory to guide (a) the variable assessed, (b) the methods and measures, and (c) the manner in which the assessment process unfolds

incremental validity: extent to which a measure adds to the prediction of a criterion above what can be predicted by other sources of data

internal consistency: extent to which all aspects of a test contribute in a similar way to the overall score

interrater reliability/ interscorer reliability: extent to which similar results would be obtained if the test was conducted by another evaluator

intervention-focused assessment services: assessments conducted in the context of intervention services

predictive validity: extent to which the test predicts a relevant outcome

prognosis: predictions made about the future course of a patient's psychological functioning based on the use of assessment data, in combination with relevant empirical literature

screening: procedure to identify individuals who may have problems of a clinical magnitude or who may be at risk for developing such problems

sensitivity: proportion of true positives identified by the assessment

specificity: proportion of true negatives identified by the assessment

standardization: consistency across clinicians and testing occasions in the procedure used to administer and score a test

test-retest reliability: extent to which similar results would be obtained if the person was retested at some point after the initial test

Key Names

Gary Groth-Marnat   Michael Lambert

ADDITIONAL RESOURCES
Books

Groth-Marnat, G. (2003). *Handbook of psychological assessment* (4th ed.). Hoboken, NJ: John Wiley & Sons.

Hersen, M. (Ed.). (2004). *The comprehensive handbook of psychological assessment* (Vols. 1–4). New York: John Wiley & Sons.

Hogan, T. P. (2007). *Psychological testing: A practical introduction* (2nd ed.). Hoboken, NJ: John Wiley & Sons.

Hunsley, J., & Mash, E. J. (Eds.). (2008). *A guide to assessments that work.* New York: Oxford University Press.

Check It Out!

The Buros Center for Testing provides listings of tests and test reviews: http://www.unl.edu/buros

Several Web sites offer information on screening for psychological problems. For example: National Alcohol Screening Day: http://www.mentalhealthscreening.org/events/nasd/

National Depression Screening Day: http://www.mentalhealthscreening.org/college/depression.aspx

Self-screening for anxiety and depression, offered by Freedom From Fear: http://www.freedom fromfear.org/screenrm.asp

CHAPTER 6

Assessment: Interviewing and Observation

INTRODUCTION

Among the myriad strategies used in clinical assessments, interviews and observations are most commonly used by psychologists. Across diverse theoretical orientations, clinical psychologists gather assessment data by talking to clients and by observing them. Interviews are used in overlapping ways for both clinical assessment and psychotherapy (see **Figure 6.1**). They are an integral component of both stand-alone assessments and assessments that are part of the delivery of psychological services. Interviews are the most common strategy for gathering information necessary to make a diagnosis, but serve many additional purposes. They are also used to obtain information for case formulation, problem definition, and goal setting. Interview data include material that cannot be easily assessed in psychometric tests and that is important in generating hypotheses and elaborating on themes that have been identified in other assessment strategies. The clinical interview is a valuable tool—not just as a source of information, but also for developing a collaborative relationship between client and psychologist.

In this chapter we will explain some of the differences between clinical assessment interviews and regular conversations. Psychologists are trained how to ask questions and how to listen. The way that questions are formulated can encourage clients to give a yes or no answer, or to elaborate and explain in greater detail. Listening skills include verbal strategies to convey understanding and to clarify what the client has said, as well as nonverbal behaviors that convey that the psychologist is attentively tracking the conversation. In this chapter we will discuss confidentiality issues that must be addressed prior to beginning any interview. We will describe strategies used in interviews to define the client's problems, formulate client goals,

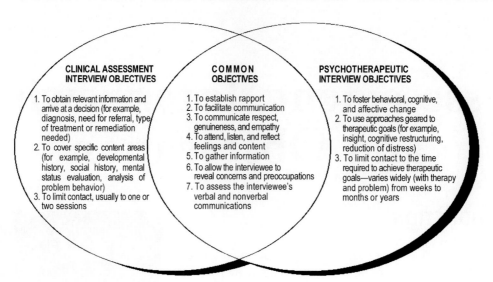

FIGURE 6.1   Differences and Similarities Between Clinical Assessment Interviews and Psychotherapeutic Interviews
From Mash & Sattler (1998) Reproduced with permission.

and obtain an accurate description of ways the client has attempted to solve these problems in the past. We will also present ways that the skills required in interviewing an individual must be adapted when the psychologist is interviewing a couple or a family. For example, you can imagine that a clinical psychologist interviewing 13-year-old Daniel and his mother would quickly lose rapport with the teenager if all the focus of the interview was on his mother. In working with more than one client, the psychologist must be adept at ensuring that each person has an opportunity to talk.

The psychologist must maintain rapport with both the teenager and the parent. (Source: Spencer Grant/PhotoEdit)

Different purposes require different types of interviews that vary in their degree of structure. In unstructured interviews, the psychologist decides what questions to ask and to follow up on as the interview unfolds. Semi-structured interviews allow the psychologist some flexibility in questioning and the order of questions. Highly structured interviews specify the precise ways that questions should be posed and queries made, as well as define the types of responses necessary to score a particular symptom as present. You may recall that in Chapter 4 we discussed the need to balance threats to internal validity and external validity; similarly, in considering interview formats the psychologist must weigh the advantages of structure with the advantages of flexibility. In practice, most clinical assessment interviews are unstructured and follow the format preferred by the individual psychologist. Even though unstructured clinical assessment interviews do not follow a set script, they are distinct from regular conversation in important ways we describe later.

For many decades children were considered to be unreliable informants, so all pertinent clinical information was gathered from the significant adults in their lives. There has been growing recognition that children can provide important information about their experiences, thoughts, and feelings. However, it is not sufficient to simply scale down an adult interview for use with children. Although face-to-face interviews are a common way for adults to gather information, this strategy poses special challenges with children. We will describe some of the developmental issues that must be taken into account when interviewing children, including their level of cognitive development, their emotional expression, and their suggestibility. Given the limitations of child interviews, diagnostic information is also obtained from adults who know the child well, such as parents, teachers, and caregivers.

Interviews offer rich opportunities for the psychologist to observe the client. The psychologist is attentive to the client's appearance, behavior, affect, and responses to questions. Couple, parent–child, and family interviews also provide the opportunity to observe the ways that family members interact, the way they take turns, how they handle disagreement, and so on. Psychologists also find it useful to observe children and families in more naturalistic environments, such as in a playroom, at home, or at school. We will discuss the types of information that can be gathered from such observations. In the final section of the chapter, we will discuss the usefulness of self-monitoring as a clinical assessment strategy, in which the client keeps track of and records the details of relevant thoughts, behaviors, or feelings.

ETHICAL ISSUES: LIMITS OF CONFIDENTIALITY

Ethical codes dictate that psychologists must provide confidential services. This means that the psychologist is required to maintain secrecy with respect to the material that is revealed in the course of providing psychological services. The psychologist is bound to respect the client's privacy and must not discuss details with other people without the client's permission. Even though privacy legislation in all jurisdictions in the United States limits the use and release of private information, there are limits to the confidentiality of information provided to a psychologist. As we discussed in Chapter 5, in some cases, a third party such as a school board, an insurance company, an HMO, or a family court judge has requested the assessment. In those circumstances, the client must give permission for the results of the assessment to be sent to the third party. There are also legal obligations to break confidentiality when a person's safety is at risk. All states have child protection laws that require professionals to inform the local child protection agency if there is a suspicion that a child may be in need of protection. Psychologists are required to take steps to ensure that clients are protected from self-harm and that others are protected if a client plans to harm someone else. Psychological reports and records can be subpoenaed by the court, and the psychologist can be required to testify with respect to the psychological services provided to the client.

Psychologists must ensure that clients understand the limits to confidentiality before they enter into an agreement to receive psychological services (which is why we are discussing ethical issues so

---

TABLE 6.1   Limits of Confidentiality: A Heavy Way to Start a Conversation, but a Professional Way to Start an Assessment Interview

"Everything that is said here is private. I will not tell other people what's talked about. However, there are some important exceptions to that rule. First, if you told me that a child was being harmed in some way, then by law I have to do something to protect the child, that is, I'd have to report the information to Child Protection Services. Second, if I heard that you were finding things so tough that you felt life just wasn't worth living anymore, then I'd have to take steps to protect you. Basically, if I hear anyone is in danger of being hurt by someone else or by him or herself, then I can't keep things private, but must do something to protect the person. Third, if there was ever some kind of a court case, then a judge could ask me to give testimony, could ask me about these sessions, or ask to see my notes.

Do you understand the limits to confidentiality that I just described? Do you have any questions? I know this is a heavy way to get started, but I believe it is important to describe this to all clients, just so you know where you stand."

---

early in this chapter!). The client has a right to know what will be kept confidential and under what circumstances confidentiality may be broken. **Table 6.1** provides an example of the way that a psychologist might introduce the **limits of confidentiality** at the beginning of a first appointment. Although it is highly unusual to begin a first conversation with a statement that sets out all kinds of unpleasant scenarios, such as child abuse, suicide, homicide, and court cases, an explanation of the limits of confidentiality gives a very clear signal that the conversation that will follow is a professional one. By calmly explaining the limits of confidentiality, the psychologist demonstrates that in the context of psychological services, the client's rights are protected, a person's safety is considered paramount, and that it is possible to talk about very difficult issues. As you can imagine, students in training sometimes wonder whether a client who has been told the limits of confidentiality will be afraid to say anything to a psychologist; however, this is not the case. Knowing that the psychologist will need to take action, clients still disclose painful experiences such as being the victim of abuse or having thoughts of suicide.

What is your reaction to the script in Table 6.1? How would this affect your views of psychological services? What kind of skills does it require to begin a conversation this way?

UNSTRUCTURED ASSESSMENT INTERVIEWS

In conducting clinical interviews, psychologists strive to create a safe environment designed to make the client more at ease to talk about the issues that are troubling to him or her. The assessment interview is conducted free from disruptions; the psychologist does not answer the phone, read text messages, or respond to email during interviews. Ideally, offices are soundproofed to limit distracting background noises. The psychologist adopts a calm and relaxed stance designed to put clients at ease. However, the clinical interview is not a social visit. It differs in important ways from the conversations a client may have with friends, with the hairdresser, or with a stranger on a long train journey. Allowing a person to simply tell his or her story is not the same as conducting a clinical assessment interview. Empathic listening may be sufficient to provide temporary relief to a distressed friend, but it is not

TABLE 6.2   Differences Between Clinical Interviews and Social Conversations

Social Conversation	Clinical Interview
Can take place anywhere	Usually in an office
May be overheard by others	Private
Variable duration	Usually 50 minutes to an hour
Details may be repeated in other conversations:	Confidential, except to protect safety or with client's written permission
Purpose is relationship maintenance	Purpose is both information gathering and establishing a collaborative relationship
Free flowing according to each person's interest	Goal directed; keeps to an agenda; clear sequence; keeps to relevant themes
Reciprocal: "something similar happened to me . . ."	Focused on the client "that reminds me of the time when I . . .."
Each person waits for an opening to make a comment:	Clinician interrupts and redirects conversation:
"now you mention worries . . ."	"Do you ever worry . . ."
Maintenance of relationship usually takes precedence over gathering information	May require persistent questioning
Commonly avoids painful topics	Clinician raises painful topics such as abuse, violence, suicide
Participants rarely take notes	Psychologist may take notes
Not documented	Notes of session are kept by the psychologist
Not recorded	With client's permission may be audio- or video-recorded

sufficient to enable the psychologist to formulate a diagnosis or to begin treatment planning. **Table 6.2** lists some of the ways that clinical interviews differ from regular conversations. Because an assessment interview is not a regular conversation, the client may feel more at ease in discussing painful or embarrassing issues than he or she would be willing to discuss in chats with friends.

 If you choose a career in clinical psychology because you have always liked talking to people and are considered by your friends and family to be a good listener, you may be surprised to discover that you will need to learn to interact in very different ways in your future role as a psychologist.

The psychologist is responsible for structuring the session to ensure that relevant topics are covered during assessment interviews. The psychologist's theoretical orientation and training determine the extent to which he or she explicitly directs the session, the manner in which the questions are asked, and the topics that are covered. In general, though, psychologists are trained to formulate questions in a manner that facilitates the client's engagement in the interview. One important distinction is between **open questions** and **closed questions.** Open questions allow the client to provide elaborate responses and cannot be answered with a simple "yes" or "no." Closed questions, on the other hand, can be answered with a single word. Each type has advantages and disadvantages. Open questions allow the client to give a more complex answer and do not

TABLE 6.3   Open and Closed Questions

Open	Closed
Who lives in your house?	Does your Dad live with you?
What was your reaction when you found out you were pregnant?	Were you pleased when you found out you were pregnant?
How do you show affection?	Do you kiss your partner?
What do your parents do when you break curfew?	Do you get grounded when you break curfew?
What happens when you argue?	Do you hit her when you argue?
Tell me about the kinds of things that make you feel anxious.	Were you anxious when you gave a presentation to the class?
How did your reactions compare to what you usually feel?	Did you feel better after taking a deep breath?
How would your life be different if you make the changes you want in therapy?	Do you think you will be able to work again when you no longer feel depressed?

suggest that a particular response is required. However, open questions may invite the client to begin a long, tangential story that may be of limited relevance, in which case the psychologist must direct the client back to the topic at hand. Closed questions, on the other hand, yield brief, less ambiguous answers, allowing the rapid coverage of many topics. **Table 6.3** gives examples of open and closed questions. Many psychologists find it useful to begin discussion of a topic with an open-ended question and to follow up with closed questions that clarify details of the response.

 Pay attention to your usual style of questioning in your conversations with friends. Do you notice any difference in the impact on the conversation when you use open and closed questions?

Although some people worry that asking questions about difficult issues such as suicide will increase the likelihood of suicidal behavior, this is not the case. Because the phrasing of the question can influence the type of answer, psychologists are careful not to ask leading questions or to put words in the client's mouth. The client's initial response to a question may be noncommittal or vague, requiring the psychologist to encourage the client to elaborate or to explain: "tell me what you mean . . . tell me more about that." Contrary to the conventions of regular conversation, the psychologist gently persists with a line of questioning until the question has been answered. For example, after Sonia changed the topic or made a joke when asked about her new relationship, a friend might conclude that she did not wish to discuss it and so would move on to other topics, whereas a psychologist might ask her if she noticed that she seemed to be having difficulty talking about the relationship. Because clinical assessment interviews are not the same as regular conversation, the psychologist may ask questions that people may find difficult to answer (e.g., "What was it like for you when you had the miscarriage?" "What went through your mind as you were forcing yourself to vomit?" "How do people respond to you when you tell them that you have schizophrenia?"). Sometimes clients are at a loss how to answer and must reflect before answering. Psychologists use silence to allow the client time to reflect and, therefore, do not feel obliged to fill in the gaps in conversation as they might in a social context.

STRUCTURED DIAGNOSTIC INTERVIEWS

In Chapter 3 we described the evolution of diagnostic systems used to categorize different types of psychopathology. You may remember that each version of the *Diagnostic and Statistical Manual of Mental Disorders* (DSM) provided more precise decision rules for the diagnosis of disorders. Researchers noted that although most mental health professionals agreed on the general features of a disorder, there was poor interrater reliability in assigning diagnoses; that is, there was low agreement between two interviewers about the precise diagnostic category. To address this problem, a number of **structured interviews** were developed. These interviews vary in their coverage of symptoms and life context. They have a specific format for asking questions and a specific sequence in which questions are asked. Based on initial client responses, the interviewer is then directed to use follow-up questions that help confirm or rule out possible diagnoses. Although structured interviews can be designed to address almost any clinical issue, the majority are designed to provide diagnostic information.

The most widely used clinical interview in North America, the **Structured Clinical Interview for Axis I Disorders** (SCID; First, Spitzer, Gibbon, & Williams, 1997) permits diagnosis of a broad spectrum of disorders. Two versions have been developed. The SCID-I is an interview designed for research that includes the entire spectrum of DSM Axis I disorders, whereas the shorter SCID-CV covers only the most common disorders. The SCID begins with an open-ended interview on demographic information, work history, chief complaint, history of present and past psychopathology, treatment history, and assessment of current functioning. This less structured format is designed to develop rapport with the client before beginning the structured symptom-focused questions that are designed to yield diagnostic information. It is clear, therefore, that the SCID is not a completely standardized instrument. The structured portion includes required probe questions as well as recommended follow-up questions. Each probe corresponds to a specific DSM criterion. For some types of disorder, such as bipolar disorder, good interrater reliability values have been reported, whereas for others, such as agoraphobia, the findings are mixed (Keller & Craske, 2008). Given the increasing use of information technology to deliver health care services, it is important to note that the SCID is as reliable when administered via videoconferencing as it is when administered in person (Shore, Savin, Orton, Beals, & Manson, 2007). The developers assumed that, because the SCID criteria parallel DSM criteria, this provided sufficient evidence of its validity. Therefore, in a sense, the validity of the SCID is tied to the validity of the DSM itself. The strength of the SCID lies in the breadth of the disorders it covers; its weakness, which may be related to the breadth of coverage, is the variable reliabilities that are obtained for different disorders and the lack of strong validity data. Because the SCID covers all of the Axis I diagnoses, it also can be very time consuming to administer—an important consideration in clinical use.

In contrast to the broad coverage of the SCID, the **Anxiety Disorders Interview Schedule for DSM-IV** (ADIS IV; Brown, Di Nardo, & Barlow, 1994) is a semistructured diagnostic interview that focuses on anxiety disorders and disorders that are commonly comorbid with anxiety disorders (mood disorders, somatoform disorders, and substance-related disorders). There are two versions for adults (one that addresses current diagnosis only and a longer version that assesses both current symptomatology and lifetime history of problems) and parallel child and parent versions for assessing anxiety disorders in youth. Like the SCID, the ADIS includes general background information as well as questions that relate directly to DSM IV criteria. There is considerable evidence of the reliability and validity of the ADIS. Its main advantage over more general diagnostic interviews lies in the depth of coverage of the disorders that are assessed (Summerfeldt & Antony, 2002).

A brief measure, the Primary Care Evaluation of Mental Disorders (PRIME-MD), was developed for use in primary health care settings (Spitzer et al., 1995). The main advantage of the PRIME-MD is as a rapid screening device (Summerfeldt & Antony, 2002). Although it cannot be considered a substitute for a full diagnostic interview, its brevity makes it very appealing for use in medical clinics. There is growing evidence of the reliability of the PRIME-MD as well as support for its validity (e.g., Jackson, Passamonti, & Kroenke, 2007). As a result, it has been translated into many languages, and research evidence supports its use in primary care settings in a wide range of countries, including France (Norton et al., 2007), Hungary (Voros et al., 2006) and Iraq (Hussein & Sa'Adoon, 2006).

Table 6.4 presents information on the diagnostic interviews we have discussed. As you can see, the comprehensive interviews take at least an hour to administer, whereas the screening measures are completed more quickly. Most of these interviews can be administered by mental health professionals who have received additional specialized training.

Some of the structured diagnostic interviews that were originally developed for adults have been modified for use with children. For example, in adapting the ADIS for use with youth (ADIS Clinician Manual for Child and Parent Versions; Albano & Silverman, 1996), visual cues such as the Feelings Thermometer were introduced. Respondents are asked to indicate on a picture of a thermometer how they are feeling. 0 might represent totally calm and 100 might represent very afraid. The Feelings Thermometer is designed to enable children to better communicate different gradations of feelings when their vocabulary

TABLE 6.4   Comparison of Features of Diagnostic Interviews

Name	Age range	Training required	Breadth	Time to administer of coverage	Correspondence to DSM-IV
Structured Clinical Interview for Axis I Disorders SCID)	Adult	Trained mental health professional	Broad	60 minutes	Yes
Anxiety Disorders Interview Schedule (ADIS) IV	Adult	Trained mental health professional	Medium	45–60 minutes	Yes
Anxiety Disorders Interview Schedule (ADIS) IV Child–Parent Version	Child	Trained mental health professional	Medium	45–60 parent; 45–60 child	Yes
Primary Care Evaluation of Mental Disorders (PRIME-MD)	Adult	Trained health professional	Narrow	10–20 minutes	Somewhat
Dominic-R	6–11 years	Trained mental health professional	Broad	10–15 minutes	For screening only; no frequency and duration data

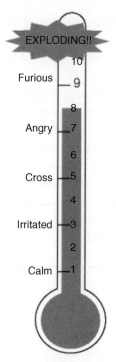

FIGURE 6.2 An Anger Thermometer: An anger thermometer allows a child to identify different intensities of anger that she or he is feeling. From: http://www.embracethefuture.org.au/resiliency/index.htm

for expressing these distinctions is limited (see Figure 6.2). For example, whereas a child might be able to verbalize only crude distinctions like "kind of scared" and "really scared," he or she may be able to convey that in some situations the level of fear is a 20, and on others it is a 60 or 80. Nevertheless, some features of diagnostic interviews are particularly problematic with children. These include the length of the interview, which often exceeds children's attention capacity, as well as questions requiring a more precise response than children are capable of providing. Diagnostic interviews for children and adolescents usually have parallel versions that are completed by parents, which of course raise the challenging issue of how to make sense of disagreements between different informants (Silverman & Ollendick, 2008).

To address some of the challenges of assessing very young children, some creative interview formats have been developed. Ablow and colleagues have used puppets in the assessment of children ages 4–8 (Ablow et al., 1999; Measelle, Ablow, Cowan, & Cowan, 1998; Measelle, John, Ablow, Cowan, & Cowan, 2005). Children are presented with two identical puppets, Iggy and Ziggy, who describe themselves in different ways. For example, Iggy says "I am not shy when I meet new people" and Ziggy says "I am shy when I meet new people." Children are then asked to indicate which puppet they are similar to. Ablow and colleagues have reported encouraging test-retest reliability and discriminant validity for the interview. Children appear to be able to reliably report on their personality traits (Measelle et al., 2005) and on basic symptoms of anxiety and depression (Luby, Belden, Sullivan, & Spitznagel, 2007).

A group of researchers have developed a diagnostic interview for children ages 6–11 years, *Dominic*, which uses cartoon drawings as cues (Valla, Bergeron, & Smolla, 2000). Children are shown a series of drawings and asked to respond to a question on whether they would or would not behave like the target child. The stimuli are available in different formats that vary in gender, age, ethnic background, and language. Given children's difficulties with the concept of time, there is no attempt to determine the frequency of behaviors, so the interview cannot yield full information required for diagnosis, nor does the information yield contextual data. Valla and colleagues have reported adequate test-retest reliability and criterion validity to support the use of *Dominic* as an effective, brief screening instrument for mental disorders. Work is currently underway to validate an interactional version in which the stimuli are presented via computer and the child responds by clicking the appropriate box (e.g., Scott, Short, Singer, Russ, & Minnes, 2006). *Dominic* is a good example of the use of computers to administer interviews to clients, a trend that is becoming increasingly popular and holds the promise of improving the quality of data collected as part of psychological assessments (cf. Garb, 2007).

Do you think you would respond differently to an interview administered by a person than to one administered by a computer? Why?

GENERAL ISSUES IN INTERVIEWING

Attending Skills

Clinical assessment requires skills not only in asking questions, but also in listening. **Table 6.5** lists a number of listening skills that are crucial for a psychologist to develop. In an assessment interview, the psychologist attends carefully to what is being said and also observes nonverbal behavior. There may be important discrepancies between what a person is saying and how he or she is behaving (e.g., Nathan agitatedly rubs his hands together while simultaneously reporting that everything is fine in his relationship). The psychologist also uses nonverbal behavior such as nods, eye contact, and vocalizations such as "Mmm ..." and "Uh huh" to communicate that he or she is tracking the conversation without interrupting the flow of what is being said. Periodically, the psychologist summarizes and paraphrases the client's statement as a way of clarifying that he or she understands what is being said. Emotional reflections are statements related to the client's nonverbal behavior and the content of the responses that focus attention on the client's affect: "it sounds as though that was very painful for you" or "you seem very angry about that."

Unlike regular conversations, clinical assessment interviews focus exclusively on the client. The psychologist does not take turns in describing similar experiences that he or she has had. In Chapter 14 you will learn that therapist self-disclosure can facilitate a positive therapeutic alliance; however, therapeutic self-disclosure is not the same as the reciprocal sharing of personal information that takes place in social relationships. In deciding whether or not to self-disclose, the therapist is guided by the client's interests, rather than by a personal need to vent or to gain approval from the client.

How do you think it would feel to have a conversation focus entirely on you for almost an hour? Would you feel comfortable, or awkward, or maybe intimidated? If you were in training as a psychologist, how easy would it be for you to modify your natural conversation style to be able to focus on someone else for such an extended period of time?

TABLE 6.5   Listening Skills Nondirective Listening Response Attending behavior

	Description	Primary Intent/Effect
Silence	Eye contact, leaning forward, head nods, facial expressions, etc.	Facilitates or inhibits spontaneous client talk
	Absence of verbal activity	Places pressure on clients to talk Allows "cooling off" time Allows interviewer to consider next response
Clarification	Attempted restating of a client's message, preceded or followed by a closed question (e.g., "Do I have that right?")	Clarifies unclear client statements and verifies the accuracy of what the interviewer heard
Paraphrase	Reflection of rephrasing of the content of what the client said	Assures clients you hear them accurately and allows them to hear what they said
Sensory-based paraphrase	Paraphrase that uses the client's clearly expressed sensory modalities	Enhances rapport and empathy
Nondirective reflection of feeling	Restatement or rephrasing of clearly stated emotion	Enhances clients' experience of empathy and encourages their further emotional expression
Summarization	Brief review of several topics covered during a session	Enhances recall of session content and ties together or integrates themes covered in a session

From Sommers-Flanagan & Sommers-Flanagan, 2003. Reprinted with permission.

It is essential that the psychologist ask questions and listen to the client's answers in a manner that is respectful and nonjudgmental. Psychologists and their clients often differ in their ethnic backgrounds, so it is important that the psychologist be aware of how this may affect the interaction during the interview. Moreover, during the course of an assessment interview clients reveal, often for the first time, painful, embarrassing, or frightening experiences they have had. They may be concerned about how they will be judged by others and how the psychologist will react to the disclosure of this sensitive information. Whether the client is someone coming to terms with his sexual identity, seeking to reconcile mixed feelings toward a parent who abandoned her as a child, or hoping that fears about going crazy are unfounded, the client requires support from the psychologist when providing details about concerns. In situations in which the client describes a behavior that the psychologist cannot condone or finds abhorrent, the psychologist must still maintain a non-blaming stance and seek to understand the client's perspective. The psychologist's goal is to gather information and convey understanding of what the client is communicating, even if the psychologist does not approve of the behavior. **Table 6.6** gives an example of the ways a psychologist might use questions and listening skills in interviewing a man who has been referred for an assessment to determine his suitability for an anger management program.

TABLE 6.6   Sample Interview Illustrating Questions and Listening Skills

Psychologist:	What happens when you argue? (Open question)
Client:	Well, it sometimes gets out of hand.
Psychologist:	Tell me what you mean by that. (Clarification)
Client:	Well, I never mean to hurt her.
Psychologist:	What is it that you do? (Open question)
Client:	I am not proud of this, I am not a bully.
Psychologist:	Sounds like you are ashamed of what happens. (Emotional reflection)
Client:	Yeah, it just gets out of hand sometimes. I don't think I am a wife-beater.
Psychologist:	When the two of you argue, you do things that you are not comfortable about, that you don't like. (Summarize)
Client:	Mmm, hmm.
Psychologist:	Tell me about the last time you argued and things got out of hand—what happened? (Open question)
Client:	She was on my case, and I said let's just leave it, I didn't want a fight, but she kept on, then when I started to walk out, she stood in my way, so I pushed her out of the way.
Psychologist:	When you pushed her, did she fall? (Closed question)
Client:	Yeah, she kind of stumbled against the fridge, I didn't mean to hurt her, I just wanted to get out.
Psychologist:	How often do your arguments end up in pushing and shoving? (Open question)
Client:	Not too often.
Psychologist:	Every day? Every week? Every month or so? (Closed question)
Client:	Probably most weeks, I guess.

Contextual Information

The assessment interview is often used to gather contextual information. This may include demographic information about the client's current context (such as age, living arrangement, family composition, school, or employment), developmental history, previous psychological services, medical history, educational background, and exposure to stressful or traumatic life events. The type of background information considered essential to an assessment depends on the theoretical orientation of the psychologist as well as on the type of services offered. For example, psychodynamically oriented psychologists typically devote more time to discussing childhood events and concerns than do psychologists with a cognitive-behavioral orientation. Regardless of orientation, many hours could be devoted to gathering information about a person's life—the challenge for clinical psychologists is to selectively focus on aspects that are most relevant for understanding the client's problems and the personal resources that could be brought to bear on the problems.

VIEWPOINT BOX 6.1

SCREENING FOR EXPOSURE TO VIOLENCE

Carl, age 12, presented at a local mental health center with symptoms of fearfulness, physiological arousal, and difficulties sleeping. He was diagnosed with generalized anxiety disorder.

Melissa, age 14, was assessed prior to sentencing for assault charges and diagnosed with conduct disorder.

Sheila, age 35, presented to her family physician with loss of pleasure in usual activities, weight loss, and difficulties concentrating. She was diagnosed with major depressive disorder.

Carl (who was introduced in Chapter 2) was not asked and did not volunteer information about the bloody scenes he had witnessed as his father was murdered in a war-torn country. As a result, the PTSD diagnosis was overlooked, and his anxiety symptoms were misinterpreted as generalized anxiety. Melissa was not asked and did not describe witnessing her father beating her mother. Similarly, she remained quiet about the violence in her current dating relationship. Sheila was not asked and was too ashamed to tell about the repeated violence she suffered from her partner.

Violence affected these three people profoundly. It caused pain, shame, self-doubt, fearfulness, and anger. It altered the way they thought about relationships, the way they thought about themselves, and their views of the world. Exposure to violence can result in feelings of numbing and avoidance. The person who has been a victim or witness to violence may avoid thinking about it, and may respond in a dull way that masks the intensity of their feelings. Repeated exposure to violence can also lead to desensitization and minimization so that the person feels that abusive treatment is to be expected and should not be complained about. The victim or witness of violence may be afraid of the repercussions of talking about the violence—fear of retribution by the perpetrator, and fear of blame by others for remaining in the relationship or for having provoked the abuse in the first place.

Psychologists and other mental health professionals are very concerned about the effects of violence. It is upsetting to discover that innocent people are harmed by strangers and also by those who are close to them. It is particularly troubling to know that nobody is immune from the threat of violence. Psychological assessment must include routine screening to determine whether the person has been a witness to and/or a victim of violence. Questions must be phrased in a sensitive and open way that allows the client to acknowledge what he or she has experienced. A client who is asked directly if she has been abused may reply that she has not, if she considers that she deserved to be slapped and pushed around for having left the house in a mess. Sensitive questioning offers a number of possible responses. The psychologist may note:

"Sometimes when couples argue, one person leaves the room. In other couples, one person may give the silent treatment; sometimes one person may say very hurtful things. In some couples, one person may treat the other like a punching bag. What kinds of things does your partner do when he is angry?"

In addition to the types of questions that are asked, it is important to consider the context in which such screening is conducted. Asking a woman about partner abuse in the presence of her partner is likely to yield denial. She may simply not be safe to disclose what she has suffered. Research conducted in emergency departments, family medicine practices, and women's health clinics found that, although women preferred to answer questions about intimate partner violence on self-report measures, such measures may be less accurate than information collected via interviews (MacMillan et al., 2006).

Learning about Carl's witnessing of his father's murder leads the psychologist to understand his difficulties in a different way. If Carl is suffering from posttraumatic stress disorder, he may benefit from exposure-based treatment. Finding out that Melissa was a child witness to violence and is now the victim of partner abuse helps us understand her aggressive behavior and underlines the necessity for her to learn ways to protect herself and assert herself appropriately in relationships. Sheila's depression may be understood differently in the context of the abuse she has suffered. Issues around her current and future safety must take priority in treatment.

Culturally Sensitive Interviewing

Given the diversity of the population of United States, it is absolutely essential that psychologists pay attention to the subtle and dramatic ways that different racial, ethnic, and linguistic groups think, act, and behave. The American Psychological Association has developed guidelines for ethical practice with diverse populations (American Psychological Association, 2002b). In interviewing clients, the psychologist must be sensitive to ethnic, socioeconomic, regional, and spiritual variables that affect the client's experience and the behavior with the psychologist (Sue & Sue, 2008; Takushi & Uomoto, 2001). For example, orthodox Jews observing *shomer negiyah* are not permitted to touch a member of the opposite sex and so may refuse to shake hands with the psychologist. The psychologist must therefore be careful not to interpret as social withdrawal, lack of engagement, or surliness what is actually observance of a religious edict. Importantly, there is growing research demonstrating that small slights, misunderstandings, and unwarranted assumptions based on stereotypes on the part of the psychologist (collectively called microaggressions) can have a substantial negative impact on the alliance with clients and on the clients' overall therapy experience (e.g., Constantine, 2007).

No psychologist can expect to be familiar with all of the cultural diversity he or she will encounter in his or her professional life, so it is necessary to be aware of any cultural blind spots. This means that the psychologist must not assume that communication patterns and styles are universal. The same behavior may have different significance in a different group. Eye contact is a good example. Whereas in the 1970s and 1980s most clinical psychology training programs taught students to maintain eye contact with clients, there is now greater sensitivity that in some cultures, too much eye contact may be perceived as intimidating. Similarly, it would be an error to interpret an averted gaze as evidence of avoidance, as it may simply represent a respectful stance toward an authority figure.

Cultures vary in the degree of importance that is paid to punctuality—arriving late to an interview may be a sign of disorganization and lack of motivation within some groups, but may simply reflect a more casual attitude toward time in others. A psychologist assessing a child who had recently arrived from Africa found that attendance at assessment appointments was sporadic, with the client and her mother often arriving late. On one occasion when the client and her mother did not show up for an appointment, the psychologist called the family to reschedule and was surprised to hear that the outgoing message on the family's answering machine was for her, announcing that as it was a beautiful day, the family had decided to go to the beach instead of coming to the psychologist's office. The psychologist also noted that during the assessment the child performed poorly on timed tasks. In understanding the challenges the child faced in adjusting to the school system, it was very helpful to appreciate culturally based differences regarding the importance of time.

There is great variability across individuals with respect to their comfort with open-ended questions. A client who expected to be asked highly structured questions might appear disorganized and confused when faced with a less structured interview. Psychologists must be aware of potential differences such as these and must be willing to ask clients to explain the

Psychologists must be sensitive to the fact that communication styles may differ across ethnic groups.
Source: Kevin Russ/iStockphoto

ways that things work in their cultural group. As psychologists expand their services to a diverse clientele, they may face challenges in assessing clients who do not speak English or Spanish. To address this, interpreters may be used. This presents new challenges in terms of confidentiality as well as in ensuring that the interpreter is competent in conveying the subtleties of what is said by both psychologist and client. There is emerging evidence that interpreter-mediated services can be successful. For example, d'Ardenne, Ruaro, Cestari, Fakhoury, and Priebe (2007) examined the effects of treatment for posttraumatic stress disorder among refugees in England: one group of patients received treatment in English, whereas a second group (who required interpreters) received the same treatment but with the involvement of trained interpreters in the treatment sessions. Refugees in both conditions obtained comparable treatment results. The use of interpreters has also been found to have no effect on the sensitivity and specificity of an interview designed to assess depression and PTSD in refugees (Eytan, Durieux-Paillard, Whitaker-Clinch, Loutan, & Bovier, 2007).

Defining Problems and Goals

Clients often arrive in psychologists' offices with vaguely defined complaints about themselves or other people. They make general statements about themselves such as "I can't get along with people" or describe their loved ones in unclear ways such as "he's irresponsible." The challenge with these labels is that they could mean anything, as we all have somewhat different standards for judging behaviors and reactions. Does the person who cannot get along with others have violent outbursts or simply wish he or she had a more active social life? Many words that are diagnostic labels are also used regularly in everyday conversation. You may hear a parent describe a child as hyperactive or anxious, a coworker describe a person as paranoid, or a television news announcer wonder whether someone is schizophrenic. In assessment interviews, the psychologist helps the client elaborate on the problem. Cognitive-behavioral psychologists, in particular, ask clients many questions designed to translate the complaint into a behavioral description of the problem. These details are essential for the psychologist to have a clear sense of the patterns within the problem area, as this information will form the basis of a treatment plan. **Table 6.7** shows questions that might be asked to help the client move from a vague description to one that clearly describes the problem, its frequency, intensity, and duration. For many clients, this is not an easy task and requires gentle persistence on the part of the clinical psychologist to obtain a clear definition of the problem, rather than a general and vague complaint.

Once the problem has been defined in specific, concrete terms, it is easier to determine whether the client meets criteria for diagnosis of a particular problem. In making these decisions, the psychologist must have a good understanding of normative behavior. For example, in assessing a child who may suffer from attention deficit-hyperactivity disorder the psychologist must decide whether the child's activity level, impulsivity, and attention span are within normal limits for a child that age or whether they are unusual.

After clarifying the definition of the problem, a cognitive-behavioral psychologist then seeks a clear definition of the client's goals. Like problems, goals are often defined in vague terms: "I'd like to feel better;" "I wish my child would be more respectful;" "I wish my partner and I could get along better." Unless goals are formulated in more concrete terms, it is impossible to determine whether there is progress toward reaching them. So the formulation of concrete goals is an essential step in determining whether psychological services may be helpful. **Table 6.8** gives examples of the types of questions psychologists ask to help clients more clearly identify their goals for treatment.

Assessing Suicide Risk

As we have mentioned several times, assessment interviews are not like regular conversations. In assessment interviews, psychologists must be alert to client difficulties. Given the special risk for suicide among those suffering from a depressive disorder, in assessing a depressed client it is customary to ask questions to determine the risk that the client will make a suicide attempt. It is essential that those questions be based on what is known about the factors that increase the risk of suicidal behavior. Psychologists ask direct questions about suicidal thoughts, plans and their lethality, and access to the means to attempt suicide. Given the strong links between a history of suicidal behavior and risk for future suicidal behavior, questions must also focus on a history of suicide attempts. Because some suicidal clients may make only a general statement about their level of unhappiness or hopelessness, it is the psychologist's responsibility to follow up such comments with questions assessing the current risk. **Table 6.9** gives examples of the kinds of questions psychologists ask in assessing suicide risk. If a

TABLE 6.7   Problem Definition Questions

Clients come to psychologists with vague complaints about themselves or other people:

- I'm a loser
- I'm depressed
- I can't get along with people
- I can't seem to get started
- s/he never listens; s/he's defiant
- s/he won't do anything; s/he's irresponsible/lazy
- s/he hurts people; s/he's aggressive
- s/he never thinks; s/he's impulsive
- s/he's so clingy; s/he's dependent
- s/he has trouble at school; s/he's dumb
- s/he has fits/tantrums

To translate the complaint into a behavioral description of the problem, psychologists ask:

Tell me what you mean by "depressed."

"Trouble" means different things to different people, what does it mean to you?

When you say s/he is aggressive, what is it that s/he does?

Give me an example of what you mean by "clingy."

I'm trying to get a picture in my head of what you mean by "defiant." Help me imagine what s/he is doing when s/he is defiant.

Questions about the frequency of the problem

How often does s/he ...?

Does it happen every day?

Many times a day ...?

Questions about the duration of the problem

When did this start?

Can you remember a time when this didn't happen?

Are there times when s/he does not ... ?

How long has s/he been ...?

Questions about the intensity of the problem

How long does it last?

What does s/he break?

How hard does s/he hit?

---

patient is determined to be at low risk for committing suicide, it would be appropriate to ensure that the person has emergency numbers for a suicide helpline and a local hospital; on the other hand, if the person appears to be at an elevated risk, the psychologist may need to accompany the patient to the emergency unit of the nearest hospital (Cukrowicz, Wingate, Driscoll, & Joiner, 2004).

TABLE 6.8   Goal Definition Questions

- Goal must be important to the client

- Goal must be expressed in terms of the ways people behave

- Goals must be small, simple, and achievable

- Goal must be in positive terms:

At the end of our sessions, what would lead you to decide that it had been worthwhile? How would you know you had not wasted your time?

If services here were to be helpful, what would be different?

If you and Pat were to get along better, what would you be doing then that you are not doing now?

How would Maro show he was happier?

If there was a change in the right direction, what would it be?

Yes, it would be great to win the lottery, but let's suppose that doesn't happen—what would have to happen for your financial worries to decrease a bit?

I understand that what you most want is to finish high school. If we were to break that down into steps, what would be the first step?

So, if Xavier was not so inattentive, what is it he would be doing? How would you know he was more attentive?

Interviewing Couples

So far, we have described interviews with an individual. In some circumstances, psychologists may interview a couple. Couple interviews may be conducted to focus on the partner's impressions of the client's problems, on couple problems, or on the problems that the couple's child is experiencing. Interviewing a couple requires the psychologist to simultaneously engage with two people. As the two partners may differ in cultural background, interpersonal style, opinions, and

TABLE 6.9   Empirically Supported Suicide Risk Assessment

Questions Used as Part of a Suicide Risk Assessment

- Have you had any thoughts of suicide recently?

- When you think about suicide, what exactly do you think about?

- Have you ever attempted suicide?

- Have you made any plans for taking your life, such as obtaining the means to commit suicide?

- Do you think that you could follow through on a suicide attempt?

- Have you ever hurt yourself intentionally, such as by cutting or burning yourself?

- What are the reasons that you would consider suicide as an option?

- Tell me about your family and friends. Do you feel supported and are you able to talk to them about your problems?

- Do you think that anything can be done about your problems?

Adapted from Cukrowicz, Wingate, Driscoll, & Joiner, 2004

willingness to attend the interview, the psychologist requires flexibility and interpersonal skills to ensure that each person has an opportunity to talk without the conversation getting out of hand. After all, it is quite likely that each person has a different view of the situation and that the views may not be at all compatible. The couple interview allows the psychologist to ask about and observe the way the couple interacts, their warmth toward one another, the way they handle differences, and the way they communicate in general (Snyder, Heyman, & Haynes, 2008). The ability to direct and structure an

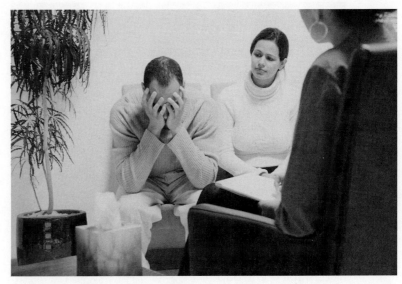

Interviews allow the psychologist to observe how a couple interacts. (*Source:* Media Bakery)

interview is very important when there is a clear power differential in the couple, which may be evident from what is said by each partner or from one partner's reluctance to engage in the discussion. However, not all couple issues are best addressed in couple sessions and, for this reason, most couples therapists routinely have at least one individual session with each partner. For example, it is impossible to screen for partner abuse in the presence of the partner. One person may be too intimidated by an abusive partner to respond honestly to questions about violence in the relationship. Screening for partner abuse must be conducted individually.

Interviewing Families

Just as couple interviews can be more challenging to conduct than individual interviews, family interviews can be even more taxing for the psychologist. The psychologist has the daunting task of establishing rapport with several people who have different styles and different agendas for the assessment. A psychologist who devoted undivided attention to Zak, who wanted greater freedom from his parents, would quickly lose rapport with Zak's parents Ethan and Lindy, who wanted to explain their worries that their son was failing in school and interacting with delinquent peers. Similarly, if the psychologist devoted undivided attention to the parents, Zak would easily become disengaged. In assessing families, the psychologist ensures that over the course of the interview, attention is devoted to each person. At the beginning of the interview, the psychologist tells family members explicitly that he or she would like to hear from each person. However, to put that into practice, the psychologist often must diplomatically cut off one family member to ensure that each has a turn: "I would like to hear more from you, but am conscious of time, and would also like to hear ideas from others in the family." The psychologist also conveys that it is normal for each person to have a different perspective. Although each person is invited to speak, each also has the right to be silent. It may be necessary to remind parents of this. Family members are invited to comment from their own perspective.

VIEWPOINT BOX 6.2

ISSUES IN INTERVIEWING OLDER ADULTS

With an aging population it is inevitable that there will be an increasing need for psychological services for older adults. Demographic forecasts predict that older adults will comprise a large percentage of the population in the coming decades. There is considerable overlap between the needs of older adults and the needs of adults in mid-life, so both

Psychologist assessing older adult. (*Source:* Tom Rosenthal/SUPERSTOCK)

geropsychologists and generalist clinical psychologists may be able to offer effective psychological services to older adults. Like younger adults, older adults seek psychological services to deal with a range of emotional, behavioral, and cognitive issues. However, as we have emphasized in other chapters, the provision of effective psychological services requires sensitivity to developmental issues that influence clients' seeking services, as well as the nature of assessment and intervention services that are appropriate.

Guidelines for psychological practice with older adults have been developed by the American Psychological Association (2004) and by the Australian Psychological Society (Pachana, Helmes, & Koder, 2006). These guidelines encourage psychologists to become knowledgeable about adult development and aging. Psychologists should be aware of the problems in daily living that are commonly faced by older adults and, in addition to general knowledge of psychopathology, they should know about patterns of psychopathology that are evident in older adults. In assessing older adults, psychologists must tailor their strategies to the specific needs of that population. This means that assessment strategies should take into account the older person's health status and cognitive and emotional functioning.

Compared with the general population, older adults are more likely to face issues around declining health, loss of autonomy, relationships with caregivers, bereavement, and issues of mortality. Older adults are usually referred to psychological services by a primary health care provider. Given their declining health, older adults have more frequent contact with primary health care providers than do younger adults (La Rue &

Watson, 1998). They may be referred to what seems to them a confusing array of health professionals. It is the psychologist's responsibility to ensure that the older adult is aware of the purpose of the psychological services and provides fully informed consent to any assessment procedure. If the older person is judged not capable of providing consent due to cognitive impairment, then consent is required from the person having legal authority for the older person, and the older person would be asked to provide a verbal assent to procedures.

Although the majority of older adults enjoy sound cognitive functioning, a significant number have some degree of cognitive impairment. APA recommends that psychologists become skilled at recognizing cognitive changes in older clients. The extent of cognitive impairment varies from one person to another, with many people remaining capable of reaching decisions and acting autonomously despite some cognitive changes. The psychologist should ensure that the client understands the reason for referral, the nature of services offered, and the likely outcome of services. In offering services to older adults with serious cognitive impairment, the psychologist must pay particular attention to whether the person is capable of consent to services.

In interviewing older adults, the psychologist must be sensitive to the possible presence of cognitive impairment and to possible cohort effects. For example, the current population of older adults grew up around the time of the economic depression of the 1930s and the Second World War. As one developmental task of later life is to reminisce about one's formative years, the sociopolitical influences these older adults experienced may figure prominently in their discussions of their lives. The interviewer must also be sensitive to the impact such events may have had on the interviewee.

The psychological assessment of older adults requires knowledge of the physical challenges that may affect the person. Issues around chronic illness and disability may be the reason that psychological services are required, but may also introduce special challenges in conducting the assessment. Psychologists must be well informed about the possible effects of medication on client functioning. Skills in health psychology may be particularly important in working with older adults.

With declining health, some older adults may need to rely increasingly on both paid and unpaid caregivers. The cooperation of these caregivers may be essential in having the older adult attend an interview. The client may be unable to attend unless a caregiver agrees to provide transportation. Furthermore, when the older person suffers confusion or memory problems, it may be necessary to also gather important information from others. Like the challenges faced in integrating data from parents and children, the psychologist may face challenges in reconciling discrepant accounts from older adults and their caregivers. Unfortunately, some older adults are vulnerable to abuse by caregivers. Sensitive psychological services should include screening for maltreatment by family members or paid caregivers. The need for effective psychological services is bound to increase in the coming years. The provision of services will rely on the psychologist's sensitivity to the many health, cognitive, and social factors that affect the older adult.

Interviewing Children and Adolescents

In contrast to early approaches to the psychological assessment of children that relied primarily on adult accounts of child behavior or on interpretations of children's play, current child assessment

strategies often include the child as an important source of information about his or her thoughts and feelings. It is now recognized that children can provide unique information about aspects of their experience that are not fully tapped by measures completed by adult informants such as parents, teachers, or caregivers (Mash & Hunsley, 2007).

Interviews with children are designed to explore the child's perspective. They also allow the psychologist to assess the way the child interacts with an unfamiliar adult. The psychologist conducts the interview in a way that makes it seem like a conversation to the child but that en-

Drawing, painting, or play may be used to facilitate rapport with children.
(*Source:* PhotoDisc, Inc./Getty Images)

sures the relevant topics are covered. Like adults, children are entitled to know about confidentiality and its limits. The psychologist must explain the purpose of the interview. Because children may associate interviews with adults as evaluative in nature, it is important to reassure the child that there are no right or wrong answers to the questions, and that everyone has a different opinion. To engage the child in conversation, the psychologist maintains a varied voice tone and relaxed posture.

Interviewing techniques must be adapted when psychologists are interviewing children. Developmental considerations affect cognitive functioning and the young clients' understanding of what is being asked. Young children differ from adults in terms of their attention span and capacity to stay focused on the interview. Furthermore, children differ from adults in their style of interaction.

Think about a visit to the home of an adult friend and the way that you and your friend might talk together, perhaps seated at the kitchen table or on the sofa. As adults, you may sustain conversation over a lengthy period of time, maintaining eye contact, asking questions, and clarifying your understanding of what was said. Now think about a conversation you might have if a child was present (perhaps your friend's younger sibling or your friend's child). In what ways would your conversation be different with the child? What if you and the child are not members of the same ethnic group—how might this make a difference? It is quite likely that the range of topics you would talk about with a child would be substantially different. In addition, you'd probably change the way you asked questions. You would be surprised if 6-year-old Sarah joined in the conversation for a lengthy period—most likely she would chat for a while, then leave to do something she found more interesting. The type of conversation you would have would also depend on the child's age. In talking to a preschool-age child, you'd probably talk about the immediate environment, such as the TV show the child had just watched, a toy the child was holding, the logo on a T-shirt, or the sport that the child was about to do. With an elementary school–age child, you would be able to ask questions about the child's life—school, friends, activities, sports, or holidays. In other words, you would be able to talk about topics that were not in the child's immediate environment or planned activities. In general, with older children it becomes increasingly possible to have them reflect on patterns in their experiences and to discuss how other people might be feeling. Conversations with adolescents can cover a range of remote and abstract topics that younger children would be unable to discuss.

In interviewing children, psychologists must be careful not to use a sophisticated vocabulary that is incomprehensible to them. Although some children may announce they do not understand and ask for clarification, others may simply lose interest and become quiet. It is the psychologist's responsibility to ensure that a child client understands the questions that are being asked. A child who fails to understand a question may stare blankly, say "I don't know" or may give an answer based on erroneous understanding of what was being asked. Children find questions that relate to time particularly difficult. For example, a young child may be at a loss to say how many times over the last 6 months he or she has felt a certain way if the child has no concept of how long 6 months is. Generally, it is helpful to use special events or occasions that are personally relevant to them such as the beginning of school, Halloween, or a birthday. However, some strategies that are effective in helping children give more detailed responses, such as using dolls, may also increase the number of errors in children's statements (Salmon, 2001).

Careful attention must be paid to ensure that the interviewer does not inadvertently influence the child to give a particular response (Bruck & Ceci, 2004). Sometimes children may mistake a word for another that sounds similar. An 8-year-old girl who was asked whether she ever thought about death, replied that she did, almost every day. When asked to tell more about this, she explained, "There's a girl in my class called Kirsten who is death and she has to sit at the front and wear a special hearing aid so she knows what the teacher says." Without this type of clarification, the psychologist might have wrongly assumed that this child felt suicidal, rather than recognize that the child did not differentiate between the words death and deaf. Nonverbal cues from an interviewer can also greatly affect children. For example, researchers have found that children interviewed by someone who gives the impression of being aloof and impatient, compared to the same

Because children do not have the same sense of time as adults do, it is helpful to anchor interview questions to special events in the child's life. (*Source:* Sonya Farrell/Image Source Limited)

interviewer who smiles and is patient, are more likely to answer questions incorrectly and less likely to tell the interviewer that they don't know the answer (Almerigogna, Ost, Akehurst, & Fluck, 2008). This response could obviously lead to considerable errors in the conclusion drawn about the children.

Although face-to-face contact and eye contact may be important ingredients of assessment interviews with most adults, we know that children and adolescents engage in some of their best conversations when they are not in eye contact. Teenagers who remain silent at the meal table may be much more talkative in the car on the way to an activity. Similarly, psychologists may invite child clients to play or draw while they are chatting. It is important to note, however, that using drawings and toys as aids to facilitate rapport is not the same as making interpretations about the child's drawings or play. In the first case, dolls and drawings are used to make the child at ease, whereas in the second they are used as projective material intended to reveal aspects of psychological functioning. We discuss issues around projective tests in Chapter 8.

Psychologists may also have challenges in understanding what the child is talking about. As children's fashions change quickly, the psychologist may be uncertain whether Yu-Gi-Oh is the child's new friend, a TV show, or a new vaccination. No psychologist can expect to remain constantly up to date with the changing trends in children's expressions, activities, games, or movies, just as no psychologist can expect to be equally knowledgeable about the mores and customs of all cultures. Instead, a psychologist must develop skills in listening to the child and in sensitively clarifying that he or she has properly understood what the child was saying. Rapport with children may be enhanced if the psychologist asks the child to explain details, whereas it may be impaired if the psychologist tries to give the impression of being familiar with all details of the child's life. Children are different from adults, but they also differ from one another at different ages and developmental stages. Strategies that may be effective in engaging a young school-age child such as bright decor, cheerful posters, and soft toys on the bookshelf may alienate the adolescent client. Psychologists must also alter their style when interviewing adolescents. If they treat the adolescent as an adult, there may be concepts and terms that the client doesn't understand (and may not admit to not understanding). On the other hand, adolescents may also be sensitive to what they perceive as simplistic baby talk, such as "When I use the word depression I mean when someone feels sad or kind of down" or a kindergarten teacher style of questioning, "Do you know what I mean when I say bulimia?"

OBSERVATIONS

During the assessment interview, the psychologist is a keen observer of the client. In addition to the answers to questions, important data can be gathered by observing the client. Although clinical assessments traditionally included comments on the client's appearance and grooming, it is only necessary to report noteworthy features that are relevant to the assessment. Comments on clients' attractiveness are often not salient to the referral question and are considered offensive by some people. The psychologist notices the client's activity level, attention span, and impulsivity. Careful attention is paid to the client's speech, noting any difficulties or abnormalities. The psychologist observes the physical movements and behaviors of clients as well as the ease of interacting with them.

PROFILE BOX 6.1

DR. STEPHANIE WOO

I earned an undergraduate degree in psychology and my master's and doctoral degrees in clinical psychology from UCLA. During my graduate studies, my research focused on the relationship between nonverbal and paralinguistic communication of individuals diagnosed with schizophrenia and their family members. I completed a 2-year postdoctoral fellowship in psychological assessment at the UCLA Neuropsychiatric Institute. During this fellowship I developed my skills in conducting neuropsychological and psychodiagnostic assessments with adult inpatients and outpatients. Currently, I am a licensed clinical psychologist and a tenured Associate Professor of Psychology at the Pepperdine University Graduate School of Education and Psychology. I am also the Director of the Masters of Arts in Psychology with an Emphasis in Marriage and Family Therapy program at Pepperdine's Malibu campus. My

Dr. Stephanie Woo

areas of teaching interest include psychopathology, psychological assessment, and cognitive and behavioral interventions, and one of my main research interests is the development of computerized diagnostic assessment methods. Additionally, I serve as a consultant to the RAND Corporation on research examining the development, implementation, and efficacy of an innovative manualized group Cognitive Behavioral Therapy intervention for depression in people with substance abuse problems, designed to be delivered by paraprofessional drug counselors.

How did you choose to become a clinical psychologist?

When I was in high school I had an opportunity to participate in a summer college program where I took an abnormal psychology class and became thoroughly fascinated by the disorders we discussed. I went on to major in psychology and as an undergraduate was fortunate to land a job as a research assistant for Barbara Fish, a prominent schizophrenia researcher at UCLA. Her longitudinal study of children born to mothers with schizophrenia provided a remarkable window into the development of this puzzling disorder and confirmed my desire to become a clinical psychologist and study this disorder further.

What is the most rewarding part of your job as a clinical psychologist?

Currently, I primarily teach and provide clinical supervision, both of which are exceptionally rewarding activities. Being able to spark and nurture students' interest in the assessment and treatment of mental disorders gives me a great sense of personal satisfaction. I also find it gratifying to help students develop skills in the treatment approaches that are relevant for the clinical populations they are most interested in. In supervising paraprofessionals in a depression treatment study for the RAND Corporation,

I also appreciate the opportunity to guide the development of counselors' clinical skills and to observe the often life-changing nature their work has on alleviating the suffering associated with depression.

What is the greatest challenge you face as a clinical psychologist?

As an educator involved in the training of future mental health professionals, a great challenge I face is ensuring that, when I teach, scientifically based information is presented in a way that emphasizes the personal or human face of the psychological disorders being discussed. In learning about disorders, it is easy for students and professors alike to emphasize symptom lists, theories, and statistics that can become abstract and separated from the experiences of people who live with these disorders. Successful work with clients requires the ability to apply scientifically based knowledge in an interpersonally adept and empathic manner—these skills are also essential for effective classroom teaching.

Tell us about your research on families using observational coding systems

This work stemmed from my interest in Expressed Emotion (EE), an index of critical and emotionally overinvolved attitudes among family members of individuals with schizophrenia. In study after study, EE has been shown to be a robust predictor of relapse among individuals with schizophrenia. I wanted to understand what might contribute to the development of these attitudes in family members. So I developed a coding system to examine nonverbal indicators of subclinical symptoms in individuals with schizophrenia and applied this to videotaped family interactions. I found that subclinical levels of hostility and unusual behavior in persons with schizophrenia were associated with higher rates of high EE behaviors among family members. This suggests that the development of EE attitudes in family members is a complex bi-directional process that is shaped by both family member factors and characteristics of their psychiatrically ill relative.

How do you integrate science and practice in your work?

One way I do this is in the classroom, where I emphasize the use of evidence-based treatments. However, we also discuss ways to modify therapy that was developed in the context of a research study in order to meet the needs of a particular client. I encourage students to use their research skills when working with clients. An important example of this is ensuring that they collect meaningful data that allows them to assess treatment progress of their clients.

What do you see as the most exciting changes in the field of clinical psychology?

For me, the most exciting change is that we are gaining an increasingly greater appreciation for the value of looking more *holistically* at the individuals, couples, and families we treat. The positive psychology movement has led to a greater appreciation of the strengths that people bring to treatment and encourages clinical psychologists not just to focus on psychopathology. Although there is still much work to be done, we are also recognizing the important role that culture and other forms of diversity play in affecting how people understand themselves, the problems they are facing, and what they find most helpful in treatment. We are also gaining a greater appreciation for the role of religion and spirituality in individuals' lives and bringing consideration of this into treatment.

Client behavior in the psychologist's office may not always be representative of the way the person behaves. For example, children with ADHD often respond well in novel situations with the undivided attention of an unfamiliar adult. Therefore, a psychologist could underestimate the extent of the child's problems by assuming that the child's behavior during an intake interview was representative of how the child generally behaves. The purpose of naturalistic observations is to gather information that could not easily be obtained in the office. It allows observation of behaviors that clients may not describe in interviews or questionnaires because they are either unaware of them or uncomfortable about them. Home observations provide information about the ways the child and parents behave in a familiar setting. School observations provide information about the school context, teaching style, and the child's behavior in a school context. Permission must be obtained to conduct observations outside the clinic. The parent (and the child if she or he is judged capable to consent) must give permission for the child to be observed. School personnel must also consent to observations at school. Naturalistic observations are scheduled at a time when the problem behavior is most likely to occur. In many families with young children the hours around supper, homework, and preparation for bed are times of conflict and difficulty. Depending on the particular assessment question, school observations may be scheduled to see the child in both preferred and nonpreferred activities, with different teachers, in quiet study periods, and at the playground.

The observer's goal is to be like the proverbial fly on the wall, noticing everything but not being noticed. Observers dress in a professional but unobtrusive style. After brief introductions, the observer invites everyone to behave as they normally do. A clipboard and pen are reminders to both adults and children that this is not like a regular social visit. Even though adults may initially try hard to make a good impression and behave at their best, children are extraordinarily effective in leading adults to behave authentically. Children comment on unusual behaviors that the adults may engage in to impress the observer: "We're having dessert tonight?" "Why do you want us to eat at the table today?" "I really like the new toy you gave me." At the end of the observation period, the observer takes a few minutes to ask how typical this day was of their usual routine. "I know it's very strange having someone watching." "How typical would you say today was?" "Was Jose's behavior the same as usual, worse than usual, or better than usual?" "In what way?" "What about your behavior?"

 Imagine having a psychologist observe your interactions during meal-time at your home. How might you behave differently? Even if you were initially self-conscious about what you were doing and saying, how long do you think this would affect you?

Data from direct observations are used to generate hypotheses about the child's functioning that can be examined in light of other assessment data. It would obviously be inappropriate to draw diagnostic decisions solely based on observations, or to conclude that because a child appeared fine during the observation period that there were no difficulties. At most these observations provide a limited window on how the child behaves with significant others at home and at school. However, when combined with information from interviews, testing, and other people's reports, observational data can provide data that confirm or attenuate the evolving picture of the child's strengths and weaknesses.

A large body of psychological research demonstrates that people are influenced by appearances (Garb, 1998). A well-known example is the assumption that people who wear glasses are more intelligent than those who do not wear glasses. Other biases relate to the way we cover or wear our hair, the formality of our clothes, levels of grooming, expressiveness of hand gestures, loudness of voice, and posture. Psychologists are not immune from these biases that may affect their decision-making. We are particularly prone to errors when interacting with an unfamiliar group. In some parts of the country a greeting may entail a barely perceptible nod of the head, whereas elsewhere it may involve a handshake (of varying types), kisses on the cheeks, air kisses, or a hug. Ethical guidelines require psychologists to become aware of the ways that their background influences their interactions with others and their interpretations of the behaviors of others.

Given the valuable insights that we have gained into parent–child and marital relationships based on research using systematic observation of interactions, you might expect that psychologists would have borrowed these systematic observation systems for use in the clinic. This is not the case at all. Although clinicians use observation as an essential tool in assessment, they rarely use observational coding systems that have been standardized or that have established reliability and validity (Mash & Foster, 2001). Although structured diagnostic interviews that were originally developed in a research context have been modified for use in clinical practice, the same transfer from research to clinical practice has not occurred in terms of observations. One major obstacle is expense. Some of the most useful research coding schemes require as much as 20 hours of coding to analyze one hour of interaction. In a cost-conscious health care system, these costs would be extremely difficult to justify.

SELF-MONITORING

In terms of data gathering, it would be ideal if a psychologist could observe a patient for many hours each day to see the precise nature of the symptoms or problems that are the focus of treatment. As this is not feasible, psychologists rely on patients' retrospective reports of events to get a sense of how frequently a problem occurs and exactly how the problem is handled. As we all know, however, memories for events become clouded over time and, despite the patient's best efforts, he or she might not remember the important details of an event that occurred 6 days prior to an appointment with the psychologist. To obtain accurate information as economically as possible, psychologists have developed a number of strategies for patients to observe themselves that collectively are known as **self-monitoring** strategies.

Self-monitoring can take many forms. The client may be asked to simply record the occurrence of an event, such as when a cigarette was smoked, a meal was consumed, or a headache occurred. This kind of self-monitoring data can provide the type of information needed to establish baseline conditions for a behavior or problem that will be the focus of treatment (such as using relaxation techniques to reduce the severity and frequency of headaches). With precise information about the frequency of these problems before and during treatment, it becomes possible to ascertain the degree to which treatment is effective or needs to be altered. Self-monitoring can also involve the client keeping daily records of thoughts or feelings. This information is particularly useful for the psychologist, as it provides access to variables that are not amenable to direct observation. A client may be asked, for example, to record pertinent details each time he or she has thoughts of being a failure. For cognitive-behavioral psychologists, obtaining information about the context in which these thoughts occur can provide useful information about factors that may provoke or maintain dysfunctional or nonproductive behaviors. In developing intervention strategies for working with a client, self-monitoring involves recording occurrences of symptoms and also the efforts made to manage or curtail the symptoms. Compared with a simple series of interview questions in the psychologist's office requiring retrospective recall, recording is likely to provide a fuller picture of the client's usual strategies, both successful and unsuccessful, for dealing with the symptoms. **Figures 6.3 and 6.4** provide examples of self-monitoring forms that might be used in the treatment of an eating disorder and an anxiety disorder, respectively.

Psychologists may choose to provide a client with a standard self-monitoring form that is appropriate for the symptom/behavior to be reported. Alternatively, the psychologist may decide to construct a form with the client that has the potential of ensuring that the client better understands the nature of the reporting task. In some clinics there may be aids used in self-monitoring. For example,

FOOD INTAKE RECORD

NAME: _____

DATE: _____

TIME	PLACE	FOOD CONSUMED	MEAL OCCASION	SITUATION
7:15 am	home	1 cup coffee, black 1 bran muffin	breakfast	For a change I actually got up in time to have breakfast.
1:30 pm	university cafeteria	Small salad, no dressing Diet coke, small	lunch	I tried putting off eating as late as possible
3:15 pm	class	Chocolate bar Bag of peanuts	snack	I was so hungry in class that I had to eat something from my backpack
6:30 pm	home	2 cheese sandwiches, (light cheese slices) 1 apple, 1 bran muffin	dinner	I tried to have a nutritious meal
11:30 pm	home	1 litre chocolate ice cream, 3 glasses skim milk	snack	I couldn't sleep and I ended up bingeing

FIGURE 6.3 Self-Monitoring of Food Consumption

MY WORRY RECORD

DATE: _____

Please record every significant worry that you have during the day. As we discussed in our sessions, this would include anything that you find upsetting, is difficult to stop thinking about, or that interferes with the things you are trying to do. Please be as specific as possible about each worry.

TIME	SITUATION	WORRY	ANXIETY LEVEL 0=calm 10=panicky	DURATION (minutes)
3:30 pm	at work	I will never get this done. I'm a failure. I won't be able to keep fooling them at work. I'm going to lose this job	8	45 minutes
7:40 pm	home, trying to relax	I know I can do it, but why do I have such a hard time with work deadlines? I spend so much time worrying and trying to understand my reaction. Why don't I just get things done! What is wrong with me!	6	30 minutes

FIGURE 6.4   Self-Monitoring Worry

a watch with a timer may be given to the client, with the alarm set to sound at a preset time, thus indicating that the client should record the target behavior. Electronic diaries are used increasingly to provide both a prompt for recording an event and a convenient tool for entering the self-monitoring data (Piasecki, Hufford, Solhan, & Trull, 2007). The use of a standard database program on a cell phone or a handheld computer also allows the client to keep track of changes over the course of treatment and even to graph treatment progress. Moving beyond the recording of thoughts, emotions, and behaviors, some self-monitoring devices, known as ambulatory biosensors, are designed to measure physiological variables. These devices require virtually no effort on the part of the client, as data are recorded automatically with no disruption in the daily activities of the person. A wide array of such devices is now available, including those designed to assess cardiovascular activity, physical activity, and cortisol levels (Haynes & Yoshioka, 2007).

Despite the obvious strengths of the self-monitoring method, there are some challenges in implementation. Self-monitoring data are not always accurate, as the client may fail to record information at the appropriate time, may not have fully grasped the nature of the task given by the psychologist, or may be reluctant to report some undesirable thoughts or behaviors (Korotitsch & Nelson-Gray, 1999). The psychologist must take the time to ensure that the client understands both the importance of obtaining self-monitoring data and how to accurately record the necessary information. As with interviews, there may need to be procedural alterations in using self-monitoring with children (Shapiro & Cole, 1999). To ensure that children are clear on the behaviors to be recorded, the self-monitoring form may include reminders, in the form of words, pictures, or stick figures. Training to do the self-monitoring properly also requires that the purpose of the task and the instructions be presented in an age-appropriate manner. The issue of **reactivity** occurs in self-monitoring regardless of the client's age. Reactivity refers to a change in the phenomenon that is being monitored that is due specifically to the process of the self-monitoring. This effect has been found for a surprisingly wide array of symptoms and problems, including hallucinations, substance abuse, worry, and insomnia (Korotitsch & Nelson-Gray, 1999). In almost all cases, such change results in a decrease in the problem behavior in question. Although this provides a therapeutic "bonus," it does undermine efforts to obtain the most accurate data possible.

VIEWPOINT BOX 6.3

ECOLOGICAL MOMENTARY ASSESSMENT

In both clinical work and research, psychologists often use self-report measures to evaluate a person's behaviors, thoughts, and emotions. (We describe such measures more fully in Chapter 8.) However, measures that ask, "How do you usually feel?" or "Which statement best describes you?" may not fully capture the complexities of daily life. For example, Verkuil, Brosschot, and Thayer (2007) asked university students to complete several commonly used self-report measures of worry and anxiety, and then to keep a self-monitoring diary of the frequency and duration of any worry they experienced over the next 6 days. Much to the researchers' surprise, there was only moderate correlation between the two types of measures, and self-report measures predicted less than half of the variance in students' experience of daily worry.

Many psychological interventions focus on altering clients' emotional distress and maladaptive behaviors as they occur in day-to-day life. Accordingly, it is important that the research used to guide such interventions provide complete and accurate information about individual patterns of psychological experience as they occur across hours, days, and weeks. Ecological momentary assessment is the term used for a set of strategies that allow research participants (and patients) to report repeatedly on what is occurring to them in real time (Shiffman, Stone, & Hufford, 2008). Using either electronic recording strategies or pencil-and-paper diaries, participants provide information on their experiences in event-based designs (e.g., describing their thoughts, behaviors, emotions, and interpersonal interactions around the time they experienced a specific problematic event, such as a panic attack) and/or time-based designs (e.g., recording their mood and physical activity levels every hour in order to obtain an accurate sense of how fluctuations in mood and activity affect each other). The results of ecological momentary assessment research allow psychologists to examine patterns in clinically relevant processes, such as efforts to quit cigarette smoking. Based on such research, we know that most smokers experience very little craving when they quit, although there may be some brief periods of intense craving; cravings experienced early in the morning are most likely to put people at risk for smoking a cigarette; and experiences of acute distress (e.g., getting angry) also lead to temptations to smoke (Shiffman et al., 2008). Bearing these findings in mind, psychologists can then help their clients be better prepared to manage the challenges of quitting smoking.

SUMMARY AND CONCLUSIONS

Interviews and observations are used by all clinical psychologists in their assessment activities. Clinical interviews are different from other types of verbal interactions, in that they are directed by one person with a specific set of goals in mind. In interviewing and observing, psychologists must be sensitive to diversity issues, including cultural, regional, and generational norms. Cognizant of these issues, psychologists must also find ways to obtain the type of information they need, even when asking about sensitive or painful topics. Because a number of factors affect the quality of an interview, structured interviews have been developed for a range of tasks, most notably for diagnostic purposes. Although these interviews provide a reliable approach to diagnosis, they can be very time consuming and limited in scope. A final assessment method used by many psychologists is self-monitoring. Instead of relying on retrospective accounts of important events or behaviors, the patient is provided with a structured format to record events shortly after they occur. This information, when combined with that available from interviews and observations, helps fill out the emerging clinical picture of the client and his or her experiences.

Critical Thinking Questions

What are some of the major goals of assessment interviews?

What are some of the advantages and disadvantages of unstructured interviews?

What are the advantages and disadvantages of structured diagnostic interviews?

How have psychologists adapted interview techniques to take into account developmental issues?

What are the major differences between assessment interviews and conversations with friends?

How can psychologists conduct culturally sensitive interviews?

How can self-monitoring strategies add useful data to an assessment?

Key Terms

closed question: question that can be answered with a single word

limits of confidentiality: situations in which the psychologist is legally obliged to break confidentiality by disclosing information provided by the patient to another person or agency

open question: question that allows elaborate responses and cannot be answered with a simple "yes" or "no"

reactivity: a change in the phenomenon being monitored that is due specifically to the process of monitoring the phenomenon

structured interview: interview with a specific format for asking questions and a specific sequence in which questions are asked

self-monitoring: strategies to monitor one's own behavior, emotions, and/or thoughts

ADDITIONAL RESOURCES

Hersen, M., & Turner, S. M. (Eds). (2003). *Diagnostic interviewing* (3rd ed.). New York: Kluwer Publishers.

Sattler, J. M. (1998). *Clinical and forensic interviewing of children and families.* San Diego, CA: Jerome Sattler.

Sommers-Flanagan, J., & Sommers-Flanagan, R. (2003). *Clinical interviewing* (3rd ed). New York: John Wiley & Sons.

Sue, D. W., & Sue, D. (2008). *Counseling the culturally different: Theory and practice* (5th ed.). New York: John Wiley & Sons.

Check It Out!

You can find information about the SCID here: http://www.scid4.org/

This site has information about the *Dominic* Interview: www.dominicinteractive.com

For information on risks for suicide and understanding more about suicide prevention: http://www.livingworks.net/ http://www.sprc.org/

There are numerous Web sites that provide examples of self-monitoring forms and procedures for personal concerns such as mood and weight loss. Here are just a few examples: http://www.cognitivebehaviourtherapy.org.uk/guides/depression/monitoring/, http://web4health.info/en/answers/bipolar-self-monitor.htm, http://health-infocenter.org/reach-your-goal/self-monitoring-the-importance-of-a-food-and-activity-diary.html

CHAPTER 7

Assessment: Intellectual and Cognitive Measures

INTRODUCTION

In 1946, an organization called MENSA was founded in England. Since its inception, membership has been restricted to people with an intelligence test score (usually referred to as an intelligence quotient or IQ) that is in the top 2% of the population. Today, more than 100,000 people worldwide are members of this organization, with national chapters on every continent except for Antarctica. For many years, people have been interested in knowing their IQ, which has led to the proliferation of many books and online tests purporting to provide valid IQ tests. One of the earliest of these products, Hans Eysenck's best-selling book *Know Your Own I.Q.*, originally published in 1962, has gone into multiple editions and can still be purchased today.

Western society has tended to place great value on intelligence but also places a great emphasis on the idea of equality. As a result, frequently there have been intense public debates around the use of intelligence tests to make decisions about people's educational and occupational choices. For example, the publication of *The Bell Curve* (Herrnstein & Murray, 1994), a review of the history of research on intelligence, ignited a lengthy debate in the media about the meaning of intelligence and the advantages and disadvantages of using intelligence tests. Although many of the research-based conclusions presented in the book were not particularly original or controversial, the authors' attempts to link the results of research on intelligence to public policy initiatives (such as rescinding affirmative action policies in education and hiring) drew the ire of many critics.

As you learned in Chapter 1, the history of assessment in clinical psychology and the history of intellectual assessment are closely connected, as both were greatly influenced by Binet and Simon's development of the first standardized test of intelligence.

Many of the criteria that are now used to evaluate the qualities of any psychological test date back to efforts to develop the first intelligence tests in the early part of the 20th century. At that time, special education services were being designed, and it was necessary to develop scientific instruments to identify those in need of such services. The vital importance of accurately identifying individuals who were unlikely to benefit from regular education led to the promotion of concepts such as standardization, reliability, validity, and norm-referenced interpretations. Another byproduct of these initial assessment efforts is that both our concepts of intelligence and our intelligence assessment instruments have heavily emphasized aspects of intelligence that are directly relevant to educational and instructional initiatives. As you will see later, some of the more recent models of intelligence have tried to balance this focus with greater attention to nonacademic skills that reflect intelligent behavior.

In the testing of intelligence and cognitive capacities there is a great deal at stake. Because of the important implications of the results of intellectual and cognitive assessment, in the latter half of the 20th century test developers made great efforts to reduce test bias and measurement error. As a result, tests of intelligence and related cognitive abilities are among the psychometrically strongest tests that psychologists have developed.

We begin this chapter by outlining theories of intelligence and some of the research relevant to understanding the influences on intelligence and intelligence tests. Psychologists working in many different settings are often asked to assess an individual's intellectual and cognitive abilities. After describing some of the more common situations in which such evaluations are required, we move to describe the most commonly used intelligence tests and other tests of cognitive functioning.

A number of Web sites purport to provide online evaluations of intelligence. Do you know the phrase "caveat emptor?" It means "buyer beware" and is as relevant for anyone taking self-administered intelligence tests as it is for purchasing yoga clothing, diet products, used cars, or anything that sounds like a deal that is just too good to pass up.

DEFINING INTELLIGENCE

We all have an intuitive idea of what intelligence is. We can point to individuals we consider highly intelligent; likewise, we can probably identify examples of intelligent behavior (and probably some examples of not so intelligent behavior). How can we define intelligence in a manner that is appropriate across skill sets, areas of performance, and cultural contexts? One option is simply to avoid the use of the term "intelligence" and to use other concepts such as ability or, more accurately, general mental ability. Although a number of theorists and test developers have taken this approach, it doesn't really get us any further in trying to tease out the meaning of intelligence, because it just substitutes one word or phrase for another.

Throughout the years, psychologists have made many attempts to define intelligence. The range has included both broad definitions, such as the ability to learn or to adapt to the environment, and narrow definitions, such as the ability to engage in abstract thinking (cf. Aiken, 2003). Because Binet was working on the development of a tool to predict school performance, his definition focused on ability related to scholastic/academic tasks. You will probably agree that this yields a limited definition.

Subsequent definitions of intelligence have focused on the context of life more generally. An influential definition was presented by Wechsler (1939), who defined intelligence as a person's global capacity to act purposefully, to think in a rational manner, and to deal effectively with his or her environment. Wechsler devoted his career to the development of scales to assess a range of problem-solving skills. He assumed that these abilities were acquired through education and life experiences. Wechsler's definition has had a profound influence on the way clinical psychologists evaluate intelligence. As we will see in the next section, theories of intelligence in the latter part of the 20th century explicitly acknowledge that intelligence is a combination of abilities in multiple areas of life.

THEORIES OF INTELLIGENCE

To provide a brief overview of the many theories of intelligence, we will categorize the dominant models into one of three domains: *factor models, hierarchical models,* and *information-processing models.* Factor models involve two or more factors that are postulated to be at more or less the same structural level. In contrast, hierarchical models are based on the assumption that there are different levels of factors, with the higher order or primary factors composed of lower order or secondary factors. Information-processing theories focus less on the organization of types of intelligence and more on identifying the processes and operations that reflect how information is handled by the brain.

The earliest and probably most influential factor model of intelligence was developed by **Charles Spearman** (1927). Based on the intercorrelations among tests of sensory abilities (sensory discriminations, reaction time, etc.), Spearman proposed that all intellectual activities share a single common core known as the *general factor* or *g.* The more highly correlated two tests of mental abilities are, the more they share a substantial loading on the g factor. However, because measures of intellectual abilities are not perfectly correlated, Spearman postulated that there are a number of *specific factors,* or *s,* that are responsible for unique aspects in the performance of any given task. The more a test is influenced by *s,* the less it represents the influence of *g.* Spearman's focus on *g* and *s* was known as the *two-factor model.*

Although the idea of *g* is retained in most theories of intelligence, other factor models have been proposed. All of them suggest that there are related, but distinct, factors that comprise intelligence. Thurstone (1938) proposed one of the first alternatives to Spearman's model. Based on his research into the relatively low intercorrelations among many ability measures, Thurstone proposed a group of factors known as *primary mental abilities,* including spatial, perceptual, numerical, memory, verbal, word, reasoning, deduction, and induction abilities. These abilities, although relatively distinct, overlap to a very small extent, and it was this small overlap that Thurstone suggested was Spearman's *g.* In contrast to the majority of researchers who developed a model of intelligence, Thurstone also developed a measure of intelligence based on his model.

Is intelligence composed of as few as 2 factors or well over 100 factors (Guilford, 1956)? One response to this question is to propose a small number of main factors that are comprised of subfactors. This is the approach taken by theorists who developed hierarchical models. One of the first and most influential of these models was proposed by **Raymond Cattell** (1963, Horn & Cattell, 1966). Cattell believed that existing intelligence tests were too focused on verbal, school-based tasks. In developing a test that assessed more perceptual aspects of intelligence, he proposed two general factors in intelligence: **fluid intelligence** (*Gf*) and **crystallized intelligence** (*Gc*). Fluid intelligence is the ability to solve problems without drawing on prior experiences or formal learning and is, therefore, best understood as representing one's innate intellectual potential. Crystallized intelligence is what we have learned in life, both from formal education and general life experiences. Other hierarchical models represented attempts to reconcile many of the differences among the previous theories of intelligence, often with Spearman's g as the highest order factor (e.g., Carroll, 1993).

In the 1980s, developments in cognitive psychology laid the groundwork for two influential information processing models of intelligence. Instead of examining intercorrelations among ability test scores (typically with some form of factor analysis), these models were based on research focused on explaining the manner in which people process information and solve problems. Unlike earlier models in which some form of g was seen as the dominant element of intelligence, Sternberg's (1985) *triarchic theory* involves three interrelated elements: componential, experiential, and contextual. The componential element deals with (a) the mental processes of planning, monitoring, and evaluating (referred to as executive functions), (b) performance, or the solving of a problem, and (c) knowledge acquisition, including encoding, combining, and comparing information. The experiential element addresses the influence of task novelty or unfamiliarity on the process of problem solving. The third element, context, involves three different ways of interacting with the environment: adaptation, alteration of the environment, and selection of a different environment. Sternberg's model suggests that consideration of all these elements is necessary to understand intelligence. The explicit inclusion of the experiential and contextual elements sets it apart from other models, as these elements underscore the need to incorporate learning history and environment in understanding intelligent behavior.

A second information processing theory, Gardner's (1983, 1999) *theory of multiple intelligences,* also

assigns less importance to g. According to Gardner, there are multiple forms of intelligence including linguistic, musical, logical-mathematical, spatial, bodily-kinesthetic, intrapersonal, interpersonal, naturalist, spiritual, existential, and moral. Not surprisingly, given the early connection of intelligence tests to academic performance, these different types of intelligence are inadequately assessed by traditional tests. Gardner argued that a culturally unbiased assessment requires recognition of the full range of different types of intelligence. His theory has been embraced by many educators and has led to the development of school curricula designed to maximize every student's potential to learn (Hogan, 2007). According to Gardner's model, instead of asking "How intelligent are you?" a better question is "How are you intelligent?"

Gardner identified multiple forms of intelligence.
(*Source:* Corbis Digital Stock)

In summary, over the past century, a range of theories of intelligence have been proposed, with earlier theories focusing on the role of g and later theories placing much more of an emphasis on information-processing skills. Because clinical psychology is usually touted as a science-based discipline, it would be reasonable to assume a strong connection between theories and measures of intelligence. However, this has not been consistently true in the realm of intellectual assessment. As you will see later in the chapter, the most commonly used measures of intelligence are not entirely based on current models of intelligence. Indeed, as we highlighted in Chapter 5 and as you will see again in many other chapters, a continuing challenge in clinical psychology is ensuring that psychological services are based on the best available research evidence.

Consider for a moment the following set of people: an Olympic athlete, an expert interpreter, a talented musician, a skilled carpenter, a popular comedian, and a successful fishing guide. To what extent are their different abilities reflective of intelligence, effort and practice, and/or biological predispositions? How broadly should we define intelligence and intelligent behavior?

ASSESSING INTELLIGENCE: THE CLINICAL CONTEXT

The assessment of intelligence is often an integral component of a psychological assessment. The following brief case examples provide an illustration of the range of situations in which an evaluation of intellectual functioning is required.

Roxanne is a 63-year-old woman who has requested an evaluation of her cognitive functioning due to concerns about what she perceives to be recent memory problems. She is a senior manager in a successful marketing company and has always derived great satisfaction from her work. In the past year, Roxanne has noticed that she often forgets her appointments and fails to complete her administrative duties on time because of a lack of attention to deadlines. Although she has purchased various aids to help her keep track of her work activities (such as a personal digital assistant), she fails to use them consistently. Occasionally she notices similar memory lapses in her home life, although they are less frequent with social appointments or activities with her husband. Roxanne is concerned that the memory lapses are becoming more frequent and is concerned that they may be the initial stages of a more serious memory or cognitive disorder.

David is a 47-year-old man who suffered a workplace accident two months ago. David is a bricklayer who was working on a job site repairing damage to the brickwork of a shopping mall when a car hit the scaffolding on which he was standing. The scaffolding collapsed and David fell from a height of two stories onto a pile of bricks on the ground, injuring his back and breaking his wrist. He was also struck on the head by a falling brick. Although he did not lose consciousness at the time, he felt a bit dizzy for a couple of days after his fall. Initially he was primarily concerned about the potential effect of his back and wrist injury on his return to work. In the past month, though, David has noticed that he often forgets where he is going and that he has a "fuzzy" feeling in his head that makes it difficult for him to concentrate. He was referred for an evaluation by the Workers' Compensation Board to determine whether he is fit to return to work or whether there are grounds for considering some form of disability pension stemming from his head injury.

Randi is an 8-year-old girl whose parents requested an assessment as part of their efforts to have her enrolled in a gifted program. Her parents report that she began reading words at the age of 2 years and that by the age of 5 she was reading books intended for those in grade 2. Randi is currently in grade 3 and is often being given additional work by her teacher

Tests to assess intellectual abilities are available for all ages. (*Source:* Laura Dwight/PhotoEdit)

because she rapidly completes the usual work assigned to the class. Despite being generally successful in school, Randi is described by her parents as being rather fearful of new situations and has a tendency to focus on her school work rather than playing with friends or getting involved in games or athletic activities.

Joaquin is a 19-year-old university student who was referred for assessment because of academic problems. Although he reports always having had difficulty getting organized and completing his work on time, he found the first year of university extremely stressful because of consistently having to work through the night to complete assignments. In class, Joaquin refrains from asking any questions and borrows other people's notes because his own are poor and incomplete. Joaquin is an avid reader who frequently forgets about his other commitments when he is in the middle of reading a novel. He reports that his friends describe him as a daydreamer. Joaquin wonders whether he has some type of learning problem that is interfering with meeting his academic goals.

In the preceding case examples, both Roxanne and David are experiencing changes in their usual level of cognitive functioning. In one instance, there is a concern that this may be due to an underlying neurological condition, and in the other there is a question about whether the changes are due to an injury. A common question addressed by psychologists in such cases is whether the current level of functioning represents a change from a previous level. Although it would be easy for a dentist to compare a person's dental status before and after an accident, people do not routinely have assessments of their intellectual functioning unless there is a problem. There can be conceptual and measurement problems associated with efforts to estimate what is known as a **premorbid IQ** (i.e., intellectual functioning prior to an accident or the onset of a neurological decline). However, psychologists have developed relatively effective strategies for making these estimates by consulting the client's achievement records, testing with measures of ability that are relatively insensitive to decline, and paying close attention to the intelligence scale subtests that are least affected by neurological impairment (Groth-Marnat, 2003). Progress has also been made in using demographic variables and scores for subtests of intelligence scales to predict premorbid IQ (Schoenberg, Lange, & Saklofske, 2007).

The cases of Roxanne and David also present a challenge for the assessor because the extent and severity of the possible changes in psychosocial functioning must be determined. In both cases the assessment will not be limited to the use of an intelligence scale because, at a minimum, self-monitoring data and interviews with relevant others will be necessary to document any decrements in functioning. The use of multiple sources of data, including intellectual test results, is relatively standard for assessment questions that involve possible alterations in cognitive functioning, whether due to an accident, disease, or dementia.

The cases of Randi and Joaquin present another common set of assessment questions that hinge on the use of intelligence tests. Questions related to giftedness, mental retardation, or learning disabilities rely heavily on the results of intelligence tests. Giftedness is defined, in most jurisdictions, as an intelligence test score in the top 2% of the population (IQ $\geq$ 130). A diagnosis of mental retardation requires that a person obtain an IQ score in the lowest 2% of the population (IQ $\leq$ 70) as well as have impairments in functioning in areas such as self-care, social skills, home living, and work. In most jurisdictions, to diagnose a learning disability or a learning disorder in DSM IV-TR terminology, there must be a substantial discrepancy between scores on a standardized achievement test and the person's age and level of intelligence.

In all cases, though, psychologists are careful to differentiate between intelligence test scores and intelligence per se. For reasons described in the following section, commonly used intelligence tests do not tap the full range of abilities that are included in modern theories of intelligence. Instead, they tend to focus on those abilities that are related to academic performance and are not designed to measure social, emotional, and other domains. Because our intelligence tests have only limited content validity for the broader construct of intelligence (as currently understood), any result on an intelligence test does not fully represent a person's total intelligence.

As you learned in Chapter 5, surveys of clinical psychologists identified the Wechsler scales as among the top five most commonly used tests in child and adolescent assessment (Cashel, 2002) and among the five tests rated as most important in assessment practice (Piotrowksi et al., 1998). We turn now to an examination of these scales.

THE WECHSLER INTELLIGENCE SCALES

There are three main Wechsler intelligence scales: the Wechsler Adult Intelligence Scale–Fourth Edition (WAIS-IV), which is designed to assess individuals in the age range of 16 to 90 years; the Wechsler Intelligence Scale for Children–Fourth Edition (WISC-IV), which is designed to assess children and adolescents in the 6–16 age range; and the Wechsler Preschool and Primary Scale of Intelligence–Third Edition (WPPSI-III), designed to assess children in the age range from 2 years 6 months to 7 years 3 months. An extended version of the WISC-IV, the WISC-IV Integrated, is available for situations in which more fine-grained testing of intellectual abilities is required. A brief test, the Wechsler Abbreviated Scale of Intelligence (WASI), is also available for testing people between 6 and 89 years of age.

In the rest of the chapter, we focus primarily on the Wechsler intelligence scales and associated cognitive tests, for four main reasons. First, the Wechsler intelligence scales are the most commonly used individually administered measures of intelligence. Second, use of these scales allows for testing of people across almost the entire age range (i.e., 2.5 to 90 years). Third, there are current versions of the three main scales that have been developed for use in a number of countries. Fourth, and most important, for the past few decades these scales have been developed in ways that have enhanced the quality of the scales' psychometric properties and norms. In the following sections, we discuss a range of issues that are relevant to all of the Wechsler intelligence tests, such as factor structure, normative sample, administration, and interpretation. We then move on to provide some specific information about each of the three main tests.

Background Issues

Figure 7.1 shows the history of the three tests that are all derived from the original Wechsler-Bellevue Intelligence Scale. As the three tests share common origins, there is overlap in the concepts assessed and in the types of items. However, as we will see in the descriptions for each test, there are also important differences between tests, which reflect not only evolving notions about how best to conceptualize intelligence but also the necessity of assessing intelligence in a developmentally sensitive manner.

For psychologists, the name of **David Wechsler,** developer of the Wechsler intelligence scales, is synonymous with intelligence testing. Wechsler had extensive experience with the early intelligence

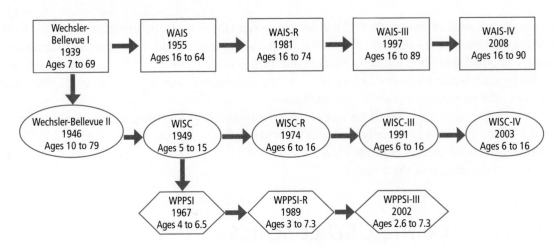

Note: WPPSI = Wechsler Preschool and Primary Scale of Intelligence; WISC = Wechsler Intelligence Scale for Children;
         WAIS = Wechsler Adult Intelligence Scale. From A.S. Kaufman & E.O. Lichtenberger, *Essentials of WISC-III and WPPSI-R Assessment*.
         Copyright 2000. John Wiley & Sons, Inc. This material was modified and used by permission of John Wiley & Sons, Inc.

FIGURE 7.1   History of the Wechsler Intelligence Scales

tests, as he studied under Spearman and was an intelligence examiner in the First World War. You may remember learning in Chapter 1 that mental abilities were tested by administering the Army Alpha test in a group format. The Army Beta test was also administered in a group format and was used to assess recruits who were unable to read or who had limited knowledge of English. In the 1930s, Wechsler became chief psychologist at Bellevue Hospital in New York, and it was in this context that he developed the Wechsler-Bellevue Intelligence Scale (1939), the first individually administered intelligence test intended for use in a general child and adult population. In constructing this intelligence scale, Wechsler's goal was to create a test that borrowed from and improved on other tests of intelligence, such as the Stanford-Binet and the Army Alpha and Beta tests (Kaufman & Lichtenberger, 1999). He did not set out to develop a test that reflected a particular theory of intelligence, but rather was motivated by the quest for an instrument that had substantial clinical utility. In his scale, similar to the Alpha and Beta tests, equal weight was accorded Verbal Intelligence subtests (i.e., those requiring verbal responses) and Performance Intelligence subtests (i.e., those relying on nonverbal responses that are often timed).

An important innovation, introduced by Wechsler, was the use of deviation scores to measure intelligence. The Stanford-Binet (briefly discussed in Chapter 1 and also later in this chapter) relied on comparisons between the chronological age (CA) and the person's mental age (MA—defined as the average age in the normative sample of those who achieved the same test score as the person). The formula for the intelligence quotient (IQ) obtained from the scale is then IQ = (MA/CA) × 100. Thus, if Krista's CA is 20 and her MA is 20 (i.e., the average age of those receiving the same test score as she did is 20 years), she will have an IQ of 100; if her father's CA is 50 and he has an MA of 50, he will also have an IQ of 100. Although this is simple enough, there is a problem with this IQ ratio approach if the standard deviation of the IQ distribution differs with age. Let's assume, for a moment, that the standard deviation is 15 IQ points for 20-year-olds and 10 points for 50-year-olds. If Krista and her father both scored one standard deviation above the age mean, this would result in an IQ of 115 for Krista and an IQ of 110 for her father. Suddenly the meaning of a ratio IQ is not quite so clear-cut.

To remedy this problem, Wechsler translated raw scores into *standard scores* based on a normal distribution with a mean of 100 and a standard deviation of 15, thus ensuring comparability in the meaning of IQ scores across ages. In other words, going back to our example, both 20-year-old Krista and her 50-year-old father who score one standard deviation above the mean receive an IQ score of 115.

VIEWPOINT BOX 7.1

IQ AND ITS CORRELATES

There is probably no more controversial area of psychological research than that of intelligence and its correlates. The controversy is partially due to a misunderstanding about psychological research. There is, for example, a common confusion about correlation and causation. The fact that a variable is correlated with an IQ score does not mean it has a causal connection with intelligence. A second source of error leading to controversy is the erroneous belief that intelligence (or any other psychological characteristic) must be due to *either* heredity *or* the environment. The results of decades of psychological research leave no question on this point: both heredity and environment interact in complex ways to influence intelligence.

Controversy and misunderstanding may also occur because of confusing an IQ score with the concept of intelligence. Remember that the content validity of most intelligence tests is related to performance in logical, educationally influenced tasks. Results of a study by Sternberg and colleagues (2001), who examined academic intelligence and practical intelligence in Kenyan children, nicely illustrate this point. These researchers used standard measures of fluid and crystallized intelligence (see the section on Theories of Intelligence near the beginning of this chapter) along with a measure assessing practical intelligence for adaptation to the environment (primarily knowledge of natural herbal medicines). The correlation between the measure of practical intelligence and crystallized intelligence (i.e., academic intelligence) was −.31. This inverse relation means that children with higher scores in terms of academic intelligence had lower scores in terms of their knowledge of natural herbal medicine. The researchers speculated that this might be because the more time children devoted to school and school work, the less time they were able to devote to developing tacit knowledge about aspects of the indigenous environment.

With these points in mind, what do we know about the correlates of intelligence? The following conclusions are based on summaries of the research literature presented by Aiken (2003) and Hogan (2007).

- Approximately 50–60% of the variance in a population's IQ scores is attributable to genetic factors. However, this does not indicate the genetic component of specific individual's intelligence, nor does it indicate how intelligent any individual is likely to be.

- Fetal and infant malnutrition is associated with persistent negative effects on IQ.
- Exposure to high levels of lead during early childhood has an adverse effect on IQ.
- Although there may be variability in a person's IQ during early childhood, it becomes relatively stable during the school years.
- Mean IQ scores increase slightly during early adulthood and, for most people, reach a plateau by the age of 30 years. However, for those with above-average IQs, small increases in IQ may be evident throughout middle age and even later.
- Declines in IQ are likely after the age of 70 years, but this does not occur for all individuals.
- Sex differences in IQ are minimal, but the variability of IQ scores is greater for men than it is for women.
- IQ is positively correlated with socioeconomic status (i.e., parental income, education, and occupation).
- There tend to be small ethnic differences in IQ, with the highest scores obtained by those whose ethnic heritage is identified as Asian, followed by Caucasian, Hispanic, and African. These differences are hypothesized to be due to a range of factors including test bias, differences in educational and social opportunities, and differences in brain structure.
- The IQ of first-born children is slightly greater than that of later-born children in a family. This may be related to the greater parental emphasis on language development for first-born children compared with later-born offspring.

The early versions of the WAIS, WISC, and WPPSI provided three main summary scores: Verbal IQ (VIQ), Performance (nonverbal) IQ (PIQ), and **Full Scale IQ** (FSIQ, the sum of Verbal and Performance scales). The FSIQ is the total score for an intelligence scale and is the value that is usually referred to simply as the IQ. Over the years, numerous factor analytic studies of the Wechsler scales have found moderate intercorrelations among the various subscales in the three scales, suggesting they tap a *g* factor (e.g., Caruso & Cliff, 1999). This finding suggests it is reasonable to use a total score that combines verbal and nonverbal scores in order to assess general intelligence. However, very few factor analytic studies have found unqualified support for two separate Verbal and Performance factors, so the research evidence does not support the use of VIQ and PIQ scores on their own.

Although there is some slight variability across the three main Wechsler scales, a four-component factor structure seems to best represent the underlying nature of the scales. Accordingly, the most recent versions of scales emphasize these factors (usually referred to as indexes or composite scores) rather than the VIQ and PIQ. For example, the four index scores for the adult test, the WAIS-IV, are Verbal Comprehension (the ability to comprehend and use verbal material), Perceptual Reasoning (the ability to use visually presented material), Working Memory (the ability to do timed tasks that require the use of information in short-term memory), and Processing Speed (the ability to quickly process and use new information). Implicitly, the Wechsler scales reflect a hierarchical model, with the FSIQ as a measure of *g* and the separate abilities represented by the four index scores.

The Wechsler-Bellevue was greatly criticized for its very limited set of norms. Since that early test, Wechsler and his collaborators have devoted enormous efforts to establishing a solid normative base for the Wechsler intelligence scales. The most recent versions of the three scales have all used normative samples of over 2,000 participants. For all scales, great care was taken to ensure that the demographic characteristics of the normative samples matched the most up-to-date American census data. Although this ensures the **representativeness** of the normative sample for testing in the United States, it does not guarantee that the norms are appropriate for testing in other countries. This is an important point for the many clinical psychologists using the Wechsler tests in English-speaking countries outside of the United States.

Tests with norms, such as the various Wechsler tests, are useful to the extent that they provide accurate information about a normative group that is relevant to the tested individual. The most salient characteristics that must be considered in making these normative comparisons are age, grade, sex, geographic region, ethnicity, and socioeconomic status (Sattler, 2001). Interpreting the test result from any individual who differs from the normative group on these characteristics may be problematic. Even though there is evidence that the Wechsler *scales* measure the same core set of cognitive abilities when used in countries other than the United States (e.g., Bowden, Lissner, McCarthy, Weiss, & Holdnack, 2007; Bowden, Weiss, Holdnack, Bardenhagen, & Cook, 2008), there is evidence that the Wechsler *norms* are not always appropriate for use outside the United States. For example, Kamieniecki and Lynd-Stevenson (2002) found that Australian children under the age of 15 obtained slightly higher IQ scores than did American children of a similar age. If the American norms were used to classify giftedness or retardation among Australian children, for example, classification errors would occur.

There is, of course, another problem that may occur when testing someone who differs from the normative sample: the test itself may not be fair. For example, questions that are specific to an American context (e.g., "How many states were there when the United States was established?") may not be appropriate for assessing the general knowledge of a non-American test-taker. To address these issues, recent editions of the Wechsler tests in other countries (e.g., Australia, Canada, the UK) have used standardization procedures to ensure that test items are appropriate and have included country-specific norms.

A final general point should be kept in mind with respect to the Wechsler intelligence scales. Wechsler modeled the original Wechsler-Bellevue scale on tests evaluating an examinee's abilities in academically related areas. This means that the tests are oriented to analytical forms of intelligence and do not measure abilities in the artistic, social, or emotional domains, among others. It also means that the focus of the Wechsler tests is on the examinee's current ability or some of the *products* of intelligence, with little or no attention directed to the *processes* that underlie intelligence. A person's performance on the Wechsler scales indicates a great deal about how well he or she can solve problems in a few important areas, but very little about exactly how he or she solves diverse problems (Groth-Marnat, 2003).

Administration, Scoring, and Interpretation Issues

Doctoral students in clinical psychology often spend an entire graduate course learning how to administer, score, and interpret the Wechsler scales. Standardized administration requires familiarity with all the subtests, ease in handling materials, and detailed knowledge of permitted prompts when an item is partially or incorrectly answered. Administration of the Wechsler scales should be conducted in a comfortable but relatively nondescript room (i.e., with no distractions that influence the person's concentration). Typically, the psychologist sits opposite the test-taker or at a 90-degree angle to

VIEWPOINT BOX 7.2

EMOTIONAL INTELLIGENCE AND ITS CORRELATES

Among the multiple intelligences defined by Gardner (1983) are the abilities to understand oneself and others, labeled intrapersonal and interpersonal intelligence. In contrast to the wealth of literature on intelligence related to academic and occupational performance, emotional intelligence received relatively little attention until the 1990s. Adopting an approach similar to that used for other types of intelligence, Salovey and Mayer (1990) proposed that emotional intelligence (EI) is composed of related abilities that enable the person to perceive, understand, and regulate emotions. As the painstaking and scholarly work of developing sound measures progressed, the publication of the popular book *Emotional Intelligence: Why It Can Matter More Than IQ* (Goleman, 1995) catapulted the concept of EI to the attention of the general public. The idea of EI has a great deal of intuitive appeal. The search to understand the qualities that enable people to be informed by emotions and to regulate their emotions in order to be well adjusted and to get along with others is clearly an important endeavor. Not surprisingly, the concept of EI has fueled a thriving industry. A Google search will reveal many ways to assess EI, to enhance EI, and to become certified in helping others to do so. Improving EI is welcomed as an important goal in both education and in the workplace. Many of the Web sites claim that their materials are scientifically validated and supported by many years of research. As you may be aware, marketing often progresses at a faster pace than science does, so some of the claims are not yet backed up by replicated scientific evidence.

It should not surprise you to learn that there are a variety of ways of defining EI, each leading to the development of different measures. For example, the Emotional Quotient Inventory, and its short form EQ-i-Short (Bar-On, 2002) are based on a definition of EI as a disposition, made up of cognitive, personality, and motivational and affective factors (Parker, Saklofske, Wood, Eastabrook, & Taylor, 2005). This measure requires participants to rate themselves on intrapersonal, interpersonal, stress management, and adaptability scales yielding a total EI score. Data suggesting that high scores on the scale can be easily faked raise concerns about its validity and practical usefulness (Grubb & McDaniel, 2007). The Mayer-Salovey-Caruso Emotional Intelligence Test (MSCEIT, Mayer, Salovey, Caruso, & Sitarenios, 2003) is an ability-based measure and contains questions that are akin to those found in intelligence tests. The model on which it is based hypothesizes that EI encompasses abilities in four areas: (a) perception of emotion, which refers to the ability to detect emotions in oneself and in others—this work developed from research on recognition of nonverbal cues; (b) use of emotional information in thinking—this refers to the ways that emotions influence our thinking and is grounded in cognitive psychology; (c) understanding emotions; and (d) managing emotions.

A recent review of the research using ability-based measures (Mayer, Roberts, & Barsade, 2008) summarized findings indicating that EI is associated with:

- Better social relations for children (as reported by children, their family members and their teachers)

- Better social relations for adults (according to self-report)
- Better family and intimate relations (reported by self and others)
- More positive perceptions by others—high EI individuals are considered more pleasant to be around, and more empathic
- Better academic achievement (reported by teachers)
- Better social relations during work performance
- Better psychological well-being (according to self-report)

There is also preliminary evidence from ability-based measures that emotional intelligence is associated with positive adjustment, as rated by the individual and by others. Overall, though, comparisons of findings across studies in the EI literature are greatly complicated by the use of different models and different measures (Mayer, Salovey, & Caruso, 2008). Undoubtedly, the burgeoning field of EI research will continue to grow in the coming years, and many of the scientific gaps and challenges in the literature will be addressed by researchers committed to enhancing our knowledge of this fascinating psychological construct.

the person—an important point if assessing an energetic youngster who is eagerly trying to peek at what the psychologist is getting ready to do next! The test-taker should be given information about the nature of the test (in an age-appropriate manner) and should be allowed to ask questions. Testing with the scales can be time consuming: Ryan, Glass, and Brown (2007) reported that about one third of administrations of the WISC-IV took more than 80 minutes and that child age, school grade, and FSIQ all correlated positively with administration time. That is, the older you are, the further along in school you are, and the higher your intelligence, the more items are administered and the longer the testing session. Unlike a coach or teacher, the assessor is not permitted to give the test-taker any feedback on performance or whether answers are correct or incorrect, so the encouragement takes the form of noticing effort, concentration, and persistence, rather than suggesting that the person is doing well. In some cases, such as with children, older adults, or individuals with brain damage, it is necessary to take breaks between subtests, otherwise the person's fatigue may interfere with the concentration necessary for the testing.

Extensive details about the administration, scoring, and interpretation of the Wechsler intelligence scales are provided in the manuals that accompany the measures. There are also many other sources available to aid psychologists in their use of these scales (e.g., Flanagan & Kaufman, 2004; Kaufman & Lichtenberger, 1999; Lichtenberger & Kaufman, 2004). Having mastered administration of the scales as part of their graduate training, clinical psychologists usually attend training sessions when a revised scale is published, so that they learn about and practice new procedures introduced in a revised edition. For the test scores to be meaningful, clinicians must follow administration guidelines scrupulously—otherwise it is not possible to accurately use the normative data to interpret a person's test scores.

Administering and scoring these tests are not easy tasks. Numerous studies have found evidence of substantial errors in the administration and scoring of all three Wechsler scales (e.g., Hopwood & Richard, 2005; Loe, Kadlubek, & Marks, 2007; Ryan & Schnakenberg-Ott, 2003). Unfortunately, the consequences of administration and scoring errors can be serious. In addition to errors related to carelessness, errors also can be caused by the complexity of accurately using the Wechsler scales. To give you a sense of this, consider the following example, similar to an item on the WAIS-IV. The test-taker is asked to indicate "In what way are a swimming pool and a baseball field alike?" The assessor must determine whether the person's response "You can have fun in both" is worth 2 points, 1 point, or 0 points. In the manual, information such as the following is provided: 2 points are awarded for answers that involve a recognition that both are used for sporting or athletic activities, 1 point is awarded for answers that indicate they are found in recreational areas or that both require maintenance, and 0 points are awarded for answers such as "You get wet in both" or "Both can be outside, but only a pool can be inside." Although the Wechsler manuals have been extensively tested and the most common responses (both good and poor) are listed, the assessor must know when to ask for more information in reaction to an answer that does not appear in the manual. If the examiner fails to ask for more information when such a prompt is required, the score may be underestimated; if however, the examiner prompts unnecessarily, it may incorrectly inflate the person's score. For testing to proceed at a reasonable rate, the psychologist must be familiar with all the scoring rules to make rapid scoring decisions. Lengthy delays while the examiner consults the manual may prolong the testing session, leading to boredom, frustration and suboptimal performance.

The general interpretive strategy, recommended by almost every source on the Wechsler tests, is to move from the general to the specific. Groth-Marnat (2003), for example, suggested that the FSIQ should always be interpreted first, followed by the factor scores (such as Verbal Comprehension, Working Memory). These steps allow the psychologist to understand the broad pattern of the examinee's IQ and the person's general strengths and weaknesses. FSIQ information, including the percentile rank, provides an overall indication of the person's mental abilities in comparison with the normative group. Interpretations of the factor scores allow for a more comprehensive picture of the examinee's cognitive abilities, including whether there are noteworthy aspects such as much superior functioning in the verbal comprehension compared with the perceptual reasoning. A difference such as this can be due to a host of different factors, including educational background and brain damage. Careful consideration of these scores in the context of other assessment information can provide valuable information for determining the person's overall cognitive functioning and possible options for vocational or educational remediation.

The next step in the interpretation of a Wechsler scale is to examine additional factorial groupings of subtests that have been identified in the research literature. A common strategy is to use Horn and Cattell's (1966) distinction between crystallized and fluid intelligence. As we indicated earlier in the chapter, crystallized intelligence is defined as education-based knowledge and abilities, whereas fluid intelligence is the ability to solve novel problems. As we describe a bit later in the chapter, the WAIS-IV now incorporates measures of fluid intelligence. Most authorities then recommend that the psychologist interpret variability between and within the subtests of the scale. To this end, sources such as Flanagan and Kaufman (2004), Kaufman and Lichtenberger (1999), and Lichtenberger and Kaufman (2004) provide detailed descriptions, for each subtest, of the clinical considerations associated with each subtest and the factors that may influence each subtest. Although widely endorsed and practiced, the analysis of subtest scatter is problematic, not least because the internal consistency reliability of each subtest is typically much lower than that associated with the summary scores (i.e., the FSIQ score and factor scores). This translates into reduced assessment precision, which in turn means an increased likelihood of false positive and false negative statements about the person's ability as measured on each subtest. Decades of research have found that information contained in subtest profiles adds little to the prediction of academic achievement or of learning behaviors (Watkins, 2003).

Wechsler Adult Intelligence Scale–Fourth Edition (WAIS-IV)

The latest edition of the WAIS, the WAIS-IV, was released in 2008 (Wechsler, 2008). This version includes extensive changes over previous versions: some new subtests were added and some long-standing subtests were eliminated, changes were made to the items in many of the subtests that were retained, the age range was enlarged to include 16- to 90-year-olds, and, for the first time, the use of index scores replaced the use of verbal and performance intelligence quotients. These changes were designed to address several goals, including making the structure of the test consistent with results of factor analytic research on previous versions of the WAIS, improving the reliability and validity of the subtests, and reducing the overall administration time. **Table 7.1** provides details on the WAIS-IV subtests.

The normative sample for the WAIS-IV included 2,200 adults, ranging in age from 16 to 90 years. These participants were selected to be representative of the population in terms of sex, education level, ethnicity, and region of the country. Subgroups of the normative sample also completed the WAIS-III, the WISC-IV, the Wechsler Individual Achievement Test-II, the Wechsler Memory Scale-III, and the soon to be released Wechsler Memory Scale-IV. This allowed the researchers to ensure that the results of the WAIS-IV were consistent with those obtained with other intellectual and cognitive measures.

Previous versions of the WAIS were noted for their generally excellent reliability values. The WAIS-IV continues this trend, with the internal consistency coefficients derived from the normative sample for the FSIQ and the four index scores all equaling or exceeding 0.90. Greater variability is evident with the individual subtests, with reliability values ranging from 0.78 to 0.93 (only one subtest, Cancellation, is below a value of 0.80). Because so many validity studies were conducted over the years for earlier versions of the WAIS, it is important to note that there are very high correlations among the IQ scores for the WAIS-IV and the WAIS-III. The pattern of subtest intercorrelations and factor analytic results reported in the test manual all support the continuing validity of the WAIS-IV. Despite all the encouraging validity data for the WAIS-IV, keep in mind that validity is not a property of a test, but rather a property that scores on a test have when used for a particular purpose with a specific group of people. The WAIS-IV (and the other Wechsler scales) must always be used and interpreted within the limits of the characteristics of the normative sample and the purposes for which it has established validity.

Early in this chapter we encouraged you to adopt an attitude of "caveat emptor" when examining self-administered IQ tests. One of the most important ways that you can evaluate the quality of any psychological test is by considering the strength and extent of the reliability and validity evidence for the test, which is why we provide this kind of technical information about the Wechsler scales. If a family member was being assessed to determine whether he or she was eligible for admission to a giftedness program, you would probably want to be sure that the person was assessed using the most valid measure possible.

TABLE 7.1   Wechsler Adult Intelligence Scale–Fourth Edition (WAIS-IV) Indexes and Subtests

Verbal Comprehension Scale

Similarities: The examinee is asked to explain how a series of pairs of words are similar.

Vocabulary: The person is asked to define a series of orally and visually presented words.

Information: The person is asked questions that address knowledge of events, objects, people, and places.

Comprehension: The person is asked questions about common concepts and problems.

Perceptual Reasoning Scale

Block Design: The person is asked to use colored blocks to create three-dimensional representations of two-dimensional geometric patterns.

Matrix Reasoning: The person is presented with incomplete patterns and, from a list of five choices, must select the choice that completes the pattern.

Visual Puzzles: The person is presented with images, like pieces of a puzzle, and must choose the images that go together to match the example given by the examiner.

Picture Completion: The person is presented with pictures of common objects and settings and must identify the missing part.

Figure Weights: The person must choose the "weight" depicted in a series of images that would be equivalent to the "weight" depicted in the example given by the examiner.

Working Memory Scale

Digit Span: The person is presented with a series of numbers and must repeat them in the same sequence or in a reversed sequence.

Arithmetic: The person solves arithmetic problems and provides the answer orally.

Letter-Number Sequencing: Sequences of letters and numbers are presented orally, and the person repeats them with the letters in alphabetical order and numbers in ascending order.

Processing Speed Scale

Symbol Search: The person must indicate, by checking a box, whether target symbols occur in the group of symbols presented.

Coding: Using a key that matches numbers to symbols, the person must rapidly provide the correct symbols to a list of numbers.

Cancellation: The person is presented with a series of shapes of different colors and is asked to cross out images that have a specific shape (e.g., circles) and a specific color.

Adapted from Wechsler (2008).

Wechsler Intelligence Scale for Children–Fourth Edition (WISC-IV)

The fourth edition of the WISC was released in 2003 (Wechsler, 2003). A description of the subtests and the four indexes is presented in **Table 7.2**. As you can see by comparing it with the information on the WAIS-IV subtests in Table 7.1, there are many similarities in the type of tasks included on the two intelligence scales. The WISC-IV is designed to provide age-appropriate

TABLE 7.2   Wechsler Intelligence Scale for Children–Fourth Edition (WISC-IV) Indexes and Subtests

Verbal Comprehension Index

Similarities: After being presented with pairs of words (describing concepts or objects) the child provides an explanation about how the two concepts or objects are similar.

Vocabulary: The child is asked to name pictures that are presented and to define words presented orally.

Comprehension: Questions about common concepts and social situations are presented orally, and the child provides the answer or solution.

Information: The child is asked questions on a wide range of general topics.

Word Reasoning: After being presented a series of clues, the child is asked to describe the underlying common concept.

Perceptual Reasoning Index

Block Design: The child is asked to use colored blocks to create three-dimensional representations of three-dimension models and two-dimensional geometric patterns.

Picture Concepts: The child chooses pictures from rows of pictures to form a group that has a characteristic in common.

Matrix Reasoning: The child is presented with incomplete patterns and, is asked to select the one that completes the pattern from five choices.

Picture Completion: The child is presented with pictures of common objects and is asked to point to or name the missing part.

Working Memory Index

Digit Span: The child is presented with a series of numbers and is asked to repeat them in the same sequence or in a reversed sequence.

Letter-Number Sequencing: Sequences of letters and numbers are presented orally, and the child is asked to repeat them with the letters in alphabetical order and numbers in ascending order.

Arithmetic: The child is asked to solve arithmetic problems and provide the answer orally.

Processing Speed Index

Coding: Using a key that matches numbers or geometric shapes to symbols, the child is asked to rapidly provide the correct symbols to a list of shapes or numbers.

Symbol Search: The child is asked to indicate whether target symbols occur in the group of symbols presented.

Cancellation: The child is asked to mark target pictures in a series of pictures that include both random arrangements and structured arrangements.

Adapted from Wechsler (2003).

assessment of children/adolescents between the ages of 6 and 17. To increase the developmental appropriateness of the scale compared to the previous version, the developers simplified the instructions, including sample and/or practice items within each subtest, and made the test material more attractive and engaging for children. Similar to the strategy used with the WAIS-IV, the WISC-

IV was developed with a stratified sample of 2,200 children and adolescents. A Spanish version of the WISC-IV is available. To ensure the validity of the instrument, test items were modified from the original WISC-IV to minimize cultural bias, and a Spanish-speaking normative sample was collected and the results calibrated to the original norms.

Based on the normative data, the mean internal consistency reliability of the WISC-IV subtests is very good, with only two of the subtests having reliability values below .80. The reliability of the FSIQ is .97, a rather remarkable accomplishment for the scale. All of the four index scores have outstanding reliability values, ranging from .88 to .94. As with previous versions of the WISC, there is a great deal of validity information reported in the manual, including the intercorrelations among subtests and the factor structure of the scale. There are also numerous findings presented on the relation between the WISC-IV and other measures, including measures of similar and dissimilar constructs (i.e., convergent and discriminant validity). For example, the FSIQ correlates .89 with the FSIQ from the previous version of the WISC and with the FSIQ from the WAIS-III (based on data from 198 sixteen-year-olds). In contrast, the correlations between a measure of emotional intelligence and the FSIQ and the four indexes ranged from .22 to .31, thus providing evidence of discriminant validity.

PROFILE BOX 7.1

DR. AURELIO PRIFITERA

I have master's degrees from the University of Chicago (social science), University of Illinois (psychology), and Northwestern University (business administration), and my doctorate in clinical psychology is from Loyola University. As a licensed psychologist, I have had a number of positions over the years, including a private practice in clinical psychology and staff psychologist positions at Northwestern University Medical Center and Duke University Medical School. Since 1985 I have been with Harcourt Assessment, joining Pearson when they acquired Harcourt Assessment in 2008. Currently I am Group President and CEO of the group that includes both domestic and international clinical businesses within Pearson. My projects have included some of the company's most well known and widely used assessments in the Wechsler family of products. Finally, I have

Dr. Aurelio Prifitera

written numerous articles and papers on psychology and assessment, co-edited three books on assessment, and I am a fellow of the American Psychological Association.

How did you choose to become a clinical psychologist?

My 6th grade teacher posed a question to the class about how human language began, which inspired me to begin thinking about human communication and interaction. In college I had a great mentor, Dr. Murray Miron, a psycholinguist who used language to study personalities, behavior, and psychopathology. This experience helped shape my interest in clinical psychology as both a science and area of professional practice.

What is the most rewarding part of your job?

Right now I would have to say the people I work with. I work with really bright, passionate, and imaginative people who are trying to improve the practice and science of psychology through their commitment to developing excellent and useful assessment tools. Through my work I also get the opportunity to meet many leaders in psychology, which makes my job very rewarding as well. There are new challenges everyday, and this keeps the job fresh, new, stimulating and rewarding.

What is the greatest challenge you face in your professional work?

The greatest challenge is the pace of change and keeping ahead of it. With the rapid pace of change in the science of psychology and the digital age, we need to keep ourselves at the leading edge of the assessment field. Balancing what is new in assessment (but not yet known to be valid or useful) with what we know works is a constant challenge in my work.

Tell us about your work on the Wechsler family of measures

I first studied the Wechsler scales in graduate school and began doing research on the Wechsler scales during my clinical internship. I quickly found that the research helped me to use the scales more effectively and the clinical work informed the research questions I worked on. In 1985 I was excited by the opportunity to take a job at The Psychological Corporation, publisher of the Wechsler scales, as this combined my interests in psychology, research, and development with business interests in working for a corporation. I was also the only licensed clinical psychologist on staff at the time, which brought a different perspective to the organization. One of the first tests I worked on was the revision of the Wechsler Memory scale, followed by the third edition of the Wechsler Intelligence Scale for Children. It had been 20–40 years since those tests had been updated and revised. Since that time, we have realized that changes in norms, items' content validity, and advances in the field in general could not justify a long time between new editions of these major instruments in the field of psychology. Accordingly, we began spending much more time and money in shorter revision cycles to keep tests up to date. In my work on these tests I learned how meticulous and detailed you had to be to create a good test, which I had taken for granted when I used them as a clinician.

How do you integrate science and practice in your work?

I spend most of my professional time running the clinical assessment business at Pearson. This gives me the opportunity to facilitate the development of scientifically sound instruments for clinicians. A major part of my role is to encourage my staff to develop products and services that will be useful tools for clinical professionals and that are designed for the demands of clinical practice in mind. I keep current in the professional aspects of psychology through publishing (e.g., the second edition of my WISC-IV book), reading journals, attending conventions and conferences, and maintaining my clinical licensure to practice psychology.

What do you see as the most exciting changes in the field of clinical psychology?

First, I think that the increased focus on evidence-based practice will enable clinicians to make better decisions about how to effectively assess and treat their clients. Over the past few years there has been enormous growth in assessment around the world, and I see great opportunities for a more global foundation to the science and practice of clinical psychology. The increased accessibility of information through digital modalities is influencing our ability to disseminate these developments in assessment and treatment, and is allowing for opportunities for research collaboration and exchange of knowledge that will quicken the pace of advancing the field. Finally, I am also seeing much more openness to the importance of clinical psychology in the treatment of medical conditions. As health care policies and funding become more open to this, we should see a greater role of clinical psychology in the mainstream care of patients.

WECHSLER PRESCHOOL AND PRIMARY SCALE OF INTELLIGENCE–THIRD EDITION (WPPSI-III)

The WPPSI-III was released in 2002 (Wechsler, 2002) and, although there are 14 subtests, psychologists are likely to use only a subset of them in assessing an individual child. Subscales are selected according to the age of the child. For the youngest children (those age 2 years 6 months to 3 years 11 months), there are four core subtests: Receptive Vocabulary, Information, Block Design, and Object Assembly, and the FSIQ is comprised of all four. For older children (those 4 years to 7 years 3 months), six subtests are used for the FSIQ: Information, Vocabulary, Word Reasoning, Block Design, Matrix Reasoning, Picture Concepts, and Coding. The subtests are similar to those described in Table 7.2 for the WISC-IV but are age appropriate in content, with even less emphasis on timed performance and reliance on verbal responses. There is also a series of subtests that can be administered to obtain index scores for Processing Speed and General Language (an index specific to the WPPSI-III).

For the younger age group, based on the data from the normative sample, the internal consistency reliability of the five core subtests is uniformly good, with the lowest value being .83. The FSIQ reliability value is .95, with the reliability values for the composite (factor) scores exceeding .88. A similar reliability profile is evident for the older age group. Based on the normative sample data, all subtests have a mean reliability value of at least .81, the composite values are all at least .90, and the FSIQ reliability is .96. The short-term test-retest reliability (over an average of 28 days) for the scale was determined in a sample of 104 children. The resulting stability values were excellent, with the values for all subtests exceeding .75 and the composite scores and FSIQ having values of at least .80. As with the other Wechsler scales, the manual reports validity data based on subtest intercorrelations and factor analytic results.

VIEWPOINT BOX 7.3

THE FLYNN EFFECT

Are you more intelligent than your parents or your grandparents? According to research conducted by **James Flynn** (1987), the answer to this question is *yes*—at least at the population level. Flynn, a professor of political studies at a New Zealand university, analyzed changes in IQ scores in developed countries over the past few decades. He found that, on average, there was an annual increase of .33 IQ score points. In other words, an average undergraduate student today has an IQ that is approximately one standard deviation higher (i.e., 15 points) than that of the average undergraduate 40 years ago. Not all IQ measures or subtests are rising at the same rate. Flynn found that measures of visuospatial abilities—usually treated as measures of fluid intelligence (see the section on Theories of Intelligence near the beginning of the chapter)—increased more than did measures of acquired knowledge (i.e., crystallized intelligence).

How can this be? Although it is always possible that part of these increases may be due to factors related to the tests themselves, this is rather unlikely. There is no evidence, for example, that people are generally aware of what the items are on IQ tests, or that they study for the tests prior to taking them, or that schools have altered their curricula to emphasize subjects related to *g*.

The span of a few decades seems too brief for such dramatic changes to be due to genetic factors. Changes stemming from genetic alterations within a population usually take centuries, not generations, to be evident. However, in the past century, we have witnessed unprecedented urbanization and mobility of human populations. As these factors have led to an increase in the human genetic variability due to the mating of individuals from genetically distinct subpopulations, Mingroni (2007) argued that such increased genetic variability is at least partially responsible for the observed changes in intelligence.

Can environmental influences be a significant driving force behind this rise in IQ? Flynn speculated that improvements in educational systems are an important contributory factor. This includes both increases in the number of people within a population who receive formal education and increases in the number of years of education completed. Flynn argued that other environmental influences must also be at work. These factors include improved nutrition, greater parental involvement with children, fewer severe childhood diseases, and rapid developments in technology that emphasize visuospatial skills such as television, video games, and computers (Neisser, 1998).

However, consider for a moment the fact that at least half of the variance in population IQ scores can be attributed to genetic factors. If these substantial rises in IQ are largely attributable to environmental factors, it might appear that alterations in these environmental factors over the past 50 years are absolutely enormous. In attempting to explain this "IQ paradox," Dickens and Flynn (2001) emphasized the importance of small but persistent alterations in the environment that, over generations, could influence IQ scores even though there is such a high genetic influence on IQ. For example, over the past century the cognitive complexity of most jobs has increased, leisure time has increased, technologies in the home have increased, and average family size has decreased (allowing more time for parents to focus their attention on each child). Cumulatively, year after year, generation after generation, these changes may be responsible for rising IQ scores by providing stimulating environments that match the intellectual potential of more and more people in a population. By optimizing the gene–environment fit, Dickens and Flynn speculated that a multiplier effect is occurring in which small environmental forces can yield large IQ effects. However, as appealing as such a model may be, it is unlikely to be the last word on the pattern of rising IQ scores.

OTHER INTELLIGENCE SCALES

Although we have focused on the Wechsler scales of intelligence because they are the most commonly used and have a strong evidence base, psychologists also use other scales to assess intellectual abilities. The Stanford-Binet intelligence scales, now in its fifth edition, is designed to assess intelligence in individuals from 2 to 85 years (Roid, 2003). Like the Wechsler scales, the Stanford-Binet scales is standardized to have a mean of 100 and a standard deviation of 15. The subtests can be summed to provide a FSIQ and various composite factor scores. A normative sample of 4,800 was selected based on 2000 American census data. The reliability data for this sample were very strong, with all subtests having internal consistency values $\geq .84$ and the composite and FSIQ scores $\geq .92$. Validity data were obtained by correlating the scores with a host of intelligence and achievement tests included in the normative sample. Although the Stanford-Binet scales has a long historical tradition, in contrast to the Wechsler intelligence scales, their value outside of the United States is limited due to the lack of content adaptations and norms necessary for the validity of the instrument when used in other countries.

In developing tests of intellectual ability, Kaufman and Kaufman took a very different theoretical approach to that used in the Wechsler scales or the Stanford-Binet. Rather than focusing on content areas that measure intellectual functioning, they constructed process-based measures (Lichtenberger, Broadbooks, & Kaufman, 2000). In other words, the Kaufman Assessment Battery for Children (Kaufman & Kaufman, 1983), now in a second edition, and the Kaufman Adolescent and Adult Intelligence Test (Kaufman & Kaufman, 1993) focus on how children and adults learn and assessed styles of learning rather than knowledge or skill areas. The subscales of the child version—Sequential Processing, Simultaneous Processing, Mental Processing Composite, and Achievement—are clearly different from those of the Wechsler scales. A comparison between scores on the processing scales with those obtained on the achievement scale identifies gaps between the person's potential to learn and what the examinee has actually learned. As is typical with intelligence scales, normative data were collected on a large nationally representative sample, and extensive psychometric data were presented in the test manuals.

Although the Kaufman scales were designed to be culturally fair and relevant to educational contexts, they do not seem to be widely used by clinical psychologists. This may be due as much to the limited number of training programs that teach the use of these scales as it is to the need for traditional IQ scores in making a range of clinical diagnoses. Additionally, for those working outside of the United States, the lack of country-specific standardized version of the scales is also a significant drawback.

SELECTED COGNITIVE ASSESSMENT SCALES

To address some of the assessment questions described earlier in the chapter, clinical psychologists usually need to supplement the results from an intelligence test with information obtained on other tests that address cognitive functioning. In this section, we describe two of the tests most commonly used for this purpose. As with our presentation of intelligence tests, we will focus on Wechsler instruments in this section. Not only do these instruments have excellent norms and psychometric properties, but also they are designed to address important clinical issues when used in combination with a Wechsler intelligence scale. The first test we consider is the Wechsler Memory Scale–Third Edition, a test that is typically used if there is a question of brain injury or brain dysfunction due to causes such as dementias, temporal lobe epilepsy, or Parkinson's disease. The second test we present is a standardized achievement test: the Wechsler Individual Achievement Test–Second Edition. An achievement test is used, along with a measure of intellectual functioning, in assessments focused on diagnosing learning disabilities and making recommendations for educational plans to address any observed learning problem.

Wechsler Memory Scale–Third Edition (WMS-III)

The original WMS was published by Wechsler in 1945, revised in 1987, and revised again in 1997 (Wechsler, 1997). A fourth edition of this scale is currently being developed. To help you understand the constructs that the WMS-III assesses, consider what we know about memory processes. Lichtenberger, Kaufman, and Lai (2002) distinguished between *procedural memory*—involving skills and complex motor actions (such as riding a bike)—and *declarative memory*—involving symbolic representations (such as a phone number). Declarative memory can be further subdivided into **semantic memory** and **episodic memory.** Semantic memory involves general knowledge of words, concepts, and events, whereas episodic memory deals with the person's direct experiences. Although all of these forms of memory may be relevant in clinical contexts, the WMS-III is designed to assess the episodic form of declarative memory. To that end, the tasks involved in the WMS-III require the examinee to respond to a number of stimuli, both auditory and visual. **Table 7.3** provides details on the scale's primary subtests (there are optional subtests, which we will not describe). For each subtest, as with the Wechsler intelligence scales, the mean is 10 and the standard deviation is 3. The index scores on the WMS-III have a mean of 100 and a standard deviation of 15, just like an IQ score.

TABLE 7.3   Wechsler Memory Scale–Third Edition (WMS-III)

INDEXES AND SUBTESTS

Immediate Memory

Auditory Immediate

Logical Memory I: A story is read aloud, and the examinee is asked to repeat back as much of the story as possible.

Verbal Paired Associates I: A set of word pairs is read out. Following this a single word is read, and the examinee is asked to provide the paired word.

Visual Immediate

Faces I: The examinee is shown a set of pictures of faces and then must indicate whether each face in a second set was in the original set of faces.

Family Pictures I: Several scenes with characters in them are shown, and the examinee is then asked who was in the scene and some questions about the activities of the characters in each scene.

General Memory (Delayed)

Auditory Delayed

Logical Memory II: The examinee is asked to recall stories presented in Logical Memory I and is then asked a series of questions about the stories (at least 25 minutes must have passed from doing Logical Memory I).

Verbal Paired Associates II: Same task as in Verbal Paired Associates I, but examinee must also indicate which word pairs were also in the Verbal Paired Associates I (at least 25 minutes must have passed from doing this subtest).

Visual Delayed

Faces II: A set of pictures of faces is presented, and the examinee is asked whether each face appeared in the original set of faces in Faces I (at least 25 minutes must have passed from doing Faces I).

Family Pictures II: The examinee is asked to recall the characters from Family Picture I, where they were and what they were doing in each scene (at least 25 minutes must have passed from doing Family Pictures I).

Auditory Recognition Delayed

Logical Memory II: See above

Verbal Paired Associates II: See above

Working Memory

Letter-Number Sequencing: Sequences of letters and numbers are read aloud, and the examinee must repeat the sequences.

Spatial Span: Blocks are touched in specific sequences, and the examinee must then repeat the sequences of touches (either forward or backward).

Adapted from Wechsler (1997).

The WMS-III was normed with the WAIS-III; similarly, the WMS-IV (scheduled for release in 2009) and WAIS-IV were normed together as well. This resulted in a representative normative sample of 1,250 adults (between the ages of 16 and 89 years) who completed both third edition scales. Based on the normative data, internal consistency values for the subtests range from .74 to .93, with short-term stability values ranging from .62 to .82. For the primary indexes, the internal consistency values range from .74 to .93 and the stability values from .70 to .88. There is clear evidence that the WMS-III differentiates between clinical groups (such as those with dementias or neurological disorders) and those with normal memory functioning; the primary index scores can distinguish among the memory-impaired clinical groups (Groth–Marnat, 2003). Evidence of validity for these tasks is especially important, as the WMS-III is the main measure used by clinical psychologists and neuropsychologists to assess memory impairment.

Wechsler Individual Achievement Test–Second Edition (WIAT-II)

The original WIAT was released in 1992. The revised test, the WIAT-II, was released a decade later (The Psychological Corporation, 2002). The WIAT-II is designed to evaluate a person's academic and problem-solving skills. The manual provides linkage with scores from the Wechsler family of intelligence tests, allowing easy identification of discrepancies between intellectual functioning and academic achievement. As a result, the WIAT-II, when used in conjunction with a Wechsler intelligence scale, can be used in the diagnosis of learning disabilities and can provide invaluable information that can be used for planning remedial educational efforts.

Table 7.4 provides information on the nine subtests of the WIAT-II. To give you a sense of the kinds of questions that are asked, a Written Expression question asks the person to write a response to a

---

TABLE 7.4   Wechsler Individual Achievement Test–Second Edition (WIAT-II)

COMPOSITE SCORES AND SUBTESTS

Reading Composite

Word Reading: Depending on age and grade, the person is required to identify letters, beginnings or ends of words, rhyming words, or to read as quickly as possible from a list of words.

Reading Comprehension: The person reads sentences and short passages, answers questions about the text, and draws conclusions and inferences from the text.

Pseudoword Decoding: The person uses phonetic skills to sound out unfamiliar or nonsense words.

Mathematics Composite

Numerical Operations: The person solves math problems of varying complexity.

Math Reasoning: The person solves problems related to areas such as time, measurement, geometry, and probability.

Written Language Composite

Spelling: The person spells a word based on its meaning as used in a sentence.

Written Expression: The person writes words, sentences, or a brief essay in response to a topic; the writing is evaluated based on spelling, punctuation, vocabulary, organization, and theme development.

Oral Language Composite

Listening Comprehension: The person must match words/sentences to pictures.

Oral Expression: The person provides words that match a topic, repeats sentences, tells a story based on presented pictures, or describes the necessary steps in completing a task.

Adapted from The Psychological Corporation, (2002).

---

statement like: *My favorite thing to do is*... and a Reading Comprehension question involves the person reading a passage about kangaroos and then answering questions about how kangaroos move, where they live, and how they are born. The nine subtests are organized into four composite scores: Reading, Mathematics, Written Language, and Oral Language. The composite scores have substantial applied value, because they map onto the four areas that are critical in assessing the precise nature of a learning disability.

As with the Wechsler scales of intelligence, data from the normative sample demonstrate that the WIAT-II has strong internal consistency values. Across the age range of 5–19 years, five of nine subtests have average reliability values $\geq .90$. For the two subtests that each yields only a single response, internal consistency cannot be calculated. For these subtests, the test-retest data provide evidence of excellent reliability ($r = .86$ for the 5–19 year range). Only the Listening Comprehension subtest has relatively poor reliability for a clinical measure, with an internal consistency value of .78. Nevertheless, the composite scores all have reliability values $\geq .87$, indicating a very high level of reliability. Although the WIAT-II included college and university students in the normative sample, the reliability data for these groups are mixed. Some subtests are highly reliable (e.g., a mean value of .90 for Numerical Operations), whereas others have unacceptably low reliability for an achievement test (e.g., a mean value of .60 for Written Expression), and even the composite scores vary greatly in reliability (from .77 to .90). Accordingly, considerable caution should be exercised when using the WIAT-II to assess college and university students.

SUMMARY AND CONCLUSIONS

Our society highly prizes intelligence. It is not surprising, therefore, that the measurement of intelligence is a sensitive topic that arouses heated debate. Decisions about access to educational and rehabilitation services are frequently made based on the results of intellectual assessment. The assessment of intellectual and cognitive functioning has been an important professional activity for clinical psychologists for almost a century. Because significant decisions are made based on the results of intelligence tests, a great deal of effort has been made to ensure that tests are fair, that adequate normative data are gathered, and that assessments are both reliable and valid. The Wechsler scales are the most commonly used scales, allowing assessment of intelligence over different developmental periods, assessment of episodic memory, and assessment of academic achievement.

Critical Thinking Questions

What are the problems in defining intelligence in terms of academic performance?

What types of questions can assessment of intelligence and cognitive functioning address?

What is the significance of having an appropriate normative group?

Why do you think psychologists developed a Spanish language version of the child intelligence test?

What are some of the limitations of the Wechsler scales?

Key Terms

crystallized intelligence: what we have learned in life, both from formal education and general life experiences

episodic memory: memories of a person's direct experiences

fluid intelligence: the ability to solve novel problems; innate intellectual potential

Flynn effect: observed trend for IQ scores in developed countries to increase over the past few decades

Full Scale IQ: total score for an intelligence scale obtained by summing scores on verbal and nonverbal scales; usually referred to simply as the IQ

g: the general factor shared by all intellectual activities

premorbid IQ: intellectual functioning prior to an accident or the onset of a neurological decline

representativeness: extent to which a sample reflects the characteristics of the population from which it is drawn

semantic memory: memory of general knowledge of words, concepts, and events

Key Names

Raymond Cattell   Charles Spearman

James Flynn   David Wechsler

ADDITIONAL RESOURCES

Sternberg, R. J. (Ed.). (2000). *Handbook of intelligence*. New York: Cambridge University Press.

The journal *Intelligence*, published by Elsevier, includes articles on the nature and function of intelligence.

Check It Out!

Information on MENSA can be found at: http://www.mensa.org/home.php and http://www.canada.mensa.org

To take the MENSA workout (not an intelligence test!), go to: http://www.mensa.org/index0.php?page=12

Learning Disabilities Association of American: http://www.ldanatl.org/

Harcourt Assessment, the current publishers of the Wechsler scales: http://harcourtassessment.com/haiweb/Cultures/en-US/Harcourt/Community/Psychology/Psychologicalhome.htm

The following Web site provides information on research on emotional intelligence. It also lets you see sample reports and learn about what a person might be encouraged to do based on the results of the Mayer-Salovey-Caruso Emotional Intelligence Test: http://www.unh.edu/emotional_intelligence/index.html

CHAPTER 8

Assessment: Self-Report and Projective Measures

INTRODUCTION

Many people take psychology courses because they are interested in better understanding the differences among people in attitudes, beliefs, behaviors, and emotionality. Psychology examines the ways that we can identify differences among people and use this knowledge to predict future behavior. Having focused on differences in intelligence in Chapter 7, in this chapter we turn our attention to differences in personality and psychosocial functioning. As social beings, people develop models for understanding and predicting other people's behavior. If you were asked to describe the key psychological characteristics of your friends and family members, you probably wouldn't have difficulty coming up with a list. As you looked over your lists for the different people you know, you'd probably find that you used descriptors such as "friendly," "trustworthy," "sociable," "honest," "serious," "caring," and "fun-loving." These concepts refer to a person's tendency to consistently behave in a specific way—otherwise known as personality traits or dispositions. Moreover, we tend to use these concepts not only for those we know well, but also for ourselves, for people we barely know, for characters in books and movies, and even for our pets. Over the course of a day, we seek patterns in the behaviors of others (*Seth is grumpy today*), generate hypotheses about why those patterns occur (*I wonder whether he's worried about the midterm*), make inferences about other personal characteristics based on these patterns (*He can really be a perfectionist at times*), and predict future behaviors from these patterns (*He'll probably be so hard on himself that he will be unbearable when he's doing his honors thesis next year*).

Over the past century, psychologists have constructed literally thousands of measures of individual differences. Many of these measures are designed to assess **personality traits**, which psychologists define as consistencies in behavior, emotions, and attitudes that are evident across situations and across time. Personality theorists and researchers work to determine the influences of genetics and life experiences on the development and expression of traits (Mischel, 2004; Mischel, Shoda, & Smith, 2004). Clinical psychologists are active in both researching personality traits and assessing personality traits for clinical purposes. As you may know from taking a personality theory course, personality measures vary in the scope of the constructs they are designed to assess. Some are intended to measure very broad constructs such as extraversion or neuroticism; others focus on highly specific constructs, such as locus of control for health or motivation for academic tasks. Most personality measures are based on self-report data and are often called **objective personality tests** because they can be scored objectively (i.e., the same scoring system is always used). Other self-report measures are less complex than personality tests and are derived from descriptive characteristics of an experience or an event rather than from a personality theory. These **behavior checklists** or symptom checklists are designed to provide information about the nature of an individual's experience (e.g., psychological distress, mood states, and feared situations) and the frequency or severity of the experience. **Projective personality tests** represent a very different approach to assessing personality characteristics. Projective tests require the test-taker either to respond to ambiguous stimuli such as pictures or incomplete sentences or to generate drawings according to the assessor's instructions. Projective tests are based on the assumption that valuable information on aspects of the test-taker's personality structure can be gleaned from responses to these ambiguous stimuli.

In this chapter we will review some of the major objective personality measures, behavior and symptom checklists, and also frequently used projective personality measures. To help you appreciate the strengths and weaknesses of these types of measures, we begin by discussing some of the factors that influence their clinical usefulness and accuracy.

THE PERSON–SITUATION DEBATE

Since the late 1960s, researchers and clinicians have struggled with a fundamental question about personality. Although most people (and most personality theorists) believe that personality traits influence the way people behave and are, therefore, responsible for the apparent stability of behavior across time and situations, others have raised the question: what if this stability is illusory? In other words, what would happen if measures of personality couldn't accurately predict individual differences among people or the behavior of an individual? This was the challenge—often called the person–situation debate—that **Walter Mischel** launched in his 1968 book *Personality and Assessment*. Mischel reviewed decades of research into personality assessment and the relation between personality and actual behavior. At that time theorists and clinicians assumed a direct connection between personality traits or dispositions and actual behavior. Therefore, it was believed that the more an individual possessed a certain trait, the more likely the person was to behave in a manner consistent with that trait in any environment or situation. For example, Kayla, who is an extraverted person, would be expected to always behave in an outgoing, confident way at home, school, and with friends. However, Mischel's literature review revealed that the link between trait scores and actual behavior rarely exceeded a correlation of .30! Moreover, he also provided examples of research demonstrating that variations across situations seemed to be more important than personality measures in accounting for behavioral variability. To demonstrate this point, think about what is more likely to influence Kayla's behavior at a party—her personality characteristics or contextual factors such as whether it was a student party, a reception given by a potential employer, or a party to celebrate her grandparents' wedding anniversary. Although she may score high on a measure of extroversion, is she likely to behave in a highly extroverted way regardless of the type of party?

How consistent is your behavior, and how consistent are your emotional reactions across various situations? In reviewing your own psychological reactions, how important do you think your personality is in determining your responses? How important are the demands of the situation you find yourself in, such as the expectations of others?

Mischel's work, combined with some other conundrums personality researchers were facing (such as the limits to self-knowledge, see **Viewpoint Box 8.1**), led many clinical psychologists to question the clinical value of personality measures. This skepticism coincided with the rising influence of behavioral approaches to treatment. Clinical psychologists using a behavioral approach to treatment did not rely on traditional personality measures, preferring instead to use situation-specific or disorder-specific checklists and rating scales. The current use of such checklists in clinical practice largely developed from the activities of these early behavioral and cognitive-behavioral clinicians. Cross-situational variability in people's actions was seen as a source of important information by psychologists with a behavioral approach to assessment. For example, if Jacob, who is depressed, feels discouraged while on the job in an information technology company but has great energy in his volunteer work at the animal shelter, it may be valuable to help him (a) learn about the conditions in which the symptoms are less severe and (b) use this knowledge to try to increase involvement in situations in which the symptoms are lower.

In the decades since the publication of Mischel's book, there have been substantial developments in the science of personality. It now appears that variability across situations and stability across time

VIEWPOINT BOX 8.1

HOW WELL DO WE (AND CAN WE) KNOW OURSELVES?

We usually take for granted that we can know ourselves fairly well. Most people feel confident in their ability to accurately describe themselves, their attitudes, and their personal preferences. Yet, for well over a century, psychological theorists and researchers have questioned the extent to which we can actually know our own mental states and the causes of our actions.

Based on early Freudian theories, many people view the nonconscious—or unconscious—aspect of our existence as something that can be accessed through a great deal of conscious effort. The metaphor often used is that of an archaeological dig that yields ever more fascinating material the deeper one digs into the past. In contrast, though, the contemporary view of the unconscious is rather less romantic than this. Most cognitive, social cognitive, and neuroscience researchers see the human mind as a collection of information processors that function largely out of our awareness and that probably developed long before consciousness emerged in our species (Wilson, 2002). According to this research-informed perspective, no amount of "digging" (i.e., introspection) is likely to result in a more accurate understanding of ourselves, our motives, or our past experiences.

Wilson and Dunn (2004) reviewed research relevant to the questions of (a) the extent to which we can know and understand ourselves and (b) the obstacles that interfere with efforts to attain greater self-knowledge. Many of their conclusions may surprise you. First, despite decades of theorizing and research, there is little compelling evidence for the existence of the Freudian concept of repression by which information is kept out of consciousness but is stored in memory. Although there is no firm evidence for repression, there is substantial evidence for the existence of conscious suppression (i.e., trying not to think about or focus on something). Most research on suppression indicates that suppression often fails to accomplish the goal of rendering information unavailable to consciousness. Ironically, efforts to suppress thoughts, memories, or feelings can frequently result in people paying even more attention than usual to the information they are attempting to ignore (Wegner, 1994). See for yourself: for the next few minutes, actively try not to think about a hippopotamus wearing a lime green ballet tutu and neon pink ballet slippers.

If the unconscious is not the repository of unwanted and undesirable urges and experiences, then what is it? Psychological research has firmly established that a great deal of nonconscious processing does occur but, according to Wilson and Dunn, this processing is largely related to matters of perception, attention, learning, and automatic judgments. Contrary to Freud's hypotheses, current research indicates that there are no motivational or emotional impediments to people easily accessing this unconscious content. Instead, much of the unconscious is simply inaccessible to conscious inspection, either because it was never processed in consciousness to begin with (for example, we are not consciously aware of what we do to perceive depth) or because a simple, repetitive task has become automatic and has been removed from conscious awareness (for example, when we learn to drive a car or to roller blade we are conscious of each action, but as our skill develops, performing the various subtasks becomes automatic or unconscious).

If introspection cannot help us better understand ourselves, can we take other steps to increase the accuracy of our self-knowledge? Wilson and Dunn suggested that we could learn much about ourselves by attending to how others view us. However, research indicates that most people are unable to accurately learn about how others see them, especially if those views do not match their own views of themselves. Social cognitive research indicates that the best route to self-knowledge is to intentionally observe our own behaviors and decisions as they occur. However, before you decide to embark down this path toward greater self-awareness, there is one caution you should consider. Decades of psychological research have convincingly shown that there are real physical and psychological benefits to positive self-illusions, such as feeling you are more attractive, more intelligent, or more skilled than you really are (Taylor & Brown, 1988).

coexist. Those arguing for the power of situational influences and those arguing for the power of personality were both correct (Fleeson, 2004; Fournier, Moskowitz, & Zuroff, 2008). Having information on both situational characteristics and personality characteristics can enhance the prediction of human behavior. However, as you will see later in the chapter, the most commonly taught and used personality measures have been available for well over 50 years. Although changes in clinical assessment tools have not kept pace with advances in personality research, these research advances appear to have influenced the way that most clinical psychologists interpret the results from personality measures. Yet, as you will see in the next chapter, there continue to be substantial concerns about how various biases—such as overestimating the influence of personality characteristics on actual behavior—affect the process of clinical decision-making.

SELF-PRESENTATION BIASES

In many circumstances people may be motivated to present themselves in a particular light. In some cases, such as those involving custody and access assessments or assessments to determine the suitability for police training, people may have a desire to downplay any personal problems and to appear as resilient and mentally healthy as possible. In other circumstances, such as when seeking compensation for work- or accident-related psychological problems, people may be inclined to overemphasize their distress and difficulties.

> Can you think of times when you deliberately underemphasized or overemphasized physical problems or emotional difficulties that you were experiencing? Did this seem justified to you at the time? Did your presentation of your problems have the effect on other people that you hoped it would have? Are there times when you think other people are downplaying or highlighting problems?

To address these possible biases, most personality inventories designed for clinical use, such as the Minnesota Multiphasic Personality Inventory (MMPI), the Millon Clinical Multiaxial Inventory (MCMI), and the Personality Assessment Inventory (PAI), include **validity scales**. Generally speaking, the scales focus on three possible tendencies that could distort the answers given by test-takers: emphasizing positive characteristics ("faking good"), **malingering** or emphasizing negative character-istics ("faking bad"), and inconsistent or random responding to test items (which can occur when the person does not take the test seriously or when the person is cognitively impaired). You will find more details on the validity of these validity scales when we present information on these inventories later in the chapter. In addition to malingering scales that are part of large-scale personality tests, there are also tests specifically designed to evaluate possible malingering. The Test of Memory Malingering (Tombaugh, 1997), for example, was designed to assess whether an individual with established or suspected neurological impairments is exaggerating his or her memory deficits. This test has been demonstrated to be highly accurate in detecting attempts to simulate memory problems (Rees, Tombaugh, Gansler, & Mocyznski, 1998). Of course, psychologists often examine other data when they have concerns about the accuracy of information provided to them by those they are assessing. Information obtained from interviews with other people who know the person being assessed (e.g., spouse, employer) and from a review of relevant records (e.g., medical records, police records, school records) can be invaluable in this regard.

To avoid the problem of intentional misrepresentation, many clinical psychologists have advocated the use of projective personality tests, arguing that their ambiguous nature makes it difficult for clients to exaggerate or minimize psychological problems. The many studies on this issue have yielded inconclusive findings. In one study, Meisner (1988) instructed half of the sample of nondepressed undergraduate student participants to act as if they were depressed when responding to psychological tests. To assist them in this, he also provided them with a clinical description of depression and offered a cash incentive for convincingly displaying depression. Compared with the control group participants who completed the measures in an honest manner, those in the malingering condition had higher scores on the Beck Depression Inventory (a symptom checklist) as well as on several Rorschach indices of depression (a projective personality test). This result suggests that the projective measure was just as susceptible to faking as the symptom checklist. In contrast, Bornstein, Rossner, Hill, and Stepanian (1994) found that, when instructed to deliberately present as dependent or independent, undergraduate student participants could do so effectively on a self-report measure of dependency but not on a Rorschach dependency scale. Thus, the research on whether projective tests are less easily faked is not conclusive.

DEVELOPING CULTURALLY APPROPRIATE MEASURES

Given the multicultural nature of most countries, personality measures must be relevant and unbiased across cultural and ethnic groups. Malgady (1996) proposed a radical change in the ways that clinical psychologists react when there is a paucity of research evidence. Rather than approaching these issues in the usual way that null hypotheses are generated—that no bias or differences exists—he argued that both practitioners and researchers should assume that measures *are* culturally biased unless there are data to suggest the opposite. Following this recommendation, psychologists have made substantial efforts to carefully examine the relevance of personality measures and lack of bias across cultural and ethnic groups. Research has shown that a growing number of measures are suitable for use across cultural and ethnic groups; however, not all commonly used clinical instruments have such evidence supporting their use.

Tests can be biased or unfair in several ways. First, the test content may not be equally applicable or relevant to all cultural groups. Test items that accurately capture the essence of the underlying psychological construct for one cultural group may not be as appropriate for other cultural groups. In an early study on the influence of ethnicity on responses to the California Personality Inventory, for example, Cross and Burger (1982) found that African American and European American university students responded differently on more than a third of the test items. Second, the pattern of validity coefficients may not be similar across groups. For example, an association between a negative attributional style and depressive symptoms may be much larger for one group than for another. Third, the use of a cut-off score on a scale to classify individuals may not be equally accurate across groups. As described in Chapter 5, many personality inventories use T scores (i.e., scores based on group means and standard deviations) of 65 or 70 to determine whether an individual's responses fall outside the normal range. Bias related to cut-off scores could mean that those in certain cultural and ethnic groups could be either over- or underidentified as having scores in the clinical range. Using the California Personality Inventory, Davis, Hoffman, and Nelson (1990) found that Native American women, compared with European American women, scored much higher on measures of passivity and assistance seeking. A clinical psychologist using this test with a Native American woman would, therefore, need to consider the impact of cultural influences when interpreting the meaning of the obtained test scores. A fourth form of bias could occur with respect to the test's underlying structure. Researchers frequently use a statistical procedure called factor analysis to explore exactly how components of a construct relate to each other. For example, a measure of anxiety may have a factor structure that has cognitive and physical components for one group and only a physical component for another. If this pattern of results occurred, it would mean that the test is actually tapping different constructs in the two groups.

Few studies examine all of these possible forms of bias, although it is common for researchers to test for more than one form. Blumentritt and Van Voorhis (2004), for example, tested for bias in the Millon Adolescent Clinical Inventory (MACI), a widely used self-report measure of adolescent psychopathology that we describe later in this chapter. In their sample of Mexican American youth, they found that the inventory had good reliability and construct validity. They also found that the cut-off scores used to determine clinical range scores provided information consistent with other available clinical data on their participants.

How should a clinical psychologist conduct an assessment with a client from an ethnic minority back-

Personality measures must be relevant and unbiased across cultural and ethnic groups. (*Source:* Media Bakery)

ground? Obviously, the best option is to use measures that have been validated for use with members of the ethnic population in question. If the best measures available do not have such validation (including evidence of lack of test bias), then caution must be exercised in interpreting the results obtained with the tests. At a minimum, the psychologist should indicate in the assessment report that the accuracy and validity of the results may be less than ideal. This might mean, for example, reporting the test score and interpreting it according to test norms, but then indicating that both the test items and the norms may not provide an optimal assessment of the client's psychological functioning. If the administration of the test was not standardized (e.g., if the psychologist translated some of the items to ensure that the client understood the questions) and/or if the psychologist has significant concerns about the accuracy of the test results, then the prudent course of action would be to not report test scores in a report and to only use the test to aid in generating hypotheses about client functioning (cf. Fernandez, Boccaccini, & Noland, 2007).

For psychologists who are able to offer services in more than one language, there is an increasing array of psychological tests that were developed in English and then translated and validated in another language. As guides to the translation and cross-cultural adaptation of tests become more commonly available (e.g., van Widenfelt, Treffers, de Beurs, Siebelink, & Koudijs, 2005), it is likely that the rate at which translated measures become available will also increase. According to the International Testing Commission (2001), translation and adaptation of a test requires five steps. First, items are translated into the second language, this version is translated back into the initial language by a second translator, and the two versions are compared. This procedure is known as back translation. Second, pilot testing should be conducted with the translated measure to ensure there are no problems with the

---

TABLE 8.1   Assessing Cultural and Linguistic Factors

Immigration History

- Length of time residing in the country
- Circumstances surrounding migration from country of origin (e.g., immigration for economic reasons, refugee)
- Current legal status in the country

Contact with Other Cultural Groups

- Ethnic composition of the area in which the client lives
- Does the client tend to stay within the area in which she or he lives?
- Frequency of changes in residence and impact on the client

Acculturative Status

- Consider elements such as cultural norms, behaviors, and values
- Evaluate the acculturation of the client, using separate dimensions of exposure-adherence to traditional culture and exposure-adherence to the dominant culture

Acculturative Stress

- Impact of acculturation on the client (i.e., stress and distress)

Socioeconomic Status

- Obtain information about financial resources (e.g., family income), interpersonal resources (e.g., educational level), and nonmaterial resources (e.g., family structure)

Language

- Client language preference and ability/fluency in language(s) used in the assessment
- Consideration of both verbal and nonverbal communication skills

Adapted from Acevedo-Polakovich et al. (2007)

---

comprehension of items. Third, evidence of good reliability should be obtained on the translated measure. Fourth, scores on the measure should be restandardized using norms specific to the translated measure. Fifth, construct validation efforts should be undertaken to determine whether the instrument measures the same psychological qualities in both languages. Of course, before a psychologist decides to use a translated test, it is critical to determine the extent to which the supporting research is relevant to the client being assessed. When assessing Spanish translations, Fernandez, Boccaccini, and Noland (2007) encouraged psychologists to consider the extent to which there is research support for a test in various Hispanic populations. This is critical, because a test adapted for use in Spain may not necessarily be appropriate for use with Hispanic Americans or residents of Latin America. Subtle linguistic differences evident among these populations might affect the way in which respondents interpret test items. Moreover, the reliability and validity data from one population may not necessarily generalize to other populations.

When using psychological tests with members of ethnic minority groups, including both translated tests and English language tests validated for use with the minority group in question, psychologists must always ensure that they take into account the client's life circumstances when interpreting the test data and integrating it with other clinical information. In particular, a large number of cultural factors must be considered. A fine example of how psychologists should approach the assessment of members of ethnic minority groups, in this instance Latinas/os, was provided by Acevedo-Polakovich et al. (2007). **Table 8.1** presents these authors' recommendations regarding the types of issues that must be considered when addressing ethnicity or culture in psychological assessments.

THE CLINICAL UTILITY OF SELF-REPORT AND PROJECTIVE MEASURES

Against the backdrop of challenges we described in the preceding sections, just how useful are self-report and projective measures in practice? The research base for personality measures and behavior/symptom checklists is simply staggering in size, involving many tens of thousands of published studies. There is replicated, cumulative research on scores of personality traits and behavior/symptom profiles that has greatly advanced our knowledge of human functioning. Whether the construct is state anxiety, sensation-seeking, ego strength, dependency, or optimism, psychologists have a wealth of empirical evidence to draw upon in understanding individual differences in human experience. In considering the impact of this research, it is essential to distinguish between basic and applied perspectives. In terms of the goals of basic research, our knowledge of personality has grown enormously in the past few decades. We now know a great deal about the manner in which personality traits are expressed and the ways in which they are reciprocally influenced by the person's life circumstances (Mischel, 2004; Mischel et al., 2004).

Addressing the applied value of this research literature is a different matter. Simply because psychologists know a great deal about personality determinants, structure, and expression, it does not follow that all (or any) of this knowledge is useful in making changes in people's daily functioning. Instead, there must be firm evidence that the measures, and the research on the measures, have **clinical**

utility. Hunsley and Bailey (1999) proposed distinct and increasingly stringent ways to define clinical utility by addressing three questions.

1. Is the tool found to be useful by clinical practitioners?
2. Is there replicated evidence that the measurement data provide reliable and valid information about clients' psychological functioning?
3. Does the use of the test and the resulting data improve upon typical clinical decision making and treatment outcome? In other words, does using the measure eventually make a difference in terms of the client's functioning?

According to the first definition of clinical utility, it is indisputable that self-report and projective tests are seen as critical for general clinical practice. **Table 8.2** summarizes surveys of APA-accredited clinical training programs (Childs & Eyde, 2002), APA-accredited internships (Clemence & Handler, 2001), and clinical psychologist members of the APA (Camara, Nathan, & Puente, 2000) with respect to the most commonly taught or used psychological tests. In all three surveys, the Wechsler intelligence tests were consistently seen as the most important measures in clinical practice. However, as illustrated in Table 8.2, there is also remarkable consistency among endorsements of the self-report and projective measures. Among self-report personality measures, knowledge of the various versions of the MMPI and the MCMI was seen as essential. Two projective personality tests, the Rorschach inkblot test and the Thematic Apperception Test (TAT), were consistently ranked as being among the most important measures for students and practitioners. One self-report symptom checklist, the Beck Depression Inventory (BDI), was viewed as being important for both internship training and general clinical practice.

Let's move now to the second question used to define clinical utility: whether there is evidence that the test can provide reliable and valid information about clients. Again, voluminous data indicate that many self-report tests and some projective tests provide psychometrically sound information. Some examples from the comprehensive report on psychological testing by Meyer and colleagues (2001) illustrate this point. These researchers drew data from more than 125 meta-analyses to illustrate the validity of a number of psychological tests. As we mentioned in Chapter 4, effect sizes in meta-analysis can be expressed as either differences between groups or as correlation

TABLE 8.2   Rank Ordering of Self-Report and Projective Measures Among All Clinical Tests

Test	Taught in Clinical Graduate Courses[a]	Recommended for Internship[b]	Used by Clinical Psychologists[c]
MMPI	3	2	2
MCMI	8	8	10 (tied)
BDI	—	4	10 (tied)
Rorschach	4	3	4
TAT	5	5	6

[a]Childs & Eyde (2002); [b]Clemence & Handler (2001); [c]Camara, Nathan, & Puente (2000)

coefficients. Meyer et al. calculated correlations and found the following: thematic apperception scores (using TAT-like stimuli) of achievement motivation and achievement behavior, $r = .22$; internal locus of control and subjective well-being, $r = .25$; attributions for negative events and depression, $r = .27$; MCMI scale scores and ability to detect depressive or psychotic disorders, $r = .37$; Rorschach-derived dependency scores and dependent behavior, $r = .37$; MMPI scale scores and conceptually relevant criterion measures, $r = .39$; MMPI validity scales and detection of known or suspected malingering, $r = .45$.

What do these numbers mean? Is this good news or bad news? It may be useful to compare these results with other validity findings in health care research. Meyer et al. (2001) reported that, for example, traditional electrocardiogram stress tests and coronary artery disease are correlated at $r = .22$, screening mammogram results and detection of breast cancer within a year are correlated at $r = .32$, and conventional dental x-rays and diagnosis of between-tooth cavities are correlated at $r = .43$. Compared with validity evidence from such other health care assessments, the results for many psychological tests appear very similar, thus suggesting that psychological tests may be just as useful as assessments commonly used in health care systems. Nevertheless, these results should be interpreted cautiously. In contrast to the situation for many medical or dental tests, there is surprisingly little evidence that psychological test results provide information that actually makes a difference in treatment provision or treatment outcome (e.g., Garb, Klein, & Grove, 2002).

This leads us to the third definition of clinical utility. Unfortunately, even though the need for evaluations of clinical utility has been apparent for many years (e.g., Mash, 1979) there are limited data supporting the clinical utility of psychological tests (Nelson-Gray, 2003). The only tools with broad supporting evidence of their utility are behaviorally oriented assessment strategies that rely on idiographic measurement and some behavioral/symptom checklists (Haynes, Leisen, & Blaine, 1997). Many of the psychological treatments that have been demonstrated to work well rely on behavior and symptom checklists in assessing patient characteristics and experiences. It would be reasonable to assume, therefore, that these checklists have substantial clinical utility. Yet there is little research that has examined the degree to which these measures are really necessary for the success of these treatments. Indeed, the same can be said of the most commonly used personality tests. Despite decades of validity research and frequent clinical use, there is no scientific evidence that results from even the MMPI or the Rorschach have a meaningful impact on the outcome of psychological services (Hunsley & Bailey, 2001).

As you will see later in the chapter, most of these instruments were designed to evaluate a person's psychosocial functioning; many of them are very good at doing this. However, as you learned in Chapter 1, over the decades clinical psychologists' principal activities have shifted from assessment to intervention. With this change, these instruments were increasingly used to inform treatment planning decisions—a purpose that they were never originally designed to serve. As you learned in Chapter 5, the validity of a test is very much conditional on the purpose for which it is being used and the population with which it is used. This means that an instrument that has scientific support for evaluating personality characteristics and psychosocial functioning is not necessarily valid for determining the optimal ways to enhance or improve problematic aspects of personality and psychosocial functioning. In other words, using the concepts we introduced in Chapter 5, instruments that may be useful for assessment-focused evaluations may not be useful for intervention-focused evaluations.

The fact that there is currently little evidence for the intervention-related utility of self-report and projective tests is of great concern and makes it difficult to justify with scientific data the need for time-consuming and expensive personality assessments conducted for intervention-focused evaluative purposes. This gap in the literature could be addressed easily using straightforward research designs. For example, in an experimental design, all patients who are about to receive treatment could complete a self-report personality measure. Half of the therapists would be randomly selected to receive the results of this test and the others would receive nothing. This design would allow the researcher to determine whether the test results influence (a) therapists to alter the nature of the treatment offered to clients and (b) the actual outcome of the treatment. Lima and colleagues (2005) used just such a design to examine the value of clinicians' having access to patient MMPI-2 data at the beginning of treatment. They found that having these data available had no impact on the number of sessions patients attended, whether therapy ended prematurely, or overall patient improvement in functioning assessed at the end of treatment.

The obvious question in all of this is why there is so little research on the utility of assessment instruments. As you may recall from Chapter 1, we introduced the distinction between efficacy and effectiveness in the context of treatment research. There is a different emphasis on internal and external validity in these two types of studies, with efficacy trials constructed to be high on internal validity and effectiveness trials high on external validity. As we will describe later in the text, researchers have tended to ensure that a treatment works at the level of efficacy trials before moving on to examine effectiveness. It is likely that the same type of decision has occurred with psychological instruments. A great deal of research effort has gone into, and continues to go into, evaluating the reliability and validity of instruments. In many ways, this is akin to the purpose of efficacy studies, inasmuch as the basic question addressed by the research is whether or not the test (or treatment) "works." The applied question of whether the test has utility in actual clinical services is similar to the question behind effectiveness trials (i.e., does this treatment work in real-world clinical settings?). Just as psychotherapy researchers are now beginning to attend more to effectiveness trials, perhaps assessment researchers will soon begin to focus more of their efforts on the very important question of the clinical utility of our assessment instruments.

SELF-REPORT PERSONALITY MEASURES

In the following sections we present the most commonly used personality inventories in clinical psychology. The original major personality inventory, the Minnesota Multiphasic Personality Inventory, is now available in forms appropriate for adults (MMPI-2) and adolescents (MMPI-A). These inventories provide broad coverage of many clinical syndromes and other characteristics relevant for typical assessment and intervention purposes. Based on a distinct theoretical approach to psychopathology and keyed to DSM conditions, the Millon Clinical Multiaxial Inventory-III (for adults) and the Millon Adolescent Clinical Inventory (for adolescents) are frequently used by clinicians because of their emphasis on personality styles and disorders. One of the newest multiscale inventories, the Personality Assessment Inventory, is gaining support among clinical psychologists because its main scales are designed to address common DSM Axis I and Axis II diagnoses. **Table 8.3** provides summary information on the basic characteristics of the MMPI-2, MCMI-III, and PAI.

TABLE 8.3 Comparing the MMPI-2, the MCMI-III, and the PAI

	MMPI-2	MCMI-III	PAI
Number of items	567	175	344
Response format	True/False	True/False	4-point scale
Age range	18 and over	18 and over	18 and over
Reading level	6th–8th grade	8th grade	4th grade
Administration time	60–90 minutes	25–30 minutes	40–50 minutes

MMPI-2 and MMPI-A

Background Issues

As described in the preceding pages, the Minnesota Multiphasic Personality Inventory (MMPI) and the revised versions of the test, the MMPI-2 (for use with adults) and the MMPI-A (for use with adolescents), are the most commonly taught and used self-report (or objective) personality measures in clinical psychology. The original MMPI was published in 1943 by **Starke Hathaway** and **J. Charnley McKinley** based on their test development research at the University of Minnesota Hospitals. Their original goal was to construct a self-report test that could provide accurate information on symptom severity and possible diagnoses for adult patients suspected of having mental disorders. Up until then, assessment data were collected via interviews by hospital staff, which entailed a great deal of time, effort, and expense. Also, as you learned in Chapter 6, interrater reliability for unstructured interviews is generally poor. In developing the MMPI, the researchers relied on a test construction strategy known as an **empirical criterion-keying approach**, which involves the generation and analysis of a pool of items. Items are retained for inclusion in the test only if they discriminate between two clearly defined groups (in this case, patients with mental disorders and a comparison group made up of patients' friends and family members, recent high school graduates, and patients with medical disorders). First, the researchers established a pool of 1,000 items from existing personality tests, clinical reports, and other sources of clinical information. Following data analyses of group differences in item responses, almost 500 items were eliminated. With the later inclusion of scales measuring masculinity–femininity and social introversion, the final version of the original MMPI consisted of 550 items. Within years, the MMPI became widely used and researched; the MMPI was also translated and validated for use in many countries outside the United States (Butcher & Beutler, 2003; Groth-Marnat, 2003).

Addressing concerns about the potential for test-takers to either intentionally or unconsciously influence the way in which they answered the items on the test, Hathaway and McKinley developed several scales to assess possible threats to the validity of responses to the MMPI (such as answering in an unrealistically positive manner). As time passed and the MMPI became the dominant self-report personality measure used by psychologists, concerns were raised about wording problems, the outdated content of some items, the nonrepresentativeness of the original normative comparison group, and the test's technical shortcomings stemming from the use of empirical criterion-keying methods.

James Butcher headed a project to revise the MMPI that was begun in 1982. The researchers in this project faced a substantial challenge in attempting to (a) improve upon the original test by using better test construction strategies and obtaining representative normative data *and* (b) ensure continuity with the original test by retaining the MMPI's main scales. After some items were updated and a number of provisional new items were added, data were collected from more than 2,500 adults. Extensive data analysis led to the elimination of some old and some new items, which resulted in the 567-item MMPI-2 (Butcher, Dahlstrom, Graham, Tellegen, & Kaemmer, 1989). The first 370 items on the test contain all of the original validity and clinical scales, with the remaining items providing information for a range of additional scales designed to supplement the information available from the original MMPI scales. Many of these new scales were formed by means of a **content approach** to test construction, which involves developing items specifically designed to tap the construct being assessed. This approach to test construction is much more consistent with current views of optimal test development strategies.

Many clinical psychologists who were familiar with the MMPI adopted the MMPI-2 slowly and cautiously. Changing from one version to the next required the purchase of new test and scoring materials, as well as learning how to interpret the new measure. Eventually, despite ongoing criticisms about weaknesses in the test construction procedures used by the restandardization committee (e.g., Helmes & Reddon, 1993), the revised test became even more popular than the original because of its improved content, coverage of psychological symptoms, and standardization sample. The MMPI-2 is now available in more than two dozen languages (Butcher & Beutler, 2003).

Over the years, problems specific to test use with adolescents became apparent: for example, the MMPI was too long for many young people to complete, the reading level was too high, and the norms were not suitable for use in interpreting the scores obtained by adolescents (Groth-Marnat, 2003). This led to the development of the MMPI-Adolescent (MMPI-A; Butcher et al., 1992). This test includes a normative sample of adolescents, fewer items (478) than the MMPI-2, as well as reworded and additional items of particular relevance to young people.

Tables 8.4, 8.5, and 8.6 provide information on the main scales found in both the MMPI-2 and the MMPI-A. As shown in **Table 8.4**, the scales can assess potential biased responding in several ways, by detecting overly negative, overly positive, and careless, random, or otherwise biased responses. The range of validity scales provide a thorough evaluation of biases in self-presentation, and even allow for the determination of whether the way in which a person responded to the test items changed as he or she took the test!

Table 8.5 provides details on the traditional clinical scales that were part of the MMPI and were retained for the revised tests. **Table 8.6** provides information about the most clinically relevant scales. These so-called Content scales were developed specifically to address some of the test users' needs (such as more thoroughly assessing anxiety and depressive symptoms and having information on factors related to family, work, and treatment contexts). Most psychologists examine the results obtained from both the basic clinical scales and the content scales.

The most recent major development with the MMPI involved the development of *restructured clinical scales*. One of the longstanding problems with the MMPI clinical scales was the high intercorrelations among scales—in some studies, the shared variance among pairs of scales has been 75% or higher (Nichols, 2006). Additionally, because small samples of patients were used in the original empirical criterion-keying approach to MMPI development, concerns about the validity and relevance of the clinical scales have often been expressed in the literature. As a result, Tellegen et al. (2003) undertook a revision of the eight main clinical scales (i.e., not including scales 5 and 0). These

TABLE 8.4   MMPI Validity Scales

Cannot Say (?): This scale is the total number of unanswered items. A large number of unanswered items indicate defensive responding.

Lie Scale (L): A measure of self-presentation that is unrealistically positive.

Infrequency Scale (F): A measure of self-presentation that is very unfavorable. This can indicate a desire to present oneself as having severe psychopathology *or* it can be an accurate report of substantial distress, disorganization, and confusion.

Defensiveness Scale (K): A measure of unwillingness to disclose personal information and problems. The scores on some of the clinical scales are adjusted based on the test-taker's *K* score.

Back *F* Scale (FB): Similar to the *F* scale, the items for this scale all occur in the final third of the inventory. The scale measures a possible change in self-presentation, which may be due to a change in test-taking strategy.

Variable Response Inconsistency Scale (VRIN): A number of items have either similar or opposite content. The *VRIN* measures the tendency to answer these item pairs inconsistently and may reflect random or confused responding to the test.

True Response Inconsistency Scale (TRIN): The *TRIN* scale is based on answers to item pairs that are opposite in content. A very high score indicates a tendency to give "True" answers indiscriminately; a very low score indicates a tendency to give "False" answers indiscriminately.

TABLE 8.5   MMPI Clinical Scales

Scale 1 (Hs: Hypochondriasis): Measures the tendency to be preoccupied with one's health and to be unlikely to connect psychological problems to the experience of some physical symptoms.

Scale 2 (D: Depression): Measures common cognitive, physical, and interpersonal symptoms of depression.

Scale 3 (Hy: Hysteria): Measures the tendency to develop physical symptoms when stressed and to minimize the extent of interpersonal problems.

Scale 4 (Pd: Psychopathic Deviate): Measures the tendency toward rebellious attitudes, conflict with authorities and family, and engagement in antisocial activities.

Scale 5 (Mf: Masculinity–Femininity): Measures gender-stereotyped interests, beliefs, and activities.

Scale 6 (Pa: Paranoia): Measures interpersonal sensitivity, feelings of being mistreated, and, at the extreme, delusions of persecution.

Scale 7 (Pt: Psychasthenia): Measures the tendency toward worry, apprehension, rumination, and fears of loss of control.

Scale 8 (Sc: Schizophrenia): Measures the tendency to withdraw and experience social alienation, feel inferior, and, at the extreme, to experience delusions, hallucinations, and extreme disorganization.

Scale 9 (Ma: Hypomania): Measures the tendency toward hyperarousal, excessive energy, low frustration tolerance, and agitation.

Scale 0 (Si: Social Introversion): Measures introversion, lack of comfort in social contexts, and overcontrolled style of coping.

TABLE 8.6   MMPI Content Scales

Anxiety (ANX): A measure of general anxiety and worry.

Fears (FRS): A measure of the fear of specific objects, events, and situations.

Obsessiveness (OBS): A measure of indecisiveness and obsessiveness.

Depression (DEP): A measure of depressive symptoms.

Health Concerns (HEA): A measure of general health concerns.

Bizarre Mentation (BIZ): A measure of very peculiar or psychotic thought processes.

Anger (ANG): A measure of anger, aggression, and lack of control.

Cynicism (CYN): A measure of beliefs related to a general lack of trust in people and little faith in their intentions.

Antisocial Practices (ASP): A measure of antisocial attitudes and a history of engaging in antisocial acts such as stealing.

Type A Behavior (TPA): A measure of the Type A personality (i.e., characteristics of impatience, irritability, and being easily annoyed).

Low Self-Esteem (LSE): A measure of general self- esteem.

Social Discomfort (SOD): A measure of social introversion.

Family Problems (FAM): A measure of reported family conflict and the tendency to have characteristics that increase the likelihood of current interpersonal conflict.

Work Interference (WRK): A measure of work-related impairments.

Negative Treatment Indicators (TRT): A measure of negative attitudes toward health care professionals and mental health treatments.

---

researchers used a factor analytic strategy to develop scales that did not overlap and had items that were specific to the construct being assessed by the scale. To do this, they first identified a group of items from across the clinical scales that formed a general distress factor, which they labeled Demoralization. Then, by removing the variance due to this demoralization factor from each of the eight clinical scales, they were able to identify a set of unique items for each scale that best represented the underlying construct of the scale. For example, on the basis of such factor analyses, items were eliminated from scale 1 to yield the new restructured clinical scale they labeled Somatic Complaints. Although guidelines for scoring and interpreting the restructured clinical scales are available, there is vigorous scientific debate on the validity and utility of these new scales (e.g., Nichols, 2006; Rogers, Sewell, Harrison, & Jordan, 2006; Tellegen et al., 2006). At this point, it is unclear whether consideration of these scales is now commonplace among psychologists who use the MMPI.

A common complaint among trainees learning to use the MMPI is that there are many possible scales to score and consider. Aside from the challenge of learning what all the different scales are meant to assess, can you see any other difficulties stemming from this "embarrassment of riches?" In conducting research, psychologists make decisions about significance levels in order to (partially) protect themselves from the errors associated with conducting multiple analyses. Unfortunately, there really isn't a comparable strategy for determining how best to use the information coming from well over three dozen scales commonly used for MMPI interpretations.

Norms, Reliability, and Validity

The normative sample for the MMPI-2 consisted of more than 1,400 women and 1,100 men. Participants were randomly selected within a sampling frame that was generally representative of the American population in terms of ethnicity, socioeconomic status, and geographical location. The only limitation is a slight underrepresentation of adults with lower education and lower income. Consequently, for these individuals, the cut-off scores for determining the presence of clinical problems may be too low. This means that the test is likely to yield a high number of false positives (i.e., inaccurately identifying substantial clinical problems) in the evaluation of patients of lower socioeconomic levels (Nichols, 2001). Clinicians therefore need to be aware of the possible tendency to **overpathologize** (i.e., exaggerate and overestimate the extent of psychopathology) such patients. As for the MMPI-A, the normative sample consists of more than 800 female adolescents and 800 male adolescents who were representative of the American population of adolescents in terms of ethnicity and geographic location. Although there often have been efforts to establish new regional norms when the tests have been translated, there is surprisingly little research on the degree to which the original MMPI-2 and MMPI-A norms are appropriate for English-speaking populations outside the United States.

Research on the original clinical scales yielded a wide range of reliability values, with some values being well below an alpha of .80. The median reliability values for the MMPI-2, as reported in the test manual, are .64 for the validity scales and .62 for the clinical scales. The higher median value for the reliability of the content scales, .86, is consistent with the improved approach to test construction used with the content scales. Nevertheless, based on data from the normative sample, it is evident that a number of MMPI scales have relatively weak internal consistency. As for test-retest reliability, the data are much more encouraging, with the median values for the validity, clinical, and content scales all exceeding .80. As we mentioned in Chapter 7, attention to these rather dry details is critically important in determining the strengths and weaknesses of the MMPI.

With respect to validity, it is extremely difficult to meaningfully summarize the voluminous research on the various MMPI scales. Meta-analyses of these scales typically find support for the validity of many scales for a range of purposes and populations (e.g., Parker, Hanson, & Hunsley, 1988; Hiller, Rosenthal, Bornstein, Berry, & Brunell-Neuleib, 1999). However, there are so many scales and so many studies that it is necessary to consider cumulative validity data on a scale-by-scale basis. For example, Gross, Keyes, and Greene (2000) reviewed the research on the validity of relevant clinical (Scale 2) and content (DEP) scales in predicting depression and found evidence of comparable validity for both scales. Further complicating the task of understanding MMPI validity is that, as we describe next, much of the interpretation of a test score involves a consideration of scale profiles (i.e., validity scale score, the highest two clinical scale scores, and the overall pattern of scores) rather than simply individual scales. **Figure 8.1** is an example of the profile obtained with the main MMPI validity and clinical scales.

Administration, Scoring, and Interpretation Issues

Administering the MMPI-2 and MMPI-A is relatively straightforward. Nichols (2001) recommended that the assessor provide information on the overall purpose of the assessment and the nature of the MMPI. In

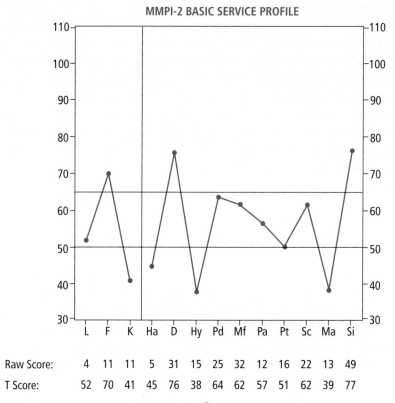

Raw Score: 4 11 11 5 31 15 25 32 12 16 22 13 49

T Score: 52 70 41 45 76 38 64 62 57 51 62 39 77

FIGURE 8.1 MMPI-2 Profile excerpted from the MMPI®-2 (Minnesota Multiphasic Personality Inventory®-2) Manual for Administration, Scoring, and Interpretation, Revised Edition. Copyright© 2001 by the Regents of the University of Minnesota. All rights reserved. Used by permission of the University of Minnesota Press. "MMPI-2" and "Minnesota Multiphasic Personality Inventory-2" are trademarks owned by the Regents of the University of Minnesota.

providing test instructions, the assessor encourages the test-taker to answer all the questions. Because the person must read the test, it is important to ensure that he or she has no visual impairment that interferes with test-taking (severely visually impaired patients typically use an audiotaped version of the test). The test requires reading comprehension at the grade 8 or 9 level. Most people complete the test in 1 to 2 hours, although some psychiatric patients may require up to 4 hours.

Several standardized and objective scoring options are available. One option is to have the patient respond to the test using a computer scanning sheet that allows for direct entry and computerized scoring. Alternatively, the completed test response form may be sent to test scoring services that provide interpretive reports based on the test-taker's response. A third option is computerized administration and scoring (which has the additional advantage of reducing the time usually required to complete the test). The final and most cumbersome option is to hand-score using templates available from the test publisher. Evaluators who use hand-scoring must check carefully to ensure they make no scoring errors.

The MMPI-2 and MMPI-A provide a wealth of information on the patient's self-presentation, symptoms, severity of distress, personality style, and social functioning (Nichols, 2001). Several options are available to clinical psychologists for interpreting the test data, including interpretation by a test scoring service, the use of MMPI interpretation software, and reference to one of several professional books on the topic (e.g., Greene, 2000; Nichols, 2001). In most instances, psychologists use a combination of these sources of interpretive information.

Interpretation begins with examination of the validity scales to determine the degree to which responses to the clinical and content scales might be affected by response biases. The next stage involves categorizing the test profile into **code types,** which are summary codes for the highest two clinical scale elevations. Interpretive guidelines provide details on the possible meaning of code types, other high clinical scale scores, high content scale scores, and high restructured clinical scale scores. Regardless of the source of the interpretative information, it is imperative that factors related to age, ethnicity, and life context be taken into account when drawing conclusions from test data. Both individual circumstances and generational factors influence the nature of the patient's response. For example, Newsom, Archer, Trumbetta, and Gottesman (2003) found that the MMPI responses of typical adolescents have become more extreme over the past few decades, reflecting shifts in attitudes and experiences rather than increased distress and psychopathology. All guidelines for test interpretation, whether text-based or computer-based, are derived from expert summaries of the research literature, which vary in terms of completeness and accuracy (Butcher, Perry, & Atlis, 2000). Hence, for all these reasons, a computer-generated test report should never be used without careful review and analysis by a clinical psychologist who is knowledgeable about the test's strengths and limitations and about the current status of MMPI research.

Other Clinical Measures of Personality Functioning

The Million Measures: MCMI-III and MACI

Personality and psychopathology researcher **Theodore Millon** has developed a set of personality inventories for use in a wide range of clinical settings. We will focus on two of these measures: the Millon Clinical Multiaxial Inventory-III (MCMI-III; Millon, 1997) and the Millon Adolescent Clinical Inventory (MACI; Millon, 1993). Both measures were developed from Millon's theory of psychopathology, are oriented toward DSM diagnostic categories, and contain scales to assess validity, clinical personality patterns, and clinical syndromes.

The MCMI-III is a 175-item, true-false self-report measure designed to assess personality styles and disorders (e.g., avoidant personality pattern, passive-aggressive personality pattern, borderline personality pathology) and major clinical syndromes (e.g., mood disorders, anxiety disorders, and substance dependency). It is intended for use with clients seeking mental health services and is not appropriate for use with adults with no psychological problems. Like the MMPI tests, the MCMI-III can be hand-scored or computer-scored. Computer interpretation software or text guidelines (e.g., Strack, 2002) can be used to interpret the test scores, including both the validity indices and the personality and syndrome scales. Normative data for the test are based on responses from almost 1,000 American and Canadian adults with psychiatric diagnoses. The normative sample underrepresents ethnic minorities but is otherwise representative in terms of demographic characteristics. A set of norms based on data from more than 1,600 inmates in correctional facilities is available for use in correctional settings. The internal consistency values based on the normative data are quite variable for the MCMI scales, with most values in the .70 to .90 range; 1- to 2-week test-retest values are typically higher than .80 (Millon, 1997). In developing and validating the third edition of the measure, Millon drew upon research on the previous two editions. This has led to substantial improvements, especially with respect to the psychometric properties of the personality disorder scales (Strack & Millon, 2007). Although research has generally supported the validity of the MCMI-III scales, two major concerns are often expressed about the test (e.g., Retzlaff & Dunn, 2003). First, there are concerns about the item overlap among scales (i.e., the same item may appear on more than one scale), which can artificially inflate correlations between scales. Second, due in part to item overlap, it is common for test-takers to have high scores on several scales and, thus, the MCMI-III has a tendency to overpathologize test-takers.

The MACI is a 175-item, self-report inventory designed to assess personality styles and disorders (e.g., inhibited personality pattern, dramatizing personality pattern, oppositional personality pattern), expressed concerns (e.g., body disapproval, peer insecurity, family discord), and major clinical syndromes (e.g., eating dysfunctions, anxious feeling, suicidal tendency). It is intended for use with adolescent clients age 13 to 19 years who are seeking mental health services. Scoring and interpretation options are similar to those described for the MCMI-III. Data from more than 1,000 American and Canadian adolescents were used to develop the test norms and provide supporting psychometric data. Separate norms are available for young adolescent girls, young adolescent boys, older adolescent girls, and older adolescent boys. Although the psychometric data published with the inventory are encouraging, there has been only limited subsequent research on the inventory (Strack, 2002). Additional research, especially studies conducted by investigators other than the test developer, is crucial for establishing the validity of the inventory. The limited research on the MACI also restricts the extent to which new information can be added to the knowledge base on which interpretation of the inventory is based.

Personality Assessment Inventory

Another broad-based personality inventory increasingly used by clinical psychologists is the Personality Assessment Inventory (PAI; Morey, 1991, 2007). The PAI is a 344-item, self-report measure designed for use with adults; a version with fewer items has been developed and normed for use with adolescents (Personality Assessment Inventory–Adolescent). Although the PAI has many items, it requires only a grade 4 reading level and can be completed in under an hour. The PAI contains 4 validity scales, 11 clinical scales (e.g., somatic complaints, antisocial features, borderline features), 2 interpersonal scales (dominance and warmth), and 5 treatment-oriented scales designed to yield provide information on respondent characteristics that might affect engagement in therapy or disrupt the process of therapy (e.g., aggression, stress, treatment rejection). It was developed using modern test construction principles with extensive attention to both content validity and discriminant validity.

The PAI norms are based on data from 1,000 adults who were representative of American census data in terms of age, gender, and ethnicity. The overall reliability of the scales is superior to the inventories described thus far. Based on data from the normative sample and samples of more than

1,000 patients and more than 1,000 university students, median internal consistency and test-retest values are above .80. There is an impressive body of research supporting the validity of many of the scales in this relatively new inventory. Research on use of the PAI in forensic, correctional, and rehabilitation services is growing dramatically. In 2007 a special issue of the *Journal of Personality* was devoted to PAI research developments (Blais & Kurtz, 2007). Like the other inventories we have presented, the PAI can be scored by hand or with computer software, and interpretations can be based on information in the manual, test interpretation guides (Morey, 2003), or via computer software. As with the MMPI tests, the interpretation process involves an examination of validity indices, two-point code types, and then individual scales.

Self-Report Measures of Normal Personality Functioning

The self-report inventories we have discussed so far are intended for use with adolescents and adults who are likely to have some impairment in their psychosocial functioning. Some measures, such as the MMPI-A, are intended to provide information to help determine the presence and nature of the distress or disorder, whereas others, such as the MACI, are only appropriate for use with individuals who have already been determined to have clinically relevant problems.

A host of inventories focused on normal personality assessment are available for use in clinical practice and research. We present two of the most commonly used measures below. These types of measures may be especially appropriate in assessing clients in vocational or counseling contexts, in which the goal of the assessment is to obtain data to help improve or optimize the client's adjustment, rather than to treat a mental disorder. For example, in dealing with a common event such as the ending of an intimate relationship, a person may seek psychological services as an aid to understanding what went wrong in the relationship and what could be done to enhance relationship functioning in the future. It may be advantageous in such a case for the psychologist to provide the client with research-based feedback on their personality as part of a discussion about personal preferences and styles that the client may wish to consider altering through treatment or through their own efforts. It is worth noting that, because of the focus on normal personality functioning, these types of inventories rarely include the types of validity scales that are common in the inventories we reviewed in the previous sections. It is assumed that respondents typically present an accurate picture of themselves, as there is little to be gained from presenting an overly positive or negative depiction of oneself in the situations in which these measures are commonly used.

The California Psychological Inventory (CPI; Gough & Bradley, 1996), now in its third edition, is a 434-item inventory with a similar structure to the MMPI. In fact, roughly one third of the CPI items also appear on the MMPI-2. Unlike the MMPI, though, the CPI largely focuses on interpersonal patterns and skills within the normal range of functioning and is composed of scales that measure constructs such as dominance, empathy, tolerance, and flexibility. The research base for the CPI is enormous, involving more than 2,000 studies (Groth-Marnat, 2003). The inventory's norms and psychometric values are all generally acceptable, and substantial information is available to assist clinicians in the use and interpretation of the CPI (e.g., Megargee, 2002).

The NEO Personality Inventory–Revised (NEO PI-R; Costa & McCrae, 1992) is based on the five-factor model of personality that is generally seen as the most scientifically supported personality theory

(Wiggins & Trapnell, 1997). This 240-item test measures the personality factors of neuroticism, extroversion, openness, agreeableness, and conscientiousness. Completion of this instrument requires sixth grade reading skills. The norms are based on data from more than 1,500 adults. Based on the normative data, the internal consistency values for the factors all exceed .85, as do the 6-month test-retest reliability values. Validity data reported in the test manual provide extensive evidence for the factor scores. The research literature on the NEO PI-R is voluminous. Because the factors assessed by the inventory tap the basic structure of personality, the evidence base for the inventory's validity continues to grow, with many studies on the NEO PI-R appearing each year. Because of its growing use in clinical contexts, researchers have developed and evaluated validity scales for the NEO PI-R. Although, to date, empirical studies on these scales have provided mixed results, there is some indication that they may be a useful addition to the scale (e.g., Morasco, Gfeller, & Elder, 2007). The widespread acceptance of the five-factor personality model has also given rise to other personality measures, including International Personality Item Pool Representation of the NEO PI-R (this can be found at http://www.personal.psu.edu/~j5j/IPIP/).

 A very brief measure of the five-factor model can be found at *http://users.wmin.ac.uk/~buchant/wwwffi/*. There is no charge to take the test and receive feedback on your scores on this personality measure.

SELF-REPORT CHECKLISTS OF BEHAVIORS AND SYMPTOMS

Despite the long history of emphasizing self-report personality inventories and (possibly) projective tests in clinical training, in their current assessment practices many clinical psychologists have made an important shift away from reliance on time-consuming broad-band tests (such as personality inventories and projective measures) toward a greater use of self-report checklists of behaviors and symptoms (Groth-Marnat, 1999; Mash & Hunsley, 2004). These changes are fueled by a number of factors, including changes in the reimbursement practices of insurance companies and health care organizations with respect to psychological assessments conducted as part of treatment provision (e.g., Stout & Cook, 1999) and clinicians' awareness of and demand for measures that aid in the formulation and evaluation of psychological services (Barkham et al., 2001; Bickman et al., 2000).

Current assessment practices of many clinicians reflect a shift to greater usage of self-report checklists of behaviors and symptoms. (*Source:* WinstonDavidian/iStockphoto)

As we discussed in the earlier section on clinical utility, there is currently little evidence that traditional psychological assessments actually improve clinical outcomes. In the absence of compelling evidence of clinical utility, psychologists must consider the value of the resulting test information in light of the expense of hours spent in administering, scoring, and interpreting self-report inventories and projective tests. It is important to also remember that, although often used for intervention-focused evaluation purposes, most of these instruments were not designed for this purpose. In contrast, behavior and symptom checklists are very inexpensive and have direct and immediate relevance to treatment planning and monitoring. For example, it may be very useful for a clinical psychologist to track week-by-week changes in a patient's bingeing and purging. Based on checklist data, the psychologist is able to determine the success of treatment strategies and, if necessary, to discuss changes in treatment with the patient if there is no symptomatic improvement after several sessions of therapy.

There are literally dozens of well-developed, psychometrically sound checklists; in the following pages we provide only a small sample of the types of measures available to clinical psychologists for both research and clinical purposes. As you will see, some of these checklists cover a range of behaviors and symptoms, whereas others are problem specific or disorder specific.

Achenbach System of Empirically Based Assessment

As we described briefly in Chapter 3, the Achenbach System of Empirically Based Assessment (ASEBA; Achenbach & Rescorla, 2000, 2001, 2003; Achenbach, Newhouse & Rescorla, 2004) is a family of questionnaires developed over many years by **Thomas Achenbach.** The original scale, the Child Behavior Checklist (CBCL), is a standardized questionnaire completed by a child's parents that includes competence items as well as diverse problems. For each item the respondent is required to note whether it does not apply, applies occasionally, or applies frequently (Achenbach & Rescorla, 2001). The CBCL is one of the most widely used measures of child adjustment and has been demonstrated to be reliable and valid over hundreds of studies. Versions are available to be completed by parents of children age 1.5–5 years and 6–18 years as well as by caregivers and teachers. The Youth Self-Report is a version of the CBCL that is completed by young people age 11–18 years. Norms based on large national American samples are available for all the child and youth ASEBA measures. The ASEBA scales yield scores in the normal, clinical, or borderline range. Scales yield a total problem score, as well as scores for two broad-band types of problems: internalizing problems and externalizing problems. Internalizing problems relate to distressed feelings, social withdrawal, worry, and sadness. Externalizing problems refer to acting-out and aggressive behaviors. In addition, scores are generated for a number of DSM-oriented scales. Most recently, the ASEBA has expanded to include measures and norms for adults (18 to 59 years; Achenbach & Rescorla, 2003) and older adults (60 to 90 years; Achenbach et al., 2004); these measures are the Adult Self-Report, Adult Behavior Checklist, Older Adult Self-Report, and Older Adult Behavior Checklist.

Computerized scoring of the ASEBA scales also provides an analysis of the degree of agreement between two raters (e.g., mother and youth), as well as a comparison of their degree of agreement about a problem with that of a normative group. This is a particularly useful feature of the ASEBA, as it is common to have parallel versions of the test completed by different informants. Using a wide range of measures, researchers have consistently found rather modest correlations among different raters rating the same individual. For example, pairs of parents rating their children have a mean correlation of .60, and correlations between youth self-ratings and parent ratings of the youth are typically not much more than .20 (e.g., Achenbach, McConaughy, & Howell, 1987). Likewise, correlations between adults' ratings of themselves and ratings of them by those who know them well are lower than you might think. For example, mean correlations for measures of substance use can be as high as .68, but mean correlation values for ratings of internalizing (.43) and externalizing problems (.44) are substantially lower (Achenbach, Krukowski, Dumenci, & Ivanova, 2005). With the ASEBA, data from different raters can be correlated and compared to normative data on what is a typical degree of concordance between raters. Thus, it is possible to determine whether there is an average level of correspondence between the ratings or whether the ratings are much more (or much less) similar than is usually found. This information aids the clinician in interpreting and integrating the information provided by all informants.

SCL-90-R

The Symptom Checklist-90-Revised (SCL-90-R; Derogatis, 1994) is probably the most widely used general measure of distress in clinical service delivery settings. It is a 90-item measure with nine subscales that cover a range of symptom dimensions, including interpersonal sensitivity, phobic anxiety, and hostility. Respondents are asked to indicate the extent to which they have been distressed by various symptoms over the past two weeks. Norms—although not nationally representative—are available for various groups, including nonpatient adults, nonpatient adolescents, psychiatric in-patients, and psychiatric outpatients. The internal consistency and test-retest reliability values (over 1 week) based on data from these normative groups all exceed .75. The SCL-90-R has been used in hundreds of research studies. Although both the individual subscales and the global indices of distress available for the test have been demonstrated to be sensitive to treatment-related changes, there is considerable evidence that most subscales do not adequately measure the constructs they are designed to assess. Moreover, a commonly voiced concern among clinicians is that the scale tends to overpathologize. Finally, there is substantial intercorrelation among the subscales and little evidence for the divergent validity of the subscales (Groth-Marnat, 2003). As a result, the SCL90-R is probably best conceptualized as a brief measure of general psychological distress.

Outcome Questionnaire 45

The 45-item Outcome Questionnaire (OQ-45; Lambert et al., 1996) is an increasingly popular measure for research and clinical purposes. The OQ-45 is composed of three subscales: symptom distress, interpersonal relations, and social role functioning. Taken together, these subscales provide a good overview of a client's psychosocial functioning that takes only 5 minutes or so to complete. Because of high interscale correlation, it is probably most appropriate that the total score be used as an indicator of client distress. Although a relatively new measure, there is growing evidence that it is psychometrically strong across a range of populations (e.g., Umphress, Lambert, Smart, Barlow, & Clouse, 1997; Vermeersch, Lambert, & Burlingame, 2000). Designed for measuring therapeutic change, there is substantial evidence that the OQ-45 can accurately assess client progress. Even more important, meta-analytic results from more than 2,500 clients indicated that the use of the OQ-45 in monitoring treatment progress can both dramatically improve treatment success rates and reduce the rates of deterioration associated with treatment (Lambert et al., 2003). Data such as these have played a major role in the widespread adoption of the OQ-45 by clinical psychologists. **Figure 8.2** is an example of a computer-generated OQ-45 report. A version of the measure is also available for use with children and

Name:	An, Adult, 2	ID:	24059
Session Date:	4/20/2005	Session:	4
Clinician:	Clinician, Randy	Clinic:	South Clinic
Diagnosis:	Depression		
Algorithm:	Empirical		

Alert Status:	**Yellow**
Most Recent Score:	100
Initial Score:	91
Change From Initial:	No Reliable Change
Current Distress Level:	Moderately High

Most Recent Critical Item Status:

8. **Suicide** - I have thoughts of ending my life. — **Frequently**
11. **Substance Abuse** - After heavy drinking, I need a drink the next morning to get going. — **Sometimes**
26. **Substance Abuse** - I feel annoyed by people who criticize my drinking. — **Frequently**
32. **Substance Abuse** - I have trouble at work/school because of drinking or drug use. — **Frequently**
44. **Work Violence** - I feel angry enough at work/school to do something I might regret. — **Rarely**

Subscales	Current	Outpat. Norm	Comm. Norm
Symptom Distress:	56	49	25
Interpersonal Relations:	27	20	10
Social Role:	17	14	10
Total:	**100**	**83**	**45**

Total Score by Session Number

Graph Label Legend:
(R) = **Red**: High chance of negative outcome   (Y) = **Yellow**: Some chance of negative outcome
(G) = **Green**: Making expected progress   (W) = **White**: Functioning in normal range

FIGURE 8.2 OQ-45 Sample Report
Reproduced from www.OQMeasures.com with permission from OQ Measures.

adolescents (Burlingame et al., 2001). Taken together, these measures hold great promise for enhancing the impact of psychotherapeutic services offered to the public.

Beck Depression Inventory-II

The Beck Depression Inventory-II (BDI-II; Beck, Steer, & Brown, 1996) is a 21-item checklist with a multiple-choice format (i.e., several response options are available to describe each symptom). It is designed to evaluate the severity of depressive symptoms experienced in the past 2 weeks. Based on normative data, cut-offs are provided to classify the symptoms as minimal, mild, moderate, or severe. Although the BDI-II more closely maps onto DSM criteria than did the original BDI, it does not provide sufficient detail to determine whether a person meets diagnostic depression for a mood disorder. As the

The BDI-II has been identified as a reliable and valid symptom checklist for use with university students. (*Source:* Digital Vision)

BDI-II is one of the most frequently used symptom checklists in clinical research, there are studies of its reliability and validity in numerous populations, including psychiatric inpatients, patients with chronic pain, and university students. Although the precise factor structure and validity of the BDI-II varies somewhat across these groups, there is compelling evidence that the measure is a psychometrically strong tool for assessing depressive symptoms in adolescents and adults. It appears, though, that scores can drop appreciably simply due to repeated administration of the test (e.g., Longwell & Truax, 2005). Such findings cause concern, as they indicate that the BDI-II may yield imprecise results when used for treatment monitoring purposes.

Children's Depression Inventory

Similar in content and structure to the BDI-II, the Children's Depression Inventory (CDI; Kovacs, 1992) is a self-report checklist designed to evaluate recent (in the past 1 or 2 weeks) symptoms of depression in children. It has been shown to have good reliability and validity, especially in community samples (Sitarenios & Kovacs, 1999). The research evidence suggests that the CDI does not distinguish between heightened levels of depressive and anxious symptoms, but no depression checklist is particularly good at making this distinction. A meta-analysis revealed no socioeconomic status effects in CDI responses, although there may be effects due to ethnicity (Twenge & Nolen-Hoeksema, 2002). Unfortunately, consistent with data from the BDI, there is evidence that repeated testing with the CDI can result in substantial decreases in reported symptoms (Twenge & Nolen-Hoeksema, 2002).

Profile Box 8.1 introduces Dr. Wendy Silverman who is an expert on assessment and treatment of anxiety in children.

PROFILE BOX 8.1

DR. WENDY SILVERMAN

I received my Ph.D. in clinical psychology at Case Western Reserve University in Cleveland, Ohio, after completing my clinical psychology internship at the University of Mississippi Medical Center in Jackson. Following positions at Stony Brook, State University of New York and Albany, State University of New York, I moved to Florida International University (FIU) in Miami, where I am currently a Professor of Psychology. My research program has been funded for the past 20 years by the National Institute of Mental Health (NIMH) and focuses on developing and evaluating evidence-based assessment and treatment procedures for use with children and adolescents who suffer from debilitating anxiety disorders. In addition to conducting research, teaching, and mentoring students, I have held a number of professional positions, including Editor of *Journal of Clinical Child and Adolescent Psychology*, Associate Editor of *Journal of Consulting and Clinical Psychology*, President of the Society of *Clinical Child and Adolescent Psychology*, and Chair of the NIMH grant review panel for Child and Adolescent Psychosocial and Psychopharmacological Intervention Research.

Dr. Wendy Silverman

How did you choose to become a clinical psychologist?

In retrospect, I can now point to some personal, though indirect experience, with mental illness in my family, especially with the adverse consequences of ineffective psychotherapy. Upon entering college, I immediately declared myself a Psychology major in college, became involved in undergraduate independent psychology research experiences with several professors, and quickly got hooked on the idea that scientific principles can be applied to alleviate the problems of children and adults who suffer from psychological difficulties.

What is the most rewarding part of your job as a clinical psychologist?

What has been most rewarding is knowing that through my research activities, I am contributing to knowledge (which is read by students like you in your textbooks!) and that this knowledge, in turn, serves to help children and families. Equally rewarding for me has been my training of the next generation of psychologists through my mentoring of undergraduate and graduate students.

What is the greatest challenge you face as a clinical psychologist?

There continue to be unacceptably high rates of psychological disturbance in young people. It continues to break my heart when I hear about children who have not received any treatment for their psychological disturbances for a variety of economic and social reasons. Just as sad, from my perspective, is when I hear about children who have received ineffective treatments so that no improvement occurs or they were worse off than before.

Tell us about your research on assessing anxiety in youth

That children and adolescents suffer from different types of anxiety disorders (e.g., social phobia, obsessive compulsive disorder) became formally recognized by the field only when the DSM-III was published in 1980. However, there existed no formal or systematic procedures to assess and diagnose the different anxiety disorders that children are likely to present with. This was a problem for a number of reasons. First, it is very common for children to present with multiple (or comorbid) disorders. Second, there is much overlap between the symptoms that comprise the various anxiety disorders, as well as other psychological disorders, such as attention deficit hyperactivity disorders and depression.

Third, there is evidence that when clinicians assess and diagnose psychological disorders in children and adolescents by asking questions through unstructured clinical interview procedures, the clinicians make errors. This is because it is difficult for clinicians to recall and ask about all the details and nuances involved in making a differential diagnosis. All of this led me to develop and evaluate the Anxiety Disorders Interview Schedule for Children (ADIS-C). The ADIS-C is a semistructured interview that allows clinicians and researchers to ask in separate interviews with the child and parent all about the different types of anxiety disorders, as well as other psychological disorders, that the child may have. By using a more structured information-gathering procedure, the likelihood is higher that correct diagnoses are made, thereby improving the likelihood that young people receive appropriate treatment. The ADIS-C for DSM-IV has now become the "gold standard" in the field.

How do you integrate science and practice in your work?

Because I run a child anxiety research clinic, there is no distinction whatsoever between science and practice in my work. All children and families who receive psychological services at my clinic are serving as participants in research projects, while at the same time receiving "state of the science" assessment and treatment procedures, including the ADIS-C for DSM-IV.

What do you see as the most exciting changes in the field of clinical psychology?

What I see as most exciting are the advances in understanding not only which psychological treatments work for given child and adolescent disorders, but also advances in understanding *why* these treatments work and for whom.

PROJECTIVE MEASURES OF PERSONALITY

A variety of personality instruments used by clinical psychologists fall under the general category of projective measures. What these instruments have in common, and what makes them projective measures, is that the items or stimuli are ambiguous with respect to content and meaning. That is, regardless of whether the measure relies on pictures, colors, incomplete sentences, drawings, or puppets, there is no inherent meaning to the stimulus material, just as there are no obvious right and wrong answers. A core assumption is that the ambiguity of the material requires the individual to make sense of the stimulus and, in the process of doing this, aspects of the individual's personality are revealed. The original concept of projection was developed by Freud and was seen as a type of defense mechanism in which people unconsciously attribute to others undesirable or negative parts of themselves. There is little evidence to support the existence of projection and little doubt that the process involved in responding to projective tests doesn't rely on projection per se—rather, the process involves responses being influenced by a person's experiences and personality (Lilienfeld, Wood, & Garb, 2000).

There is some similarity between the methods used with projective measures and some of the techniques now used in cognitive sciences to examine unconscious mental processes (Westen, Feit, & Zittel, 1999). What is lacking, though, in the clinical use of projective measures is the standardization and rigorous attention to scientific principles that are the hallmarks of cognitive science techniques. As we noted in Chapter 1, projective tests such as the Rorschach inkblot test, the Thematic Apperception Test, and projective drawings were not developed in a manner consistent with psychological test construction guidelines. Consequently, most projective tests used in clinical settings do not have standardized administration, scoring, or interpretation guidelines, and only the Rorschach has normative data (Hunsley, Lee, & Wood, 2003).

Projective measures can be subdivided into five broad, but overlapping, categories (Lilienfeld et al., 2000). In the following sections we will present two examples from measures involving association techniques (i.e., those requiring people to report what a stimulus looks like) and construction techniques (i.e., those requiring the individual to produce a story or a drawing). Other categories of projective measures are completion techniques (e.g., sentence completion tasks), arrangement/selection techniques (e.g., color tests that require the rank-ordering of preferred colors), and expression techniques (e.g., handwriting analysis). There is no denying the intuitive appeal of many of these techniques. For some clinical psychologists with a psychodynamic orientation, projective measures hold a special appeal because they are assumed to provide information on unconscious processes. However, after many decades of research, there is no other assessment topic in clinical psychology as controversial as the use of projective techniques. Although some clinical psychologists are likely to view these tests as indispensable clinical tools, many others view them as invalid and potentially damaging measures.

Rorschach Inkblot Test

The Rorschach inkblots, developed by Swiss psychiatrist Hermann Rorschach, consist of 10 cards, each containing symmetrical inkblots, some colored and some in black and white. Patients are asked to report what they see in these ambiguous stimuli. For much of the 20th century, several distinct approaches to the administration and scoring of the Rorschach existed, and many clinicians tended to use elements of different systems and to "personalize" the scoring and interpretation of the Rorschach based on their own experiences. However, **John Exner**'s Comprehensive System (CS; Exner, 1993) is now considered the principal scoring system for the Rorschach. The Rorschach is a very complex measure to administer, score, and interpret. The CS offers very clear information on administration and scoring, with extensive tables and computer software available to aid the interpretation of the test results. Directions specify the seating arrangements, the instructions to be given to examinees, the sequence of card administration, as well as permissible responses to examinee's questions. Unfortunately, research indicates that even if these standards are followed, relatively innocuous contextual factors

An inkblot pattern similar to those used in the Rorschach test. (*Source:* Stefan Klein/iStockphoto)

in Rorschach administration, such as the layout of the testing room and the appearance of the assessor, affect the responses produced by examinees (Masling, 1992).

After developing the CS, Exner published norms for different age groups that have become a cornerstone of the system's scientific basis (e.g., Exner, 1993). For the adult norms, convenience sampling strategies were used to obtain Rorschach protocols from approximately 1,300 volunteers over a 20-year period. From this pool, 700 protocols were selected in an attempt to match key demographic variables reported in the 1980 U.S. census. Although members of some minority groups were included in this selected sample, this is not sufficient to ensure that the norms are relevant for the clinical use of the Rorschach with members of minority groups (Gray-Little & Kaplan, 1998).

A major problem for the CS norms is the likelihood that nonpatient norms overpathologize normal individuals—a phenomenon found for both child and adult samples (Wood, Nezworski, Garb, & Lilienfeld, 2001). The extent of this problem is vividly apparent in Hamel, Shaffer, and Erdberg's (2000) study involving data from 100 children who were selected for the absence of psycho-pathology and behavior problems based on historical information and assessment of current function-ing. When the Rorschach data from these children were scored and interpreted according to CS norms, a considerable number of children scored in the clinical range on Rorschach indices of psychopathology. As the authors wrote (p. 291): "(T)hese children may be described as grossly misperceiving and misinterpreting their surroundings and having unconventional ideation and significant cognitive impairment. Their distortion of reality and faulty reasoning approach psychosis. These children would also be described as having significant problems establishing and maintaining interpersonal relation-ships and coping within a social context." According to the interpretation of their responses to the Rorschach inkblots, these children sound very troubled, but remember—none of these children had had psychological problems in the past, none were currently experiencing psychological distress, and all were doing very well in school and in social activities.

Because of the concerns about the quality of the CS norms, considerable efforts have been devoted to developing norms that meet the standards expected of psychological tests. To that end, a series of norms (called the International Reference Samples) have been published for the CS that draw on data from more than 5,800 people from 16 countries (Shaffer, Erdberg, & Meyer, 2007). Taken together, these norms are now recommended for scoring and interpreting adults' responses to the Rorschach (Meyer, Erdberg, & Shaffer, 2007). However, major problems arose in trying to develop norms for data from youth, because substantial and erratic differences in CS scores occurred both within and across samples from the various countries. As a result, the primary researchers behind this international norming effort recommended against using available norms for Rorschach responses from children and adolescents (Meyer et al., 2007)—in other words, the Rorschach should not be used as a psychological test with youth. This scientifically sound position stands in direct contrast with frequent claims that using the Rorschach with youth is consistent with ethical and professional standards for psychological test usage (Hughes, Gacono, & Owen, 2007).

Moving now to issues of scoring reliability, Acklin, McDowell, Verschell, and Chan (2000) reported interrater reliability values for most CS scores, for both normal and clinical samples. The median reliability value was slightly above .80, thus indicating (as with some of the self-report personality inventories described previously) that many, but not all scores meet the level commonly seen as indicative of good reliability. Of concern, Guarnaccia, Dill, Sabatino, and Southwick (2001) found that both graduate students and practicing psychologists made numerous errors in scoring

Rorschach data. These errors were so extensive that the overall mean accuracy in scoring the major components of the CS was only 65%! As you will recall from Chapter 7, scoring errors on intelligence tests can also greatly affect the accuracy of the results obtained with these tests.

The literature on the validity of the Rorschach, in general, and the CS, in particular, is so large that it is impossible to review it within a few paragraphs. There have been very heated debates over the past 50 years about the quality of Rorschach research and its adequacy for supporting the widespread clinical use of the test. A number of clinical psychology journals, such as *Psychological Assessment* (Meyer, 1999, 2001), have published special sections on this topic. Some general conclusions can be drawn, however, about the scientific status of the Rorschach. For example, global meta-analyses of Rorschach validity (Parker et al., 1988; Hiller et al., 1999) have demonstrated that some Rorschach scales have reasonable validity, although typically lower than that found for MMPI scales. There is consensus that the Rorschach should not be used to provide diagnostic information. Wood, Lilienfeld, Garb, and Nezworski (2000) reviewed more than 150 studies on the use of the Rorschach and diagnoses of mental disorders and found almost no evidence that the Rorschach could consistently detect major depressive disorder, posttraumatic stress disorder, antisocial personality disorder, or many other psychiatric diagnoses. On the other hand, even the harshest critics of the Rorschach agree that the test can provide valid information about intelligence and thought disorder, although evidence of validity does not suggest that the Rorschach is necessarily the best method to assess these constructs (Wood, Nezworski, & Garb, 2003).

The Rorschach is likely to have some continuing value in research examining personality structure and correlates. However, as we have emphasized throughout the text, clinical psychologists have a responsibility to evaluate their assessment and treatment services in light of professional standards and scientific evidence. As we discuss in the next chapter, even when used with other measures, the Rorschach is likely to overpathologize patients. The evidence of both substantial problems with scoring accuracy and the significant limitations of the youth norms suggest that the Rorschach simply has too many shortcomings to be clinically useful.

VIEWPOINT BOX 8.2

WHY DO QUESTIONABLE PSYCHOLOGICAL TESTS REMAIN POPULAR WITH SOME CLINICAL PSYCHOLOGISTS?

As we described in Chapter 5, for decades projective tests have been among the assessment tools most commonly used by clinical psychologists and most commonly taught in graduate programs. Clearly, a large number of professionals believe that these tests are valuable in assessing patients' psychosocial functioning. Yet, as we have presented in this chapter, the research support for these tests is, at best, mixed, and often nonexistent. So the question that inevitably arises is: why have these tests remained relatively popular among clinicians?

In addressing this question, Lilienfeld, Wood, and Garb (2006) have drawn upon a number of sources, including research on decision-making processes, in suggesting that five main factors are responsible for the continuing use of projectives (and other tests with weak or nonexistent research support). The first factor is that of clinical tradition: many psychologists have been trained to use these measures and, not surprisingly, they continue to use them when they graduate from doctoral programs. Of course, if a program provides training in projective testing, it is highly likely that the scientific weaknesses of these tools are ignored, downplayed, or explained away as irrelevant to "real" clinical practice. Thus, many psychologists who use these instruments may not be fully aware of just how problematic these tests are.

Lilienfeld and colleagues suggested that two forms of decision-making errors, illusory correlation and the P. T. Barnum effect, also play a role in the continued use of projective tests. Illusory correlation is a phenomenon that involves the belief that there is a stronger statistical association between variables than there actually is. For example, patients whose projective drawings of human figures included overly large eyes have often been considered as being highly suspicious, even though there is almost no research evidence to support such an association. Of course, the proper way for a psychologist to consider the validity of a hypothesis of covariation between two variables is to search the research literature to evaluate the accuracy of the hypothesis. The P. T. Barnum effect, named after the 19th century circus entrepreneur, is a phenomenon in which an individual finds something of personal relevance in a generic statement that could apply to almost anyone. For example, the statement "There are times when you find it difficult to make certain decisions" probably applies to almost everyone. As Lilienfeld et al. reported, research has found that a person is much more likely to rate such statements as a more accurate reflection of his or her personality if the person was tested with the Rorschach rather than a self-report measure or an interview. In the context of clinical work, this suggests that patients may reinforce the clinician's belief that information of particularly high value is only available from projective tests.

Overperception of psychopathology is an issue that we have discussed repeatedly in this chapter and is the fourth factor viewed as contributing to the popularity of projectives. As clinical psychologists, most of our work is with people who have considerable problems. Therefore, in most assessment tasks, we go into the evaluation process expecting to find problems. If the Rorschach, for example, tends to classify too many people as having psychological problems, this may appear to be "evidence" consistent with clinicians' typical expectations. Rather than cause them to question the accuracy of the Rorschach, these results are much more likely to reinforce the clinicians' belief in the value of the Rorschach.

The final factor that Lilienfeld et al. proposed as contributing to the popularity of projectives is something they called the alchemist's fantasy. As you probably know, alchemy was based on the belief that, with the right processes and ingredients, base metals could be transmuted into gold. Well, according to Lilienfeld and colleagues, those who use projectives have a comparable belief—namely, that, despite the lack of research evidence for the validity of projectives, there is something special that clinicians can do to take projective data and turn it into clinical "gold." Indeed, one can find many examples in the literature on projective tests in which authors claim special clinical "powers" to discern patterns in projective data that sophisticated research designs and methods have been unable to detect.

Thematic Apperception Test

The Thematic Apperception Test (TAT; Murray, 1943) is a projective measure composed of 31 cards. The person being assessed is asked to tell stories about pictures printed on cards. The principle underlying the TAT is that, in creating these stories, the dominant needs, emotions, and conflicts of the person's personality are revealed. Moreover, it is assumed that at least some aspects of personality cannot be assessed by self-report, because they may not be consciously accessible to the person being assessed. Although the TAT was the first apperceptive measure developed, there are a number of other such measures, including some designed for use with children, the elderly, and minority groups (Bellak & Abrams, 1997; Costantino, Malgady, Rogler, & Tsui, 1988).

There is little survey information available on the extent to which practitioners follow or modify the original instructions developed by Murray for the TAT. What is clear, though, is that there is little consistency across clinicians and researchers in terms of how many cards are used in an assessment, which cards are used, the order in which the cards are presented, the instructions used in administering the test, and the scoring and interpretive principles used with the test (Groth-Marnat, 2003; Keiser & Prather, 1990). Unlike the Rorschach, there is no single dominant scoring system for the TAT and no norms are available for the measure. Even ardent proponents of the TAT admit that most clinicians using the TAT have abandoned a scientific approach to its use (Rossini & Moretti, 1997). Given this, any psychometric data on the measure available in the research literature are irrelevant to determining its actual reliability and validity as it is used by clinical psychologists. The current clinical status of the TAT is, therefore, that it is best characterized as a measure taught and used in a manner that ignores scientific and professional standards (Hunsley et al., 2003).

The neglect of science in the routine clinical use of the TAT is very unfortunate. Most importantly, for those assessed with the TAT, there is absolutely no evidence to support the validity of the conclusions drawn by the psychologist. Nevertheless, there is substantial research to suggest that standardized apperceptive methods have the potential to provide valid personality information. For example, using selected TAT cards and adding other specially developed picture stimuli, McClelland and colleagues conducted a programmatic series of studies on achievement, power, and affiliative needs. This pioneering research has been continued by a number of researchers (e.g., Langan-Fox & Grant, 2006). The results of this research provided compelling evidence that, by using a standard set of cards and empirically supported scoring criteria, data from the modified TAT often outperformed self-report measures in predicting subsequent behavior (McClelland, Koestner, & Weinberger, 1989; Spangler, 1992). Similarly Westen (1991) developed a psychodynamically oriented scoring system for TAT responses that focuses on the assessment of interpersonal relations (e.g., the complexity of representations of people, the capacity for emotional investment in relationships, and the understanding of causal factors in social relations). Using a detailed scoring manual and data from five to seven TAT cards, high interrater reliability has been obtained in several studies for this system, and data from both nonpatient and patient samples have provided evidence of convergent validity with a range of self-report, interview, and other projective measures (Westen, 1991). Such findings with a carefully designed and validated scoring system stand in stark contrast to the repeated negative finding in the literature that many approaches to scoring the TAT are incapable of differentiating between research participants with mental disorders and those with no mental disorders (Lilienfeld et al., 2000). Although potentially useful systems are used in research contexts, they have not been adopted in clinical practice.

SUMMARY AND CONCLUSIONS

The self-report and projective measures described in this chapter represent some of the key measures within the clinical psychologist's kit of assessment tools. In graduate training, psychologists learn how to administer, score, and interpret various instruments that are used in the objective assessment of personality and in projective assessment. Although the scoring of objective assessment measures is more standardized and straightforward than the scoring of projective measures, it is not immune from administrative errors that can distort scores. In the interpretation of both objective and projective personality assessment measures, clinical psychologists are faced with a complex array of interpretation methods that vary in their degree of empirical support. Unfortunately, important advances in research on personality have not been reflected in comparable advances in the clinical assessment of personality. There has been an important shift in measure validation in the recognition of the need to determine the suitability of measures developed in one population for use with another population. In addition to issues of standardization, reliability, validity, and norms, we must add the criterion that a test must be shown to be reliable and valid for the population in which it will be used. Without attention to these issues, there is a danger that psychological tests will overpathologize those who take the tests and, thus, have iatrogenic effects. Another fundamental question about the value of psychological tests relates to the clinical utility of these assessment tools. Although limited utility data are available, there is growing recognition of the usefulness of cost-effective, brief measures that allow tracking of symptoms in treatment planning and monitoring.

Critical Thinking Questions

What are the main differences between objective personality tests and symptom checklists?

How do some tests overpathologize test-takers, and why is that a problem?

How can we ensure that tests are culturally sensitive and appropriate?

What criteria can we use to judge whether a test is useful?

What are the shortcomings of current practice in projective assessment?

Key Terms

behavior checklists: list of behaviors that are rated for frequency, intensity, or duration

clinical utility: extent to which a test and the resulting data improve upon typical clinical decision-making and treatment outcome

code types: summary codes for the highest two clinical scale elevations on the MMPI scales

content approach: method of test construction that involves developing items specifically designed to tap the construct being assessed

empirical criterion-keying approach: method of test construction that involves the generation and analysis of a pool of items; those items that discriminate between two clearly defined groups are retained in the scale

malingering: emphasizing negative characteristics and deliberately presenting a more problematic picture

objective personality tests: tests that can be scored objectively, always using the same scoring system

overpathologize: exaggerate and overestimate the extent of pathology

personality traits: consistency in behavior across situations and across time

projective personality tests: tests requiring drawings or a response to ambiguous stimuli, based on the assumption that responses reveal information about personality structure

validity scales: scales designed to detect whether a person is "faking good," "faking bad," or responding randomly

Key Names

Thomas Achenbach

James Butcher

John Exner

Starke Hathaway

J. Charnley McKinley

Theodore Millon

Walter Mischel

ADDITIONAL RESOURCES

BOOKS

Weiner, I. B., & Greene, R. L. (2008). *Handbook of personality assessment.* New York: John Wiley & Sons.

Wood, J. M., Nezworski, M. T., Lilienfeld, S. O., & Garb, H. N. (2003). *What's wrong with the Rorschach? Science confronts the controversial inkblot test.* New York: John Wiley & Sons.

JOURNALS

Assessment

Journal of Personality Assessment

Journal of Psychopathology and Behavioral Assessment

Psychological Assessment

Check It Out!

MMPI-A, the publisher's site:
http://www.pearsonassessments.com/tests/mmpia.htm

MCMI-II, the publisher's site:
http://www.pearsonassessments.com/tests/mcmi_3.htm

MACI, the publisher's site:
http://www.pearsonassessments.com/tests/maci.htm

PAI, the publisher's site:
http://www.parinc.com/product.cfm?ProductID¼148

ASEBA, the publisher's site:
http://www.aseba.org/

CHAPTER 9

Assessment: Integration and Clinical Decision Making

All assessments are conducted to address a question. The psychologist refers to the question that prompted the assessment as a framework to guide the process of drawing together the various pieces of information available about the client. A question about a client's intellectual capabilities leads to the preparation of a report that highlights general intellectual functioning and more specific cognitive strengths and weaknesses. Emotional and interpersonal factors that affect the client's ability to achieve his or her potential also receive attention in such an assessment, but they are secondary to a clear presentation of the client's intellectual skills. On the other hand, an assessment report summarizing data relevant to the question of whether a depressed teacher is able to return to work would have a very different focus and structure. Symptom and diagnostic information would have to be discussed first. After that, the psychologist would address the factors that led to the teacher's burnout, the teacher's motivation and readiness to return to work, and possible impediments (both psychological and interpersonal) that could affect the return to work. Cognitive correlates of the depression, such as difficulty in decision making and planning that would affect her teaching abilities, would be addressed as secondary to the emotional issues.

In Chapter 5 we described some of the general issues in psychological testing and assessment. Psychological assessment involves gathering and integrating multiple forms of information from multiple sources and perspectives. Based on the purposes of the assessment and the initial hypotheses to be explored, the clinical psychologist selects the most appropriate assessment methods and tools to conduct the assessment. As the psychologist gains a better understanding of the person (or couple or family) being assessed, additional assessment procedures may be used to narrow or expand the focus of the assessment.

In Chapters 6, 7, and 8 we presented information on the most commonly used assessment methods and tools: interviews, observations, intellectual assessment measures, cognitive assessment measures, self-report measures, and projective measures. Now we turn our attention to the final phases of the assessment process—namely, the integration of the diverse data collected about the client and the clinical use of the completed assessment.

As we described in Chapter 5, the clinical psychologist must examine all the assessment information, consider both consistencies and contradictions in the information, generate final hypotheses about the client, and formulate conclusions or clinical recommendations about the client based on the overall picture emerging from the assessment. These tasks are necessary whether the psychologist is providing an assessment-focused service or an intervention-focused assessment service. In this chapter we consider the process by which psychologists integrate assessment data and the product of this integration. To do this, we will examine research on the process of case formulation, threats to the validity of psychological assessments, and the use of assessment reports and feedback about the assessment findings. Because much of the focus of the chapter is on integrating data and addressing factors that can affect the assessment's accuracy, we will use an extended example, the case of Teresa whom we introduced in Chapter 3, to illustrate how clinical psychologists work to achieve an assessment that is comprehensive, accurate, and clinically useful. Our goals are to convey to you both the challenges in integrating assessment data and the potential value for clients of an integrated psychological assessment.

You have probably heard of postpartum depression, a form of depression that can develop due to the many psychosocial and physical changes related to pregnancy, birth, and caring for a newborn. Researchers and clinicians have begun to pay increasing attention to anxiety disorders that develop or become more severe around the postpartum period. As illustrated by the case of Teresa, these anxiety problems can become very debilitating.

---

 case example **TERESA**

In Chapter 3 we described some of the problems that Teresa was experiencing; in this chapter we present the results of the evaluation of Teresa's problems. A new mother who had recently left her nursing career, Teresa reported a number of complaints related to worries about inadvertently injuring other people. These worries began in her work life after hearing media reports about errors in dispensing medication that had led to numerous deaths in hospitals in North America. She became increasingly preoccupied with the possibility of making such an error and spent excessive amounts of time checking and rechecking all of her work. Not surprisingly, this led to her becoming very inefficient at work and, consequently, receiving a poor annual evaluation from her supervisor. Teresa tried to follow through on the supervisor's recommendations to work faster, but this led her to become even more concerned about the likelihood of making critical errors. Her anxiety mounted, she became irritable with patients and colleagues, and she no longer looked forward to her workday. During her time away from work, she became increasingly agitated and anticipated a call from work telling her that one of the patients in her care had died because of a mistake she had made. When Teresa became pregnant, she and her husband Jeff decided that the stress she was experiencing at work was simply not worth the effect it was having on her—she quit the job that, only two years previously, she had cared so much about.

Both Teresa and her husband, Jeff, had noticed that her concerns about hurting other people through inattention had spread to her life outside of work. They had assumed that her worries about hitting someone while driving would disappear once the stress of work was removed from her life. Unfortunately, this did not occur. If anything, her fears seemed to worsen, for she was frequently worried about how minor alterations in her diet, activities, and emotional state might injure the developing fetus. Although she would have preferred to stop driving altogether, she forced herself to continue driving because Jeff sometimes had business trips away from home.

Preparations for the baby's room and for the birth filled her with dread, for she imagined all the accidents that could occur during the birth and the baby's first weeks of life. Although the delivery was uneventful and Teresa and Jeff had the help of family members in making the adjustment to their roles as new parents, Teresa became even more anxious and distressed. Teresa worried about the baby's eating and sleeping patterns. She was concerned about her capacity to feed the baby and was anxious that her diet might cause the baby gastric problems. Teresa was also vigilant for risk of sudden infant death syndrome. If she had to leave the baby's room, she turned the baby monitor on and, if she heard the slightest sound, she rushed back to check the baby. Teresa laundered the baby's clothes and bed linens on noticing the slightest mark. Exhausted from giving birth and from looking after a newborn, she spent much of her time when the baby was asleep going over the house to ensure that it was "baby proof." Although the couple had already done this prior to the birth, Teresa was convinced that they had forgotten something. She started using baby gates to block off access to the stairs in the house. The couple argued repeatedly about this, with Jeff pointing out that the baby was only a few weeks old and they were months away from needing to use the gates. Teresa also checked and rechecked all the cabinets in the kitchen, the bathrooms, the laundry room, and even the garage to make sure that all cleaning products, matches, and other hazardous materials were tightly sealed and stored at eye level.

Jeff's concern about his wife's health mounted during the first months after the birth of their child. He saw Teresa's distress and exhaustion grow. Although he felt that she was a wonderful and caring mother, he was starting to worry that her fatigue and distractibility might actually lead her to make the kind of mistake that she dreaded. As checking for possible problems consumed more and more of her time, her involvement in pleasurable activities diminished and the number of arguments between the couple increased. Following a tearful discussion, Jeff and Teresa agreed she needed to talk to their family physician about her worries.

Teresa and Jeff met with the physician the following week. Ten minutes into their appointment, the physician was convinced that the situation they were describing went beyond the typical cautiousness of new parents. She then asked questions about whether Teresa's anxiety was evident in other areas of her life. When she heard the litany of concerns, she knew that Teresa needed to be assessed by a specialist. She asked Teresa whether she would be willing to meet with a psychologist who would be better able to diagnose her difficulties and possibly help her overcome them. Teresa quickly agreed to this, and the physician said that she would make a referral to a psychologist. The physician then suggested that Jeff check about the behavioral health coverage he had through his work and, that afternoon, Jeff contacted someone in his company's human resources department and learned that he did have coverage for services with a psychologist. The next day, the receptionist in the physician's office phoned Teresa to tell her that a referral had been made for her to see a psychologist the following month.

INTEGRATING ASSESSMENT DATA

The clinical psychologist has many tasks in integrating data obtained during an assessment. At the simplest level, it requires providing a descriptive account of the client's present psychological

functioning. Even providing this "simple" account may be a very complex task for a clinical psychologist. Depending on the nature of the assessment, a simple account might involve a consideration of the client's personality structure, level of emotional distress, coping resources, and/or intellectual capacity. In many instances this description includes diagnosis using a classification system such as the DSM-IV. Because comorbidity is common in clinical diagnoses, with many clients receiving more than one diagnosis, the psychologist must indicate how these diagnoses are related to each other and to the person's overall psychosocial functioning. It is possible for someone to receive one or more diagnoses but to still function relatively well in many life domains. Psychological assessment requires an understanding of the person in his or her social and interpersonal environment. For example, the examination of the impact of diagnostic status on global psychosocial functioning is an important aspect of assessments conducted to determine a person's suitability to return to work or a parent's fitness to have primary physical custody of a child.

Psychological assessments are conducted to answer a question—for example, determining a person's suitability to return to work. (*Source:* Media Bakery)

Unlike pieces of a jigsaw puzzle, data obtained in psychological assessments only infrequently fit together smoothly and neatly—rarely does one piece of information perfectly conform to a related piece of information. As described in the previous chapters, it is important for the psychologist to gather information using different methods and, often, from different informants. Yet each source of

data has its own strengths, limitations, and potential biases that must be taken into account when integrating the data and drawing conclusions. Assessments of children and adolescents typically require that, in addition to the information gathered directly from the young client, information is also obtained from significant others such as parents and teachers. In assessing adults, it is less common to obtain data from multiple informants, although for some assessment purposes (such as treatment planning for couples therapy or evaluating the daily impact of dementia on a patient) obtaining information from others can also be critical. **Viewpoint Box 9.1** describes some of the challenges in meaningfully integrating data obtained from different informants.

Think of what it is like for you to collect and use information necessary for writing a term paper. You need to get material from a number of sources, often including books, journal articles, and Web sites. Once you have all the necessary material, you have to sift through it to determine what is useful, what isn't, and what is redundant. Then, you have to find a way to put all of the various pieces of information together in a manner that makes sense. This should give you a bit of an idea of the challenges involved in integrating data gathered as part of a psychological assessment.

VIEWPOINT BOX 9.1

INTEGRATING DATA FROM MULTIPLE INFORMANTS

The psychological assessment of children and adolescents often involves collecting data from multiple informants. For example, in assessing 12-year-old Ahmed, who has been suspended from school for aggressive behavior, data may be gathered from Ahmed, his parents, and his teachers. The computer-generated profile based on Ahmed's responses reveals that he does not consider himself to have any problems with aggression, although he acknowledges feeling sad and having difficulties paying attention. In contrast, his father's profile shows that he sees Ahmed as having externalizing problems in the borderline range; his mother's profile indicates that she sees her son as having clinically significant attentional problems and borderline problems with anxiety, depression, and externalizing behaviors; and his teacher's profile suggests that she perceives Ahmed as having clinically significant attentional problems and borderline problems with externalizing behaviors. It sounds as though we have four different descriptions of the same youth. How do we make sense of these apparently conflicting reports? Is Ahmed 'faking bad' by exaggerating his worry and sadness to avoid punishment? Is his father's perspective realistic or is he minimizing the problem? Is the mother realistic or is she oversensitive to her son's distress? Did the teacher rate the correct child or did she perhaps mix Ahmed up with someone else in her class?

As we have described in previous chapters, it is common for there to be only limited correspondence between the ratings of different informants regarding a target individual. Likewise, informant ratings and the self-ratings of the individual are typically only moderately correlated. Given the low concordance between raters, how does a clinical psychologist proceed to make sense of the differing information provided by these reports? Should the psychologist ignore some of the reports or try, somehow, to integrate the various perspectives?

One way in which researchers have addressed this important clinical problem is to examine the value of different decision-making rules in using multiple sources of data. For example, if a psychologist uses the "or" rule, it is based on the assumption that the variable targeted in the assessment is present if any informant reports it. On the other hand, the use of the "and" rule means that the psychologist requires evidence of the presence of the variable from two or more informants before assuming that the variable is actually present. Perhaps not too surprising, which rule to follow appears to depend on the variable being assessed.

In their research on youth bipolar disorder, Youngstrom et al. (2004) compared the diagnostic accuracy of six different instruments designed to screen for bipolar disorder in children and adolescents. Three of these instruments involved parent reports, two involved youth self-reports, and one relied on teacher reports.

Across all measures, the parent-based measures consistently outperformed the other measures in identifying bipolar disorder among youth (as determined by a structured diagnostic interview of the youth and parent). In addition, the researchers found that the prediction of bipolar disorder was not improved by combining data from other informants with the parent-based reports.

However, a different picture emerges when considering ADHD in youth. Pelham, Fabiano, and Massetti (2005) synthesized the results of several years of research on the use of multi-informant data in diagnosing ADHD. Among their conclusions: (a) consistent with diagnostic criteria, confirmatory data from both teachers and parents are necessary for the accurate diagnosis of ADHD (i.e., the "and" rule) and (b) in ruling out an ADHD diagnosis, it is not necessary to use both parent and teacher data, because if either informant does not endorse ADHD items, the youth is unlikely to have a diagnosis of ADHD (i.e., a variation of the "or" rule). In the case of Ahmed, this would suggest that, based on the nature of the information provided by the various informants, the psychologist should definitely assess for the presence of ADHD. Additionally, although there are no clear research findings to guide this decision, it would also be prudent for the psychologist to more fully explore the extent to which aggressive, depressive, and anxious symptoms are present.

Combining information from multiple psychological tests or even from multiple scales within a self-report personality test can be a daunting task. Common psychological practice is to begin by examining the client's test responses at the most global level. This would mean, for example, that on the MMPI-2 the psychologist would first consider scores on the various validity scales and then move to examine the MMPI-2 code type (i.e., the highest two scores on the clinical scales). The validity score data allow the psychologist to evaluate the extent to which the other scale scores are likely to accurately reflect the client's personality and psychosocial functioning. With this in mind, the code type information serves as the foundation for generating hypotheses about the client, with other MMPI-2 scales and other sources of assessment data added to this foundation (Lewak & Hogan, 2003). Psychologists must be aware that data from other self-report tests and interviews are not independent sources of information that can be used to confirm initial hypotheses. Whether the client provides information about himself or herself during an interview, on one psychological test, or on many psychological tests, these data sources all represent client self-report. Additional assessment data from sources other than self-report (such as reports by significant others, clinical observation, or archival records such as hospitalization data) have the potential to independently corroborate or nuance hypotheses based on self-report data. However, if all the sources of assessment data are based on what is essentially the same source or form of information (such as different self-report measures completed by the same person) then the apparent convergence of data can lead to misplaced confidence regarding the validity or accuracy of the hypotheses or conclusions (Hunsley & Meyer, 2003).

VIEWPOINT BOX 9.2

INTEGRATING SELF-REPORT AND PROJECTIVE TEST DATA

In Chapter 5 we reported that, for many decades, the Rorschach inkblot test and the MMPI have been among the most commonly taught and used assessment tools in clinical

psychology. Over this same period, the empirical literature on these two measures has been remarkably consistent in demonstrating little or no meaningful relation between the two; even scales supposedly measuring the same construct have little in common (Archer, 1996). For example, Krishnamurthy, Archer, and House (1996) examined the convergent validity of conceptually related MMPI-A and Rorschach scales in a sample of 152 adolescents. From a total of 237 correlations computed among conceptually related scales, only 8 (or 3.4%) were significantly correlated. Keeping in mind that the error rate typically set for statistical analyses is 5% (i.e., $p < .05$), it is highly likely that these significant correlations were simply due to chance.

In light of this lack of convergent validity, some psychologists have argued that combining MMPI and Rorschach data should lead to better assessments, as each test could contribute independent, nonredundant information to be used in addressing the assessment goals. The question of whether the addition of test data to other assessment information actually improves the outcome of the assessment is one of incremental validity. A number of studies have examined the incremental validity of the two measures relative to each other and, in general, the results suggest that adding Rorschach data to MMPI data does not improve assessment accuracy. For example, using the same sample of adolescents as Krishnamurthy et al. (1996), Archer and Krishnamurthy (1997) reported that in no instance did adding data from a Rorschach variable to that of an MMPI-A scale improve the accuracy of the assessment. Moreover, the MMPI-A scales were consistently the best data to use in obtaining accurate assessment results.

Despite these empirical findings, many psychologists continue to advocate the conjoint use of the two tests in clinical assessments. Finn (1996), for example, suggested that three important outcomes could occur when the two tests are used: (a) the results of the two tests could agree, thus providing strong evidence for the validity of the assessment; (b) the Rorschach could show more disturbance than the MMPI, thus indicating underlying psychopathology in clients; or (c) the MMPI could show more disturbance than the Rorschach, thus indicating that clients are overemphasizing problems and symptoms in order to draw attention to their situation. In most examples in the clinical literature, though, the dominant emphasis is on the ability of the Rorschach to "detect" psychopathology when the MMPI has failed to do so (e.g., Weiner, 1999). The problem with this stance is that it flies in the face of the empirical evidence regarding the incremental validity of the Rorschach. Most importantly, when psychologists use Rorschach data to augment the findings obtained from MMPI data, they are greatly increasing the likelihood that their assessment results yield false positives (i.e., inaccurately concluding that a problem exists). Remember that, in Chapter 8, we described the study by Hamel, Shaffer, and Erdberg (2000) in which many of the 100 children screened for an absence of psychopathology and behavior problems were determined to have significant psychological impairments when data from the Rorschach were considered. Because the Rorschach is likely to "detect" pathology when in fact no problems exist, there is a very real danger that those assessed with the test will be improperly diagnosed and unfairly described as having clinically significant psychological problems, even when their MMPI-A results are in the normal range.

Case Formulation

Many assessment questions require the psychologist to go beyond a descriptive account of the client. Often, the purpose of the assessment is to provide directions for possible alleviation or remediation of problems. Included are assessments to address educational concerns (e.g., does the client require some form of special education services?), vocational questions (e.g., are the client's career aspirations realistic in light of his or her intellectual abilities, personality, and interests?), rehabilitation services (e.g., does the client need assistance in developing new strategies for daily living to cope with the effects of a severe closed head injury?), and possible referrals for psychotherapy (e.g., are the client's problems amenable to treatment, and how motivated is the client to engage in therapy?). In such cases the psychologist needs to formulate hypotheses about how the problems developed and the factors that maintain them. Typically, the clinical psychologist is also expected to develop a fuller perspective on how the client's current functioning fits with his or her life history and how well the client may be able to function in the future. Then, based on these hypotheses and conclusions, the psychologist provides recommendations of ways to improve the client's functioning. These recommendations frequently, but not necessarily, include suggestions for psychological services. Other suggestions may include obtaining further assessment data from other health care specialists (such as internists, neurologists, or audiologists) or involving health care specialists or other professionals (e.g., teachers, lawyers, and residential care staff) in service planning.

As described in Chapter 5, the term **case formulation** refers to the task of both describing the patient in his or her life context and developing a set of hypotheses that pull together a comprehensive clinical picture in sufficient detail that the psychologist can make decisions about treatment options. **Table 9.1** summarizes the ways in which a good case formulation can aid in planning clinical services. A detailed case formulation is particularly useful when a patient has numerous or complex clinical problems, for it allows the psychologist to make informed decisions about the timing, sequence, duration, and specific focus of interventions (Mumma, 1998; Tompkins, 1999). Even when assessment is followed by treatments that are evidence based, case formulations are critical. They may provide, for example, information to assist the psychologist in choosing among evidence-based treatment options. Once the option has been chosen (in consultation with the client, of course), the case formulation will

---

TABLE 9.1 The Benefits of a Clinical Case Formulation

- Provides a way of understanding the connections between a patient's various problems

- Provides guidance on the type of treatment to consider (including whether the treatment should be conducted in an individual, couple, family, or group modality)

- Predicts the patient's future functioning if treatment is not sought and how this functioning will be different if treatment is successful

- Provides options to consider if difficulties are encountered in implementing and following through on treatment

- Indicates options, outside of psychological services, for the patient to consider

- Provides alternative treatment options to consider if the initial treatment is unsuccessful

Adapted from Persons (1989)

---

guide the psychologist in determining what issues should be emphasized in treatment and how the steps in a treatment manual can be individualized to match client needs.

Clinical psychologists of all theoretical orientations use assessment data to develop case formulations. Eells, Kendjelic, and Lucas (1998) found that, across orientations, case formulations tended to include four major components: symptoms and problems, events or stressors that led to the symptoms and problems, predisposing life events or stressors (i.e., preexisting vulnerabilities), and a hypothesized mechanism that linked the first four components together to offer an explanation for the development and maintenance of the problems and symptoms. **Table 9.2** summarizes the steps that Mariush (2002) suggested all psychologists should follow in developing a case formulation.

A major challenge in case formulation is that the psychologist must accurately detect patterns in the wealth of data gathered during an assessment, including patterns that may be primarily attributable to cultural factors (Ridley & Kelly, 2006). Even if the assessment is limited to an interview with the client and some self-report measures completed by the client before the interview, it is not an easy task to detect patterns. Then, assuming that the psychologist has been able to recognize patterns in the data, he

---

TABLE 9.2 Steps in Developing a Case Formulation

Step 1: Develop a comprehensive problem list, including the patient's stated problems and other problems indicated by referral agents or identified by other informants during the assessment.

Step 2: Determine the nature of each problem, including its origin, current precipitants, and consequences.

Step 3: Identify patterns or commonalities among the problems; this may yield an indication of previously unidentified factors that serve to maintain, exacerbate, or lessen the problems.

Step 4: Develop working hypotheses to explain the problems.

Step 5: Evaluate and refine the hypotheses, using all information gathered during the assessment and the patient's feedback on the hypotheses.

Step 6: If the psychologist moves from conducting an assessment to providing treatment, the hypotheses should be reconsidered, reevaluated, and revised (as necessary) based on data gathered during treatment.

Adapted from Mariush (2002)

---

or she must try to relate these patterns to specific causes and outcomes. We address the challenges of this exercise more fully in the next section. At this point we will illustrate the difficulty of these tasks with one example. O'Brien (1995) presented clinical psychology graduate students with a very limited but clear set of assessment data: daily self-monitoring data (for 14 days) from a client who presented with frequent and severe headaches. Each day of self-monitoring data included information on the client's overall stress level, hours of sleep, interpersonal conflicts, number of headaches, severity and duration of the headaches, and the number of analgesics taken to deal with the headaches. The students' task was to estimate the magnitude of the relation between precipitating factors (such as reduced sleep, high stress, and frequency of arguments) and headache symptoms (such as frequency, severity, and duration). Across the 14 days of self-monitoring data, the students were able to accurately detect the factors most highly correlated with symptoms only 50% of the time!

Thus far we have not directly addressed the influence of the clinical psychologist's theoretical orientation in the elaboration of a case formulation. Theoretical orientation plays a central role in all aspects of the assessment process, from the nature of the initial hypotheses made about the client, to the selection of assessment tools, to the manner in which the assessment data are used to build a full clinical picture of the client. Berman (1997) described case formulation as having two key features. The first is a succinct analysis of the client's core strengths and weaknesses, which she called the premise. The second is the supporting material, which involves an in-depth analysis of these strengths and weaknesses. Berman indicated that the premise of the case formulation is tied to the clinician's theoretical perspective. Indeed, the type of constructs to be included in both the premise and the supporting material are enormously influenced by orientation. Interpersonally oriented psychodynamic case formulations are likely to focus on dysfunctional relationship styles (called "cyclical maladaptive patterns") as the premise for the formulations, whereas process-experiential formulations are likely to use information about the client's emotional processing and insight into emotional issues in developing the main premise (Berman, 1997; Eells, 2006).

Given exactly the same clinical information, clinicians of differing orientations are likely to develop very different formulations. For example, Plous and Zimbardo (1986) found that in developing hypotheses about the development of psychological symptoms, psychoanalysts emphasized dispositional and personality factors, whereas behavior therapists focused on either situational influences or on the interaction of situational and dispositional influences. Of course, this raises the question of just who is right: unfortunately, there is very limited research on the validity of case formulations (Garb, 1997). There is, however, growing research on the reliability of case formulations. This line of research provides evidence on the extent to which clinical psychologists within an orientation are likely to formulate the same case formulation for a given patient. **Jacqueline Persons** has devoted considerable effort to develop an approach to case formulation that clinical psychologists can easily learn and use. Her *cognitive-behavioral case formulation approach* emphasizes the importance of identifying the patient's overt problems (such as psychological symptoms, interpersonal conflicts, or legal problems) and the longstanding beliefs (called "schemas") that, when activated by life events, are believed to cause the overt problems (Persons, 1989). She found that, when presented with detailed case information, clinicians accurately identified about two thirds of a client's main presenting problems and that the mean interrater reliability of patient schemas was $r = 0.72$ (Persons & Bertagnolli, 1999). Similar reliability results have been reported for psychodynamic case formulations that focus on core relationship conflicts (Barber & Crits-Christoph, 1993). Such findings suggest that, within an orientation, there can be considerable similarity in the case formulations developed by clinicians. There is also growing evidence that, regardless of orientation, some basic training in developing case formulations can greatly enhance the quality of clinicians' formulations (Kendjelic & Eells, 2007).

 c a s e   e x a m p l e   **TERESA**

The clinical psychologist to whom Teresa was referred specialized in providing cognitive-behavioral treatments for anxiety and related problems. Based on the referral from the physician, the psychologist assumed that a major part of the assessment would involve an evaluation of obsessive-compulsive symptoms. However, knowing from the empirical literature that patients who have an anxiety disorder often have a comorbid mood disorder or another anxiety disorder, the psychologist was prepared to assess a full range of potential anxiety and mood symptoms. As people with anxiety disorders often use alcohol or other drugs in an attempt to moderate their symptoms, the evaluation would also cover the possibility of a substance abuse problem. Finally, because individuals with obsessive compulsive disorder (OCD) may not be fully aware of the extent or severity of their problems, the psychologist planned to briefly interview Jeff as part of the assessment. (More details on these assessment issues can be found in Abramowitz [2008] and McLean and Woody [2001].) An interview with Jeff would also provide an opportunity to determine (a) Jeff's perspective on the extent to which the baby might be in any significant danger because of Teresa's symptoms leading her to neglect or forget about the baby and (b) his willingness to assist in his wife's treatment (with his wife's agreement, of course). Accordingly, based on knowledge of both the psychopathology and treatment literatures, the psychologist planned to use the following assessment tools: an interview with Teresa, an interview with Jeff, self-monitoring diaries with Teresa (and possibly with Jeff), the MMPI-2, the Yale-Brown Obsessive Compulsive Scale (YBOCS; Goodman et al., 1989), the BDI-II, the Penn State Worry Questionnaire (Meyer, Miller, Metzger, & Borkovec, 1990), and the Fear Questionnaire (Marks & Mathews, 1979). Of course, tools might be dropped or added based on the psychologist's initial case formulation following the interviews.

Having reviewed criteria for OCD, major depressive disorder, and generalized anxiety disorder prior to the interview, the psychologist conducted an interview with Teresa that focused largely on her symptoms. Questions were also asked about her understanding of the development of her problems, her efforts to cope with her symptoms, and her concerns regarding the symptoms' effects on her baby and Jeff. After approximately 45 minutes, the psychologist concluded this first interview with Teresa. The importance of using standardized symptoms measures was then explained to Teresa, and she was asked to complete the four symptom checklists (not including the MMPI-2) while Jeff was interviewed. During his interview, Jeff was asked about how Teresa was coping with her problems, his understanding of her problems, and how his life was affected by Teresa's distress. The psychologist also made a point of asking Jeff how they were both dealing with the demands of being new parents and how Jeff saw Teresa in her role as a mother. After 30 minutes or so the psychologist concluded the interview with Jeff, checked that Teresa had completed the measures, and invited her to join Jeff in the psychologist's office.

At this point the psychologist shared some initial impressions with the couple. After commenting on how well they were dealing with the challenges they both faced, the psychologist stated that it appeared Teresa was indeed suffering from OCD. Although the tests would need to be scored and further information would be required to determine whether other clinical problems were evident, it was clear that Teresa should consider treatment for this anxiety disorder. The psychologist briefly described the main evidence-based psychological and pharmacological treatments for OCD but emphasized that Teresa would not need to make any treatment-related decisions until the assessment was concluded. As a final step in this initial feedback session, the psychologist provided Teresa with a simple self-monitoring form to record some information (duration of anxiety, level of anxiety, and efforts to cope with the anxiety) each time she noticed that she was anxious about inadvertently harming someone and about the possibility of having left dangerous materials in the house. Teresa understood that recording these details would help the psychologist better understand the nature of her anxiety and readily agreed to do the self-monitoring each day until the next assessment appointment 6 days later.

Between the first and second appointments with Teresa, the psychologist scored the symptom measures and summarized diagnostic hypotheses from the interviews. Teresa clearly met criteria for OCD, and both the obsessions and the compulsions subscales of the YBOCS were in the OCD range. There were a number of situations that Teresa indicated on the Fear Questionnaire that she tended to avoid but, other than trying to avoid thoughts of injury or illness, none of the items indicated evidence of a clinical problem. On the worry measure she scored above the 70th percentile, but the interview data suggested that she did not meet criteria for generalized anxiety disorder, as all of her worries were better accounted for by the OCD diagnosis. Teresa scored in the moderately depressed range on the BDI-II, but the interview data indicated that she did not currently meet criteria for a mood disorder—it did seem likely to the psychologist that such a disorder might develop if her OCD was not treated.

At the second appointment, the psychologist met with Teresa for 30 minutes to review the self-monitoring data and to ask Teresa about her symptoms over the past few days. The psychologist also checked whether she had any questions about the information discussed in their first meeting. After the interview, Teresa completed the MMPI-2. To allow sufficient time for the psychologist to review the assessment data, a full feedback session was scheduled for 2 weeks later. Teresa asked if Jeff could attend the meeting— the psychologist immediately agreed to this.

In interpreting the MMPI-2, the psychologist was particularly interested in the code type of Teresa's responses (i.e., her highest scores on the Clinical scales) and the scores on some of the Content scales. All Validity scale scores were in the normal range, indicating that she had responded in a consistent and forthright manner to the MMPI-2 items. This was in line with observations of Teresa during the two interviews, for she clearly took all the interview questions seriously and tried to give full and accurate answers even when she became upset in describing some of her difficulties. With respect to code type, Teresa's highest two scores in the clinical range were 7 (Pt) and 8 (Sc), with 7 being much higher than 8. This code type is typically found among people who are having problems with ruminations, obsessions, anxiety, and depression, who have frequent health concerns, and who are feeling stressed-out. On the Content scales, there were elevations with Anxiety, Obsessiveness, and Health Concerns—the Depression scale did not quite reach the clinical level. Finally, the psychologist scored the test for the supplemental scores available to evaluate addiction and substance abuse: consistent with interview data there was no indication that Teresa was relying on alcohol or other substances to alleviate her anxiety.

THREATS TO THE VALIDITY OF ASSESSMENTS AND CASE FORMULATIONS

Patient/Client Factors

As you know from Chapter 8, clinical psychologists are well aware that people may selectively choose how they depict themselves during a psychological evaluation. To achieve certain ends, people may consciously highlight either their strengths or their weaknesses. Some people who are required to undergo an evaluation for court-mandated reasons may attempt to render their results invalid by purposely responding to test items in a random manner. As we described previously, there are measures to detect such attempts at impression management. There are also more subtle biases that can affect the validity of patient-provided data. These biases are not necessarily consciously intended and, therefore, are much less likely to be detected by responses to validity scales or measures of malingering.

A basic assumption underlying the use of interviews and self-report measures is that people accurately recall and report events in their lives. The truth of this assumption seems so obvious that, in our daily lives, we rarely have any reason to question it. After all, we are usually certain about what we were doing when important events occurred in our lives, whether they be events of personal significance (such as learning of the death of a family member) or of more global significance (such as what we were doing when we learned that planes had struck the World Trade Center in New York City in 2001). However, when psychologists study the accuracy of these recalled memories, it appears that there is good reason to be skeptical about the general accuracy of memory. We will examine several lines of research bearing on the accuracy of self-report data that relies on **retrospective recall.**

Gosling, John, Craik, and Robins (1998) videotaped research participants in a group discussion. Following the interaction, each participant was asked to recall how frequently he or she had engaged in specific acts such as "I persuaded others to accept my opinion on the issue." Using the videotapes, observers recorded each instance of the participant engaging in these acts. Across 12 different acts that were coded with high reliability (an alpha > .80), the average correlation between participants' recall and observers' records was only .40! For highly observable acts (e.g., "The participant reminded the group of their time limit") there was much greater agreement than there was for acts that required some inference on the part of observers (e.g., "The participant took the opposite point of view just to be contrary"). The desirability of the acts also seemed to have an effect on the correlation between participant and observer data. Compared with observer act counts, participants tended to overreport the frequency with which they engaged in socially desirable acts (e.g., "Participant settled the dispute among other members of the group") and to underreport engaging in less desirable acts (e.g., "Participant yelled at someone"). Taken together, these results, which are consistent with prior research findings, suggest that there may be considerable variability in the accuracy of people's reports of how they acted in a particular situation, even when the reports are given shortly after the situation occurred. The clinical implications are clear: first, we should not assume complete accuracy when using checklists that ask clients to indicate the frequency of occurrence of behaviors, symptoms, or other experiences and, second, we should expect that the desirability of the experience being reported may influence the accuracy of the information provided by the client.

A second line of research relevant to the issue of memory effects on self-report measures compares people's recording of events as they happen (or shortly after they happen) with their later recall of the events. For example, Shiffman and colleagues (1997) asked people who recently had quit smoking to record on a hand-held computer their smoking lapses and temptations to smoke. Twelve weeks later, participants were asked to provide retrospective accounts of these events. The overall pattern of results suggested that recalled information was highly inaccurate: only 57% of participants were able to accurately recall whether they had a lapse within a 2-week period, and the recalled number of cigarettes smoked was three times greater than the number reported during the lapses. Perhaps most strikingly, people were highly confident in the accuracy of their recall, but there was no statistically significant relation between confidence ratings and accuracy. Stone and colleagues (1998) also used hand-held computers to examine the relation between immediate reports of participants' attempts to cope with daily stressors and recall of their coping efforts two days later. On average, approximately one third of people failed to retrospectively report coping efforts they recorded using during the actual occurrence of their efforts; a similar number retrospectively reported using coping strategies that they did not report using during the events in question. As a final example, Halford, Keefer, and Osgarby (2002) asked 60 heterosexual couples to keep a daily diary of events in their relationship for one week. At the end of the week, all participants were asked to describe the week overall, and their descriptions were then coded in terms of positive and negative comments about the relationship. The researchers were particularly interested in whether participants' satisfaction with their relationship would color their recall of events. Consistent with their hypotheses, when these summary comments were compared with the daily diaries, low relationship satisfaction was significantly related to a tendency to recall the relationship events in an overly negative manner.

Studies suggest that peoples' recall memory is not as accurate as they would believe when compared to their recording of events as they occurred. (*Source:* Vuk Vukmirovic/iStockphoto)

Research indicates that it is not only minor daily events that are difficult to accurately recall. As part of an ongoing project based in New Zealand to track health and development, Henry, Moffit, Caspi, Langley, and Silva (1994) used data from more than 1,000 young adults to compare retrospectively recalled events at age 18 with data on these events that were obtained throughout the participants' childhood and adolescence. The researchers found enormous variability in the accuracy of the recollections, with correlations between recalled events and actual details of the events ranging from −.02 to .77! Although correlations were relatively high for such reports on the number of housing moves ($r = .76$) and height and weight just prior to puberty ($r \geq .59$), accuracy was very poor for recall of psychosocial variables such as the extent of conflict in the family prior to age 15 ($r \geq .25$), maternal depression prior to age 15 ($r \leq .20$), and the extent of depressive or hyperactive symptoms in participants prior to age 11 ($r \leq .12$). As these psychosocial variables are the ones that clinicians typically ask about during initial assessments, it appears that there are considerable grounds for doubting the veracity of these reports.

As we described in previous chapters, clinical psychologists may be asked to assess individuals to determine their level of ability or functioning prior to an event such as a workplace injury or a motor vehicle accident. Many studies suggest that it is important to gather archival information, such as medical, school, or police records, as part of this assessment rather than relying on patient self-report. Greiffenstein, Baker, and Johnson-Greene (2002), for example, compared self-reported and actual academic performance among people with head injuries who were or were not involved in legal suits based on the accident that led to the injuries. Compared with the nonlitigating group, those who had filed legal suits showed a much greater tendency to overestimate their scholastic performance.

 Does it seem to you that your memories of recent and more distant events might be flawed? Can you think of examples of memories that you have that seem very clear but that you know are not entirely accurate?

Clinician Factors

Since the groundbreaking work of cognitive psychologists Tversky and Kahneman (1974), there has been dramatic growth in our knowledge of how subtle influences can affect judgment, reasoning, and decision-making processes. We now know a great deal about how experience, expectations, attributions, and stereotypes all shape the ways in which people make both relatively minor and major decisions. For example, hundreds of studies have examined the tendency for people to see themselves in a generally positive light, even when such positivity may not be warranted. A meta-analysis conducted by Mezulis, Abramson, Hyde, and Hankin (2004) included 266 studies of the **self-serving attributional bias.** This bias involves people making more internal, stable, and global attributions for positive events in their lives than they do for negative events (e.g., "I got an A on the paper because I worked hard for it. I am always a hard worker, in every area of my life, so it is no wonder that good things occur in my life." versus "I really didn't deserve a C on the paper. It really wasn't my fault that my computer crashed. I usually get things done on time—I know that I left things late this time, but if my hard drive hadn't crashed I would have been fine."). Health care professionals are not immune to this bias, which can lead to substantial overestimates about one's competence and the quality of the services one provides (Brosnan, Reynolds, & Moore, 2008; Davis et al., 2006).

PROFILE BOX 9.1

DR. HOWARD GARB

I received a B.A. from the University of Illinois at Urbana-Champaign and a double-major Ph.D. in clinical psychology and statistics from the University of Illinois at Chicago. This was followed by a postdoctoral fellowship in clinical psychology and program evaluation at Northwestern University. For 19 years I worked at the Pittsburgh V.A. Healthcare System evaluating and treating veterans, while also teaching at the University of Pittsburgh and conducting research on clinical judgment and test validity. Currently, I am the director of the largest and most rigorous mental health screening program for the United States Air Force (USAF), with more than 35,000 trainees screened a year. In helping the USAF decide who to recruit and with ongoing research to help them decide who to select for work with nuclear weapons, I have introduced an actuarial approach that relies on the collection of extremely large databases and extensive statistical analyses. By conducting program evaluations, I have helped program managers accept more responsibility and become more accountable for their programs. I was elected President of the Society for a Science of Clinical Psychology for 2008–2009.

Dr. Howard Garb

How did you choose to become a clinical psychologist?

Many of my relatives had severe mental disorders, and others were mental health professionals. My father's brother became psychotic and died in a mental health hospital as a young man. In the 1940s, effective treatments were not available, and my uncle died because of the inappropriate use of shock treatment. When I entered college, I hoped to discover the cause of schizophrenia using psychodynamic or psychoanalytic theory. It was a fanciful notion, but one that fit with the dominance of Freudian theory in the 1970s. My professors steered me in a different direction. The University of Illinois has a celebrated undergraduate honors program that I was lucky to get into, and my thesis was on mathematical models of judgment and decision making.

What is the most rewarding part of your job as a clinical psychologist?

Psychologists get to do interesting things. I have worked with clients, taught at a major university, conducted research and written scholarly articles and books, and I am now involved with changing policy and practices in the military. Throughout my career, my work has been absorbing and meaningful.

What is the greatest challenge you face as a clinical psychologist?

Resistance to change. We would all like to help clients change, but I would also like to see mental health providers and organizations change by incorporating more science in their services.

Tell us about research on clinical decision making

Much of the research describes whether mental health professionals' judgments are correct or incorrect, and many of the results are surprising. For example, appropriate training is generally more important than clinical experience in ensuring accurate and

valid judgments. Psychologists who use invalid psychological tests often believe the tests are valid because of their clinical experiences with the tests. These professionals need to be more responsive to research findings and not base their decisions primarily on their clinical experiences. On a somewhat different note, psychologists typically do a good job of describing clients' psychological characteristics, but they do less well with the task of case formulation. The research on case formulation shows that it is more difficult to accurately explain something than to describe it.

How do you integrate science and practice in your work?

As a staff psychologist at the V.A., I was guided by research findings. For example, I initially used projective tests including the Rorschach. I stopped using them not because of my clinical experiences but because of research findings that reflected badly on the tests. In my time working for the USAF, we have collected large data sets on the USAF and have developed statistical prediction rules to help decision-making. Mental health staff still have a role in the judgment-making process (e.g., to clarify recruits' responses on questionnaires), but the use of statistical prediction rules and large databases are becoming increasingly important in efforts to accurately predict human behavior.

What do you see as the most exciting changes in the field of clinical psychology?

Advances in judgment and decision making continue to be made. For example, only in recent years have clinical psychologists been able to successfully predict events and behaviors such as violence, psychosis, and sexual offenses. In addition, the use of computer-administered interviews and rating scales may lead to improved judgments and decisions because they allow clinicians to obtain comprehensive information in a systematic and economical manner.

The field of clinical psychology will also change as a result of the war in Iraq. Since the beginning of the Iraq War, clinical psychologists have played an increasingly prominent role in the military by addressing mental health issues through screening, assessment, and treatment. The war in Iraq is likely to have a powerful effect on the field of psychology, if only because there will be substantial numbers of veterans who will be in need of mental health treatment.

Generally speaking, **biases** involve judgments that are systematically different from what a person should conclude based on logic or probability. **Heuristics** are mental shortcuts that people often use to ease the burden of decision making but that also tend to result in errors in decision making and, thus, are at the heart of cognitive biases. Since the 1980s, **Howard Garb** has contributed much to our understanding of how biases and heuristics influence routine clinical tasks (e.g., Garb, 1997, 2005), and his 1998 book provides an excellent summary of the large literature indicating that even those trained to provide psychological services are prone to human information processing biases. **Profile Box 9.1** introduces Dr. Howard Garb who is an expert on decision-making errors.

Table 9.3 provides a summary of common biases and heuristics that can affect clinical decision making. Although we present this table in the section on clinician factors that affect the validity of assessment, these biases and heuristics apply equally to patient reports.

By definition, biases and heuristics lead to errors in decision making. However, not all errors are created equal: some are potentially more damaging than others, and small errors may not really make much of a difference. For example, inaccurately scoring one item on an intelligence test will definitely affect the overall total score, but it is unlikely to affect the global interpretation of the client's score as being average or above average. In other words, not all errors result in mistakes that have real-world consequences. We do know, however, that some clinician errors can have substantial consequences. Kim and Ahn (2002) found that when determining a diagnosis, clinical psychologists and graduate clinical psychology students are more likely to be influenced by their own causal theories than they are by the actual DSM criteria relevant to the diagnostic category. As another example, compared with actual occurrences of violence, clinicians typically overpredict the violence of male patients and underpredict the violence of female patients; likewise, African American psychiatric inpatients and prison inmates are predicted to be more violent than are White psychiatric inpatients and prison inmates (Garb, 1997, 2005). Other ethnic biases have also been found in clinical practice: for example, minority patients diagnosed with schizophrenia are almost twice as likely as White patients to receive excessive dosages of antipsychotic medication (Wood, Garb, Lilienfeld, & Nezworski, 2002).

If some clinical errors are so important, what gets in the way of clinicians—psychologists, physicians, psychiatrists, and others—identifying and correcting their mistakes? One of the main obstacles seems to be that people tend to be overconfident in the accuracy or correctness of their decisions (Griffin, Dunning, & Ross, 1990). Ryan and Schnakenburg-Ott (2003), for example, found that despite making substantial errors in scoring a WAIS-III protocol, both experienced psychologists and graduate students were very confident about the accuracy of their scoring efforts. In an attempt to understand the factors that lead to overconfidence in clinical decisions, Smith and Dumont (2002) asked 36 clinical psychologists to "think aloud" while they read case file material about a patient (including life history data and information about current events in the patient's life). The researchers coded several aspects of the thoughts reported by participants during the task, including the confidence expressed in the accuracy of their conclusions. Among the variables they investigated, the sole factor that predicted psychologists' confidence was the extent to which dispositional (as opposed to contextual) information was used. In other words, it appears that the fundamental attribution error (see Table 9.3) may play a powerful role in leading clinicians to be overconfident in their interpretations, decisions, and conclusions.

TABLE 9.3   Common Decision-Making Biases and Heuristics

Fundamental Attribution Error: In attempting to understand why a person acted in such a manner, there is a tendency to overestimate the influence of personality traits and to underestimate the influence of situational effects on the person's behavior.

Inattention to Base Rates: A psychologist may believe that a certain pattern of responses on a test is indicative of a specific diagnosis and supports this belief with information on some relevant cases. However, without full knowledge of the base rate of (a) the pattern of test responses and (b) the diagnosis, it is not possible to determine the extent to which the test responses accurately predict the diagnosis.

Belief in the Law of Small Numbers: Results drawn from small samples are likely to be more extreme and less consistent than those obtained from large samples. Nevertheless, the clinical psychologist may be tempted to attend more to information gained from two or three patients with a specific disorder than to the results of research on the disorder. Direct experience with a small number of patients may feel more relevant and compelling, even though it is less likely to yield accurate information compared with data drawn from research samples.

Regression to the Mean: Because of the nature of measurement error, a person who obtains an extreme score on a test at one point in time is likely to obtain a less extreme score when next taking the test. This apparent change in test scores has nothing to do with real alterations in the person's life. (The standard error of measurement is available for many psychological tests so that psychologists can take this into account when comparing test scores from two time points.)

Inferring Causation From Correlation: A psychologist may note that there appears to be substantial co-occurrence of certain patient characteristics (such as a history of sexual abuse and the presence of borderline personality disorder) and infer that the earlier of the two characteristics causes the later characteristic (i.e., the abuse led to the development of the personality disorder). Before drawing causal inferences, though, other factors must be considered, including whether the later characteristic may influence the information provided about the earlier characteristic and the possibility that both characteristics stemmed from a third variable (e.g., severely dysfunctional family environment).

Hindsight Bias: As the saying goes, "Hindsight is 20/20." Most decisions (including clinical decisions) must be made without the benefit of all the pertinent information. After a decision has been made and, as a consequence, a certain course of action has been taken, new information may become available. It is tempting to validate or question the initial decision based on data gathered after the fact even though it was not possible to have these data inform the original decision.

Confirmatory Bias: Once a clinical hunch has been formed, it is tempting to gather information to support it. However, in testing a hypothesis it is important to evaluate evidence both for and against the hypothesis. The clinical psychologist must avoid simply looking for evidence to support the hypothesis (such as a diagnosis or an emerging case formulation) and must also actively look for evidence that would refute or temper the strength of the hypothesis.

Representativeness Heuristic: Relying on biases such as the belief in the law of small numbers to draw conclusions about the degree to which a symptom or behavior is representative of an underlying disorder or condition.

Availability Heuristic: Making a decision based on easily recalled information, such as recent or extreme or unusual examples that are relevant to the decision. Using only easily recalled examples (such as the last person assessed with similar symptoms) will lead to an incomplete evaluation of the elements that must be considered in the decision; by definition, extreme examples are atypical and likely to bias a decision.

Affect Heuristic: When reaching a decision, the affective qualities (such as likeability, negativity, disgust, or pleasure) of cognitive representations of people or objects are rapidly considered. This usually occurs at an unconscious level and can lead to a judgment based solely on emotional considerations (such as the attractiveness of an individual), with only minimal attention paid to the full range of factors relevant to the decision.

Anchoring and Adjustment Heuristic: Initial conditions or characteristics determine a starting point for considering the nature of an individual or task (such as using the dealer's price when negotiating to buy a car). In clinical contexts this means that, for example, first impressions may serve as the (possibly inaccurate) basis for considering and integrating all subsequent information gathered about a person.

Improving the Accuracy of Clinical Judgment

In light of the kinds of errors we have just described, it seems obvious that psychologists and other clinicians should be more cautious in their decision making. Simply being aware of decision-making biases and the resultant errors is insufficient—clinical psychologists (and others who wish to reduce the role of biases in their decisions) must take concrete steps to tackle the potential for bias and error. In this regard, the evidence is overwhelming that the use of informal, unstructured strategies to integrate assessment data is inferior to strategies that rely on the structured application of empirical evidence (Ægisdóttir et al., 2006; Grove, Zald, Lebow, Snitz, & Nelson, 2000). This was the conclusion reached in the middle of the last century by Meehl (1954), who launched the so-called clinical versus actuarial debate; the conclusion has been repeatedly supported since then. Accordingly, no one should interpret an MMPI-A profile by looking at individual items to generate a clinical formulation: the formulation should be informed by code type interpretations based on research studies. Measures designed to systematize clinical observations are being developed, which holds the possibility for structuring the data obtained from even the most unstructured clinical interviews (Westen & Weinberger, 2004).

Table 9.4 describes a host of other simple, practical strategies that psychologists can follow in order to minimize the impact of bias and error in their work. Unfortunately, based on a review of courses offered in APA-accredited clinical psychology programs, very few graduate students in clinical psychology receive much classroom training in these strategies. Harding (2007) found that, in these programs, issues related to decision making were most likely to be covered in nonrequired courses in cognitive psychology. Only 9% of these programs had required courses that included material on decision improvement strategies. That being said, psychologists who learn and routinely applying the the strategies listed in Table 9.4 will do a great deal to enhance the quality of their decision making and reduce the likelihood of errors affecting the services they offer to the public.

TABLE 9.4   Ways to Improve the Accuracy of Clinical Judgment

- Use psychological tests that are directly relevant to the assessment task and that have strong psychometric qualities.
- Check for scoring errors when using test data.
- Use computers as aids in the collection, scoring, and interpretation of clinical data whenever possible.
- Use normative data and base rate information whenever available.
- Use DSM criteria when making diagnostic decisions.
- Use decision aids, such as decision trees or clinical guidelines.
- In unstructured tasks, such as conducting interviews and reviewing assessment data, be as systematic and structured as possible in obtaining, considering, and using all relevant information.
- Be aware of relevant research in psychological assessment, psychopathology, and prevention/intervention.
- Be aware of personal biases and preconceptions.
- Be self-critical: search for alternative explanations for hypotheses and challenge evolving case formulations.
- Seek consultation from other professionals when unsure of the accuracy of conclusions.
- Don't rely on memory, and don't rush any conclusion or decision.

A friend has just told you that someone she knows named Chris is interested in switching to psychology as a major. Without asking your friend any questions, do you assume that Chris is female or male? Obviously, the person's name can be either a man's name or a woman's name, so this doesn't give you any clues. However, you do know something about the base rate of men and women in psychology courses. For many years now, the majority of students majoring in psychology are women. Using this base rate information, your best guess about Chris' gender should be that Chris is a woman.

case example TERESA

Teresa's psychologist was concerned about a number of possible biases that might affect the validity of the assessment information. To deal with the possibility that Teresa might unwittingly underestimate the extent of her problems, symptom-related information was also collected from Jeff. As Teresa might consciously downplay her difficulties, a measure with established validity scales was used (the MMPI-2). Because both Teresa and Jeff's memories of her symptoms might be influenced by her most recent episodes of anxiety or by her most extreme episodes of anxiety, Teresa was asked to self-monitor her anxiety for a week. Finally, because both Teresa and Jeff might have concerns about how Teresa's anxiety was influencing her ability as a parent, the psychologist asked each of them separately about this issue. This point was particularly important, as the psychologist had a duty to contact the child protection services if it appeared that the baby was in need of protection. After interviewing both parents, it was the psychologist's opinion that the baby was not in need of protection.

Several steps were taken to guard against biases that might affect the clinical psychologist's judgment; for example, DSM-IV-TR criteria were used to make diagnostic decisions. Because the psychologist specialized in anxiety disorders, it was important to address the possibilities of overestimating the likelihood of an anxiety diagnosis and underestimating other diagnoses. To this end, several self-report measures were used to establish the nature of the anxiety and depressive symptoms. The MMPI-2 would also provide indications if other clinically significant disorders might be present. With respect to the possibility of errors in the assessment, standardized psychological tests were used that had relevant norms and solid psychometric properties. The psychologist checked all scoring of the measures and used software to generate interpretive statements for the MMPI-2. The psychologist obtained information from multiple informants and looked for independent confirmation of the main hypotheses generated early in the assessment with Teresa.

PSYCHOLOGICAL ASSESSMENT REPORTS AND TREATMENT PLANS

The assessment process culminates in writing a report and, usually, presenting the assessment findings to the individual or individuals who were the focus of the assessment. In addition to providing information to the agency or professional (or the client), the report serves as a record of the assessment that can be referred to subsequently and, in some instances, can also be a document used for legal purposes. In situations in which some form of treatment will follow the assessment, the report records the client's functioning prior to intervention. This baseline information is crucial in accurately determining the impact of any intervention.

Assessments may be requested by many people including clients, the parents of young clients, physicians, insurance companies, employers, lawyers, or the courts. Accordingly, when conducting the assessment and writing the report, the psychologist must be cognizant of the potential uses of the report and the "audiences" for the report (Groth-Marnat & Horvath, 2008). This is especially important when the person being assessed is in a potentially adversarial position with the agency that requested the assessment. As described previously in the text, this can happen when an individual is making a claim for compensation based on injuries suffered and the agency responsible for adjudicating the claim seeks an independent evaluation of the individual's psychological state. Issues of informed consent and confidentiality are always important in the provision of psychological services. However, when there may be competing interests involved, it is crucial for the psychologist to emphasize and reiterate the rights and options available to the person who is being assessed.

In almost all jurisdictions, privacy legislation allows clients access to their psychological records, so the psychologist should write a report with this in mind. Although this should not change any conclusions or recommendations, it should affect how the report is written. Care must be taken to minimize or eliminate any stigmatizing or objectionable terms or descriptions in the report. Moreover, in integrating information from multiple sources, it is also crucial that the psychologist clearly attribute who said what. Reports are always potential legal documents that may have ramifications far beyond the original reasons for which the assessment was conducted. If based solely on client self-report, a statement such as "His father physically assaulted him on numerous occasions" should be written as "The client reported that his father had physically assaulted him on numerous occasions." Likewise, ambiguous terms should be avoided: in describing marital arguments, for example, the phrase "the couple often fights" could refer either to frequent arguments or physical violence. **Table 9.5** highlights some principles that clinical psychologists typically follow in order to maximize the validity and usefulness of their assessment reports.

TABLE 9.5   Report-Writing Principles

- Identify common themes, integrating the findings across assessment procedures.

- Use all relevant sources of information about the client (including reliable and valid test results, behavioral observations, individual test responses, interview data, and case history) in generating hypotheses, formulating interpretations, and making recommendations.

- Be definitive when the findings are clear; be cautious when the findings are inconsistent or problematic.

- Use concrete examples to enhance the report's readability.

- Interpret the meaning and implications of a test score rather than simply citing test names and scores.

- Refrain from making diagnoses solely on the basis of test scores; consider all sources of information.

- Communicate clearly and eliminate unnecessary technical material in order to enhance the report's readability.

Adapted from Sattler (1992)

Earlier in the chapter we described how computers could be used to improve the accuracy of some aspects of clinical decision making. Despite the numerous benefits of using computers for various assessment-related tasks, clinical psychologists need to exercise considerable caution with **computer-based interpretations** (CBIs) when integrating the assessment data and writing the assessment report. Because CBIs are based on research using group-level data, not all interpretative comments associated with, say, a specific MMPI-2 code type applies to the patient being assessed. The clinician needs to review the CBI and select only those narrative statements that accurately describe the patient in question. Next, the psychologist must examine the relevance of any statement given the reasons for the assessment (Kvaal, Choca, & Groth-Marnat, 2003). In most jurisdictions the regulatory bodies for psychologists have clear guidelines on the use of CBIs in psychological assessment. Most typically, these include the need to ensure the relevance of the interpretations to the patients and to clearly identify any statements that come directly from the computer report and that are the sole source of information for a specific point or conclusion. For these reasons, including an unedited computer report in an assessment report is not considered appropriate or responsible in routine practice.

Table 9.6 presents the sections typically found in most psychological assessment reports. There are no standards dictating the necessary components of a report; the content and structure depends on the reasons for the assessment. Most reports are several single-spaced pages in length, although reports prepared for legal or forensic purposes tend to be substantially longer.

Table 9.7 presents the sections usually included in assessment reports prepared for intervention purposes. These treatment plans differ from the typical assessment report: they primarily focus on using the assessment data to develop and structure a plan for intervening with the patient. Treatment plans should also include some consideration of whether psychological treatment is warranted or appropriate at this time. Both types of reports serve to document the client's psychological functioning and to provide clinically informed formulations that draw on the assessment data. A treatment plan report involves problem identification, delineation of the aims and goals of treatment, and the strategies and tactics involved in the planned treatment (Mariush, 2002). Specific attention is also paid to the need for ongoing evaluation of the patient's functioning, because the monitoring of treatment impact is

---

TABLE 9.6   Sections of a Typical Psychological Report

- Patient/client information
- Reason for referral
- Background information (including, as relevant, developmental history, educational history, employment history, family history, relationship history, medical history, history of symptoms and disorders)
- Assessment methods (including tests administered)
- Interview data and behavioral observations
- Test results (including interpretation of test scores)
- Diagnostic impressions
- Summary
- Recommendations

TABLE 9.7   Elements of a Typical Treatment Plan

- Identifying patient/client information (i.e., name, age, gender, etc.)

- Reason for referral

- Evaluation of primary symptoms and problems

- Diagnosis

- Patient strengths

- Treatment-related goals and objectives

- Proposed treatment(s)

- Potential barriers to treatment

- Criteria for treatment termination or transfer to other service provider

- Service provider responsible for treatment implementation and evaluation of treatment

Adapted from Mariush (2002)

---

important in determining whether treatment should be discontinued or alternative treatment options should be considered. A growing number of agencies now require a treatment plan prior to the commencement of therapy and sometimes require an updated plan if the clinical psychologist requests additional sessions for the patient's treatment. **Viewpoint Box 9.3** deals with one of the challenges psychologists are likely to encounter in developing a treatment plan.

VIEWPOINT BOX 9.3

MULTIPLE PERSPECTIVES ON TREATMENT GOALS

One of the first steps in offering intervention services is for the psychologist to help the client establish treatment goals (Nezu & Nezu, 1993). Psychological interventions for adult clients involve at least two perspectives: that of the client and that of the therapist. The psychologist asks questions to discover what the person hopes to get out of psychological services. Clients vary in the extent to which they have clear ideas about what needs to change to resolve the problem. The goals identified by the psychologist depend on the way the psychologist formulates the case, which in turn is influenced by the theoretical model that the psychologist uses in understanding problems. The core of an effective therapeutic alliance is the agreement on goals by client and therapist (Horvath & Luborsky, 1993). Agreement on goals is even more of a challenge in the delivery of psychological services to children and families. Children rarely refer themselves for services (Kazdin, 1988). Over years of clinical practice, we have yet to receive a call from a young person saying "I realize that I am pretty tough to live with; my distractibility is getting in the way of meeting my academic goals and my impulsiveness leads to all kinds of trouble, so I think

I need to see a psychologist." Adults are the ones to request psychological services for children. As you saw in Viewpoint Box 9.1, there is often limited overlap in the ways that young people and their parents view their behavior. If parents and children do not agree on what the problem is, how can they agree on treatment goals?

Hawley and Weisz (2003) asked 315 children and their parents attending community mental health centers about the problem for which services were being sought. They also asked the children's therapists to identify the presenting problem. All three raters identified disobedience, temper tantrums, poor schoolwork, and difficulties getting along with other children as the most common reasons for seeking services. However, beyond such generalities, the level of agreement among children, parents, and therapists was low. Only 23.2% of triads (child–parent–therapist) agreed on the target problem for therapy; less than half of the triads agreed on the general area that needed to be addressed. Agreement was significantly higher for externalizing, or acting-out, problems (41.3%) than it was for internalizing problems, for which there was only 6.7% agreement. In general, there was higher agreement between therapists and parents than between children and either therapists or parents. Therapists offering services to children and families therefore face a dilemma: if they act according to the parents' identification of the problem, they are likely to set treatment goals that are not endorsed by the child. On the other hand, if they set goals according to what the child thinks is a problem, they risk alienating the parents, who may see the focus as misplaced. To engage both child and parents in psychological services, the psychologist first must find a way to formulate goals that are meaningful to both the child and parents. If the child does not see the point in services, he or she is unlikely to cooperate, and although parents may sometimes force the child's attendance, they cannot force meaningful involvement. As the parents are the ones who control access to services, it is essential that they be convinced that the services offered are relevant. Psychologists working with children and families must therefore be sensitive to the different perspectives of those seeking services and of those child clients who are referred to them.

Assessment Feedback

For much of the history of psychological assessment, the results of the assessment process were delivered primarily to the medical or educational personnel who requested the assessment. In the assessment of child clients, parents often received some feedback on the results of the assessment. Opportunities to present assessment feedback are invaluable in assisting other professionals in developing remedial or intervention strategies to use with the assessed client. However, with changes in ethical codes and legislation since the 1970s, it is now commonplace for those who were assessed to also receive feedback from the clinical psychologist involved. Indeed, current ethical requirements underscore the importance of psychologists providing such feedback in most circumstances. As indicated in **Table 9.8**, not only do clients have the right to receive feedback, but also the provision of feedback yields an opportunity for the psychologist to verify assessment findings and conclusions and to help clients begin to use the assessment findings in making modifications in their lives. For an assessment designed to address elements of a treatment plan, it is essential that client and psychologist work collaboratively during the initial assessment phase and throughout the following treatment phases. Therefore it is crucial that the

---

TABLE 9.8   The Purposes of Providing Assessment Feedback

- Verify the general accuracy of the assessment results

- Refine the interpretation of the results to ensure an optimal fit with the individual's life circumstances

- Put the individual's symptoms, problems, and experiences in the context of his or her life history and current life circumstances

- Provide some psychological relief for the individual by presenting an integrated picture that helps make sense of the individual's difficulties

- Provide concrete information about steps the individual can take to address personal difficulties

- Help the individual identify potentially stressful situations that can exacerbate difficulties

- Collaborate with the individual in creating therapeutic goals that build on personal strengths

Adapted from Lewak and Hogan (2003)

---

psychologist explain the results of all assessments, including the initial assessment data and the data that are collected as part of the treatment monitoring and evaluation process.

In 2007, Smith, Wiggins, and Gorske published data from a survey of over 700 psychologists who frequently conducted either personality assessment or neuropsychological assessments for clinical purposes. Their survey included questions on a range of issues dealing with the psychologists' practices in providing assessment feedback and the value of providing assessment feedback. Despite differences in the focus of their assessment activities, there were relatively few statistically significant differences between the data on assessment feedback reported by the two groups of psychologists. Overall, the researchers found that most psychologists were likely to provide in-person feedback to the person who had been evaluated: over 70% indicated that they usually or almost always provided this kind of direct verbal feedback. On the other hand, less than a quarter of the psychologists routinely provided clients with a copy of the actual assessment report. With respect to the benefits of providing assessment feedback to clients, most psychologists believed that receiving feedback allowed clients to (a) better understand their problems, (b) be more motivated to follow any recommendations that resulted from the assessment, and (c) actually feel better. Interestingly, the more strongly that psychologists believed in these positive effects of feedback, the more likely they were to spend an extended time (i.e., an hour or more) providing assessment feedback to their clients.

Building on a range of research evidence suggesting that assessment feedback can influence client emotional functioning, **Stephen Finn** developed a **therapeutic model of assessment** (e.g., Finn & Tonsager, 1997). In this model, clients are active participants in all phases of the assessment. This active involvement includes discussing the reasons for assessment, observing the test results, and interpreting the test scores. Particular efforts are made to (a) develop a strong working alliance with the client, (b) work collaboratively in defining the client's goals for the assessment, and (c) explore the assessment data with the client. Research evaluating aspects of this model has been encouraging: compared with assessment procedures focused solely on information gathering (i.e., little active collaboration with clients), clients receiving therapeutic assessment developed stronger working alliances with the psychologists and were less likely to prematurely terminate treatment (Hilsenroth & Cromer, 2007). Most of these studies were conducted in the context of providing short-term psychodynamic treatment to clients, but the results may also be relevant to other treatment forms. Therapist–client collaboration is a cornerstone of cognitive-behavioral treatments, and findings such as these suggest that the collaborative approach to assessment and treatment may be instrumental in the well-documented success of the cognitive-behavioral therapies (see Chapter 14).

 case example **TERESA**

The psychologist drafted a report to be sent to Teresa and Jeff's family physician and to the company that managed Jeff's health care benefits. The psychologist summarized the reason for the assessment and Teresa's history of anxiety symptoms. The results of the testing, interviews, observations, and self-monitoring were described, and a diagnosis of obsessive-compulsive disorder was indicated. Based on the nature of Teresa's symptoms and the treatment literature on OCD, the psychologist recommended that Teresa begin cognitive-behavioral treatment emphasizing exposure and response prevention. It was also recommended that, if the couple were willing, Jeff should participate in some sessions in order to assist Teresa with some of the exposure steps she would need to undertake.

The psychologist met with Teresa and Jeff to provide feedback on the full assessment and to review details of the report. The couple were encouraged to ask questions about the results—they had very few, as the findings were consistent with their own views. They were also encouraged to ask questions about the treatment options, including medication and partner-assisted exposure and response prevention. They had many questions on these matters, and the psychologist took considerable time to explain the nature of the psychological treatment. They discussed, in particular, the symptoms that would be targeted in the treatment (e.g., thoughts about injuring people, checking for dangerous materials around the house, checking about pedestrian injuries when driving). The psychologist also emphasized that the treatment required substantial commitment from both Teresa and Jeff to work on anxiety-related assignments between treatment sessions.

After noting two minor errors in the information in the draft report (concerning the dates of work-related events), Teresa indicated that she felt comfortable with the report being sent to the physician and the health care company. Although the psychologist indicated that the couple could take their time to discuss treatment options between themselves, very little discussion was needed for Teresa and Jeff to decide to go ahead with the psychological treatment. Accordingly, the psychologist booked an initial treatment appointment for both of them. Teresa was also asked to continue her self-monitoring activities, as these data would provide an important baseline for examining changes in anxiety symptoms during treatment.

SUMMARY AND CONCLUSIONS

In this chapter we have described the final stage of the assessment process in which the psychologist integrates diverse material from different sources into a sound formulation. The task of drawing together information requires the same kind of scientific thinking needed to make sense of research results. The psychologist draws on a wealth of knowledge about psychological functioning, psycho-pathology, risk, and protective factors, as well as solid understanding of psychometric issues in reaching a meaningful conclusion about a particular client. Like other types of decision making, clinical decision making is prone to a host of biases and errors. The psychologist must be flexible in generating hypotheses and cautious in weighing the evidence in support of them or against them. Overconfidence in one's own wisdom and experience may lead to a premature conclusion that fails to take into account all relevant data. Even-handed consideration of confirming and disconfirming data is as essential in clinical practice as it is in conducting research.

Students of clinical psychology may initially feel discouraged to learn of all the potential pitfalls in clinical decision making. However, it is important to remember that these decision-making errors apply to everyone: they apply in our personal lives and they occur in other types of decision making. Clinical psychologists are not immune from the same kinds of errors in decision making that affect other people. However, awareness of these pitfalls can lead to the use of strategies that minimize the likelihood of errors. As we discussed in earlier chapters, the different types of assessment information all have advantages and disadvantages. There is no single test that will yield a meaningful clinical formulation—the task of the clinical psychologist is much more complex. Research has established that clinical psychologists can effectively combine data from several imperfect methods to reach a clinically meaningful formulation that can guide services. The move toward greater transparency and account-ability in the delivery of health services fits well with the clinical psychology practices of providing feedback to clients following psychological assessment. A psychological assessment report is the product of careful analysis of a specific client: it draws on research evidence developed on large groups of individuals with particular attention to the client's specific circumstances.

Critical Thinking Questions

What common heuristics are operating when we assume that a person who has been exposed to trauma is likely to be psychologically vulnerable?

What are the challenges involved for psychologists in synthesizing all of the information collected as part of a psychological assessment?

In what ways is the process of developing a case formulation a scientific endeavor?

What are the advantages of reviewing reports with clients?

Key Terms

biases: judgments that are systematically different from what a person should conclude based on logic or probability

case formulation: a description of the patient that provides information on his or her life situation, current problems, and a set of hypotheses link psychosocial factors with the patient's clinical condition

computer-based interpretations: reports generated by computer programs that match a patient's general pattern of responses on a psychological test to summaries of research evidence about the typical characteristics of people with such a pattern of test responses

heuristics: mental shortcuts that make decision making easier and faster but often lead to less accurate decisions

retrospective recall: using data that rely on people to remember events that happened to them at some point in the past

self-serving attributional bias: a tendency to take more personal credit for successes than for failures by attributing success, but not failure, to internal, stable, and global causes

therapeutic model of assessment: an approach to psychological assessment in which clients are actively encouraged to participate in discussions about the reasons for the assessment, the results of the testing, and ways the assessment data should be integrated and interpreted

Key Names

Stephen Finn   Howard Garb   Jacqueline Persons

ADDITIONAL RESOURCES

BOOKS

Antony, M. M., & Barlow, D. H. (2002). *Handbook of assessment and treatment planning for psychological disorders*. New York: Guilford Press.

Eells, T. D. (Ed.). (2006). *Handbook of psychotherapy case formulation* (2nd ed.). New York: Guilford Press.

Garb, H. N. (1998). *Studying the clinician: Judgment research and psychological assessment*. Washington, DC: American Psychological Association.

Check It Out!

For more information on decision-making biases and heuristics, including some examples you can try that illustrate various biases and heuristics, visit these Web sites: http://www.nku.edu/~garns/165/pptj_h.html, http://www.prioritysystem.com/reasons1.html

In 2002, the cognitive psychologist Dr. Daniel Kahneman won the Nobel Prize for economics for his research on how people make decisions under conditions of uncertainty. You can read his Nobel Prize lecture on his research here: http://nobelprize.org/nobel_prizes/economics/laureates/2002/kahne-mann-lecture.pdf

There are many Web sites that provide examples of psychological assessment reports written for different purposes. Here are some of them, including some sites that have computer-based interpretative reports for specific assessment instruments:

http://www.msresource.com/format.html

http://www.behaviordat.com/sample.htm

http://www.self-directed-search.com/sdsreprt.html

https://www3.parinc.com/uploads/samplerpts/PAI_A_SAMPLE1.pdf

http://www.harcourt-au.com/media/products/NEO_PIR_Sample%20Interpretive%20Report.pdf

http://www.psycan.com/ecms.aspx/2d3a1847-a5f5-4886-a908-50cf7985fd6e/Documents/WRAT4-IR_Interpretive_Report.pdf

http://www.stoneandassociates.us/samples/peFail.pdf

CHAPTER 10

Prevention

INTRODUCTION

Harry sits in a comfortable chair watching the clock. Since the death of his wife 5 years ago, Harry has lived alone. An avid reader and expert horticulturalist, Harry spends many hours reading and tending his plants. His adult children maintain regular contact with weekly phone calls, but live too far away to allow frequent visits. Over the years Harry, now 83, has been troubled by rheumatoid arthritis that causes him pain and debilitation. He has found it increasingly difficult to manipulate small objects as the joints in his hands are stiff and inflamed. Pain in his knees and hips makes walking difficult, although he attempts to be as active as possible. Harry adjusts his clothing, smoothing his tie and brushing lint off his jacket. He checks his watch, shaking it to make sure it has not stopped. On hearing a noise outside his door, Harry grasps his cane and pulls himself painfully to a standing position. As the door opens with a creak, Harry grumbles, "I'm hungry, I thought you were supposed to be here at 12:30." The cheery face at his door belongs to Anne, a sprightly 76-year-old who has been a volunteer since her retirement from teaching 11 years ago. Anne sets out Harry's lunch, asks how he's enjoying the book he's reading, admires the blooms on his azalea, commiserates with his disappointment that his daughter has had to postpone her next visit, gathers up the tray and dishes from yesterday's meal, and leaves to deliver other meals.

The *Meals on Wheels* organization operates in many countries to provide wholesome meals to older adults whose nutrition might otherwise be poor. The benefits to recipients of *Meals on Wheels* may extend beyond the physical advantages of having a good meal. For Harry, the regular brief visits punctuate his day, reducing his isolation. For Harry's adult children who live far away, they provide reassurance that he is having at least one good meal a day and that he is seen by an informed and caring person on days that meals are delivered. For volunteers such as Anne, there may be a sense of satisfaction in contributing to the well-being of others. The *Meals on*

Wheels program is a nonprofit, volunteer-based organization in different countries. It is a good example of a program designed to offer services to a vulnerable population and prevent the development of serious problems. *Meals on Wheels* is committed to offering a sustainable service that is accountable to government and is sensitive to the needs of a diverse population. This model program provides benefits for both physical and mental health.

Prevention programs were first established to prevent physical health problems. Programs to prevent the spread of infectious diseases involve simple practices such as hand-washing, more intrusive procedures such as quarantining and wearing masks, and challenging tasks such as the development and use of vaccines. According to the World Health Organization, the provision of clean drinking water and the development of vaccination programs have been effective in preventing illness and death for millions of people worldwide every year (World Health Organization, 2003). Although scientists have developed vaccinations that are cost-effective in preventing virulent diseases, tragically, these vaccines are underused, and two million children die each year from diseases that could be prevented at low cost (World Health Organization, 2003). Furthermore, although vaccines in general are effective, a particular vaccine might not be effective for a given individual.

Because lifestyle factors are associated with many health problems, many prevention efforts also focus on encouraging the development of healthy habits such as good nutrition, regular exercise, and adequate sleep. Efforts to introduce a healthy lifestyle are usually referred to as **health promotion**. Health promotion is usually designed to increase activities that are beneficial to many aspects of physical health. As we discussed in Chapter 1, until recently clinical psychologists were not very involved in prevention activities. Another branch of psychology, **community psychology**, focuses on the reciprocal relations between individuals and the community in which they live. Community psychologists have a long history of developing services that are offered to a vulnerable population. For many years, the training of clinical psychologists focused on understanding problems at the level of the individual—it made sense then that interventions would also be designed at that level. Clinical psychologists reasoned that if problems were related to the way a person thought, felt, or acted, then it made sense to help the person by finding ways to change the dysfunctional thoughts, feelings, or behaviors. Consequently, clinical psychologists developed interventions at the level of the individual, couple, or family. Efforts to evaluate the effectiveness of those psychological services showed that the services were definitely helpful for some people.

Health promotion programs are designed to increase beneficial activities. (*Source:* Purestock)

Services to help parents manage their children's behavior are a good example. We know from studies of species from flatworms to humans, that (a) when a behavior is followed by a positive outcome, that behavior is likely to be repeated and (b) when a behavior is followed by a negative outcome it is less likely to be repeated. Early parent education programs based on these simple reinforcement principles were helpful to many parents. Nevertheless, some people do not come for psychological services, some drop out after the first session, and others fail to do the between-session assignments designed to improve their parenting. Even though clinical psychologists know effective ways to help parents encourage appropriate behavior, to help children manage their angry feelings and learn to share, and so on, they were unable to reach some parents. Who are these people who are so difficult to reach? Parents who argued a lot tended to drop out of treatment, as did depressed mothers and women who felt isolated (Reyno & McGrath, 2006). The recognition that potentially effective strategies were not accessible to parents who needed them the most forced clinical psychologists to develop innovative ways to prevent problems and to head off more serious problems. Increasingly, therefore, clinical psychologists have begun to develop programs that utilize the results of decades of community psychology research.

You may remember learning in Chapter 1 of the vast numbers of people who suffer from mental disorders, the severe psychological toll of these disorders on affected individuals and their families, and the escalating financial costs of mental health problems. Estimates for the United States suggest that the annual costs of mental disorders were at least $147 billion—more than the costs of cancer, respiratory disease, or AIDS (World Health Organization, 2004). Mental disorders also increase the risk of physical illness. Experts agree, therefore, that the only sustainable way to reduce the burden of mental disorders is through prevention (World Health Organization, 2004). Clinical psychologists working with people suffering from specific disorders are increasingly aware of the need to develop prevention programs (Dozois & Dobson, 2004). We admire the apparent simplicity of vaccination programs that allow the body to develop immunity to a virus before exposure to the actual virus. A trip to the clinic, tears of protest, and an afternoon with a slightly cranky child seem a small price to pay to protect a child from the dangers of smallpox! There is, however, no vaccine for child abuse, bullying, suicide, or eating disorders. Although we can all agree that prevention is a desirable goal, it is much more difficult to determine the most appropriate prevention program to develop, how it will be implemented, who will pay for it, and how we will measure its effectiveness.

Although intervention programs are much more common than are prevention programs, we have chosen to place the chapter on prevention before the chapters describing therapeutic intervention (like the old adage, "an ounce of prevention is worth a pound of cure"). It is clear that clinical psychology has the potential to help many people and to reduce the burden of care by the development and evaluation of programs for those at risk to prevent the development of mental disorders. You will notice that prevention programs are often delivered by service providers who are not clinical psychologists—the role of the clinical psychologist is more likely to be in program development, training, supervision, and evaluation than it is in front-line service provision.

In this chapter we outline different models that have guided the development of prevention programs. We present some key concepts in prevention science and illustrate them by briefly describing effective programs. Because prevention is based on the principle of early intervention, much of the work we highlight focuses on children and youth (Weissberg, Kumpfer, & Seligman, 2003). Although there are many innovative and promising prevention programs that target adults (Dozois & Dobson, 2004; Le, Muñoz, Ippen, & Stoddard, 2003; Zabinski, Wilfley, Winzelberg, Taylor, & Calfas, 2004), in this chapter we highlight programs that target children and youth. We follow a developmental path, first addressing programs to promote effective parenting, to prevent various types of violence, to prevent internalizing disorders, to prevent substance abuse, and to prevent problems in those exposed to trauma or loss. As prevention programs are not limited to the very young, **Viewpoint Box 10.2** (later in this chapter) describes a program designed to promote physical activity in the elderly. First, though, **Viewpoint Box 10.1** discusses the role that poverty plays in the mental health of children.

Have you considered a professional role in which you would not necessarily be the direct service provider? Do you find it appealing to think of ways your work could affect a large number of people?

VIEWPOINT BOX 10.1

POVERTY

In 2003, UNICEF released troubling results indicating that more than one billion children worldwide suffer the severe effects of poverty and are deprived of basic human rights such as adequate shelter, food, water, sanitation, and education. There is, however, no internationally agreed on definition of poverty. As politicians and scholars point out, the definition of poverty varies according to a country's level of affluence. There are basically two ways to identify and track those who are vulnerable to the effects of poverty: in relative terms or in absolute terms. Relative definitions identify the proportion of the population whose income is significantly below the median income. This is a statistical definition. Absolute terms identify those people whose incomes are insufficient to purchase goods and services that are considered essential. Critics argue that official poverty statistics drastically underestimate the numbers of children who live in poverty. The Luxembourg Income Study (2000), a landmark international initiative, adopted relative definitions to compare poverty rates across 25 countries by calculating the proportions of people whose income was 50% of the median income. Data for 1994 indicated that the highest proportion of children living in poverty among the 25 countries evaluated was Mexico (26.1%), followed by the United States (24.5%). Levels of child poverty were similar in Australia (15.8%), Canada (15.4%), Ireland (14.6%), and the United Kingdom (13.9%). In the years since the publication of the Luxembourg Income Study, there has been a significant decrease in the rate of child poverty in the United Staqtes, so that in 2007 17% of children, or 13 million, lived in families that are considered poor (National Center for Children in Poverty, 2007).

For decades, social scientists have recognized the deleterious consequences of child poverty on children's mental and physical health status. Scholars now see that children living in poverty are subject to multiple risk factors that have cumulative negative effects on their well-being. Poverty is harmful to the physical, socio-emotional, and cognitive well-being of children, youth, and their families (Evans, 2004). Compared with other children, children living in poverty are more likely to be exposed to family disruption and violence, and they have parents who are less responsive, read to them less frequently, and are less involved with their school activities. These children are more likely to be exposed to environmental pollutants, live in more crowded housing, and attend poorer quality day care.

How is all of this relevant to clinical psychology? The most important message is that children living in poverty are being challenged on multiple fronts. They are compromised in all areas of their lives. Consequently, any efforts to prevent negative outcomes for these vulnerable children must take into account the effects not simply of one stressor or disadvantage but of the pileup of stressors. Although it may be conceptually easier to study the effects of children witnessing violence in one study and the children of alcoholic parents in another study, we now understand that there is tremendous overlap in the different populations—the child whom we identify as exposed to violence in one study may be the same child identified as the child of an alcoholic parent in another study and as an aggressive child in a third study. The serious, cumulative, and chronic risks to which children in poverty are exposed require high dosage prevention programs to buffer children from the pileup of challenges these children face. A meta-analysis of the effectiveness of preschool prevention programs (Nelson, Westhues, & MacLeod, 2003) provided encouraging data indicating that positive effects of intensive preschool interventions for multiply disadvantaged children are sustained in the short, medium, and long term. Not surprisingly, the longer and the more intense the intervention, the greater the gains.

APPROACHES TO PREVENTION

The Commission on Chronic Illness (1957) identified three different types of intervention with respect to illness: primary, secondary, and tertiary. Primary intervention occurs before a disorder has developed and is designed to prevent the development of the disorder. Secondary intervention occurs when a disorder is evident; we usually refer to this type of intervention as treatment. Tertiary intervention occurs with respect to a chronic disorder and focuses on rehabilitation and long-term adaptation. The model of primary, secondary, and tertiary intervention that was originally designed to categorize services with respect to physical illness was then applied to mental disorders. Traditionally, the focus of psychological services has been at the level of secondary intervention or treatment. As described in Chapter 1, clinical psychologists also have extended their services both toward primary intervention in the prevention of problems and toward tertiary intervention in rehabilitation services.

It is also useful to think of distinctions among prevention programs. One distinction involves universal preventive interventions, selective preventive interventions, and indicated preventive interventions (Mrazek & Haggerty, 1994). As the name implies, **universal preventive interventions** are applied to an entire population. As a member of the general public you will have been exposed to several universal preventive interventions. You may, for example, remember television advertising campaigns designed to reduce undesirable activities such as wife assault or smoking or to promote healthy activities such as regular physical exercise. Your parents probably remember the initial advertising campaigns to encourage the wearing of seat belts while driving. During the flu season, universal programs remind the public to reduce contagion by frequent and thorough hand-washing. **Selective preventive interventions,** on the other hand, target people who are at elevated risk of developing a particular disorder or problem. For example, during an outbreak of a contagious disorder, selective prevention programs might require people entering hospitals to wear masks. **Indicated preventive interventions** target people who do not meet criteria for a disorder but who have elevated risk and may show detectable but subclinical signs of the disorder. Those who have come into contact with a confirmed case of an infectious disorder may be targets for indicated preventive interventions requiring a period of quarantine. We can probably all agree that the goal of preventing a debilitating, contagious, and potentially fatal disease is a good one. Nevertheless, there is controversy about the most effective prevention efforts. If you were a nurse in a hospital caring for patients with the disease, you would want compelling evidence that the prevention strategies were effective in protecting you from potentially fatal infection. Similarly, if your life was effectively put on hold for almost two weeks by imposed quarantine (missing school, recreation, and social life), you would probably want reassurance that this sacrifice was necessary to help contain the spread of the disease. Thus, prevention programs should be evaluated to determine whether they are meeting their goals.

Some prevention scientists consider that these categories of universal, selective, and indicated prevention rely too much on a disease model and have proposed that psychologists think instead in terms of promoting health (e.g., Kaplan, 2000). This of course raises the question of what we mean by health. Health is not simply the opposite of illness. There is no universal definition of health—it all depends on the person's context. Younger people often consider health in terms of fitness, energy, and strength. Older people tend to see health in terms of their inner strength and their ability to meet life's challenges (World Health Organization, 2004). There are similar challenges in defining mental health and the promotion of mental health. To this end, the World Health Organization defines mental health promotion activities as those designed to increase well-being and resilience.

Different types of prevention programs are designed to reduce the symptoms and burden of mental disorders. **Primary prevention** is based on a behavioral model of functioning and does not rely on the concept of disease. Primary prevention is focused on the provision of conditions conducive to good health. Primary prevention is similar to the concept of health promotion. **Secondary prevention** is more similar to selected and indicated prevention programs because it focuses on prevention in groups of people who are identified as being at high risk. The **risk reduction model** of prevention relies heavily on research to guide interventions (Mrazek & Haggerty, 1994). **Risk factors** are characteristics of the individual or the environment that render a person more vulnerable to the development of a problem or disorder or that are associated with more severe symptoms. Once at-risk individuals are identified, they are the target of prevention programs designed to protect them from developing the problem or disorder. The other side of the coin is the identification of factors associated with resilience—**protective factors** are those characteristics that protect high-risk individuals from developing the problem or disorder. If we understand the variables that are protective, then we can use such knowledge in developing effective prevention programs.

The science of prevention requires knowledge of a problem, its prevalence, variables that are causally involved in its development, the mechanisms of risk transmission, and particular subgroups that are at high risk. Obviously not all risk factors are equally malleable, so it makes sense to target those risk factors that can be changed. Some risk and protective factors are specific to disorders, whereas others are generic. Potential risk and protective factors associated with the development of psychopathology in children and youth are listed in **Table 10.1** and **Table 10.2**.

 If you were asked to design a program to prevent the development of behavioral problems using a risk reduction model, you would need to target risk and protective factors that are modifiable. Which of the factors listed in Table 10.1 and Table 10.2 are most likely to be modifiable?

TABLE 10.1   Risk Factors for the Development of Psychopathology in Children and Youth

Individual Factors

- Complications in pregnancy and/or birth
- Physical health problems or disability
- Difficult temperament
- Poor nutrition
- Intellectual deficit or learning disability
- Attachment problems
- Poor social skills
- Low self-esteem
- Impulsivity
- Attention deficits

School Context

- Bullying
- Peer rejection
- Deviant peer group
- Inadequate behavior management

Family/Social Factors

- Parental isolation
- Single parent
- Antisocial role models in family
- Exposure to family or community violence
- Harsh or inconsistent discipline
- Inadequate supervision and monitoring
- Parental abuse or neglect
- Long-term parental unemployment
- Criminality in family
- Parental psychopathology

Life Events and Situations

- Abuse
- Family disruption

(Continued)

TABLE 10.1 *(Continued)*

- Chronic illness or death of family member
- Poverty
- Unemployment
- Homelessness
- Parental imprisonment
- War or natural disasters
- Witnessing trauma
- Migration
- High-density living
- Poor housing conditions
- Isolated from support services including transport, shopping, recreational facilities

Community and Cultural Factors

- Socioeconomic disadvantage
- Social or cultural discrimination
- Isolation
- Exposure to community violence or crime

Adapted from Barrett and Turner, 2004

Once a program has been designed, the prevention scientist must carefully monitor its implementation to ensure that it is conducted as planned. This is especially important, as the prevention program is likely to be implemented in numerous agencies that vary in their resources and staff skills. Both the program's short- and long-term outcomes must be monitored in order to fully evaluate its impact. **Table 10.3** describes the process that a researcher follows in developing a prevention program.

In assessing the effects of a treatment intervention, it is relatively easy to determine whether the treatment made a difference. We can assess whether those who received the service had a different outcome than those who did not receive the service: we can test whether there was a clinically significant reduction in their symptoms, determine whether or not they meet criteria for a diagnosis, or whether they now score in the normal range on a particular measure. Determining the efficacy of a prevention program presents a greater challenge; researchers must assess whether the program resulted in fewer people developing a problem than would have been the case without the prevention program. **Incidence rates** are used to describe the number of new cases of a specific problem—so some prevention researchers measure the success of their program by examining the extent to which the incidence rate is reduced. Although more than 1,000 controlled studies have examined the effectiveness of programs designed to prevent mental health problems, very few have examined whether these programs are effective in reducing the incidence of new cases of a disorder (Cuijpers, 2003). One reason why this strategy is rarely used is that in order to have the statistical power to detect a difference in the incidence of

TABLE 10.2 Protective Factors for the Development of Psychopathology in Children and Youth

Individual Factors

- Easy temperament
- Adequate nutrition
- Positive attachment
- Above-average intelligence
- School achievement
- Problem-solving skills
- Social competence
- Optimism
- Positive self-esteem

Family/Social Factors

- Supportive, caring parents
- Authoritative parenting
- Family harmony
- Supportive relationship with another adult (aside from parents)
- Strong family norms and prosocial values

School Context

- Prosocial peer group
- Required responsibility and helpfulness
- Opportunities for some success and recognition of achievement
- School norms against violence
- Positive school–home relations

Life Events and Situations

- Adequate income
- Adequate housing

Community and Cultural Factors

- Attachment to networks within the community
- Participation in church or other community groups
- Strong cultural identity and ethnic pride
- Access to support services
- Community/cultural norms against violence

Adapted from Barrett and Turner (2004)

TABLE 10.3   Designing and Evaluating Prevention Research

- Identify the target: What do you want to prevent?

- Determine how serious the problem is. How many people are affected? What are the costs of the problem, in human suffering, health care costs, etc.?

- Review the research evidence about the problem. What do we know about how the risk factors develop? What variables make it more likely that a problem will develop?

- Identify high-risk groups. These are the factors that have been shown to moderate risk.

- What is known about protective factors?

- Design the intervention: How will the target condition be prevented? Is there an evidence-based prevention program for this problem? If so, does it need to be modified for my community?

- Design the study: How will you know whether the intervention is efficacious?

---

disorder, it is necessary to have studies with very large samples. Alternative research strategies are to target high-risk samples, to offer the program at high intensity, or to rely on accumulating samples from different studies. Although used with increasing frequency, these strategies remain underutilized in evaluating the impact of prevention efforts. Yet another way to measure the success of a prevention program is by calculating the **number needed to treat**, which refers to the number of people who need to receive the intervention in order to prevent one person from developing the condition. Perhaps the best example of this is the well-known practice of regular use of aspirin to lower the risk of heart attack, for which the number needed to treat is 130—that means that for every 130 people who regularly take aspirin, one person will be saved from having a heart attack. As you can see, this commonly used prevention strategy must be used by many people in order to have an effect on a single person.

Meta-analytic reviews of prevention programs are very useful in identifying the types of programs that have demonstrated effectiveness—in the following sections we will describe the results of meta-analyses of programs designed to prevent a range of disorders. You may recall from Chapter 4 the distinction between efficacy and effectiveness. These concepts apply to the science of prevention just as they do to intervention research. Once a prevention program has been shown to be efficacious in controlled studies, it is likely to be adopted in other less strictly controlled settings. Effectiveness refers to the extent to which a prevention program achieves desired outcomes when used in an applied setting rather than in the original research conditions. Even if a program has been demonstrated to be effective in other settings and meta-analyses have yielded positive results, it is important that the program be evaluated to determine its usefulness in each setting in which it is applied.

PROMOTING EVIDENCE-BASED PARENTING

Parents play a key role in their children's socialization. The task of parenting children is a demanding one that requires no license, training, or supervision. As you saw in Table 10.1, harsh or inconsistent discipline, poor supervision and monitoring of a child, parental abuse, and neglect are risk factors for the development of child and adolescent psychopathology. On the other hand, the availability of supportive, caring parents can protect children and youth from the development of psychopathology (Table 10.2). Although the responsibilities of child rearing can be daunting at times to all parents, some parents are particularly vulnerable due to their age, isolation, distress, conflict, or limited socioeconomic resources. There is strong evidence that children's functioning is challenged by poor parenting, conflict in the family, and parental psychopathology (Biglan, 2003; World Health Organization, 2004). We describe below three evidence-based programs that have been developed to promote good parenting and therefore to decrease the risk factors for diverse child problems.

Home Visiting Programs

A number of programs have demonstrated impressive results in targeting at-risk parents. In a 25-year research program, Olds and his colleagues have developed, implemented, tested, and replicated a program offering services to low-income teenage single mothers expecting their first child (Olds, 2002). Home visits were conducted by trained nurses beginning during the pregnancy and continuing after the child's birth. During these visits nurses addressed women's concerns about the pregnancy, delivery, and care of the child. They taught skills in both self-care and child care and promoted women's use of the health care system. **Figure 10.1** illustrates the model of program influences on maternal and child health and development.

In randomized controlled trials, Olds and his colleagues have found that the home visit program is effective in achieving the immediate goal of improving parental care. In the middle term, this has benefits for children in terms of reducing child abuse and neglect, and in the long-term, reducing the number of arrests, convictions, substance abuse problems, and sexual promiscuity in the children when they reached the age of 15. Furthermore, the program improves a young mother's life course by increasing labor force participation and her economic self-sufficiency. These positive effects are all the more remarkable as nurses completed only an average of 8 visits during pregnancy and 25 visits during the child's first two years of life. Visits lasted up to an hour and a half. These short- and long-term gains were accomplished in a very high-risk group with the investment of under 50 hours of direct contact between nurses and teenage mothers. In general, the most beneficial effects were found for the families who were at greatest risk.

Triple P

Developed by psychologist **Matthew Sanders** and his colleagues in Australia, the Triple P Positive Parenting Program is an evidence-based parenting program designed to: (a) enhance knowledge, skills, and confidence of parents; (b) promote safe environments for young people; and (c) promote children's competence through positive parenting practices (Bor, Sanders, & Markie-Dadds, 2002; Sanders, 1999; Sanders, Cann, & Markie-Dadds, 2003; Sanders, Markie-Dadds, Turner, & Ralph, 2004). Consistent with the idea of adapting programs to offer different "dosages" of intervention according to participants' needs, the Triple P program is a multilevel system that provides interventions of gradually increasing intensity, according to the level of need (Collins, Murphy, & Bierman, 2004).

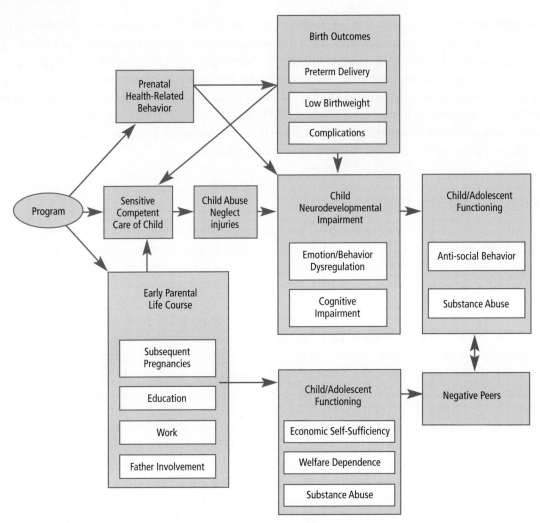

FIGURE 10.1   Model of Influences of a Home Visit Program on Maternal and Child Health and Development
Adapted from Olds (2002), with permission from Springer Science and Business Media

The Universal Triple P program is offered to all interested parents using a variety of media to provide evidence-based information about general parenting strategies to deal with everyday issues and challenges. The next step in the program hierarchy is to offer brief (one- or two-session) individualized services by phone or face to face to address parents' specific concerns. Moving one step further, parents of children with mild to moderate problems may benefit from a program delivered over four sessions by a primary health care provider. Parents of children with more severe behavior problems may require the Standard Triple P offered in either a group or self-directed format. The most intensive intervention is the Enhanced Triple P, which includes not only parenting skills, but also additional sessions focused on parents' mood, coping, and partner support.

Program materials are designed for five different developmental stages (infants, toddlers, preschoolers, children in elementary school, and teenagers). The program is designed to enhance protective factors and to decrease risk factors for children's problems. Consequently, parents are trained to develop positive relationships with their children, encourage desirable behavior, teach new skills, and manage misbehavior. Parents are encouraged to adopt developmentally appropriate expectations about their child's behavior. The importance of taking care of oneself as a parent is also stressed. The Triple P approach involves intense training of practitioners as well as continuing education for those who deliver the program.

The developers of the Triple P approach have conducted a series of randomized controlled trials comparing Triple P interventions with wait-list control groups, as well as comparing different formats of Triple P (Sanders et al., 2004; Sanders, 2008). Results of this research indicate that Triple P is effective in helping parents adopt positive parenting practices, which in turn is associated with fewer child problems, greater parental confidence, and enhanced parental well-being (Sanders et al., 2004). Meta-analytic results support the efficacy of Triple P in reducing child behavior problems (Thomas & Zimmer-Gembeck, 2007). Currently, the Triple P program is being adapted for use in diverse populations in several countries, and evaluations of those programs are under way (Prinz & Sanders, 2007).

Incredible Years

Developed and refined over 20 years of research by psychologist **Carolyn Webster-Stratton**, the Incredible Years training program was originally designed to help children ages 3–8 who had been identified as having conduct problems (Webster-Stratton & Reid, 2003). As the program was found to be successful in treating conduct problems, it has been expanded to cover a wider age range and has been offered as a prevention program (Baydar, Reid, & Webster-Stratton, 2003). The program uses group discussion, videotaped modeling, and behavioral rehearsal techniques to promote adult–child interactions that will facilitate children's development of social competence. The primary goal of the Incredible Years program is to train parents in skills so that they can effectively play with their child, provide praise for positive behaviors, and set limits on unacceptable behaviors using time-out, ignoring, appropriate consequences, and problem solving. The basic program is available for different age ranges and includes a minimum of 12 sessions (although additional sessions may be required). An advanced 9- to 12-session program targets parents' interpersonal difficulties by teaching problem solving, anger management, communication, emotional regulation skills, and support-seeking skills. A supplementary program, Supporting Your Child's Education, helps parents whose children are experiencing school difficulties. Complementary programs involve training teachers (Webster-Stratton, Reid, & Hammond, 2001) and a 22-week child training program (Webster-Stratton & Reid, 2004) that teaches emotional literacy, perspective taking, friendship skills, anger management, and problem solving. The effectiveness of this selective prevention program has been tested with more than 1,000 multiethnic, socioeconomically disadvantaged families. Results support the program's effectiveness in promoting good parenting, enhancing children's social competence, and preventing the development of conduct problems (Gross et al., 2003; Webster-Stratton & Reid, 2003). For more about Dr. Webster-Stratton, see **Profile Box 10.1.**

PROFILE BOX 10.1

DR. CAROLYN WEBSTER-STRATTON

Dr. Carolyn Webster-Stratton

I started my career with my bachelor's degree in Nursing from the University of Toronto. After spending some time practicing nursing in Africa, I took a Masters as a Pediatric Nurse Practitioner and a Masters in Public Health at Yale University. Following graduation I worked for 4 years as a nurse practitioner, first with three pediatricians in Connecticut, then for a year at University of Toronto Health Clinic, and finally for 2 years in private practice in Alaska. My experience in Alaska providing counseling to depressed mothers and children with behavior problems and suicidal adolescents prompted me to pursue my psychology degree. I moved to Seattle, where I received my Ph.D. in Educational Psychology at the University of Washington. I then completed a self-designed internship and was licensed as a Clinical Psychologist in Washington. My current position is Professor and Director of the Parenting Clinic at the University of Washington. My research program has been funded for the past 25 years by the National Institute of Mental Health (NIMH), National Center for Nursing Research (NCNR), National Institute for Drug Abuse (NIDA), and Head Start and has focused on the development of programs to prevent and treat young children with Oppositional Defiant Disorder, Conduct Disorders, and Attention Deficit Disorder. I have been fortunate to have been recipient of an NIMH research scientist award for 10 years, which has allowed me to focus on my clinical work with families and teachers along side research and teaching of graduate students.

How did you choose to become a clinical psychologist?

After my masters degree, I worked for several years as a nurse practitioner doing work that involved running mother and baby groups in hospitals, evaluating children's development, teaching Lamaze classes, helping parents manage children's behavior problems, and working with depressed adolescents. I became intrigued with the idea of how to work most effectively and collaboratively with families in order to reduce behavior problems and enhance children's social and emotional competence. I felt that combining my nursing knowledge with what I could learn from psychology would help me understand more effective behavior-change strategies for working with families and others caring for children.

What is the most rewarding part of your job as a clinical psychologist?

The ability to help parents from many diverse cultures as well as teachers of young children to feel more confident in their ability to provide developmentally appropriate and nurturing interaction and discipline strategies, which result in more socially, and emotionally competent children. It is amazing and extremely rewarding to me to find that, at this point in my career, I now have the opportunity to help other clinicians and teachers from many different countries to offer these evidence-based programs to families in their communities.

What is the greatest challenge you face as a clinical psychologist?

Fewer than 10% of young children with conduct problems get any intervention, and even fewer of those get an evidence-based intervention. This is especially true for socioeconomically disadvantaged families and those without health care insurance. I find this lack of evidence-based services for this age group unacceptable given the consistent research showing that young children who are the "early starters" of conduct problems and antisocial behaviors are those who are most likely to become delinquent, drug abusers, and violent in later years. We still have a long way to go to get agencies and schools to deliver evidence-based programs with fidelity using the recommended treatment dosage and methods researched in studies and recommended by developers.

Tell us about the development of the Incredible Years Programs to prevent externalizing and internalizing problems

The Incredible Years Programs started with the development of parent prevention and treatment programs using DVDs of unrehearsed video interactions to provide modeling and to stimulate group discussion and practice of appropriate child-directed play, communication interactions, and discipline strategies. This video-based, group discussion strategy was later expanded to develop new programs for teachers designed to teach them how to strengthen student's social and emotional self-regulation and problem-solving skills as well as how to manage children's behavior problems including both externalizing and internalizing problems. Finally, a third DVD program was also developed for direct use with children so that teachers could show their students video models of how to be friendly, express emotions and manage anger, problem solve, and handle conflict. These video programs are based on the social learning theory, and relationship and cognitive theories of Patterson, Rogers, and Bandura and others. They are used in a group discussion format in order to foster support networks and stimulate sharing and collaboration between participants.

How do you integrate science and practice in your work?

For 30 years I have been developing and researching different interventions for young children, and I have always participated as a clinician delivering all of these interventions. As I have learned firsthand about the strengths and limitations of these programs and how they do or do not reduce risk factors or strengthen protective factors, I have continued to try to refine these programs and develop new programs focused on those risk factors amenable to change. It is this process of working clinically myself with families and teachers that provides me with the necessary "fuel" that motivates my ongoing research.

What do you see as the most exciting changes in the field of clinical psychology?

One of the most exciting changes is to develop further understanding of the biological, physiological, and developmental aspects of children's mental health problems and how this interplay with their environment (at home and at school) makes a difference in children's eventual outcomes. This research is on the cusp and will help us to refine interventions for the future.

PREVENTION OF VIOLENCE

Physical Abuse of Children

Physical abuse of children refers to the deliberate infliction of injury on a child. Estimates of the incidence of physical abuse vary, as there is considerable variability in the definition of the boundaries between acceptable discipline and abuse. For example, although a growing number of countries have banned the use of physical punishment, in the United States parents are permitted to punish their children physically, as long as they do not inflict physical harm. A meta-analysis of 23 methodologically sound studies of programs designed to prevent parents' physical abuse of children found that home visiting programs, behavioral parent training programs, and multimodal programs were effective in modifying the risk of physical abuse (Lundahl, Nimer, & Parsons, 2006).

The risk of child abuse by poor, single teenage mothers who participated in the home visiting programs described in the previous section (Olds, 2002) was half that of comparison mothers who did not participate. Both behavioral training and stress management training were effective in improving maternal reports of their own well-being and child welfare; these positive effects were evident both in the short-term and at long-term follow-up. Unfortunately, improvements in parenting skills were evident in the short-term only and were not maintained at follow-up. Multimodal programs appear to blend the benefits of both home visits and skills-based programs and have the advantage of minimizing participant attrition (O'Riordan & Carr, 2002).

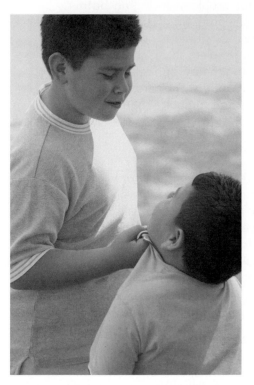

School-based anti-bullying programs can be very effective in altering the frequency of bullying behavior.
Source: Media Bakery

Youth Violence: Bullying and Delinquency

One of the most common reasons children are referred to mental health clinics stems from problems with aggressive and noncompliant behavior (Miller & Prinz, 1990). A subgroup of children exhibits risk factors for the development of aggression from a very early age (Nagin & Tremblay, 1999). By the time these young people reach adolescence, their aggressive behavior has brought them into conflict with the law, and they are alienated from the school system (Fisher, 2003). Intervention at that stage has only limited success, as these young people are very resistant to efforts to change their behavior (Fisher, 2003). If we have such limited success in treating conduct disorder once it has developed, it makes much more sense then to try to prevent its development in the first place (Biglan, 2003; World Health Organization, 2004).

There is some overlap between the types of programs designed to prevent violence and delinquency and those designed to treat oppositional defiant disorder and conduct disorder in young children. In a previous section we described programs for families with very young children such as home visits, Triple P, and Incredible Years that have been successful in promoting parenting, enhancing child competence, and reducing child aggression. School-based interventions that directly target aggression and violence by training students in anger management and conflict resolution have reported mixed success (Prinz & Dumas, 2004). For example, observers may note improvements in prosocial behaviors, but there may be no change in parent or teacher ratings of the youth's aggression. In other studies, youth knowledge of socially appropriate responses increases, but there is limited change in violent behavior after participation in the program.

More encouraging results were found in a comprehensive school-based program to reduce bullying in children ages 6–15 years developed in Norway following the suicide of two youth who were the victims of bullying (Olweus, 1993). The program is designed to reduce both the opportunities and the rewards for bullying. This comprehensive program encourages changes in the school (anti-bullying policy) and in the classroom (anti-bullying rules and discussion of alternatives to antisocial behavior), and promotes links between family and schools. The program is effective not only in reducing bullying, but also in reducing antisocial behavior in general and in enhancing student satisfaction with school. A study of 37 schools and 89 teachers who used the Olweus Bullying Prevention Program to varying degrees revealed that teachers are the key agent of change: their recognition of a problem with bullying and their commitment to the program are essential to its effective implementation (Kallestad & Olweus, 2003). The Olweus program has been applied in many countries. McCarthy and Carr (2002) reviewed four studies of its effectiveness, including data from 110 schools and almost 20,000 youths. They concluded that the program is effective in reducing reports of bullying as well as reducing reports of being bullied. These effects are evident in the short term and, importantly, are sustained over longer periods. Consistent with our previous comments about prevention program implementation, program effectiveness is determined by the extent to which program integrity is maintained. When the program is diluted, effects are reduced (McCarthy & Carr, 2002).

A multicomponent prevention program, the Fast Track Project was launched in 1990 by the Conduct Problems Prevention Research Group (CPPRG; 2002a). This trial project was based on available research on risk and protective factors in the development of conduct disorder. The program was designed to assess the feasibility of (a) engaging community stakeholders in the project, (b) maintaining the program's fidelity while responding to local needs, and (c) maintaining community engagement so that the program would be sustainable (CPPRG, 2002a). The Fast Track program expanded on a program developed to target high-risk children in kindergarten (Tremblay, Pagani-Kurtz, Mâsse, Vitaro, & Pihl, 1995). Screening of more than 9,000 kindergarten children identified a very high-risk sample of 891 children who were then randomly assigned to an intervention group or to a control group. A multiyear program was offered in the schools attended by the intervention group children. The intervention included a child component designed to increase academic competence, emotion regulation, and social skills. Discipline, support of constructive behavior, and monitoring of activities were targeted in the parent component. Group discussions were followed up by home visits. The classroom component involved a curriculum designed to promote self-control, emotional awareness, and social problem solving. At the end of the first year, the program had been delivered successfully to most families, and the results were encouraging (CPPRG, 2002b). Compared with the control group, children in the intervention had more positive interactions with their peers and were less frequently rejected. Parents in the intervention group were more involved with their children, were more consistent in their discipline strategies, and were less reliant on harsh physical punishment. Teachers rated intervention parents as more involved with their children's education. School observations revealed that the intervention children had fewer behavioral problems than did the

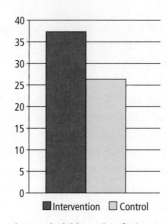

FIGURE 10.2   Proportion of Intervention and Control Children Classified as Problem-Free

Adapted from Conduct Problems Research Group (2002b); reproduced with permission from Springer Science and Business Media.

untreated control children. As the goal of a prevention program is to reduce the incidence of problems in the future, longer-term assessment is essential. An assessment of children at the end of grade 3 revealed that some of the gains had been maintained, but some effects had disappeared. Children who received the intervention were less likely to show signs of serious conduct problems than were children in the control group. **Figure 10.2** shows that more than a third of the children in the intervention group (37%) were classified as "problem-free" at the end of grade 3, whereas just over a quarter of children in the control group were considered problem-free.

At first glance these results may seem disappointing, as almost two thirds of the children in the program were classified as having conduct problems. However, there is another way to look at these data. Although the total elimination of disorders or illnesses would be ideal, prevention programs usually have a more realistic goal of reducing the incidence of disorders. Thus, another way to think of the results is that the children who received the program were 37% less likely to have serious problems than were children in the control group. Follow-up at the end of grades 4 and 5 indicated that high-risk children who participated in the program had better social competence, fewer problems in social cognition, less involvement with deviant peers, and fewer conduct problems than did high-risk children who did not participate (CPPRG, 2004). Although significant, these effects were small. Ongoing evaluation of this program as the children progress toward adolescence will assess the long-term effectiveness of this intervention for children at very high risk of developing conduct problems.

PREVENTION OF INTERNALIZING DISORDERS

You may recall from Chapter 3 that researchers have found it useful to consider problem behaviors along two dimensions: internalizing problems and externalizing problems. So far in this chapter we have focused most of our discussion on the prevention of externalizing problems and on the promotion of good parenting. Externalizing problems are often dramatic and, when they result in injuries or damage to property, can yield sensational newspaper headlines. Internalizing problems, such as anxiety and mood disorders, by definition, are more private. The person with internalizing problems may suffer quietly on his or her own without coming to anyone's attention. Internalizing problems are no less serious, however, and recent prevention efforts have also focused on ways to prevent the development of problems such as anxiety and depression. In addition to their psychological toll, these disorders incur substantial costs to the health care system and to the economy. Internalizing problems are also evident in childhood. Some research suggests that anxiety problems in childhood may be related to the development of depression in young people (Cole, Peeke, Martin, Truglio, & Seroczynski, 1998). Psychologists have therefore been at the forefront of efforts to prevent anxiety and depression in children.

Anxiety Disorders

Risk factors for the development of anxiety include individual factors such as inhibited temperament and an avoidant coping style, as well as overprotective parenting practices and parental anxiety (Barrett & Turner, 2004). A group of Australian researchers, led by **Paula Barrett,** developed a prevention program that was adapted from an effective treatment program for children with anxiety disorders (Barrett & Turner, 2001; Dadds, Holland, Barrett, Laurens, and Spence, 1999; Lowry-Webster & Barrett, 2001). In a selected prevention program, schoolchildren were screened to identify those with mild to moderate anxiety problems ($n = 128$) who were randomly assigned to an intervention group or to a monitoring group. The intervention was based on the Coping Koala program with 10 sessions offered to children in a group format as well as three sessions offered to parents, followed by booster sessions. Children who received the intervention were found to have lower rates of anxiety disorder at the end of treatment. At 12-month follow-up, differences between the intervention group and the comparison group had diminished, but by the 24-month follow-up, 39% of children in the untreated group met criteria for an anxiety disorder, whereas only 20% of children in the intervention group did so (Dadds et al., 1999). This means that participation in the program was associated with almost a 50% reduction in the incidence of anxiety disorders at 2-year follow-up.

Barrett and Turner (2001) adapted the Coping Koala program to a format that could be used in a universal prevention program delivered by teachers (Friends for Children and Friends for Youth). Within a sample of 489 children, assignment was made to one of three conditions: psychologist-led preventive intervention, teacher-led preventive intervention, or standard curriculum. The intervention included 10 weekly sessions and two booster sessions as well as four parent sessions. Assessment at the end of the program revealed positive effects in both intervention conditions. These data suggest that the program can be effectively delivered by teachers. Longer-term follow-up evaluations and replications in other cultures are under way (Barrett & Turner, 2004).

Depression

Risk factors for the development of depression include individual variables such as interpersonal skills deficits and cognitive errors, family variables such as parental depression and marital conflict, as well as contextual factors such as negative life events (Lee & Asgary-Eden, 2009). Horowitz and

Garber (2006) examined a wide range of programs designed to prevent depressive symptoms in children and adolescents. Horowitz and Garber found little evidence that universal programs are effective in preventing depression, but observed small yet significant effects for indicated and selective intervention. Studies with a greater percentage of female participants had larger effect sizes. Their recommendations include a focus on at-risk groups, such as being a female adolescent, offspring of depressed parents, with elevated levels of depressive or anxious symptoms, and being exposed to family-related stress such as divorce or bereavement. Interestingly, a meta-analysis that examined prevention programs across the life span found that preventive interventions reduce the incidence of depressive disorders by 22%. The number needed to treat is 22—recall that for the preventive effects of aspirin the comparable figure is 130 (Cuijpers, van Straten, Am Smit, Mihalopoulos, & Beekman, 2008).

To date, universal prevention programs have been found to have little impact on the incidence of depression. (*Source:* zhang bo/iStockphoto)

Overall, these studies suggest that there is merit to developing programs to prevent the development of internalizing problems. Programs based on cognitive-behavioral and interpersonal principles are promising strategies to promote individual and interpersonal skills that will protect children and youth from developing internalizing disorders. School-based programs offer an appealing avenue to circumvent adolescents' avoidance of the stigma of mental health services. Researchers are working hard to identify the most cost-effective strategy to convey these skills to young people and to solicit the collaboration of their parents.

PREVENTION OF SUBSTANCE ABUSE

The societal costs of smoking, alcohol abuse, and drug abuse are enormous. Alcohol, tobacco, and drug use during pregnancy are associated with a host of deleterious consequences such as premature delivery, low birth weight, perinatal mortality, and long-term neurological and cognitive-emotional problems (World Health Organization, 2004). It is estimated that tobacco is responsible for 4.1% of the total global economic costs due to disability, with alcohol accounting for another 4.0% (World Health Organization, 2004). Substance abuse is a leading cause of adolescent morbidity and mortality due to its links with motor vehicle accidents and with sexual behavior leading to unplanned pregnancies and HIV infection (Essau, 2004). Problems with smoking, alcohol, and drug abuse emerge during adolescence. There is evidence that the early onset of consumption is associated with higher risk of abuse (Essau, 2004).

Although alcohol use is common in society, not all those who drink alcohol go on to abuse it. What factors are associated with greater risk? Risk can be considered at the level of the individual, the family, peer group, and community, and at a provincial or national level according to the laws governing access to cigarettes and alcohol. Individual-level risks include temperamental factors, coping skills, psychopathology, and exposure to negative life events. Unfortunately, some high-risk youth may also be at risk of school dropout and may therefore not receive a prevention or health promotion program if it is delivered in school (Zucker, 2003). Those at risk for one problem behavior may also be at risk for others. For example, adolescent smoking is highly correlated with engagement in other problem behaviors including alcohol abuse, antisocial behavior, high-risk sexual behaviors, and academic failure (Biglan & Severson, 2003).

Problems of substance abuse are particularly acute in some indigenous populations. Although risk and protective factors for the development of substance abuse may be similar in Native American populations and in the general population, there has been little systematic study of any culture-specific risk and protective factors or of the effectiveness of prevention programs in these populations (Marlatt et al., 2006). As a step toward addressing this shortcoming in our

Problems with smoking, alcohol, and drug abuse emerge during adolescence. (*Source:* Media Bakery)

knowledge, a group of researchers from the University of Washington has collaborated with the Seattle Indian Health Board to develop a program based on empirically supported principles that is congruent with the culture of urban native youth (Hawkins et al., 2004). Evaluations of the Journeys of the Circle program are under way.

Universal preventive interventions can focus on regulating young people's access to tobacco and alcohol as well as on education about their harmful effects. A series of meta-analyses by Tobler and colleagues (Tobler et al., 2000) distinguished between two types of programs: interactive and noninteractive. *Interactive programs* that foster the development of interpersonal skills yielded higher effect sizes than did lecture-based *noninteractive programs*. The effective programs begin by providing multiple sessions early in adolescence and follow them with booster sessions in midadolescence (Coughlan, Doyle, & Carr, 2002). In addition to directly targeting youth, prevention programs can be designed to influence the behavior of significant others and, indirectly, the behavior of children and adolescents. A meta-analysis of 20 studies that examined parenting programs to reduce misuse of tobacco, alcohol, and drugs by youth found evidence that efficacy was associated with active parental involvement in developing social competence and self-regulation (Petrie, Bunn, & Byrne, 2007). Based on the results of years of research, **Table 10.4** summarizes the features of efficacious drug abuse prevention programs.

Although it makes sense to think that in choosing a prevention program, organizations would be guided by the results of the scientific literature, unfortunately, this is not always the case. For example, Ennett and colleagues (2003) surveyed a national sample of public and private schools about the programs they used to prevent substance abuse. Although Tobler's series of meta-analyses clearly identified that programs are most effective when they include interactive teaching strategies, only 17.4% of surveyed programs delivered material in an interactive style. It is possible that sufficient time had not passed for Tobler's work to influence these school programs. On the other hand, the majority of the studies used in the meta-analyses had been available for many years with, apparently, limited effect on the nature of school-based prevention efforts. Psychologists' ethical codes dictate that they should

TABLE 10.4   Key Elements of Efficacious Drug Abuse Prevention Programs

Resistance Skills and Normative Education

- Skills to identify social pressure to use drugs, and skills to resist such pressure
- Accurate knowledge about prevalence of drug use to help develop conservative drug use norms

Life Skills

- Assertiveness skills
- Skills for improving self-control and self-esteem
- Stress management skills
- Social communication and problem-solving skills
- Decision-making skills
- Skills for developing social alternatives to drug use

Multisystemic Involvement

- Peer-leader involvement in program delivery
- Peer group projects exploring alternatives to drug use
- Home-school liaison about drug use prevention policy
- Parent–child homework assignments about drug abuse prevention
- Parent training in parent–adolescent communication, limit-setting, and supervision
- Community involvement in a drug abuse prevention task force

General Design Features

- Adequate training, support, and supervision of teachers, peer leaders, and program staff
- Manualized program curricula
- Monitoring of accurate program implementation
- Active training methods (modeling, rehearsal, corrective feedback, reinforcement, and extended practice)
- Begin at the transition from primary to secondary school when youngsters are ages 11–13
- Extend over at least a school year and include booster sessions annually throughout high school
- Incorporated into the existing school curriculum
- Developmentally staged
- Socially and culturally acceptable to the community, particularly where youngsters are from ethnic minorities
- Rigorously evaluated, and feedback of evaluation given to implementation team and participants

Adapted from Coughlan, Doyle, and Carr, 2002

strive to deliver programs that work, and taxpayers expect that funds should be directed toward those programs that are most cost-effective. It is essential therefore that priority be given to developing scientifically based programs that are effective in preventing problems and in promoting health.

VIEWPOINT BOX 10.2

HEALTH PROMOTION AND PREVENTION PROGRAMS FOR OLDER ADULTS

Although most of the prevention and promotion programs we have presented target very young children, it would be a mistake to conclude that health promotion and the prevention of mental disorders focus exclusively on very young participants. With an aging population, there have been growing efforts to identify ways to promote resilience and decrease the risk of problems in older adults. These include programs to promote exercise and social support, early screening efforts, and programs to support caregivers (World Health Organization, 2004).

Studies have provided evidence of the multiple mental and physical benefits of regular exercise for older adults. Li, McAuley, Chaumeton, and Harmer (2001), for example, reported from a randomized controlled trial of the effects of tai chi that participants scored higher than did controls on measures of life satisfaction and positive affect and had fewer depressive symptoms. Various factors contribute to the social isolation of older adults, including their lack of involvement in the labor force, decreased mobility due to disability, and bereavement due to the death of a spouse or friend. Although befriending programs are believed to have positive effects on the well-being of older women, there have been few systematic attempts to assess whether such programs are effective in enhancing social support (World Health Organization, 2004). Early screening programs are designed to identify older adults requiring additional services. A small, randomized controlled trial (Shapiro & Taylor, 2002) reported that provision of early in-home geriatric assessment to older adults at moderate risk for losing their ability to remain in their own homes was associated with higher subjective well-being and lower likelihood of institutionalization.

Family caregivers of older adults shoulder a significant financial, physical, and emotional burden in caring for their loved ones. Because the toll of such care giving is substantial, a number of programs have been designed to ease caregiver burden. Sörensen, Pinquart, and Duberstein (2002) conducted a meta-analysis of 78 caregiver intervention studies. Sörensen and colleagues found that interventions yielded small to moderate effect sizes. Overall, programs were more effective in increasing knowledge than they were in reducing burden or depressed symptoms. The field of prevention of problems for older adults is an emerging one, with promising interventions. However, with the growing need for such programs to meet the demands of an aging population, it is essential that the evaluation of the usefulness of such programs be a priority.

PREVENTION OF PROBLEMS IN THOSE EXPOSED TO TRAUMA OR LOSS

Within the mental health field, it is a commonly held belief that it is necessary to express and *work through* difficult experiences. This conviction has its origins in Freudian theories and has led to the widespread belief that mental health services are required by everyone who is the victim of or witness to an unpleasant event (Bonanno, 2004). News reports of tragedies such as high school shootings, train derailments, or murder-suicides inevitably end with the phrase "counselors will be available on site to assist the survivors." The strategy of *critical incident stress debriefing* was introduced as a preventive strategy to ensure that survivors and witnesses to tragedies had assistance in processing the details of the traumatic event at the time in order to avoid the dangers of a delayed stress reaction. In critical incident stress debriefing, counselors work with groups of up to 15 participants, whom they instruct to recount details of the event they have witnessed. Participants are then asked to describe their thoughts, emotional reactions, and symptoms in response to the event. Finally, counselors provide psychoeducation on coping skills before sharing a snack and returning participants to their regular environment (Enright & Carr, 2002). The rationale for critical incident stress debriefing has an intuitive appeal. If, indeed, it were possible to protect people from developing posttraumatic stress disorder by devoting a couple of hours to hearing their stories, then it would certainly be time well invested. Unfortunately, outcome data do not support the effectiveness of critical incident stress debriefing and suggest that sometimes it may even be harmful as it may impede natural recovery processes (Bonanno, 2004; World Health Organization, 2004). The basic problem with an approach such as critical incident stress debriefing is that it is based on the faulty assumption that there is only one path to recovery and that beneficial effects can be obtained by imposing the same solution on everyone. There is, however, ample evidence that there are multiple pathways to healthy functioning and that it is ineffective and sometimes harmful to insist that everyone be treated the same.

We see similarly faulty logic with respect to services for the bereaved. Although we assume that the death of a parent would be an appalling blow that would provoke serious mental health problems for children, research suggests that a substantial minority of bereaved children are resilient in the face of such deaths and do not show any signs of adjustment problems (Lin, Sandler, Ayers, Wolchik, & Luecken, 2004). Nevertheless, it is common for bereaved children to be offered psychological services to prevent the development of problems. A meta-analysis of bereavement interventions with children found no evidence that they generate positive outcomes (Currier, Holland, & Neimeyer, 2007). The majority of bereaved children are resilient in the face of their loss, and so services offered to bereaved children are likely to show little effect simply because many children simply do not need any intervention.

The assumption that grief is resolved in a similar fashion by everyone led to the assumption that a person who does not show an overt grief reaction is an emotional time bomb who will inevitably one day experience a delayed grief reaction. There is no scientific evidence to support this assumption (Bonanno, 2004). It is clear that in our efforts to identify those who are suffering psychological pain, we have inadvertently overlooked the many people who are resilient in the face of adversity. By searching to better understand the qualities, behaviors, and resources of these individuals—who despite enduring suffering maintain their equilibrium and lead satisfying lives—we may be in a better position to mount effective prevention programs.

On the other hand, there are certainly people who are adversely affected by life-threatening or traumatic events. Such individuals may well, indeed, benefit from psychological services designed to minimize the effects of these events. A meta-analysis that examined the effects of different types of psychological services on children exposed to traumatic events found strong evidence for the helpfulness of individual and group cognitive-behavior therapy (Wethington et al., 2008). Additionally, the researchers found that there was simply not sufficient evidence to conclude that the other interventions (play therapy, art therapy, medication, psychodynamic therapy, or psychological debriefing) were effective in reducing psychological harm in children exposed to trauma.

VIEWPOINT BOX 10.3

UNSUNG HEROES

It is easy to get discouraged when we read the data from the World Health Organization that despite the development of effective vaccines, millions of children die every year from infectious diseases and that, despite the development of effective programs for the prevention of substance abuse, most programs are not delivered in an effective way. If you are contemplating a career in prevention science, you may be overwhelmed by the thought of having to master knowledge and skills not only in clinical psychology but in public health as well. You may doubt that you would have the charisma, vision, or persistence to become a member of a team that was successful in securing funding and getting cooperation from stakeholders in government, education, and the community. Does this mean you cannot contribute to the prevention of mental health problems? Let's consider Rachel's story.

Rachel's father, Daniel, was a Holocaust survivor, embittered by his suffering and haunted by guilt that he alone of all his family had survived the concentration camps of Nazi Germany. Daniel married, had two children, and built a life in America, working hard to provide safety for his son and daughter. His grief prevented him from ever experiencing much joy, and he was a hard taskmaster to his children. He punished his son harshly with a strap and was critical and demanding toward Rachel. Rachel grew up with low self-esteem and poor coping skills. She married early and found herself in a relationship that mirrored the emotional abuse she suffered as a child. Nevertheless, she was a resourceful woman who was a devoted and loving mother to her own two children. Rachel sought psychological services for depression after leaving her abusive husband. During the intake assessment, the psychologist asked her about other adults who might have been sources of support during her childhood and adolescence. Sadly, Rachel saw her mother as having failed to protect her from her father's rages. The person she remembered was the father of a friend of hers. On a rare free evening after school in grade 9, Rachel had gone home with her friend Hillary. As the girls prepared a snack in the kitchen, they heard Hillary's father call up from the basement: "Is that you Hillary? Could you give me a hand please?" To Rachel's horror, Hillary yelled back, "Sure Dad, in a few minutes when we're done with our snack." Rachel felt her heart pound and her hands get clammy as she braced for Hillary's dad to burst out of the basement in a rage because Hillary had not immediately complied with his request. She could not believe her ears when he replied, "OK, honey, no rush." Rachel treasured the opportunities to visit Hillary—she found Hillary's relationship with her father amazing. Hillary's father may have shaken his head sadly at his daughter's shy friend and may have felt helpless to make a difference in the life of this young woman whose home life was overshadowed by the suffering of the Holocaust. Although he did not know it, Hillary's father provided a lifeline for Rachel. He gave her hope that young people could be treated respectfully by parents. Rachel nurtured that hope and acted on it with her own children, treating them as she had seen Hillary's father behave, rather than as she had been treated.

Even if you do not choose a career in preventing mental health problems, you will have many opportunities to contribute to the prevention of emotional and behavioral difficulties. The principles for healthy development are relatively simple. You already learned in other psychology courses about the importance of positive reinforcement, social support, modeling prosocial behavior, and clear communication. As you put those principles into practice in your job, your family, your friendships, and your community, you will be making an important step in preventing problems. The protective factors listed in Table 10.2 include many ways that you can contribute to mental health promotion.

SUMMARY AND CONCLUSIONS

We have summarized research on some of the many programs designed to prevent emotional and behavioral problems and to promote positive psychological functioning. The most successful programs have several features in common (Biglan, Mrazek, Carmine, & Flay, 2003). First, they are evidence-based. Each effective program was designed to target known risk and protective factors in the development of psychopathology. These prevention programs drew on psychological research that has identified those factors that make a person vulnerable to develop psychopathology as well as those factors that act as a buffer against the development of problems. Second, many programs work to promote the same relatively simple principles such as promoting positive adult–child relationships; allowing children ample opportunities to be rewarded for appropriate behavior; providing adequate monitoring and supervision; providing mild corrective feedback for inappropriate behavior; helping children manage emotions, treat one another with respect, and act assertively rather than aggressively; and facilitating the development of supportive networks (Biglan, 2003; Carr, 2002). Third, they are usually multifaceted, involving different components or modules that operate at the level of the individual, family, school, community, or legal system. This allows the same message to be conveyed by parents, teachers, peers, community leaders, and government (Biglan, 2003; Weissberg et al., 2003).

A fourth common feature among some of the most successful programs is that they were developed as an expansion of an efficacious treatment intervention that was modified and offered in a slightly diluted format to those with subclinical problems. Programmatic research is then carried out over many years to determine the program's effectiveness (Nation et al., 2003). Fifth, successful programs are offered in convenient contexts. Services are offered in a milieu that minimizes obstacles to participation, by using schools, community centers, and home visits, as well as by offering child care services so that parents can participate (Carr, 2002). Finally, the developers of effective prevention programs all stress the importance of program fidelity in adopting their interventions (e.g., Webster-Stratton, 2006). This means that it is necessary to use the same materials and protocols and to deliver the same number of sessions as the original program.

To ensure that people are receiving effective services, it is necessary to conduct outcome assessments of both competence and symptoms/risk factors. These programs are designed to reduce problems in the future, so it is essential that evaluations extend beyond the conclusion of a program in order to evaluate longer term functioning. Because those who receive preventive services are led to believe that these services will make a difference in their lives, we owe it to them to be certain that this is really the case.

Critical Thinking Questions

Compared with prevention programs for physical health problems, what are the special challenges faced in prevention programs for mental health problems?

How do primary and secondary prevention programs differ in their focus? Are these approaches incompatible with one another?

Why is long-term systematic evaluation so important in prevention science?

Prevention programs seem to be relatively effective for many psychological problems, so why aren't they more commonly used in our health care and educational systems?

Key Terms

community psychology: a branch of psychology that focuses on research and practice on the reciprocal relations between individuals and the community in which they live

health promotion: programs designed to increase activities that are beneficial to many aspects of physical health

incidence rates: the number of new cases of a specific problem

indicated preventive interventions: prevention program that targets people who do not meet criteria for a disorder, but who have elevated risk and may show detectable but subclinical signs of the disorder

number needed to treat: the number of people who need to receive the intervention in order to prevent one person from developing the condition

primary prevention: the provision of conditions conducive to good health

protective factors: characteristics of the individual or the environment that render a person less vulnerable to the development of a problem or disorder

risk factors: characteristics of the individual or the environment that render a person more vulnerable or that are associated with more severe symptoms

risk reduction model: approach to prevention that reduces risks and promotes protective factors

secondary prevention: prevention that targets groups of people who are identified as being at high risk (similar to selected and indicated prevention)

selective preventive interventions: prevention program that targets people who are at elevated risk of developing a particular disorder or problem

universal preventive interventions: program applied to an entire population, such as a media awareness campaign on the dangers of drinking and driving risk factors

Key Names

Paula Barrett   Matthew Sanders

Carolyn Webster-Stratton

ADDITIONAL RESOURCES

Dozois, D. A., & Dobson, K. S. (Eds). (2003). *The prevention of anxiety and depression: Theory, research, and practice.* Washington, DC: American Psychological Association Press.

Greenwood, C. R., Kratochwill, T. R., & Clements, M. (Eds). (2008). *Schoolwide prevention models: Lessons learned in elementary schools.* New York: Guilford.

Tolan, P., Szapocznik, J., & Sambrano, S. (Eds). (2006). *Preventing youth substance abuse: Science-based programs for children and adolescents.* Washington, DC: American Psychological Association Press.

Check It Out!

This Web site provides information on the Incredible Years Program: http://www.incredibleyears.com

This Australian Web site provides information on the Triple P program: http://www.triplep.net/

Web site for the Blueprints for Violence Prevention program, which identifies programs that have been demonstrated to prevent violence: http://www.colorado.edu/cspv/blueprints/

The Web site of the Substance Abuse and Mental Health Services Administration: http://www.samhsa.gov/

CHAPTER 11

Intervention: Overview

INTRODUCTION

In previous chapters you have learned about the ways that psychologists conduct assessments (Chapters 5 to 9) as well as efforts to prevent the development of psychological disorders (Chapter 10). In this chapter and the following three chapters, we discuss psychological interventions to help people like Anwar, Braden, and Genevieve's father Allan. As we described in Chapter 2, a major part of most psychologists' workload is devoted to providing psychological treatment; the vast majority of clinical psychologists report providing psychotherapy as part of their practices. Throughout the text we have drawn attention to the ethical principles that guide the delivery of psychological services. In this chapter we will discuss ethical issues in the selection of treatments, in informed consent to services, and in the requirement for ongoing assessment of treatment usefulness. We will also highlight issues related to confidentiality. Then we will examine some major models that inform current evidence-based psychological interventions.

Rather than provide comprehensive coverage of theoretical approaches to psychotherapy, in this chapter we present therapies that have been shown to work. Although there are hundreds of different forms of psychotherapy offered by mental health professionals, most of them have not been empirically evaluated—and so are not covered here. Instead, in keeping with both the scientific and ethical evolution of the field of clinical psychology, we focus on evidence-based approaches to psychotherapy. Accordingly, you will notice that we do not present any information on two large categories of therapy: those that have a long history but scant empirical support (e.g., psychoanalysis, Jungian analysis) and more recently developed therapies that, likewise, are lacking empirical support and are largely discredited (e.g., primal scream therapy, thought field therapy; for more examples of discredited treatments, see Norcross, Koocher, & Garofalo, 2006).

To provide you with a broad sense of the nature of psychotherapeutic services, we will consider the characteristics of people who seek and receive psychological services. Some psychologists refer to these individuals as "patients" and others use the term "clients," so we will use the terms interchangeably in this and subsequent chapters. We will look at the paths by which people are referred (or self-refer) for psychological services. Although the majority of psychological interventions are delivered in one-to-one sessions in the psychologist's office, there is evidence that other modes of treatment delivery—such as couples therapy, family therapy, and group therapy—are also efficacious. Because of the diversity of the clientele, as well as concerns to offer the most cost effective services, psychologists are developing menus of treatments that can be calibrated according to the level of need. We will discuss the principles of this "stepped care" approach. Finally, we will highlight recent innovations in the use of computer technology and the Internet in the delivery of psychological interventions.

THE ETHICS OF INTERVENTION

In Chapter 5 you learned about ethical issues in obtaining consent to psychological assessment, and in Chapter 6 we described confidentiality and the limits to confidentiality in psychological services. Given the central importance of these ethical principles in the delivery of all psychological services, it is critical to recognize their applicability in psychological interventions. A core ethical issue is that the psychologist cannot proceed with any psychological services without the client's agreement to receive the services. Furthermore, this agreement must be based on a reasonable understanding of what the services will entail and the likely outcomes of receiving or not receiving services. The process of obtaining informed consent recognizes the consumer's rights regarding psychological services. It is insufficient to simply obtain the client's signature at the bottom of a jargon-filled description of services; the psychologist must provide a comprehensible account so that the client can make an informed decision on whether to pursue services. Each person who is involved in services must understand the nature of those services and must consent. As an illustration of this, guidelines developed for the United Kingdom by the National Institute for Health and Clinical Excellence for the treatment of anxiety and depression (NICE 2004a, 2004b) indicate that patients should be informed of the treatment options and invited to choose the one with which they are most comfortable. According to these guidelines, in the treatment of anxiety, patients should be informed that in descending order of long-term effectiveness, the treatment options are psychological therapy such as cognitive-behavioral therapy (CBT), medication such as a selective serotonin reuptake inhibitor (SSRI) approved for the treatment of generalized anxiety disorder, and self-help based on CBT principles.

 The next time you seek health services, pay attention to informed consent issues. How does the service provider explain the options to you? Does it make a difference to you whether the service provider ensures that you understand your choices?

In different jurisdictions the issue of obtaining consent from children is treated in various ways, including setting chronological ages at which children are presumed competent to give consent, or

TABLE 11.1   Questions to Ask About Psychotherapy Services

- What kind of training and experience do you have in dealing with problems like the ones I have?
- What type of treatment is most effective for the kinds of problems I have, and do you provide this treatment?
- Are there any disadvantages or side-effects associated with the most effective treatment?
- Are there other effective treatment options that I should consider?
- What is the hourly rate for sessions?
- Do you offer a sliding fee based on individual or family income?
- Will my health insurance cover the costs of these services?
- How many sessions will treatment likely take? How often will we need to meet?

requiring the psychologist to determine in each case whether a child is competent to give consent (Fisher, 2004). A child who is not competent to give consent still has a right to have procedures explained in a simple manner and is asked to give assent, which is the verbal form of consent. Obviously, the onus is on the psychologist to know and follow the legal requirements relevant to the jurisdiction in which he or she practices. Ability to provide consent can also be an issue in working with older clients who are experiencing significant cognitive impairment, such as can occur with dementia. Careful evaluation of the client's capacity to understand options and make decisions is required in such situations.

As you learned in Chapter 6, clients must be assured of the confidentiality of the services they receive, as well as the limits to confidentiality when a person's safety is at risk. They must also receive clear descriptions of the steps taken by the psychologist to protect their privacy. Many potential clients do not ask about confidentiality issues, financial arrangements, or treatment alternatives (Braaten, Otto, & Handelsman, 1993). When seeking psychological services, it is wise to prepare a list of questions to ask potential service providers. **Table 11.1** provides some of the questions all clinical psychologists should be prepared to answer for potential clients.

Ethical issues are prominent at the beginning of psychological services, but they do not end once consent has been obtained, confidentiality explained, and a course of services begun. As we have emphasized many times, the psychologist has an ethical responsibility to monitor the effectiveness of services. It would be unethical to persist in offering services to a client if those services did not prove helpful in addressing the problem. Although there is great merit in adopting an approach that has been shown to be effective in treating similar problems, the psychologist must be vigilant in monitoring its usefulness for each client. Ethical practice requires that the psychologist be attentive to the ongoing and potentially changing fit between the treatment plan, the client's needs, and the client's responses to treatment.

Think of health services you have received recently. They might be treatment for an infection, orthodontic services, or chiropractic services. How did the health care provider monitor the effectiveness of the services in helping you? Is it important to you to know that the services are making a difference in your life?

Many people ask what a psychologist should do if there is no evidence-based treatment for the problem presented by a client. Fortunately, at this point in time, there is research evidence that is relevant to the treatment of almost all psychosocial problems. Although there may no randomized controlled trials relevant to the problem, there are likely to be other types of pertinent research data, including uncontrolled treatments trials and case reports. Evidence-based practice does not require that treatments be based on highly controlled, internally valid, replicated studies—it requires that the psychologist base treatment for a client on the *best available evidence*. In other words, there is little justification for psychologists or other mental health professionals to offer treatments that are not informed by research evidence. In situations in which there is limited evidence about treatment efficacy, the client should be informed of this and asked to consent to treatment with full knowledge about the limited scientific basis for the treatment.

Another commonly encountered question is whether there are forms of intervention that should *not* be provided to clients. Although most psychological therapies do not have harmful side effects, there is a growing awareness, and research base, on psychological treatments that can cause harm. Two examples provided by Lilienfeld (2007) illustrate the general concern about some widely available treatments. "Scared straight" programs that try to frighten adolescents at risk for ongoing criminal behavior actually increase the odds of subsequent criminal offending. Rebirthing therapy, in which children are wrapped and blankets and squeezed repeatedly to "simulate" the "trauma" of birth, has resulted in a number of deaths. These examples clearly demonstrate that some psychological treatments can cause harm and underscore the need for psychologists to provide services that are strongly based in science.

THEORETICAL APPROACHES

Consistent with our commitment to evidence-based services, we will present the forms of psychological therapies that have the strongest empirical support. These include **short-term psychodynamic therapy**, **interpersonal therapy**, **process-experiential therapy**, and **cognitive-behavioral therapy**. As you will see, each approach is based on a distinct theory of psychological functioning and change processes. All of these approaches have at least a moderate amount of supporting data for use in the treatment of specific DSM IV Axis I disorders. All have also been applied to DSM IV Axis II disorders, although the evidence of their impact is limited at this time. In Chapters 12 and 13 we will provide more details about specific evidence-based versions of each approach. Because it is clear that treatments based on different theoretical approaches can be helpful in dealing with the same problem, in Chapter 14 we provide information on ways in which efficacious treatments may have many elements in common.

As you read through the following sections on the different theoretical orientations, we encourage you to try to imagine what it would be like to receive the different forms of treatments and how you might respond to the different emphases in treatment that are evident across orientations.

Short-Term Psychodynamic Psychotherapies

In response to concerns about the cost and effectiveness of extended psychoanalytic and psychodynamic interventions, a number of short-term psychodynamic psychotherapies (STPPs) have been developed. STPPs are grounded in psychodynamic principles that originated in the work of Sigmund Freud (Messer, 2001). As you may recall from Chapter 1 and from other psychology courses, Freud's drive theory emphasized the importance of innate, biological drives that the individual must control in order to adapt to society. Building on this theory, a number of psychodynamic models developed in the twentieth century. Ego psychology, developed by Anna Freud among others, focused on the process by which the very young child learns to construct a model of the world (Vakoch & Strupp, 2000). Themes from both drive and ego theories were blended in object relations theories, which noted that infants tend to categorize their experiences into good and bad. As children mature, they learn that each person has both positive and negative qualities. However, if they do not learn this, they are prone to chaotic relationships, because they act as though people are either all good or all bad (Vakoch & Strupp, 2000).

Psychodynamic theories also assume that individuals are prone to conflicts between id and ego. These conflicts are resolved when the ego learns to accept and tolerate the id impulses. However, there is a tendency for these impulses to be suppressed, so that they are not within conscious awareness and tend to be reenacted throughout the client's life. According to psychodynamic theorists, it is inevitable that the client's core interpersonal conflicts will be repeated in the relationship with the therapist through a process known as **transference** (Vakoch & Strupp, 2000). Most current forms of psychodynamic treatment use transference to assist clients in understanding their problems and making changes in their lives. Generally speaking, clients are helped to see how their core interpersonal conflicts are influencing the relationship with the therapist, how these conflicts developed, and how these conflicts have affected, and continue to affect, their lives. Psychodynamic theorists believe that by repeatedly attending to these issues, clients are able to make choices about their interpersonal style and behave in a manner that is less determined by their unconscious conflicts.

Brief psychodynamic therapies were championed in the 1960s and 1970s by psychiatrists Malan, Davanloo, and Sifneos, who proposed theoretical models in which change is proposed to occur by the therapist challenging the client's defenses. The 1980s witnessed the development of another generation of brief therapies, including **Lester Luborsky**'s supportive-expressive therapy (Luborsky, 1984) and Strupp's time-limited dynamic therapy (e.g., Strupp & Binder, 1984). Although there are currently several forms of psychodynamic therapy that have different emphases and assign differing importance to various intervention strategies, the various psychodynamic therapies have a great deal in common. Across the different types of STPPs, therapy is considered a process of understanding stages of psychological development, bringing to awareness unconscious processes, and reenacting in the relationship with the therapist issues that have troubled the client in the past (Messer, 2001). Luborsky's research on core conflictual relationship themes has been studied with people diagnosed with a range of Axis I and II disorders, and this research has greatly influenced the manner in which contemporary STPP is conducted.

STPPs involve face-to-face sessions conducted once or twice a week for between 16 and 30 sessions (Leichsenring, Rabung, & Lebing, 2004). By limiting the number of sessions, the therapist encourages the client to anticipate that change will occur relatively quickly (Messer, 2001). Compared with traditional psychoanalytic therapists, STPP therapists are active, engaging in dialogue and challenging the client. The therapist's first task is to foster the development of a therapeutic alliance and positive transference, by adopting an open-minded, nonjudgmental stance and displaying interest in the client's experience (Cutler, Goldyne, Markowitz, Devlin, & Glick, 2004). Among the techniques used by the STPP therapists to alter maladaptive patterns are reflection (paraphrasing clients' statements or commenting on emotional states in order to enhance their awareness of current experiences), clarification (asking clients to attend more closely to some aspects of their experience in order to see connections or patterns), interpretation (commenting on a problem or experience and relating it to the use of defense mechanisms or underlying core conflictual themes), and confrontation (challenging clients to recognize that defense mechanisms are interfering with their optimal functioning or that core conflictual themes are responsible for aspects of their experience) (Messer, 2001).

Like most forms of psychodynamic therapy, examination of the transference relationship is a central theme of STPP; however, attention is paid to the present relationship, without necessarily connecting patterns to the client's past (Leichsenring et al., 2004). Examination of the transference relationship is considered an important tool in understanding how the client views the world; it is designed to bring to awareness unconscious fantasies and to reveal the ways that the client thinks about relationships (Blagys & Hilsenroth, 2000). Counter-transference refers to the therapist's emotional reaction to the client. Although Freud viewed counter-transference as a breach in therapeutic neutrality caused by the therapist's unconscious conflicts, STPP therapists take a more benign view, seeing counter-transference as providing useful information about the way the client's interpersonal behaviors affect others (Vakoch & Strupp, 2000). **Table 11.2** lists the therapeutic tasks of the different STPP stages.

Early in therapy, the STPP therapist identifies specific themes or conflicts that will be the focus of attention. This theme is individualized to capture the therapist's formulation of the conflict that underlies the presenting problem (Messer, 2001). Throughout therapy, the therapist maintains a focus on these themes, treatment goals, and termination issues. The therapist identifies defensive patterns that interfere with the client's life (Cutler et al., 2004). Consistent with their Freudian roots (Blagys & Hilsenroth, 2000), STPP theorists accord a central role to evoking emotions and to facilitating change through a process of catharsis (i.e., the release of previously suppressed emotional reactions). Goal-setting plays an important part of STPP, setting it apart from long-term psychodynamic therapy and making it similar to other short-term treatment approaches (Messer, 2001).

As therapy moves toward termination, gains are consolidated. During this phase, the client faces issues of loss (of the therapist), separation (from the therapeutic relationship), and individuation (moving toward independence from the therapist). As STPP is, by definition, brief and time limited,

---

TABLE 11.2   The Therapeutic Tasks of Short-Term Psychodynamic Psychotherapy

Phase 1:   Developing a positive transference relationship
Identifying themes that are important for the patient

Phase 2:   Analyzing the transference relationship
Exploring themes through clarification and confrontation

Phase 3:   Terminating therapy
Dealing with loss
Dealing with expectable challenges in life

Adapted from Vakoch and Strupp (2000)

---

issues of termination of services cannot be avoided. Theorists have proposed that the time-limited nature of therapy raises awareness of the time-limited nature of human life, making it particularly salient for clients who are dealing with mortality issues (Messer, 2000). There is strong evidence that STPP is efficacious in the treatment of depression and initial evidence that specific forms of psychodynamic therapy can be efficacious in the treatment of panic disorder, substance abuse, and borderline personality disorder (Gibbons, Crits-Christoph, & Hearon, 2008).

Interpersonal Psychotherapy for Depression

Departing from the intrapsychic focus of psychodynamic theories, Sullivan (1953) drew attention to interpersonal factors in psychopathology, suggesting that psychiatric problems were often related to difficulties in communication and to dysfunctional relationships. This theoretical framework laid the foundation for studies of the interpersonal context of a wide range of disorders. Compelling evidence regarding the interpersonal difficulties experienced by those with depression fueled interest in developing a therapy that addressed interpersonal factors associated with this disorder (Klerman, Weissman, Rounsaville, & Chevron, 1984). Interpersonal psychotherapy (IPT) for depression focuses on changing interpersonal problems that are related to the onset, maintenance, and relapse of depressive symptoms.

IPT is a brief therapy that involves weekly meetings over 3 to 4 months. IPT is divided into distinct phases that are described in **Table 11.3**. The first phase involves assessment of the symptoms of depression as well as an examination of the patient's relationships. The construction of an inventory of current and past relationships is essential in identifying the interpersonal themes that will be the focus of therapy. At the end of this assessment phase, the IPT therapist diagnoses the patient and provides an interpersonal formulation of the patient's difficulties. The patient is explicitly absolved of responsibility for symptoms as these are ascribed to the disorder of depression. The IPT therapist explains the ways that interpersonal issues maintain the depression and invites the patient to participate actively in changing current relationships.

The focus of subsequent IPT sessions is tailored to the client's specific needs and may include addressing one or all of the following themes: grief, role disputes, role transitions, and interpersonal deficits. In addressing grief issues, the therapist facilitates mourning of a lost relationship as well as the development of a new social network. If role disputes are identified as contributing to depressive symptoms, the patient and therapist collaborate on a plan for resolving the difficulty, by renegotiating the problem, reaching an agreement that the dispute is insoluble, or dissolving the relationship. The patient is assisted in developing effective communication patterns and in developing realistic expectations about relationships. Both IPT and STPPs address aspects of interpersonal functioning. An important difference is that IPT is designed to alter relational functioning, whereas STPPs use information about relationships to alter intrapsychic variables.

Dysfunction family relationships can be addressed in IPT for depression. (*Source:* Media Bakery)

TABLE 11.3   Interpersonal Psychotherapy for Depression

Initial sessions (1–3):

Assessment of symptoms
Diagnosis and explanation of depressive disorder
Assessment of interpersonal context (current and past)
Presentation of IPT formulation of patient's problems

Intermediate sessions (4–12) addressing one or more of the following themes:

Grief

- help patient deal with a loss; promote healthy mourning
- facilitate the development of new relationships

Role disputes

- identify dispute
- formulate plan for dispute resolution
- modify communication and/or change expectations to resolve dispute

Role transitions

- leave old role and mourn its loss if necessary
- develop skills, coping strategies, and support for transition

Interpersonal deficits

- build social skills
- increase social involvement

Termination phase sessions (13–16)

Acknowledge worries and sadness related to ending therapy
Encourage awareness and practice of new skills
Anticipate future challenges in which new skills will be employed

Adapted from Weissman, Markowitz, and Klerman (2000)

Imagine that you were seeking services to deal with conflicts that you are experiencing with one of your parents. How would the focus of services in STPP differ from those in IPT? Which one would focus more on altering the way you interact with your parents? Which one would focus more on how you feel about your parents and how being with them makes you feel?

Research has established that people are often vulnerable at times of role transition. Even though some transitions such as marriage, the birth of a child, or starting a new job are considered positive and may be welcomed, they create a challenge as the person adapts to new role demands. In IPT, the patient is first encouraged to leave the old role (e.g., moving from being a student to a professional, from being single to married, or from being employed to retired). Next, the client is aided in developing skills that are required in the new role (e.g., adopting a more formal style, focusing on the challenges of living with another person, or finding ways to maintain an active social life). Some depressed patients may not be troubled by grief, role disputes, or role transitions, but may have an impoverished interpersonal network with few contacts and little opportunity for pleasant or supportive exchanges. In that case, the therapist focuses on the development of communication and relationship skills that are likely to promote closer interpersonal ties. Within IPT, the termination phase of therapy offers an opportunity to consolidate gains made in previous phases. The therapist helps the client recognize and take credit for the changes that have occurred as well as prepare for future challenges. In therapy, the client communicates any misgivings and anxieties about ending the therapeutic relationship.

As interpersonal difficulties are found in all ages, **Myrna Weissman** and her colleagues have modified the treatment protocol to address the needs of people of various ages (Weissman, Markowitz, & Klerman, 2000). IPT-LL was developed to meet the needs of adults in late life (Sholomskas, Chevron, Prusoff, & Berry, 1983) by having brief sessions that included help with practical matters and that focused on ways to tolerate negative effect in relationships rather than withdraw from them. Mufson and her colleagues (Mufson & Dorta, 2004; Mufson, Dorta, Moreau, & Weissman, 2004) developed IPT-A for adolescents by including attention to developmental issues such as separation from parents, exploration of parental authority, the development of dyadic relationships, and peer pressure. In addition to strong evidence of efficacy in the treatment of depression, there is also good evidence for a form of IPT (combined with behavior therapy elements) in the treatment of bipolar disorder (Frank, 2005). Finally, IPT has been adapted for use in different cultures (e.g., group treatment for depression in rural Uganda; Bolton et al., 2003) and has been modified for use with eating disorders, anxiety disorders, and substance use disorders (Weissman, Markowitz, & Klerman, 2000).

Process-Experiential Therapies

With their origins as alternatives to psychodynamic and behavioral psychology, humanistic and experiential approaches to psychotherapy include client-centered therapy (Rogers, 1951), Gestalt therapy (Perls, Hefferline, & Goodman, 1951), and existential therapy (May, Angel, & Ellenberger, 1958). These approaches are based on the assumption that human nature is fundamentally growth oriented, trustworthy, and guided by choice (Elliott, Greenberg, & Lietaer, 2004). You may recall learning in Chapter 1 that Rogers was committed to psychotherapy research. During the 1970s and the 1980s, however, research on humanistic and experiential approaches dwindled. Given the emphasis on the uniqueness of each individual's subjective experience, humanistic and experiential approaches have not been the subject of much psychotherapy outcome research. For many decades, humanistic and experiential theorists and therapists actively rejected any attempts to evaluate their treatments with experimental designs. Consequently, by the early 1990s there was only one experiential therapy (emotion-focused therapy for moderately distressed couples, Johnson & Greenberg, 1985) that was considered to have a strong evidence base (Elliott, 2001).

In recent years, largely through the efforts of **Robert Elliott** and **Leslie Greenberg**, there has been a resurgence of well-designed research on the process-experiential (PE) approach that draws together elements of client-centered and Gestalt approaches into a strongly emotion-focused approach to treatment (Elliott et al., 2004). Combining these humanistic and experiential approaches with basic psychological research on emotions, Greenberg (2008) has proposed that PE treatment should include the following elements: increasing the client's awareness of emotion, encouraging the client to express emotion, enhancing the client's emotion regulation abilities, aiding the client to reflect on emotions, and helping the client to transform maladaptive emotions into adaptive emotions. Solid evidence exists for the efficacy of PE in treating depression and couple distress, and there is growing evidence of its value in treating adult survivors of childhood abuse (Greenberg, 2008).

A central characteristic of PE therapies is the emphasis on in-session experiencing of affect. These therapies are based on the assumption that changes can be attained by facilitating experiential processing by guiding clients to focus their attention on their in-session experiences. In order to make these emotions more intense and vivid, PE emphasizes using the therapeutic relationship to help clients process their emotions and, subsequently, to create new meaning for their emotional experiences. The therapeutic relationship is considered to provide both support and guidance in the client's exploration of his or her experience. PE is a 12- to 20-session treatment in which the therapist facilitates the client's role as an active agent of self-change. This approach is clearly intrapsychic, placing emphasis on the client's self-exploration and understanding, rather than on relationships with others. In contrast to early client-centered approaches, the PE therapist takes a more task-focused approach, largely emphasizing emotional content (Elliott, 2001). **Table 11.4** describes general features of process-experiential therapy.

Cognitive-Behavioral Therapies

The many forms of behavioral, cognitive, and cognitive-behavioral therapies can be considered a single orientation. Behavioral approaches are based on the assumption that problem behaviors are learned and that faulty learning can be reversed through the application of learning principles. The earliest application of behavior therapy (BT) was the use of operant conditioning in treating patients who were considered untreatable: those with psychotic disorders and those with mental retardation. From its roots in the application of classical and operant conditioning, the field of BT has advanced to include procedures based on research findings from areas such as perception, cognition, and the biological bases of behavior. Therapists focus on present functioning as opposed to childhood history. Accordingly, behavioral interventions focus on specific targets by reducing undesirable behaviors (e.g., intrusive thoughts about a traumatic event, self-harming behaviors, and avoidance), as well as increasing desirable

Dr. Albert Bandura's research has influenced the development of CBT. (*Source:* Jon Brenneis/Life Magazine/Time & Life Pictures/Getty Images, Inc.)

behaviors (e.g., engaging in pleasant activities, calmly presenting a seminar, or assertively dealing with an angry customer). An essential feature is the application of scientifically derived principles in the treatment of problems. Throughout therapy, progress is assessed to determine whether the strategy should be modified. BT requires clear identification of goals and is oriented toward the future (Emmelkamp, 2004).

Albert Bandura's seminal findings that learning could take place by observation and imitation have been applied in the treatment of both adults and children (Naugle & Maher, 2003). **Self-efficacy**, which refers to a person's sense of competence to learn and perform new tasks, is often found to be the best predictor of behavior, such as approaching a phobic stimulus or attempting a new behavior. Bandura's work laid the foundation for approaches that

---

TABLE 11.4   The Principles of Process-Experiential Therapy

Fostering a Therapeutic Relationship

- Enter and track client's experiencing
- Express empathy and genuine valuing of the client and the client's experience
- Facilitate mutual involvement in setting the goals and tasks of therapy

Facilitating Work on Therapeutic Tasks

- Facilitate optimal client experiential processing
- Foster client growth and self-determination
- Facilitate client completion of key therapeutic tasks

Experiential Response Modes

- Utilize simple empathy responses
- Engage in empathic exploration of client experiencing
- Guide the client in exploring the experience
- Encourage the client to stay "in the moment" to focus on the experience

Therapeutic Tasks

- Aid the client in exploring emotions and experiences
- Use reflection and active expressions of client emotional states
- Use the therapeutic relationship to support and facilitate client exploration

Adapted from Elliott (2001)

---

emphasize the importance of cognitions in mediating behavioral responses (Craighead, Hart, Craighead, & Ilardi, 2002). Using models developed to understand information processing, D'Zurilla and Goldfried (1971) introduced a problem-solving approach that was applied in the treatment of diverse problems such as weight control, clinical depression, and social skills deficits. The key elements of problem solving in cognitive-behavioral treatments are defining and formulating the problem, generating alternative solutions to deal with the problem, deciding on the best solution to implement, and implementing and evaluating the solution (D'Zurilla & Nezu, 1999).

Cognitive approaches, such as Ellis's rational-emotive behavior therapy and **Aaron Beck's** cognitive therapy, are based on the assumption that an individual's perception of events, rather than the events themselves, affect adjustment. Consequently, these approaches focus on identifying automatic thoughts and changing maladaptive patterns of thinking that are associated with distress, anxiety, and depression (Hollon & Beck, 2004). Cognitive approaches foster a collaborative relationship in which the therapist and client work together to identify problems, test hypotheses, and reevaluate beliefs. Like their behavioral relatives, cognitive and cognitive-behavioral approaches rely on the application of empirically derived strategies in the treatment of diverse disorders.

TABLE 11.5   Phases of Cognitive Behavioral Therapies

Assessment phase:
  Integration of data from interview, direct observation, rating scales, and self-monitoring
  Establishment of concrete, collaboratively agreed-upon treatment goals

Intervention phase:
  1. Possible skills learned in session:
  Behavioral skills could include assertiveness, relaxation, engaging in enjoyable activities, using self-reinforcement to develop and maintain behaviors, or exposing oneself to feared stimuli.
  Cognitive skills could include developing strategies to dispute automatic negative thoughts and using cognitive restructuring strategies to challenge and evaluate the accuracy one's beliefs, assumptions, and expectations.
  Cognitive-behavioral skills could include developing problem-solving skills, stress management skills, and communication skills to improve interpersonal relationships.
  2. Skills are practiced in-session and then as homework assignments that are reviewed in the following session.
  3. There is an emphasis on ensuring that skills learned in-session are generalized to the client's day-to-day life context.
  4. Included is session-by-session review of progress toward agreed-upon treatment goals.

Termination phase:
  Review of treatment goals and the extent to which they were achieved
  Review of skills learned in therapy and their application to daily life
  Anticipation of future challenges and how they could be handled

Booster sessions:
  Review of treatment goals and the extent to which they were achieved
  Review of skills learned in therapy and their application to daily life
  Anticipation of future challenges and how they could be handled

CBT emphasizes the use of psychopathology research in understanding the problems experienced by clients. Although relevant research is the starting point for understanding the client's difficulties (e.g., identifying the likely causes and concomitants of panic disorder), a cornerstone of all CBT approaches is the tailoring of assessment and treatment to the needs of the individual client. Another core element of CBT is the continuous monitoring of the client's responses to treatment in order to evaluate the effect of intervention and alter treatment plans if necessary. Perhaps because of the use of the psychopathology research evidence to develop treatments that are specific to a disorder, there is strong evidence that CBT is efficacious in treating a multitude of youth and adult disorders and conditions, including mood disorders, anxiety disorders, eating disorders, sleep disorders, somatoform disorders, substance abuse disorders, marital distress, and anger and stress-related problems (Butler, Chapman, Forman, & Beck, 2006; Nathan & Gorman, 2007). **Table 11.5** describes the typical phases of CBT, usually provided over 8–30 sessions.

CBT therapists assume a very active role in service provision. They probe the precise nature of the problem, seeking information on its intensity, frequency, and duration as well as contextual factors that are associated with variation in the problem. They collaborate with clients in establishing concrete treatment goals and in translating vague complaints into measurable outcomes toward which the client will work. CBT therapists provide information about the process of treatment, explaining the central role of homework assignments in gathering data, carrying out experiments, and practicing new skills.

CBT therapists take responsibility for structuring each session, setting an agenda, and teaching new skills. Throughout treatment, the therapist uses a blend of didactic teaching methods (i.e., directions and instructions) and Socratic questioning (i.e., asking questions that encourage the client to examine his or her beliefs and to be self-directed in skill acquisition) to help the client. To promote changes, the therapist engages in a process of collaborative empiricism with the client. This means that the client and therapist develop strategies to concretely test the client's dysfunctional beliefs. By encouraging self-examination and then working with the client to test the validity of his or her beliefs, the therapist actively encourages a process of guided discovery for the client. Thus, in contrast to many other forms of therapy, the most important changes are presumed to take place not in sessions but *between* sessions as the client completes and learns from homework assignments (Blagys & Hilsenroth, 2002).

The other theoretical orientations we have discussed consider termination at the end of the therapeutic relationship. In CBT the termination phase is seen as a time for consolidating skills, anticipating future challenges, and preparing the client to face inevitable slip-ups. Termination is future-oriented. CBT also allows for the possibility of clients requiring one or two future "booster" sessions to help them get back on track.

VIEWPOINT BOX 11.1

THE CASE OF MICHAEL

Cutler et al. (2004) described a client, Michael, who was referred for treatment of depression. Experts of different theoretical orientations (long-term psychodynamic, interpersonal, and cognitive-behavioral) described how they would understand and treat Michael.

Although he had been a successful student as an undergraduate, in law school Michael developed a habit of procrastination and poor class attendance that led to him having to cram at exam time. He found this extremely stressful and started to feel increasingly depressed, began overeating and oversleeping, and had increasing trouble concentrating. Michael experienced prolonged feelings of sadness as well as decreased sexual desire and diminished pleasure in activities he used to enjoy.

After his parents divorced when he was an infant, Michael's father remarried and began a new family; his mother did not date or remarry. His father maintained contact twice a year, but did not engage in any meaningful parenting. As a preadolescent, Michael was cared for by his grandmother while his mother sought training in another city. The only times in which his father became engaged in Michael's life were when he was in trouble for skipping classes. As a student, Michael had a supportive mentoring relationship with a professor, but felt disappointed that the professor did not maintain the relationship when Michael moved to law school. During law school Michael was troubled by phone calls from his mother expressing her distress and reproving him for not spending enough time with her. Another current stressor in his life was an unsatisfactory relationship with a student he had dated. Although the woman broke off the romantic relationship with Michael, she maintained regular contact with him.

Michael's style toward the therapist was deferential. He apologized for arriving late for some of the intake assessment interviews. After a couple of sessions Michael reported that he had begun to feel better, had thrown away his prescription for antidepressant medication, and wished to engage in psychotherapy.

Dr. Glick, whose orientation is psychodynamic, assumes that Michael's depressive problems stem from conflicts of which he is not fully aware. The goal of therapy would be to promote Michael's exploration of the underlying meaning of his feelings. Dr. Glick would strive to respond to Michael in an open-minded manner to facilitate Michael's curiosity about himself and, eventually, his insight into the source of his problems. Dr. Glick assumes that in the context of a nonjudgmental therapeutic relationship, Michael will learn to tolerate painful feelings. Exploration of the transference relationship is designed to facilitate greater awareness of defensive responding. The therapist would comment on aspects of Michael's behavior toward him, offering possible interpretations of their significance. For example, "You missed a big part of each session. And today you seem to be staying on the surface of things. Might you be avoiding painful or troubling feelings about you?" (Cutler et al. 2004, p. 1571). Dr. Glick assumes that a core issue is Michael's unconscious feelings of unresolved anger toward his parents, whom he perceives as rejecting. His ambivalence toward his mother is then played out in his current romantic relationship. Examination of the transference relationship allows exploration of Michael's need for a nurturing father-figure and his fears of being seen as needy and weak.

Dr. Markowitz, the interpersonal psychotherapist, is sensitive to Michael's various relational difficulties and their relation to his depression. He would probe Michael's emotions in reaction to perceived rejection or disappointment and ask whether Michael has communicated his reactions to the people in his life. The therapist would explicitly present an interpersonal formulation of Michael's problems in which his reactions are normalized. "Coming to terms with losses can be hard, especially when you've had as many dislocations as you've already had . . . I suggest we work . . . on solving your law school role transition; as you gain greater comfort in your situation there, not only will that improve your life, but your mood symptoms should improve as well." (Cutler et al. 2004, p. 1570). Dr. Markowitz predicts that over the course of interpersonal psychotherapy, Michael would learn to respond more effectively to interpersonal challenges. Although no formal homework is given, Michael would be encouraged to increase his activity level. The final phase of services would allow Michael to consolidate his gains, taking credit for the new skills he has mastered. Termination would be a time to celebrate his gains as well as to be aware of the loss associated with ending the therapeutic relationship.

Dr. Devlin, the cognitive behavior therapist, would establish goals and collaborate to help Michael better understand his depression and the links between his thoughts, feelings, and behaviors. Homework tasks would be assigned to help track links between different feelings and procrastination behaviors, as well as to identify exceptional occasions on which Michael experiences pleasure. Michael would be encouraged to conduct behavioral experiments to determine whether his thoughts are accurate. For example, the thought that *I don't enjoy anything anymore* could be tested by monitoring his mood as he engages in different activities. Michael would be encouraged to shift from making character-based statements about himself to recognizing the choices that he makes to behave in specific ways. As he became more active, Michael would be in a position to identify and challenge his core beliefs about his inadequacy.

SEEKING PSYCHOLOGICAL TREATMENT

People seek the services of a clinical psychologist for many reasons. Some people desire assistance and advice in managing the expectable challenges in life, such as problems in settling in at college, the pain of a relationship break-up, or handling workplace difficulties. The transition from one phase of life to another, such as becoming a parent, brings new demands as well as new joys. Dealing with other expectable but painful life events such as the death of a parent or a spouse may also lead some people to initiate therapy. In many cases the person is seeking relief from emotional distress that interferes with daily functioning. Individuals often suffer from mental disorders for months or years before seeking professional services. Finally, some people who engage in therapy have only minimal levels of distress. These individuals are often seeking to address questions related to personal identity, values, or self-knowledge.

Psychotherapy is often defined as a process in which a professional systematically applies techniques derived from psychological principles to relieve another person's psychological distress or to facilitate growth. This rather broad definition also defines psychological counseling and, as we described in Chapter 1, there is a blurring of boundaries between counseling and psychotherapy. To clarify this situation—for clients, psychologists, and others working in the health care system—Barlow (2004) suggested that the term *psychological treatments* be used for the growing number of specific, evidence-based interventions designed to treat clinically significant problems (i.e., Axis I and II diagnoses). It is important to recognize that psychotherapy is practiced by professionals from many disciplines, including psychology, psychiatry, social work, medicine, and nursing. In most jurisdictions, the title *psychotherapist* is not

The increased use of mental health services can be accounted for by dramatic growth in the prescription of psychoactive medication. (*Source:* Photo Disc, Inc.)

licensed or restricted in any fashion. Accordingly, anyone can advertise his or her services as a psychotherapist. Those seeking psychotherapeutic services would be well advised, therefore, to obtain treatment from a licensed health care professional. The following statement from the California Board of Psychology document, *A Consumer Guide to Psychological Services* (n.d., p. 9), nicely captures the reasons for seeking services from a licensed psychologist.

> "The Board strongly recommends that you choose a licensed psychologist. A license ensures the psychologist has met stringent educational and experience standards and passed comprehensive written examinations. It also ensures he or she has gone through a criminal background check. It is important to verify the psychologist has a current, valid license. This means he or she is up-to-date on continuing education requirements and can legally practice psychology. What's more, a current license is required for your insurance company to accept the psychologist as a valid provider."

Evidence suggests that the overall use of mental health services has been increasing in recent decades; however, much of this increase is associated with the use of medication rather than psychotherapy. For example, in the United States in the past twenty years, the percentage of patient visits to psychiatrists involving psychotherapy declined from almost half of all visits to less than a third of visits (Mojtabai & Olfson, 2008). Similar data were obtained by Esposito et al. (2007), who conducted a telephone survey to determine the pattern of treatment for depression in Alberta, Canada. They found that, among those meeting diagnostic criteria for major depression, approximately 40% reported using antidepressant medication, whereas only 14% reported receiving some form of counseling or psychotherapy. Based on a population survey in Great Britain in 1993, 6.7% of women and 6.2% of men reported receiving psychotherapy for an Axis I disorder (Brugha et al., 2004). In 2000, there was no statistically significant change in this: 7.9% of women and 9.8% of men reported receiving psychotherapy. In stark contrast, the rates of psychotropic medication use during this period rose sharply for both women (9.6% to 20.1%) and men (9.7% to 19.1%).

Who are the people who decide to seek therapy as either an alternative or an adjunct to medication? Epidemiological surveys indicate that a number of sociodemographic characteristics are related to the use of psychotherapy (Hunsley, Lee, & Aubry, 1999; Vessey & Howard, 1993). Across all approaches to psychotherapy, the majority of psychotherapy clients are female and are young to middle-age adults. Unfortunately, consistent with the information we presented early in the book, these surveys also suggest that many of those most in need of such services (i.e., those with a diagnosable condition) never seek professional help of any kind.

There are many routes to receive treatment from clinical psychologists. In some countries, services provided by psychologists in hospitals or community clinics are covered by the national health care system; in other countries, such services may be covered by private insurance for most individuals, with only those in the lower income brackets receiving state-supported services. Across most health care systems, it is possible to obtain services from clinical psychologists in private practice settings. Typically, this requires that clients directly pay for services; some clients have health care benefits through their workplace that may cover part or all of the costs. A referral from a physician may be necessary for psychological services delivered in publicly funded settings (such as a hospital) and may be required by some insurance plans; however, clients may be able to self-refer when seeking the services of a private practitioner. The financial costs of psychological services are a major obstacle for many potential clients. This economic burden comes on top of the multiple obstacles that many people face when making a decision to seek therapy. Saunders (1993) conceptualized the process of seeking psychotherapy as involving a series of four interrelated decisions: realizing that there is a problem, deciding that therapy might be of value, actually deciding to seek therapy, and then contacting a therapist or a clinic. In Saunders' research, the majority of those who eventually sought therapy reported that it took several months to move from recognizing that a significant problem existed to deciding that therapy might be useful. Even then, over half of the clients indicated that it took at least several weeks to make the decision to seek treatment. The extent to which the potential client feels supported by significant others in this process can also influence decisions around seeking therapy (Saunders, 1996).

THE DURATION AND IMPACT OF PSYCHOTHERAPY

Mention the word psychotherapy to most people, and their initial associations probably include a couch and a nodding therapist who says very little but grunts enigmatically. As mentioned in Chapter 2, movies and television series frequently depict psychotherapy as a life-long form of treatment. Even if images such as these were accurate at one time, they do not correspond to current reality. The vast majority of people who receive psychotherapy attend fewer than 10 sessions, and evidence-based treatment, across orientations, requires a very active therapist. Across practice settings, countries, and clients presenting problems, the duration of psychotherapy has been remarkably consistent for decades (Garfield, 1994; Phillips, 1991): a substantial minority of clients attend only one or two sessions, and the median number of therapy sessions is typically in the range of 5 to 13 sessions. Over the years, several studies have examined clients' and therapists' expectations for a number of treatment-related factors, including the duration of treatment and reasons for therapy termination (e.g., Hunsley, Aubry, Vestervelt, & Vito, 1999; Steenbarger, 1994). Ironically, compared with therapists' expectations, clients' expectations for treatment duration seem to be more in line with the actual duration of therapy. Likewise, clients generally report more benefits from treatment—even treatment of a brief duration— than do therapists.

Findings reported by Hansen, Lambert, and Forman (2002) nicely illustrate several aspects of what is known about the duration and impact of psychotherapy as it is typically practiced, based on data from more than 6,000 adult patients seen in a range of settings including employee assistance programs, university counseling centers, community mental health clinics, and health maintenance organizations. Fully one third of these patients attended only a single session of psychotherapy, with the median number of therapy sessions being three! Using data from the Outcome Questionnaire (OQ-45, see Chapter 8), across settings, 8.2% of patients deteriorated during treatment, 56.8% experienced no change, and 35% had improved or recovered. Similar findings were reported by Wampold and Brown (2005) based on their analyses of data from more than 6,100 American adults, all of whom were diagnosed with an Axis I disorder and who received therapy from a managed care company. They found that the median number of sessions attended was 8. Using outcome data from this sample, 29% of patients were seen as improved or recovered at the end of therapy.

Much more promising results were obtained in two large-scale studies conducted on those receiving psychotherapy services from National Health Service sites in the United Kingdom. Evans, Connell, Barkham, Marshall, and Mellor-Clark (2003) and Stiles, Barkham, Connell, and Mellor-Clark (2008) obtained improvement rates at least twice the size of estimates from the two American data sets. However, in both British reports, the only patients included in analyses were those for whom data were available for both the first and final treatment sessions (roughly a third of all patients). By excluding from analysis all other patients, including those who dropped out of treatment, it is highly likely that the treatment outcome estimates are overly positive with respect to the likely effects of therapy for everyone who began treatment.

The general results for psychotherapy outcome may seem very discouraging and, in many ways, they are. At first glance the data seem to suggest that psychotherapy, as routinely practiced (at least as evaluated in the two American studies), only benefits about a third of those who enter treatment. Viewed with a skeptical eye, it is likely that results of all four large-scale studies we described are overestimates: without the use of an experimental design that includes a randomly assigned untreated control group it is not possible to attribute changes in functioning solely to the impact of therapy. On the other hand, if you take into account that the median number of therapy sessions reported in the American studies was in the single digits, it is not entirely surprising that psychotherapy has such a limited impact. As you will see in Chapters 12 and 13 when we discuss specific evidence-based psychological treatments, most current treatments are designed to be short term, ranging from 10 to 30 sessions. It seems obvious that, just as with medication, if most people are not receiving the full treatment, any therapeutic benefits are likely to be minimal. The two British studies may provide a better indication of what may be possible with an appropriate "dose" of psychotherapy. Keep in mind, however, that the data we just described came from the results of psychotherapy as it is usually delivered in practice settings. It is likely that only some of this therapy is evidence based, an issue we will return to in later chapters. In other words, the observed impact of routine psychotherapy may be weak for two separate reasons: most patients attend too few sessions and many therapists do not provide evidence-based treatments.

In contrast to these findings, it is informative to look at other data summarized by Hansen et al. (2002) based on data extracted from randomized controlled trials (RCTs) of evidence-based treatments. Across 28 studies and more than 2,100 patients, the average dose of therapy was 12.7 sessions, with 57.6% of patients meeting criteria for recovery (and 67.2% meeting criteria for improvement or recovery). Because of the use of untreated control groups in these studies, these positive results can be attributed directly to the effects of treatment. Hence, with more treatment, and treatment that is evidence based, the success rate of psychotherapy improves substantially compared with treatment as usual. The discerning reader might question whether the RCTs obtain better results because they are dealing with a less distressed sample of patients. In actual fact, the exact opposite is true: Stirman, DeRubeis, Crits-Christoph, and Brody (2003) reported that the average severity of symptoms reported in RCTs of evidence-based treatments is greater than that found in the patients seeking routine psychotherapy services. Evidence-based treatments do better than treatment as usual, even though the patients receiving the evidence-based treatments are more severely distressed. It is also important to note that there is growing evidence that evidence-based treatments are efficacious for clients who are members of ethnic minority groups (Miranda et al., 2005) and that modifying treatments to better fit clients' cultural contexts may be important in enhancing treatment outcomes (Griner & Smith, 2006).

ALTERNATIVE MODES OF SERVICE DELIVERY

Although the vast majority of psychological interventions are delivered in individual sessions in the psychologist's office, psychological services are also delivered in other formats. For example, a variety of structured, brief couples therapies have been developed from different theoretical orientations including behavioral marital therapy, cognitive-behavioral marital therapy, insight-oriented marital therapy, and emotionally focused couple therapy. Although some of these approaches were originally labeled "marital therapies," the term "couple therapy" is now used as these approaches apply to intimate relationships in married and cohabiting heterosexual, gay, and lesbian couples. Based on results of the efficacy of couple therapy, many approaches have been modified. For example, behavioral marital therapy was modified from a solely skill-based, behavioral exchange model designed to improve unsatisfactory relationships into an approach that also includes tasks designed to facilitate acceptance of an imperfect but adequate relationship (Jacobson, Christensen, Prince, Cordova, & Elridge, 2000).

Couple therapy is offered to treat distressed relationships and also to address psychological disorders that are associated with relationship dysfunction, such as depression (Baucom, Epstein, & Gordon, 2000; Birchler & Fals-Stewart, 2002). Couple therapy is delivered primarily by means of conjoint sessions in which both partners are present but may also include individual sessions with each partner. Although there is a wealth of research on couple therapy, there are no systematic data on the effectiveness of these approaches with ethnic minority couples (Gray-Little & Kaplan, 2000).

Like couple therapy, family interventions are practiced by clinical psychologists of different orientations as well as by other mental health professionals such as social workers and psychiatrists. However, whereas advocates of different theoretical approaches to couple therapy agree on a common goal of therapy such as reduced conflict and increased satisfaction, there is no single type of family outcome that is sought across different approaches (Sexton, Alexander, & Mease, 2004). Family therapy may be sought to address difficulties associated with transitions, as well as to address Axis I problems in one or more family members. Although early family approaches viewed the family as the source of a family member's problems, many current family approaches make no such assumption but consider the family an important part of the solution to problems. A common aspect of family approaches is to identify interactions between family members that may inadvertently contribute to problems. Research supports the usefulness of a number of methods that integrate behavioral and family approaches in the treatment of serious problems in adolescence (e.g., Henggeler, Schoenwald, Borduin, Rowland, & Cunningham, 1998).

Given concerns over mounting health care costs, there are increasing pressures to find innovative ways to deliver services in as cost efficient a manner as possible. One obvious solution is to bring together a group of people who are facing the same types of difficulties and to treat them as a group. Like all other forms of psychotherapy, group approaches are based on a variety of theoretical models, including psychodynamic, interpersonal, experiential, and cognitive-behavioral. It is useful to make a distinction between *process* groups that are designed to capitalize on the dynamics of the group and *structured* group approaches that are extensions of treatments that are also offered in an individual format (Burlingame, MacKenzie, & Strauss, 2004). Group approaches should not be seen simply in terms of cost savings, as they also offer unique opportunities to promote change by exchanges between participants (Yalom, 1995). Group therapy is offered both as a primary form of treatment for diverse types of problems, as well as an adjunct to individual therapy, as in the case of the treatment of substance abuse (Burlingame et al., 2004). Groups are offered at different stages of the lifespan to children, adolescents, adults, and the elderly (Brabender, Fallon, & Smolar, 2004).

Group therapy offers many promising mechanisms of change, including universality, support, and modeling. Universality refers to the experience of recognizing that one is not alone in facing a particular difficulty and that others share similar challenges and reactions. Support, both emotional and instrumental, may be provided in a group format, not only by the therapist but also by others in the group. Group contexts allow opportunities for modeling of behaviors, so that a client may learn new ways of coping by observing the efforts of another person. Unfortunately, groups allow the modeling of both positive and negative behaviors. Dishion, McCord, and Poulin (1999) reviewed evidence suggesting that when adolescents with significant problem behaviors received peer-group interventions, they learned aggressive behaviors from one another. Thus, group treatment had an iatrogenic effect, in that youth who received the group treatment did more poorly than did youth who did not receive the treatment. This finding underlines the essential requirement to continuously evaluate the effects of therapy, to determine that therapy is helpful, and to ensure that, if therapy is harmful, it is terminated immediately.

Thus far we have discussed what might be termed "traditional" alternative modes of intervention. Since the 1980s, there has been dramatic growth in a new wave of alternative intervention options.

These include **self-administered treatment** (also known as self-help), **computer-based treatment** (including virtual reality treatments), and computer-based treatment delivery systems.

It may seem strange to consider self-help books as a new development in treatment. After all, the shelves of any bookstore are replete with self-help books, with advice from a host of health care professionals, famous and formerly famous celebrities, and self-promoting lifestyle gurus. Whereas the sales of some of these books may lead to improvements in the financial well-being of their authors, there is little evidence that they do much for improving the quality of the readers' lives. What has changed, though, is that there is now a new generation of self-help materials that has been demonstrated to have a meaningful clinical impact. What these books have in common is that they are based on both well-established psychological principles and treatment protocols for psychotherapies that are evidence based.

Self-help materials can be used in different ways in treatment (Newman, Erickson, Przeworski, & Dzus, 2003). At one end of the continuum, treatment can be entirely self-administered, with the only therapist contact being an initial assessment of patient suitability. Alternatively, treatment can be predominantly self-administered, with occasional therapist contact beyond an initial assessment to teach patients how to use the materials and check on their progress. The degree of therapist involvement can be further increased—but still below the level found in traditional therapy—in minimal-contact therapy, where the therapist actively aids the patient in using the self-help materials (which still remain the central focus of therapy). Finally, at the other end of the continuum, in traditional, predominantly therapist-administered treatments, self-help materials can be used as an adjunct to treatment. There is evidence that self-administered treatments, across this continuum, can be clinically effective in treating depression, anxiety disorders, and substance abuse disorders (Menchola, Arkowitz, & Burke, 2007; Scogin, 2003). Malouf and Rooke (2007) reviewed the empirical support available for self-help books readily available from bookstores. They found that there were books with some empirical support for several disorders, including depression, panic disorder, social anxiety, binge eating, and chronic fatigue. The book with the greatest empirical support, by far, was Burns' (1980) book on CBT techniques, *Feeling Good: The New Mood Therapy*.

Since the early 1980s, researchers have experimented with the possibility of delivering individual treatments via computers. Early programs were rather primitive and limited in scope but, with the rapid growth in computing power in personal computers, more recent programs are incredibly sophisticated and flexible. In fact, in a number of experimental trials, computer-based treatments have been found to have efficacy comparable to that of traditional individual psychotherapy for some people and conditions (Marks, Shaw, & Parkin, 1998). For example, Proudfoot et al. (2004) reported on a large randomized controlled trial in England in which 274 primary care patients with anxiety and/or depression received, with or without medication, either computerized CBT or treatment as usual as directed by the patient's primary care physician. The *Beating the Blues* program involves a brief video introduction followed by eight 50-minute computer sessions, with assigned homework to be completed between sessions. Compared with the treatment as usual condition, the patients who followed the *Beating the Blues* program evidenced significant improvements in depression, anxiety, work adjustment, and social adjustment. Interestingly, even though the cost of the computer-based treatment was $70 higher per patient than the usual treatments, lost employment costs were $730 less per patient (McCrone et al., 2004). Overall, the research on computer programs for treating depression clearly indicates their success in alleviating symptoms, but it also appears that the rate of premature termination from these treatments is higher than for patients receiving traditional therapy services from a mental health professional (Kaltenthaler, Parry, Beverley, & Ferriter, 2008).

How would you feel about receiving psychological treatment based on a computer program provided under the supervision of a psychologist? Would your reactions changed if you were able to start the computer-based treatment immediately, rather than having to wait weeks or months on a waiting list to receive therapy from a psychologist?

Other computer-based treatments are now available through the Internet, thus greatly expanding service delivery options for those who are far from a psychologist or who are too impaired by anxiety symptoms to travel for treatment (Kenwright & Marks, 2004). This use of information technology and telecommunications to provide health care services at a distance is known as **telehealth** (mentioned in Profile Box 11.1). Telehealth covers a range of delivery options, including telephone, videoconferencing, and computer-mediated communications (including email, chat rooms, and Internet-based services). The possibility of providing appropriate evidence-based services at a distance is extremely exciting and opens up countless opportunities for reaching people who might otherwise be unable or unwilling to seek necessary psychological services. In **Profile Box 11.1,** you will learn more about the work of Dr. Robert Glueckauf, whose research investigates the promise and challenges of telehealth.

PROFILE BOX 11.1

DR. ROBERT GLUECKAUF

I earned a Ph.D. in clinical psychology from Florida State University (FSU). Currently I am a Professor in the Department of Medical Humanities and Social Sciences at the FSU College of Medicine. Before moving to FSU in 2003, I directed the Center for Research on Telehealth and Healthcare Communications at the University of Florida. I have served as the President of the American Psychological Association's Division of Rehabilitation Psychology and as Associate Editor of the division's journal, *Rehabilitation Psychology*. I am a licensed psychologist in Florida. My research and clinical interests lie in (a) the development and evaluation of telehealth delivery systems for underserved individuals with chronic illnesses and their family caregivers, (b) measurement of rehabilitation and health outcomes, and (c) the family system's interventions for persons with disabilities. My research has

Dr. Robert Glueckauf

been supported by numerous federal and state grants. I have authored over 80 empirical and theoretical articles, books, and chapters in the field of health care and rehabilitation.

How did you choose to become a clinical psychologist?

During my last two years of undergraduate studies I developed strong interests in family psychology and applied behavior analysis. In pursuing graduate studies, I wanted to be in a program that would allow me to have clinical training opportunities in combination with excellent research training. Consequently, I chose a clinical psychology program that had a strong concentration in applied behavior analysis, a variety of clinical practica, and an option to have a minor in family studies. As a result of my graduate training and early postgraduate work, I learned that I greatly enjoyed providing psychological services in the context of intervention research.

What is the most rewarding part of your job as a clinical psychologist?

As a professor, my major responsibility is conducting applied research. My research program focuses on evaluating the effects of family intervention programs for under-served rural and ethnic minority populations with chronic illnesses and their caregivers. Most rewarding to me is finding ways to adapt interventions to the needs, beliefs, and sociocultural characteristics of the target population, and after these interventions are established, determining how to make them easily accessible, user friendly, and cost effective through the use of telehealth technologies and other creative delivery strategies. Telehealth is an innovative approach to delivering health care by using telecommunication and information technologies to provide access to health information and services across a geographical distance, including (but not limited to) consultation, assessment, intervention, and follow-up programs to ensure maintenance of treatment effects.

What is the greatest challenge you face as a clinical psychologist?

I enjoy providing psychological treatment and developing services that make a difference in people's lives. As my research requires ongoing grant support, I need to write grant applications, regularly monitor grant budgets, and perform numerous other management activities. Although critical to our projects' success, such activities remove me from direct provision of psychological services. Therefore, my greatest challenge is finding ways to remind myself that spending time on administrative tasks is necessary in order for me to accomplish what is most meaningful for me. One of my major life goals is to help enhance the quality of life of persons with chronic illnesses and their family caregivers.

Tell us about developments in the provision of telehealth services by psychologists

I am interested in finding ways to make psychological services accessible to individuals with chronic illnesses and their family caregivers. I am particularly concerned to make sure they are available to the economically disadvantaged and those underserved by the health care system. This has led me to focus my research efforts on the development and evaluation of telehealth-based family intervention programs. This field of research has grown considerably over the past decade, and a range of randomized control trials now support the efficacy of telehealth-based interventions. However, the lack of insurance reimbursement remains a major obstacle to the provision of telehealth services in the United States. Although some headway has been made in subsidizing rural telehealth services, most insurers do not cover telehealth-based psychological services to individuals with chronic illnesses and their family caregivers. I believe it is essential that the U.S.

government, particularly the Center for Medicare and Medicaid Services, recognize the shift in the health care delivery landscape and reorganize its funding priorities. As the baby boomer generation ages, Internet and other computer-based technologies are likely to become vehicles of choice for provision of health information and health promotion services for those at risk for chronic illnesses.

How do you integrate science and practice in your work?

My clinical practice and research activities are inextricably linked. All clinical interventions my research team and I provide are guided by a conceptual framework and are typically grounded in previous telehealth and/or family intervention research. When implementing new, untested interventions, we gather data on their impact before advocating their use in future research protocols or in clinical practice.

What do you see as the most exciting changes in the field of clinical psychology?

One promising change is the increased recognition of the importance of adapting clinical interventions to the characteristics of the population. This requires considerable effort on the investigator's part to understand the sociocultural characteristics, needs, and values of the population of interest, and then to modify or develop interventions that take these factors into account. In my opinion, clinical psychology has tended to be overly narrow in its approach to research on factors influencing health and emotional functioning, so I am quite excited by the burgeoning interest in clinical research and practice in considering the influence of spirituality on people's health.

To date, most of the research on telehealth treatments has involved adapting forms of CBT, and encouraging results have been obtained for the treatment of a number of disorders, especially depression and anxiety disorders (e.g., Carlbring et al., 2007; Litz, Engel, Bryant, & Papa, 2007; Mohr et al., 2005). However, the use of these technologies also opens a host of ethical, legal, and training questions (Glueckauf, Pickett, Ketterson, Loomis, & Rozensky, 2003; Jerome & Zaylor, 2000). What additional training is required to allow a psychologist who is competent at delivering evidence-based therapy to be prepared to deliver the same types of treatment via videoconferencing? Is it legal for a psychologist to deliver Internet-based treatment to a patient who lives in a jurisdiction other than the one in which the psychologist is licensed?

With this growing range of treatment options, models of **stepped care**, long available in medicine, are now being applied to psychological treatments. In an attempt to make the most of scarce health care resources, lower cost interventions are offered first, with more intensive and more costly interventions provided only to those for whom the first-line intervention was insufficient (Haaga, 2000; Scogin, Hanson, & Welsh, 2003). Following a thorough assessment of the patient and the state of the research evidence for the available treatment options, self-help or computer-based treatments may be worth considering as initial treatments. If symptoms persist after the completion of such treatments, then individual therapy might be considered. If the likelihood is low that a patient will complete a treatment that does not involve ongoing contact with a health care professional, minimal contact treatments (i.e., 3 or 4 sessions) or group treatments might be the best initial options. With respect to providing services to children and families, less intense interventions may involve the use of therapeutic feedback, large group parenting training, or psychoeducational school-based programs (Stormshak & Dishion, 2002; also see Table 10.6 for a description of the different dosages of the Triple P program). Many details need to be worked out, and much research needs to be done, before stepped care models will be viable and widely accepted by patients and psychologists. What is clear, though, is that individual, face-to-face psychotherapy is no longer the only choice for many individuals seeking psychological services.

SUMMARY AND CONCLUSIONS

In this chapter we have provided an introduction to psychological intervention. We described a number of psychological treatments that have empirical support. These therapies share some features, such as their short-term nature, the establishment of treatment goals, and the active role played by the therapist. Similarly, they share the view that the therapist must establish a positive relationship with the client. Most important, there have been efforts to evaluate the efficacy and effectiveness of these approaches. They differ, however, in their assumptions about the nature of problems, the process by which change occurs, the importance of examining the past, and the relative benefits of insight, experimentation, and skills. These approaches also differ in the role ascribed to the therapeutic relationship—whether it is seen as a mirror of the problems the client experiences, as a support in exploration, or as a resource to aid in experimenting and learning new skills.

Although there has been an increase in the number of people seeking treatments for psychological problems, this is largely accounted for by increased psychopharmacology rather than increased psychotherapy or other psychological services. It is clear that the majority of people who require psychological services do not have access to them. The popular stereotype of long-term psychotherapy does not match the data on the provision of psychotherapy, as important changes are made by many clients after weeks or months of psychological services. The short-term therapies we described are intended to create an expectancy of change as well as encouragement to think, behave, or feel in different ways. In addition to individual therapy, encouraging findings are reported from couple, family, and group therapy. Psychologists are also exploiting the enormous potential of virtual reality and Internet technologies to extend services to sections of the population who have been underserved in the past. Rigorous evaluation of the effectiveness of psychological services allows the development of a range of interventions that can be offered according to clients' needs and preferences. Rather than imposing a "one size fits all" approach to psychotherapy, it makes sense to tailor approaches to meet the needs of a diverse population.

Critical Thinking Questions

What may account for the difficulty many people experience in deciding to seek psychological services?

Once people have decided to begin therapy, what kinds of questions should they raise in the first appointment with a psychologist?

Four main evidence-based approaches to therapy are presented in the chapter. Where would you place them on a continuum, with intrapsychic and interpersonal as endpoints?

Compared with individual treatment, do you think that there are some disorders for which group treatment might be especially appropriate?

For someone considering psychological treatment, what might be the advantages in considering self-administered treatments? What drawbacks might there be?

Key Terms

cognitive-behavioral therapy: a treatment approach that emphasizes the role of thoughts and behavior in psychological problems and, therefore, focuses on altering beliefs, expectations, and behaviors in order to improve the client's functioning

computer-based treatment: psychological interventions that are delivered via a computer program, typically based on principles underlying an evidence-based treatment

interpersonal therapy: a treatment approach that emphasizes interpersonal elements in the development, maintenance, and alteration of psychological problems (especially grief, role disputes, role transitions, and interpersonal deficits)

process-experiential therapy: a treatment approach that emphasizes the importance of becoming aware of emotions, understanding and expressing emotions, and transforming maladaptive to adaptive emotions

self-administered treatment: treatments that the client administers without direct input from a mental health professional

self-efficacy: a person's sense of competence to learn and perform new tasks

short-term psychodynamic therapy: a treatment approach that emphasizes bringing to awareness unconscious processes, especially as they are expressed in interpersonal relationships, and helping the client to understand and alter these processes

stepped care: an approach to health care service delivery in which lower cost interventions are offered first, with more intensive and more costly interventions provided only to those for whom the first-line intervention was insufficient

telehealth: the delivery of health care services via telephone, videoconferencing, or computer-mediated communications

transference: the unconscious application of expectations and emotional experiences based on important early relationships to subsequent interpersonal relationships

Key Names

Albert Bandura	Leslie Greenberg
Aaron Beck	Lester Luborsky
Robert Elliott	Myrna Weissman

ADDITIONAL RESOURCES

BOOKS

Norcross, J. C., Santrock, J. W., Campbell, L. F., Smith, T. P., Sommer, R., & Zuckerman. (2003). *Authoritative guide to self-help resources in mental health* (rev. ed.). New York: Guilford Press.

Wood, J. C. (2007). *Getting help: The complete and authoritative guide to self-assessment and treatment of mental health problems.* Oakland, CA: New Harbinger Publications.

JOURNALS

Annual Review of CyberTherapy and Telemedicine

CyberPsychology and Behavior

Journal of Telemedicine and Telecare

Psychotherapy

Psychotherapy Research

Check It Out!

For more on *Beating the Blues*, acomputer-based treatment of anxiety and depression: http://www.thewellnessshop.co.uk/products/beatingtheblues/

For more information on the *FearFighter*, an Internet-based treatment of phobias and panic, and other Internet-based treatments: http://www.ccbt.co.uk/

Some additional Web sites describing virtual reality treatments and treatment-related research follow. Keep in mind the importance of empirical evidence in reviewing self-help books and Web sites offering treatment options: http://www.virtuallybetter.com
http://www.vrphobia.com/
http://w3.uqo.ca/cyberpsy/en/index_en.htm

CHAPTER 12

Intervention: Adults and Couples

INTRODUCTION

There has been a dramatic evolution in the nature of psychological treatment since the middle of the twentieth century. Significant questions about whether or not psychotherapy works provoked a veritable explosion of research on the impact of psychological treatments, which, in turn, led to the establishment of efficacious and (often) effective treatments for a wide range of disorders and presenting problems. In the first part of this chapter we summarize these important events in the evolution of effective psychological treatments and describe strategies to accurately review treatment studies. We outline recent initiatives to establish criteria for evidence-based treatments. In a growing number of countries, these efforts have culminated in the development of clinical practice guidelines that set out treatments of choice for both adult and child disorders.

In addition to presenting the big picture regarding the history and current state of research-based efforts to develop and promote psychological intervention, we will also provide several detailed examples of current evidence-based treatments for a number of disorders. This will give you a sense of what is involved in state of the art treatments for common debilitating conditions such as depression, posttraumatic stress disorder (PTSD), and couple conflict. Because of the great volume of research and scholarly activity involved, it is not possible to do justice to all of this work in a single chapter. Accordingly, in this chapter we focus on treatments for adults and couples; Chapter 13 addresses treatments for children, adolescents, and families.

DOES PSYCHOTHERAPY WORK? A CONTROVERSY AND ITS IMPACT

PsycINFO, the searchable database of psychological literature developed by APA, covers the period from the second half of the 1800s to the present. If you search this database for empirical studies on psychotherapy for adults that were published in peer-reviewed journals prior to 1950, you will find zero entries. If you rerun the search for the years 1950 to 1980, you will find hundreds of entries, and if you search from 1980 to the present, you will find thousands of additional entries! Many scholars attribute the beginning of this astonishing growth in empirical attention to the effects of psychotherapy to a single controversial paper. In 1952, Hans Eysenck published an article in which he argued that the rates of improvement among clients receiving psychodynamic or eclectic therapy were comparable to, or even worse than, rates of remission of symptoms among untreated clients. At that time, there were no randomized controlled trials (RCTs) of psychotherapy. Instead, proponents of various schools of psychotherapy authoritatively proclaimed the efficacy of their treatments on the basis of clinical experience and, occasionally, case histories of successfully treated patients. Eysenck, an early proponent of applying learning principles to alleviate psychological distress, reviewed data from 24 uncontrolled evaluations of psychoanalytic and eclectic therapies. Summing across data sets, he concluded that 44% of patients receiving psychoanalysis improved and 64% of those receiving eclectic treatments improved. He compared these results with two data sets in which *spontaneous recovery* occurred for 72% of *untreated* patients.

As we discussed in Chapter 4, internal validity is an important aspect of any psychological research. If you look back at Table 4.7, you can see that Eysenck's analysis of the data probably suffered from several threats to internal validity, including history, maturation, statistical regression, and selection biases. Without the use of appropriate control groups, in which participants are randomly assigned to treatment conditions, it is incorrect to compare the results from the different data sets. Without randomization there is no way to determine whether the patients in the different samples were comparable in terms of disorder or severity of distress. It is also important to note that the so-called *untreated* groups were patients in residential treatment settings and patients making psychologically based disability claims who were treated by general medical practitioners. In other words, although they did not receive formal psychotherapy services, these *untreated* patients would have received some guidance and suggestions on their psychological difficulties as part of their treatment regimen. Critics of Eysenck's work, such as Luborsky (1954), also claimed that Eysenck's criteria for establishing clinical improvement were arbitrary and biased against finding positive therapeutic effects.

From the late 1950s to the early 1970s, a number of competing reviews of the impact of psychotherapy were published. Those who advocated the use of learning principles in developing psychological interventions, such as Eysenck (1966) and Rachman (1971), maintained that there was no compelling evidence supporting the efficacy of psychodynamic and other "traditional" forms of treatment. In stark contrast, proponents of the traditional psychotherapies conducted reviews showing that not only did these therapies have positive effects, but also that their effects were comparable to those reported for the newly developed behavioral therapies (Bergin, 1971; Luborsky, Singer, & Luborsky, 1975). Because each research group used different criteria to select studies for review, there was little overlap in the studies on which conclusions were based. Furthermore, different criteria were used to evaluate whether therapy worked. On top of that, interpretation of results was colored by preexisting biases for and against the value of traditional psychotherapies. For example, Bergin (1971) concluded that significant results in 22 out of 60 studies indicated that psychotherapy had a moderately positive effect, whereas critics of traditional therapy claimed the opposite, noting that 38 out of 60 studies failed to demonstrate clear evidence of positive treatment effects.

How important is it to you that psychological treatments be empirically evaluated? If you were considering seeking treatment (or were making recommendations to family members or friends about therapy), would it matter to you whether or not the treatment you received had a solid evidence base?

META-ANALYSIS AND PSYCHOTHERAPY RESEARCH

Throughout the 1970s, as the debate about the impact of psychotherapy grew, so did the number of published treatment studies. The literature became so vast that anyone attempting to understand and integrate the research evidence on various forms of psychotherapy faced the daunting task of qualitatively reviewing hundreds of published studies. The publication of the first **meta-analysis** of the psychotherapy literature by **Mary Smith** and **Gene Glass** (1977) was a landmark in efforts to review scientific literature on treatment outcome.

Dr. Gene Glass co-authored the first meta-analysis of the psychotherapy literature in 1977.

As you learned in Chapter 4, meta-analysis is a method for quantitatively reviewing research studies. We have mentioned results of meta-analytic studies in several preceding chapters. In this chapter and the remaining chapters, we will be providing a bit more detail about the results of the meta-analytic studies we present. In order to for you to be able to understand these results, you need a sense of the statistics used in meta-analyses. To allow for the meaningful integration of data across studies, researchers convert the results of studies into **effect sizes**. When based on group comparison statistics (such as t or F), effect sizes are expressed in standard deviation units: an effect size of $d = .5$ means that there is a difference of one half standard deviation between groups. When correlational analyses are used (e.g., r or R), the effect size is expressed as an r statistic. It is also possible to convert d effect sizes into r effect sizes, and vice versa.

Effect sizes using the d statistic can also be represented in another way that is even more compelling. Let's consider a psychotherapy outcome research study with a treated and an untreated group, and let's assume that the distribution of outcome scores for each group is normal in shape. If there were no group difference, then d would equal 0, and the two group distributions would overlap perfectly. However, if the treated group had better outcomes than did the untreated group (for example, $d = .5$), then the distributions would only overlap partially, as there is a half standard deviation difference between the

TABLE 12.1   Equivalencies for Meta-Analytic Statistics

d	r	Percentage of untreated participants below the mean of treated participants
0.0	.00	50
0.2	.10	58
0.4	.20	66
0.6	.29	73
0.8	.37	79
1.0	.45	84
1.5	.60	93
2.0	.71	98

means of the two groups. It is possible, therefore, to represent the d statistic as the percentage of participants in the untreated group whose scores are lower than that of the average participant in the treated group. **Table 12.1** provides information on the equivalency among d, r, and the percentage of those in the untreated group falling below the level of the mean treated participant.

By current standards, the first attempt to employ meta-analytic techniques was rather crude. Nevertheless, based on data from more than 370 published and unpublished studies, Smith and Glass (1977) reported the average effect of psychotherapy to be $d = .68$. In percentage terms, this means that the average person receiving treatment was better off at the end of treatment than 74% of those who had not received treatment. Psychotherapy, in general, certainly seemed to have a substantial impact. In 1980, Smith, Glass, and Miller published a more extensive and more sophisticated meta-analysis of the psychotherapy literature. They reviewed 475 controlled studies of psychotherapy, including studies published in scientific journals and unpublished dissertations. Their overall finding was that psychotherapy had an average effect size of $d = .85$ (i.e., the average person receiving therapy was better off after therapy than 80% of people who did not receive therapy).

Smith and colleagues calculated the efficacy of various types of treatment. Cognitive and cognitive-behavioral treatments had the largest effect sizes (d values of 1.31 and 1.24, respectively), followed by behavioral (.91), psychodynamic (.78), and humanistic treatments (.63). These effect sizes cannot be directly compared, however, as clients treated within each type of treatment were not necessarily equivalent in the type and severity of problems. Smith and colleagues also examined the effects of psychotherapy across different disorders. Some of the largest effect sizes were for anxiety and mood problems and, again, some significant differences between treatments were evident. A subset of the studies they reviewed included direct comparisons of different forms of treatment (i.e., comparative treatment outcome studies in which participants were randomly assigned to different treatments). We will discuss these and other findings from this landmark meta-analysis in Chapter 14.

Criticisms of meta-analysis emerged rapidly (e.g., Eysenck, 1978; Wilson & Rachman, 1983). One criticism referred to the problem of *garbage in, garbage out;* in other words, if poor-quality studies were included in a meta-analysis they could negatively influence the results. Similarly, the *apples and oranges* argument raised concern about the meaningfulness of including different treatments and different measures in a meta-analysis. For example, in considering the general effect of treatment, meta-analysts might give as much weight to a measure of patients' satisfaction with treatment as they did to data on whether a diagnosable condition was still present after treatment. In early meta-analyses, some researchers made other mistakes such as not controlling for differences in sample sizes across studies or using all results from each study rather than an average of all results (which meant that studies with a large number of analyses had more influence on the results of the meta-analysis). Fortunately, meta-analysts took these concerns seriously, and current practices in meta-analysis address such shortcomings.

Throughout the 1980s and 1990s, the number of meta-analyses grew. Because Smith and colleagues' (1980) general findings on the effectiveness of psychotherapy were replicated by other researchers (e.g., Landman & Dawes, 1982), meta-analyses became more focused in nature. Instead of dealing with whether or not therapy had an effect, questions were refined to: How effective are the treatments for a specific disorder? and How effective is a specific treatment for a specific disorder? Dobson (1989) and Robinson, Berman, and Neimeyer (1990), for example, examined research on treatments for depression and found that cognitive therapy had a very large effect size compared with waiting-list controls ($d > 1.5$) but only a small relative advantage over other treatments such as behavior therapy. Chambless and Gillis (1993) reviewed research on the treatment of anxiety disorders, including agoraphobia, panic disorder, social phobia, and generalized anxiety disorders. Cognitive-behavioral treatments were, in general, very efficacious compared with no-treatment conditions, but the extent to which treatments differentially emphasized cognitive or behavioral elements had little impact on treatment outcome.

Today, a PsycINFO search would reveal hundreds of meta-analyses published in the adult psychotherapy literature. This quantitative approach to reviewing research is now the gold standard for evaluating treatment effects. However, sometimes even gold has impurities that mar its value—as we discussed previously, the quality of meta-analytic results is largely dependent on methodological decisions made by researchers who conduct the meta-analyses. In a series of *multidimensional* meta-analyses, **Drew Westen** and his colleagues examined treatment research for depression, bulimia nervosa, generalized anxiety disorder, panic disorder, PTSD, and obsessive-compulsive disorder (Bradley, Greene, Russ, Dutra, & Westen, 2005; Eddy, Dutra, Bradley, & Westen, 2004; Thompson-Brenner, Glass, & Westen, 2003; Westen & Morrison, 2001). These meta-analyses were designed to improve on previous meta-analyses by analyzing a number of other treatment-related variables in addition to treatment outcome. For example, in order to consider the external validity and the clinical utility of treatment studies, Westen and colleagues also examined variables such as the number of patients excluded from the RCTs for failure to meet inclusion criteria, recovery rates (not just symptom change), and the persistence of treatment benefits over time. By examining these types of variables, the researchers' intention was to determine (a) the clinical significance of obtained treatment results and (b) the applicability of the research results to the general population of patients receiving therapy.

To illustrate these points, we will consider their multidimensional meta-analysis on bulimia nervosa (Thompson-Brenner et al., 2003). These researchers found that, on average, more than 80% of patients who began the RCT completed the treatment—an important aspect to consider in understanding the potential impact of the treatments studied. When the usual effect sizes across treatments were calculated from 26 clinical trials, the average effect of therapy compared with no treatment was substantial, with *d* values in the range of .9 to 1.0. Just how big an effect was this in the patients' lives? Approximately 40% of patients recovered completely, with the others continuing to experience some symptoms. Thirty-two percent of patients maintained their recovery a year after treatment. Although these findings indicated that treatments for this eating disorder can have a substantial impact on patients' functioning, it is clear that many patients continued to manifest some aspects of the disorder despite having received treatment.

Thompson-Brenner and colleagues were also concerned to find that, on average, 40% of patients were excluded from the RCTs they examined. Potential participants were excluded for a variety of reasons, including the presence of psychotic disorders, substance abuse, or other major psychiatric problems. This raises an important issue: is it possible that the RCTs routinely exclude from treatment too many patients who normally seek treatment, thereby greatly reducing the generalizability of findings? Fortunately, this does not appear to be the case. As we mentioned in Chapter 11, Stirman and colleagues (2003) found that the average severity of symptoms reported in RCTs of evidence-based treatments is greater than that found in the patients seeking routine psychotherapy services. Moreover, it appears that, even if a potential research participant might be excluded from an RCT because of the presence of a comorbid diagnosis, it is highly likely that the patient would meet commonly used inclusion criteria used in the RCTs for the comorbid diagnosis (Stirman, DeRubeis, Crits-Christoph, & Rothman, 2005). Thus, for example, someone excluded from an RCT for depression because of a comorbid panic disorder could be included in an RCT for panic disorder. The implications of this are that (a) there are likely to be efficacious treatment options (based on RCTs) for most patients, even those with comorbid diagnoses and (b) in working with patients with comorbid diagnoses psychologists must decide which diagnosis or condition should be addressed first and which problems should be addressed only after some initial changes in functioning have occurred. For example, in treating a client experiencing both PTSD and bulimia nervosa, the psychologist might determine that the eating problem needs to be stabilized before initiating treatment for the trauma.

Should authors of treatment studies be required to report on the proportion of potential participants who were excluded from the studies and the proportion of participants who failed to complete treatment? What differences might these data make in interpreting the results of the study? Do you think that clinical psychologists should use this type of information when they decide what kind of treatment to offer a patient?

EVIDENCE-BASED TREATMENTS: INITIATIVES AND CONTROVERSIES

Based on the efforts of psychotherapy researchers in many countries, there is now compelling evidence that psychotherapy has the potential to improve the psychosocial functioning of adult patients with a wide range of disorders. These include common psychological disorders—mood disorders, anxiety disorders, eating disorders, sleep disorders, sexual disorders, and substance-related disorders—and diseases and disorders that are routinely seen in primary care medical practices but that are typically difficult to medically manage, including type 1 diabetes, chronic tension-type headaches, rheumatoid arthritis, chronic low-back pain, and chronic fatigue syndrome (First & Tasman, 2004; Hunsley, 2003a). Given this research, it is surprising that so little has been done to promote the use of treatments found to be efficacious.

Clinical practice guidelines, based on the best available empirical evidence, are a common way in which empirical evidence is used to assist clinicians in making assessment and treatment decisions. Many health professions, such as medicine, nursing, and psychiatry, have developed expert review panels to translate the knowledge gained from research into concrete guidelines intended to inform clinical practice. The American Psychiatric Association, for example, has over a dozen practice guidelines listed on its Web site that address the treatment of dementias, mood disorders, several anxiety disorders, borderline personality disorder, eating disorders, and schizophrenia.

Despite the extent and strength of psychotherapy research, organized clinical psychology has been very slow and seemingly reluctant to develop clinical practice guidelines. The first initiative in this direction in clinical psychology began in the early 1990s, when the APA Society of Clinical Psychology struck a task force on the promotion and dissemination of psychological procedures. The goal of the task force was to set a standard for defining treatment efficacy that was comparable to standards used in other areas of health care, such as approval criteria for pharmaceuticals. The impetus for this work came from increasing pressure for health care practices to be both demonstrably effective and cost effective (Beutler, 1998). Legislation and state case law were being used to shape the nature of both federal and state health care policy, and there appeared to be a very real danger that access to mental health and behavioral health care services might be curtailed because of perceptions that such services were both expensive and relatively ineffective.

Members of the original task force, chaired by **Dianne Chambless,** came from a range of employment settings and espoused a variety of theoretical orientations. The task force's strategy was to examine treatment research for specific disorders and conditions according to a number of criteria. For a treatment to be designated as an **empirically supported treatment** (EST), the task force required, among other things, that there must be evidence of symptom reduction and/or improved functioning either from at least two independently conducted RCTs or from a large series of single-case studies. A report of the task force criteria and an initial list of ESTs was published in 1995 (Task Force on Promotion and Dissemination of Psychological Procedures, 1995). As the task force continued its work, the member-ship was expanded and additional issues were addressed in subsequent reports (Chambless et al., 1996; Weisz, Hawley, Pilkonis, Woody, & Follette, 2000). In a related effort in 1998, a special section in the *Journal of Consulting and Clinical Psychology* was devoted to the topic of ESTs. To guide authors in reviewing the literature for the special section, Chambless and Hollon (1998) refined the criteria for designating ESTs; their criteria are presented in **Table 12.2**. As you can see, one of the Chambless and Hollon criteria for ESTs is that the treatment be shown to be helpful on the basis of an RCT or equivalent design. As you learned earlier in the text, evidence-based treatments vary in the extent and nature of their supporting data—so a treatment could have an evidence base but, because no RCTs have been conducted on the treatment, it would not meet the criteria to be an EST. Therefore, the term evidence-based is broader than the term EST.

TABLE 12.2　Chambless and Hollon's (1998) Criteria for Empirically Supported Treatments

Methodological and Statistical Criteria for Treatment Studies

1. There must be a comparison of the treatment with no-treatment control group, alternative treatment group, or placebo in an RCT, controlled single-case experiment, or an equivalent time-series research design.
2. The treatment must be statistically significantly superior to the comparison groups described above *OR* the treatment is equivalent to another treatment that is already of established efficacy.
3. The research must have sufficient statistical power to detect moderate differences.
4. The research must have been conducted with (a) a treatment manual or its equivalent, (b) a population treated for specified problems, for whom inclusion criteria have been delineated in a reliable and valid manner, (c) reliable and valid treatment outcome measures that, at a minimum, assess the problems addressed in the treatment, and (d) appropriate data analysis.

Designation Criteria for Treatments

Efficacious: The superiority of the EST must have been shown in at least two independent research settings (for single-case experiments the sample size must have been at least 3 at each site). If the data from all studies of the treatment are conflicting, the preponderance of the well-controlled data must support the EST efficacy.

Possibly Efficacious: One study is sufficient for this designation, in the absence of conflicting evidence (for single-case experiments the study must have had a sample size of at least 3).

Efficacious and Specific: The EST must have been shown to be statistically significantly superior to pill, psychological placebo, or alternative bona fide treatment in at least two independent research settings. If there is conflicting evidence, the preponderance of the well-controlled data must support the EST's efficacy and specificity.

 What do you think of these criteria? Do they seem too demanding, or not demanding enough? Why do you think the requirements for efficacious treatments include the need for supporting evidence from at least two independent research groups?

Many vocal critics of the EST initiative expressed concerns about a multitude of issues, ranging from the scientific soundness of the endeavor to the potential negative impacts on practicing clinicians (e.g., Garfield, 1996; Henry, 1998; Silverman, 1996; Wampold, 1997). **Table 12.3** provides a summary of concerns and objections raised most frequently by these and other commentators, along with a set of responses typically offered by EST proponents.

The series of meta-analyses by Westen and colleagues raised the question of the appropriateness of reliance on statistically significant differences on symptom measures between treated and untreated patients to determine the strength of a treatment. As we described earlier in the chapter, even a large effect size (such as $d = 1.0$) does not guarantee that the majority of patients are symptom free by the end of treatment or that they remain symptom free for years after treatment. On the other hand, the standard used by most health care professions in defining preferred treatments is evidence of significant group differences from RCTs. At a minimum, clinical psychologists, along with other health care providers, need to remain aware of the important difference in all health care treatment research between *statistically significant differences* and *clinically significant differences* (as represented by such concepts as *improved quality of life, cure,* and *recovery*).

TABLE 12.3   The EST Initiative: Criticisms and Responses

- It is premature to come up with list of treatments with empirical support. *Given (a) the pressing need for services that work, (b) hundreds of treatment studies, and (c) the millions of dollars spent on psychotherapy research to date, it is time for greater professional and public awareness of what works.*

- The EST criteria—for example, requiring RCTs and treatment manuals—are a disadvantage for some therapeutic orientations. *The criteria may require some psychotherapy researchers to provide more details about the nature of the treatments they study, but researchers from psychodynamic, experiential, interpersonal, and cognitive-behavioral approaches have been able to develop treatment manuals and conduct RCTs.*

- Patients in RCTs are not representative of patients in the "real world" who seek therapy. *This is an important issue that requires further empirical attention. Initial indications are that, by and large, patients in RCTs may have more severe problems than those typically found in clinical practice.*

- EST designations are based on efficacy trials, but do we really know that these treatments can work in the "real world" (i.e., what about effectiveness trials)? *This is an extremely important point, as effectiveness trials are critical for ensuring that treatments can be appropriately delivered in clinical practice. However, the relation between efficacy and effectiveness trials should be seen as evolutionary, because it only makes sense to mount an effectiveness trial for a treatment that has been shown to work in efficacy trials.*

- Treatment manuals can never capture the subtle nuances necessary for clinical services. *True, but manuals are not intended to do this. Thorough clinical training is necessary for the appropriate application of treatment manuals.*

- Doesn't using an EST require the clinician to follow, step-by-step, the treatment manual, thus leaving no room to tailor therapy to the clients' individual needs? *This criticism may have been valid for the first wave of treatment manuals developed in the 1970s and 1980s. However, most manuals now outline the key elements of treatment and explicitly encourage clinicians to adjust treatment to clients' needs.*

- Why the exclusive emphasis on treatment techniques—what about the therapeutic relationship or client characteristics? *A good point—one that led to the development of a task force looking at these issues (see Chapter 14).*

- What about diversity issues—for example, have ESTs been developed for all ethnic groups? *This, too, is a good point, and one for which current research is inadequate. A growing number of RCTs include patients/clients from various ethnic groups, and some granting agencies will only fund studies with samples that are broadly representative of the population in the area in which the study is conducted. Nevertheless, at this point in time, psychologists must rely on their clinical skills and sensitivity to determine how best to tailor ESTs to the realities of individual patients, including attention to all forms of diversity.*

Within an evidence-based approach to treatment, it is critical to distinguish between a treatment that is untested (which by definition could not meet EST criteria) and a treatment that has been demonstrated to be ineffective or harmful. Treatments that have been shown to be harmful should not be used. It is highly likely that some existing, but as yet untested, treatments work for some patients. No doubt the next edition of this text will include new treatments that are currently being evaluated. According to the principles of evidence-based care, health care professionals and patients should consider a treatment with existing research support *before* they turn to untested treatments. This is true whether the clinical condition requiring treatment is depression, back pain, or diabetes, and whether the health care provider is a psychologist, a physician, or an occupational therapist. When an evidence-based treatment is chosen as the first line of care, because even the best evidence-based treatments are not 100% efficacious for all people, it may be necessary to consider other available treatments that do not yet have strong research support. Based on research evidence, ESTs are likely to be the best treatment option for most people, but they are not a panacea.

The EST initiative inspired other divisions within APA to examine the issue of evidence-based treatments. In Chapter 13 we describe some of the efforts to designate treatments for children and youth as empirically supported. Related to these efforts, the APA accreditation criteria require that clinical training programs and internships include training in ESTs.

In addition, there have been evidence-based treatment initiatives in other countries. For example, in Germany, the federal government commissioned an expert report on psychotherapy that was used to guide the writing of laws to regulate psychotherapy. An important element of this expert report was the emphasis on ensuring access to psychotherapy services for which there is empirical evidence of efficacy (Schulte & Hahlweg, 2000). Another example comes from Australia and New Zealand, where the Quality Assurance Project has published several guidelines for the treatment of psychological disorders. These guidelines are based on the combined results of meta-analytic reviews of the empirical literature, surveys of practitioners, and the opinions of experts. Another approach was developed in the United Kingdom, where the National Health Service (NHS) commissioned a report to guide the strategic policy review of psychotherapy services. The authors of this report used similar, but less stringent, criteria to those used by the Society of Clinical Psychology (Roth & Fonagy, 1996, 2005). Three criteria were used to determine whether there is evidence of treatment efficacy, each of which is less demanding than the EST criteria presented in Table 12.2. First, there must be a minimum of a single, high-quality RCT showing treatment efficacy. Second, there must be a clear description of the treatment, preferably but not necessarily in the form of a therapy manual. Third, there must be a clear description of the recipients of the therapy.

Over a series of editions, Nathan and Gorman (1998, 2002, 2007) adopted a different approach to reviewing and evaluating the therapy literature. Expert contributors were asked to provide indications of the methodological adequacy of outcome studies that supported the various treatments for a specific disorder. This approach allowed experts to provide evidence-based guidance on the treatment of conditions for which the research was limited or was in an early stage of development. Three types of clinical trials were identified. In descending order of quality, Type 1 studies are high-quality RCTs, Type 2 studies are imperfect RCTs (e.g., very limited treatment duration, incomplete patient randomization), and Type 3 studies are **open trials** or pilot studies in which there are no control conditions. Additionally, experts could draw on the conclusions from quantitative literature reviews such as meta-analyses (Type 4), qualitative literature reviews (Type 5), and case studies or professional consensus statements not based on research evidence (Type 6).

Nathan and Gorman's consideration of all types of treatment studies is consistent with the approach to evidence-based practice that we have described in previous chapters. Indeed, most efforts to operationalize the concept of evidence-based practice rely heavily on a ranking system such as the one used by Nathan and Gorman (2007) to establish a hierarchy of evidence. This is an important feature of evidence-based practice because, as we described in Chapter 4, research designs vary in the extent to which they address threats to internal and external validity. Accordingly, basing treatment recommendations for a patient on the results of a single, non-replicated study is less desirable than basing the recommendations on the results from numerous studies of the same treatment. Similarly, though, making treatment decisions based on uncontrolled or correlational research is better than basing it solely on professional opinion. The establishment of a hierarchy of research evidence allows decisions to be made using the best available data with respect to a given disorder or condition.

Table 12.4 provides a summary of Nathan and Gorman's (2007) review of psychological treatments for adult DSM-IV disorders. In order to provide a sense of the range of evidence-based treatment options available, we provide information on treatments that have the highest level of empirical support (primarily Type 1 and 2 studies). Psychopathology research about each disorder informed the development of the treatments listed and, subsequently, each treatment was evaluated for its efficacy. This means that these therapies were designed to treat a specific disorder. Thus, for example, although interpersonal therapies for bipolar disorder and bulimia share many elements in common (such as a focus on how others' reactions to the disorders affect those who have the disorders), each treatment has been uniquely tailored to address the key aspects of each of the disorders (such as symptoms, interpersonal problems, and cognitive distortions). In many ways, psychopathology research forms the foundation for all of these evidence-based treatments.

In examining this list, we encourage you to keep several points in mind. First, for some of the disorders listed in the table, there are additional treatment options that have empirical support, although the support is not as strong as that for the treatments presented in the table. For example, in the treatment of opiate dependence, there is evidence that short-term psychodynamic treatment can be efficacious and, in the treatment of depression, both short-term psychodynamic and process-experiential treatments have empirical support (Gibbons, Crits-Christoph, & Hearon, 2008; Greenberg, 2008). Second, there are many psychological disorders and problems not reviewed in Nathan and Gorman's (2007) work. For example, we know that CBT is efficacious in the treatment of body dysmorphic disorder (Williams, Hadjistavropoulos, & Sharpe, 2006) and that CBT, insight-oriented marital therapy, and emotionally focused couples therapy are all efficacious in treating couple conflict (Chambless & Ollendick, 2001). There are also efficacious psychological treatments for health problems and illnesses, such as irritable bowel syndrome, chronic fatigue syndrome, Raynaud's disease, tinnitus, and smoking, to name only a few (you will learn more about clinical health psychology in Chapter 15). Third, although there is growing awareness of the need to examine the efficacy of treatments for a diverse population, to date there is relatively limited research on efficacious psychotherapy options for ethnic minority clients. Although the evidence generally indicates that treatments found to be efficacious for patients with White European ancestry can be efficacious for patients with other ethnic backgrounds, there may be a need to adapt these treatments in culturally appropriate ways (Horrell, 2008; Miranda et al., 2005). Finally, no matter how thoroughly the scientific literature was reviewed in developing a list of evidence-based treatments, the publication of new studies means that such a list must be frequently updated. Updating is especially

TABLE 12.4 Evidence-Based Treatments for Adults

Mood Disorders

Major Depressive Disorder

- Behavioral marital therapy
- Cognitive-behavioral therapy
- Interpersonal psychotherapy

Bipolar Disorder

- Psychoeducation (including family members)
- Cognitive-behavioral therapy
- Interpersonal and social rhythm therapy
- Some forms of marital and family therapy

Anxiety Disorders

Specific Phobias

- Cognitive-behavioral therapy

Social Phobia

- Cognitive-behavioral therapy

Panic Disorder With and Without Agoraphobia

- Cognitive-behavioral therapy

Generalized Anxiety Disorder

- Cognitive-behavioral therapy

Obsessive-Compulsive Disorder

- Cognitive-behavioral therapy

Posttraumatic Stress Disorder

- Cognitive-behavioral therapy
- Eye movement desensitization and reprocessing

Eating Disorders

Anorexia Nervosa

- Cognitive-behavioral therapy

Bulimia Nervosa

- Cognitive-behavioral therapy
- Interpersonal therapy

Binge-Eating Disorder

- Cognitive-behavioral therapy
- Interpersonal psychotherapy

Substance-Related Disorders

- Psychoeducation (including motivational interviewing)
- Cognitive-behavioral therapy
- Marital and family therapy (CBT)
- 12-step programs

Sleep Disorders

- Cognitive-behavioral therapy

Sexual Disorders

- Cognitive-behavioral therapy

Schizophrenia

- Cognitive-behavioral therapy
- Psychoeducation (including family members)

Personality Disorders

Avoidant Personality Disorder

- Cognitive-behavioral therapy

Borderline Personality Disorder

- Dialectical behavior therapy
- Some forms of long-term psychodynamic therapy

Adapted from Nathan and Gorman (2007)

important for treatments that have received little research attention, as data from one or two newly published studies may provide supporting evidence for a treatment that previously had none.

Two features in this table are striking. The first is the range of conditions: there are evidence-based therapies for almost all commonly encountered Axis I disorders for adults. Axis II conditions fare less well in this regard. This is partially due to the difficulties in treating personality disorders (which by definition are chronic and pervasive problems) and partially due to the difficulty in obtaining research funds and conducting clinical trials that are of a duration sufficient to address these disorders (i.e., typically over 1 year). A second striking feature is the strength of the evidence supporting the use of CBT treatments. Indeed, in many instances more than one form of CBT has been demonstrated to be efficacious in treating a disorder. Despite this, it is clear that process-experiential, interpersonal, and psychodynamic treatments have also been demonstrated to be efficacious in the treatment of some clinical conditions. In some instances, the results achieved in efficacy studies with these approaches are comparable to those obtained with CBT. Treatment evaluation research has always been a central aspect of CBT, which explains, at least in part, why so many evidence-based treatments are cognitive-behavioral in nature. As this evaluation ethos is adopted by psychologists espousing other orientations, it is likely that there will be more non-CBT therapies added to the list of evidence-based treatments. Indeed, one could argue that one of the most important spin-offs from the movement toward evidence-based practice is that proponents of non-CBT approaches to psychotherapy are attending more to the need to empirically determine the impact of their treatments (cf. Elliott, Greenberg, & Lietaer, 2004). Psychoanalysts, too, have been urged to conduct RCTs to establish an empirical basis for their treatment (Gabbard, Gunderson, & Fonagy, 2002).

As described in Chapter 1, an APA presidential task force was constituted to determine APA policies and practices with respect to evidence-based practice (APA Presidential Task Force on Evidence-Based Practice, 2006). Members of the task force were selected from academic, institutional health care, and private practice settings to provide representation for all views on evidence-based practice issues. In its report, the task force defined evidence-based practice in psychology as the integration of the best available research and clinical expertise within the context of patient characteristics, culture, values, and treatment preferences. In contrast to most statements about evidence-based practice issued by health care professional organizations, the statement was extremely cautious about the use of research evidence in planning psychological services and said little about how different forms of research evidence should be weighted in making treatment decisions. The task force's position that treatment should be *informed by* research evidence but *determined on* the basis of other clinical information, patient choice, and the likely costs and benefits of available treatment options suggests that research evidence is possibly the least important factor to consider in practicing in an evidence-based manner (Stuart & Lilienfeld, 2007). With respect to patient values, the statement was silent on the need for psychologists to ensure that patient views were based on accurate information and not on mistaken assumptions about the nature of psychological disorders and psychological treatments. Regardless of these shortcomings, the fact that principles of evidence-based practice have been adopted as APA policy should increase the likelihood that greater numbers of psychotherapy clients will be receiving evidence-based treatments in the future.

VIEWPOINT BOX 12.1

THE EMDR CONTROVERSY

As indicated in **Table** 12.4, there is sufficient research on Eye Movement Desensitization and Reprocessing (EMDR) to list it as an evidence-based treatment for PTSD. What is EMDR? In essence, it involves the patient imagining aspects of the traumatic event while visually tracking a quickly moving stimulus that goes back and forth across the patient's visual field. That stimulus is usually the therapist's first two fingers. Shapiro (1989) developed this treatment after a personal experience in which she found that, while thinking of an anxiety-provoking stimulus, her eyes made rapid, saccadic movements and, shortly thereafter, her anxiety was eliminated (Shapiro, 1995). Many thousands of mental health professionals have now been trained to provide EMDR. Although originally used to treat traumatic memories, EMDR has been promoted as a rapid cure for a host of psychological problems, including substance abuse, sexual dysfunction, dissociative disorders, and personality disorders (Devilly, 2002).

What is the controversy about EMDR? There are several areas of debate, including (a) the theory behind EMDR, (b) the utility or necessity of eye movements in EMDR, (c) the efficacy of EMDR, and (d) the likely mode of action responsible for treatment efficacy. With respect to theory, Shapiro initially claimed that the eye movements in EMDR were similar to those occurring in rapid eye movement sleep and that somehow these eye movements trigger a change in neurological functioning that allows the traumatic memories to be fully processed. There is no scientific evidence to support this position. Moreover, several studies have demonstrated that EMDR without the accompanying eye movements has results comparable to those obtained with EMDR with eye movements (e.g., Feske & Goldstein, 1997). In response to this research (which seems to call into question the main underlying premise of EMDR), proponents of EMDR then claimed that any external stimuli (such as finger snapping or finger tapping) were sufficient to achieve successful treatment outcomes (Devilly, 2002).

Within a decade of the introduction of EMDR, numerous case reports and single-subject studies were published, along with approximately two dozen group treatment studies. Many studies found evidence for the efficacy of EMDR in treating trauma and other anxiety problems. In their review of the literature, Lohr, Lilienfeld, Tolin, and Herbert (1999) concluded that (a) eye movements were not necessary in EMDR, (b) EMDR was not more efficacious than existing exposure-based treatments, and (c) it was likely that the mode of therapeutic action in EMDR was through exposure (i.e., by repeatedly thinking about the trauma) rather than through any direct alterations in neurological functioning caused by the external visual or auditory stimuli. A subsequent meta-analytic review of this research substantiated these conclusions (Davidson & Parker, 2001).

The weight of evidence at this time is that EMDR is, at best, comparable in clinical impact to exposure-based treatments for PTSD and that it probably works because of the inclusion of some exposure elements in the treatment (e.g., repeatedly thinking about and imagining the traumatic events for extended periods). Despite substantial empirical evidence to the contrary, proponents of EMDR continue to claim that the treatment works better and faster than CBT treatments utilizing exposure (see the claims on the EMDR Institute's Web site at http://www.emdr.com). Based on a review of the scientific evidence, critics of EMDR conclude that what is new and innovative about EMDR (i.e., eye movements triggering neurological changes) is not effective, and what is effective (i.e., exposure) is not particularly new or innovative.

CLINICAL PRACTICE GUIDELINES

As we indicated earlier in the chapter, clinical practice guidelines are used increasingly by many health care professions to promote evidence-based practice. Health care professionals in the United Kingdom have been at the forefront of efforts to promote evidence-based health care. It is hardly surprising, therefore, that the UK National Health Service (NHS) has been actively involved in efforts to translate research evidence into recommendations and priorities for health care services. Compared with the limited attention accorded mental health issues in most countries, the inclusion of mental health services in these efforts is especially noteworthy. We have already briefly described the work of Roth and Fonagy (1996). Following that, a multidisciplinary guideline development group led by the British Psychological Society (BPS) developed lists of effective treatments and factors shown to affect treatment outcome. The report was designed to identify the main therapies that are most appropriate for specific adult patients (U.K. Department of Health, 2001). **Table 12.5** summarizes some of the conclusions from this group.

TABLE 12.5   Treatment Choice in Psychological Therapies and Counseling

Principal Recommendations

- Psychotherapy should be routinely considered as an option when assessing mental health problems in patients.

- Patients adjusting to difficult life events, illnesses, disabilities, or losses may benefit from brief therapies, including counseling.

- Posttraumatic stress symptoms may be helped by psychotherapy, with most evidence supporting the use of CBT. The routine use of debriefing techniques following traumatic events is not recommended.

- A number of brief, structured therapies may be used to treat depression, including CBT, interpersonal therapy, and psychodynamic therapy.

- Patients with anxiety disorders are likely to benefit from CBT.

- Psychological intervention should be considered for somatic complaints having a psychological component. The strongest evidence is for the use of CBT in treating chronic pain and chronic fatigue.

- The best evidence for treating bulimia nervosa is for CBT, interpersonal therapy, and family therapy for adolescents. There is little evidence regarding the best treatment for anorexia nervosa.

- Structured psychological therapies delivered by skilled clinicians can contribute to the longer-term treatment of personality disorders.

Adapted from U.K. Department of Health (2001)

This group also identified treatments that should not be used, based on replicated evidence of nonsignificant effects and possible harm to clients. The identification of *stress debriefing* (also known as *critical incident stress debriefing,* described in Chapter 10) as a contraindicated treatment has been controversial but is consistent with research evidence. Subsequent to the British report, McNally, Bryant, and Ehlers (2003) reviewed the scientific evidence for what is known about trauma, the development of PTSD, and debriefing strategies. They found that, although many people receiving debriefing services described them as helpful, the research evidence indicates that (a) those not receiving debriefing do not subsequently exhibit worse psychosocial functioning than do those who received debriefing, (b) debriefing does not reduce the incidence of subsequent PTSD, and (c) in some instances, debriefing may have an iatrogenic effect (i.e., result in decreased psychosocial functioning). Such results underscore the importance of an evidence-based approach to health care, because well-intentioned interventions delivered by caring and committed professionals can be ineffective or even harmful.

Because of a commitment to the translation of scientific findings into the provision of health care services, the NHS in England and Wales developed the National Institute for Health and Clinical Excellence (NICE) to guide health care professionals and patients in making decisions about health care treatment options. Interestingly, the Institute of Medicine (2008) has called for the development of an American-based organization similar to NICE that would provide unbiased reviews of health care research. Independent from the NHS, NICE conducts extensive consultations with stakeholder organizations (both professional and consumer groups) in developing evidence-based clinical guidelines. Guidelines are reviewed and updated after several years to ensure their accuracy and completeness. There are clinical guidelines for assessment and treatment services for dozens of conditions.

With respect to psychological/psychiatric conditions, there are currently guidelines for the treatment of anxiety disorder, mood disorders, eating disorders, substance abuse disorders, schizophrenia, self-harm, and violence with several others in development (e.g., personality disorders). To develop guidelines related to these conditions, NICE draws upon the expertise of the National Collaborating Centre for Mental Health, which is a joint venture between the BPS and the Royal College of Psychiatrists that also involves consumer groups and other professional organizations (e.g., those representing occupational therapists, nurses, pharmacists, and general medical practitioners). The involvement of a wide range of stakeholders is intended to ensure that the guidelines are comprehensive and professionally viable. NICE serves as an exemplary model that could be adopted by health care systems in other countries.

Because of the prevalence of depression, we have selected the NICE guideline for the management of depression to illustrate the essence of an evidence-based clinical guideline (NICE, 2007). **Table 12.6** provides details on the evidence-based steps recommended in the model. It is important to note the variability in the strength of evidence supporting each of these recommended steps, ranging from relatively strong (meta-analyses of RCTs) to relatively weak (expert committee reports or opinions of respected authorities). Moreover, there is currently no evidence to support the entire stepped care model. It is essential that as guidelines such as these are disseminated, researchers evaluate the validity and usefulness of recommended steps within the model and the service models themselves (cf. Bower & Gilbody, 2005).

TABLE 12.6 Stepped Care Model for the Management of Depression

Step 1. Screening in primary care and general hospital settings

- Screening for depressive symptoms should be undertaken for patients with a past history of depression, significant physical illnesses causing disability, or other mental health problems.

Step 2. Treatment of mild depression in primary care

- For patients with mild depression, there are a number of possible options to consider.
- For those who do not want an intervention or who, in the opinion of the health care professional, may recover with no intervention, a further assessment should be arranged, normally within 2 weeks ("watchful waiting").
- Advice on sleep hygiene, anxiety management, and mild exercise may be appropriate.
- A guided self-help program or computer program based on cognitive-behavioral therapy (CBT) could be offered.
- Problem-solving therapy, brief CBT, or generic counseling may be appropriate.
- Antidepressants are not recommended for the initial treatment of mild depression.

Step 3. Treatment of moderate to severe depression in primary care

- For patients with moderate depression:
  - Offer antidepressant medication (usually a selective serotonin reuptake inhibitor) to all patients and consider switching to another medication if there is no response within 1 month.
  - Offer CBT or IPT to patients who refuse medication or do not have an adequate response to other treatments (e.g., antidepressants, brief psychological interventions).
- For patients with severe depression:
  - A combination of antidepressants and individual CBT should be considered (consider this combination also for patients with chronic depression).

Step 4. Treatment of depression by mental health specialists

- For patients referred for specialist care, the following options should be considered:
  - Offer treatments previously received if they were inadequately delivered or adhered to.
  - Consider a combination of individual CBT and antidepressants for people with treatment-resistant depression.
  - Augment one antidepressant with another type of antidepressant medication.
  - Continue medication for 2 years, or offer CBT, for people with recurrent depression.

Step 5. Inpatient care for depression

- Inpatient treatment should be considered for patients at elevated risk of self-harm or suicide.
- Electroconvulsive therapy should be considered for severe symptoms only after adequate trials of other treatments have been ineffective or the severe depression is considered to be potentially life threatening.

Adapted from NICE (2007)

❗ What do you think of the NICE depression guidelines, especially in terms of the emphasis on the provision of counseling and psychotherapy? What about the recommendations with respect to the use of antidepressants? If a friend of yours was looking for information about treatment of depression, would you find this kind of information helpful?

EVIDENCE-BASED TREATMENTS: SOME EXAMPLES

CBT for Depression

In the previous chapter we provided details on interpersonal psychotherapy for depression. We now turn to a brief presentation of another efficacious treatment for depression: cognitive-behavioral therapy. Many variants of CBT for depression have been extensively researched, ranging from those that are predominantly behavioral to those that are primarily cognitive (Emmelkamp, 2004; Hollon & Beck, 2004). A good example is a general form of CBT for depression described by Persons, Davidson, and Tompkins (2001).

The focus of CBT for depression is on altering the behaviors, negative automatic thoughts, and dysfunctional beliefs that are associated with the condition. In working with a depressed individual client using CBT, the psychologist conducts an initial assessment to determine the client's diagnostic status (including comorbid conditions) and to obtain a sense of the client's current life circumstances. Particular attention is paid to the client's relationships and social functioning, the client's psychological resources and strengths, recent events that may have precipitated the depressive episode, and the potential for suicidal behavior. For example, Persons et al. (2001) described the case of Garrett, a musician who had lost a recording contract and a series of concert bookings. Based on initial assessment information and in order to guide treatment, a case formulation was developed that related precipitating life events (e.g., loss of the contract and concert dates) to longstanding dysfunctional beliefs (e.g., *I'm a loser*). The case formulation also provided a framework for understanding Garrett's affective, cognitive, and behavioral symptoms. By spending time at home alone, instead of his usual socializing, and by spending hours watching television, instead of working on his music, Garrett felt increasingly depressed, discouraged, and listless.

Early in the treatment process the client is provided basic information about the nature of depression, the evolving case formulation, and the possible treatment options for addressing the depressive symptoms. As we described in Chapter 11, a CBT model emphasizes a collaboration in which the client participates actively in decision making throughout treatment, which means that the therapist frequently provides information and lays out the options for addressing the agreed-upon targets for treatment. Throughout treatment, the client is asked to monitor symptoms and changes in functioning to determine the impact of therapy.

Initial sessions tend to focus primarily on behavioral activation tasks, such as getting the client to reengage in some of the pleasurable activities that he or she used to do prior to the depressive episode. In order to do this, clients are first asked to self-monitor their activities during the day. In the typical case, the resulting information indicates that the client engages in very few pleasurable activities of any kind. To combat the lethargy and dysphoria common in depression, clients are encouraged to actively plan to increase their daily involvement in pleasant activities. Such activities might include exercise, going to a movie with a friend, reading a book, or making a special meal. Engaging in any of these pleasant activities is likely to reduce depressed feelings, whereas dwelling on past failures and ruminating about current problems are likely to increase depressed feelings.

As clients attempt to follow through on activity scheduling assignments, they typically express doubts about the point of the assignments and/or their abilities to carry them out. Their doubts provide an opportunity for the psychologist to point out the tendency to automatically focus on negative aspects of experiences and reasons for not attempting activities. Usually, in the first few sessions this leads to the development of another form of homework assignment for clients that involves thought monitoring, which is recording the types of thoughts that typically occur around upsetting or difficult situations. Persons et al. (2001) suggest the use of a thought record that includes a description of the situation (e.g., an event, a memory, or an attempt to do something), associated behaviors (e.g., getting into an argument and yelling at someone), associated emotions (e.g., frustration, sadness, and discouragement), and associated thoughts (e.g., *What's the point, I'm such a pushover, I'm such a total failure*). You can find some examples of self-monitoring records in Figures 6.4 and 6.5. At the next stage in treatment, the therapist and client work together to examine how these thoughts influence decisions around behaviors (e.g., yelling

Self-monitoring is an important element of CBT for depression. (*Source:* Media Bakery)

rather than acting in a more assertive manner) and the resulting emotional states. The client is then coached to challenge the accuracy of these negative thoughts. Usually, it is easy for clients to acknowledge the link between thoughts such as *I'm a loser* and feelings of discouragement and disengagement from an activity. It takes a great deal of effort and repeated practice, however, for a client to counter these thoughts with a response such as *No, I'm not a loser, I'm just not very comfortable about handling conflict*. However, once the client is able to do this, it usually opens up a whole range of options for responding differently to a situation than was previously evident. At this point, depending on the client's needs, the psychologist may help the client develop skills in areas such as assertiveness, problem solving, or time management.

In the next stage of treatment, the primary focus is on examining and challenging the long-standing beliefs or schemas held by the client that render the client vulnerable to depression when confronted by negative life events. This involves helping the client to see patterns in the assumptions they make about themselves and events in their lives. These assumptions are often along the lines of beliefs such as *There is something basically wrong with me, Good things never happen to me, I can never succeed at anything important*, and *I'm not a loveable person*. Building on the behavioral and cognitive skills honed earlier in treatment, the client is encouraged to challenge these beliefs both cognitively and by engaging in personal experiments to test the accuracy of the assumption.

The final stage of treatment focuses on relapse prevention. The gains achieved by the client are reviewed, as are the specific skills the client learned or rediscovered. The clinician encourages the client to imagine events that might cause self-doubt and helps the client explore the most adaptive ways (both behavioral and cognitive) to respond to such events.

PROFILE BOX 12.1

DR. JEANNE MIRANDA

I received my BA from Idaho State University and my PhD in Clinical Psychology from the University of Kansas. I completed a one-year clinical internship at the University of California, San Francisco, and then spent three years there doing of postdoctoral work in health services research (an area that addresses issues relevant to providing good mental health care to those in need). I stayed on at University of California, San Francisco, for seven years as a faculty member in the Department of Psychiatry and then moved to the Department of Psychiatry at Georgetown University Medical Center. For the past six years, I have been in the Department of Psychiatry at

Dr. Jeanne Miranda

University of California, Los Angeles. My work examines the provision of quality care for depression to young, minority women. Many of these women are single mothers and have many responsibilities, so we have learned that we need to provide babysitting and transportation to help them get to services. It is also essential that services are provided through community connections the women already have, such as through county entitlement programs.

How did you choose to become a clinical psychologist?

I grew up in a small town in rural Idaho. No one was a clinical psychologist, and very few women even attended college. I went to my local junior college and took an initial course in psychology. I was hooked! I have enjoyed studying clinical psychology ever since.

What is the most rewarding part of your job as a clinical psychologist?

The most rewarding part of my job is being able to identify helpful treatment for women who need services. My research has grown directly from my clinical work. I helped start a clinic to treat depression in patients at the San Francisco General Hospital. When I was in graduate school, I was taught that poor people were too busy with their difficult lives to benefit from psychotherapy. This made no sense to me. If someone who is middle class becomes depressed, we all think they need treatment. If someone who is poor becomes depressed, I firmly believed that they too need treatment. The highlight of my career was publishing a paper in the *Journal of the American Medical Association* demonstrating that poor young women do benefit from depression treatment.

What is the greatest challenge you face as a clinical psychologist?

The greatest challenge I have faced in my career has been the lack of funding for new areas of inquiry. The research agencies that fund our studies typically fund work that builds directly on prior research in an area. It was very challenging to get funding to move into an area with little prior scientific study, such as providing traditional depression care to an underserved population. I am now turning my attention to the fact that there is no evidence base for treating adopted children and families adopting children. We are working to be the first to work in this area, so it is very challenging and very exciting.

Tell us about your research on providing evidence-based psychological treatments to ethnic minority clients

For many years, we all thought we would need to adapt all psychological treatments so they would be appropriate for different cultural groups. Our work has found that traditional treatments appear to work very well for African American and Hispanic Americans in need of services. We do find that getting these populations into services is very difficult, as they often don't trust mental health providers. The importance of providing mental health care within medical settings they do trust has been one of the most important findings in our studies.

How do you integrate science and practice in your work?

I have had the wonderful opportunity to use science to verify that the clinical work we do is appropriate for different populations. In my new adoption work, we will be working to examine scientifically whether the clinical care we believe is helpful truly works.

What do you see as the most exciting changes in the field of clinical psychology?

Many people in the field of clinical psychology are now working to see that appropriate services are provided to people in need in our country. For many years, researchers identified efficacious treatments, but they were rarely used in practice. At this time, exciting work is under way to figure out the best ways to get these services to those in need.

Prolonged Exposure (CBT) for PTSD

There are some general similarities in the CBT approach to treating depression and PTSD (and other conditions for that matter). These include the importance of a thorough initial assessment to develop a case formulation to guide treatment, the provision of information to the patient throughout treatment (both about the patient's condition and the rationale for specific treatment strategies), the development of a collaborative relationship between psychologist and patient, the use of between-session assignments, the ongoing monitoring of treatment impact, and attention to relapse prevention issues. Beyond these similarities, there are several treatment components that are different in the prolonged exposure treatment of PTSD (Cook, Schnurr, & Foa, 2004; Rothbaum & Schwartz, 2002).

Treatment typically begins with an assessment of the patient's condition and the provision of psychoeducational information about the nature of PTSD and the nature of the CBT approach. There are three broad components to CBT for PTSD: use of relaxation skills, imaginal exposure, and in vivo exposure. Because patients are asked to confront images and

Relaxation strategies are useful in dealing with anxiety. (*Source:* Media Bakery)

situations that cause them severe emotional upset, it is important that the psychologist help patients develop or enhance their relaxation skills. This can involve the use of progressive muscle relaxation, breathing retraining, and/or cognitive strategies for self-soothing. In many instances, patients are given reading materials or audiotapes and CDs to assist them in practicing these relaxation skills at home. In most cases, treatment then moves to the use of imaginal exposure. As part of the initial assessment process, patients will have already described the events, situations, and memories that are most disturbing to them. During treatment sessions, patients are asked to close their eyes and to recount these traumatic experiences for an extended period (typically more than 30 minutes), using the present tense and providing as much contextual details as possible (e.g., smells, sounds, their own thoughts and physical reactions). This imaginal exposure encourages the patient to begin to fully emotionally process the trauma that was experienced. This procedure allows patients to (a) revisit details of the trauma and gain new perspective on what happened and what might have occurred, (b) distinguish between remembering the event (which is not inherently dangerous) and reencountering the event (which could be dangerous), (c) develop a consistent, organized narrative of what occurred, (d) learn that remembering the events can lead to an overall reduction in anxiety and other symptoms, and (e) develop a new appreciation for what they did to survive the trauma (Cook et al., 2004). These imaginal exposure sessions are usually audiotaped, and the patient is asked to listen to the tape repeatedly between sessions in order to promote emotional processing.

In vivo exposure is used to assist patients in reducing distress associated with encountering stimuli that remind them of the trauma. Such stimuli could include sounds (for a patient traumatized in a car accident, this could be hearing a car braking hard) and smells (for a patient who was raped, this could be the smell of the rapist's cologne), as well as common situations such as driving a car (for the car accident victim) or walking by a body of water (for someone who almost died in a flash flood). The psychologist develops a hierarchy of feared stimuli with the patient and encourages the patient to intentionally expose himself or herself to increasingly fearful stimuli. By having patients repeatedly expose themselves to these stimuli, anxiety is reduced, a sense of self-efficacy is developed, and the opportunity for engaging in a broader range of activities (instead of avoiding certain situations) is enhanced.

EFT for Couple Distress

Emotionally focused therapy (EFT) is a process-experiential treatment combining an experiential approach to affect with a systemic focus on the way in which relationship behaviors can develop into cyclical, self-perpetuating interactional patterns. The key factors in relational distress are assumed to be the ongoing construction of absorbing states of negative affect and destructive interactional sequences that arise from, reflect, and then prime this distressing affect (Johnson, Hunsley, Greenberg, & Schindler, 1999). Accordingly, the main goals of EFT for couple distress are to (a) modify emotional responses and constricted, rigid interactional patterns and (b) foster the establishment or enhancement of a secure emotional bond in the couple (Johnson, 2004).

EFT is an efficacious treatment for couple distress.

The psychologist providing EFT for couple distress must address each partner's affect and each partner's perspective on interactional problems. Partners are not seen as deficient in their ability to manage interpersonal issues but, rather, as needing assistance in formulating and presenting their attachment-related needs and fears to each other. To bring about change in the couple's relationship, the psychologist must find ways to generate new emotional experiences and new interactional experiences for both partners. As with any form of couple treatment, this can be very challenging, as partners in distressed relationships typically develop habitual strategies for protecting themselves and attributing the lion's share of responsibility for their problems to the other partner.

There are nine steps in EFT designed to bring about the necessary changes in the couple's relationship. In mildly distressed couples, it is common for both partners to work quickly through the nine steps at a similar pace. In couples with greater distress, the more withdrawn or passive partner is encouraged to go through the steps ahead of the other partner. It is assumed that as the more passive partner becomes engaged in the process, it will be easier for the more active or critical partner to trust that the passive partner is truly committed to the change process.

The first four steps involve assessment and the deescalation of problematic interpersonal cycles. Step 1 involves the formation of an alliance with each partner and the development and presentation of a case conceptualization of the couple's core conflicts from an attachment perspective. Step 2 is devoted to the identification of the problematic interpersonal cycle that maintains the insecure attachment and the affective distress. The third and fourth steps focus on accessing the emotions underlying each partner's position in the relationship and then presenting their core relationship conflicts as stemming from these underlying emotions and attachment needs.

The next three steps are designed to promote change in each partner's interactional position. In Step 5, each partner is encouraged to identify and accept psychological needs that they have disowned or suppressed and to integrate these needs into their relationship. Step 6 requires each partner to learn to accept the other's new approach to their relationship. As partners adjust to these changes, Step 7 focuses on facilitating this adjustment by ensuring emotional engagement in the couple. The final two steps focus on developing new solutions to old relationship problems (Step 8) and consolidating these new solutions and the partners' new relationship positions (Step 9).

EFFECTIVENESS TRIALS

Throughout the text we have highlighted the distinction between efficacy and effectiveness several times. As we mentioned earlier in the book, it is important to know about the effectiveness of usual clinical treatments (Hansen, Lambert, & Forman, 2002). So far, we have presented a sample of the substantial literature on treatment efficacy. However, it is vital to consider evidence that efficacious treatments (developed in controlled research studies) are effective in clinical settings. As we discussed previously, reservations have been voiced about the representativeness of the patients included in typical efficacy trials (e.g., Westen & Morrison, 2001).

It is encouraging that accumulating data indicate many treatments demonstrating positive results in efficacy trials also have a substantial impact in effectiveness trials. In other words, contrary to some initial concerns, it now appears that many efficacious treatments can be transported into routine clinical practice without much loss of treatment impact. Equally important, there is accumulating evidence that these treatments can be effective for patients from differing ethnic backgrounds (e.g., Miranda et al., 2005). The strongest evidence for the transportability of a treatment to clinical settings is for CBT for depression. A number of studies, both in the United States (e.g., Merrill, Tolbert, & Wade, 2003; Persons, Bostrom, & Bertagnolli, 1999) and the United Kingdom (e.g., Cahill et al., 2003), have found that the treatment can be as effective in clinical settings (such as community mental health clinics and private practice settings) as it is in efficacy trials. These studies were conducted with patients who were seeking treatment for depression, and services were provided by clinicians who differed in (a) their background training (including both doctoral and master's level clinicians) and (b) their experience in providing CBT for depression.

In effectiveness studies it is common to use what is known as a **benchmarking strategy** to evaluate the impact of a treatment. This involves using the results of efficacy trials to form a standard (or a benchmark) against which the services provided to *regular* patients by *regular* clinicians can be compared. Using benchmarks for treatment completion and treatment outcome derived from efficacy studies, Hunsley and Lee (2007) examined the results of effectiveness studies. For the treatment of adult depression and anxiety disorders, in most effectiveness studies, they found that more than 75% of patients followed the course of services to completion. This was comparable to completion rates reported in efficacy trials. In terms of the outcome of treatment, most of the effectiveness studies reported results that were comparable or superior to those obtained in the efficacy studies relevant to each condition. Thus, based on the benchmarking strategy, there is evidence from various countries that evidence-based treatments can very effective when used in routine practice settings.

 Do you think it is important to know that a treatment has supporting evidence in effectiveness studies? Are such data more important than data from efficacy studies? How do you think practicing clinicians might view the relevance of effectiveness data?

VIEWPOINT BOX 12.2

DEVELOPING TREATMENTS FOR BORDERLINE PERSONALITY DISORDER

The treatment of personality disorders has traditionally posed a major challenge to clinicians. By definition, patients with these disorders have considerable self-concept problems and difficulties in interpersonal relationships. Not surprisingly, it can be a serious challenge to engage them in psychotherapy and have them remain for a complete course of treatment. Similar challenges are faced in developing and evaluating treatments for Axis II disorders. Attrition is always a concern for psychotherapy researchers but is even more problematic in examining treatments that are long term in nature (i.e., at least a year).

Over the years, the clinical lore surrounding people with borderline personality disorder (BPD) has been especially negative and, until recently, clinicians had limited treatment options with supporting empirical evidence. Fortunately, there now are at least three distinctly different types of long-term therapy that have evidence supporting their value in the treatment of BPD.

Of the three approaches, dialectical behavior therapy (DBT) has the most extensive empirical support. Several RCTs have been conducted, including an effectiveness study in which DBT was found to be more effective than treatment provided by therapists recognized as community experts in the treatment of BPD (Linehan et al., 2006). DBT is based on a theory emphasizing disturbances in affect regulation as the underlying feature of the disorder. Two main treatment components are provided concurrently: an individually based form of CBT (in which the client and clinician meet weekly to address commonly encountered problems such as self-harm, disruptions in the therapeutic relationship, and chaotic relationships) and a group psychoeducational format (weekly meetings in which information and skill development is emphasized, especially with respect to self-awareness, interpersonal style, tolerance of distress, and emotional regulation).

Data from both open trials and a small number of RCTs have provided support for two other treatment options. Transference-focused psychotherapy is a psychodynamic treatment based on an object relations theory of BPD (e.g., Clarkin, Levy, Lenzenweger, & Kernberg, 2007). Individual therapy sessions are held twice a week, with the primary focus on the transference relationship. However, unlike other psychodynamic treatments, much of the early work by the clinician involves establishing a clear contract with the client outlining the nature of what will transpire and the boundaries of what is deemed to be acceptable treatment-related behavior. The third treatment with empirical support is a form of cognitive therapy called schema-focused therapy (e.g., Giesen-Bloo et al., 2006). It is based on a cognitive theory that emphasizes the role of maladaptive schemas developed early in life. In schema-focused therapy, there are two main treatment phases. In the first phase, schemas are assessed and clients are educated about how their maladaptive schemas developed and how they negatively influence day-to-day functioning. In the second phase, the clinician engages the client in emotional expression, cognitive restructuring, and an examination of the therapeutic relationship.

ADOPTION OF EVIDENCE-BASED TREATMENTS

Rarely a day goes by without a media announcement of a breakthrough in the treatment of some health condition or disease. Hearing such news reports, you probably realize that it will take time for the breakthroughs to trickle down so that they are available in routine health services. It is unlikely, however, that the average person realizes all of the barriers that can impede the introduction of innovations into health care systems. In some cases, such as the introduction of a new vaccine, there are established laboratory and public health systems that can facilitate the relatively rapid development and distribution of the vaccine. Unfortunately, this is rarely the case for evidence-based innovations in psychological interventions.

There are a number of reasons for this state of affairs. One reason is that psychological interventions, unlike pharmaceutical interventions, cannot be patented. Pharmaceutical companies typically devote enormous sums of money to advertising and promoting their treatments. This includes targeting the health care professionals who prescribe the product and, in some countries, directly advertising to potential consumers. When a psychological treatment has been found to be efficacious (and even effective), there is no comparable process for disseminating the information and rapidly training psychologists to provide the treatment. Ethical codes and professional guidelines also prohibit most types of advertising of psychological services. A second reason is that there is often more to learning how to provide an efficacious psychological treatment than there is to learning how to appropriately prescribe a new medication. In this regard, the training necessary to appropriately provide the intervention is akin to what is required for surgeons to learn and use new surgical procedures. Reading the research reports and details on the indications and contraindications for a new drug may be sufficient for responsible prescribing, but such steps are unlikely to be sufficient for surgery or psychotherapy.

To effectively provide psychological services, the clinician requires background preparatory work, specialized training, and closely supervised experience in providing the intervention. Calhoun, Moras, Pilkonis, and Rehm (1998), for example, recommended that a clinical psychologist wishing to attain adequate skill in the delivery of a psychological treatment should be supervised in providing the treatment to at least three or four *typical* patients and a comparable number of *atypical* (i.e., those with more complex or chronic problems) patients. At this time, even though many jurisdictions require clinical psychologists to engage in continuing education activities, there are few structured opportunities for practicing psychologists to obtain this intensity of training (cf. Arnow, 1999). In a survey of 206 clinical psychologists and other mental health professionals, Nelson and Steele (2008) asked respondents about the treatment factors that influenced their selection of treatments to offer clients. As shown in **Table 12.7**, among the most influential factors were whether a treatment had empirical support in an efficacy or effectiveness study. Importantly, factors associated with learning a treatment were very influential in clinicians' decision to use a treatment. This type of finding underscores the critical need for access to training opportunities in evidence-based treatments.

TABLE 12.7   Treatment Factors Influencing Clinicians' Treatment Selection Decisions

1. Treatment flexibility

2. Research support in an effectiveness study

3. Recommendation by trusted colleague(s)

4. Past success with the treatment in own practice

5. Easy to learn and implement

6. Easy access to training and supervision in the treatment

7. Research support in an efficacy study

8. A focus on the therapeutic relationship

9. Reimbursement for treatment by insurance company

10. Short treatment duration

Adapted from Nelson and Steele (2008)

Beyond the issue of the availability of training, there are myriad potential barriers to the adoption of evidence-based treatments by psychologists and other health care professionals. These include systems-level factors such as the extent of organizational support for learning and providing cutting-edge interventions, and individual level factors such as motivation, knowledge, and skill. Given the clear indication that there are evidence-based treatments for many (if not most) disorders, it is important to understand the barriers to their application. At the systems level, many institutions employing clinical psychologists are under great pressure to reduce waiting lists. There is, as a result, often a tension between the need to devote time to developing new skills and the need to devote this professional time to immediate patient care.

Even in doctoral training, where the expectation is that proportionally more time is devoted to skill development than to patient services, students may face significant challenges in learning about evidence-based treatments. Weissman et al. (2006) found that, in a survey of accredited doctoral programs in clinical psychology, 44% of Ph.D. programs and 67% of Psy.D. programs did not require any training in evidence-based treatments. Hays et al. (2002) reported that, in their survey of APA accredited internships, 19% of internships reported little or no time spent on providing training and supervision in ESTs, with only 28% reporting that they spent more than 15 hours of training and supervision in ESTs during the internship year. Finally, and perhaps of greatest concern, in a survey of almost 1,200 graduate students in clinical psychology programs, Luebbe, Radcliffe, Callands, Green, and Thorn (2007) found that the nature of a treatment's empirical support was among the least important factors influencing students' treatment planning decisions. As guidance from supervisors was the most important factor in these decisions, this underscores the central roles that program requirements and faculty modeling of sound professional practices must play in the dissemination of evidence-based treatments.

 Now that you know that clinical programs differ in the extent to which they provide training in evidence-based practice, how important would it be for you to find a program that has a strong commitment to training in evidence-based practice?

Addis, Wade, and Hatgis (1999) summarized many of the individual-level factors that obstruct the widespread adoption oxf evidence-based treatments by psychologists. These factors include concerns about the feasibility of implementing manual-based treatments, the possible lack of fit between client needs and available evidence-based treatments, the impact that manual-based treatments might have on the therapeutic relationship with clients, and the possibility for decreased job satisfaction among psychologists. In a survey of almost 900 psychologists, Addis and Krasnow (2000) found consistent associations between experience with offering manual-based treatments and attitudes toward such treatments: the psychologists with the strongest negative views on these treatments were those least likely to have familiarity with the nature of manual-based treatments.

Despite individual- and systems-level challenges, many psychologists provide evidence-based treatments and are motivated to learn to use such treatments. For example, in a survey of clinical psychologists who provide treatments for eating disorders, Mussell et al. (2000) found that, although 70% of respondents reported using empirically supported therapy techniques, approximately 75% of these psychologists reported having received no formal training in the provision of CBT or IPT for eating disorders. For many of these psychologists, this probably indicated a commitment on their part to learn these treatments on their own after graduation. Importantly, though, more than 80% of respondents indicated a desire to obtain formal training in the approach. Commitment to the use of evidence-based treatments appears to be influenced by the nature of the clients' presenting problems and the nature of the treatment. As discussed earlier in the chapter, exposure is a key component of efficacious treatments for PTSD. A survey of psychologists providing PTSD treatments found that only 1 in 4 had received training in the use of exposure and only 17% reported using any form of exposure in their treatments of clients with PTSD (Becker, Zayfert, & Anderson, 2004). Numerous reasons for not using exposure were reported, including lack of familiarity with the technique, concerns about the appropriateness of the technique (e.g., clients presenting with comorbid disorders), and concerns about complications that could arise from using exposure (e.g., increased symptoms, dissociation). Although concerns about client suitability and well-being strongly influenced psychologists' perceptions about the usefulness of exposure, few, if any, of their concerns are likely to be valid when exposure is used in a clinically sensitive manner (Cook et al., 2004). Indeed, exposure-based treatment for PTSD has been successfully adapted for use in other cultures, such as in the treatment of traumatized Ugandan refugees (Neuner, Schauer, Klaschik, Karunakara, & Elbert, 2004).

Clearly, much more must be done in the education and continuing education of clinical psychologists to promote the use of evidence-based practices. Accreditation requirements for training in these practices should continue to influence what is taught in both doctoral training programs and internships. Beyond that, many psychologists are working on developing models to develop, disseminate, and implement evidence-based treatments (e.g., Gotham, 2004; Stirman, Crits-Christoph, & DeRubeis, 2004). A key element of such models is that both psychologists who conduct treatment research and psychologists who provide real-world services must be involved as active and equal participants in efforts to adapt and implement these treatments in clinical settings. Psychological science has much to offer patients suffering from diverse health conditions, but efforts to disseminate treatment breakthroughs must take into account the challenges facing the frontline clinicians who, ultimately, have the task of providing psychological services.

SUMMARY AND CONCLUSIONS

The second half of the twentieth century was a period of rapid growth in psychological interventions for a variety of disorders. Passionate debates pitted proponents of one school of thinking against another. All of this occurred against a backdrop of shrinking health care budgets, increasing concerns about accountability, and growing reliance on practice guidelines. Psychologists used a range of strategies of varying methodological sophistication to examine whether or not their treatments worked. Meta-analysis became an important tool in integrating findings from the growing body of literature. Because meta-analysis requires an explicit statement about the decision rules for including a study and for weighting its findings, meta-analysis itself has been the subject of fierce debate, and many of the original criticisms of meta-analysis have led to important modifications of the procedure.

There are many interdisciplinary efforts that have focused on achieving consensus about (a) the criteria for determining when a treatment is evidence-based and (b) routes for disseminating information about efficacious treatments. Overall, the results with respect to psychological treatments are encouraging, as there appear to be effective treatments for many Axis I disorders and other health and mental health conditions. Cognitive-behavioral approaches are prominent in the lists of evidence-based treatments. This prominence can be explained in part by CBT's emphasis on establishing clear treatment goals and requiring the ongoing monitoring of treatment efficacy. The armamentarium of effective treatments for some conditions also includes interpersonal, psychodynamic, and process-experiential interventions. Despite the encouraging data on treatment efficacy and growing evidence from effectiveness studies, it is premature to conclude that evidence-based approaches are now the routine standard of care in clinical psychology services. Barriers to the implementation of evidence-based services occur at many levels, including the lack of graduate and postgraduate training opportunities.

Critical Thinking Questions

How has meta-analysis affected the field of psychotherapy?

What are the advantages to the client of receiving evidence-based services?

What are the challenges in establishing a list of evidence-based treatments?

How can the results of effectiveness studies add to our knowledge of the impact of psychological treatments?

For a treatment that is successful in research studies, what are the barriers to its routine implementation?

Key Terms

benchmarking strategy: the use of data from empirical studies to provide a comparison against which the effectiveness of clinical services can be gauged

clinical practice guidelines: a summary of scientific research, dealing with the diagnosis, assessment, and/or treatment of a disorder, designed to provide guidance to clinicians providing services to patients with the disorder

effect size: a standardized metric, typically expressed in standard deviation units or correlations, that allows the results of research studies to be combined and analyzed

empirically supported treatment: psychotherapy that has been found, in a series of randomized controlled trials or single participant designs, to be efficacious in the treatment of a specific condition

meta-analysis: a set of statistical procedures for quantitatively summarizing the results of a research domain

open trial: a type of initial, exploratory treatment study in which no control group is used and, typically, few participant exclusion criteria are applied

randomized controlled trial: an experiment in which research participants are randomly assigned to one of two or more treatment conditions

Key Names

Dianne Chambless   Hans Eysenck

Gene Glass   Mary Smith

Drew Westen

ADDITIONAL RESOURCES

BOOKS

First, M. B., & Tasman, A. (2004). *DSM-IV-TR mental disorders: Diagnosis, etiology, and treatment.* New York: John Wiley & Sons.

Nathan, P., & Gorman, J. M. (Eds.). (2007). *A guide to treatments that work* (3rd ed.). New York: Oxford University Press.

Roth, A., & Fonagy, P. (2005). *What works for whom? A critical review of psychotherapy research* (2nd ed.). New York: Guilford Press.

JOURNALS

American Journal of Psychiatry

Archives of General Psychiatry

Behavior Therapy

Clinical Psychology: Science and Practice

Journal of Consulting and Clinical Psychology

Check It Out!

There are many reputable sources of information on evidence-based psychotherapies. Here are some of the best Web sites available.

Empirically supported treatments: http://www.apa.org/divisions/div12/rev_est/index.html

Treatment choice in psychological therapies and counseling; evidence-based clinical practice guideline: http://www.dh.gov.uk/assetRoot/04/05/82/45/04058245.pdf

NICE clinical guidelines: http://www.nice.org.uk/page.aspx?o=guidelines.completed

American Psychiatric Association practice guidelines: http://www.psych.org/psych_pract/treatg/pg/prac_guide.cfm

Centre for Evidence-Based Mental Health: http://www.cebmh.com/

Best treatments (for mental health conditions, from the *British Medical Journal*): http://www.besttreatments.org/btus/health-topic/mental-health.jsp

CHAPTER 13

Intervention:
Children and Adolescents

INTRODUCTION

In Chapter 12 we described the debates over the efficacy and effectiveness of psychotherapy for adults, the development of psychotherapy research, issues and controversies over evidence-based practice, as well as the emergence of clinical practice guidelines. Many issues in the psychological treatment of childhood disorders mirror the themes that were presented with respect to adults. Because we assume that you are now familiar with the material in Chapter 12, we will first explore ways that child services are different from services for adults. Next, we will highlight landmarks in the evolution of evidence-based psychological treatments for childhood disorders. We will illustrate some evidence-based treatments for common childhood problems and, finally, we will consider issues related to generalizing from efficacy trials to regular clinical practice.

In this chapter we return to the case of Carl, whom we introduced in Chapter 3. He is the adolescent boy who had been traumatized by the genocide in his country of origin. By describing the psychological treatment Carl received, we explain how evidence-based strategies can be applied in situations for which there is currently no comprehensive evidence-based treatment package.

WHO IS THE CLIENT IN PSYCHOLOGICAL SERVICES FOR CHILDHOOD DISORDERS?

Adult psychotherapy usually involves an individual client working with a mental health professional to address an identified problem. In most cases, the adult seeks services after recognizing that there is a problem. As you may remember learning in Chapter 11, psychological services cannot be imposed on a client: informed consent is required. Children and youth rarely refer themselves for psychological services. It is highly unlikely that 12-year-old Raheem would ask for psychological services because he realized that his inattentiveness, impulsiveness, and distractibility were interfering with his capacity to learn, that he was disrupting the class, and that the series of infractions at school seemed to be cascading toward expulsion. Similarly, it is unlikely that Sara, who has stayed home from school with a series of physical ailments that have no physiological basis and who is fearful of harm befalling her mother, would take the initiative to seek psychological help. Instead a young person is brought for psychological services by one or more adults who are troubled or concerned by the young person's behavior.

In Chapter 9 (Viewpoint Box 9.1), we pointed out that there is an imperfect match between the views of young people, their parents, and their teachers on the nature of the problem. Similarly, there is poor agreement between parents and youth about the goals for psychological services (Viewpoint Box 9.2). The child or youth may not believe there is a problem: according to 9-year-old Tyler, for example, the only problem is that his mom is picky and his teacher is strict and, if only both those adults would get off his case and stop grumbling about the importance of tidying up his room and doing his homework, then there would be no problem. For his mother and teacher, though, Tyler's noncompliance has reached the point where both are frustrated in their search for ways to positively influence him. Fifteen-year-old Jia, who has been feeling very low and who cuts her arms when she is distressed, may know that there is a problem. Despite her parents' insistence that she see some doctor they found, she is far from confident that it would make any difference to talk to some old person of 35 who has a boring office with certificates on the wall and who couldn't possibly understand what she is feeling.

Children and youth do not have the resources to seek, attend, and pay for psychological services independently. Unless services are provided within the school context or parents facilitate attendance by seeking a referral, arranging transportation, and paying for services, it is unlikely that children and youth will receive outpatient psychological services. For example, data from the Great Smoky Mountain study of 1420 adolescents revealed that only one in three adolescents requiring services for psychopathology received them (Costello, Copeland, Cowell, & Keeler, 2007).

Parents generally serve as gatekeepers for psychological services for their children. This can have some important implications. Miller and Prinz (2003) found that when treatment of childhood conduct problems did not match parents' understanding of the child's problem, parents were less likely to engage in treatment. Furthermore, even though parent motivation seems to be a necessary condition for a young person to attend psychological services, it is not sufficient for positive change to be achieved. This was underscored in a study in which young people receiving outpatient mental health services and their parents rated the alliance with the therapist (Hawley & Weisz, 2005). The *parent*-therapist alliance was related to participation in therapy, with those parents who reported a stronger alliance participating more in services and cancelling fewer sessions. The *youth*-therapist alliance was related to reports of improvements in symptoms. The results of this study illustrate that unless parents are convinced that the therapy is useful, it will be difficult for the youth to participate, but unless the young person is collaboratively engaged with the therapist, there will be limited change in his or her symptoms.

Legal issues around consent for psychological services for a child or adolescent are complex. Depending on the context in which services are offered (e.g., through schools, mental health clinics, hospitals, child protection agencies, or the offices of private psychologists), consent laws may be included in legislation that deals with education services, health services, or child protection. That means that the psychologist must be knowledgeable about the specific legislation that covers psychological services in the type of agency in which he or she works. In many states, consent procedures are determined by the young person's chronological age; according to an age criterion, for example, children under 12 can only receive psychological services with the consent of a parent or legal guardian. The psychologist must also be knowledgeable about consent laws concerning separated or divorced parents.

Jorge's situation illustrates how difficult these issues can be. Jorge is a 14-year-old who suffers from moderately severe symptoms of Tourette's disorder (frequent facial and vocal tics). He has developed severe social phobia because of his embarrassment about his tics. His parents, who are very concerned about his emotional and social functioning, brought him to see a clinical psychologist. Jorge's diagnostic status was clear to the psychologist based on interviews with the parents and an interview with Jorge. It was also clear to the psychologist, however, that Jorge generally understood the nature of his problems and was not willing to be involved in any treatment aimed at ameliorating his distress. The psychologist explained both the likely benefits of therapy and the likely prognosis if his problems went untreated. Again, Jorge understood these things. According to the laws regarding competency to consent to health services in the jurisdiction, the psychologist had no choice but to explain to the distraught parents that their son was not willing to engage in treatment. The only option available for the family at that point was for the parents to consider involvement in a local family support group for Tourette's disorder or involvement in family-focused services (without Jorge) aimed at helping them encourage Jorge to increase his social activities.

Parents and youth often have different views about the need for treatment. (*Source:* Media Bakery)

It should not surprise you to learn that although legal consent to receive services is a necessary condition for treatment, it is not sufficient to ensure cooperation with the services. You can probably easily imagine the scene in which Jia's parents have insisted that she come to a mental health clinic; not wanting to create a scene in front of a stranger, Jia has signed a consent to services, but she effectively communicates disinterest in the process by sitting hunched in the chair, her hoodie and hair concealing most of her face, rolling her eyes, and answering most questions with "I dunno." Confidentiality issues are often complex in services with children and youth. The psychologist must clarify from the outset of services the circumstances under which confidentiality will be maintained and what information will be shared with parents. As you learned in Chapter 6, child protection laws require the psychologist to report situations in which a child is in need of protection. At the outset of services, the psychologist also explains who has access to material in the client's file.

In Chapter 10 (Table 10.1), we presented risk factors for the development of psychopathology in children and youth. As you can see, many of the risk factors involve conditions over which the young person has very limited control, such as antisocial role models in the family, inadequate supervision and monitoring, parental psychopathology, bullying, or poverty. The protective factors (Table 10.2) suggest some possible avenues for psychological services in the development of problem-solving skills, social competence, supportive family relationships, positive school–home relations, strong cultural identity, and ethnic pride. An examination of risk and protective factors influencing the development of psychopathology underlines that psychological services for children's psychological disorders must address the context in which the child's problem developed and is maintained. In Chapter 10 you learned about how knowledge of risk and protective factors informs the development of prevention programs. In this chapter, we focus on services for the treatment of diagnosable psychopathology in a child or adolescent. Child psychotherapy has traditionally focused on intrapsychic factors but, as you will see later in the chapter, decades of research on developmental psychopathology have led to the development of treatments that attend to both intrapsychic and interpersonal factors.

LANDMARKS IN THE EVOLUTION OF EVIDENCE-BASED PSYCHOLOGICAL SERVICES FOR CHILDREN AND ADOLESCENTS

In general, the literature on psychological services for childhood disorders has followed a similar path to the one you learned about in Chapter 12 with respect to treatments for adults. Unfortunately, progress in the psychological treatment of children and adolescents has generally lagged behind the progress in psychological treatments for adults. There are simply fewer studies to examine in meta-analyses and, accordingly, compared with the adult literature, more limited and tentative conclusions must be drawn from the youth literature.

Do Psychological Treatments for Children and Adolescents Work?

Echoing Eysenck's 1952 report, Levitt (1957, 1963) concluded that there was no evidence for the efficacy of child psychotherapy. During the subsequent two decades, a variety of new approaches to the treatment of disorders of childhood was developed and numerous studies examined the efficacy of different types of child psychotherapy. In the 1980s and 1990s, four large-scale meta-analyses examined the child psychotherapy outcome literature. Casey and Berman (1985) examined data from 75 studies covering services to treat diverse clinical problems using a large range of therapeutic approaches for young people under the age of 13. Across all techniques, they reported an effect size comparable to that reported by Smith and Glass (1977) in their review of the adult psychotherapy literature. A subsequent meta-analysis by Weisz, Weiss, Alicke, and Klotz (1987) examined 108 controlled studies (less than a third of which were also reviewed by Casey and Berman, 1985). Psychotherapy researcher John Weisz and his colleagues reasoned that if a treatment uses an artificial activity (like a computer task) to train a skill (like paying attention), then it is simply not fair to use a score on that same computer activity as a measure of treatment outcome. However, if the therapy is designed to treat fear of dogs, then a behavioral approach would focus on helping the child to approach dogs, and an appropriate outcome measure would be the extent to which the child was able to comfortably interact with dogs. Using this reasoning, they excluded from analyses of outcome any artificial or analogue activities that had been used in the treatment but retained as outcome measures real-world activities that had been targeted in treatment. Based on their analyses, Weisz and his colleagues reported a mean effect size of .79, with larger effects found for behavioral approaches than for no behavioral approaches. **Profile Box 13.1** introduces Dr. Weisz.

PROFILE BOX 13.1

DR. JOHN WEISZ

I grew up in Mississippi and received a BA from Mississippi College. After serving as a Peace Corps volunteer in Nairobi Kenya, I studied at Yale, where I received MS and PhD degrees. I am Professor of Psychology in the Harvard Faculty of Arts and Sciences and in Harvard Medical School. I am also President and CEO of the Judge Baker Children's Center, affiliated with Harvard Medical School. My work combines research—especially on the development of evidence-based practices and transporting those practices into community clinic and school settings—with university teaching and with administrative leadership of an organization that combines research and direct services for children and families. I was previously on the faculty of Cornell University, then University of North Carolina at Chapel Hill, and then University of California at Los Angeles, where I served

Dr. John Weisz

for a term as Director of the Graduate Program in Clinical Psychology and Director of the Psychology Clinic. I have been licensed to practice clinical psychology in North Carolina, California, and Massachusetts. My written work includes books and articles focused primarily on child mental health care. My most recent book is *Psychotherapy for Children and Adolescents: Evidence-Based Treatments and Case Examples,* published by Cambridge University Press.

How did you choose to become a clinical psychologist?

I was blessed with an engaging teacher of Intro Psychology in college, who made the subject seem vital and exciting. As I learned more about the field, I loved the idea of a career that could combine research, teaching, and clinical intervention.

What is the greatest challenge you face as a clinical psychologist?

Time management! There are so many things I would love to do as a clinical psychologist, and not enough time to do them all.

Tell us about advances in evidence-based services for children and adolescents through schools and community centers

We live in exciting times. The past few decades have been a season of ferment in intervention science, with an array of increasingly robust prevention and treatment programs for kids. A current challenge is to find the best ways to get these programs out of the universities where they were created and into everyday clinical and school settings where the kids are, and to ensure that the programs work well in these settings and with children from diverse cultural backgrounds. Fortunately, scores of very bright people are now at work addressing this challenge.

How do you integrate science and practice in your work?

The research my colleagues and I do is inspired and informed by clinical questions, such as how to alleviate depression in children. Most of the clinical supervision and services activities I am involved in are guided by intervention science; I try to support only those interventions that have been shown to be effective. In our service outreach programs at the Judge Baker Children's Center we gather evidence on our service programs to assess how well they are working, child by child.

What do you see as the most exciting changes in the field of clinical psychology?

- The shift in clinical practice to an emphasis on evidence-based intervention and on assessment of outcome
- Advances in research on the biology of psychopathology, from studies of brain activity to gene–environment interaction
- Development of quantitative methods for tracking trajectories of change (e.g., during treatment) and for testing multivariate models
- The beginning of research testing the separate and combined effects of psychotherapies and pharmacotherapies

A subsequent meta-analysis by Kazdin, Bass, Ayers, and Rodgers (1990) yielded a very similar effect size to those reported by Casey and Berman (1985) and Weisz et al. (1987). However, although the effect sizes looked encouraging, **Alan Kazdin** and his colleagues drew attention to a troubling discrepancy between the nature of psychotherapy research and the nature of clinical practice. They found that treatment studies often relied on volunteer samples recruited through schools and treated in a group format. In contrast, surveys indicated that clinical practice more commonly involved individual treatment of referred patients in outpatient clinics. Furthermore, Kazdin and his colleagues recommended that treatment researchers pay greater attention to characteristics of the child, parent, family, or therapist that might influence treatment outcome.

You learned in Chapters 4 and 12 that the use of meta-analysis has revolutionized the field of psychology by offering an explicit set of decision rules for synthesizing data from diverse studies and reporting findings using a common metric. Like other research tools, meta-analysis is not perfect. As problems in the procedure are identified, refinements are introduced. The fourth major meta-analysis of the effects of child psychotherapy (Weisz, Weiss, Han, Granger, & Morton, 1995) introduced a more conservative way of calculating effect sizes, using a statistical technique known as the *weighted least squares method*. As you know from your statistics courses, when sampling data from a population, there is always error (i.e., deviations from the true population values). Generally speaking, data from larger samples have less error variance and, therefore, are closer to population values. The weighted least squares method takes this into account by assigning less weight in the meta-analysis to studies with greater error variance and more heavily weighting those with less error variance. Based on a meta-analysis of 150 outcome studies that had not been previously reviewed, Weisz et al. (1995) reported a similar effect size to all the previous meta-analyses when they used unweighted least squares methods, but a lower effect size of .54 using the weighted strategy. Weisz and colleagues also examined data from follow-up studies and found encouraging evidence that treatment effects were evident not only at the end of services, but at follow-up 6 months later as well.

All of the meta-analyses described thus far relied on published studies. Unfortunately, this may bias the results because journals are more likely to publish studies that report statistically significant findings than those that report nonsignificant results. McLeod and Weisz (2004) compared 134 published studies with 121 dissertations in terms of both their methodological adequacy and their findings. Overall, they found that the unpublished dissertations were stronger methodologically but obtained lower effect sizes than did the published studies. This suggests that meta-analyses based on published studies may lead us to overestimate the effect sizes from child psychotherapy studies. McLeod and Weisz therefore recommended that future meta-analyses also include data from unpublished dissertations.

Although it is encouraging to know that psychological treatments can be efficacious in treating childhood disorders, the most important questions need much more precise answers. Researchers have focused, therefore, on examining the research on efficacious treatments for different types of childhood disorders. We now turn our attention to this research literature.

Which Treatments Work for Specific Disorders?

Psychotherapy researchers in various countries have developed psychosocial interventions and have demonstrated that they can help children and adolescents who are dealing with diverse disorders and problems. These include DSM-IV Axis I disorders such as autism (Rogers & Vismara, 2008); anxiety disorders (Silverman, Pina, & Viswesvaran, 2008; Silverman, Ortiz. et al., 2008), depression (David-Ferdon & Kaslow, 2008; Watanabe, Hunot, Omori, Churchill, & Furukawa, 2007), ADHD (Pelham & Fabiano, 2008), disruptive behavior disorders (Eyberg, Nelson, & Boggs, 2008), and substance abuse (Waldron & Turner, 2008), as well as issues in primary care or medical practice such as adherence to treatment of chronic health conditions (Kahana, Drotar, & Frazier, 2008). Unfortunately, although there are numerous efficacious psychological treatments for various problems of childhood and adolescence, they are not routinely offered in standard care (Connor-Smith & Weisz, 2003). A meta-analysis of 32 studies comparing evidence-based treatments to usual clinical care found that evidence-based care consistently outperformed usual clinical care; furthermore, evidence-based treatment was also superior among minority youth and among youth with the most severe problems (Weisz, Jensen-Doss, & Hawley, 2006).

You may recall from Chapter 12 that critics of EBP suggest that patients in RCTs have less severe problems and fewer comorbid disorders than do patients seen "in the real world" (Table 12.3). Jensen-Doss and Weisz (2006) examined this issue in 325 clinically referred young people ages 7–17 and found no evidence of poorer outcome in youth with multiple problems. Similarly, Kazdin and Whitley (2006) found that the presence of comorbidity was associated with greater change in young people with disruptive behavior disorders who received evidence-based parent training or problem-solving treatments. If evidence-based approaches seem to work better than care as usual, to be helpful to those with more serious problems, and to be helpful to minority youth, why are they not used by all mental health professionals? One obstacle to the adoption of efficacious treatments is that clinicians may simply be unaware of them. The field of clinical psychology is constantly evolving, with exciting new research findings published daily. The average clinician is unable to consult the literature and synthesize new findings into meaningful recommendations on a regular basis. In addition, the average parent who is a potential consumer of psychological services can be faced with a bewildering array of contradictory messages about the most appropriate solution to the child's problem. If you browse through the parenting sections of bookstores or search the term *children's behavior* on the Internet, you will see books advocating diverse ways to address children's problems. It is a challenge for parents to distinguish between experts whose message is based on solid research and those who are simply proposing something that makes sense to them but that lacks a solid empirical foundation.

To get a sense of the challenges faced by those seeking information about efficacious treatments for young people, check out the self-help sections of your local bookstore. Pick a childhood problem that interests you. How easy is it for you to tell whether the treatment discussed in the book is evidence based?

Among the health disciplines, psychology is not alone in facing this dilemma of how to translate research findings into practice. Similar challenges are faced by clinicians trying to keep up to date with rapid advances in the knowledge base in professions such as nursing and medicine. As we explained in Chapter 12, a number of expert review panels have been set up to evaluate research findings and to develop clear evidence-based practice guidelines. Some of these review panels are organized within a particular discipline, whereas others are multidisciplinary. Some are sponsored by a professional organization, and others are the independent enterprise of a small number of researchers.

Over a decade ago, an influential review of children's mental health services was initiated in response to a class action lawsuit on behalf of children with special needs. The settlement of the lawsuit involved an agreement by the state of Hawaii to develop a comprehensive system of care for those ages 0–20 years with mental health needs (Chorpita et al., 2002). As a first step, the Hawaii Department of Health established a task force to identify the empirical basis for services. This multidisciplinary group included health administrators, parents of children with special needs, clinical service providers, and academics in psychology (including anxiety and depression researcher **Bruce Chorpita**), psychiatry, nursing, and social work. The task force conducted a literature review of studies in psychology, psychiatry, and related mental health disciplines. The mandate of the Hawaii task force was to identify which treatments would work in the challenging context of isolated rural areas with multiethnic populations.

You learned in Chapter 12 of the APA division task forces that reviewed psychosocial treatments for adults. Similarly, the Society of Clinical Child and Adolescent Psychology (Division 53 of the American Psychological Association) commissioned a series of reviews on psychosocial treatments for disorders of childhood and adolescence that were published in the late 1990s. The large body of research that was published in the following decade on psychosocial treatments for a variety of disorders of childhood and adolescence was reviewed in a special series of the *Journal of Clinical Child and Adolescent Psychology* (Silverman & Hinshaw, 2008). Authors examined the research using the criteria established by Nathan and Gorman (2002) as well as by Chambless and Hollon (1998) (see Chapter 12 for details on these criteria).

Over the last 15 years, there have been concerted efforts in different countries and across different disciplines to identify the most helpful psychological treatments for childhood disorders. **Table 13.1** presents a list of the major evidence-based treatments for children and adolescents identified in the reviews in the special series in the *Journal of Clinical Child and Adolescent Psychology* as "well-established" or "probably efficacious" (Silverman & Hinshaw, 2008). You must remember that like all such lists, this should be considered to reflect the state of knowledge in the area at the time of writing. The field is constantly evolving, so the list in the next edition of this book may look somewhat different. We have not included in the table approaches that have promise and were labeled by the special series authors as "possibly efficacious"—as evidence accumulates, some of them will have stronger support in the future.

You will notice that many of the evidence-based approaches are behavioral and cognitive-behavioral. Moreover, in contrast to treatments for adults that are offered to individuals, many of the efficacious treatments involve parents learning strategies to respond to their children's behavior. As you can imagine, many parents who bring their children for psychological services are surprised to find

---

TABLE 13.1 Evidence-Based Psychological Treatments for Child and Youth

Autistic Disorder

- Intensive behavioral treatment

Attention-Deficit/Hyperactivity Disorder

- Behavioral parent training
- Behavior classroom management
- Intensive peer-focused behavioral interventions

Disruptive Behavior Disorders

- Individual behavioral parent training
- Group behavioral parent training
- Individual CBT
- Group CBT

Exposure to Traumatic Events

- Individual trauma-focused CBT
- School-based group CBT

Depression

- Individual interpersonal therapy
- Individual CBT

- Individual CBT with parent/family involvement
- Group CBT
- Group CBT with parental involvement

Obsessive-Compulsive Disorders

- Individual CBT

Phobic and Anxiety Disorders

- Individual CBT
- Group CBT
- Group CBT with parental component

Substance Abuse

- Group CBT
- Individual CBT
- Multidimensional family therapy
- Functional family therapy
- Behavioral family therapy
- Multisystemic therapy

that they are asked to participate by changing their behavior toward the child or adolescent. Treatments for externalizing problems often include others who are trained to respond in a way that encourages desirable behavior. Although treatments for internalizing problems usually focus directly on the child, many approaches also include parents in services (Barrett, Farrell, Pina, Peris, & Piacentini, 2008). In the treatment of adolescent depression, attention is also focused on interpersonal issues. Thus, most effective treatments of childhood disorders fall under the umbrella of behavioral, cognitive-behavioral, and interpersonal approaches. The involvement of parents is consistent with our earlier discussion of the importance of attending to protective factors in designing psychological interventions for youth. Due to developmental changes, in examining the usefulness of different treatment strategies (such as parental involvement), it is also important to take into account the child's age. However, as you may recall from Chapter 10, parental psychopathology may make it more difficult for parents to engage in and complete psychological services for their children.

Imagine that you are a parent whose child is having psychological problems. How would you feel when the psychologist informs you that you will be expected to play an important role in the services your child will receive? What would you see as the advantages and disadvantages of being involved in the services?

The special series on evidence-based treatments also included a meta-analysis of studies that had examined efficacy in samples of ethnic minority youth (Huey & Polo, 2008). These authors found evidence that a number of treatments are probably efficacious in the treatment of minority youth, including combined medication and behavioral treatment for African American and Latino youth with ADHD, CBT for depressed Puerto Rican youth, Multisystemic Therapy (MST) for African American juvenile offenders, Lochman's CBT Coping Power program with aggressive African American youth, brief strategic family therapy for Latino youth with conduct problems, and multidimensional family therapy for diverse groups of ethnic minority youth. Additionally, in the treatment of traumatized minority youth, various CBT and peer-modeling approaches appear efficacious. Huey and Polo also examined the empirical question of whether treatments demonstrate "ethnic invariance" or "ethnic disparity." A finding of **ethnic invariance** implies that an evidence-based treatment yields equivalent results for ethnic minority youth. **Ethnic disparity**, on the other hand, implies that the treatment is not as powerful when applied to ethnic minority youth and, therefore, the treatment requires adaptation. Huey and Polo examined five studies that examined whether ethnicity moderated treatments effects. The results demonstrated ethnic disparity, but the disparity was not always

Interventions may need to be adapted for clients with different ethni backgrounds. (*Source:* Blend/Image Source Limited)

in favor of the majority youth. In fact, for three studies, stronger effects were found for ethnic minority youth than for European American youth, whereas in two studies, better outcomes were obtained for European American youth than for ethnic minority youth.

Clinical Practice Guidelines

In Chapter 12 you learned about the wealth of treatment guidelines that are available with respect to adult disorders; in contrast, the development of treatment guidelines for childhood disorders has lagged behind significantly. A number of professional organizations have sponsored reviews of the scientific literature to identify efficacious treatments that should be offered as routine care in the treatment of a specific problem. Unfortunately, no guidelines have yet been developed by psychological organizations. Since 1997, the American Academy of Child and Adolescent Psychiatry has published 25 practice parameters and guidelines in the *Journal of the American Academy of Child and Adolescent Psychiatry* that address topics including the treatment of anxiety disorders, ADHD, autistic disorder, conduct disorder, obsessive-compulsive disorder, and PTSD.

If you check practice guidelines you will notice that, like many products in the grocery store, these guidelines are identified with a "best before" date. This is an explicit acknowledgement that although they represent the best recommendation based on available knowledge at the time they are released, research is ongoing, our understanding is constantly evolving, and guidelines must not be seen as the final word. Thus, ongoing updates of clinical practice guidelines based on new research are essential to the promotion of evidence-based practice.

It is inevitable that guidelines developed by one professional body may be seen to promote the approach favored by that profession and downplay the benefits of other approaches. There are, therefore, benefits to collaboration between different disciplines in identifying practices that are most helpful. One of the earliest multidisciplinary review panels on children's mental health was convened by the National Institutes of Health (NIH) to identify evidence-based treatment of ADHD (NIH, 1998). This resulted in the *NIH Consensus Statement on the Diagnosis and Treatment of Attention-Deficit/Hyperactivity Disorder*, which sets out standards for the evidence-based assessment and treatment of this condition. In Chapter 12 we described the development in England and Wales of the National Institute for Health and Clinical Excellence (NICE) whose mandate is to guide health care professionals and patients in making decisions about health care treatment options. Although to date, the bulk of the work in the mental health field has focused on adult disorders, NICE has published guidelines on the treatment of conduct disorder (NICE, 2006), depression in children and adolescents (NICE, 2005), and attention-deficit/hyperactivity disorder (2008). Consultation is under way for guidelines on the treatment of autism and nocturnal enuresis. Although in its infancy, the movement to develop interdisciplinary, evidence-based guidelines for the assessment and treatment of diverse childhood disorders has the potential to inform policy-makers, consumers, and the mental health professionals who serve children with emotional and behavioral problems. The widespread application of research-based services has the potential to streamline those services so that a greater proportion of the children in need can be helped.

EXAMPLES OF EVIDENCE-BASED TREATMENTS

It is clearly beyond the scope of this chapter to present all the evidence-based interventions that are listed in Table 13.1. Instead, we will examine some of the evidence-based treatments for different types of common problems of childhood. As disruptive behavior disorders are the most frequent reason for referral to mental health services, we will examine some treatments that are helpful in the treatment of oppositional defiant disorder and conduct disorder. Next, we will examine a treatment for adolescent depression.

Disruptive Behavior Disorders

As we discussed earlier in the chapter, children do not refer themselves for treatment. It is perhaps not surprising that disruptive behavior constitutes the most common reason for which adults refer children and youth for mental health services (Kazdin, 2004). Oppositional defiant disorder (ODD) reflects a pattern of persistent negativistic and hostile behavior that is usually evident before the age of 8 years (American Psychiatric Association, 2000). Although all children sometimes fail to comply with parental requests, argue with adults, and are easily upset, children diagnosed with ODD behave like this consistently and their behavior interferes with normal functioning. Children with ODD have problems in several contexts, such as home and school. ODD often precedes conduct disorder (CD), which involves a pattern of serious violation of the rights of others including aggression, destructiveness, deceitfulness, and serious violation of rules (American Psychiatric Association, 2000). Young people diagnosed with ODD and CD are at risk for other mental health problems such as ADHD, learning problems, depression, and substance abuse. There is evidence that left untreated, these problems persist into adolescence and adulthood.

The research on treatment for disruptive behavior disorders has been the subject of many reviews. Eyberg, Nelson, and Boggs (2008) identified 16 evidence-based programs, many of which are behavioral parenting programs inspired by *parent management training* (PMT), developed and refined by **Gerald Patterson** and his colleagues at the Oregon Research Institute (Patterson, 1982). We will focus in this chapter on Patterson's PMT program. We will also describe *multisystemic therapy* (MST) for seriously disordered adolescents, developed by Scott Henggeler and his colleagues (Henggeler & Lee, 2003; Henggeler, Schoenwald, Borduin, Rowland, & Cunningham, 1998).

Parent Management Training

Parent management training (PMT) is based on social learning theory and the assumption that oppositional child behavior can be changed by modifying the child's social environment rather than by working directly with the child. According to this theory, maladaptive patterns of parent–child interaction inadvertently encourage both parents and children to engage in inappropriate behaviors. During **coercive exchanges**, the parent unintentionally rewards the child for whining or aggression (by withdrawing a demand or providing attention) and the child rewards the parent for giving in to his or her complaints (by ceasing the aversive behavior). Patterson's team has conducted more than 30 years of systematic observations of families (Chamberlain & Smith, 2003; Patterson, 2005) and has found that in all families there are disagreements and conflicts that must be managed. In well-functioning families, children learn prosocial ways to resolve conflict (such as discussion and compromise), whereas in families with aggressive children, the child learns coercive ways to get what he or she wants. You have probably observed the classic example of a coercive exchange at the grocery store checkout. You first see a child grab a chocolate bar. The parent reminds the child that it is soon time for a meal, or that he or she has already had enough sugar. The child then launches into a routine that begins with wheedling, "Please, just one. . ." then rapidly escalates in volume and aversiveness as the parent repeats quietly "I said no." The child may protest loudly that he or she is hungry, that the parent had promised, or that the parent allowed another sibling to have a chocolate bar the last time they were in the grocery store. The child may also demand an explanation for the parent's refusal ("Why are you always so mean to me?"). As the child's protests draw the attention of a growing number of onlookers, the parent's embarrassment mounts, and he or she gives in to the child's demands. This sequence has rewarded the child for grabbing, whininess, yelling, and persistence as well as increasing the likelihood that the child will do the same thing the next time. The parent's giving in is briefly rewarded by the short-term relief of the child's tantrum ending. Unfortunately, the coercive behaviors reinforced in the home are then applied in other contexts, so that the child behaves in a noncompliant and disruptive way with teachers, babysitters, coaches, and other children.

In their research, Patterson and his colleagues observed five parenting practices that are associated with the development of prosocial or deviant behavior: skill encouragement, discipline, monitoring, problem solving, and positive involvement (Patterson, 2005). The idea behind the treatment is simple—to train parents who have children with behavior problems to parent in the same way as parents whose children do not have problems. Patterson and his colleagues developed a program designed to train parents to encourage appropriate behavior and to discourage unacceptable behaviors. Parents meet with a therapist who teaches them the core skills listed in **Table 13.2**. An essential aspect of behavioral training is that complex skills are broken into small steps. First, parents must establish a few simple rules on which they agree and which they are willing to impose consistently. Rules for child behavior are basic guidelines about daily living, including the child's responsibilities and chores, daytime routines, and respectful ways of interacting. Lists of rules must be realistic, taking into account the child's developmental level, circumstances, and any special needs.

 The grocery store provides a great opportunity for naturalistic observation of parenting. The next time you are shopping, keep in mind the core skills and see whether you can identify examples of parents using any of the five core skills of effective parenting.

Because research has consistently found that distressed families engage in fewer positive interactions than do nondistressed families, an important goal in treatment is to increase reinforcement for positive behavior. As you have learned in other psychology courses, **positive reinforcement** is any consequence that increases the likelihood of a behavior being repeated. Parents seeking mental health services for their children's oppositional behaviors often report that their interactions with their children are very negative. They feel at a loss in coming up with potential reinforcers. In fact, the list of potential reinforcers is very long. The benefits of social reinforcement through smiles, attention, verbal encouragement, and touch are often overlooked. In coming up with other potential reinforcers, the

TABLE 13.2   Core Parenting Practices

Skill encouragement

- Breaking behaviors into small steps
  Put your coat on
  Now do up the buttons
  Slip on your boots
  Close the tab

- Prompting appropriate behavior through clear rules and cues
  Put your toys away

- Contingent positive reinforcement (praise and incentives)
  Wow, you tidied up your toys—that's great!
  I like the way you played with Tyler and shared your toys. Would you like to pick a sticker?
  You've done your homework carefully, now you can have 30 minutes on the computer.

Discipline

- Limit setting
  Complete your homework after school.
  No hitting.

- Mild sanctions (time out, removal of privileges)
  Because you did not complete your homework, you cannot have screen time.
  Because you hit your brother, you must take a time out for 10 minutes.

Monitoring

- Tracking the child's whereabouts and activities

Problem solving

- Establishing clear rules

- Establishing consequences

- Negotiating

Positive involvement

- Loving attention

parents must put themselves in the child's position, so that they can appreciate the range of stickers, activities, and freedoms that can possibly serve as reinforcers of desirable behavior. Parents may also worry about the long-term consequences of what they see as paying their children to behave well. By learning to use social reinforcers and by understanding the importance of fading out the use of material reinforcers, parents learn to intentionally use reinforcers without being haunted by the unrealistic fear of turning their child into a monster who will only behave well if bribed.

Although establishing a system of positive reinforcement can go a long way toward resolving some behavior problems, parents need to also develop skills in dealing with noncompliance. Patterson's approach offers mild punishment as an effective response to misbehavior. Basically, punishment involves the withdrawal of reinforcers—this can include a range of losses according to the child's age and preferences. Punishment for a very young child may involve not being allowed to play with a favorite toy that he or she has just used to hurt another child or turning off the TV after the child has yelled and disturbed a sibling; for an older child, punishment may include an earlier curfew, or loss of computer time or Internet access. Parents learn to use **time out** procedures in which the child does not have access to reinforcers for a brief period following misbehavior.

Just as engaging in a restricted diet is not a permanent solution to weight problems (only a regular routine of healthy eating and exercise provide sustained effects), so PMT is not offered as a quick fix for child behavior problems. It is an approach to parenting in which the adult assumes an active role in monitoring and responding to the child's behaviors. Once the child's behavior is more acceptable, parents cannot abandon this type of parenting or the problems will quickly return. With very young children, monitoring may include close physical supervision of the child's activities. As the child grows older, parental monitoring shifts so that parents learn to maintain a relationship with the young person, who informs the parents about his or her whereabouts and activities. An essential component of parenting is recognizing that as children get older they should become more involved in decision making. Therefore, parents learn negotiation and how to alter their expectations based on developmental changes.

PMT is delivered in a structured format, using a treatment manual and repeated practice. The number of sessions varies according to the child's age and the severity of the disruptive behavior: from 4–8 weeks with young mildly oppositional children, to 12–25 weeks for clinically referred youth diagnosed with conduct disorder (Kazdin, 2003). During sessions, parents practice skills through behavior rehearsal and role-playing. Between sessions, they complete homework assignments related to the skills they have learned. Patterson's work has also inspired many variations of parenting programs that were described in Chapter 10, including the Incredible Years program and the Triple P program.

PMT also highlights the importance of cognitive and affective variables that are related to treatment outcome. For example, if parents believe that the young person *intentionally* engages in misbehavior, then they are less likely to adopt effective discipline strategies and are more likely to continue with strategies that actually increase the likelihood of misbehavior. It is therefore necessary for PMT to focus not only on parents' behaviors toward the child, but also on the ways that parents understand the child's misbehavior (Patterson, 2005). A core element of PMT is to increase the amount of positive interaction between parent and child. The importance of this affective dimension has been underlined in recent studies that have shown that parent–child warmth is associated with **parental monitoring** and that adolescent–parent contempt is associated with inconsistent and disrupted parental monitoring, which in turn is associated with delinquency (Patterson, 2005).

A randomized controlled trial conducted in Norway demonstrated that this program was effective in improving parental discipline practices, improving teacher-rated social competence, and decreasing parent-rated externalizing problems in 112 children with conduct problems (Ogden & Hagen, 2008). Children in foster care are a vulnerable population that has a high rate of externalizing problems. A study of 700 foster families caring for children ages 5–12 compared outcomes in families randomly assigned to receive 16 weeks of parent management training and those assigned to usual care (Price et al., 2008). The investigators found that among an ethnically diverse, vulnerable population, the intervention increased the chances of a successful outcome of the foster placement; that is, children were more likely to be successfully reunited with their parents.

Multisystemic Therapy

Multisystemic therapy (MST) is an approach designed to treat seriously disturbed delinquent adolescents by intervening in an integrated way in the multiple systems in which they are involved (Henggeler et al., 1998). These youth, who are at risk of being placed in out-of-home care, require costly services that consume a disproportionate amount of mental health resources (Henggeler & Lee, 2003). Grounded in an **ecological theory** of psychosocial functioning (Bronfenbrenner, 1979), MST works with these youth within the context of numerous systems including the nuclear family, extended family, neighborhood, school, peer, community, juvenile justice, child welfare, and mental health (Henggeler et al., 1998). This treatment approach is consistent with research findings that delinquent behavior is not simply caused by one factor but, rather, is multiply determined. Within this model, the caregiver (usually, but not always, a parent) plays a key role in the young person's short- and long-term adjustment. **Table 13.3** describes the nine principles that guide MST. The goals of the approach are positive and future-oriented. MST uses a behavioral approach that is designed to integrate services, so that gains in one area will generalize to other contexts. A fundamental characteristic of this approach is that treatment effectiveness is evaluated continuously from the perspective of multiple stakeholders, including the youth, parents, and others in the educational, health, and justice systems.

MST therapists work in teams of three to five people. Each therapist works with a very small caseload of four to five families. The therapist coordinates all the services that the youth and family receive. To reduce barriers to participation, services are offered in homes, schools, and neighborhood centers rather

---

TABLE 13.3   MST Treatment Principles

Principle 1:	The primary purpose of assessment is to understand the fit between the identified problems and their broader systemic context.
Principle 2:	Therapeutic contacts emphasize the positive and use systemic strengths as levers for change.
Principle 3:	Interventions are designed to promote responsible behavior and decrease irresponsible behaviour among family members.
Principle 4:	Interventions are present focused and action oriented, targeting specific and well-defined problems.
Principle 5:	Interventions target sequences of behavior within and between multiple systems that maintain the identified problems.
Principle 6:	Interventions are developmentally appropriate and fit the developmental needs of the youth.
Principle 7:	Interventions are designed to require daily or weekly effort by family members.
Principle 8:	Intervention effectiveness is evaluated continuously from multiple perspectives, with providers assuming accountability for overcoming barriers to successful outcomes.
Principle 9:	Interventions are designed to promote treatment generalization and long-term maintenance of therapeutic change by empowering caregivers to address family members' needs across multiple systemic contexts.

Adapted from Henggeler, Schoenwald, Borduin, Rowland, and Cunningham, (1998)

---

than in hospitals or court clinics. Treatment is time limited, lasting only 3 to 5 months. It is, however, very intense, with therapists available 24 hours a day and 7 days a week to respond to crises.

The first phase of services involves an explanation of the MST model. The therapist works hard to develop a collaborative relationship with the caregiver. Assessment involves identification of the risk factors that contribute to the problem, as well as strengths that can be drawn upon in every system in which the young person is involved. As you learned in Chapter 10, risk factors include low caregiver monitoring, low warmth, ineffective discipline, high conflict, caregiver psychopathology, and family criminal behavior. Protective factors include secure attachment, a supportive family environment, and a harmonious couple relationship between the parents. At an early stage in services, the therapist works with the family to establish measurable long-term goals that can be broken down into measurable weekly goals. The therapist makes contact with any person or system that can affect the attainment of these goals in order to ensure their cooperation. In collaboration with the caregiver and youth, the therapist then selects evidence-based treatments for each goal. As you can imagine, services to establish clear rules, to reward prosocial behavior, and to encourage appropriate monitoring are very similar to PMT approaches. Caregivers are not always able to implement the recommendations, and their stress or psychopathology may pose a serious obstacle to successful treatment. Therefore, the MST therapist also targets for intervention any caregiver characteristics that significantly limit the capacity to parent effectively.

Interventions that target the peer system depend on the nature of the problem. Peers can serve as a risk factor if they are antisocial or as a protective factor if they are socially competent. Youth lacking in social skills or assertiveness receive training in these areas. On the other hand, if the peer group is an antisocial one that encourages delinquent behavior, the intervention focuses on limiting access to those peers, increasing parental monitoring, and developing more appropriate peer contacts through other activities.

Risk factors in the school system include learning problems, a chaotic school environment, and poor contact between family and school. Protective factors include strong intellectual functioning, a commitment to education, and good contact between family and school. MST therapists can play a key role in facilitating the development of a collaborative relationship between school and family to ensure a consistent approach between the two environments.

Individually oriented services target specific difficulties the youth may be experiencing using evidence-based approaches. For example, cognitive-behavioral strategies may be used to address problems with anxiety or depression. A referral may be made for a trial of medication in the treatment of ADHD in addition to parenting interventions and classroom interventions. Because MST is a short-term intervention, considerable emphasis is placed on developing a supportive network so that the youth and family will be able to maintain the gains that they made when working directly with the therapist, after the therapist is no longer actively involved.

The developers of MST have established a quality assurance system to ensure that the approach is faithfully applied according to a manual by trained therapists who receive adequate supervision and consultation. Given the promising data on the efficacy of MST in reducing delinquent behavior among seriously troubled youth, it is encouraging to learn that licensed MST programs operate in 30 of the U.S. states and in several countries (Henggeler & Lee, 2003). Ongoing research is examining the usefulness of this approach to treat other serious problems in adolescents.

VIEWPOINT BOX 13.1

TREATMENT OF CHILDHOOD ATTENTION-DEFICIT/HYPERACTIVITY DISORDER

ADHD is a neurological disorder, reviews have consistently found evidence for the efficacy of stimulant medication in reducing symptoms of inattention, hyperactivity, and impulsivity (NICE, 2008; NIH, 1998; Schachar et al., 2002). You may wonder, therefore, why there is any need for psychosocial interventions to treat children with ADHD. There are many significant reasons why psychosocial treatment should be considered. First, although problematic parent–child interaction does not cause ADHD, there is evidence that the presence of child ADHD is associated with disrupted parenting, and this in turn affects the management of ADHD symptoms and the development of oppositional symptoms. Second, stimulants should not be prescribed to children under age 6 (NICE, 2008; Paykina, Greenhill, & Gorman, 2007. Third, a number of parents are unwilling to consider giving their children medication (Waschbusch & Hill, 2003). Fourth, although stimulant medication is effective in suppressing the symptoms of ADHD, the effect lasts only while the child is taking medication, with a return to regular functioning within 3–10 hours of ingesting a dose (Paykina et al., 2007; NICE, 2008). Fifth, 30% of children with ADHD do not respond to the medication (Paykina et al., 2007). Sixth, although stimulants are associated with reduction of core symptoms of ADHD, there is little evidence that medication is associated with improvement in academic or social skills (NIH, 1998). Seventh, although stimulants are not associated with serious side effects, there are minor unpleasant physiological symptoms, the most common of which is appetite suppression (NICE, 2008). Eighth, over time, there is a gradual decline in the numbers of children who adhere to their medication (Charach, Ickowicz, & Schachar, 2004). Unfortunately, it is impossible to predict which children will respond positively to medication (Paykina et al., 2007).

Because medication is not suitable for all children and its positive effects are limited to the hours shortly after it has been administered, it is not surprising that behavioral approaches that have been used to treat other disruptive behavior disorders have also been used to treat childhood ADHD. Similar to PMT for oppositional behavior, behavioral treatments for children with ADHD are designed to help adults (parents and teachers) provide a structured, consistent environment in which the child is reinforced for appropriate behavior and misbehavior is ignored or mildly punished. Pelham and Fabiano (2008) found evidence of positive treatment effects both at home and school regardless of whether the intervention used parents, teachers, or behavioral experts. However, echoing the findings for medication, although behavioral approaches have been demonstrated to be efficacious in the short term, sustaining treatment effects in the long run remains a challenge, and treatment effects only generalize to other settings if efforts are made to ensure that they are applied in different contexts (Hinshaw et al., 2003; Waschbusch & Hill, 2003). Furthermore, not all parents benefit from behavioral parent training (Chronis, Chacko, Fabiano, Wymbs, & Pelham, 2004). Similar to findings with respect to treatment of children with oppositional behavior, parents facing environmental stressors such as low family income, single parenthood, marital discord, and parental psychopathology are least likely to benefit from standard behavioral parent training. For example,

Sonuga-Barke, Daley, and Thompson (2002) found that mothers who themselves had high levels of ADHD symptomatology demonstrated no improvement in parenting following training, whereas mothers with low or moderate ADHD symptoms demonstrated substantial improvement in parenting.

Given the promising but imperfect results from studies examining the separate effects of medication and of psychosocial treatment, a large group of researchers launched the Multimodal Treatment Study of Children with Attention Deficit/Hyperactivity Disorder (MTA; Richters et al., 1995). In this collaborative study, 579 children diagnosed with ADHD-combined type were recruited across six sites. Children were randomly assigned to 14 months of treatment in one of four treatment conditions: (1) medication management only (in which the dose of medication was adjusted in double-blind trials); (2) behavioral treatment with parents, child, and school; (3) a combination of medication management and behavioral treatment; and (4) a comparison of regular treatment in the community (which included medication for about two thirds of the group).

The results from the MTA study are complex and vary according to the type of outcome measure as well as to characteristics of the child and family, suggesting that there is there is no "one size fits all" treatment for all children with ADHD, but there is a menu of options from which to choose. Quite simply, because ADHD is a chronic disorder that causes serious debilitation in multiple contexts, as well as frequent comorbidity (oppositional behavior, learning problems, and depression), it is unlikely that a single approach to treatment will be sufficient to address the problem for all children. A multidimensional approach is therefore recommended (NICE, 2008; Pelham & Fabiano, 2008). Researchers continue to develop enhancements to psychosocial interventions that will help a greater number of families benefit from this approach (Chronis et al., 2004; Hoza, Kaiser, & Hurt, 2007).

Adolescent Depression

Epidemiological studies indicate that major depressive disorder is almost as common in adolescence as it is in adulthood (Lewinsohn & Clarke, 1999). By the age of 18, 1 in 5 young people will have experienced an episode of major depressive disorder (Clarke, DeBar, & Lewinsohn, 2003). Depression is a chronic recurrent disorder that is associated with difficulties in peer relationships, poorer school functioning, and troubled family relationships (Seligman, Goza, & Ollendick, 2004). It is also associated with an increased rate of suicide (Clarke et al., 2003). Although adolescent depression is a serious problem, in contrast to the wealth of research on the treatment of adult depression, the literature with respect to depression in young people is less extensive. Reviews of this literature have concluded that there is support for CBT and for interpersonal therapy (IPT) (David-Ferdon & Kaslow, 2008; Watanabe et al. 2007;Weisz, McCarty, & Valeri, 2006).

Guidelines for the treatment of depression in children (NICE, 2005) recommend that the initial assessment address risk and protective factors in the child's social networks. If there is evidence that the young person is exposed to bullying, school and health professionals should develop strategies to deal with the bullying. Mental health professionals should consider whether it is necessary that parental psychopathology be treated in parallel with the services offered to the young person. The young person should be advised of the benefits of lifestyle factors, including regular exercise, adequate sleep, and good nutrition. The NICE guidelines recommend that antidepressant medication *not* be prescribed to treat mild depression. Instead, monitoring, nondirective supportive therapy, or group CBT is recommended. The first line of treatment for youth with moderate or severe depression is individual CBT, IPT, or short-term family therapy. According to the guidelines, antidepressant medication should only be offered in combination with a psychological treatment.

In Chapter 11 we described the ways that IPT, which was originally developed to treat depression in adults, has been modified to meet the needs of adolescents (Mufson & Dorta, 2003; Mufson, Weissman, Moreau, & Garfinkel, 1999). In Chapter 12 we described CBT for adult depression. In order to give you a sense of how CBT can be provided to youth, we will describe a CBT approach developed for adults that has been modified specifically to treat adolescent depression.

Coping with Depression in Adolescence

Coping with Depression in Adolescence (CWDA) is a program developed by **Peter Lewinsohn** and his colleagues (Lewinsohn & Clarke, 1999; Clarke et al., 2003) as an adaptation of the *Coping with Depression Course* (Lewinsohn, Antonuccio, Steinmetz, & Teri, 1984) that had been found to be efficacious in the treatment of depressed adults. The two coping programs are based on a model of depression that applies to both adults and adolescents. It is assumed that there are genetic risk factors for depression that, when combined with maladaptive learned thoughts and behaviors, heighten the chances of experiencing clinically significant depressive symptoms (Clarke et al., 2003). In CWDA, treatment focuses on behaviors, cognitions, and management of affect. Behavioral interventions include increasing pleasant activities and developing problem-solving skills, assertiveness skills, communication skills, and conflict resolution skills. Cognitive techniques include promoting the use of positive self-talk, self-monitoring, coping, and cognitive restructuring. The affective component involves learning strategies for dealing with negative emotions, including relaxation and anger management. Parents may be involved to develop their parenting, conflict resolution, and communication skills. Just as with CBT for adult depression, **mood monitoring** is a central activity that is introduced at the beginning of the program and is continued throughout the course of services. The focus of initial sessions is on behavioral change, with an emphasis on the practice of social skills and an increase in pleasant activities. This flows logically into an examination of dysfunctional cognitions. The end of the program focuses on strategies to ensure the maintenance of gains, progress toward goals, and the prevention of relapse. Participants are told that not every skill will be equally useful to all participants, but they are required to attempt every activity. Booster sessions can be offered at 4-month intervals for 2 years after completing the program.

The CWDA program is delivered according to a treatment manual in a group format. Between 6 and 10 depressed adolescents (ages 13–18) take part in each group. The **psychoeducational** approach presents material in a similar way to the way other subjects are taught in school. This style of conveying material is assumed to be less stigmatizing to young people who may feel very uncomfortable with the idea of receiving treatment of a mental disorder. Treatment includes 16 two-hour sessions that are scheduled over an 8-week period. The course uses a workbook with readings, quizzes, and forms for homework. Materials are designed to be engaging for young people, using popular newspaper cartoons

to illustrate common dysfunctional thoughts. Therapists are active and engage participation by seeking examples and facilitating the exchange of ideas between group members. Skills are presented in the session and are practiced using role plays. Participants are then assigned homework tasks that involve the application of the skills in their everyday lives. As you can see, there are more similarities than dissimilarities between the treatment of adult and youth depression. The major difference is in adapting the psychoeducational material to make it more engaging to young people and in developing modules that include parents.

VIEWPOINT BOX 13.2

PSYCHOLOGICAL TREATMENT FOR CARL

In Chapter 3 we introduced Carl, a 12-year-old boy exposed to the trauma of genocide. Carl suffered from diverse symptoms, including anxiety, persistent re-experiencing of the events, avoidance of stimuli associated with the trauma, somatic complaints, and sleep disturbance. Carl's symptoms were consistent with a diagnosis of PTSD. The initial assessment led to a formulation of Carl's problems in terms of his initial exposure to genocide when he was 3 years old, as well as the reemergence of threat when he was 9 years old. Counterbalancing these serious risk factors were the protective factors of his strong attachment to his mother and twin sister. Carl's mother did not connect her son's symptoms of anxiety to his horrific experiences. She was bewildered that, now the family was safe in North America, her son was showing signs of "craziness." In understanding the mother's reaction, it is important to bear in mind that she, too, had been exposed to trauma, with the murder of her husband and threats to herself and her children. She, too, suffered from PTSD and experienced characteristic numbing and avoidance of stimuli that made it hard for her to acknowledge the source of Carl's difficulties.

In treatment planning, psychologists must first consider whether there are evidence-based treatments for the client's problem. Although there are efficacious treatments for adults with PTSD, the treatment of childhood and adolescent PTSD is not as well developed (Feeny, Foa, Treadwell, & March, 2004; Silverman et al., 2008). There is evidence of the usefulness of some approaches in treating childhood PTSD resulting from a single traumatic event such as a car accident (Scotti, Morris, Ruggiero, & Wolfgang, 2002). However, Carl was exposed to unremitting trauma over the course of months. There is evidence of the usefulness of CBT approaches in treating children who suffer PTSD as a result of sexual abuse (Silverman, Ortiz, et al. 2008), and case studies of exposure in the treatment of Lebanese children suffering war-related PTSD (Feeny et al., 2004), but no studies on the treatment of children and adolescents exposed to genocide. As you learned in Chapter 12, efficacious treatments for adults with PTSD include relaxation, imaginal exposure, and in vivo exposure. Important prerequisites for treatment are that the person must be safe and there must be people available to support him or her during the painful period of habituation to the stimuli associated with symptoms. Although Carl was safe at present, his refugee claim was pending. In the event that his family's claim for refugee status was denied and they were forced to return to their home country, he would again be exposed to danger. Carl's mother was devoted to her children's well-being, but she also suffered from PTSD, so her capacity to support him emotionally was diminished.

In the absence of an evidence-based treatment package that matches the client's needs, the psychologist must consider whether there are elements of evidence-based approaches that are relevant (Connor-Smith & Weisz, 2003). Fortunately, the treatment of anxiety disorders in childhood includes many efficacious strategies (Cartwright-Hatton, Roberts, Chitsabesan, Fothergill, & Harrington, 2004; Kazdin, 2003; Roberts, Lazicki-Puddy, Puddy, & Johnson, 2003). Accordingly, the treatment goals for Carl included the development of relaxation and stress management strategies, as well as the accurate identification of emotions and changes in his belief systems. A critically important goal was the reduction of avoidance of stimuli associated with the trauma. In a feedback session with Carl and his mother, the psychologist provided information about PTSD, linking it to the events they had experienced. Carl and his mother agreed to parallel services in which each would work on PTSD symptoms and develop effective stress management skills.

Carl attended 13 sessions. Initial sessions focused on the development of a collaborative relationship through nonthreatening activities. For example, Carl learned to expand his vocabulary of emotions by Internet-based activities in which he had to match facial expressions to emotion labels (e.g., scared, disappointed, frustrated, grumpy, worried). Next, he worked to generate possible explanations for emotions (e.g., worried because a test is coming up, embarrassed because he does not want to look stupid). Carl agreed to keep a sleep log in which he recorded his nighttime routine and any awakening as well as the thoughts he had when unable to sleep. Subsequently, he learned relaxation activities including both breathing exercises and progressive muscle relaxation; at the same time, his mother was also learning relaxation strategies. Carl then practiced these relaxation activities when he went to bed and whenever he awoke in the night. Carl observed that the relaxation strategies were helpful in reducing the time spent awake.

In the next phase of services, Carl's cognitions were targeted. Following an episode in which he lay awake for hours having heard what he thought was an intruder in the house, Carl learned to distinguish between "real" emotional alarms and "false" emotional alarms. The therapist used the example of firefighters to illustrate this. Carl learned that when the bell sounds in the fire hall, the firefighters get ready to fight a fire; as they put on their gear and travel to the possible fire, they are ready for action. Once at the site, they check carefully whether there is a fire. In the event that there is a fire, they work to extinguish it. However, in the event that there is a false alarm, they return to the fire hall and resume their activities. Applying this analogy in his own life, Carl was able to remind himself that, like the firefighters, he should check to see whether there was a reason for the alarm by checking that the doors were locked and that no one had access to the house; once he had established that it was a false alarm, he could use the relaxation strategies to fall back to sleep.

As the anniversary of the genocide approached, Carl talked about his ambivalence in participating in memorial activities. Equipped with his expanded vocabulary of feelings, he communicated his desire to avoid the extreme sadness and anger of remembering the horror, balanced by his desire to connect to other people who had shared the experience. Carl recognized that participation did not have to be an all-or-nothing decision, and chose to be involved in some activities, such as a candlelight vigil, but to limit others, such as watching hours of television footage of the carnage. With the psychologist, Carl practiced communicating his preferences to his mother. Subsequently, Carl reported satisfaction that he was able to make choices, exhaustion at the emotional toll of the memorial, but appreciation of a greater feeling of connectedness with others in his extended family and community. At the end of services, Carl reported that he no longer suffered from sleep disturbance or somatic complaints. The persistent reexperiencing of the trauma had diminished, and he was less avoidant of stimuli associated with it.

In adapting treatment for this young client, it was essential to deliver material in a developmentally appropriate fashion; whereas a younger child might be engaged in cutting pictures from a magazine and pasting a collage that illustrates different emotions, Carl found it cool to point and click at images on a Web site. As a young man on the verge of adolescence, Carl was most comfortable with individual services in which he could enjoy privacy with the therapist. Nevertheless, from the provision of information about PTSD that reduced the mother's intolerance of her son's anxious behavior, to the encouragement that both practice relaxation exercises, the coordination of services for mother and youth was essential.

EFFICACY, EFFECTIVENESS, AND THE DISSEMINATION OF EVIDENCE-BASED TREATMENTS

In Chapter 12 we discussed the challenges of moving from efficacy in clinical trials to establishing effectiveness in clinical practice. The issues raised with respect to adults are equally important with respect to children and adolescents. In the previous sections of this chapter, we described the progress that has been made in identifying efficacious psychological treatments for children and adolescents. There is growing evidence that standard community care for child and adolescent disorders is generally not effective (Ollendick & King, 2004). For example, Weersing and Weisz (2002) compared the outcomes of depressed youth receiving care in community mental health centers with those obtained in clinical trials. It is very troubling that the effects of community-based services were more similar to the results found for youth in no-treatment control conditions than to the results found in the treatment condition of RCTs. The two crucial issues confronting the field are therefore: (1) whether efficacious treatments established in methodologically sound studies are also effective when they are applied as part of regular clinical practice; and (assuming the first question is answered affirmatively) (2) how these evidence-based treatments can be disseminated so that they are more widely available.

In Chapter 12, you learned about the Hunsley and Lee (2007) review that compared data from effectiveness studies to benchmarks from meta-analyses. All of the effectiveness studies for children and youth included in that review found that more than 75% of patients followed the course of services to completion. The majority of studies reported completion rates comparable or superior to those reported in efficacy trials. In terms of the outcome of treatment, most of the effectiveness studies reported results that were comparable to those obtained in the efficacy studies relevant to each condition. Thus, based on the benchmarking strategy, there is evidence from various countries that evidence-based treatments for children and youth can be very effective when used in routine practice settings.

A growing body of research indicates that evidence-based treatments for anxiety, depression, ADHD, and disruptive disorders appear to be equally effective for African American and Latino youths as they are for European American youths (Miranda et al., 2005). Unfortunately, despite progress in the identification of efficacious treatments, dissemination of those treatments appears slower for childhood disorders than for adult disorders (Herschell, McNeil, & McNeil, 2004). For example, Herschell and colleagues found twice as many journal articles devoted to treatment dissemination for adult disorders than for disorders of childhood and adolescence. **Table 13.4** lists some of the strategies proposed by Herschell and colleagues to improve dissemination of evidence-based treatments. As you can see, some of the strategies require action on the part of the developers of interventions (e.g., making treatment manuals widely available, providing opportunities for training and supervision). Other recommendations target graduate training programs and licensing bodies. It is clear that the process of learning does not end with the awarding of the PhD but is a career-long endeavor.

The concerns first raised by Kazdin and his colleagues in their 1990 meta-analysis (Kazdin et al., 1990) are still applicable today. Kazdin (2003) highlighted the ongoing need to conduct research to identify the ingredients in treatment that are responsible for change, as well as for research identifying particular subgroups for which a treatment is helpful. Weisz, Doss, and Hawley (2005) reviewed published, methodologically sound RCTs for anxiety (82 studies), depression (18 studies), ADHD (40 studies), and conduct problems (96 studies). These authors highlighted a number of threats to both internal validity and external validity that limited the extent to which results could be generalized. For example, in many studies there was no reliable determination of the diagnosis. Most studies were

---

TABLE 13.4   Strategies to Facilitate the Dissemination of Evidence-Based Treatment

- Development of manuals that allow flexible implementation
- Graduate education in evidence-based treatment
- Continuing education in evidence-based treatment
- Training protocols such as workshops, supervision, and consultation
- Increased research on effective dissemination strategies

Adapted from Herschell, McNeil, and McNeil, 2004

underpowered: they had too few participants in each condition to provide the statistical power to detect meaningful group differences. Few studies were clinically representative: in the majority of studies, participants were recruited rather than drawn from contexts in which they were seeking treatment. Furthermore, the authors reported that learning-based treatments were 8 to 10 times more likely to be studied than were insight-based treatments (i.e., psychodynamic treatments). Thus, although there has been progress in the study of psychological treatments for children and adolescents, it is essential that research be conducted to determine the extent to which promising treatments are useful for the populations who require services.

SUMMARY AND CONCLUSIONS

Compared with the evidence base for adult treatments, far less is known about the effects of psychotherapy for children and adolescents. Nevertheless, meta-analytic estimates do indicate that treatments for youth can have substantial effects on psychological symptoms, with some estimates indicating almost comparable treatment effects for adults and youth. Various organizations have worked to develop listings of evidence-based interventions for children and adolescents and, at present, there are scientifically supported psychosocial treatments for the most commonly occurring Axis I disorders. Clinical practice guidelines for addressing mood disorders, anxiety disorders, ADHD, and externalizing disorders are now available for both clinicians and patients and their families. Despite these advances, much more work needs to be done to encourage treatment research that is more clinically representative, to understand exactly what the ingredients of successful treatment are, and to promote the use of evidence-based treatments in real-world settings.

Critical Thinking Questions

What are some of the major differences between services for children and adolescents and services for adults?

Why has there been less treatment research for youth than for adults to date?

Is there currently evidence that psychotherapy can work in the treatment of childhood and adolescent disorders?

Why is it so important to have parents involved in many forms of child treatment?

How do services for children and services for adolescents differ?

Key Terms

coercive exchanges: parent–child interactions in which the parent unintentionally rewards the child for whining or aggression (by withdrawing a demand or providing attention) and the child rewards the parent for giving in to his or her complaints (by ceasing the aversive behavior).

ecological theory: theory that examines a young person's functioning within the multiple contexts in which he or she lives—family, school, neighborhood, and so on.

ethnic disparity: the finding that evidence-based treatment is not as powerful when applied to ethnic minority youth as it was found to be with youth from the dominant ethnic background—suggesting that the treatment needs to be modified to meet the needs of minority youth.

ethnic invariance: the finding that evidence-based treatment yields equivalent results for ethnic minority youth as for youth from the dominant ethnic background—suggesting that the treatment does not need to be modified.

mood monitoring: tracking mood on a regular basis, usually using a chart.

parental monitoring: parents' awareness and tracking of the child's activities; the way the parent monitors shifts as the child develops.

positive reinforcement: any consequence that increases the likelihood of a behavior being repeated.

psychoeducation: teaching psychological concepts to clients in a manner that is accessible to them.

time out: parenting strategy in which the child does not have access to reinforcers for a brief period following misbehavior.

Key Names

Bruce Chorpita

Peter Lewinsohn

John Weisz

Alan Kazdin

Gerald Patterson

ADDITIONAL RESOURCES

Fonagy, P., Target, M., Cottrell, D., Phillips, J., & Kurtz, Z. (2002). *What works for whom? A critical review of treatments for children and adolescents.* New York: Guilford.

Kazdin, A. E., & Weisz, J. R. (Eds). (2003). *Evidence-based psychotherapies for children and adolescents* (pp. 101–119). New York: Guilford.

Weisz, J. R., McCarty, C. A., & Valeri, S. M. (2006). Effects of psychotherapy for depression in children and adolescents: A meta-analysis. *Psychological Bulletin, 132,* 132–149.

Check It Out!

The APA's Society of Clinical Child and Adolescent Psychology: http://www.effectivechildtherapy.com/

The *British Medical Journal*, for reviews of the literature on the treatment of physical and mental disorders: http://www.clinicalevidence.org

The American Academy of Child and Adolescent Psychiatry, providing practice parameters: http://www.aacap.org/clinical/parameters/index.htm

To learn more about multisystemic therapy: http://www.mstservices.com/

CHAPTER 14

Intervention: Identifying Key Elements of Change

INTRODUCTION

Consistent with our emphasis that clinical psychology is an evidence-based profession, Chapters 12 and 13 examined the empirical evidence on interventions that work in the treatment of a variety of disorders and problems. However, it is important also to consider the large body of evidence that focuses on patient/client, therapist, and therapeutic process variables that influence treatment outcome. As we described in the previous chapters, hundreds of studies have examined the outcome of treatments and the comparative outcome of different types of treatment. There are also, however, hundreds of studies that examine elements of psychotherapy, such as the alliance between patient and therapist, and how these process elements are related to the impact of treatment. Such approaches to studying psychotherapy are known as, respectively, process research and process-outcome research. In the first part of this chapter, we illustrate what can be learned about psychotherapy from **process research** and **process-outcome research**.

As we mentioned in Chapter 2, many clinical psychologists describe their theoretical orientation as combining two or more of the major approaches to treatment, such as experiential and cognitive-behavioral. When asked to explain their use of multiple approaches to treatment, these psychologists may indicate that there are **common factors** in successful treatment that cut across specific approaches to therapy (e.g., Garfield, 1994a; Norcross & Goldfried, 1992). In the latter part of the chapter we examine both theories and research on these common (or nonspecific) factors. Common factors are sometimes presented as responsible for most of the impact of any form of psychotherapy, so we review evidence with respect to the claim that all forms of psychotherapy have equivalent effects.

As you learned in Chapters 12 and 13, findings from treatment outcome research have been used to develop evidence-based recommendations for the treatment of specific disorders and conditions. The results of process research and process-outcome research have also been used to formulate clinical guidelines for psychologists and, in the final part of this chapter, we examine these guidelines in detail. The first initiative involved explicitly emphasizing client characteristics and therapy relationship factors that have been found to be related to treatment outcome. The second and more integrative initiative involved combining research findings on client, therapist, client–therapist relationship, and treatment characteristics to develop evidence-based principles of therapeutic change that can be applied to all forms of treatment.

PSYCHOTHERAPY PROCESS AND PROCESS-OUTCOME RESEARCH

To understand the relation between treatment outcome research and process-outcome research, it is useful to consider a sports analogy. A team's performance over a season can be analyzed in a number of ways. For example, you can count the number of wins during a season, the number of wins when a team plays at home, the number of wins when a team plays on natural or synthetic surfaces, or the team's record against specific opponents. Like treatment outcome research, all of these examples focus on *outcomes*, outcomes under varying conditions, or how the team fared compared with other teams. None of this reveals much about *how* the team achieved its record. To do this, we need to examine *processes* within each game and then examine the consistency of these processes across all games the team played. For example, how well does the team do if they score first, what happens if the star offensive player has a poor game, or what is the effect on the outcome if there are a greater than average number of penalties called against the team? All of these questions explore the issue of what is occurring during a game that is associated with the team being relatively successful or unsuccessful. Such questions are similar to those posed by process-outcome psychotherapy researchers.

These ways of examining the record of a sports team (or of psychotherapy) address different questions. Similarly, different types of psychotherapy research can address different questions. Treatment outcome research addresses the question of *which* intervention is more efficacious, whereas process research and process-outcome research ask about *how* an intervention works. Identifying the best team or comparing teams

Psychotherapy, like sports, can be analyzed in terms of how you win as well as whether you win. (*Source:* Graham Winterbottom/Image Source Limited)

TABLE 14.1   Levels of Analysis for Psychotherapeutic Process and Outcome Studies

TIMEFRAME	TIME SCALE	PROCESS FOCUS	OUTCOME FOCUS
Liminal	Split-seconds	Facial expressions, shifts in gaze	None
Momentary	Minutes	Specific statements, changes in direction of conversation	Emergence of specific experiences such as insight or catharsis
Situational	Hours	Changes in dynamics across sessions, dealing with alliance problems	Immediate improvements in mood or motivation
Daily	Days	Homework assignments, between-session experiences	Change in functioning, improved handling of problems
Monthly	Weeks	Development of alliance, phases of treatment	Ongoing improvements in functioning and reduction of symptoms
Seasonal	Months	Addressing recurrent themes in treatment, entire course of treatment	Changes in adaptation and identity
Perennial	Years	Long-term treatment events	Personality change

Adapted from Orlinsky, Rønnestad, and Willutzki (2004)

to one another requires different data and a different approach to data analysis than does determining the factors that contribute to a team's success or whether these same factors account for the performance of all the teams in the league. In a review of the history of process-outcome research, **David Orlinsky** and colleagues (Orlinsky, Rønnestad, & Willutzki, 2004) traced the development of this line of psychotherapy research over the past 50 years. In the 1950s and 1960s, psychologists interested in the process of psychotherapy began using two important sources of data: recordings of psychotherapy sessions and standardized measures of clients' and therapists' experience of the treatment process. Since then, the strategies for studying what transpires in therapy (process research) and how it is related to client change (process-outcome research) have grown dramatically and become more complex. **Table 14.1** provides an overview of the different levels at which psychotherapy researchers have addressed these important questions.

As you will see throughout this chapter, by examining process questions and then relating this information to treatment outcome, psychotherapy researchers have learned a great deal about how therapy works. For example, many studies have examined the ways in which the behavior of therapists during treatment sessions varies across different theoretical orientations. In general, even though there is considerable similarity across therapist behaviors, therapists tend to behave in ways that are consistent with the theoretical orientations they espouse (e.g., Blagys & Hilsenroth, 2000). In the following pages we describe some of the interesting results obtained in process-outcome research. By using this research to influence therapeutic practices, clinical psychologists can improve the services they offer clients. Our description of the research on sudden client gains in treatment in **Viewpoint Box 14.1** is an example of the important discoveries that have been made in process-outcome research.

VIEWPOINT BOX 14.1

SUDDEN GAINS IN THERAPY

After reading the chapters on psychological treatment you may be wondering what the process of therapeutic change looks like. How can you tell whether the client is improving? Is it a steady progression of small, barely perceptible but important changes that cumulatively result in altered psychosocial functioning? Or is it the case that, as often portrayed in movies, after weeks of nonproductive sessions, a client experiences a dramatic breakthrough that results in a qualitatively different view of him- or herself?

This was the question that Tang and DeRubeis (1999) addressed when they undertook a session-by-session review of the treatment progress of depressed patients in two cognitive-behavioral therapy (CBT) efficacy trials. Although they found different patterns of progress across patients, they noticed that more than one third of patients experienced large reductions in depressive symptoms early in treatment. Closer examination revealed that these patients made sudden large gains in functioning around session 4, 5, or 6. The sudden gains in functioning were very large—they involved at least a 25% reduction in pretreatment symptom levels—and were made during a single period of time between two sessions. Those who experienced these sudden gains were less depressed than other patients at the end of treatment, and they tended to maintain their gains up to 18 months after treatment. Using a different CBT efficacy trial data set, Tang, DeRubeis, Beberman, and Pham (2005) replicated their original findings. They found clear evidence of the same pattern of sudden gains and also found evidence that, prior to the sudden gains, substantial cognitive changes occurred among the patients who experienced sudden gains. Consistent with the cognitive theory of change proposed by cognitive therapists (Chapter 11) it appears that changes in the way in which patients thought about themselves and their life situations were causally related to the observed changes in symptoms.

Sudden gains have also been found in depressed patients receiving other forms of treatment. Tang, Luborsky, and Andrusyna (2002), for example, reported sudden gains in an efficacy trial of short-term psychodynamic treatment. These sudden gains were of similar magnitude to those originally reported by Tang and DeRubeis (1999) and occurred for a similar percentage of patients early in treatment. Although patients with sudden gains were, in comparison with those without sudden gains, significantly better at the end of treatment, the two groups had similar levels of depression 6 months after treatment ended. Using data from patients receiving cognitive therapy for depression, Tang, DeRubeis, Hollon, Amsterdam, and Shelton (2007) reported that patients who experienced sudden gains were far less likely than other patients to experience relapse in the 2 years following treatment. Sudden gains have also been found in interpersonal psychotherapy for depression, but the experience of sudden gains did not affect the likelihood of patients achieving a remission of symptoms at the end of treatment (Kelly, Cyranowski, & Frank, 2007). Evidence of sudden gains has also come from two British studies using data from routine treatment settings. Hardy et al. (2005) examined the progress of clients receiving cognitive therapy for depression in a National Health Service clinic: 40% of clients experienced changes almost identical to those reported by Tang and

DeRubeis (1999). Stiles et al. (2003) examined data from 135 clients with a variety of disorders and problems who were treated with a variety of approaches (including cognitive therapy, psychodynamic therapy, and experiential therapies). Seventeen percent of clients experienced the sudden gains, with half of the clients achieving them by the fifth treatment session. As in most other studies, by the end of treatment these clients had significantly improved relative to the clients who did not experience sudden gains. Finally, Vittengl, Clark, and Jarrett (2005) found evidence of sudden treatment gains in two data sets that involved cognitive therapy of major depressive disorder. Sudden gain patterns similar to those reported by Tang and DeRubeis (1999) were found using both patient data and therapist data. What is particularly noteworthy, though, is that Vittengl and colleagues also found evidence of sudden gains in patients who received pill placebos and those who received antidepressant medication.

The repeated independent replication of the sudden gains pattern lends credibility to the validity of the phenomenon. However, the fact that effect of sudden gains on treatment outcome is evident in many, but not all, forms of intervention has raised the question of whether there might be different mechanisms of change operating in different types of treatment. In future studies, researchers will attempt to address the important questions of what is responsible for the sudden gains and whether the outcome-related impact of sudden gains may occur for different reasons in different psychotherapies.

Think about an "intervention" you have begun recently—it could be yoga for relaxation, physiotherapy for knee pain, strips to whiten your teeth, or spinning to improve your cardiovascular fitness. If you were to experience sudden gains after a few sessions, how would that affect the likelihood of persisting with the intervention?

Examining Client Factors

As you learned in Chapters 12 and 13, the vast majority of randomized controlled trial (RCT) psychotherapy research examines treatment outcomes for different groups of clients classified on the basis of diagnoses or presenting problems. However, there is far more to people than just their psychological symptoms. No psychotherapy researcher believes that diagnosis is the primary factor that determines treatment outcome. Client characteristics other than diagnosis may be very important predictors of treatment success or failure. Consequently, a large literature has examined the influence of client variables on psychotherapy. Much of this research comes from studies of treatments provided in real-world clinic settings, but a growing number of studies are derived from RCTs in which investigators have sought to identify mediators and moderators (discussed in Chapter 4) of treatment efficacy (Kazdin, 2007).

The first challenge in examining client variables is determining which variables to evaluate. Which client characteristics should be taken into account? Among the many potential variables are personality characteristics, current life circumstances, life experiences, family of origin characteristics, ethnicity and cultural factors, beliefs about psychological problems, and expectations regarding treatment. If we know the impact such characteristics can have on therapy, we can formulate a treatment plan that is likely to be optimally responsive to the needs of the client. Efforts to synthesize results of the voluminous research on client factors in therapy have been hampered by the nonsystematic nature of the studies. In other words, different researchers have tended to examine a variable, such as clients' treatment expectations, in different ways across studies. It is extremely difficult to detect patterns across studies that used different types of measures (e.g., completion of a self-report measure versus coding of statements made during a therapy session) and different timing of the assessment (e.g., prior to commencing treatment or after one session of therapy). As succinctly summarized by Petry, Tennen, and Affleck (2000) the unfortunate consequence of this variability is that despite thousands of empirical studies we have only a rudimentary appreciation of how client variables affect treatment responses. **Table 14.2** provides a summary of the most consistent findings in the empirical literature.

TABLE 14.2   Client Variables That Influence Treatment

Sociodemographic Characteristics
Socioeconomic Status
- Higher socioeconomic status is associated with a greater likelihood of engaging in and staying in treatment.

Ethnicity
- Similarity in client and therapist ethnicity is associated with a greater likelihood of clients staying in treatment and of making therapeutic change.

Gender
- Women are more likely to seek therapy than are men, but there is no gender difference in premature termination of services.
- Matching of client and therapist gender has little influence on treatment outcome or treatment satisfaction.

Age
- Client age is unrelated to treatment outcome.

Psychological Functioning
Symptom Severity
- Greater severity of psychological symptoms is related to poorer treatment outcome.

Functional Impairment
- Greater overall impairment in functioning (i.e., in various social roles and health status) is related to poorer treatment outcome.

Personality Characteristics
Personality Disorders
- Presence of an Axis II diagnosis is associated with premature termination, problems in the process of therapy, and less therapeutic change during treatment.

Ego Strength
- Ego strength (broadly defined as the capacity to use personality resources to manage negative emotional states and threats to personal identity) is related to positive treatment outcome.

(Continued)

TABLE 14.2 *(Continued)*

Psychological Mindedness

- Psychological mindedness (broadly defined as the ability to understand people and problems in psychological terms) is related to positive treatment outcome.

Psychological Reactance

- Clients low in reactance (broadly defined as the tendency to react against attempts to influence or limit one's behaviors or options) tend to experience greater therapeutic gains in more directive treatments, whereas clients high in reactance tend to experience greater therapeutic gains in less directive treatments.

Treatment Expectations

- Positive expectations for treatment are associated with remaining in treatment and achieving greater therapeutic gains.

Adapted from Clarkin and Levy (2004) and Petry, Tennen, and Affleck (2000)

The information in Table 14.2 provides clear guidance to help therapists tailor their treatment plans for the individual client. Let's take the example of socioeconomic status. Knowing that a client with a lower socioeconomic status is at heightened risk for premature termination, psychologists can take steps early in treatment to enhance the likelihood that the client will engage in treatment. For example, in providing services to Shari, a single mother of two young children who has a part-time job with irregular working hours, the psychologist could explicitly discuss options to help Shari fit therapy appointments into her schedule. Rather than scheduling a regular appointment during standard office hours, the psychologist could offer appointments that do not require Shari to take time off work or to make arrangements for extra child care. Furthermore, many psychologists in private practice have sliding fee scales that allow patients with lower incomes (and limited private insurance coverage) to pay reduced fees. Access to affordable services may make the difference between Shari engaging in therapy and prematurely ending services.

It is important to keep in mind that preexisting client variables, such as current life context, life experiences, and personality, may have their greatest impact on client decisions about seeking and engaging in therapy. Once treatment starts, however, the dynamic interplay between client and therapist is likely to generate a far more powerful influence on the course and outcome of treatment (cf. Clarkin & Levy, 2004). The ultimate outcome of treatment is affected by the way the client feels about the therapist, therapist response to client questions and challenges, the degree of benefit the client experiences early in treatment, and the extent to which treatment influences the client's daily life. In a large-scale study of the treatment of depression, for example, patients who initially expected treatment to be effective remained in therapy and engaged actively and constructively in therapy sessions, which resulted in reductions in their symptoms (Elkin et al., 1999; Meyer et al., 2002).

Given what you learned in Chapter 9 about the possible effects of heuristics and biases in clinical decision making, do you think that there are any dangers associated with using research on client factors to guide treatment planning for a specific client? What steps can a psychologist take to ensure that the research information is used in an appropriate manner?

Examining Therapist Factors

Just as researchers have explored the impact of *client* variables on treatment processes and outcome, so too have they addressed the ways in which *therapist* characteristics affect aspects of psychotherapy. This research has yielded subtle and nuanced findings about the impact of the psychotherapist on the patient's response to treatment. As mentioned previously with respect to client variables, this is partly because of (a) the manner in which interactions between patient and therapist occur and evolve over the course of treatment and (b) the power such interactions exert on the process of therapeutic change. **Table 14.3** summarizes the main findings on the contribution of therapist factors to psychotherapy process and outcome.

The research described in Table 14.3, like that summarized for client variables in Table 14.2, is based on an examination of the individual contribution of specific therapist variables on the therapeutic process. However, many therapist variables may interact in therapy. It seems intuitively obvious that the "sum" of the therapist's personal qualities should be an important ingredient in any recipe for good therapy. After all, a good psychotherapist must have considerable knowledge, technical skills, interpersonal sensitivity, and tolerance for distress. For example, Lafferty, Beutler, and Crago (1989) studied trainee therapists in clinical psychology, psychiatry, clinical social work, and psychiatric nursing working in an outpatient clinic. Based on the treatment results for two randomly selected clients for each trainee, they selected 30 therapists for whom both clients improved and 30 for whom neither client improved. Data from patients and therapists were used to examine differences in the therapists between these two groups. Although there were only small differences between the groups of therapists in terms of their emotional adjustment or general life values, analyses revealed an important group difference in what transpired during treatment. Specifically, patients of the more effective therapists reported feeling more understood in treatment than did the patients of the less effective therapists.

What do we know about overall differences in therapeutic effectiveness among fully qualified and practicing therapists? Two large-scale studies examining the success of individual practicing therapists have found that 5–8% of the variance in client improvement can be attributed to therapist effects (Lutz, Leon, Martinovich, Lyons, & Stiles, 2007; Wampold & Brown, 2005). Moreover, in examining the various components responsible for patient change in RCTs, Lyons and Howard (1991) found that the effects on patient outcome due to specific therapists are typically greater than the effects due to specific treatments. Even though systematic training based on explicit treatment manuals improves the overall effectiveness of therapists, it does not eliminate important variability among specific therapists (Teyber & McClure, 2000).

Unfortunately, we know very little about the characteristics that differentiate more and less effective therapists or what sets the exceptional therapist apart from his or her colleagues. For example, in a large-scale study of treatment for alcohol problems (more than 1,700 patients), 4 out of 54 therapists accounted for most of the poorest treatment outcomes (Project MATCH Research Group, 1998). However, the researchers were unable to identify characteristics that discriminated these 4 therapists from the others. As there is evidence of important variability in therapist impact, even in RCTs, psychotherapy researchers are increasingly concerned to examine therapist characteristics and behaviors that may be responsible for variability in patient outcome. Evidence of differences in the effectiveness of therapists has also led to suggestions that, rather than focusing on defining treatments as

TABLE 14.3   Therapist Variables That Influence Treatment

Sociodemographic Characteristics

Ethnicity

- There is very limited systematic research examining the main effect of therapist ethnicity or cultural background on treatment outcome, with no consistent pattern of effects yet apparent.

Gender

- Therapist gender has no consistent effect on treatment outcome.

Age

- Therapist age is unrelated to treatment outcome.
- Similarity in age between client and therapist does not contribute significantly to treatment outcome.

Professional Background

Professional Discipline

- Therapists trained in a mental health discipline tend to have better treatment outcomes than those trained in a health discipline (i.e., general practitioners).
- Research is inconclusive regarding the relative effectiveness of therapists trained in different mental health disciplines (i.e., clinical psychologists, psychiatrists, social workers, marriage and family counselors).

Professional Experience

- Although the variability in the evidence is considerable, overall the research indicates that therapist experience (measured in years or number of clients treated) is positively related to treatment outcome.

Personality Characteristics

Personality Traits

- Therapist personality traits have little association with treatment outcome.

Emotional Well-Being

- Therapist emotional well-being is consistently positively associated with treatment outcome.

Values, Attitudes, and Beliefs

- No consistent pattern of results has been found regarding the influence of therapists' values, attitudes, and beliefs on the process and outcome of therapy.

Use of Self-Disclosure

- Self-disclosure (broadly defined as the therapist's judicious sharing of personal experiences or views in the process of therapy) has been found to have a small but positive effect on treatment outcome.

Adapted from Beutler et al. (2004) and Teyber and McClure (2000) empirically supported or evidence based, the emphasis should be on empirically certifying *therapists* as effective based on results obtained in actual practice (Krause, Lutz, & Saunders, 2007).

Examining Treatment Factors

In previous chapters we described some of the characteristics of the current main approaches to psychotherapy and presented evidence for their efficacy and effectiveness in treating specific conditions. Researchers have examined, both within specific treatment orientations and across orientations, whether some aspects of therapy are especially important in achieving therapeutic change. Is it important for therapists to explicitly interpret clients' behavior? Is it better to focus on reducing symptoms or on achieving insight? Does the use of between-session assignments make any difference in treatment? Process-outcome researchers have investigated these questions and many others. In this section we consider some of the main findings from this line of inquiry.

Interpretation

Interpretation of client behavior often occurs in psychodynamic and experiential approaches to therapy. This can include explanations for the client's problems as well as the labeling of unconscious processes that are believed to influence thoughts, emotions, and behaviors. In their review of the research on interpretations, Beutler and colleagues (2004) found no consistent pattern of results across studies. Although the weighted average effect size was a nonsignificant $r = .07$, there were a number of studies in which interpretations were strongly correlated with positive outcome. In general, these studies suggested that therapist interpretations were most successful with clients who had good interpersonal skills. You can well imagine the mixed reactions people would have to frequent comments on the reasons for their behaviors and emotions. A high degree of interpersonal competence would probably be important in helping the client to openly discuss such affectively charged therapist comments.

Directiveness

How directive should the therapist be? Is it better to have an active, guiding therapist, or is a neutral, reflective stance more conducive to positive outcomes? Based on their review, Beutler et al. (2004) reported a weighted average effect size of $r = .06$, which was statistically nonsignificant. However, the range of effect sizes across studies varied enormously, from $-.17$ to $.79$. With such wide variation, it is obvious that calculating the mean across studies is likely to obscure some important information. In all likelihood, in this instance, there are moderating variables that influence the extent to which therapist directiveness is appropriate. When we consider the evidence summarized in Table 14.2, it seems likely that the optimal degree of therapist directiveness is determined, at least in part, by the client's level of psychological reactance. Psychological reactance is the tendency to react against attempts to directly influence one's behavior. Low-reactant clients usually experience greater therapeutic gains in more directive treatments, whereas clients high in reactance tend to experience greater therapeutic gains in less directive treatments.

Across all treatment approaches, it is possible for therapists to flexibly adjust their interactional style in order to differentially emphasize the provision of direct guidance versus client self-exploration and self-directedness. What would this actually mean for psychologists in providing services? Let's consider the initial appointment for Florio, a middle-aged man referred because of recent panic attacks. When the clinic receptionist called to make the appointment with Florio, he insisted on talking to the psychologist directly. When the psychologist later phoned him back, Florio proceeded to ask a series of questions about the psychologist's training, her experience with treating people with problems similar to his, and whether she could guarantee that the treatment would help. During the first session, the psychologist's attempts to structure the interview and to gather information about his anxiety and panic and his family history were met with frequent comments such as "Just let me tell you my story in my own time," "Not so fast, I don't think I want to answer that question," and "So why do you want to know that?" Whenever the psychologist made an empathic statement about how Florio seemed to be feeling, he rebuffed her with statements such as "Not at all" and "You're off the mark there, doc." Halfway through the session, the psychologist concluded that her usual approach to gathering information was simply not going to work with Florio. She told Florio that, in order to try to help him with his panic attacks, she needed precise information about what was going on in his life that seemed to be related to the panic. She said that, although she normally asked a series of questions to help gather this information, as he was a "take charge" kind of person she was willing to be guided by Florio in how she gathered this information. She invited Florio to tell her what he thought was important and stated that she would only ask an occasional question if she needed something clarified. At this point Florio laughed and said "Well, you've got my number doc. I just don't like being bossed around and told what to do. But don't worry—I don't bite, just ask whatever you want when you want. Don't push too hard though." The interview then proceeded more smoothly, with the psychologist gathering less information than was usual in a first session, but with Florio making a commitment to come to a second assessment session.

Insight Versus Symptom Reduction

For the relative merits of treatments focused on achieving patient insight or patient symptom reduction, Beutler et al. (2004) reported overall effect sizes of zero in this literature. However, patient coping style may be an important moderator of the relation between the focus of treatment and treatment outcome. By and large, focusing on enhancing patient self-awareness and understanding of their problems works best for patients who are introspective or introverted. In contrast, patients who are impulsive and undercontrolled respond best to a focus on symptom alleviation. That being said, most current treatments focus on helping the client to both (a) better understand his or her experiences and problems *and* (b) make changes in his or her day-to-day life. As with the degree of therapist directiveness, regardless of orientation, it is possible for therapists to adjust the focus of treatment to take into account individual differences in client styles and preferences.

 If you were seeking psychological services, how important would it be to gain an understanding of why you were having a particular problem? If you were able to get over the problem without fully understanding why it occurred, would that be sufficient for you?

Between-Session Assignments

Between-session assignments (also known as homework assignments) are used by many clinical psychologists and other psychotherapists of various theoretical orientations (Kazantzis, Busch, Ronan, & Merrick, 2007; Kazantzis, Lampropoulos, & Deane, 2005). Does it really matter whether a therapist assigns homework in order to consolidate something addressed in the session, and does it matter whether the clients actually do the homework? The answer to both these questions is "yes." In a meta-analysis of 27 CBT studies, Kazantzis, Deane, and Ronan (2000) reported an effect size of $r = .36$ for the association between the use of homework assignments and positive treatment outcomes and an effect size of $r = .22$ for the association between the degree of patient completion of assignments and positive treatment outcomes. Research conducted by Westra, Dozois, and Marcus (2007) suggests that patient compliance in completing homework acts as a moderator on the relation between positive treatment expectations and initial improvement in functioning. In other words, getting involved in between-session assignments appears to be critical in turning hope for improvement into actual improvement.

 Does doing homework between sessions fit with your ideas of what clients do in psychotherapy? Can you think of reasons why completion of between-session assignments is related to a positive treatment outcome?

Some Methodological Cautions Regarding Process-Outcome Research

Almost all of the research we have discussed thus far in the chapter has examined ways in which some characteristic of the client, therapist, or treatment is related to the outcome of therapy. In other words, the researchers are examining correlations between the variables of interest. As we discussed in Chapter 4, it is important to avoid assuming that a significant correlation means that one variable causes the other—one should always carefully examine the study to determine whether some aspects of the study's theoretical framework, methodology, or statistical analyses may hold information critical to understanding what a significant correlation might mean. In the following example, we illustrate the importance of not immediately assuming that a significant correlation indicates that one variable causes another.

Jones and Pulos (1993) reported intriguing results from their analysis of the therapeutic process in psychodynamic and cognitive-behavioral treatments. Based on expert judges' ratings of therapy transcripts from treatment studies using these two forms of therapy, the researchers developed a list of descriptors that characterized each treatment. For example, descriptors of psychodynamic techniques included "Therapist is neutral," "Therapist points out patient's use of defensive maneuvers," "Therapist interprets warded-off or unconscious wishes, feelings, or ideas," and "Memories or reconstructions of infancy and childhood are topics of discussion." Some of the descriptors of cognitive-behavioral techniques were "Therapist explains rationale behind his/her technique or approach to treatment," "Therapist acts to strengthen defenses," "Therapist self-discloses," and "Therapist gives explicit advice and guidance." So far this should seem consistent with our descriptions of these treatment approaches in Chapter 11. The incongruence arose, however, when the researchers correlated the ratings of these techniques with patient outcome. Generally speaking, the two treatments were successful in treating the majority of patients. In the cognitive-behavioral treatment, the use of cognitive-behavioral techniques was not significantly associated with any of the five patient outcome measures, but the use of psychodynamic techniques (by the cognitive-behavioral therapists) was significantly correlated with patient change on four of the five measures. In the psychodynamic treatment, the use of psychodynamic techniques was significantly correlated with change on only one of four measures, and similarly, use of CBT techniques (by the psychodynamic therapists) was correlated with one of four patient outcomes.

How can this be? How is it possible that the use of psychodynamic techniques—but not cognitive-behavioural techniques—by cognitive-behavioral therapists is related to patient improvement? How is it possible that the use of psychodynamic techniques (or CBT techniques either, for that matter) in psychodynamic treatment was unrelated to patient improvement? A careful reading of the study reveals two methodological issues that may explain the rather strange pattern of results. First, researchers rated transcripts from the first, fifth, and fourteenth therapy sessions. Like any other relationship, the therapy relationship evolves over time. Just as you would expect to see different behaviors on a first date compared with a date in an established relationship, what transpires during the first therapy session is likely to be very different from what occurs at the fifth or fourteenth. By combining information about what therapists and patients do when starting treatment with information about what they do partway through and when they have almost completed treatment, the researchers are likely to end up with "averages" of therapist and client behaviors that are not at all representative of what occurs during any specific treatment session. For example, it might be a good thing for a psychodynamic therapist to frequently point out a patient's use of defense mechanisms in the fifth session of therapy, but if the therapist still needs to do this in one of the final sessions, this may actually be an indication that treatment is *not* going well.

A second questionable assumption made in this research is that the more therapists or clients engage in a specific strategy, the better it is for client outcome. By correlating the use of specific techniques with client outcome, that is essentially what the researchers assumed. Is this a valid assumption about therapy? Returning to the date analogy, although you may appreciate your date self-disclosing on some topics, you would probably not respond positively to a person who spent the entire evening providing a revealing account of himself or herself. Likewise, in the realm of psychotherapy, it is relevant to ask whether more therapist self-disclosure in cognitive-behavioral treatment is always better than less. Similarly, is more therapist neutrality in psychodynamic treatment always better than less?

Unfortunately, such methodological problems are relatively common in the process-outcome treatment literature. As pointed out by Stiles (1988) and Stiles and Shapiro (1989), it is inappropriate to assume that a significant correlation necessarily means that a process component (such as a cognitive-behavioral therapist explaining the rationale for the treatment) is crucial in achieving the desired outcome. Likewise, they argued that a nonsignificant correlation does not necessarily mean that the process component is irrelevant to successful outcome. Clinical skill involves adapting the frequency and strength of certain techniques to match the patient's individual needs. Jones and Pulos (1993) found that explaining the rationale for an intervention was characteristic of CBT—but if the patient clearly understands the rationale, why would frequent (and unnecessary) explanations of the rationale be expected to correlate positively and significantly with patient outcome? Presumably, repeated explanations would be necessary only if there were consistent indications that the patient had not fully grasped the nature of the treatment.

It is always important to read carefully the methods and results sections of research articles. The information contained in these sections is crucial for a complete understanding of the nature of the data and analyses used in the study. Because the results of treatment research (whether process-outcome research or treatment outcome research) can have a significant impact on the provision of clinical services, it is essential that consumers of the scientific literature exercise critical and informed judgments in evaluating the relevance and applicability of this research.

Have you developed the habit of carefully reviewing the method and results sections of scientific articles? How easy is it for you to generate hypotheses about the ways that the methods of the study may have influenced their results?

COMMON FACTORS IN PSYCHOTHERAPY

Despite clear differences in guiding theory and preferred intervention techniques among the major approaches to psychotherapy, many clinical psychologists maintain that the effectiveness of all approaches stems from a common set of therapeutic factors. Rosenzweig (1936) is credited with being the first to identify a common set of therapeutic factors. He presented two broad propositions about psychotherapy: first, all therapies share common therapeutic elements that are responsible for client improvement (in particular, the therapeutic relationship and an explanation for the existence of the client's problems) and, second, because all therapies rely on these common factors to bring about change, all therapies should be equivalent in outcome. In considering Rosenzweig's assertion, it is important to note that treatments at that time were all variations on psychoanalytic treatment and that Rosenzweig provided no evidence supporting his claim. Nevertheless, both of these claims have greatly influenced subsequent psychotherapy researchers. We examine the common factors proposition first and consider the equivalency proposition in a later section.

For much of the middle of the twentieth century, the common factors proposition lay dormant and, as described in Chapter 1, there was a proliferation of new theoretical approaches to treatment. In the 1970s, **Jerome Frank** revisited the common factors perspective. Drawing on such diverse sources of data as studies of psychiatric practices, the placebo effect, and anthropological reports of the practices of shamans (or "witch doctors"), Frank developed an intriguing and compelling model to explain all treatment effects (Frank, 1973, 1982). His model begins with a demoralized individual who is distressed and unable to resolve his or her problems. The individual seeks help from a socially sanctioned healer, who provides the healing services that, if successful, result in the restoration of the individual's morale. This occurs by virtue of the healer working in a recognized healing setting, providing a rationale for the person's difficulties, instilling hope that improvement is possible, and using a set of healing rituals to resolve the problems. Frank argued that this model applies to all health care treatments, irrespective of differences in healers (psychologists, mystics), settings (hospitals, religious shrines), or rituals (free association while reclining on a couch, doing between-session assignments, or sacrificing animals to appease angry spirits).

Inspired by Frank's model, psychologists began to develop generic models of psychotherapy that cut across theoretical orientations, to develop lists of possible common factors shared by psychotherapies, and to search for evidence of the influence of these factors. By the 1990s, the common factors perspective had become so popular that Weinberger (1995) identified an interesting dilemma: few

TABLE 14.4   Common Factors in Psychotherapy

Support Factors	Learning Factors	Action Factors
Reduce isolation	Advice	Practice
Provide reassurance	Cognitive learning	Modeling
Therapeutic alliance	Emotional experiencing	Reality testing
Therapist expertise	Insight	Facing fears
Therapist respect, empathy,	Feedback	Working through issues
acceptance, warmth	Exploration of assumptions,	Development of mastery
Catharsis	beliefs, expectations	Behavioral regulation
Release of tension		

Adapted from Lambert and Ogles (2004)

proponents of the common factors explanation for psychotherapeutic changes agreed on what actually constituted the set of hypothesized common factors. As Weinberger wryly noted in the title of his literature review, "common factors aren't so common." In attempting to bring order to the common factors perspective, Weinberger emphasized the importance of the therapeutic relationship, client expectations, confronting problems in therapy, the client's development of a sense of mastery, and the client's attributions for the treatment outcome. Taking a different approach, Lambert and Ogles (2004) used three main dimensions of common factors (support factors, learning factors, and action factors) to categorize the most commonly suggested common factors. Their framework is presented in **Table 14.4**.

The intuitive appeal of the common factors approach and its potential to harness the power of psychotherapy led to the promotion of **integrative treatment models**. These models borrow theories and techniques from the major therapeutic approaches to optimize the influence of the common factors, regardless of the nature of the patient's problems or characteristics (e.g., Hubble, Duncan, & Miller, 1999; Lampropoulos, 2000). There is little doubt that many of the common factors are found in a variety of treatments, but how do we know that they are the *main* elements of treatment responsible for client improvement? The diversity evident among the list of common factors and the inconsistencies in operationalizing the factors have resulted in little cumulative research addressing the importance of these common factors in achieving treatment outcome. There is one notable exception to this state of affairs, a *common* common factor that has received extensive attention from researchers—the **therapeutic alliance**—and it is to this research that we now turn.

Research Perspectives on Common Factors: The Therapeutic Alliance

The therapeutic alliance refers to the quality and strength of the collaborative relationship between client and therapist (Horvath & Bedi, 2002). It includes positive affective bonds (e.g., mutual trust, liking, respect, and caring), consensus about and commitment to the goals of therapy, and a shared sense of partnership in the therapeutic process. Although originally developed within psychodynamic approaches, the construct of therapeutic alliance applies to all approaches to psychotherapy. A series of meta-analyses on the relation between therapeutic alliance, typically measured in the first few sessions of treatment, and treatment outcome have all found the alliance to be a consistent predictor of the impact of treatment. This holds for treatments for adults (e.g., Beutler et al., 2004; Horvath & Bedi, 2002; Martin, Garske, & Davis, 2000) and for adolescents (Shirk & Karver, 2003). The alliance can be assessed from the perspective of the patient, the therapist, and an observer rating videotaped sessions. Although there is little evidence that the numerous measures of the therapeutic alliance are highly intercorrelated, meta-analyses yield essentially the same general effect size, typically close to a weighted r of .20.

To continue with the caution we introduced earlier in the chapter, one of the problems in interpreting the research on the alliance–outcome link is the importance of not inferring causation from correlation. Although it seems obvious that a good alliance is necessary for a good outcome, methodological factors may temper this conclusion. First, a poor alliance can lead to the premature termination of treatment by clients—this has been found, for example, with both cognitive and psychodynamic treatments for borderline personality disorder (Spinhoven, Giesen-Bloo, van Dyck, Kooiman, & Arntz, 2007). Because clients with good alliances are more likely to complete therapy, researchers have a greater chance of obtaining data on treatment effects in clients reporting a strong alliance. As a result, most of what we know about the effect of the therapeutic alliance on treatment outcome is based on data from those who experienced relatively positive therapeutic alliances. Second, as alliance is typically assessed after initial treatment sessions, it is possible that early client improvement may confound the relation between alliance and treatment outcome. In general, studies that were designed specifically to test this possibility have found that early alliance significantly predicts outcome even after statistically controlling for the effects of early improvement (e.g., Barber, Connolly, Crits-Christoph, Gladis, & Siqueland, 2000).

Before leaving this section on the therapeutic alliance, there is a final point to consider. The research on the alliance–outcome link appears compelling, which lends credence to claims about the power of common factors in therapy. However, think back to Chapter 11, in which we described alternatives to traditionally delivered psychotherapy such as telehealth, self-administered, and computer-administered treatments. As we indicated in that chapter, there is growing evidence that these forms of psychological intervention, when grounded in evidence-based therapist-administered treatments, can be very helpful treatments for many people. Is it possible to build an alliance without being physically present with the client? One could make the case that a therapeutic alliance can be established with a health service provider who is hundreds of miles away and who is known to the patient only by video link or a voice on the telephone line. What about the user of a self-help manual or a computer therapy program—can there be a form of therapeutic alliance with the materials or the "invisible" developer of the materials? If there is a sense of connection with the computer program, does this come from the material being presented in an engaging and empathic manner in order to enhance the active involvement of the client? Is it meaningful to consider this type of connection to be a form of therapeutic alliance, or is it something else?

How do you make sense of this situation? It is fairly easy to understand how a good alliance can positively influence the outcome of treatment. How is it possible that treatments without any apparent therapeutic alliance can be successful? What does this mean, if anything, about the role of therapeutic alliance in promoting change in therapy?

Research Perspectives on Common Factors: Psychotherapy Equivalence

As mentioned previously in the chapter, Rosenzweig (1936) proposed that, because all psychotherapies are based on common curative factors, they must be equivalent in their effects. He referred to this hypothesized equivalence of psychotherapies as the **Dodo bird verdict**. This is an allusion to Lewis Carroll's *Alice in Wonderland*, in which an argument about who had won a race was resolved by the Dodo bird, who announced: "*Everybody* has won, and *all* must have prizes." Lewis Carroll's Dodo bird verdict was a satirical jab at political committees, as it described the outcome of a caucus race in which competitors started at different points and ran in different directions for half an hour.

Like the common factors perspective itself, the concept of psychotherapy equivalence received little attention during the decades in which many forms of psychotherapy were being developed. However, the Dodo bird verdict was revitalized by Luborsky, Singer, and Luborsky's (1975) review of treatment research in which they concluded there was no substantial evidence of differential treatment effects. In subsequent literature reviews, **Lester Luborsky** and colleagues (Luborsky et al., 1993; Luborsky et al., 1999; Luborsky et al., 2002) reiterated this position and concluded there was overwhelming evidence that all therapies were equal and that psychotherapies did not have distinct, specific effects. As efforts to establish empirically supported treatments began, some psychologists argued that psychotherapy itself is empirically supported (e.g., Elliott, 1998) and that, for effective treatment, all that is needed is a therapeutic alliance and efforts to mobilize the client's capacity to resolve problems and distress (Bohart, O'Hara, & Leitner, 1998).

To properly consider the evidence on the impact of different psychotherapies, it is important to impose some rules. Otherwise, like Carroll's caucus race, it is comparable to having competitors in a race start at different points and run in different directions. The first rule in evaluating the accuracy of the Dodo bird verdict is that empirical evidence must be considered. Rosenzweig's claim of general therapy equivalence was based solely on the hypothesis that all curative effects in therapy are due to common factors. By applying this first rule to current forms of psychotherapy, it is easy to see that this broad claim of equivalence (i.e., that any treatment provided by a psychotherapist, regardless of the nature of the client's problem or life context, is likely to be as effective as any other possible treatment) is simply untenable because not all forms of psychotherapy have been empirically evaluated. The second rule deals with the type of evidence that can be considered in evaluating the impact of different psychotherapies. In this regard, both treatment outcome studies and comparative treatment studies are relevant. Treatment outcome studies are experiments in which the impact of a treatment is compared with a control condition in which no services are provided (typically, a wait-list control group). In contrast, comparative treatment studies are experiments in which the differential impact of at least two treatments are compared, and a no-treatment control group may or may not be included. Of course, if there was evidence for psychotherapy equivalence from these types of studies it would mean that only the

Lewis Carroll's Dodo bird. (*Source:* Hulton Archive/ Getty Images, Inc.)

psychotherapies that were evaluated in the studies could be assumed to be equivalent, as the subset of therapies that have been evaluated are by no means a representative sample of those therapies offered by clinicians (Kazdin, 1995).

As described at several earlier points in the book, to accurately consider the huge amount of treatment research we must use meta-analyses. In Chapter 12, we described the general findings from the important Smith, Glass, and Miller (1980) meta-analysis. As we indicated, Smith et al. calculated the efficacy of various types of treatment based on treatment outcome studies and reported that cognitive and cognitive-behavioral treatments had the largest effect sizes (d values of 1.31 and 1.24, respectively), followed by behavioral (.91), psychodynamic (.78), and humanistic treatments (.63), and, finally, developmental treatments (including vocational-personal development counseling and "undifferentiated counseling" (.42). This evidence certainly suggests that treatments are not equivalent.

Proponents of the psychotherapy equivalence perspective point to the importance of other analyses conducted by Smith et al., specifically comparisons of therapy "classes" in which behavioral ($d = .98$) and verbal ($d = .85$) treatments were found to produce comparable effects. In their categorization system, Smith et al. included cognitive-behavioral, behavior modification, systematic desensitization, and other behavioral treatments in the behavioral class; they included psychodynamic, humanistic, and cognitive treatments in the verbal class. As the researchers themselves noted, this categorization scheme was arbitrary but, they argued, defensible (e.g., all behavioral treatments focused primarily on attaining behavioral change). Given our description of the various orientations in Chapter 11 and the fact that cognitive therapies routinely include behavioral elements, it is extremely difficult to justify not including cognitive treatments with behavioral treatments. In other words, the apparently compelling evidence for equivalence of therapy classes in the Smith et al. meta-analysis is undermined by the reliance on a questionable classification of the classes of treatment.

Smith and colleagues also conducted analyses on data from 56 comparative outcome studies of the behavioral and verbal classes of treatment. Even with the classification error, there were significant differences between the two classes of therapy ($d = .96$ for behavioral treatments and $d = .77$ for verbal treatments). However, when the researchers then adjusted results for something they called *measurement tractability* (measures of anxiety, self-esteem, and global adjustment were rated as more tractable than were such measures as somatic complaints and life adjustment), the group differences disappeared. The basis for this statistical adjustment is hard to determine, as the researchers did not make this adjustment in any of the hundreds of other analyses they reported. Although frequently cited as evidence in support of the Dodo bird verdict, the influential meta-analysis published by Smith et al. yielded numerous results that do not support a verdict of psychotherapy equivalence. Whether examined by therapy subclasses (i.e., cognitive, cognitive-behavioral, behavioral, psychodynamic, humanistic, and developmental) or by client conditions within therapy subclasses, clear differences among treatment effects were evident.

The results of other meta-analyses are relevant to an examination of the possibility of psychotherapy equivalence. As we described in Chapter 13, meta-analyses examining treatment effects in the child and adolescent treatment literature have found clear orientation differences, with behavioral treatments being more effective than other treatments (e.g., Weiss & Weisz, 1995). In a meta-analysis focused specifically on ensuring the clinical representativeness of their results, Shadish, Matt, Navarro, and Phillips (2000) selected studies in which clients, treatments, and therapists were representative of typical clinical settings. In the 90 studies they examined, the cognitive-behavioral family of treatments was more efficacious than other treatment approaches. There have also been numerous focused meta-analyses dealing with the treatment of such specific conditions as depression, insomnia, smoking cessation, and pain, the majority of which have shown evidence of differential treatment effects (Westmacott & Hunsley, 2007).

Like Luborsky, **Bruce Wampold** has been a vocal proponent of the psychotherapy equivalency position. He has been highly critical of evidence-based treatment initiatives because, in his view, they have tended to overemphasize differences among treatments (e.g., Wampold, 2007; Wampold & Bhati, 2004). In a direct test of the Dodo bird verdict, Wampold et al. (1997) conducted a meta-analysis with data from adult treatment studies published between 1970 and 1995 that compared at least two treatments. Wampold et al. reported an average d of .19, which, despite statistical significance, was described as a small and relatively unimportant difference. Accordingly, they interpreted their results as strongly supporting the Dodo bird verdict. They did explicitly caution, however, that their results should not be taken as evidence that all psychotherapies are equally efficacious or as efficacious as those included in their sample. It has been pointed out, though, that the majority of the studies included in their analyses were comparisons among different forms of CBT, not different orientations (Crits-Christoph, 1997). Additionally, as emphasized by Chambless (2002), it is erroneous to conclude that a relatively small average difference among treatments necessarily indicates that the difference between treatment options for a specific disorder is also small. Even if the average effect is relatively small, Chambless pointed out that there could be considerable variability in the size of differential treatment effects for a specific disorder. Finally, to put Wampold and colleagues' results into context, using the concept of number needed to treat (introduced in Chapter 10), a d of .19 means that nine patients would need to be treated with the more efficacious treatment to have one more treatment success than would occur if the less efficacious treatment was used.

A focused meta-analysis conducted by Siev and Chambless (2007) nicely illustrates that some treatments are more efficacious than others. There is evidence that both CBT and a much simpler form of treatment, relaxation therapy, can help with a number of anxiety disorders. Siev and Chambless examined all published studies in which these two therapies were compared specifically for the treatment of (a) generalized anxiety disorder and (b) panic disorder. With respect to generalized anxiety disorder, both treatments were comparable in improving symptoms of anxiety and anxiety-related thoughts; they were also equivalent in their ability to help patients achieve clinically significant changes in functioning (about 45% of patients for each treatment). A very different picture emerged with the treatment of panic disorder. In these studies, patients receiving CBT achieved significantly greater reductions in panic symptoms and panic-related thoughts compared to patients receiving relaxation therapy. In terms of achieving clinically significant changes in functioning, CBT significantly out-performed relaxation therapy: 72% of CBT patients versus 50% of relaxation therapy patients achieved clinical significant changes. Obviously, some efficacious treatments can be more efficacious than others!

We now return to the rules we originally described to evaluate the Dodo bird verdict, because there is an important hidden issue about comparative treatment studies that warrants attention. In order to mount a comparative treatment study, researchers need adequate financial resources to cover the cost of training and/or paying therapists, paying for the work of research assistants over several years, and the cost of equipment (e.g., computers, recording equipment) used in the study. In most instances these costs amount to at least many tens of thousands of dollars, which means that researchers need financial support from a granting agency. This need is likely to exert a critical, but typically unrecognized, effect on the nature of the study. For a granting agency to approve the funds for a comparative treatment study, there must be convincing evidence that the proposed study is worthwhile—it must address a relevant question with a set of methods that are appropriate. Accordingly, to build the strongest possible case for the study, plans for comparative treatment studies almost always involve the head-to-head comparison of treatments that have already been shown to be efficacious. After all, the research is intended to determine which treatment is the best one. Research comparing a treatment with established efficacy to one that has no empirical support, on the other hand, is unlikely to be funded—in addition to being unethical it would be seen as a waste of time and money to compare a strong treatment with one that has no existing empirical support. The net result of this is that the comparative treatment literature largely consists of comparisons among treatments that are known to be efficacious. If all the studied treatments are efficacious, it is hardly surprising that only small differences among the treatments emerge from comparative treatment studies.

Even though there is no consensus on the question of psychotherapy equivalence, there is an alternative to the diametrically opposed positions of absolute equivalency or absolute specificity (Chambless, 2002; Westmacott & Hunsley, 2007). The evidence seems to indicate that for most conditions, the outcomes of different treatments are not equivalent. However, in a small number of cases, such as adult depression, several different treatments have sufficient evidence to be considered as first-line options for clients, including several forms of cognitive-behavioral treatment, interpersonal therapy, short-term psychodynamic therapy, and process-experiential therapy. For the treatment of other disorders, even if there is strong evidence that some treatments are more efficacious than others, the less efficacious treatments should not be dismissed out of hand. Evidence-based practice emphasizes first using the intervention that has the greatest support, but if the intervention proves to be unsuccessful with a given patient, turning to treatments with less empirical support (i.e., second- and third-line treatments) is entirely appropriate. The strategy of turning to other treatment options when a first-line treatment has not worked is used routinely in medicine, and there is no reason that the full range of evidence-based psychotherapy options should not be considered with psychotherapy patients.

EMPIRICALLY SUPPORTED THERAPY RELATIONSHIPS

As we described at the outset of the chapter, research on psychological interventions comprises both studies of treatment outcome and studies of the relation between process and outcome. If you look back at the evidence-based treatment initiatives we presented in Chapters 12 and 13, you will see that all of these efforts have been based solely on the results of treatment outcome studies. To highlight the relevance of process-outcome research for evidence-based psychological practice, the APA Psychotherapy Division (Division 29) established a task force in 1999 to identify, operationalize, and disseminate information on **empirically supported therapy relationships** (ESRs). The two aims of the task force were to (a) identify elements of effective therapy relationships and (b) determine methods of tailoring therapy to individual patient characteristics. The results of the task force, chaired by **John Norcross**, were published in a special issue of the division's journal, *Psychotherapy* (Norcross, 2001a), with a more detailed report subsequently published as a book (Norcross, 2002).

As with other evidence-based initiatives, some of the key decision points addressed by the task force involved determining what type of evidence (experimental studies, correlational studies, or both) and how much evidence was required to conclude that a treatment element was empirically supported. In the end, the decision was made to include both experimental and correlational studies and to categorize treatment elements as *demonstrably effective, promising and probably effective,* and *insufficient research to judge* (Norcross, 2001b). Unfortunately, as with most process-outcome research, this initiative was limited to studies of treatments for adults. **Table 14.5** presents the listings developed by this task force for general elements of the therapy relationship. Given the evidence presented previously in this chapter, some of the elements listed in these tables will already be familiar to you.

Alliance and Cohesion

With respect to the general elements of the therapy relationship (Table 14.5), there is little doubt that the quality of the therapeutic alliance can influence treatment outcome. As you know from our earlier discussion, the extent to which alliance and outcome are causally linked is a matter of intense investigation. Nevertheless, evidence indicates that efforts to establish and maintain a good working relationship with clients are important for all therapists. In group therapy, there are numerous relationships—between each client and the therapist, as well as among clients. The totality of all these relationships is referred to as **cohesion.** Thus, the promotion of cohesion in a group treatment modality

---

TABLE 14.5   Empirically Supported Therapy Relationship Task Force Listing of General Elements of the Therapy Relationship

Demonstrably Effective Elements

- Therapeutic alliance
- Cohesion in group therapy
- Empathy
- Goal consensus and collaboration

Promising and Probably Effective Elements

- Positive regard (treating clients in a warm and accepting manner)
- Congruence/genuineness (the therapist being himself/herself in the therapy and being fully involved in the treatment process)
- Feedback
- Repair of alliance ruptures (addressing any problems that develop in the therapeutic relationship)
- Self-disclosure
- Management of countertransference (therapist appropriately managing both negative and positive feelings toward the client)
- Quality of relational interpretations (the accuracy and appropriateness of the therapist's interpretations of interpersonal themes in the client's life)

Adapted from Norcross (2002)

---

also makes good sense. Unresolved interpersonal conflicts, unexamined tensions between group members, and feelings of exclusion or rejection among group members can all undermine the impact of group treatment.

Empathy

Empathy is typically defined as the ability to understand another person's experience. The meta-analytic finding that effect size of therapist empathy on outcome is $r = .32$ (Greenberg, Elliott, Watson, & Bohart, 2001) underlines the importance of the therapist's interpersonal sensitivity in both understanding patients and effectively communicating with them. This is true regardless of therapeutic orientation or the nature of the patient's presenting problem. As discussed in relation to the Lafferty et al. (1989) study, the patient's sense of being understood by the therapist appears to be directly related to the effectiveness of the therapist.

Goal Consensus and Collaboration

The final demonstrably effective element, goal consensus and collaboration, highlights the critical need for patient and therapist to work together to set and achieve the goals of therapy. Explicit agreement on the nature and direction of treatment seems essential if therapy is to have an optimal influence on the patient.

Client Reactance and Functional Impairment

The ESR task force concluded there were two main client characteristics that require the tailoring of treatment in order to achieve therapeutic gains. Resistance or reactance, as already discussed, requires that the therapist adapt a style that either emphasizes therapist directiveness (for low-reactant clients) or client self-direction (for high-reactant clients). Skillful therapists should be able to make such modifications to treatment, assuming of course that they have accurately gauged the client's level of reactance. When dealing with clients presenting with significant functional impairment (i.e., severe distress and disruptions in functioning that are likely manifested across several life domains), therapists must appreciate the limits that such impairment may place on whatever gains are possible in treatment. However, the negative effects of functional impairments can be partially overcome by increasing the frequency or the duration of treatment (Beutler, Rocco, Moleiro, & Talebi, 2002). This increase allows the client and therapist expanded opportunities to address specific client concerns and to ensure the generalization of gains across problematic life situations.

Recommendations

As a final step, the task force issued a number of practice, training, research, and policy recommendations based on its findings. For our purposes, we will highlight the practice and training recommendations from the task force, which are listed in **Table 14.6**. Consistent with the strength of evidence they found in the literature, the task force recommended that mental health training programs, including

TABLE 14.6 Empirically Supported Therapy Relationship Task Force Practice and Training Recommendations

For Practice

1. Create a therapy relationship characterized by the elements found to be demonstrably and probably effective.
2. Adapt the therapy relationship to specific patient characteristics shown to enhance therapeutic outcome.
3. Evaluate patients' responses to the therapy relationship and ongoing treatment in order to improve the process and outcome of treatment.
4. Use both empirically supported therapy relationships and empirically supported treatments to obtain the best outcomes for the patient.

For Training

1. Explicitly train students in the effective elements of the therapy relationship.
2. Develop accreditation and certification criteria for assessing the adequacy of training in empirically supported therapy relationships.

Adapted from the Steering Committee of the ESR Task Force (2001)

those in clinical psychology, provide specific training on elements of ESRs. Likewise, they encouraged mental health practitioners, including clinical psychologists, to actively use ESRs in their clinical work. It is especially noteworthy that the task force encouraged clinicians to (a) routinely monitor their treatment services and (b) strive to integrate aspects of ESRs and ESTs in their clinical work in order to provide the best services possible to clients. This integrated approach to intervention brings together much of what research on clinical psychology has to offer patients seeking help for psychological problems. It also avoids the unnecessary tendency, sometimes evident in clinical psychology, to pit evidence for common or nonspecific treatment factors against what we have learned from treatment outcome research.

PROFILE BOX 14.1

DR. JOHN C. NORCROSS

I received my baccalaureate in psychology from Rutgers University and earned my doctorate in clinical psychology at the University of Rhode Island after completing an internship at Brown University School of Medicine. Currently I am a professor of psychology and Distinguished University Fellow at the University of Scranton, a clinical psychologist in part-time practice, and the editor of *Journal of Clinical Psychology: In Session.* Thus far in my career I have authored more than 300 publications on psychotherapy and behavior change, including cowriting or editing 17 books (e.g., *Clinician's Guide to Evidence-Based Practice in Mental Health and Addictions, Psychotherapy Relationships That Work,* and the *Insider's Guide to Graduate Programs in Clinical and Counseling Psychology*). I have

Dr. John C. Norcross

served as president of the APA Division of Clinical Psychology, the APA Division of Psychotherapy, and the International Society of Clinical Psychology. My professional awards include APA's Distinguished Career Contributions to Education and Training Award, Pennsylvania Professor of the Year from the Carnegie Foundation, and election to the National Academies of Practice. My wife, two children, and I live in northeast Pennsylvania with our deranged cat.

How did you choose to become a clinical psychologist?

As a college student, I was torn among psychology, English, and philosophy. In the end, psychology won out because of its pragmatic purpose and my fascination with human behavior. How can one not be fascinated by human behavior, what makes us tick, and how to improve life?

What are the most rewarding parts of your job as a clinical psychologist?

I enjoy a bounty of rewards, but three stand out: Contributing to a healthier and happier world; integrating teaching, research, and practice; and learning more about human behavior and myself. In all of these pursuits, I am blessed to work with fabulous students, colleagues, and clients every day. Several recent studies have identified psychologist and professor as two of the 10 best jobs in the United States. I absolutely concur.

What is the greatest challenge you face as a clinical psychologist?

Time—finding the time to do all the things I enjoy. Like other busy professionals, clinical psychologists are constantly juggling the demands of their professional careers and their private lives. In addition, I am challenged to balance the hours I devote to teaching, research, writing, psychotherapy, supervision, administration, and my other responsibilities. It can be exhausting, but always interesting and rewarding.

What do you see as the most important elements in successful psychotherapy?

The research is clear here. The lion's share of successful psychotherapy is determined by the patient's contribution—severity of the disorder, positive expectations, motivation to change, desire to work in therapy, and so on. Next is the therapist's contribution in the form of cultivating a positive therapeutic relationship and employing an evidence-based treatment method. Then there is the person of the therapist in the form of his/her interpersonal skills, emotional health, and capacity to care. We need to look at optimal combinations of all these elements—patient, therapy relationship, treatment method, and therapist—in enhancing the effectiveness of psychotherapy.

How do you integrate science and practice in your work?

By thinking with the mind of a scientist and feeling with the heart of a humanist, it comes easy to me. The results of scientific research inform my clinical practice, and my practice helps me to formulate my research questions. My research on the effectiveness of therapeutic relationships and the psychotherapist's own personal therapy, for two examples, came directly from my clinical work. The historical gap or rift between science and practice is narrowing.

> *What do you see as the most exciting changes in the field of clinical psychology?*
>
> Lots of exciting changes: the ascendancy of evidence-based practices; the incorporation of technology (virtual reality, computer-based programs) into clinical work; the attention now directed to the mental health needs of traditionally marginalized populations (such as ethnic minorities, gay and lesbian, and the physically disabled); the discovery of effective means to match clients to particular relationships and treatments that work best for them; the rise of neuroscience and what it can tell us about psychotherapy; and the movement toward psychologists securing prescription privileges.

EMPIRICALLY BASED PRINCIPLES OF THERAPEUTIC CHANGE

In an effort to provide clear and unambiguous guidance to clinicians on how best to integrate the EST and the ESR perspectives, psychotherapy researchers **Louis Castonguay** and **Larry Beutler** developed an initiative to identify **empirically based principles of therapeutic change** (Castonguay & Beutler, 2006a). Their starting point was the assumption that psychotherapy research is sufficiently advanced to allow definition of the basic principles of therapeutic change in a manner that is not tied to any specific orientation or narrowly defined set of concepts. According to Beutler and Castonguay (2006), such principles should be general statements that identify participant characteristics (i.e., both therapist and patient), relational conditions, therapist behaviors, and types of intervention that are likely to lead to therapeutic change. Principles should be more general than a description of techniques and more specific than theoretical models.

In forming their task force, Castonguay and Beutler went to great lengths to ensure representation of a variety of perspectives by selecting experts in the adult treatment of each of four problem areas (mood disorder, anxiety disorders, personality disorders, and substance abuse disorders) who were also strongly affiliated with either the ESR or the EST perspectives. To adequately cover the relevant literature, they planned a 3 x 4 matrix with the domains of participant factors, relationship factors, and treatment factors cutting across the four problem areas. Those experts focusing on participant factors were asked to review what was known about the patient and therapist characteristics covered in the ESR report (Norcross, 2002) and other relevant reviews of this literature. Task force members working on relationship factors were also asked to assess the status of research by reviewing these sources of information. Finally, those working on treatment factors were asked to review Nathan and Gorman's books (1998, 2002), the EST chapter by Chambless and Ollendick (2001), and other relevant sources.

On completion of these reviews, members discussed the principles of change that emerged from the work. By comparing these emergent sets of principles, members distinguished between principles that were similar across the problem areas and those that were relatively unique to a specific problem area. Once common principles were identified, task force members worked on identifying and refining the list of principles that were specific to each problem area. Beutler and Castonguay (2006) cautioned that none of these principles has been empirically tested, which is why the term *empirically based* rather than *empirically supported* was used to describe them. The main common principles that resulted from this process are presented in **Table 14.7**.

TABLE 14.7   Common Empirically Based Principles of Therapeutic Change

Client variables hypothesized to *reduce* the likelihood of benefiting from therapy

- Greater pretreatment impairment
- Presence of a personality disorder
- Financial/occupational difficulties
- Significant interpersonal problems during early development
- Unfavorable expectations about problems and their treatment

Relational conditions hypothesized to *increase* the likelihood of benefiting from therapy

- Strong therapeutic alliance established and maintained during treatment
- Strong level of group cohesion developed and maintained during group therapy

Therapist behaviors hypothesized to *increase* the likelihood of benefiting from therapy

- High degree of collaboration with clients
- Empathic response
- Attitude of authenticity, caring, warmth, and acceptance
- Limited number of accurate relational interpretations
- Sensitivity to alliance ruptures and addressing these ruptures in an empathic and flexible way
- Provision of a structured treatment and a consistent but flexible focus on the application of his/her interventions
- Skillful use of nondirective techniques

Intervention targets hypothesized to *lead* to therapeutic change

- Intrapersonal issues
- Interpersonal issues related to client's clinical problems
- Problematic cognitions
- Maladaptive behavioral, emotional, or physiological responses
- Client self-exploration
- Acceptance, tolerance, and full experience of emotions
- Control over extreme emotions

Adapted from Castonguay and Beutler (2006b)

Although lengthy and, at times, rather too general in nature, the information presented in Table 14.7 is the first attempt in the history of clinical psychology to use empirical evidence in fully considering the roles of participant, relationship, and techniques in therapy. This will serve as an important starting point for future evidence-based initiatives and could be applied to the research on treatments for children and adolescents. As Castonguay and Beutler (2006b) cautioned, the principles governing these factors do not operate in isolation, as the successful implementation of an effective technique is based on a collaborative process within a well-established relationship in which the therapist is empathic and genuine. Researchers have just begun to examine these complex interactions, and the future of psychotherapy research holds the promise of many exciting findings that will lead to improvements in the quality and impact of our treatments.

To date, there has been no attempt to develop comparable empirically based principles of change relevant to services for children, adolescents, and families. Steps have been taken, however, to examine the components of evidence-based treatments in order to develop a repertoire of evidence-based treatment strategies for clinicians to use. Rather than focus on the treatment of a disorder *per se*, the emphasis here is on matching specific strategies (originally developed as part of an evidence-based treatment for a disorder) to specific problems that may occur across disorders or even when a diagnosis is not warranted (Chorpita, Daleiden, & Weisz, 2005). For example, in many evidence-based treatments for youth there are a common set of strategies to help improve assertiveness or problem-solving skills. A psychologist trained in using these strategies should be able to apply them whenever they are appropriate for a client, not just as part of an established evidence-based treatment. In a related way, McCarty and Weisz (2007) advocated determining whether there are common components across evidence-based treatments, regardless of the treatment orientation (McCarty & Weisz, 2007). For example, a range of evidence-based treatments for depressed youth, including cognitive-behavioral therapy, interpersonal therapy, and attachment-based family therapy, address issues of social relationship and communication skills. Therefore, when treating a depressed adolescent, it may be critical to (a) include some focus on these skills in treatment and (b) use treatment strategies that match the client's characteristics and needs in addressing these skills.

SUMMARY AND CONCLUSIONS

Having identified in Chapters 12 and 13 that there are evidence-based psychological interventions that are helpful in treating diverse disorders in adults and children, in this chapter we considered the elements of psychotherapy that facilitate change. The identification of common factors that cut across treatments holds an intuitive appeal. However, the task of examining these common factors in a systematic and consistent fashion has proved challenging. Over time, research has become more sophisticated in attending to the relative significance of different factors in influencing the change process at different stages. In general, clients with long-standing serious interpersonal difficulties and current acute stressors face greater challenges in benefiting from psychotherapy. Considerable progress has been made in identifying other client characteristics that moderate the effects of different therapeutic approaches. In matching interventions to best meet client needs, psychologists must be sensitive to psychological variables such as reactance. Among the many variables examined in process-outcome research, one robust finding stands out: across all types of psychotherapy, the nature of the therapeutic relationship is an important ingredient facilitating change. The establishment of a collaborative relationship in which the client feels understood and in which therapist and client agree on goals sets the stage for facilitating change.

We have highlighted some of the intense debates over interpretation of meta-analytic findings concerning the equivalence or differential effectiveness of different types of therapy. As with all research, a careful analysis of the research methods and statistical analyses used in these meta-analyses is necessary to fully and accurately understand the empirical findings. Even though these debates will continue, an evidence-based approach to treatment recognizes that all treatments with established efficacy may play in a role in the services provided to clients. Based on exhaustive reviews of the process-outcome literature and the treatment outcome literature, there are a number of treatment principles that reflect the combined wisdom and expertise of proponents of ESRs and ESTs. Efforts such as these enable us to better understand the ways that psychological interventions can assist a diverse clientele with diverse problems.

Critical Thinking Questions

How important is it that clients and therapists are similar in terms of key demographic variables? Can a male therapist possibly help a female client, or can a young therapist possibly help an elderly client?

How should the therapeutic alliance evolve over the course of successful psychological intervention?

Are good therapists born or trained?

How can we explain the apparent effectiveness of different types of treatments for some specific disorders (such as depression)?

Key Terms

cohesion: the interpersonal connectedness that occurs among participants in group therapy

common factors: therapeutic elements that occur in all or most treatments that are believed to be critical for successful client outcomes

Dodo bird verdict: in the context of psychotherapy research, this is the view that all psychotherapies are equally effective

empirically based principles of therapeutic change: client, therapist, therapeutic relationship, and treatment factors that research has found to be associated with successful treatment

empirically supported therapy relationships: aspects of the therapeutic relationship that research indicates has found to be associated with successful treatment

integrative treatment models: theoretical models that explicitly incorporate into their framework aspects of other theoretical approaches (such as psychodynamic and experiential) and, frequently, common factors

process research: this type of research examines patterns, using therapist and/or client data, that are evident within therapy sessions

process-outcome research: research that examines the relation between variables related to the process of providing psychotherapy and the outcome of therapy

reactance: the tendency to react against attempts to directly influence one's behavior

therapeutic alliance: a concept that encompasses the quality and strength of the collaborative relationship between client and therapist

Key Names

Larry Beutler

Louis Castonguay

Jerome Frank

Lester Luborsky

John Norcross

David Orlinsky

Bruce Wampold

ADDITIONAL RESOURCES

BOOKS

Castonguay, L. G., & Beutler, L. E. (Eds.). (2006a). *Principles of therapeutic change that work*. New York: Oxford University Press.

Lambert, M. J. (Ed.). (2004). *Bergin and Garfield's handbook of psychotherapy and behavior change* (5th ed). New York: John Wiley & Sons.

Norcross, J. C. (Ed.). (2002). *Psychotherapy relationships that work: Therapist contributions and responsiveness to patients*. London: Oxford University Press.

Norcross, J. C., Beutler, L. E., & Levant, R. F. (Eds). (2006). *Evidence-based practices in mental health: Debate and dialogue on the fundamental questions*. Washington, DC: American Psychological Association.

JOURNALS

Journal of Clinical Psychology

Journal of Consulting and Clinical Psychology

Psychotherapy

Psychotherapy Research

Check It Out!

For more information on empirically supported therapy relationships, go to: http://academic.scranton.edu/faculty/NORCROSS/relations.html

The Web site of the Society for Psychotherapy Research (a multidisciplinary organization that encourages research on all forms of psychotherapy) can be found at: http://www.psychotherapy-research.org/

The Web site of the Society for the Exploration of Psychotherapy Integration (an organization for mental health professionals interested in exploring the interface between differing approaches to psychotherapy) can be found at: http://www.cyberpsych.org/sepi/

CHAPTER 15

Clinical Health Psychology, Clinical Neuropsychology, and Forensic Psychology

The practice of psychology is the observation, description, evaluation, interpretation and or modification of human behavior by the application of psychological principles, methods, or procedures, for the purpose of preventing or eliminating symptomatic, maladaptive, or undesired behavior, and of enhancing interpersonal relationships, work and life adjustment, personal effectiveness, behavioral health, and mental health.

Association of State
and Provincial Psychology Boards

INTRODUCTION

Throughout this book we have emphasized the diversity of issues addressed by clinical psychologists, the range of settings in which they are employed, and the growing number of populations with which they work. Across all these types of work, clinical psychologists rely on their knowledge of normal functioning, research methods, professional issues, assessment, diagnosis, case formulation, and intervention. As you learned in earlier chapters, clinical psychology has expanded its boundaries from an early focus on mental health to address a broad array of issues including physical health (Belar, 2008; Leventhal, Weinman, Leventhal, & Phillips, 2008), brain–behavior links (Boake, 2008; Wilson, 2008), and forensic work

(Magaleta & Verdeyen, 2005; Packer, 2008). In this chapter, we will examine in greater depth three areas of clinical practice: clinical health psychology, clinical neuropsychology, and forensic psychology. There is great variability in the definitions and scope of these areas of practice. Some jurisdictions have specialty requirements to practice in these areas, whereas in other jurisdictions, practice in these areas is subsumed under the umbrella of clinical psychology. Psychologists with advanced training in these specialized areas can earn board certification from the American Board of Clinical Health Psychology, the American Board of Clinical Neuropsychology, and the American Board of Forensic Psychology.

We have touched on some of these areas of practice in earlier chapters. In the chapter on intellectual assessment (Chapter 6), we introduced cognitive assessment, a central component of many clinical neuropsychological services; and in the chapter on prevention (Chapter 10), we described health promotion activities. All clinical psychologists must be knowledgeable about the links between physical and mental health, be sensitive to the possibility of organic problems contributing to psychological impairment, and be aware that their work may be subpoenaed and they may be required to testify in court. In this chapter, we profile psychologists in health psychology (Dr. Alexandra Quittner), clinical neuropsychology (Dr. Tony Strickland), and forensic psychology (Dr. Stephen Lally). Practice in these three areas involves collaboration with other professionals, including physicians, occupational therapists, lawyers, and judges. Psychologists must work collaboratively with other professions while maintaining their professional autonomy. Depending on the setting in which the psychologist works, this collaboration may entail infrequent contact via phone or reports, or may involve regular team meetings and case conferences (Belar, 2008).We briefly address assessment and intervention issues in each area.

CLINICAL HEALTH PSYCHOLOGY

Twentieth-century advances in sanitation and medicine dramatically reduced the effects of infectious diseases on morbidity and mortality, so that lifestyle factors replaced germs as the major threat to a person's health (Poole, Hunt Matheson, & Cox, 2005). Health is affected by individual behaviors and habits, including diet, sleep, level of physical activity, and consumption of alcohol and tobacco. In addition, it is affected by moods such as anger, anxiety, and sadness. The links between exposure to psychosocial stress and health outcomes are also well established (Schneiderman, Ironson, & Siegel, 2005). Finally, advances in medical technology greatly increased the life expectancy of people living with serious illnesses such as cardiovascular disease, cancer, and HIV/AIDS. All of these developments within public health, medicine, and psychology have set the stage for psychologists to play a significant role in health promotion, treatment of disease, and rehabilitation (Leventhal et al., 2008).

Lifestyle factors have replaced germs as the major threat to health. (*Source:* Blend/Image Source Limited)

Definitions of Health and Disability

In 1980, the World Health Organization (WHO) developed the *International Classification of Functioning, Disability and Health* (ICF) to provide a standard language to describe health (see Chapter 3). The most recent update of the ICF defines *functioning* in terms of body functions, activities, and participation. In parallel, the ICF defines **disability** as impairment, activity limitation, and participation restriction (WHO, 2002). Within a medical model, disability is considered a characteristic of a person, requiring treatment of that person to correct the problem. In contrast, within a social model, disability is viewed as a function of both the physical environment and the social environment. WHO has adopted an integrated or **biopsychosocial model** that takes into account biological, individual, and social factors associated with the individual's participation in various activities. According to this model, an individual's functioning or disability is determined by the interaction between health conditions (diseases, disorders, and injuries) and contextual factors. Contextual factors include individual characteristics such as gender, age, coping style, social background, education, occupation, temperament, and behavior, as well as variables that are external to the individual including climate, physical environment, societal attitudes, and finally, legal and social structures. Impairment can, but does not necessarily, lead to restrictions in activity and in diminished participation. For example, Chantalle, who has juvenile diabetes, has a bodily impairment (pancreatic dysfunction) that is controlled by insulin injections, so she has no limitation in activities. However, because she is anxious about independently monitoring her blood sugar levels (individual contextual variable) and no teacher has offered to support her (environmental contextual variable), she is unable to participate in a school trip. Interventions to help Chantalle could focus on diminishing her anxiety as well as on strategies to mobilize environmental supports. Edward, who sustained a spinal injury in a motorcycle accident, has a serious impairment (paralysis) as well as an activity limitation in that he is unable to drive or to use public transport; however, he is a determined person who uses a specially adapted transportation system as he participates in a wide range of activities.

To get an idea of the scope of health-related problems, it is useful to look at national data on the numbers of people whose lives are affected by health problems. Data from the 2006 National Health Interview Survey (NHIS) conducted by the Centers for Disease Control and Prevention National Center for Health Statistics provided estimates for the noninstitutionalized U.S. civilian population (Adams, Lucas, & Barnes, 2008). NHIS data revealed that 34.4 million people reported that their usual activities were limited by one or more chronic health conditions. Not surprisingly, the disability rate increases with age. The rate of activity limitation was lowest among children under 12 (7%); in adults ages 45–64 the rate rose to 16%. In adults over 75, the rate rose sharply to 42%. Those with least education and lowest family income were most likely to report an activity limitation.

Although it is important to recognize the extent of disability, it is also important to consider the positive aspects of functioning. The concept of quality of life has been used by many health professions to assess various aspects of well-being for those living with diverse disorders, as well as for their caregivers. Many quality of life assessment tools have been developed for use with people suffering from mental and physical problems and for people of different ages. Although there is concern over the lack of standardization of these measures (Barbotte, Guillemin, Chau, & the Lorhandicap Group, 2001), quality of life measures appear to be sensitive to change (Selwood, Thorgrimsen, & Orrell, 2005) and to have predictive validity in some populations (Frisch et al., 2005). **Profile 15.1** presents Dr. Alexanda Quittner, a health psychologist who has developed a quality of life measure for children living with cystic fibrosis.

PROFILE BOX 15.1

DR. ALEXANDRA L. QUITTNER

I earned a Ph.D. in Clinical Psychology from the University of Western Ontario, Canada, in 1987, and am currently a Professor of Psychology and Pediatrics at the University of Miami and an Associate Editor for *Health Psychology*. I have been continuously funded by NIH and other granting agencies over the past 22 years and have published over 70 articles and book chapters.

Dr. Alexandra L. Quittner

My research focuses on the measurement of adherence and health-related quality of life in children and adolescents with chronic illnesses. I have developed a health-related quality of life measure for cystic fibrosis (CF) that has now been translated into 25 languages and is being used in international clinical trials. In addition, I am completing two NIH-funded grants evaluating family-based interventions to improve adherence to treatment regimens for adolescents and school-age children with CF. Finally, I am conducting an international epidemiological study of depression in children and adults with cystic fibrosis and parent caregivers. This project has connected me with colleagues from all over the world! You can check out the protocol, measures, and template for informed consent and assent at www.tides-cf.org.

As I began conducting research on adherence to medical regimens, it became clear that we did not have good measures of adherence behaviors, and that without solid measures, we could not select the appropriate targets for intervention or determine whether our interventions were effective. I therefore developed a Daily Phone Diary (DPD) that tracked all activities, companions and mood over a 24-hour period. We have used the DPD to measure: (1) differences in activity patterns (e.g., recreation in and outside the home) in families with and without a child with a chronic illness, (2) division of parenting and care-giving responsibilities among mothers and fathers caring for a child with a chronic illness, (3) parental differential treatment of siblings with and without a chronic illness, and (4) the frequency and duration of treatment-related behaviors. The DPD has now been modified for use in studies of children with diabetes, asthma, epilepsy, and it will soon be used with children and adolescents receiving evidence-based treatments for anxiety disorders.

My second area of research focuses on childhood deafness and its effects on child development and family functioning. I am evaluating the effects of cochlear implants on deaf infants and toddlers' cognitive, emotional, and social functioning at seven centers. We have funding for the next 5 years to follow these children as they enter school.

How did you choose to become a clinical health psychologist?

During my practicum training, I became interested in studying the stress experienced by parents of children with serious, chronic illnesses. My interest in clinical health psychology was strengthened during my internship, when I was able to focus my training on children with various chronic conditions, including cystic fibrosis, epilepsy, and cancer, and their families. The complex issues faced by children and adolescents with chronic conditions have presented incredible challenges as a clinical researcher, including the need to develop new, contextually focused measures and interventions that promote adherence and disease management in the context of specialty medical care. We are now translating our interventions for "real world" clinical settings.

What is the most rewarding part of your job as a clinical health psychologist?

Developing evidence-based interventions for children with chronic illnesses and their parents. This is an area in which psychologists have excelled and have contributed most significantly to the literature. The other very rewarding part of my job is mentoring undergraduate and graduate students. They are the next generation of clinical researchers, and getting them excited about research is critically important.

What is the greatest challenge you face as a clinical health psychologist?

The greatest challenge is interfacing with the medical system, which tends to be slow to innovate and often does not fully recognize what health psychologists can do. I think this is changing, as health care providers recognize the role that behavior in the management of a chronic illness.

Tell us about developments in research on adherence to medical regimens

We have now developed some very effective interventions to improve adherence and some very sophisticated measures of adherence behaviors, but the major challenge that remains is to implement these interventions in busy specialty clinics. We are now in the process of "translating" these interventions for use in these settings. One of our new intervention efforts, the ICARE study (*I* change adherence, *r*aise *e*xpectations), will involve randomizing 20 CF Centers in the United States to either prescription refill histories for their adolescent patients or a comprehensive adherence program we have developed that is founded on cognitive behavioral approaches (i.e., problem solving about key barriers to adherence). Centers randomized to prescription refill history only will then roll into the comprehensive program after 1 year to see whether we can replicate any positive effects. In our role as psychologists, we developed this intervention, but we are training Master's level social workers to implement it in the real-world clinical setting. This collaboration has been working really well!

How do you integrate science and practice in your work?

The integration of science and practice is relatively easy for me because my research is clinically focused. My major aim is to develop and evaluate new interventions for children with chronic illnesses, and this requires clinical and research skills. I also enjoy training health care professionals to implement these interventions, and we train a broad array of specialties: nurse practitioners, social workers, respiratory therapists, and nutritionists.

> *What do you see as the most exciting changes in the field of clinical health psychology?*
>
> There is now greater recognition that the research and clinical work we do is valuable to patients and families. For example, health-related quality of life measures are now accepted by the FDA as primary or secondary outcomes in clinical trials and can be used in the approval of new medications. This shift is also important because it acknowledges the importance of the *patient's perspective* in evaluating the benefits of new treatments.

Activities of Clinical Health Psychologists

Although various definitions of health psychology are used in different countries, all reflect a biopsychosocial view of health. Common to all the definitions is a reliance on knowledge of psychological research with respect to health in efforts to promote healthy lifestyles as well as to help people adjust to health problems. To conduct health psychology research it is not necessary to have clinical training; however, within North America, clinical health psychologists have generalist training in clinical psychology as well as knowledge of psychological issues related to health. The role of health psychologists in Britain and Ireland can also include elements related to the improvements in health care systems. In these countries, psychologists may receive training that focuses entirely on health psychology, rather than on training in health psychology as a practice area within clinical psychology. Health promotion activities include efforts to reduce smoking, reduce obesity, and encourage regular exercise. Initiatives to promote a healthy lifestyle and to prevent the development of health problems are key activities for a growing number of health psychologists. As we discussed issues related to health promotion in Chapter 10, we focus our discussion here on the activities of psychologists in providing psychological services to individuals with health problems, especially problems related to pain.

Clinical health psychologists can work with patients dealing with any type of health problem, including essential hypertension, coronary heart disease, cancer, diabetes, arthritis, recurrent headaches, asthma, end-stage renal disease, peptic ulcers, irritable bowel syndrome, women's reproductive health (menstruation, fertility, pregnancy, birth, and menopause), organ transplant, genetic testing, and somatoform disorders. Because it would be impossible to address the research in all of these areas in a single chapter, we will focus on the general issue of pain that applies across the spectrum of health problems.

Like clinical psychologists, some health psychologists engage in assessment and intervention. **Table 15.1** describes variables that would be taken into account in assessment and intervention in the clinical application of the biopsychosocial model. Health psychologists must be knowledgeable about the physical disorders from which their patients suffer. They need to know about the characteristics of the disorder, risk factors, and prognosis, as well as diagnostic and treatment procedures. In addition to these biological variables, the health psychologist must also consider psychological issues—whether the patient meets diagnostic criteria for a mental disorder in addition to a physical disorder, the patient's understanding of the condition, and how it is likely to affect his or her life. The social context determines the demands that will be placed on the patient and his or her resources, so the health psychologist must consider the quality of the person's

TABLE 15.1   Clinical Application of the Biopsychosocial Model

I. Illness variables
  A. Symptoms and course of the illness
  B. Factors that elevate the risk of the illness
  C. Diagnostic procedures
  D. Treatment procedures

II. The patient
  A. Mental health and disorder
  B. Personality traits and coping styles or mechanisms
  C. Educational and vocational issues
  D. Impact of illness on subjective distress, social functioning, activity level, self-care, and overall quality of life

III. Social, family, and cultural contexts
  A. Quality of couple and family relationships
  B. Social support
  C. Relationship with health care providers
  D. Patient's cultural background

IV. The health care system
  A. Medical organization
  B. Insurance coverage for diagnostic and treatment procedures
  C. Geographical, social, and psychological barriers to accessing health services
  D. Existence of disability benefits for medical condition

Adapted from Smith, Nealey, and Hamann (2000)

relationships, the extent to which others are available to provide instrumental and emotional support, and the nature of the relationship with health care professionals, as well as cultural issues. Finally, the patient's concerns must be considered in the context of the health care system to which the patient has access.

Clinical health psychologists may be employed within a hospital, a community health clinic, or a private practice setting—issues related to health problems don't occur only in hospitals. For example, a family sought private services from a psychologist due to concerns about their 7-year-old daughter, Laila, who was becoming fearful and reluctant to attend school. Laila's father, David, had had an unsuccessful kidney transplant and had recently been diagnosed with cancer. Physicians had informed him that he could expect to deteriorate steadily over the coming months and that there was virtually no hope of slowing the rate of his decline. Although David was resigned to having a terminal illness, he felt guilty and anxious at the thought of leaving his daughter. Laila's mother, Anna, was a tower of strength for the entire family. Since her husband's diagnosis, she had supplemented the family income by additional hours at work. A psychological assessment revealed that David was suffering from a dysthymic disorder, Laila met criteria for a diagnosis of separation anxiety disorder, and Anna, although fatigued and distressed, did not meet criteria for any mental disorder. The psychologist identified three foci for intervention: (a) addressing David's depressive symptoms, (b) addressing Laila's anxious symptoms and facilitating regular attendance at school, and (c) helping Anna to mobilize supports by reducing her work hours and taking care of her emotional needs.

Assessment and Intervention Related to Pain

Pain serves a useful function in alerting us to potential harm. The sharp pain you feel when you twist an ankle is an important signal that you need to take weight off the ankle, a scorching sensation warns you to move away from a fire, chafing lets you know that clothing is too tight, and stinging reminds you to keep away from certain plants or insects. Although most of us consider pain an unpleasant experience that we would rather avoid, the very rare individual who is insensitive to pain is vulnerable to life-threatening injuries because he or she does not experience the warning signals of pain. Because pain is a subjective experience, we rely on individual reports to let us know how much pain a person is suffering: there is no objective way in which we can judge another person's pain. This poses an important challenge in understanding the pain experiences of those who are incapable of verbalizing pain. Until relatively recently, many health care professionals assumed that babies and very young children did not feel pain (Poole et al., 2005). Consequently, it was considered reasonable to conduct procedures such as circumcision on male infants without using local anesthesia, whereas such procedures would not be applied to an older male without some intervention to block or dull the pain. **Patrick McGrath** and his colleagues have developed innovative strategies to measure pain in infants and children, as well as in adults who are incapable of expressing pain verbally (McGrath & Finley, 2003; McGrath & Unruh, 1999). These include research-based strategies for asking children about pain, observing their behavior, and watching facial expressions (Breau, McGrath, Camfield, & Finley, 2002; Chambers, Finley, McGrath, & Walsh, 2003).

It is important to distinguish between **acute pain** and **chronic pain**. Acute pain is a short-term sensation that serves an unpleasant, but useful, function; it can usually be relieved in different ways, including the application of heat or cold, rest, distraction, or the administration of analgesics. In contrast, pain that persists for more than six months is considered chronic. All people experience acute pain due to injuries, illness, and medical procedures. For example, all children are exposed to procedures such as vaccination, many experience minor surgery, and a few must face pain associated with invasive procedures associated with the treatment of serious conditions such as cancer. Pain management is multidimensional, including physical measures such as the administration of medication and psychological interventions such as training in distraction strategies. Because children usually are discharged from the hospital very rapidly following minor surgery, parents are often responsible for managing the child's pain. McGrath and his colleagues (McGrath, Finley, Ritchie, & Dowden, 2003) prepared a booklet to help parents help children. **Table 15.2** includes strategies they suggest can be helpful in addressing children's acute pain and some commonly used strategies that are not helpful.

Chronic pain is associated with a host of other problems, including sleep disturbances, depression, and anxiety (Ohayon, 2005). Chronic pain from low back problems, migraine or severe headache, and joint pain is a fact of life for more than one in ten adults (Centers for Disease Control National Center for Health Statistics, 2006). **Dennis Turk** and his colleagues have highlighted the psychological aspects of chronic pain. The person's beliefs about pain influence the experience of pain: those who attribute their pain to a traumatic injury, who are fearful of causing further pain by engaging in activity, and who feel unable to control their pain report more intense pain symptoms (Turk & Okifuji, 2002). Psychological factors play an important role in determining whether the person will recover from the pain or will experience long-term disability (Keefe,

---

TABLE 15.2   Methods to Manage Children's Acute Pain

Psychological

- Presence of a parent or other special person

- Encouragement to ask questions and express feelings

- Provision of simple, accurate information about a medical procedure

- Provision of some control (e.g., sit on a lap or in a chair)

- Distraction: talking, video games, music, books

- Imagination: thinking of activities associated with being relaxed and calm

- Suggestion that the child let the pain slip away

- Play and silliness

- Encouragement that the child is doing well

Physical

- Deep breathing

- Comforting touch: stroking, swaddling, holding, rocking, cuddling

- Medication

Unhelpful strategies

- Denying the pain: *you won't feel a thing*

- Ridiculing or shaming: *only babies cry*

- Giving false reassurance: *it only takes a second*

- Focusing too much on pain: *I know you are worried it will hurt a lot*

Adapted from McGrath, Finley, Ritchie, and Dowden (2003)

Abernethy & Campbell, 2005). Dysfunctional beliefs about pain, lack of social support, heightened emotional reactivity, low job satisfaction, and the possibility of compensation are associated with the experience of chronic problems (Turk & Okifuji, 2002). Psychologists may be consulted to conduct assessments in claims for disability due to pain-related injuries. This type of work involves knowledge of health psychology and forensic issues.

Psychological services to deal with pain may be offered within interdisciplinary services that include physicians and physiotherapists (Keefe, Abernethy, & Campbell, 2005). Psychological treatment may be directed at various goals, including the adoption of active coping strategies to manage pain, reduction of avoidance behaviors, improved sleep (see **Viewpoint Box 15.1**), adherence to a medication regimen, stress management, reduction of anxiety related to pain, resolution of interpersonal issues related to pain (e.g., communication difficulties and conflict with family members), and vocational issues (Hadjistavropoulos & Williams, 2004). **Table 15.3** lists cognitive-behavioral strategies frequently used in managing chronic pain. These interventions can be offered individually or in a group format. Treatment in interdisciplinary services for pain is as effective as pharmaceutical and surgical alternatives and is associated with a greater number of people being able to work (Turk & Burwinkle, 2005).

VIEWPOINT BOX 15.1

INSOMNIA: NO NEED TO LOSE SLEEP OVER IT!

We all need sleep. As you may know from direct experience, without adequate sleep, both children and adults suffer cognitive and physical impairments (Streisand & Efron, 2003). Sleep can be affected by many variables, including age, parental status, stress, and shift work (Williams, 2001), as well as by a host of physical variables including chronic pain (Ohayon, 2005). Results of the 2008 *Sleep in America Poll* revealed that 15% of respondents said a health care provider told them they have a sleep disorder (National Sleep Foundation, 2008).

Everyone occasionally suffers from insomnia triggered by life events, stressors, or an illness. Normal sleeping patterns usually return once the stressor or illness is over. However, an occasional bout of insomnia can develop into a chronic sleep disorder that takes on a life of its own, independent of the original trigger. Within the DSM-IV system, insomnia is a disorder of initiating and/or maintaining sleep that is accompanied by fatigue-related impairment during the day (American Psychiatric Association, 2000). Chronic insomnia is often maintained by problematic behaviors and beliefs (Morin, 2004). Although the problem of insomnia is well recognized by the medical profession, the topic is not routinely covered in training in clinical psychology (Streisand & Efron, 2003). With roots in basic psychological research and its existence on the boundary between general clinical psychology and health psychology, the topic of sleep disorders can be overlooked by applied psychologists (De Koninck, 1997). Nevertheless, there is increasing evidence that psychological interventions may be very useful in the treatment of this common disorder, especially when the insomnia is chronic. Because pharmacological interventions can lead to poor quality sleep, possible addiction, and rebound insomnia on withdrawal of the medication, there is a pressing need for effective psychological interventions.

Dr. Charles Morin (see Profile 4.1) has been at the forefront of research in this area (Morin, Colecchi, Stone, Sood, & Brink, 1999; Morin, 2004). CBT interventions include three components: educational, behavioral, and cognitive (Morin, 2004). Educational strategies focus on knowledge of the physiology of sleep and on understanding the mechanics of how insomnia develops into a chronic problem. Education also focuses on the principles of **sleep hygiene** (i.e., good sleep practices): avoid caffeine and other stimulants in the evening; avoid smoking close to bedtime; avoid exercising too close to bedtime; and reduce noise, light, and excessive temperature (Morin, 2004). Behavioral strategies focus on stimulus control with five simple instructions: (a) go to bed only when sleepy; (b) use bed or bedroom only for sleeping; (c) get out of bed when unable to sleep and return only when sleepy; (d) get up at the same time every day no matter how little you have slept; and (e) do not take daytime naps. Two additional behavioral strategies include restricting sleep time and learning relaxation strategies. Cognitive interventions target and attempt to alter dysfunctional beliefs about sleep, including unrealistic expectations, feelings of lack of control, and catastrophic thinking about the consequences of being unable to sleep. Cognitive-behavioral interventions yield an average of 50–60% symptom reduction in those suffering from insomnia, a figure comparable with that obtained with pharmacotherapy (Morin, 2004). Furthermore, the effects of cognitive-behavioral interventions are better maintained over time.

A meta-analysis of studies comparing cognitive-behavioral interventions to pharmacotherapy revealed that, whereas medication produced superior results in terms of sleep *duration*, cognitive behavioral interventions were associated with greater improvement in *quality* of sleep (Smith, Perlis, et al., 2002). Despite evidence that psychological interventions are efficacious, they have been underused, as some people consider medication an easier alternative. Researchers have therefore focused their efforts on delivering psychological interventions in brief and inexpensive ways. For example, a randomized controlled trial found that a brief (2-hour) cognitive-behavioral intervention for young and middle-aged adults was more efficacious than either pharmacotherapy or combined cognitive-behavioral treatment and pharmacotherapy in the treatment of insomnia (Jacobs, Pace-Shott, Stickgold, & Otto, 2004). Bastien, Morin, Ouellet, Blais, and Bouchard (2004) compared three different ways to deliver a cognitive-behavioral intervention to middle-aged adults with insomnia. These investigators found that participants who received services via individual sessions, groups, or telephone consultation all reported improvements in sleep that were maintained 6 months after completion. This preliminary study suggests that CBT can be effectively delivered in inexpensive ways to address a common and troubling disorder.

TABLE 15.3   Cognitive-Behavioral Approaches to the Management of Chronic Pain

Intervention	Strategy	Goal
Education about pain	Provide a rationale for the treatment	Motivate patients to take an active role in treatment
Goal setting	Short- and long-term goals; activity scheduling; pacing	Realistic goals; recognition of gradual progress
Relaxation	Training and rehearsal of skills and achieving a calm state	Develop capacity to reduce muscle tension
Contingency management	Self-reinforcement of healthy behaviors	Reduce use of analgesics; increase appropriate exercise; increase balanced response to pain
Exercise and fitness	Collaborate with physiotherapist/trainer	Address fears and avoidance of more active lifestyle
Cognitive restructuring	Identify and challenge catastrophizing thoughts	Realistic appraisals of pain
Problem solving	Address limitations and conflicts	Awareness of choices; capacity to activate support; clear communication
Generalization and maintenance	Practice skills in relation to diverse issues; anticipate difficulties	Lifestyle changes so that skills are applied consistently

Adapted from Hadjistavropoulos and Williams (2004)

In sum, the application of psychological knowledge to address issues related to health, including pain, is a growing area of practice. Over the relatively brief history of behavioral medicine and health psychology, psychologists have made an important contribution to the understanding of health, the promotion of healthy lifestyles, and the adjustment to health problems. Given the aging of our population and the increasing need for services to help people adjust to chronic health problems, it is highly likely that health psychology will become an even more important psychological service area in the coming years (Leventhal et al., 2008). Indeed, psychological services delivered in medical settings may dramatically enhance quality of life and reduce the financial burden on the health care system (Blount et al., 2007).

CLINICAL NEUROPSYCHOLOGY

Neuropsychology is the study of brain–behavior relationships; clinical neuropsychology is the application of this knowledge in the assessment and remediation of problems associated with the central nervous system (Boake, 2008). Clinical neuropsychology addresses the effects on functioning of neurological problems, including genetic problems such as Williams syndrome, birth-related injuries, head injuries resulting from sports accidents and car accidents, brain tumors, infections, demyelinating diseases such as multiple sclerosis, cerebrovascular diseases, epilepsy, neurodegenerative diseases such as Alzheimer's disease or Parkinson's disease, the effects of exposure to environmental toxins, and the effects of chemotherapy (Cairns, 2004).

Clinical neuropsychology developed after the Second World War, building on the work of **Ward Halstead** and **Ralph Reitan** in the United States and **Aleksandr Luria** in the Soviet Union (Groth-Marnat, 2000). Halstead, who was trained in physiological psychology, studied the behavior of patients with neurological impairment. Dissatisfied with the academic focus of intelligence tests, he developed tests to assess specific adaptive deficits (Broshek & Barth, 2000). Over the course of his career, Reitan conducted numerous studies comparing performance on these tests between patients with brain damage and nondisordered individuals and examining the usefulness of the battery in identifying the precise area of the brain that had been damaged (Broshek & Barth, 2000). The Halstead–Reitan battery is the most extensively investigated neuropsychological test and is widely considered a useful tool in evaluating cognitive functioning (see Table 15.6 below). However, the Halstead–Reitan is not without its flaws. Criticisms include the length of time required for administration; the failure to take into account differences according to age, education, and gender; and the lack of studies on diverse populations (Broshek & Barth, 2000). Luria's assessment approach was a qualitative one that yielded a profile of the patient's strengths and weaknesses but lent itself less readily to standardization in administration or scoring (Golden, Freshwater, & Vayalakkara, 2000). Current neuropsychological practices reflect an integration of the two traditions so that use of tests is complemented by careful analysis of functioning (Groth-Marnat, 2000).

Activities of Clinical Neuropsychologists

In addition to the knowledge base required for all clinical psychologists to practice clinical neuro-psychology, one must understand normal brain functioning (**neuroanatomy**); the ways that environmental toxins, chemotherapy, or recreational drugs affect brain functioning (pharmacology); and the ways that injuries and diseases affect the brain (**neuropathology**). In addition, clinical neuropsychologists must be knowledgeable about a wide array of assessment strategies to identify neuropsychological problems, as well as ways to adapt to these limitations.

Training in clinical neuropsychology can be obtained in several ways: within generalist training in clinical psychology, in a small number of specialist clinical neuropsychology doctoral programs, or in postdoctoral training. The Division of Clinical Neuropsychology of the American Psychological Association identifies fulfillment of the requirements of the American Board of Clinical Neuropsychology as clear evidence of competence. The Division of Neuropsychology of the British Psychological Society (BPS) has also developed professional practice guidelines, such as that chartered clinical psychologists who have met the criteria for membership in the Division of Neuropsychology are considered competent as clinical neuropsychologists (BPS, 2003).

Clinical neuropsychologists work with clients across the lifespan and must be sensitive to issues in working with children (Middleton, 2004) and older adults (American Psychological Association Working Group on the Older Adult, 1998; Morris, 2004). Those working with children require knowledge of assessment and intervention that is suitable for children and must have a strong background in developmental psychology. In assessing older adults, the clinical neuropsychologist must take into account the physical and sensory changes that accompany aging, in addition to the cognitive changes that are the focus of the assessment (APA Working Group on the Older Adult, 1998; Lichtenberg, Murman, & Mellow, 2003). **Profile Box 15.2** describes Dr. Tony Strickland, a neuropsychologist who provides services to athletes who have sustained head injuries.

PROFILE BOX 15.2

DR. TONY L. STRICKLAND

I received my doctorate in clinical psychology (behavioral medicine) from the University of Georgia. Following this, I completed postdoctoral fellowship training in clinical neuropsychology at the Neuropsychiatric Institute, David Geffen School of Medicine at UCLA and a postdoctoral clinical research fellowship in psychopharmacology at Harbor-UCLA Medical Center. I am the founder and chairman of the Sports Concussion Institute, the program director of the Memory Disorders and Concussion Management Clinics, and an Associate Clinical Professor of Neurology in the Semel Neuroscience Institute, David Geffen School of Medicine at UCLA. I am a diplomate of the American Board of Professional Neuropsychology and a fellow of the National Academy of Neuropsychology, the American

Dr. Tony L. Strickland

Psychological Association Division 50 (Addictions), and the American College of Professional Neuropsychology. My clinical and research experience is in the areas of neurobehavioral sequelae of traumatic brain injury, substance abuse, ethnobiologic variations in response to psychotropic medication, cross-cultural neuropsychology, and forensic neuropsychological evaluations. Funded by NIH for a number of projects, I have authored numerous research articles on a range of topics related to the neurosciences.

How did you choose to become a clinical neuropsychologist?

I was born and reared in Los Angeles, California, in a community that had experienced a dramatic surge in the abuse of drugs and their pernicious consequences. I had the unfortunate experience of seeing many promising lives curtailed by drug abuse and associated traumas. This fueled my interest in a career in health care in order to contribute to some solutions. I reasoned that a career as a neuropsychologist, which has as its core the study of brain–behavior relationships, would allow me to make the broadest impact upon underserved populations. Technologies in the fields of neuroimaging, pharmacokinetics, neuropsychometrics, and molecular biology allow me to evaluate potential drug-induced neurobehavioral and psychosocial phenomena and explore similarities and differences among and between select underserved groups, comparing them on the basis of gender, SES, and ethnic background.

Early in my career I noticed that it was not uncommon for a patient to have passed out as a result of consumption of drugs, and consequently to have been involved in an accident in which brain injuries were sustained. I chose, therefore, to orient my career to addressing traumatic brain injury outcomes within a population at high risk for head trauma. Athletes constitute such a high-risk group, and their desire to continue to compete often leads them to significantly underreport their injuries. After some initial work with athletes, I decided to specialize in sports neuropsychology.

What is the most rewarding part of your job as a clinical neuropsychologist?

When I awake each morning, I can hardly wait to get to work. To have created a work environment focused on sports-induced concussive disorders is very rewarding. At the Sports Concussion Institute, following evaluation and diagnosis, patients receive prompt treatment that may include medical care from our staff neurologist, ongoing services (e.g., mild head injury education, counseling, cognitive therapy) from a psychologist or neuropsychologist, and/or a referral to our extensive network of physical specialists and ancillary medical professionals. Being able to both evaluate and treat patients, and then to see them improve, are the most rewarding aspects of my job.

What is the greatest challenge you face as a clinical neuropsychologist?

The greatest challenge that I encounter is balancing the demands for escalating clinical service against the realities of decreasing reimbursement for these services. In the current economic climate I have less time available for patient interaction, so I do not have as much opportunity as I would like to educate individuals about their disorders and follow through on my treatment recommendations.

Tell us about recent developments in clinical neuropsychological assessment

The evolution of sports neuropsychology as a rapidly growing subspecialty has driven a number of new developments. For example, our clinic uses computerized neuropsychological assessments that facilitate evidenced-based evaluation of neurobehavioral status across the life span. The use of computerized neuropsychological assessment enables our clinicians to conduct a simple, 25-minute evaluation of an athlete's neurocognitive status (i.e., memory, processing speed, and other related functions) following concussion. Athletes/patients in this clinic also undergo a broader neurologic and neuropsychological examination in order to ensure that all the information needed for the proper evaluation and treatment of mild head trauma is obtained. In addition, treatment of postconcussive syndrome focuses on individual responsibility, patient education, symptom reduction, and promoting a return to previous lifestyle and function. Treatment/evaluation of sports concussions, in addition, focus on safe return to play and reducing the possibility of second impact syndrome and other injuries.

How do you integrate science and practice in your work?

I have always embraced the principle of evidenced-based practice. That being said, I also believe that one needs to be sensitive to contextual factors (e.g., patient characteristics, availability of health care options) when integrating science and practice. When I supervise students, I emphasize the importance of attending to the results of psychological science, but I also help students to generate scientifically informed hypotheses and make decisions when there is limited evidence that bears directly on the clinical issues being addressed.

What do you see as the most exciting changes in the field of clinical neuropsychology?

As mentioned previously, the evolution of sports neuropsychology represents a rapidly growing subspecialty that has driven a number of new developments. Additionally, options for facilitating evidenced-based evaluation and treatment of sports/recreation-induced neurobehavioral disorders across the life span, with a focus on outpatient neurorehabilitation, have expanded significantly. Neuropsychology provides an opportunity to focus on the evaluation and treatment needs of individuals with a wide range of acquired and degenerative brain disorders (e.g., stroke, traumatic brain injury), as well as to meet their rehabilitation needs (e.g., cognitive rehabilitation, treatment of pain and emotional disorders, addressing interpersonal and family issues).

Like other areas of clinical psychology, clinical neuropsychology has expanded and evolved over recent decades (Hayman-Abello, Hayman-Abello, & Rourke, 2003). As noted above, early clinical neuropsychology was primarily a diagnostic activity in which tests were developed to aid in the localization of lesions. Neuropsychological assessment was used to determine whether there was an organic basis for observed psychological and behavioral problems, and if so, to identify the precise area of the brain that was affected (Goldstein & McNeil, 2004). With the development of effective imaging techniques such as magnetic resonance imaging (MRI) and functional magnetic resonance imaging (fMRI), there are now alternative ways to identify the precise nature of brain dysfunction (Mellers, 2004). Clinical neuropsychology, in turn, has expanded its focus to also address cognitive, emotional, psychosocial, and behavioral difficulties that result from an insult to the brain (Laatsch et al., 2007; Livingston et al., 2005; Wilson, 2008).

Assessment

Neuropsychological assessment examines memory, abstract reasoning, problem solving, spatial abilities, and the emotional consequences of brain dysfunction (Groth-Marnat, 2000). In Chapter 5 we noted that psychological assessment can be conducted for screening, diagnosis and case formulation, prognosis, treatment design and planning, treatment monitoring, and treatment evaluation (cf. Hunsley, Crabb, & Mash, 2004). Similarly, neuropsychological assessment can address many different questions, as outlined in **Table 15.4**.

Screening for organic problems may be conducted by a generalist clinical psychologist, who then refers the patient for a full neuropsychological assessment if the screening indicates possible neuropathology. As you can see in Table 15.4, the most common reasons for neuropsychological assessment are to address issues around diagnosis, prognosis, treatment planning, and legal issues. An increasing number of clinical neuropsychologists conduct assessments that are used in a forensic context (Boake, 2008). Diagnostic issues include determining whether the person's problem is primarily neurological or psychological. To conduct such an assessment, the clinical neuropsychologist must understand neuropathology and psychopathology.

TABLE 15.4   Purposes of Neuropsychological Assessment

- Diagnosis
  Does this child show signs of having been exposed to a toxic substance? Are this patient's memory complaints related to dementia or to depression?

- Prognosis
  To what extent will this child's acquisition of language be affected by her head injury?
  How long is it reasonable to expect this person to live alone, given his declining memory and executive functioning?

- Treatment Planning and Rehabilitation
  What kind of special learning aids will this child with a learning disability require?
  If this patient who has had a stroke returns to work, what kinds of adaptations will need to be made to compensate for deficits related to the stroke?
  What can be done to help this person with mild memory loss?

- Legal Proceedings
  Is there evidence of brain dysfunction that could be related to the person committing a violent act? What is the extent of damage to this employee who sustained an electric shock?

Neuropsychologists are often requested to predict a patient's prognosis (Lemsky, 2000). For example, the neuropsychologist may be asked whether or not a person can return to work following a brain injury, and if so, to identify the types of tasks that may be difficult. Prediction of future functioning requires an understanding of the neuropathology and its course, as well as the person's developmental level. Some forms of neuropathology are progressive, so that the person can expect a process of deterioration.

Other problems, such as those caused by a blow to the head, may lead to different problems at different ages. For example, following a mild concussion, a child may exhibit fewer symptoms than an adult would. However, there is some evidence that damage occurring at times of rapid development causes more harm than does damage occurring at times of slow development (Middleton, 2004). Counterbalancing this is the fact that the child's brain is in the process of development, so it may be possible for a child to recover from some types of injuries more easily than an adult could (Middleton, 2004). In assessing an adult who had difficulties with language following a head injury, the clinical neuropsychologist predicts the extent of recovery of functioning that can be expected. In assessing a 3-year-old with a similar injury, the child clinical neuropsychologist predicts whether the child will acquire language at the same rate as noninjured peers or whether language delays can be expected (Middleton, 2004). In conducting neuropsychological assessment for the purposes of planning treatment and rehabilitation, the clinical neuropsychologist draws on knowledge of normal processes in memory, language, and executive functioning to make predictions that a person with a particular deficit could benefit from a particular intervention (Lemsky, 2000).

In Chapter 5 we emphasized that psychological assessment and psychological testing are not synonymous. Similarly, neuropsychological assessment includes, but is not limited to, neuropsychological testing. The toolkit of the clinical neuropsychologist contains assessment strategies and instruments that we presented in earlier chapters, including interviews (Chapter 6) and psychometric tests such as the Wechsler Adult Intelligence Scale IV, Wechsler Memory Scale IV, and Wechsler Individual Achievement Test II (Chapter 7). In choosing a neuropsychological test, the psychologist must consider the core psychometric elements that are required for all types of psychological tests: standardization (of stimuli, administration, and scoring), reliability, validity, and norms. There is no simple correspondence between performance on a neuropsychological test and performance of the activities of daily living (Goldstein & McNeil, 2004). The context of neuropsychological testing may actually mask some types of deficits (Lemsky, 2000). For example, an individual may perform better in the brief, structured one-to-one environment of a testing session than in the home setting with multiple distractions and simultaneous demands on attention. Therefore, it is essential that data be gathered from the individual and from others who are knowledgeable about his or her functioning, to determine his or her functional status in various domains.

In interpreting a score on a particular test, the clinical neuropsychologist refers to normative data. However, the usefulness of this comparison depends on the appropriateness of the normative group. Some widely used tests have norms for older adults. The WAIS IV (Wechsler, 2008), for example, provides normative data for the 70- to 90-year age range. Unfortunately, other commonly used neuropsychological tests were normed on small samples of convenience, so that an extreme score may represent a difference between the individual and the normative sample, rather than a clinically meaningful difference (Crawford, 2004). It is of particular concern that many norms for neuropsychological tests are based on samples that underrepresent minority groups (Boake, 2008). **Viewpoint Box 15.2** describes the development of new scales for use with diverse populations of older adults.

VIEWPOINT BOX 15.2

SENAS: A TOOL FOR THE ASSESSMENT OF COGNITIVE FUNCTIONING IN OLDER ADULTS OF VARYING ETHNIC BACKGROUNDS

With an aging population, there is an urgent need for sound tools to assess cognitive functioning and dementia in the elderly. Many commonly used tools were developed for use with an English-speaking population. Over the years, as tests have been translated into other languages, little attention has been focused on ensuring that the translation has the same psychometric properties as the original version. Furthermore, performance on tests of cognitive functioning is affected by language and education. It is possible to overestimate cognitive impairment when testing an elderly person with limited education using a translated version of a neuropsychological test. It is essential that tools be developed for use with an ethnically and linguistically diverse population. Such tools must also allow for equally sensitive and reliable measurement in different domains (Crawford, 2004).

To address these psychometric concerns, Mungas and colleagues began developing the *Spanish and English Neuropsychological Assessment Scales* (SENAS; Mungas, Reed, Crane, Haan, & González, 2004). The SENAS were designed as tests of cognitive abilities in older individuals from diverse ethnic groups. Mungas and his colleagues used sophisticated test construction techniques to develop and systematically test a set of new scales. Mungas, Reed, Marshall, and González (2000) developed 12 new neuropsychological scales that included both verbal and nonverbal measures. Item selection was guided by the research literature on cognition and intelligence, cognitive effects of aging, and cognitive effects of neuropathology. The instrument was designed to assess six areas: conceptual thinking, semantic memory, attention span, episodic memory, nonverbal spatial ability, and verbal ability. For each scale, 90–100 potential items were generated. Verbal items were translated into Spanish and then back-translated from Spanish to English to ensure that the translation was sound. Items were then tested with 21 English-speaking and 21 Spanish-speaking individuals age 60 and over. Results from pilot testing led to refining the items and the translation. Next, the items were administered to 408 community-dwelling elderly participants (208 in English and 200 in Spanish). Item response theory was used to identify and eliminate linguistically biased items, yielding scales with 40–50 items that were (a) well-matched across English and Spanish forms, (b) reliable, and (c) sensitive to cognitive impairment.

Mungas et al. (2004) reported on additional evaluations of the SENAS. The scales developed with the previous sample were modified to address shortcomings, and an additional scale was added. The 13 scales were then tested in a sample of 1,374 participants over the age of 60 (Study 1: 345 Caucasian Americans tested in English, 353 Hispanic Americans tested in English, and 676 Hispanic Americans tested in Spanish). Once again, item response theory was used to ensure the scales were well matched in terms of the psychometric properties of the English and Spanish versions and that the scale had strong psychometrics at different levels of ability. Matching within language groups was good for 7 of the 13 scales; minor differences were found in the precision of measurement across language groups for 4 of the scales; 2 scales did not yield similar psychometric properties across language groups. Analyses in a second study provided support for the model of functioning on which the scales were based. Results suggested that the different domains were correlated with one another, reflecting an underlying dimension of cognitive ability. Nevertheless, the degree of correlation was moderate, suggesting that each scale contributes unique measurement variance. Finally, in a third set of analyses using data from Study 1, the researchers examined the possibility that responses would be affected by demographic characteristics. They found that responses were relatively unaffected by education, ethnicity, gender, and age, suggesting that the SENAS will be useful in evaluating both Caucasian and Hispanic older adults.

The work of Mungas and his colleagues is noteworthy for the scrupulous application of state of the art test construction techniques in the development of sound tools that can be used in diverse populations. They have continued to collect construct validation data for the scales (e.g., Mungas, Reed, Haan, & González, 2005).

Intervention

Brain injuries affect approximately 1 million children a year in the United States (Laatsch et al., 2007). In addition, with an aging population, there are increasing numbers of people living with dementia (Turner, 2003). Furthermore, due to improvements in medical care, many people now survive strokes and serious head injuries. There is a clear need to offer effective services to help the growing numbers of people who are faced with the challenge of living with the effects of neurological problems (Wilson, 2004). Compared with the history of treatments for mental disorders, the history of interventions for individuals with neurocognitive impairment is relatively brief. Although these interventions include services to deal with the psychological consequences of the impairment, such as depression, a growing number of interventions are designed to remediate the problems identified in neuropsychological assessment. **Viewpoint Box 15.3** provides a case example of neuropsychological assessment conducted to aid in treatment planning.

Despite the potential usefulness of neuropsychological assessment in treatment planning, it is not routinely available to all patients with neurological problems. A survey of rehabilitation programs within the American Hospital Association (Stringer, 2003) revealed that most patients were under 65 and had been hospitalized for a stroke or a brain injury. The majority of these patients received individualized cognitive rehabilitation services over a period of 1 to 6 months, at a cost of $130 per session. These services were often delivered by speech therapists and occupational therapists. Few of these programs incorporated the results of neuropsychological assessment into services offered.

Different theoretical models of cognitive rehabilitation lead to different strategies to help a person deal with the real-life problems caused by neurological problems (Lemsky, 2000). Rehabilitation is an interactive process between the patient and service providers designed to enable the person to function as adequately as possible. Using the terminology of the World Health Organization, some interventions are designed to overcome impairments by teaching the patient new strategies; other interventions are designed to compensate for impairments by modifying the environment or by using aids so that the patient is capable of carrying out an activity; and others address social, psychological, and physical barriers to the person's participation (Lemsky, 2000). Treatment planning involves collaborating with the client to identify desired outcomes. Wilson (2008) used the acronym SMART to underline the importance of establishing goals that are specific, measurable, achievable, realistic, and timely.

VIEWPOINT BOX 15.3

NEUROPSYCHOLOGICAL ASSESSMENT TO AID IN DIFFERENTIAL DIAGNOSIS AND TREATMENT PLANNING

Peter (age 25) was referred for a neuropsychological assessment by a neurologist. He had difficulties with memory and concentration, slept poorly, suffered headaches, and felt anxious. Six months earlier, Peter had been a passenger in a car accident in which he sustained a mild head injury with loss of consciousness for 10–15 minutes. His close friend, who was the driver, was killed in the accident. A neuropsychological assessment was requested to determine whether Peter's symptoms were related to posttraumatic stress disorder (PTSD), a psychological disorder related to the effects of the severe accident in which a friend died, or to postconcussion syndrome (PCS), a physiological disorder due to a brain injury during the accident.

The neuropsychological assessment included an interview, as well as tests of intelligence, memory, perceptual and visual skills, and executive functioning. Results revealed that Peter experienced some symptoms of anxiety related to the accident, as well as grief over the death of his friend. However, he did not meet criteria for a diagnosis of PTSD, as he did not report reexperiencing the accident or intrusive thoughts about it. He did evidence significant cognitive difficulties in formal testing that were consistent with the problems he reported in daily living. These cognitive symptoms were more pronounced than those that would be seen after exposure to a traumatic event. The clinical neuropsychologist therefore concluded that Peter's symptoms reflected the residual effects of the brain injury (i.e., PCS), which were compounded by his emotional reaction to the accident and his friend's death. To address these issues, Peter was provided with information about head injury and given strategies to address his memory and attention difficulties. He was advised to attempt a gradual return to work and was offered counseling to address the emotional sequelae of the accident.

Adapted from Goldstein and McNeil (2004).

The development of effective interventions relies on a solid understanding of cognitive processes such as memory and learning. In the treatment of memory deficits, efforts to retrain memory have been found to be ineffective, and external memory aids such as lists, calendars, electronic agendas, pagers, and personal digital assistants are widely used (J. J. R. Evans, 2004). It is clear that much more intervention research is needed to evaluate the impact of the wide range of available intervention. The Committee on Empirically Supported Programs (COESP) of the Division of Clinical Neuropsychology of the American Psychological Association commissioned a review of literature on treatments for attentional problems (Riccio & French, 2004). Across all treatment programs and populations reviewed, methodologically adequate research has not yet been conducted to demonstrate that the treatments make a difference. Similarly, a review of cognitive rehabilitation for people with early-stage Alzheimer's disease concluded that although single-case reports provided encouraging data, no randomized control trials have been conducted, so there is only a limited empirical basis that individualized cognitive rehabilitation programs are efficacious for people with early-stage Alzheimer's disease (Clare & Woods, 2004).

A systematic review of studies of cognitive and behavioral interventions for children with acquired brain injury (Laatsch et al., 2007) also found few high-quality randomized control trials and few studies with a large number of participants. However, Laatsch and colleagues concluded that there was sufficient evidence to justify practice guidelines that children with acquired brain injury receive services to remediate memory and attention, and they also concluded that comprehensive rehabilitation services should consider involving family members as active treatment providers. In addition, Laatsch et al. found preliminary evidence of the usefulness of providing an information booklet on traumatic brain injury to parents and caregivers of children seen in an emergency department for such injuries. There is clearly an urgent need for increased research on neuropsychological rehabilitation so that we can identify the most efficacious programs for people dealing with impairment and disability related to neurological injury and disease.

FORENSIC PSYCHOLOGY

Forensic psychology, broadly defined, is the application of psychology in the legal and criminal justice systems. Like other types of clinical psychology, forensic psychologists engage in services related to prevention, assessment, treatment, and research. In earlier chapters we raised issues that are important in forensic psychology, such as assessing whether a person making an insurance claim for injuries sustained in an accident is accurately reporting symptoms or is malingering (Chapter 8), developing programs to prevent the emergence of delinquent behavior (Chapter 10), and treating victims of accidents or abuse (Chapters 12 and 13). We indicated that the work of psychologists may be subpoenaed and that before beginning any services psychologists must explain the limits of confidentiality to clients (Chapter 6). Forensic psychologists provide services to many stakeholders, including victims of crime, witnesses of crimes, offenders, parties in a legal dispute, police forces, and the courts. Other mental health professionals such as psychiatrists also offer forensic services based on interviews and examination of collateral data such as reports from schools, employers, or previous therapists. With their expertise in using data from psychological tests, psychologists are well positioned to offer expert opinion (Lally, 2003). The expert testimony of psychologists is presented in court on both civil and criminal matters (Packer, 2008).

Forensic psychologists are employed in many settings, including hospitals, private practice, court clinics, maximum security federal penitentiaries, provincial jails, provincial correctional centers, minimum security camps (both adult and youth), specialized treatment facilities, community probation and parole offices, and Aboriginal healing lodges. The vast majority of these psychologists are directly engaged in providing psychological services, but others are research psychologists or psychologists who work in the fields of policy and administration (Magaletta & Verdeyen, 2005). The nature of clinical psychologists' work in correctional facilities is greatly affected by high incarceration rates, overcrowding in prisons, and limited resources for psychological services. In their efforts to develop evidence-based clinical practice, psychologists in correctional settings must be acutely aware of the constraints associated with the environment in which they work (Clements et al., 2007).

Activities of Forensic Psychologists

Most forensic psychologists have a doctorate in clinical psychology and field training in forensic psychology. Given the nature of the problems with which they work, forensic psychologists must be knowledgeable about strategies for assessing and managing risk. In addition, those working with children must understand the criminal justice and legal systems with respect to children. Training in corrections is available through a few clinical psychology programs and in several clinical internship sites. Research forensic psychologists do not require training in clinical psychology. Certification by the American Board of Forensic Psychology indicates that the person has demonstrated advanced competencies in forensic psychology.

Table 15.5 lists some of the activities in which forensic psychologists engage. As you can see, the potential scope of activities is very broad. Few psychologists would be involved in offering all of these

---

TABLE 15.5 The Scope of Forensic Psychology Services

Prevention Programs
To reduce violence and bullying

Court-Related Assessment
Assessment of witnesses

- Credibility issues

Assessment of victims

- Impact of an assault or injury

- Credibility versus malingering

Assessment of the accused

- Evaluation of mental status at the time of an offense

- Competence to stand trial

Assessment of disputing parties

- Child custody evaluation

Assessment of Offenders
Risk of violence
Risk of sexual violence

Treatment Services for Offenders
To address mental health issues such as depression and anxiety
To address criminal behaviour

Research
To identify the best strategies to predict criminal behavior
To identify the most effective treatments

---

services, and it would be common for them to specialize in offering a small set of psychological services (e.g., assessment-focused work or offering treatment to offenders). As noted above, within the field of forensic psychology, a number of psychologists are employed within the correctional system.

Assessment

Lally (2003) surveyed expert forensic psychologists to identify the psychological assessment measures considered appropriate for different types of assessments. **Table 15.6** lists the measures that were deemed *recommended, acceptable,* or *unacceptable* in evaluating risk of violence and in evaluating competency to stand trial. Many of the assessment tools should be familiar to you from previous chapters. You will also notice that an instrument designed specifically for an offender population, the Psychopathy Checklist–Revised (Hare, 1991), is the most highly recommended tool for assessing risk of violence. This checklist uses information gathered from a semistructured interview and a review of the person's history and police/prison files. The majority of expert forensic psychologists who responded to the survey did not consider projective tests acceptable in assessing the risk of violent behavior or in determining competence to stand trial. A similar survey about instruments used in assessing young offenders' competence to stand trial indicated that (a) intelligence tests such as the Wechsler scales were used by the majority of experts in juvenile forensic assessment (82%), (b) around half of the survey respondents (56%) reported using the MMPI-A, and (c) only a small minority reported using projective tests such as the Rorschach (16%), TAT (12%), or sentence completion tests (10%) (Ryba, Cooper, & Zapf, 2003).

TABLE 15.6   Expert Opinion on Tests for Forensic Evaluations

	Risk for Violence	Competency to Stand Trial
Recommended	Psychopathy Checklist–Revised	WAIS III
		MacArthur Competence Assessment Tool
Acceptable	MMPI-2	MMPI 2
	Psychopathy Checklist– Screening version	Halstead–Reitan
	Violence Risk Appraisal Guide	Stanford–Binet
	WAIS III	Luria–Nebraska
	Personality Assessment Inventory	Interdisciplinary fitness interview
		Personality Assessment Inventory
Unacceptable	Projective drawings	Projective drawings
	TAT	TAT
	Sentence completion	Sentence completion
	Rorschach	Rorschach
	16 PF	16 PF
		MCMI II

Adapted from Lally (2003)

There are important similarities and differences between regular clinical practice and clinical practice within the corrections system. For example, correctional psychologists, like other clinical psychologists, should use evidence-based strategies in their assessment, treatment, and prevention activities. Any psychological assessment can have serious consequences for the well-being of the individual and of society. However, one of the differences in a correctional context is that assessments usually involve public safety issues. This is especially evident in the context of risk assessments that focus on the likelihood of an individual reengaging in violent criminal behavior. **Viewpoint Box 15.4** highlights issues in conducting these assessments.

VIEWPOINT BOX 15.4

RISK ASSESSMENT

One of the primary reasons for requesting a psychological assessment is to obtain a scientifically informed prediction about a person's behavior. Psychological assessments may be used in predicting diverse outcomes such as suicidal risk, the ability to benefit from a social skills group, or the likelihood that the person will adhere to a medical regimen. When making predictions, the psychologist draws on research knowledge of risk and protective factors. The risks associated with making errors are carefully weighed. Although most psychological predictions are important, they are rarely the focus of public scrutiny. However, in the case of predictions of violent behavior, the repercussions of errors are very serious. You may recall the media outcry that occurs when news breaks of a violent offense perpetrated by someone recently released from prison or on parole. There are often recriminations that mental health professionals have failed to predict and prevent the violent behavior. The failure to predict that a person with a violent history will reoffend can have deadly consequences. On the other hand, overly conservative predictions based on single episodes of violence that are unlikely to be repeated can lead to the prolonged and unjust incarceration of an offender beyond the time that a sentence has been served.

A few decades ago, mental health professionals were ill-equipped to predict dangerousness (Monahan, 1981). Since that time a number of effective, evidence-based approaches have been developed to aid psychologists in making predictions (Hanson, 2005; Webster & Bailes, 2004). Armed with research-based assessment tools that allow reasonably accurate prediction of violent behavior, numerous correctional policies have been introduced in North America to protect the public from dangerous offenders. Psychologists such as **Robert Hare** have been at the vanguard of these research efforts. Hare's groundbreaking work on the construct of psychopathy has described the capacity of charming psychopaths to manipulate others without remorse. Hare's Psychopathy Checklist–Revised (PCL-R) is considered the single best predictor of violent behavior (Fulero, 1995; Lally, 2003). The PCL-R has also been demonstrated to be useful in diverse cultural contexts (Hare, Clark, Grann, & Thornton, 2000). Another commonly used measure, the Violence Risk Appraisal Guide (VRAG; Harris, Rice, & Quinsey, 1993), uses empirically derived combinations of common clinical variables to predict long-term recidivism. Specialized measures have also been developed for subpopulations such as young offenders or men who assault their wives (Hanson, 2005). There is a high degree of correlation between the different measures, and many are moderately accurate in predicting recidivism in violent offenders (Hanson, 2005). Profile Box 15.3 introduces Dr. Stephen Lally who is an expert in forensic assessment.

PROFILE BOX 15.3

DR. STEPHEN LALLY

I earned a Ph.D. in clinical psychology with a minor in anthropology at the University of North Carolina, Chapel Hill, having completed my internship at St. Elizabeth's Hospital, Washington, DC. After finishing my training, my first job was at a mental health center providing psychological services to individuals with serious, persistent mental illness. I then accepted a position at the forensic unit of St. Elizabeth's, where I worked for 7 years conducting evaluations for the court, providing treatment to inpatients, and supervising interns and residents. It was during this period that I received my license in psychology and completed the board certification for forensic psychology (American Board of Professional Psychology). Subsequently, after teaching as an adjunct professor, I accepted a full-time faculty position at Argosy University in Washington, DC. Currently I am a professor in the clinical psychology program

Dr. Stephen Lally

for the local campus and an associate dean for Argosy University. In addition to teaching, I conduct research and publish in the areas of assessment, ethics, and forensic psychology. I have a part-time private practice that is primarily focused on forensic psychology, and I am active in local and national professional associations.

How did you choose to become a forensic psychologist?

During graduate school, I had not considered becoming a forensic psychologist, but while on internship I had the opportunity to work on a forensic unit conducting evaluations and providing treatment. I found the work exciting and challenging. After my internship I took advantage of an opportunity to return to the forensic program as a psychologist. The following years in which I worked on both pretrial and posttrial wards set me on the path to having a career in forensic psychology.

What is the most rewarding part of your job as a forensic psychologist? What is the greatest challenge you face as a forensic psychologist?

I think what is rewarding in this area of practice is that it challenges and encourages me to develop and grow as a psychologist. In forensic psychology, one needs to be knowledgeable in the fields of both law and psychology, and to remain aware of the developments with both fields. Although the two fields have very different ways of looking at and conceptualizing phenomena (e.g., motivation, issues of probability), the recent trend has been for both fields to increasingly focus on the scientific foundation of practice, professional opinions, and expert testimony.

Tell us about recent developments in forensic assessment

Within psychology there has been a growth in assessment tools focused on legally relevant issues (e.g., competency to stand trial, risk of future violence) and an increase in research on the forensic applications of other psychological assessment tools. As a result, rather than just basing one's opinions on a clinician's unsubstantiated impression, forensic mental health professionals have access to data based on evidence-based procedures and instruments. This trend is especially true for forensic psychologists, as they are trained in the scientific method and can apply this knowledge when conducting or reviewing psychological assessments.

How do you integrate science and practice in your work?

The concept of "local clinical scientist" has been used to describe how one can apply the scientific method of hypothesis testing and evidence collection to guide practice. This concept is particularly relevant for forensic psychology. To illustrate, I may be retained to evaluate whether an individual who is accused of murder meets the legal standard of insanity. This is a retrospective evaluation of a person's mental state at the time the crime was perpetrated, but because I cannot go back in time I may be evaluating the person now and then trying to generalize to that earlier time period. To do this I need to have records from that earlier time and talk to other people who may have had contact with the individual at the time of the offense. I also need to know how certain mental disorders persist or change over time. The process of hypothesis development and testing continues throughout the evaluation as I consider issues such as whether the person is now attempting to feign a mental illness (i.e., malingering).

What do you see as the most exciting changes in the field of forensic psychology?

The training clinical psychologists receive is particularly relevant for conducting forensic evaluations, and the courts appear to be increasingly using and valuing the services provided by forensic psychologists. This exciting change must be tempered with the recognition that, although our tests and methods are becoming increasingly reliable and valid, we must continue to acknowledge our limitations and the role of uncertainty in answering legally relevant questions.

Intervention

Correctional psychology is not simply clinical practice with people who happen to live in a prison (Magaletta & Verdeyen, 2005). For example, for a correctional psychologist, treatment outcome is more likely to be measured in terms of recidivism (committing crimes after release from incarceration) than reduction in symptoms. Thus, programs have traditionally been more likely to target factors associated with risk of criminal behavior (e.g., association with delinquent peers, antisocial attitudes, anger and impulse control) than to target variables that are distressing to the offender but unrelated to criminal behavior (e.g., low self-esteem) (Dowden & Andrews, 2004). For example, Greg has a history of violent behavior and has been incarcerated for physical assaults. Helping him learn to better control his anger may be an important goal for him, but it is also a critical aspect of reducing the likelihood that he will pose a threat to others when he has served his sentence. In the 1970s and 1980s, it was assumed that offender treatment had little chance of facilitating change. However, with the introduction of cognitive-behavioral programs that target risk factors, the picture has changed considerably. A series of meta-analyses have supported the utility of CBT interventions for offenders (Dowden & Andrews, 2004).

Unfortunately, the methodological quality of many outcome studies in this area is relatively poor. There are few randomized control trials, and the use of strategies to address the substantial problem of high dropout rates is inconsistent (Wormith et al., 2007). A meta-analysis by Wilson, Bouffard, and MacKenzie (2005) examining studies on a range of cognitive-behavioral interventions including problem-solving, social skills training, cognitive restructuring, and impulse control found that the methodologically strongest studies yielded a moderate effect size ($d = .51$). Translating this effect size into recidivism rates: treated offenders had a recidivism rate of 46%, whereas for untreated offenders, the rate was 54% (Wilson et al., 2005). However, as in all therapy outcome research, it is important to move beyond examining the efficacy of research treatment programs to determine the effectiveness of these programs when they are widely applied.

A number of challenges face forensic psychologists who offer treatment services. These challenges can stem from the context in which services are delivered as well as from the clients themselves. Dowden and Andrews (2004) emphasized the importance of considering correctional staff practices in the delivery of effective treatment. It is clear that the considerable impact of environmental constraints and influences (e.g., restrictiveness of the setting, staff practices, what constitutes normative behavior in a correctional setting) sets clinical practice in corrections apart from other types of mental health services provided by clinical psychologists. With respect to client issues, a prominent concern has to do with treatment drop out. Wormith (2002), for example, underlined the importance of developing effective programs for offenders of Native American ancestry who are particularly likely to drop out of treatment programs. Having debunked the notion that "nothing works" in the treatment of offenders, emerging approaches are moving beyond a simple risk-reduction model to also address offender motivation for positive change in their lives (Day, Gerace, Wilson, & Howells, 2008; Wormith et al., 2007).

SUMMARY AND CONCLUSIONS

In addition to offering traditional mental health services, a growing number of clinical psychologists work in clinical health psychology, clinical neuropsychology, and forensic psychology. Practice in these areas is based on the core skill set found in clinical psychology, with additional specific knowledge and skills taught in graduate training, in internships, and on the job. Health psychologists, with their focus on health maintenance, illness prevention, assessment, and intervention, have a broad scope of practice potentially applicable to all age groups in all health care settings. Clinical neuropsychologists, with their knowledge of brain–behavior connections, have been and continue to be key contributors to the health care of people with a wide range of neurological impairments. Forensic psychologists, working within and outside correctional facilities, have developed an increasingly efficacious and effective set of assessment and intervention procedures. Across these areas of practice, psychologists strive to apply the science of psychology to the improvement of the lives of young and old alike.

C r i t i c a l   T h i n k i n g   Q u e s t i o n s

Across the different applied areas of practice described in the chapter, what knowledge and skill elements are common to all?

Do you think it could be possible for a clinical psychologist to be a generalist who covers the areas of health psychology, neuropsychology, and forensic psychology? What would be the challenges involved for such a professional?

How does the role of a health psychologist differ from that of a physician?

With the advent of advanced imaging techniques in neurology, what can clinical neuropsychologists contribute to the care of those with neurological impairments?

What are the roles for psychologists in dealing with those involved in the criminal justice system?

K e y   T e r m s

acute pain: a short-term sensation that serves an unpleasant, but useful, function; it can usually be relieved in different ways, including the application of heat or cold, rest, distraction, or the administration of analgesics

biopsychosocial model: model that that takes into account biological, individual, and social factors

chronic pain: pain that persists for more than 6 months

disability: impairment, activity limitation, and participation restriction

neuroanatomy: normal brain functioning

neuropathology: the ways that injuries and diseases affect the brain

recidivism: reoffending

risk assessments: prediction of the likelihood of an individual reengaging in violent criminal behavior

sleep hygiene: engaging in good sleep habits, such as avoiding stimulants before bedtime, developing presleep routines, and so on

Key Names

Ward Halstead

Robert Hare

Aleksandr Luria

Dennis Turk

Patrick McGrath

Charles Morin

Ralph Reitan

ADDITIONAL RESOURCES

BOOKS

Boyer, B. A., & Paharia, M. I. (Eds). (2008). *Comprehensive handbook of clinical health psychology*. New York: John Wiley & Sons.

Goldstein, L. H., & McNeil, J. E. (Eds.). (2004). *Clinical neuropsychology: A practical guide to assessment and management for clinicians*. Chichester, UK: John Wiley & Sons.

Hollin, C. R. (Ed.). (2004). *The essential handbook of offender assessment and treatment*. Chichester, UK: John Wiley & Sons.

McConroy, M. A., & Murrie, D. C. (2007). *Forensic assessment of violence risk: A guide for risk assessment and risk management*. New York: John Wiley and Sons.

Check It Out!

The Web site of the American Board of Professional Psychology is: http://www.abpp.org/

Information on the IWK Health Centre and the Pediatric Pain Laboratory of the Psychology Department of Dalhousie University is available at: http://www.pediatric-pain.ca

The Web site of the American Board of Clinical Neuropsychology is: http://www.theabcn.org/

The Web site of the American Board of Forensic Psychology is: http://www.abfp.com/

The Oliver Zangwill Centre for Neuropsychological Rehabilitation Web site provides resources on assessment and rehabilitation: http://www.ozc.nhs.uk/

Center for Disease Control national Center for Health Statistics. (2006). *New report finds pain affects millions of Americans*. Retrieved on June 23rd 2009 from http://www.cdc.gov/nchs/PRESSROOM/06facts/hus06.htm

Major Journals Relevant to Clinical Psychology

American Journal of Psychiatry

This journal is the official publication of the American Psychiatric Association. It includes articles on developments in biological psychiatry as well as on treatment innovations and forensic, ethical, economic, and social topics.

American Psychologist

This is the official journal of the American Psychological Association. Articles address current issues in psychology, the science and practice of psychology, and psychology's contribution to public policy.

Annual Review of Clinical Psychology

The journal provides reviews of major developments in clinical psychology, including theory, research, and application of psychological principles to the assessment and treatment of psychological disorders. Additionally, it addresses reviews of broader issues in the field, such as public policy and diversity issues.

Annual Review of Psychology

This journal presents authoritative, analytic reviews by eminent psychologists covering the entire range of psychological research.

Archives of Clinical Neuropsychology

Included in this journal are articles in psychological aspects of the etiology, diagnosis, and treatment of disorders arising out of dysfunction of the central nervous system.

Archives of General Psychiatry

This journal contains studies and commentaries of general interest to clinicians, scholars, and research scientists in psychiatry, mental health, behavioral science, and allied fields.

Assessment

Included in this journal are studies on the use of assessment measures within the domain of clinical and applied psychology, including practical applications of measurement methods, test development and interpretation strategies, and advances in the description and prediction of human behavior.

Behavior Therapy

One of the two official publications of the Association for Behavioral and Cognitive Therapies, this journal includes reports and reviews of studies on the application of behavioral and cognitive sciences to clinical problems.

Behavioral Sciences and the Law

Covered in this journal are topics at the interface of the law and the behavioral sciences, with theoretical, legal, and research articles on psycholegal topics, including mental health.

Behaviour Research and Therapy

This journal contains articles on cognitive behavior therapy applied to clinical disorders, behavioral medicine, and medical psychology.

British Journal of Clinical Psychology

Published by the British Psychological Society, this journal includes original contributions to scientific knowledge in clinical psychology. Articles include descriptive studies as well as studies of the etiology, assessment, and amelioration of disorders of all kinds, in all settings, and among all age groups.

British Journal of Psychiatry

Published by the Royal College of Psychiatrists, this journal includes editorials, review articles, and commentaries on contentious articles. The target readership is psychiatrists, clinical psychologists, and other mental health professionals.

Clinical Case Studies

Devoted entirely to the presentation of case studies, this journal includes cases involving individuals, couples, and families. All articles use a standard case presentation format that presents assessment, conceptualization, and treatment.

Clinical Child and Family Psychology Review

This journal includes research reviews and conceptual and theoretical papers related to infants, children, adolescents, and families. Topics covered include etiology, assessment, description, treatment and intervention, prevention, methodology, and public policy.

Clinical Psychology Review

Presented in this journal are reviews of research on topics such as psychopathology, psychotherapy, behavioral medicine, community mental health, assessment, and child development.

Clinical Psychology & Psychotherapy

Articles in this journal focus on the integration of theory, research, and practice across different theoretical orientations.

Clinical Psychology: Science and Practice

The official publication of the Society of Clinical Psychology (Division 12) of the American Psychological Association, it includes reviews of research related to assessment, intervention, service delivery, and professional issues.

Cognitive and Behavioral Practice

One of the two official publications of the Association for Behavioral and Cognitive Therapies, it contains clinically rich accounts of assessment and intervention procedures that are clearly grounded in empirical research.

Cognitive Therapy and Research

This is an interdisciplinary journal on the role of cognitive processes in human adaptation and adjustment. The journal includes experimental studies; theoretical, review, technical, and methodological articles; case studies; and brief reports.

Criminal Justice and Behavior

The official publication of the American Association for Correctional and Forensic Psychology includes scholarly evaluations of assessment, classification, prevention, intervention, and treatment programs.

Evidence Based Mental Health

This multidisciplinary journal provides a digest of the most important clinical research relevant to clinicians in mental health.

Health Psychology

This journal is designed to further an understanding of the links between behavioral principles and physical health and illness.

Journal of Abnormal Child Psychology

This is the journal of the International Society for Research in Child and Adolescent Psychopathology. It includes research on psychopathology in childhood and adolescence with an emphasis on empirical studies of the major childhood disorders (the disruptive behavior disorders, depression, anxiety, and pervasive developmental disorders).

Journal of Abnormal Psychology

Included in this journal are articles on basic research and theory in psychopathology, normal processes in abnormal individuals, pathological or atypical features of the behavior of normal persons, experimental studies relating to disordered emotional behavior or pathology, the influence of gender and ethnicity on pathological processes, and tests of hypotheses from psychological theories that relate to abnormal behavior.

Journal of Behavioral Medicine

This interdisciplinary journal is devoted to furthering our understanding of physical health and illness through the knowledge and techniques of behavioral science.

Journal of Clinical Child and Adolescent Psychology

This is the official journal of the Society of Clinical Child and Adolescent Psychology (Division 53) of the American Psychological Association. It includes research on development and evaluation of assessment and intervention techniques, studies on the development and maintenance of problems, cross-cultural and sociodemographic variables that influence clinical child and adolescent psychology, training and professional practice issues, and child advocacy.

Journal of Clinical Psychology

Included in this journal are research studies, articles on contemporary professional issues, single case research, dissertations in brief, notes from the field, and news and notes. Topics include psychopathology, psychodiagnostics, and the psychotherapeutic process, as well as articles focusing on psychotherapy effectiveness research, psychological assessment and treatment matching, and clinical outcomes.

Journal of Consulting and Clinical Psychology

This journal includes articles on the development, validity, and use of techniques of diagnosis and treatment of disordered behavior; studies of populations of clinical interest, such as hospitals, prison, rehabilitation, geriatric, and similar samples; cross-cultural and demographic studies of interest for behavior disorders; studies of personality and of its assessment and development where these have a clear bearing on problems of clinical dysfunction; studies of gender, ethnicity, or sexual orientation that have a clear bearing on diagnosis, assessment, and treatment; and methodologically sound case studies pertinent to the preceding topics.

Journal of Family Psychology

The official publication of the Division of Family Psychology of the American Psychological Association (Division 43), this journal is devoted to the study of the family system from multiple perspectives and to the application of psychological methods to advance knowledge related to family research, intervention, and policy.

Journal of Marital and Family Therapy

The official journal of the American Association of Marital and Family Therapy, it has articles on research and clinical innovations in the areas of marital and family services.

Journal of Personality Assessment

This is the official publication of the Society for Personality Assessment. It contains articles dealing with the development, evaluation, refinement, and application of personality assessment methods. Articles address empirical, theoretical, instructional, and professional aspects of using psychological tests, interview data, and the applied clinical assessment process.

Journal of Psychopathology and Behavioral Assessment

Included in this journal are research investigations and clinical case summaries on psychopathology and mental disorders applicable to all ages, deviant or abnormal behaviors (including those related to medical conditions and trauma), and personality constructs.

Journal of Social and Clinical Psychology

This journal publishes research that applies theory and research from social psychology to the understanding of human functioning, including the alleviation of psychological problems and the improvement of psychological well-being.

Neuropsychology

The focus of this journal is on basic research, the integration of basic and applied research, and improved practice in the field of neuropsychology.

Professional Psychology: Research and Practice

Included in this journal are articles on the application of psychology, including data-based and theoretical articles on techniques and practices.

Psychological Assessment

This journal presents empirical research on measurement and evaluation relevant to the broad field of clinical psychology. Topics include clinical judgment and the application of decision-making models; paradigms derived from basic psychological research in cognition, personality–social psychology, and biological psychology; and development, validation, and application of assessment instruments, observational methods, and interviews.

Psychological Bulletin

Included in this journal are evaluative and integrative research reviews and interpretations of issues in scientific psychology.

Psychotherapy

This official publication of the Division of Psychotherapy of the American Psychological Association (Division 29) includes theoretical contributions, research studies, novel ideas, controversies, and examples of practice-relevant issues. The journal is designed to be of interest to theorists, researchers, and/or practitioners.

Psychotherapy Research

The official publication of the Society for Psychotherapy Research, it includes research findings relevant to practice, education, and policy formulation. The journal presents reports of original research on all aspects of psychotherapy, as well as methodological, theoretical, and review articles of direct relevance to psychotherapy research.

Scientific Review of Mental Health Practice

This journal is devoted exclusively to distinguishing scientifically supported claims from scientifically unsupported claims in clinical psychology, psychiatry, social work, and allied disciplines.

Training and Education in Professional Psychology

A joint publication of the American Psychological Association and the Association of Psychology Postdoctoral and Internship Centers, this journal publishes articles contributes to the advancement of professional psychology education and training.

Applications to Graduate School

DO YOU WANT TO BE A CLINICAL PSYCHOLOGIST?

We hope that the descriptions we have provided of the diverse activities in which clinical psychologists engage help you imagine what it would be like to be a clinical psychologist. As you have learned, the term "clinical psychologist" covers many different types of professional activities, so that, for example, Dr. Persons' week is very different from a week in the life of Dr. Maddux, whose work is different again from that of Dr. Alexander. Nevertheless, the work lives of these three psychologists have many features in common: (a) their work is based on a foundation of knowledge about human psychological functioning; (b) their work activities are diverse—they spend their work days in a variety of professional activities; (c) their work is demanding, and they rarely feel they have enough hours in the day to do everything they want to do; and most important, (d) their work is rewarding, and they feel a passionate commitment to what they do. These three psychologists are characterized by dynamism, energy, and a commitment to lifelong learning.

As you read the other chapters in this book, you will meet many clinical psychologists at different stages of their careers. When we asked them to tell us how they chose clinical psychology as a career, many described having discovered a passion for this field when they were undergraduates. They were drawn to clinical psychology by the promise it offered to understand and treat health and mental health problems using research-based tools. All the clinical psychologists profiled in this book have jobs that require balancing the various activities in learning about new research developments, delivering services, training others, and contributing to the administration of the agency in which they work, as well as serving the broader community. If this appeals to you, then you may be interested in a career in clinical psychology. If your career goal is to spend a much larger proportion of your professional time delivering direct services to clients, you may wish to consider other professions, including social work, counseling, or psychiatric nursing.

Many undergraduate students taking a course in clinical psychology are attracted to career possibilities in other areas of psychology. If you find that you have a passion for social psychology or cognitive psychology, you should follow the steps we suggest in this appendix, but adapt them for the area of psychology that most interests you. If you are interested in a career in clinical psychology but decide to pursue training in a different area of psychology, you should be fully aware that your chances of switching to work as a clinical psychologist are extremely limited. The best option for becoming a clinical psychologist is to complete a doctorate in an accredited clinical program.

DO YOU WANT TO GO TO GRADUATE SCHOOL?

Some students apply to graduate school without really taking the time to think about whether it is something that they want to do. Training in clinical psychology usually requires around 6 years of further training after completion of an undergraduate degree, so it is not something to be taken lightly. If you have high grades, you may have been encouraged by professors to apply to graduate school; however, you need to carefully consider whether this is something that you wish to do. Ideally, you should start thinking about applying to graduate school before the final year of your undergraduate program. This will allow you the time to consider different career options and to begin the process of gathering information about applying to graduate programs in clinical psychology.

You must consider your short- and long-term goals for both career and personal life. Are you willing to move? Are you willing to delay earning a good salary? Although clinical psychologists are typically well paid, there will be many years during graduate school when you will probably be earning much less than your peers who decided to enter the workforce. What kind of job do you hope to have 10 years from now? Graduate training does not occur in a vacuum. At the same time you are considering whether or not you wish to go to graduate school, you may also be reflecting on other decisions—for example, about relationships and when (or whether) you wish to become a parent. Although you may be fairly confident that parenthood is not in your plans in the next year or so, you may be less sure about your plans in 3 or 4 years' time. The decision to go to graduate school does not rule out having a family for the next 6 years. However, it does introduce challenges. Some programs have explicit policies with respect to parental leaves so that, for example, students are allowed one year longer to complete the program for each parental leave taken. Some scholarships now allow students to take a maternity leave. If you are a mature student who already has a family, you will no doubt be considering the ways that you can meet the financial and time demands of your multiple roles.

ARE YOU ELIGIBLE FOR ADMISSION TO A PROGRAM IN CLINICAL PSYCHOLOGY?

Competition for places in clinical psychology programs is fierce. Programs accept only around 15% of the people who apply, and all programs have demanding academic standards. Because research is such a strong component of the training in many programs, these programs ensure that candidates they admit have the intellectual capacity to conduct original research. The selection system can be an unforgiving one: a bad grade in a single course may not sink your application, but a bad year just might. Most programs prefer to accept students who are likely to receive major scholarship funding, which means that places are offered to those candidates who have earned high grades in the undergraduate degree. As we mentioned early in the book, programs in counseling psychology are often slightly less demanding in terms of the academic grades required.

The honors thesis provides an excellent opportunity to learn about the various steps in conducting research. If you enjoy the process of reviewing the literature to formulate meaningful hypotheses, the intellectual challenge of designing a feasible study that will test those hypotheses, the careful consideration of ethical issues involved in the study, painstaking data collection, rigorous data analysis, and the satisfaction of writing it all up in a coherent report, then the chances are good that you will savor the opportunity to conduct a doctoral dissertation. If, on the other hand, you find completing the honors thesis a tedious process, then you should think very carefully about whether you are attracted to a graduate program in clinical psychology in which one of the key requirements is the completion of a doctoral dissertation. Good grades and research experience are necessary but do not guarantee acceptance into graduate programs. Students with good grades can improve their chances of success if they also have varied research experience beyond the research requirements of the undergraduate program.

FINDING OUT ABOUT PROGRAMS IN CLINICAL PSYCHOLOGY

What do you need to know about clinical training programs? The American Psychological Association Committee on Accreditation (CoA) requires accredited programs to make available information that will be useful to you in selecting the programs to which you wish to apply. Specifically, the CoA requires accredited programs to provide information on the program's goals, objectives and training model, requirements for admission and graduation, curriculum, faculty, students, facilities and other resources, administrative policies and procedures, the kinds of research and practicum experiences it provides, its education and training outcomes, as well as evidence of accreditation. All of this information should be helpful to you in choosing the programs to which you will apply.

The Web site of the American Psychological Association provides lists of accredited clinical programs (http://www.apa.org/ed/accreditation/clinpsyal.html). Reviewing a program Web site is probably the best strategy to get a general sense of what the program is like. Although all programs include training in the basics of clinical psychology, programs differ in their areas of strength and whether they offer a Ph.D. or a Psy.D. For example, some programs offer separate training in adult or child clinical psychology, whereas other programs offer combined training in both adult and child clinical psychology. Some programs have faculty members with a strong profile in clinical health psychology, others have special expertise in issues related to older adults, and some provide opportunities to learn about forensic psychology.

Accredited clinical psychology programs differ in the process by which students are selected. In some universities, students are accepted into the program and during the first year of study are matched to work with a particular thesis supervisor. In other programs, there must be a match with a thesis supervisor at the time of admission. You should become aware of the process for each program and tailor your application to each one you are considering. You should also be aware that there are differences among training programs in the sequence of degrees granted. Some universities accept students into a master's program that is then followed by a doctoral program; other universities accept students directly into a doctoral program. Both sequences require comparable course work, research training, practica, and internship. The main difference is that students in the former programs must complete a master's thesis, which is required for the awarding of a master's degree.

THE APPLICATION PROCESS

The process of applying to graduate school consumes both time and money. The process consists of several phases, including gathering information and deciding whether you wish to apply to graduate school, choosing the programs to which you will apply, studying for and completing the Graduate Record Examination, preparing the application materials, obtaining letters of reference and submitting a full application, and finally, (hopefully) making a decision about offers you have received. It is probably fair to say that the application process will take the same amount of your time as a one-semester course.

Gathering Information

The information-gathering stage begins in your second or third year of undergraduate study. You can probably gather enough information from Web sites to generate a list of programs that you want to consider. You can increase your chances of obtaining a place by applying to several different programs. However, it is probably a waste of your time to apply to any programs that you know you do not want to attend. In addition to the information from Web sites, you can gather informal information by asking professors for their opinion about different programs.

The Graduate Record Examination

Once you have decided to apply to graduate school and have selected a number of programs that interest you, you will have a better idea of the application requirements for each program. Most programs require candidates to submit scores on the Graduate Record Examination (GRE). The GRE includes both a general test, which can be completed at any time of the year, and a subject test, which can be completed only in October, November, or April. The tests are completed at a licensed test center either via computer or in a paper and pencil format. The general test takes up to 3 1/2 hours and assesses verbal reasoning, quantitative reasoning, critical thinking, and analytical writing skills. Practice material is available to applicants for the general test. The subject test lasts up to 4 hours and includes about 205 multiple choice questions, of which 40% are oriented to natural science aspects of psychology, 43% are oriented to social science aspects of psychology, and 17% are general psychology. In preparation for taking the GRE you should review materials from psychology courses and download a practice test from the GRE Web site.

Curriculum Vitae

Your curriculum vitae (CV) should provide contact information and detail educational accomplishments, honors and awards, scholarly conference presentations, publications, manuscripts submitted for publication, as well as work and volunteer experience. Volunteer experience in the mental health field can provide important opportunities to learn about different populations, the challenges they face, and the resources available to them. Paid or volunteer research experience provides the opportunity to learn research methods, to work more closely with a professor, and in some cases to gain valuable experience in conference presentations and the submission of manuscripts to scholarly journals.

Application Forms and Transcripts

Although many universities use an online application system, universities and programs all have different application forms. Ensure that your form is completed accurately. Printed or typed application forms are preferable to handwritten forms. There is also variability in the deadline by which all materials should be submitted ranging from early December to the end of January, so check each date carefully. Most programs require you to arrange for official transcripts to be forwarded to the admission office. Allow plenty of time so that the materials arrive prior to the application deadline. Universities with online applications often have automated systems that will inform you about the status of your application. If you have not received a confirmation of receipt of all the necessary documents, it is prudent to contact the admissions office a couple of weeks before the final deadline to request confirmation that all the application materials have arrived safely and that your file is complete. This is a busy time of year for all admissions offices, so it is probably easiest to do this via email rather than by phone.

Statements of Interest and Research Plans

Many programs ask candidates to submit a written statement about the areas in which they are interested, as well as their research plans. Programs do not expect candidates to have mapped out the study they will conduct for the doctoral dissertation. These written statements should describe your general areas of interest. If your statements are too specific, then you reduce the likelihood of finding a good match with a professor. It probably makes more sense to think in terms of whether you can imagine yourself joining in a professor's research group, than whether you can find someone whose ideas match yours perfectly. It is useful to tailor your statement of interest to match each program to which you are applying.

Letters of Reference

All applications for graduate school require reference letters. In general, these letters should be from psychology professors. Although you may obtain a glowing letter from a person in a community agency in which you have volunteered, the opinions of psychology professors are usually given greater weight in the selection process. Professors in small universities may know undergraduate students by name, but in larger universities this occurs less frequently. Therefore, in your second or third year, you need to plan to make contact with professors who will be potential referees. You may wish to consider volunteering your services in a research project. Inform the professor that your goal is to apply to graduate programs in clinical psychology and that you are eager to obtain relevant experience.

TABLE 1 Letters of Reference

Who to Ask

Psychology professors who are familiar with your work

- Supervisor of thesis
- Instructor in a small class
- Supervisor of research assistantship or volunteer research

When to Ask

- Once the professor is familiar with your work
- At least 2 months in advance

What to Provide

- Full list of programs to which you are applying with addresses and deadlines
- Your curriculum vitae
- Copy of your transcript
- Copy of the form to be completed or link to download it

Before the Deadline

- Politely inquire whether the letter is prepared

After You Receive Results

- Inform the professors who have written letters of the results and thank them

---

Table 1 highlights issues in obtaining a letter of reference. It is to your advantage to ask the professor whether she or he is willing to write a reference letter well ahead of the deadline. As you are aware, professors have many responsibilities, so if you make a request for a letter that is due in a week's time, you risk getting a brief letter, a late letter, or none at all. Once the professor has agreed to write the letter, you must prepare a complete package that contains all the material the professor will need in order to prepare letters to be sent to the various programs to which you are applying. It is beneficial for you to make the professor's task as straightforward as possible. Avoid asking for a series of letters as you decide to apply to different programs—make sure that you give the professor a complete list of programs you are applying to, rather than giving "updated" lists as you go through the process of deciding which programs to apply to. A week or so before the earliest application deadline, contact the professor to inquire politely whether the letters are ready. Most professors who have gone to the trouble of preparing letters of reference for you will appreciate receiving a message of thanks and a message reporting the final outcome of the application process.

Universities have different policies concerning letters of reference. Some require the referee to send a letter directly to the university, others require the letters of reference to be given to the candidate in signed, sealed envelopes and included in the application package. Check the required procedure for each university.

Contacting Potential Supervisors

Email is a very easy way to contact potential supervisors. However, prior to contacting the potential supervisor, do your homework: find out all you can about the program in general and the work of that professor in particular. **Table 2** describes possible contact with potential supervisors. Professors often receive many email messages a week in the fall term from potential students, so it is helpful to keep an initial email message relatively brief. It is wise to verify whether the supervisor is planning on accepting a new student that year. It is important to know, for example, whether the professor is on parental leave, sabbatical leave, or close to retirement and not accepting a student.

Because published material is easily available electronically, it does not make sense to request copies of the professor's publications. You should do a bit of homework and read several of the professor's recent publications. If you are truly interested in working with this person you may wish to ask to see a copy of work that is in press. Avoid clogging a professor's inbox with documents such as a transcript, your CV, and a copy of your honors thesis. However, it may be helpful to offer to send any of those materials if the professor would like to read them.

If you live within easy traveling of the university to which you are applying, you may wish to express your willingness to come for an interview. Many professors do not conduct interviews until after the

---

TABLE 2   Contacting Potential Supervisors

Prior to Application

- Gather information from university Web site
- Search for materials on PsycINFO
- Express interest via email
- Confirm that professor is eligible to take a new student
- Offer to send materials (CV, transcript)
- Ask for copies of articles that are in press
- Inquire about future research planned by the professor
- Inquire about interviews
- Ask specific questions if the information is not available elsewhere

If You Are Contacted by a Potential Supervisor

- Ask questions that would give information to help you choose between two offers
- Ask about supervision style
- Ask to speak to current or recent graduate students

Once You Have Made a Decision

- Inform professor that you intend to accept offer
- Inform professor if you have accepted a place elsewhere

---

deadline for admission (they simply do not have time to interview all potential candidates, so they focus their energies on a few candidates who have met all the eligibility criteria and who are interested in research in their area). You may wish to ask a professor whether it is possible to meet or contact other graduate students.

FINANCING YOUR TRAINING

Unless you are independently wealthy, your planning should include consideration of how you will finance the years you will be in graduate school. On average, students take over 6 years after the bachelor's degree to complete a doctoral degree in clinical psychology. Expenses include tuition fees as well as living expenses. Accredited programs in clinical psychology usually require full-time registration as a student for at least 4 years. That means that you are not allowed to work more than a small number of hours a week (e.g., 10 hours a week in many universities). Part of your planning and decision making should include finding out about all your potential sources of income.

In considering offers from different universities, it is often a challenge to know which university is offering the best financial support. For example, some universities offer generous funding in the first and second year, with lower amounts as the student progresses. Other universities may offer a lower amount, but guarantee to provide it over the entire course of the program. It is useful to distinguish between money that is given to the student (i.e., scholarship) and money that the student must earn (i.e., working as a teaching assistant). In some cases, you might find that the doctoral program is not offering you any financial support and you are expected to fully finance your studies. As with most things in life, be sure to read the "fine print"!

Scholarships and Bursaries

You may be eligible to receive scholarships and bursaries from diverse sources, including the university in which you will be enrolled and from state or federal funding agencies. You can find a comprehensive list of A–Z funding opportunities at http://www.apa.org/ppo/funding/atoz.html. Most scholarships are awarded on the basis of merit, which means that they are given to the students who have high grade point averages; if you have made a presentation at a scholarly conference, or have submitted a manuscript for publication, that will also strengthen your application. It is important to gather information and submit your application in plenty of time.

In addition to major funding, there may be many small scholarships for which you may be eligible. Some of these may be offered to students whose work is in a certain area or to those in serious financial need. Some students are proficient in finding out about potential sources of funding and become competent at preparing application packages. Although a $500 scholarship will not solve all your financial concerns, it will help, and will of course be an important item to add to your CV.

Research Assistantships

You may be eligible to work part-time as a research assistant. The rates for research assistants vary from university to university. In addition to earning money, you will also be gaining experience in various research tasks. In addition, the professor who supervises your research assistantship will be in a good position to observe your research skills and may be a good person to ask to prepare letters of reference for you in the future.

Teaching Assistantships and Teaching Courses

Many graduate students work part-time as teaching assistants with responsibilities in conducting laboratories, marking assignments, and even teaching a class or two. In some universities, graduate students also have the opportunity to teach a full course. If your long-term plans include considering an academic job, this will be a great opportunity to develop your teaching skills.

Practica and Internships

In a number of doctoral programs, students receive stipends for completing some or all of their practica. Accredited clinical programs also require a full 1-year accredited paid internship. The salaries for internships vary tremendously from site to site. You will not be able to retire on your year's salary, but it will probably pay your living expenses for the internship year.

DECISION MAKING

Unsuccessful Applications

The number of qualified applicants to programs in clinical psychology far exceeds the number of spaces available in accredited clinical psychology programs. That means that each year a number of candidates with high grade point averages, excellent letters of reference, and a passionate commitment to become a clinical psychologist fail to receive an offer of admission to an accredited clinical program. This is often a very disheartening experience—it may be the first sense of academic failure that you have experienced.

If your application is unsuccessful, it is important that you carefully examine the base rates. Across clinical programs there may be as many as 10 applicants for every position. In deciding what to do next, you must consider your chances for future years. If, for example, your grade point average is above the official cut-off, but much lower than that of students admitted to clinical programs, then you may wish to consider alternative programs of study that are less stringent in terms of academic criteria. If you have highly specialized research interests in an area in which there are few supervisors, you may wish to broaden your interests. If you have applied to only one program, then you have seriously limited the odds of acceptance. If you decide to reapply next year, it makes sense to investigate strategies to enhance the chance of success next year. You may wish to consider ways to boost your GPA or perhaps study harder and retake the GRE. You may want to consider a position in a research laboratory, or you might inquire about opportunities to become involved in a conference presentation or a manuscript submission.

Successful Applications

Although receiving a rejection letter is stressful, so too is receiving more than one offer of admission. Unfortunately, there are sometimes chains of people waiting: candidate A has an offer from university 1, but really wants to go to university 2; candidate B has an offer from university 2, but really wants to go to university 3, and candidate C has an offer from university 3, but is not sure whether she or he wants to go into psychology or to law school. Although there is no foolproof way to avoid this kind of situation, it can be minimized if candidates gather all the information they need to make informed choices and develop a list of preferences.

ADDITIONAL RESOURCES

Web Sites

Listing of all clinical psychology programs accredited by the CoA: http://www.apa.org/ed/accreditation/clinpsyal.html
The Graduate Record Examination: http://www.gre.org

Books

American Psychological Association. (2010). *Graduate study in psychology: 2010 edition.* Washington, DC: Author.

Sayette, M. A., Mayne, T. J., & Norcross, J. C. (2010). *Insider's guide to graduate programs in clinical and counseling psychology: 2010/2011 edition.* New York: Guilford.

References

Ablow, J. C., Measelle, J. R., Kraemer, H. C., Harrington, R., Luby, J., Smider, N., et al. (1999). The MacArthur three-city outcome study: Evaluating multi-informant measures of young children's symptomatology. *Journal of the American Academy of Child and Adolescent Psychiatry, 38,* 1580–1590.

Abramowitz, J. S. (2008). Obsessive-compulsive disorder. In J. Hunsley & E. J. Mash (Eds.), A guide to assessments that work (pp. 275–292). New York: Oxford University Press.

Acevedo-Polakovich, I. D., Reynaga-Abiko, G., Garriott, P. O., Derefinko, K. J., Wimsatt, M. K., Gudonis, L. C., & Brown, T. L. (2007). Beyond instrument selection: Cultural considerations in the psychological assessment of U.S. Latinas/os. *Professional Psychology: Research and Practice, 38,* 375–384.

Achenbach, T. M. (2002). *Manual for the Assessment Data Management Program (ADM) CBCL, YSR, TRF, YASR, YCBCL, SCICA, CBCL/2-3, CBCL/1.5-5 and C-TRF*. Burlington, VT: University Medical Associates.

Achenbach, T. M., Krukowski, R. A., Dumenci, L., & Ivanova, M. Y. (2005). Assessment of adult psychopathology: Meta-analyses and implications of cross-informant correlations. *Psychological Bulletin, 131,* 361–382.

Achenbach, T. M., McConaughy, S. H., & Howell, C. T. (1987). Child/adolescent behavioral and emotional problems: Implications of cross-informant correlations for situational specificity. *Psychological Bulletin, 101,* 213–232.

Achenbach, T. M., Newhouse, P. A., & Rescorla, L. A. (2004). *Manual for ASEBA older adult forms & profiles*. Burlington, VT: University of Vermont, Research Center for Children, Youth, & Families.

Achenbach, T. M., & Rescorla, L. A. (2000). *Manual for ASEBA preschool forms & profiles*. Burlington, VT: University of Vermont, Research Center for Children, Youth, & Families.

Achenbach, T. M., & Rescorla, L. A. (2001). *Manual for ASEBA school-age forms & profiles*. Burlington, VT: University of Vermont, Research Center for Children, Youth, & Families.

Achenbach, T. M., & Rescorla, L. A. (2003). *Manual for ASEBA adult forms & profiles*. Burlington, VT: University of Vermont, Research Center for Children, Youth, & Families.

Ackerman, M. J., & Ackerman, M. C. (1997). Custody evaluation practices: A survey of experienced professionals (revisited). *Professional Psychology: Research and Practice, 28,* 137–145.

Ackerman, S. J., Hilsenroth, M. J., Baity, M. R., & Blagys, M. D. (2000). Interaction of therapeutic process and alliance during psychological assessment. *Journal of Personality Assessment, 75,* 82–109.

Acklin, M. W., McDowell, C. J., Verschell, M. S., & Chan, D. (2000). Interobserver agreement, intra-observer reliability, and the Rorschach Comprehensive System. *Journal of Personality Assessment, 74,* 15–47.

Adams, P. F., Lucas, J. W., & Barnes, P. M. (2008). *Summary health statistics for the U.S. populations: National Health Interview Survey, 2006. Vital Health*

Statistics 10(236). Washington, DC: National Center for Health Statistics.

Addis, M. E., & Krasnow, A. D. (2000). A national survey of practicing psychologists' attitudes towards psychotherapy treatment manuals. *Journal of Consulting and Clinical Psychology*, *68*, 331–339.

Addis, M. E., Wade, W. A., & Hatgis, C. (1999). Addressing practitioners' concerns about manual-based psychotherapies. *Clinical Psychology: Science and Practice*, *6*, 430–441.

Ægisdóttir, S., White, M. J., Spengler, P. M., Maugherman, A. S., Anderson, L. A., Cook, R. S., et al. (2006). The meta-analysis of clinical judgment project: Fifty-six years of accumulated research on clinical versus statistical prediction. *The Counseling Psychologist*, *34*, 341–382.

Aiken, L. R. (2003). *Psychological testing and assessment* (11th ed.). Toronto: Pearson.

Albano, A. M., & Silverman, W. K. (1996). *Anxiety Disorders Interview Schedule for Children for DSM-IV (ADIS IV): Clinician manual for parent and child versions*. San Antonio, TX: Psychological Corporation.

Almerigogna, J., Ost, J., Akehurst, L., & Fluck, M. (2008) How interviewers' non-verbal behaviors can affect children's perceptions & suggestibility. *Journal of Experimental Child Psychology*, *100*, 17–39.

American Educational Research Association, American Psychological Association, & National Council on Measurement in Education. (1999). *Standards for educational and psychological testing*. Washington, DC: American Educational Research Association.

American Psychiatric Association. (1952). *Diagnostic and statistical manual of mental disorders*. Washington, DC: Author.

American Psychiatric Association. (1968). *Diagnostic and statistical manual of mental disorders* (2nd ed.). Washington, DC: Author.

American Psychiatric Association. (1980). *Diagnostic and statistical manual of mental disorders* (3rd ed.) Washington, DC: Author.

American Psychiatric Association. (1987). *Diagnostic and statistical manual of mental disorders* (3rd ed., revised). Washington, DC: Author.

American Psychiatric Association. (1994). *Diagnostic and statistical manual of mental disorders* (4th ed.). Washington, DC: Author.

American Psychiatric Association. (2000). *Diagnostic and statistical manual of mental disorders* (4th ed., text revision). Washington, DC: Author.

American Psychological Association. (1994). Guidelines for child custody evaluations in divorce proceedings. *American Psychologist*, *49*, 677–680.

American Psychological Association. (2002a). Ethical principles of psychologists and code of conduct. *American Psychologist*, *57*, 1060–1073.

American Psychological Association. (2002b). *Guidelines on multicultural education, training, research, practice, and organizational change for psychologists*. Washington, DC: Author.

American Psychological Association. (2003a). Guidelines on multicultural education, training, research, practice, and organizational change for psychologists. *American Psychologist*, *58*, 377–402.

American Psychological Association. (2003b). PracticeNet survey: Clinical practice patterns. Retrieved April 8, 2005, from http://www.apapracticenet.net/results/Summer2003/1.asp.

American Psychological Association. (2004). Guidelines for psychological practice with older adults. *American Psychologist*, *59*, 236–260.

American Psychological Association Center for Workforce Studies. (2007). *Doctorates awarded in 2005-2006: Subfield by degree type*. Retrieved on August 7, 2008, from http://research.apa.org/doctoraled11.html.

American Psychological Association, Division 12 Presidential Task Force. (1999). Assessment for the twenty-first century: A model curriculum. *The Clinical Psychologist*, 52(4), 10–15.

American Psychological Association Practice Directorate. (2003). PracticeNet survey: Clinical practice patterns. Retrieved April 8, 2005, from http://www.apapracticenet.net/results/.

American Psychological Association Presidential Task Force on Evidence-Based Practice. (2006). Evidence-based practice in psychology. *American Psychologist*, 61, 271–285.

American Psychological Association Working Group on the Older Adult. (1998). What practitioners should know about working with older adults. *Professional Psychology: Research and Practice*, 29, 413–427.

Anastasi, A., & Urbina, S. (1997). *Psychological testing* (7th ed.). Upper Saddle River, NJ: Prentice-Hall.

APA Presidential Task Force on Evidence-Based Practice. (2005). *Draft policy statement on evidence-based practice in psychology*. Retrieved on March 3, 2005, from http://forms.apa.org/members/ebp/

Archer, R. P. (1996). MMPI-Rorschach interrelationships: Proposed criteria for evaluating explanatory models. *Journal of Personality Assessment*, 67, 504–515.

Archer, R. P., & Krishnamurthy, R. (1997). MMPI-A and Rorschach indices related to depression and conduct disorder: An evaluation of the incremental validity hypothesis. *Journal of Personality Assessment*, 69, 517–533.

Arnow, B. A. (1999). Why are empirically supported treatments for Bulimia Nervosa underutilized and what can we do about it? *Journal of Clinical Psychology*, 55, 769–779.

Association of Family and Conciliation Courts. (2006). Model standards of practice for child custody evaluations. Retrieved on February 5, 2008, from http://www.afccnet.org/pdfs/.

Association of Psychology Postdoctoral and Internship Centers (2008). Match statistics. Retrieved on July 10, 2008, from http://appic.org/match/5_2_2_match_about_statistics.html.

Association of State and Provincial Psychology Boards. (2005). *ASPPB code of conduct*. Montgomery, AL: Author.

Ax, R. K., Bigelow, B. J., Harowski, K., Meredith, J. M., Nussbaum, D., & Taylor, R. R. (2008). Prescriptive authority for psychologists and the public sector: Serving underserved health care consumers. *Psychological Serivces*, 5, 184–197.

Barber, J. P., Connolly, M. B., Crits-Christoph, P., Gladis, L., & Siqueland, L. (2000). Alliance predicts patients' outcome beyond in-treatment change in symptoms. *Journal of Consulting and Clinical Psychology*, 68, 1027–1032.

Barber, J. P., & Crits-Christoph, P. (1993). Advances in measures of psychodynamic formulations. *Journal of Consulting and Clinical Psychology*, 61, 574–585.

Barbotte, E., Guillemin, F., Chau, N., & the Lorhandicap Group. (2001). Prevalence of impairments, disabilities, handicaps and quality of life in the general population: A review of the literature. *Bulletin of the World Health Organization*, 79, 1047–1055.

Barkham, M., Margison, F., Leach, C., Lucock, M., Mellor-Clark, J., Evans, C., et al. (2001). Service profiling and outcomes benchmarking using the CORE-OM: Toward practice-based evidence in the psychological therapies. *Journal of Consulting and Clinical Psychology*, 69, 184–196.

Barkley, R., et al. (2002). International Consensus Statement on ADHD. *Clinical Child and Family Psychology Review*, 5, 89–111.

Barlow, D. H. (2004). Psychological treatments. *American Psychologist*, 59, 869–878.

Barlow, D. H., Allen, L. B., & Choate, M. L. (2004). Toward a unified treatment for emotional disorders. *Behavior Therapy*, 35, 205–230.

Barnett, J. E., & Johnson, W. B. (2008). *Ethics desk reference for psychologists*. Washington, DC: American Psychological Association.

Bar-On, R. (2002). *BarOn Emotional Quotient Short Form (EQ-i: Short). Technical manual*. Toronto: Multi-Health Systems.

Barrett, P. M., & Ollendick, T. H. (Eds.). (2004). *Interventions that work with children and adolescents: Prevention and treatment*. New York: John Wiley & Sons.

Barrett, P. M., & Shortt, A. L. (2003). Parental involvement in the treatment of anxious children. In A. Kazdin & J. R. Weisz (Eds.), *Evidence-based psychotherapies for children and adolescents* (pp. 101–119). New York: Guilford.

Barrett, P., & Turner, C. (2001). Prevention of anxiety symptoms in primary school children: Preliminary results from a universal school-based trial. *British Journal of Clinical Psychology, 40*, 399–410.

Barrett, P., & Turner, C. (2004). Prevention of child-hood anxiety and depression. In P. M. Barrett & T. H. Ollendick (Eds.), *Interventions that work with children and adolescents: Prevention and treatment* (pp. 429–474). Chichester, UK: John Wiley & Sons.

Barrett, P. M., Farrell, L., Pina, A. A., Peris, T. S., & Piacentini, J. (2008). Evidence-based psychosocial treatments for child and adolescent obsessive-compulsive disorder. *Journal of Clinical Child and Adolescent Psychology, 37*, 131–155.

Bastien, C. H., Morin, C. M., Ouellet, M-C., Blais, C., & Bouchard, S. (2004). Cognitive-behavioral therapy for insomnia: Comparison of individual therapy, group therapy, and telephone consultations. *Journal of Consulting and Clinical Psychology, 72*, 653–659.

Baucom, D. H., Epstein, N., & Gordon, K. C. (2000). Marital therapy: Theory, practice and empirical status. In C. R. Snyder & R. E. Ingram (Eds.), *Handbook of psychological changes: Psychotherapy processes and practices for the 21st century* (pp. 280–308). New York: John Wiley & Sons.

Bauer, S., Lambert, M. J., & Nielsen, S. L. (2004). Clinical significance methods: A comparison of statistical techniques. *Journal of Personality Assessment, 82*, 60–70.

Baydar, N., Reid, J., & Webster-Stratton, C. (2003). The role of mental health factors and program engagement in the effectiveness of a preventive parenting program for Head Start Mothers. *Journal of Consulting and Clinical Psychology, 74*, 1433–1453.

Beach, S. R. H., & Amir, N. (2006). Self-reported depression is taxonic. *Journal of Psychopathology and Behavioral Assessment, 28*, 171–178.

Beck, A. T., Rush, A. J., Shaw, B. F., & Emery, G. (1979). *Cognitive therapy of depression*. New York: Guilford.

Beck, A. T., Steer, R. A., & Brown, G. K. (1996). *Beck Depression Inventory manual* (2nd ed.). San Antonio, TX: Psychological Corporation.

Becker, C. B., Zayfert, C., & Anderson, E. (2004). A survey of psychologists' attitudes towards and utilization of exposure therapy for PTSD. *Behaviour Research and Therapy, 42*, 277–292.

Bekhit, N. S., Thomas, G. V., Lalonde, S., & Jolley, R. (2002). Psychological assessment in clinical practice in Britain. *Clinical Psychology and Psychotherapy, 9*, 285–291.

Belar, C. D. (2008). Clinical health psychology: A health care specialty in professional psychology. *Professional Psychology: Research and Practice, 39*, 229–233.

Bellak, L., & Abrams, D. M. (1997). *The Thematic Apperception Test, the Children's Apperception Test, and the Senior Apperception Technique in clinical use* (6th ed.). Boston: Allyn & Bacon.

Benjamin, L. T., Jr. (2005). A history of clinical psychology as a profession in America (and a glimpse at its future). *Annual Review of Clinical Psychology, 1*, 1–30.

Benton, S. A., Robertson, J. M., Tseng, W. C., Newton, F. B., & Benton, S. L. (2003). Changes in counseling center client problems across 13 years. *Professional Psychology: Research and Practice, 34,* 66–72.

Bergin, A. E. (1971). The evaluation of therapeutic outcomes. In A. E. Bergin & S. L. Garfield (Eds.), *Handbook of psychotherapy and behaviour change* (pp. 217–270). New York: John Wiley & Sons.

Berman, P. S. (1997). *Case conceptualization and treatment planning.* Thousand Oaks, CA: Sage.

Beutler, L. E. (1998). Identifying empirically supported treatments: What if we didn't? *Journal of Consulting and Clinical Psychology, 66,* 113–120.

Beutler, L. E., & Castonguay, L. G. (2006). The task force on empirically based principles of therapeutic change. In L. G. Castonguay & L. E. Beutler (Eds.), *Principles of therapeutic change that work* (pp. 1–10). New York: Oxford University Press.

Beutler, L. E., Malik, M., Alimohamed, S., Harwood, T. M., Talebi, H., Noble, S., et al. (2004). Therapist variables. In M. J. Lambert (Ed.), *Bergin and Garfield's handbook of psychotherapy and behavior change* (5th ed., pp. 227–306). New York: John Wiley & Sons.

Beutler, L. E., Rocco, F., Moleiro, C. M., & Talebi, H. (2002). Resistance. *Psychotherapy 38,* 431–442.

Bickman, L. (1996). A continuum of care: More is not always better. *American Psychologist, 51,* 689–701.

Bickman, L., Rosof-Williams, J., Salzerm M. S., Summerfelt, W. T., Noser, K., Wilson, S. J., et al. (2000). What information do clinicians value for monitoring adolescent client progress and outcomes? *Professional Psychology: Research and Practice, 31,* 70–74.

Biglan, A. (2003). The generic features of effective childrearing. In A. Biglan, M. Wang, & H. J. Walberg (Eds.), *Preventing youth problems* (pp. 145–162). New York: Kluwer Academic.

Biglan, A., Mrazek, P. K., Carnine, D., & Flay, B. R. (2003). The integration of research and practice in the prevention of youth behaviour problems. *American Psychologist, 58,* 433–440.

Biglan, A., & Severson, H. H. (2003). The prevention of tobacco use. In A. Biglan, M. Wang, & H. J. Walberg (Eds.), *Preventing youth problems* (pp. 63–85). New York: Kluwer Academic.

Birchler, G. R., & Fals-Stewart, W. S. (2002). Marital dysfunction. In M. Hersen (Ed.), *Clinical behavior therapy with adults and children* (pp. 216–235). New York: John Wiley & Sons.

Blagys, M. D., & Hilsenroth, M. J. (2000). Distinctive features of short-term psychodynamic interpersonal psychotherapy: A review of the comparative psychotherapy process literature. *Clinical Psychology: Science and Practice, 7,* 167–188.

Blagys, M. D., & Hilsenroth, M. J. (2002). Distinctive activities of cognitive-behavioral therapy: A review of the comparative psychotherapy process literature. *Clinical Psychology Review, 22,* 671–706.

Blais, M. A., & Kurtz, J. E. (2007). Personality Assessment Inventory [Special issue]. *Journal of Personality Assessment, 88*(1).

Blanton, H., & Jaccard, J. (2006). Arbitrarymetrics in psychology. *American Psychologist, 61,* 27–41.

Blashfield, R. K. (1991). Models of psychiatric classification. In M. Hersen & S. M. Turner (Eds.), *Adult psychopathology and diagnosis* (2nd ed., pp. 3–22). New York: John Wiley & Sons.

Blount, A., Schoenbaum, M., Kathol, R., Rollman, B. L., Thomas, M., & O'Donohue, W., & Peek, C. J. (2007). The economics of behavioral health services in medical settings; A review of the evidence. *Professional Psychology; Research and Practice, 38,* 290–297.

Blumentritt, T. L., & VanVoorhis, C. R. W. (2004). The Millon Adolescent Clinical Inventory: Is it valid and reliable for Mexican American youth? *Journal of Personality Assessment, 83,* 64–74.

Boake, C. D., (2008). Clinical neuropsychology *Professional Psychology: Research and Practice, 39*, 234–239.

Bohart, A. C., O'Hara, M., & Leitner, L. M. (1998). Empirically violated treatments: Disenfranchisement of humanistic and other psychotherapies. *Psychotherapy Research, 8*, 141–157.

Bolton, P., Bass, J., Neugebauer, R., Verdeli, H., Clougherty, K. P., Wickramaratne, P., et al. (2003). Group interpersonal psychotherapy for depression in rural Uganda. *Journal of the American Medical Association, 289*, 3117–3124.

Bonanno, G. A. (2004). Loss, trauma, and human resilience. *American Psychologist, 59*, 20–28.

Bonanno, G. A. (2005). Resilience in the face of potential trauma. *Current Directions in Psychological Science, 14*, 135–138.

Bongers, I. L., Koot, H. M., van der Ende, J., & Verhulst, F. C. (2003). The normative development of child and adolescent problem behavior. *Journal of Abnormal Psychology, 112*, 179–192.

Boothby, J. L., & Clements, C. B. (2000). A national survey of correctional psychologists. *Criminal Justice and Behavior, 27*, 716–732.

Bor, W., Sanders, M. R., & Markie-Dadds, C. (2002). The effects of the Triple-P Positive Parenting Program on preschool children with co-occurring disruptive behaviour and attentional/hyperactive difficulties. *Journal of Abnormal Child Psychology, 30*, 571–587.

Bornstein, R. F., Rossner, S. C., Hill, E. L., & Stepanian, M. L. (1994). Face validity and fakability of objective and projective measures of dependency. *Journal of Personality Assessment, 63*, 363–386.

Bowden, S. C., Lissner, D., McCarthy, K. A. L., Weiss, L. G., & Holdnack, J. A. (2007). Metric and structural equivalence of core cognitive abilities measured with the Wechsler Adult Intelligence Scale-III in the United States and Australia. *Journal of Clinical and Experimental Neuropsychology, 29*, 768–780.

Bowden, S. C., Weiss, L. G., Holdnack, J. A., Bardenhagen, F. J., & Cook, M. J. (2008). Equivalence of a measurement model of cognitive abilities in U.S. standardization and Australian neuroscience samples. *Assessment, 15*, 132–144.

Bower, P., & Gilbody, S. (2005). Stepped care in psychological therapies: Access, effectiveness, and efficiency. *British Journal of Psychiatry, 186*, 11–17.

Braaten, E. B., Otto, S., & Handelsman, M. M. (1993). What do people want to know about psychotherapy? *Psychotherapy, 30*, 565–570.

Brabender, V. A., Fallon, A. E., & Smolar, A. I. (2004). *Essentials of group therapy*. New York: John Wiley & Sons.

Bradley, R., Greene, J., Russ, E., Dutra, L., & Westen, D. (2005). A multi-dimensional meta-analysis of psychotherapy for PTSD. *American Journal of Psychiatry, 162*, 214–227.

Breau, L. M., McGrath, P. J., Camfield, C. S., & Finley, G. A. (2002). Psychometric properties of the non-communicating children's pain checklist-revised. *Pain, 99*, 349–357.

British Psychological Society. (2003). *Professional Practice Guidelines: Division of Neuropsychology*. Retrieved January 15, 2005, from http://www.bps.org.uk.

Brockington, I., & Mumford, D. (2002). Recruitment into psychiatry. *British Journal of Psychiatry, 180*, 307–312.

Bronfenbrenner, U. (1979). *The ecology of human development: Experiments by design and by nature*. Cambridge, MA: Harvard University Press.

Broshek, D. K., & Barth, J. T. (2000). The Halstead-Reitan Neuropsychological Test Battery. In G. Groth-Marnat (Ed.), *Neuropsychological assessment in clinical practice* (pp. 223–263). New York: John Wiley & Sons.

Brosnan, L., Reynolds, S., & Moore, R. G. (2008). Self-evaluation of cognitive therapy performance: Do therapists know how competent they are? *Behavioural and Cognitive Psychotherapy*, 36, 581–587.

Brown, G. W., & Harris, T. O. (1978). *The social origins of depression: A study of psychiatric disturbance in women*. London: Tavistock Institute.

Brown, T. A., Campbell, L. A., Lehman, C. L., Grisham, J. R., & Mancill, R. B. (2001). Current and lifetime comorbidity of the DSM-IV anxiety and mood disorders in a large clinical sample. *Journal of Abnormal Psychology*, 110, 585–589.

Brown, T. A., Di Nardo, P. A., & Barlow, D. H. (1994). *Anxiety Disorders Interview Schedule for DSM-IV (ADIS IV)*. San Antonio, TX: Psychological Corporation.

Bruck, M., & Ceci, S.J. (2004). Forensic developmental psychology: Unveiling four scientific misconceptions. *Current Directions in Psychology*, 13, 229–232.

Brugha, T. S., Bebbington, P. E., Singleton, N., Melzer, D., Jenkins, R., Lewis, G., et al. (2004). Trends in service use and treatment for mental disorders in adults throughout Great Britain. *British Journal of Psychiatry*, 185, 378–384.

Buchanan, T. (2002). Online assessment: Desirable or dangerous? *Professional Psychology: Research and Practice*, 33, 148–154.

Burlingame, G. M., MacKenzie, K. R., & Strauss, B. (2004). Small-group treatment: Evidence for effectiveness and mechanisms of change. In M. L. Lambert (Ed.), *Bergin and Garfield's Handbook of psychotherapy and behavior change* (5th ed., pp. 647–696). New York: John Wiley & Sons.

Burlingame, G. M., Mosier, J. I., Wells, M. G., Atkin, Q. G., Lamber, M. J., Whooery, M., et al. (2001). Tracking the influence of mental health treatment: The development of the Youth Outcome Questionnaire. *Clinical Psychology and Psychotherapy*, 8, 361–379.

Burns, D. D. (1980). *Feeling good: The new mood therapy*. New York: Signer.

Butcher, J. N., & Beutler, L. E. (2003). The MMPI-2. In L. E. Beutler & G. Groth-Marnat (Eds.), *Integrative assessment of adult personality* (2nd ed., pp. 157–191). New York: Guilford Press.

Butcher, J. N., Dahlstrom, W. G., Graham, J. R., Tellegen, A., & Kaemmer, B. (1989). *Manual for administration and scoring: MMPI-2*. Minneapolis: University of Minnesota Press.

Butcher, J. N., Perry, J. N., & Atlis, M. M. (2000). Validity and utility of computer-based test interpretations. *Psychological Assessment*, 12, 6–18.

Butcher, J. N., Williams, C. L., Graham, J. R., Archer, R., Tellegen, A., Ben-Porath, Y. S., et al. (1992). *MMPI-A: Manual for administration, scoring, and interpretation*. Minneapolis: University of Minnesota Press.

Butler, A. C., Chapman, J. E., Forman, E. M., & Beck, A. T. (2006). The empirical status of cognitive-behavioral therapy: A review of meta-analyses. *Clinical Psychology Review*, 26, 17–31.

Cahill, J., Barkham, M., Hardy, G., Rees, A., Shapiro, D.A., Stiles, W.B., et al. (2003). Outcomes of patients completing and not completing cognitive therapy for depression. *British Journal of Clinical Psychology*, 42, 133–143.

Cairns, N. J. (2004). Neuroanatomy and neuropathology. In L. H. Goldstein & J. E. McNeil (Eds.), *Clinical neuropsychology: A practical guide to assessment and management for clinicians* (pp. 23–55). Chichester, UK: John Wiley & Sons.

Calhoun, K. S., Moras, K., Pilkonis, P. A., & Rehm, L. P. (1998). Empirically supported treatments: Implications for training. *Journal of Consulting and Clinical Psychology*, 66, 151–162.

California Board of Psychology (n.d.). *A consumer's guide to psychological services*. Retrieved September 23, 2008, from http://www.psychboard.ca.gov/formspubs/consumer-brochure.pdf.

Camara, W. J., Nathan, J. S., & Puente, A. E. (2000). Psychological test usage: Implications in professional psychology. *Professional Psychology: Science and Practice, 31,* 141–154.

Carlbring, P., Gunnarsdottir, M., Hedensjo, L., Andersson, G., Ekselius, L., & Furmark, T. (2007). Treatment of social phobia: Randomised trial of internet-delivered cognitive-behavioural therapy with telephone support. *British Journal of Psychiatry, 190,* 123–128.

Carr, A. (2002). Conclusions. In A. Carr (Ed.), *Prevention: what works with children and adolescents? A critical review of psychological prevention programmes for children, adolescents and their families* (pp. 359–372). Hove, UK: Brunner-Routledge.

Carroll, J. B. (1993). *Human cognitive abilities: A survey of factor analytic studies.* New York: Cambridge University Press.

Cartwright-Hatton, S., Roberts, C., Chitsabesan, P., Fothergill, C., & Harrington, R. (2004). Systematic review of the efficacy of cognitive behaviour therapies for childhood and adolescent anxiety disorders. *British Journal of Clinical Psychology, 43,* 421–436.

Caruso, J. C., & Cliff, N. (1999). The properties of equally and differentially weighted WAIS-III factor scores. *Psychological Assessment, 11,* 198–206.

Casey, R. J., & Berman, J. S. (1985). The outcome of psychotherapy with children. *Psychological Bulletin, 98,* 388–400.

Cashel, M. L. (2002). Child and adolescent psychological assessment: Current clinical practices and the impact of managed care. *Professional Psychology: Research and Practice, 33,* 446–453.

Caspi, A., Moffitt, T. E., Newman, D. L., & Silva, P. A. (1996). Behavioral observations at age 3 years predict adult psychiatric disorders. *Longitudinal evidence from a birth cohort. Archives of General Psychiatry, 53,* 1033–1039.

Cassin, S. E., Singer, A. R., Dobson, K. S., & Altmaier, E. M. (2007). Professional interests and career aspirations of graduate students in professional psychology: An exploratory study. *Training and Education in Professional Psychology, 1,* 26–37.

Castonguay, L. G., & Beutler, L. E. (Eds.). (2006a). *Principles of therapeutic change that work.* New York: Oxford University Press. (New edition in press).

Castonguay, L. G., & Beutler, L. E. (2006b). Common and unique principles of therapeutic change: What do we know and what do we need to know? In L. G. Castonguay & L. E. Beutler (Eds.), *Principles of therapeutic change that work* (pp. 353–369). New York: Oxford University Press.

Cattell, R. B. (1963). Theory of fluid and crystallized intelligence: A critical experiment. *Journal of Educational Psychology, 54,* 1–22.

Center for Disease Control national Center for Health Statistics. (2006). New report finds pain affects millions of Americans. Retrieved on June 23rd 2009 from http://www.cdc.gov/nchs/PRESSROOM/06facts/hus06.htm.

Chamberlain, P., & Smith, D. K. (2003). Antisocial behaviour in children and adolescents: The Oregon multidimensional foster care model. In A. E. Kazdin & J. R. Weisz (Eds.), *Evidence-based psychotherapies for children and adolescents* (pp. 282–300). New York: Guilford.

Chambers, C. T., Finley, G. A., McGrath, P. J., & Walsh, T. M. (2003). The parents' postoperative pain measure: replication and extension to 2-6-year old children. *Pain, 105,* 437–443.

Chambless, D. L. (2002). Beware the dodo bird: The dangers of overgeneralization. *Clinical Psychology: Science and Practice, 9,* 13–16.

Chambless, D. L., Baker, M. J., Baucom, D. H., Beutler, L., Calhoun, K. S., Crits-Christoph, P., et al. (1998). Update on empirically validated therapies, II. *The Clinical Psychologist, 51,* 3–16.

Chambless, D. L., Caputo, G., Jasin, S. E., Gracely, E. J., & Williams, C. (1985). The Mobility Inventory for Agoraphobia. *Behaviour Research and Therapy, 23,* 35–44.

Chambless, D. L., & Gillis, M. M. (1993). Cognitive therapy of anxiety disorders. *Journal of Consulting and Clinical Psychology, 61,* 248–260.

Chambless, D. L., & Hollon, S. D. (1998). Defining empirically supported therapies. *Journal of Consulting and Clinical Psychology, 66,* 7–18.

Chambless, D. L., & Ollendick, T. H. (2001). Empirically supported psychological interventions: Controversies and evidence. *Annual Review of Psychology, 52,* 685–716.

Chambless, D. L., Sanderson, W. C., Shoham, V., Bennett Johnson, S., Pope, K. S., Crits-Christoph, P., et al. (1996). An update on empirically validated therapies. *The Clinical Psychologist, 49*(2), 5–18.

Chambless, D. L., et al. (1998). Update on empirically validated therapies, II. *The Clinical Psychologist, 51,* 3–16.

Charach, A., Ickowicz, A., & Schachar, R. (2004). Stimulant treatments over five years: Adherence, effectiveness, and adverse effects. *Journal of the American Academy of Child and Adolescent Psychiatry, 43,* 559–567.

Cherry, D. K., Messenger, L. C., & Jacoby, A. M. (2000). An examination of training model outcomes in clinical psychology programs. *Professional Psychology: Research & Practice, 31,* 562–568.

Childs, R. A., & Eyde, L. D. (2002). Assessment training in clinical psychology doctoral programs: What should we teach? What do we teach? *Journal of Personality Assessment, 78,* 130–144.

Chorpita, B. F., Daleiden, E. L., & Weisz, J. R. (2005). Identifying and selecting the common elements of evidence based interventions: A distillation and matching model. *Mental Health Services Research, 7,* 5–20.

Chorpita, B. F., Yim, L. M., Donkervoet, J. C., Arensdorf, A., Amundsen, M. J., McGee, C., et al. (2002). Towards large-scale implementation of empirically supported treatments for children: A review and observations by the Hawaii Empirical Basis to Services Task Force. *Clinical Psychology: Science and Practice, 9,* 165–190.

Chronis, A. M., Chacko, A., Fabiano, G. A., Wymbs, B. T., & Pelham, W. E. (2004). Enhancements to the behavioural parent training paradigm for families of children with ADHD: Review and future directions. *Clinical Child and Family Psychology, Review, 7,* 1–27.

Clare, L., & Woods, R. T. (2004). Cognitive training and cognitive rehabilitation for people with early-stage Alzheimer's disease: A review. *Neuropsychological Rehabilitation, 14,* 385–401.

Clark, L. A., & Watson, D. (2006). Distress and fear disorders: An alternative empirically based taxonomy of the 'mood' and 'anxiety' disorders. *British Journal of Psychiatry, 189,* 481–483.

Clark, L. A., Watson, D., & Reynolds, S. (1995). Diagnosis and classification of psychopathology: Challenges to the current system and future directions. *Annual Review of Psychology, 46,* 121–153.

Clarke, G. N., DeBar, L. L., & Lewinsohn, P. M. (2003). Cognitive-behavioural group treatment for adolescent depression. In A. E. Kazdin & J. R. Weisz (Eds.), *Evidence-based psychotherapies for children and adolescents* (pp. 120–134). New York: Guilford.

Clarke, G., Hornbrook, M., Lynch, F., Polens, M., Gale, J., Beardslee, W., et al. (2001). A randomized trial of group cognitive intervention of preventing depression in adolescent offspring of depressed parents. *Archives of General Psychiatry, 58,* 1127–1134.

Clarkin, J. F., & Levy, K. N. (2004). The influence of client variables on psychotherapy. In M. J.

Lambert (Ed.), *Bergin and Garfield's handbook of psychotherapy and behavior change* (5th ed., pp. 194–226). New York: John Wiley & Sons.

Clarkin, J. F., Levy, K. N., Lenzenweger, M. F., & Kernberg, O. F. (2007). Evaluating three treatments for borderline personality disorder: A multiwave study. *American Journal of Psychiatry, 164*, 922–928.

Clemence, A. J., & Handler, L. (2001). Psychological assessment on internship: A survey of training directors and their expectations for students. *Journal of Personality Assessment, 76*, 18–47.

Clements, C. B., Althouse, R., Ax, R. K., Magaletta, P. R., Fagan, T.J., & Wormith, J. S. (2007). Systemic issues and correctional outcomes: Expanding the scope of correctional psychology. *Criminal Justice and Behavior, 34*, 919–932.

Cohen, J. (1992). A power primer. *Psychological Bulletin, 112*, 115–159.

Cole, D. A., Peeke, L. G., Martin, J. M., Truglio, R., & Seroczynski, A. D. (1998). A longitudinal look at the relation between depression and anxiety in children and adolescents. *Journal of Consulting and Clinical Psychology, 66*, 451–460.

Cole, D. A., Tram, J. M., Martin, J. M., Hoffman, K. B., Ruiz, M. D., Jacquez, F. M., et al. (2002). Individual differences in the emergence of depressive symptoms in children and adolescents: A longitudinal investigation of parent and child reports. *Journal of Abnormal Psychology, 111*, 156–165.

Collins, L. M., Murphy, S. A., & Bierman, K. L. (2004). A conceptual framework for adaptive preventive interventions. *Prevention Science, 5*, 185–196.

Commission on Chronic Illness. (1957). *Chronic illness in the United States.* (Vol. 1) Cambridge, MA: Harvard University Press.

Conduct Problems Prevention Research Group. (2002a). The implementation of the Fast Track Program: An example of a large-scale prevention science efficacy trial. *Journal of Abnormal Child Psychology, 30*, 1–17.

Conduct Problems Prevention Research Group. (2002b). Evaluation of the first 3 years of the Fast Track prevention trial with children with high risk for adolescent conduct problems. *Journal of Abnormal Child Psychology, 30*, 19–35.

Conduct Problems Prevention Research Group. (2004). The effects of the Fast Track program on serious problem outcomes at the end of elementary school. *Journal of Clinical Child and Adolescent Psychology, 33*, 650–661.

Connor-Smith, J. K., & Weisz, J. R. (2003). Applying treatment outcome research in clinical practice: Techniques for adapting interventions to the real world. *Child and Adolescent Mental Health, 8*, 3–10.

Constantine, M. G. (2007). Racial microaggressions against African American clients in cross-racial counseling relationships. *Journal of Counseling Psychology, 54*, 1–16.

Cook, J. M., Schnurr, P. P., & Foa, E. B. (2004). Bridging the gap between Posttraumatic Stress Disorder research and clinical practice: The example of exposure therapy. *Psychotherapy, 41*, 374–381.

Cook, T. D., & Campbell, D. T. (Eds.). (1979). *Quasi-experimentation: Design and analysis issues for field settings.* Chicago: Rand McNally.

Copeland, W. E., Keeler, G., Angold, A., & Costello, E. J. (2007). Traumatic events and posttraumatic stress in childhood. *Archives of General Psychiatry, 64*, 577–584.

Costa, P. T., & McCrae, R. R. (1992). *Revised NEO Personality Inventory (NEO PI-R) and NEO Five-Factor Inventory (NEO-FFI) professional manual.* Odessa, FL: Psychological Assessment Resources.

Costantino, G., Malgady, R. G., Rogler, L. H., & Tsui, E. C. (1988). Discriminant analysis of clinical outpatients and public school children by TEMAS:

A thematic apperception test for Hispanics and Blacks. *Journal of Personality Assessment, 52*, 670–678.

Costello, E. J., Copeland, W., Cowell, A., & Keeler, G. (2007). Service costs of caring for adolescents with mental illness in a rural community, 1993–2000. *American Journal of Psychiatry, 164*, 36–42.

Coughlan, B. J., Doyle, M., & Carr, A. (2002). Prevention of teenage smoking, alcohol use and drug abuse. In A. Carr (Ed.), *Prevention: what works with children and adolescents? A critical review of psychological prevention programmes for children, adolescents and their families* (pp. 267–286). Hove, UK: Brunner-Routledge.

Council on Social Work Education. (2008). *Accreditation News, Reports and Archives*. Retrieved on June 19, 2008, from www.cswe.org.

Craighead, W. E., Hart, A. B., Craighead, L. W., & Ilardi, S. (2002). Psychosocial treatments for major depressive disorder. In P. E. Nathan & J. M. Gorman (Eds.), *A guide to treatments that work* (2nd ed., pp. 245–261). New York: Oxford University Press.

Crawford, J. R. (2004). Psychometric foundations of neuropsychological assessment. In L. H. Goldstein & J. E. McNeil (Eds.), *Clinical neuropsychology: A practical guide to assessment and management for clinicians* (pp. 121–140). Chichester, UK: John Wiley & Sons.

Creamer, M., O'Donnell, M. L., & Pattison, P. (2004). The relationship between acute stress disorder and posttraumatic stress disorder in severely injured trauma survivors. *Behaviour Research and Therapy, 42*, 315–328.

Crits-Christoph, P. (1997). Limitations of the dodo bird verdict and the role of clinical trials in psychotherapy research: Comment on Wampold et al. (1997). *Psychological Bulletin, 122*, 216–220.

Cross, D. T., & Burger, G. K. (1982). Ethnicity as a variable in responses to California Psychological

Inventory items. *Journal of Personality Assessment, 46*, 153–158.

Cuijpers, P. (2003). Examining the effects of prevention programs on the incidence of new cases of mental disorders: The lack of statistical power. *American Journal of Psychiatry, 160*, 1385–1391.

Cuijpers, P., van Straten, A., Smit, F., Mihalopoulos, C., & Beekman, A. (2008). Preventing the onset of depressive disorders: A meta-analytic review of psychological interventions. *American Journal of Psychiatry, 165*, 1272–1280.

Cukrowicz, K. C., Wingate, L. R. W., Driscoll, K. A., & Joiner, T. E. (2004). A standard of care for the assessment of suicide risk and associated treatment. *Journal of Contemporary Psychotherapy, 34*, 87–100.

Currier, J. M., Holland, J. M., & Neimeyer, R. A. (2007). The effectiveness of bereavement interventions with children: A meta-analytic review of controlled outcome research. *Journal of Clinical Child and Adolescent Psychology, 36*, 253–259.

Cutler, J. L., Goldyne, A., Markowitz, J. C., Devlin, M. J., & Glick, R. A. (2004). Comparing cognitive behaviour therapy, interpersonal psychotherapy, and psychodynamic psychotherapy. *American Journal of Psychiatry, 161*, 1567–1573.

Dadds, M. R., Holland, D. E., Barrett, P. M., Laurens, S. K., & Spence, S. (1999). Early intervention and prevention of anxiety disorders in children: Results at 2-year follow-up. *Journal of Consulting and Clinical Psychology, 67*, 145–150.

d'Ardenne, P., Ruaro, L., Cestari, L., Fakhoury, W., & Priebe, S. (2007). Does interpreter-mediated CBT with traumatized refugee people work? A comparison of patient outcomes in East London. *Behavioural and Cognitive Psychotherapy, 35*, 293–301.

David-Ferdon, C., & Kaslow, N. J. (2008). Evidence-based psychosocial treatments for child and adolescent depression. *Journal of Clinical Child and Adolescent Psychology, 37*, 62–104.

Davidson, P. R., & Parker, K. C. H. (2001). Eye movement desensitization and reprocessing (EMDR): A meta-analysis. *Journal of Consulting and Clinical Psychology, 69,* 305–316.

Davis, D. A., Mazmanian, P. E., Fordis, M., Van Harrison, R., Thorpe, K. E., & Perrier, L. (2006). Accuracy of physician self-assessment compared with observed measures of competence: A systematic review. *Journal of the American Medical Association, 296,* 1094–1102.

Davis, G. L., Hoffman, R. G., & Nelson, K. S. (1990). Differences between Native Americans and Whites on the California Personality Inventory. *Psychological Assessment, 2,* 238–242.

Day, A., Gerace, A., Wilson, C., & Howells, K. (2008). Promoting forgiveness in violent offenders: A more positive approach to offender rehabilitation? *Aggression and Violent Behavior, 13,* 195–200.

De Koninck, J. (1997). Sleep, the common denominator for psychological adaptation. *Canadian Psychology, 38,* 191–195.

Del Vecchio, T., & O'Leary, D. (2004). Effectiveness of anger treatments for specific anger problems: A meta-analytic review. *Clinical Psychology Review, 24,* 15–34.

Derogatis, L. R. (1994). *SCL-90-R: Administration, scoring, and procedures manual.* Minneapolis, MN: National Computer Systems.

Devilly, G. J. (2002). Eye movement desensitization and reprocessing: A chronology of its development and scientific standing. *Scientific Review of Mental Health Practice, 1,* 113–138.

Dickens, W., & Flynn, J. R. (2001). Heritability estimates versus large environmental effects: The IQ paradox resolved. *Psychological Review, 108,* 346–369.

Dishion, T. J., McCord, J., & Poulin, F. (1999). When interventions harm: Peer groups and problem behavior. *American Psychologist, 54,* 755–764.

Dobson, K. S. (1989). A meta-analysis of the efficacy of cognitive therapy for depression. *Journal of Consulting and Clinical Psychology, 57,* 414–419.

Dowden, C., & Andrews, D. A. (2004). The importance of staff practice in delivering effective correctional treatment: A meta-analytic review of core correctional practice. *International Journal of Offender Therapy and Comparative Criminology, 48,* 203–214.

Doyle, A. B., Edwards, H., & Robinson, R. W. (1993). Accreditation of doctoral training programmes and internships in professional psychology. In K. S. Dobson & D. G. Dobson (Eds.), *Professional psychology in Canada* (pp. 77–105). Toronto, ON: Hogrefe & Huber.

Dozois, D. J. A., & Dobson, K. S. (Eds.). (2004). *The prevention of anxiety and depression: Theory, research, and practice.* Washington, DC: American Psychological Association.

D'Zurilla, T. J., & Goldfried, M. R. (1971). Problem solving and behaviour modification. *Journal of Abnormal Psychology, 78,* 101–126.

D'Zurilla, T. J., & Nezu, A. M. (1999). *Problem-solving therapy: A social competence approach to clinical intervention* (2nd ed.). New York: Springer.

Eaton, W. W., Shao, H., Nestadt, G., Lee, B. H., Bienvenu, J., & Zandi, P. (2008). Population-based study of first onset and chronicity of major depressive disorder. *Archives of General Psychiatry, 65,* 513–520.

Eddy, K. T., Dutra, L., Bradley, R., & Westen, D. (2004). A multidimensional meta-analysis of psychotherapy and pharmacotherapy for obsessive-compulsive disorder. *Clinical Psychology Review, 24,* 1011–1030.

Eells, T. D. (Ed). (1997). *Handbook of psychotherapy case formulation.* New York: Guilford Press.

Eells, T. D., Kendjelic, E. M., & Lucas, C. P. (1998). What's in a case formulation? Development and use of a content coding manual. *Journal of Psychotherapy Practice and Research*, 7, 144–153.

Eells, T. D. (Ed.). (2006). Handbook of psychotherapy case formulation (2nd ed.). New York: Guilford Press.

Elkin, I., Yamaguchi, J. L., Arnkoff, D. B., Class, C. R., Sotsky, S. M., & Krupnick, J. L. (1999). "Patient-treatment fit" and early engagement in therapy. *Psychotherapy Research*, 9, 437–451.

Ellenberger, H. F. (1970). *The discovery of the unconscious: The history and evolution of dynamic psychiatry*. New York: Basic Books.

Elliott, R. (1998). Editor's introduction: A guide to the empirically supported treatments controversy. *Psychotherapy Research*, 8, 115–125.

Elliott, R. (2001). Contemporary brief experiential psychotherapy. *Clinical Psychology: Science and Practice*, 8, 38–50.

Elliott, R., Fischer, C. T., & Rennie, D. L. (2003). Evolving guidelines for the publication of qualitative research studies in psychology and related fields. *British Journal of Clinical Psychology*, 38, 215–229.

Elliott, R., Greenberg, L. S., & Lietaer, G. (2004). Research on experiential psychotherapies. In M. L. Lambert (Ed.), *Bergin and Garfield's Handbook of psychotherapy and behavior change* (5th ed., pp. 493–539). New York: John Wiley & Sons.

Emmelkamp, P. M. G. (2004). Behavior therapy with adults. In M. L. Lambert (Ed.), *Bergin and Garfield's Handbook of psychotherapy and behavior change* (5th ed., pp. 393–446) New York: John Wiley & Sons.

Ennett, S. T., Ringwalt, C. L., Thirne, J., Rohrbach, L. A., Vincus, A., Simons-Rudolph, A., et al. (2003). A comparison of current practice in school-base substance use prevention programs with meta-analysis findings. *Prevention Science*, 4, 1–14.

Enright, S., & Carr, A. (2002). Prevention of post-traumatic adjustment problems. In A. Carr (Ed.), *Prevention: what works with children and adolescents? A critical review of psychological prevention programmes for children, adolescents and their families* (pp. 314–335). Hove, UK: Brunner-Routledge.

Esposito, E., Wang, J. L., Adair, C. E., Williams, J. V., Dobson, K., Schopflocher, D., et al. (2007). Frequency and adequacy of depression treatment in a Canadian population sample. *Canadian Journal of Psychiatry*, 52, 780–789.

Essau, C. A. (2003). Primary prevention of depression. In D. J. A. Dozois & K. S. Dobson (Eds.), *The prevention of anxiety and depression: Theory: research, and practice* (pp. 185–204). Washington, DC: American Psychological Association.

Essau, C. A. (2004). Prevention of substance abuse in children and adolescents. In P. M. Barrett & T. H. Ollendick (Eds.), *Interventions that work with children and adolescents: Prevention and Treatment* (pp. 517–539). Chichester, UK: John Wiley & Sons.

Evans, C., Connell, J., Barkham, M., Marshall, C. & Mellor-Clark, J. (2003). Practice-based evidence: Benchmarking NHS primary care counselling services at national and local levels. *Clinical Psychology & Psychotherapy*, 10, 374–388.

Evans, G. W. (2004). The environment of child poverty. *American Psychologist*, 59, 77–92.

Evans, J. J. R. (2004). Disorders of memory. In L. H. Goldstein & J. E. McNeil (Eds.), *Clinical neuropsychology: A practical guide to assessment and management for clinicians* (pp. 143–163). Chichester, UK: John Wiley & Sons.

Exner, J. E. (1993). *The Rorschach: A comprehensive system. Vol. 1. Basic foundations* (3rd ed.). New York: John Wiley & Sons.

Eyberg, S. M., Nelson, M. M., & Boggs, S. R. (2008). Evidence-based psychosocial treatments for children and adolescents with disruptive behaviour. *Journal of Clinical Child and Adolescent Psychology*, 37, 215–237.

Eysenck, H. J. (1952). The effects of psychotherapy: An evaluation. *Journal of Consulting Psychology*, 16, 319–324.

Eysenck, H. J. (1962). *Know your own I.Q.* London: Penguin Books.

Eysenck, H. J. (1966). *The effects of psychotherapy.* New York: International Science Press.

Eysenck, H. J. (1978). An exercise in meta-silliness. *American Psychologist, 33,* 517.

Eytan, A., Durieux-Paillard, S., Whitaker-Clinch, B., Loutan, L., & Bovier, P. A. (2007). Transcultural validity of a structured diagnostic interview to screen for major depression and posttraumatic stress disorder among refugees. *Journal of Nervous and Mental Disease, 195,* 723–728.

Feeny, N. C., Foa, E. B., Treadwell, K. R. H., & March, J. (2004). Posttraumatic stress disorder in youth: A critical review of the cognitive and behavioural outcome literature. *Professional Psychology: Research and Practice, 35,* 466–476.

Feifel, D., Moutier, C. Y., & Swerdlow, N. R. (1999). Attitudes toward psychiatry as a prospective career among students entering medical school. *American Journal of Psychiatry, 156,* 1397–1402.

Fernandez, K., Boccaccini, M. T., & Noland, R. M. (2007). Professionally responsible test selection for Spanish-speaking clients: A four-step approach for identifying and selecting translated tests. *Professional Psychology: Research and Practice, 38,* 363–374.

Feske, U., & Goldstein, A. (1997). Eye movement desensitization and reprocessing treatment for panic disorders: A controlled outcome and partial dismantling study. *Journal of Consulting and Clinical Psychology, 65,* 1026–1035.

Finn, S. E. (1996). Assessment feedback integrating MMPI-2 and Rorschach findings. *Journal of Personality Assessment, 67,* 543–557.

Finn, S. E., & Tonsager, M. E. (1997). Information-gathering and therapeutic models of assessment: Complementary paradigms. *Psychological Assessment, 9,* 374–385.

First, M. B., Pincus, H. A., Levine, J. B., Williams, J. B. W., Ustun, B., & Peele, R. (2004). Clinical utility as a criterion for revising psychiatric diagnoses. *American Journal of Psychiatry, 161,* 946–954.

First, M. B., Spitzer, R. L., Gibbon, M., & Williams, J. B. W. (1997). *Structured Clinical Interview for Axis I DSM-IV Disorders (SCID-I), Clinician Version.* Washington, DC: American Psychiatric Press.

First, M. B., & Tasman, A. (2004). *DSM-IV-TR mental disorders: Diagnosis, etiology, and treatment.* New York: John Wiley & Sons.

Fisher, C. B. (2004). Informed consent and clinical research involving children and adolescents: implications of the Revised APA Ethics Code and HIPAA. *Journal of Clinical Child and Adolescent Psychology, 33,* 832–839.

Fisher, P. A. (2003). The prevention of antisocial behaviour: Beyond efficacy and effectiveness. In A. Biglan, M. Wang, & H. J. Walberg (Eds.), *Preventing youth problems* (pp. 5–31). New York: Kluwer Academic.

Flanagan, D. P., & Kaufman, A. S. (2004). *Essentials of WISC-IV assessment.* New York: John Wiley & Sons.

Fleeson, W. (2004). Moving personality beyond the person-situation debate: The challenge and opportunity of within-person variability. *Current Directions in Psychological Science, 13,* 83–87.

Flynn, J. R. (1987). Massive IQ gains in 14 nations: What IQ tests really measure. *Psychological Bulletin, 101,* 171–191.

Fonagy, P., Target, M., Cottrell, D., Phillips, J., & Kurtz, Z. (2002). *What works for whom? A critical review of treatments for children and adolescents.* New York: Guilford.

Fournier, M. A., Moskowitz, D. S., & Zuroff, D. C. (2008). Integrating dispositions, signatures, and the interpersonal domain. *Journal of Personality and Social Psychology, 94,* 531–545.

Frank, E. (2005). *Treating bipolar disorder: A clinician's guide to interpersonal and social rhythm therapy.* New York: Guilford Press.

Frank, J. D. (1973). *Persuasion and healing*. Baltimore: Johns Hopkins University Press.

Frank, J. D. (1982). Therapeutic components shared by all psychotherapies. In J. H. Harvey & M. M. Parks (Eds.), *The Master Lecture Series: Vol. 1. Psychotherapy research and behavior change* (pp. 5–38). Washington, DC: American Psychological Association.

Frisch, M. B., Clark, M. P., Rouse, S. V., Rudd, M. D., Paweleck, J. K., Greenstone, A., et al. (2005). Predictive and treatment validity of life satisfaction and the Quality of Life Inventory. *Assessment, 12,* 66–78.

Fulero, S. M. (1995). The Psychopathy Checklist-Revised. In J. C. Conoley & J. C. Impara (Eds.), *Twelfth mental measurements yearbook* (pp. 453–454). Lincoln, NE: Buros Institute.

Gabbard, G. O., Gunderson, J. G., & Fonagy, P. (2002). The place of psychoanalytic treatments within psychiatry. *Archives of General Psychiatry, 59,* 505–510.

Galea, S., Brewin, C. R., Gruber, M., Jones, R. T., King, D. W., King, L. A., et al. (2007). Exposure to hurricane-related stressors and mental illness after Hurricane Katrina. *Archives of General Psychiatry, 64,* 1427–1434.

Garb, H. N. (1997). Race bias, social class bias, and gender bias in clinical judgment. *Clinical Psychology: Science and Practice, 4,* 99–120.

Garb, H. N. (1998). *Studying the clinician: Judgment research and psychological assessment*. Washington, DC: American Psychological Association.

Garb, H. N. (2005). Clinical judgment and decision making. *Annual Review of Clinical Psychology, 1,* 67–89.

Garb, H. N. (2007). Computer-administered interviews and rating scales. *Psychological Assessment, 19,* 4–13.

Garb, H. N., & Boyle, P. A. (2003). Understanding why some clinicians use pseudoscientific methods: Findings from research on clinical judgment. In S. O. Lilienfeld, S. J. Lynn, & J. M. Lohr (Eds.), *Science and pseudoscience in clinical psychology* (pp. 17–38). New York: Guilford Press.

Garb, H. N., Klein, D. F., & Grove, W. M. (2002). Comparison of medical and psychological tests. *American Psychologist, 57,* 137–138.

Gardner, H. (1983). *Frames of mind: The theory of multiple intelligences*. New York: Basic Books

Gardner, H. (1999). *Intelligence reframed: Multiple intelligences for the 21st century*. New York: Basic Books.

Garfield, S. L. (1994a). Eclecticism and integration in psychotherapy: Developments and issues. *Clinical Psychology: Science and Practice, 1,* 123–137.

Garfield, S. L. (1994b). Research on client variables in psychotherapy. In A. E. Bergin & S. L. Garfield (Eds.), *Handbook of psychotherapy and behavior change* (4th ed., pp. 190–228). New York: John Wiley & Sons.

Garfield, S. L. (1996). Some problems associated with "validated" forms of psychotherapy. *Clinical Psychology: Research and Practice, 3,* 218–229.

Gibbons, M. B. C., Crits-Christoph, P., & Hearon, B. (2008). The empirical status of psychodynamic therapies. *Annual Review of Clinical Psychology, 4,* 93–108.

Giesen-Bloo, J., van Dyck, R., Spinhoven, P., van Tilburg, W., Dirksen, C., van Asselt, T., et al. (2006). Outpatient psychotherapy for borderline personality disorder: Randomized trial of schema-focused therapy vs transference-focused psychotherapy. *Archives of General Psychiatry, 63,* 649–658.

Glueckauf, R. L., Pickett, T. C., Ketterson, T. U., Loomis, J. S., & Rozensky, R. H. (2003). Preparation for the delivery of telehealth services: A self-study framework for expansion of practice. *Professional Psychology: Research and Practice, 34,* 159–163.

Golden, C. J., Freshwater, S. M., & Vayalakkara, J. (2000). The Luria-Nebraska Neuropsychological

Battery. In G. Groth-Marnat (Ed.), *Neuropsychological assessment in clinical practice* (pp. 263–289). New York: John Wiley & Sons.

Goldstein, L. H., & McNeil, J. E. (2004). General introduction: What is the relevance of neuropsychology for clinical psychology practice? In L. H. Goldstein & J. E. McNeil (Eds.), *Clinical neuropsychology: A practical guide to assessment and management for clinicians* (pp. 3–20). Chichester, UK: John Wiley & Sons.

Goleman, D. (1995). *Emotional intelligence: Why it can matter more than IQ.* New York: Bantam.

Goodman, W. K., Price, L. H., Rasmussen, S. A., Mazure, C., Delgado, P., Heninger, G. R., et al. (1989). The Yale-Brown Obsessive Compulsive Scale. II: Validity. *Archives of General Psychiatry, 40,* 1012–1016.

Gosling, S. D., John, O. P., Craik, K. H., & Robins, R. W. (1998). Do people know how they behave? Self-reported act frequencies compared with on-line codings by observers. *Journal of Personality and Social Psychology, 74,* 1337–1349.

Gosling, S. D., Vazire, S., Srivastava, S., & John, O. P. (2004). Should we trust web-based studies? *American Psychologist, 59,* 93–104.

Gotham, H. J. (2004). Diffusion of mental health and substance abuse treatments: Development, dissemination, and implementation. *Clinical Psychology: Science and Practice, 11,* 160–176.

Gøtzsche, P. C., Hróbjartsson, A., Marić, K., & Tendal, B. (2007). Data extraction errors in meta-analyses that use standardized mean differences. *Journal of the American Medical Association, 298,* 430–437.

Gough, H. G., & Bradley, P. (1996). *California Psychological Inventory manual* (3rd ed.). Palo Alto, CA: Consulting Psychologists Press.

Gray-Little, B., & Kaplan, D. (2000). Race and ethnicity in psychotherapy research. In C. R. Snyder & R. E. Ingram (Eds.), *Handbook of psychological changes: Psychotherapy processes and practices for the 21st century* (pp. 591–613). New York: John Wiley & Sons.

Gray-Little, B., & Kaplan, D. A. (1998). Interpretation of psychological tests in clinical and forensic evaluations. In J. Sandoval, C. L. Frisby, K. F. Geisinger, J. D. Scheuneman, & J. R. Grenier (Eds.), *Test interpretation and diversity: Achieving equity in assessment* (pp. 141–178). Washington, DC: American Psychological Association.

Greenberg, L. (2008). Emotion and cognition in psychotherapy: The transforming power of affect. *Canadian Psychology, 49,* 49–59.

Greenberg, L. S., Elliott, R., Watson, J. C., & Bohart, A. C. (2001). Empathy. *Psychotherapy, 38,* 380-384.

Greene, R. L. (2000). *The MMPI-2: An interpretive manual* (2nd ed.). Boston: Allyn & Bacon.

Greiffenstein, M. F., Baker, W. J., & Johnson-Greene, D. (2002). Actual versus self-reported scholastic achievement of litigating postconcussion and severe closed head injury claimants. *Psychological Assessment, 14,* 202–208.

Griffin, D. W., Dunning, D., & Ross, L. (1990). The role of construal processes in overconfident predictions about the self and others. *Journal of Personality and Social Psychology, 59,* 1128–1139.

Griner, D., & Smith, T. B. (2006). Culturally adapted mental health interventions: A meta-analytic review. *Psychotherapy, 43,* 531–548.

Gross, D., Fogg, L., Webster-Stratton, C., Garvey, C., Julion, W., & Grady, J. (2003). Parent training with multi-ethnic families of toddlers in day care in low-income urban communities. *Journal of Consulting and Clinical Psychology, 71,* 261–278.

Gross, K., Keyes, M. D., & Greene, R. L. (2000). Assessing depression with the MMPI and MMPI-2. *Journal of Personality Assessment, 75,* 464–477.

Groth-Marnat, G. (1999). Financial efficacy of clinical assessment: Rational guidelines and issues for future research. *Journal of Clinical Psychology, 55,* 813–824.

Groth-Marnat, G. (2000). Introduction to neuropsychological assessment. In G. Groth-Marnat (Ed.), *Neuropsychological assessment in clinical practice* (pp. 3–25). New York: John Wiley & Sons.

Groth-Marnat, G. (2003). *Handbook of psychological assessment* (4th ed.). Hoboken, NJ: John Wiley & Sons.

Groth-Marnat, G., & Horvath, L. S. (2008). The psychological report: A review of current controversies. *Journal of Clinical Psychology, 62,* 73–81.

Grove, W. M., Zald, D. H., Lebow, B. S., Snitz, B. E., & Nelson, C. (2000). Clinical versus mechanical prediction: A meta-analysis. *Psychological Assessment, 12,* 19–30.

Grubb, W. L., & McDaniel (2007). The fakability of Bar-On's Emotional Quotient Inventory Short Form: Catch me if you can. *Human Performance, 20,* 43–59.

Guarnaccia, V., Dill, C. A., Sabatino, S., & Southwick, S. (2001). Scoring accuracy using the Comprehensive System for the Rorschach. *Journal of Personality Assessment, 77,* 464–474.

Guilford, J. P. (1956). The structure of intellect. *Psychological Bulletin, 53,* 267–293.

Gunderson, J. G., Bender, D., Sanislow, C., Yen, S., Rettew, J. B., Dolan-Sewell, R., et al. (2003). Plausibility and possible determinants of sudden "remissions" in borderline patients. *Psychiatry, 66,* 111–119.

Haaga, D. A. F. (2000). Introduction to the special section on stepped care models in psychotherapy. *Journal of Consulting and Clinical Psychology, 68,* 547–548.

Hadjistavropoulos, H., & Williams, A. C. (2004). Psychological interventions and chronic pain. In T. Hadjistavropoulos & K. D. Craig (Eds.), *Pain: Psychological treatment perspectives* (pp. 271–301). Mahwah, NJ: Lawrence Erlbaum Associates.

Halford, W. K., Keefer, E., & Osgarby, S. M. (2002). "How has the week been for you two?" Relationship satisfaction and hindsight memory biases in couples' reports of relationship events. *Cognitive Therapy and Research, 26,* 759–773.

Hamel, M., Shaffer, T. W., & Erdberg, P. (2000). A study of nonpatient preadolescent Rorschach protocols. *Journal of Personality Assessment, 75,* 280–294.

Hammen, C., Shih, J. H., & Brennan, P. A. (2004). Intergenerational transmission of depression: Test of an interpersonal stress model in a community sample. *Journal of Consulting and Clinical Psychology, 72,* 511–522.

Hankin, B. L., Fraley, R. C., Lahey, B. B., & Waldman, I. D. (2005). Is depression best viewed as a continuum or discrete category? A taxometric analysis of childhood and adolescent depression in a population-based sample. *Journal of Abnormal Psychology, 114,* 96–110.

Hansen, N. B., Lambert, M. J., & Forman, E. M. (2002). The psychotherapy dose-response effect and its implications for treatment delivery services. *Clinical Psychology: Science and Practice, 9,* 329–343.

Hanson, R. K. (2005). Twenty years of progress in violence risk assessment. *Journal of Interpersonal Violence, 20,* 212–217.

Harding, T. P. (2007). Clinical decision-making: How prepared are we? *Training and Education in Professional Psychology, 1,* 95–104.

Hardy, G. E., Cahill, J., Stiles, W. B., Ispan, C., Macaskill, N., & Barkham, M. (2005). Sudden gains in cognitive therapy for depression: A replication and extension. *Journal of Consulting and Clinical Psychology, 73,* 59–67.

Hare, R. D. (1991). *The Hare Psychopathy Checklist-Revised.* Toronto, ON: Multi-Health Systems.

Hare, R. D., Clark, D., Grann, M., & Thornton, D. (2000). Psychopathy and the predictive validity of the PCL-R: an international perspective. *Behavioral Sciences and the Law*, *18*, 623–645.

Harris, C. (2003). Editorial. *Psychological Bulletin*, *129*, 3–9.

Harris, G. T., Rice, M. E., & Quinsey V. L. (1993). Violent recidivism of mentally disordered offenders: The development of a statistical prediction instrument. *Criminal Justice and Behavior*, *20*, 315–335.

Harvey, A. G., & Bryant, R. G. (2002). Acute Stress Disorder: A synthesis and critique. *Psychological Bulletin*, *128*, 886–902.

Hathaway, S. R., & McKinley, J. C. (1943). *Minnesota Multiphasic Personality Inventory*. New York: Psychological Corporation.

Hawkins, E. H., Cummins, L. H., & Marlatt, G. A. (2004). Preventing substance abuse in American Indian and Alaska native youth: promising strategies for healthier communities, *Psychological Bulletin*, *130*, 304–323.

Hawley, K. M., & Weisz, J. R. (2003). Child, parent, and therapist (dis)agreement on target problems in outpatient therapy: The therapist's dilemma and its implications. *Journal of Consulting and Clinical Psychology*, *71*, 62–70.

Hawley, K. M., & Weisz, J. R. (2005). Youth, versus parent working alliance in usual clinical care: Distinctive associations with retention, satisfaction, and treatment outcome. *Journal of Clinical Child and Adolescent Psychology*, *34*, 117–128 .

Hayes, S. C., Barlow, D. H., & Nelson-Gray, R. O. (1999). *The scientist practitioner: Research and accountability in the age of managed care* (2nd ed.). Needham Heights, MA: Allyn & Bacon.

Hayman-Abello, B. A., Hayman-Abello, S. E., & Rourke, B. P. (2003). Human neuropsychology in Canada: The 1990s (A review of research by Canadian neuropsychologists). *Canadian Psychology*, *44*, 100–138.

Haynes, S. N., Leisen, M. B., & Blaine, D. D. (1997). Design of individualized behavioral treatment programs using functional analytic clinical case methods. *Psychological Assessment*, *9*, 334–348.

Haynes, S. N., & Yoshioka, D. T. (2007). Clinical assessment applications of ambulatory biosensors. *Psychological Assessment*, *19*, 44–57.

Hays, K. A., Rardin, D. K., Jarvis, P. A., Taylor, N. M., Moorman, A. S., & Armstead, C. D. (2002). An exploratory survey on empirically supported treatments: Implications for internship training. *Professional Psychology: Research and Practice*, *33*, 207–211.

Hearn, M. T., & Evans, D. R. (1993). Applications of psychology to health care. In K. S. Dobson & D. G. Dobson (Eds.), *Professional psychology in Canada* (pp. 248–284). Toronto, ON: Hogrefe & Huber.

Helbok, C. M., Marinelli, R. P., & Walls, R. T. (2006). National survey of ethical practices across rural and urban communities. *Professional Psychology: Research and Practice*, *37*, 36–44.

Helmes, E., & Reddon, J. R. (1993). A perspective on developments in assessing psychopathology: A critical review of the MMPI and the MMPI2. *Psychological Bulletin*, *113*, 453–471.

Henggeler, S. W., & Lee, T. (2003). Multisystemic treatment of serious clinical problems. In A. E. Kazdin & J. R. Weisz (Eds.), *Evidence-based psychotherapies for children and adolescents* (pp. 301–324). New York: Guilford.

Henggeler, S. W., Schoenwald, S. K., Borduin, C. M., Rowland, M. D., & Cunningham, P. B. (1998). *Multisystemic treatment of antisocial behaviour in children andadolescents*. New York: Guilford.

Henry, B., Moffitt, T. E., Caspi, A., Langley, J., & Silva, P. A. (1994). On the "Remembrance of Things Past": A longitudinal evaluation of the retrospective method. *Psychological Assessment*, *6*, 92–101.

Henry, G. T. (1990). *Practical sampling*. Newbury Park, CA: Sage.

Henry, W. P. (1998). Science, politics, and the politics of science: The use and misuse of empirically validated treatment research. *Psychotherapy Research, 8,* 126–140.

Herrnstein, R. J., & Murray, C. A. (1994). *The bell curve: Intelligence and class structure in American life.* New York: Free Press.

Herschell, A. D., McNeill, C. B., & McNeil, D. (2004). Clinical child psychology's progress in disseminating empirically supported treatments. *Clinical Psychology: Science and Practice, 11,* 267–288.

Hersen, M., & Gross, A. M. (Eds.). (2007a). *Handbook of clinical psychology. Volume 1, Adults.* New York: John Wiley & Sons.

Hersen, M., & Gross, A. M. (Eds.). (2007b). *Handbook of clinical psychology. Volume 2, Children and adolescents.* New York: John Wiley & Sons.

Hiller, J. B., Rosenthal, R., Bornstein, R. F., Berry, D. T. R., & Brunell-Neuleib, S. (1999). A comparative meta-analysis of Rorschach and MMPI validity. *Psychological Assessment, 11,* 278–296.

Hilsenroth, M. J., Peters, E. J., & Ackerman, S. J. (2004). The development of therapeutic alliance during psychological assessment: Patient and therapist perspectives across treatment. *Journal of Personality Assessment, 83,* 332–344.

Hilsenroth, M. J., & Cromer, T. D. (2007). Clinician interventions related to alliance during the initial interview and psychological assessment. *Psychotherapy, 44,* 205–218.

Himelein, M. J., & Putnam, E. A. (2001). Work activities of academic clinical psychologists: Do they practice what they teach? *Professional Psychology: Research and Practice, 32,* 537–542.

Hinshaw, S. P., Klein, R. G., & Abikoff, H. B. (2002). Childhood Attention-Deficit Hyperactivity Disorder: Nonpharmacological treatments and their combination with medication. In P. E. Nathan & J. M. Gorman (Eds.), *A guide to treatments that work* (2nd ed., pp. 3–55). New York: Oxford University Press.

Hogan, T. P. (2007). *Psychological testing: A practical introduction.* Hoboken, NJ: John Wiley & Sons.

Hoge, M. A., Tondora, J., & Stuart, G. W. (2003). Training in evidence-based practice. *Psychiatric Clinics of North America, 26,* 851–865.

Hollifeld, M., Hewage, C., Gunawardena, C. N., Kodituwakku, P., Bopagoda, K., Weerarathnege, K., et al. (2008). Symptoms and coping in Sri Lanka 20-21 months after the 2001 tsunami. *British Journal of Psychiatry, 192,* 39–44.

Hollon, S. D., & Beck, A. T. (2004). Cognitive and cognitive behavioral therapies. In M. L. Lambert (Ed.), *Bergin and Garfield's Handbook of psychotherapy and behavior change* (5th ed., pp. 447–492). New York: John Wiley & Sons.

Holmbeck, G. N. (1997). Toward terminological, conceptual, and statistical clarity in the study of mediators and moderators: Examples from the child-clinical and pediatric literatures. *Journal of Consulting and Clinical Psychology, 65,* 599–610.

Hopwood, C. J., & Richard, D. C. S. (2005). Graduate student WAIS-III scoring accuracy is a function of Full Scale IQ and complexity of examiner tasks. *Assessment, 12,* 445–454.

Horn, J. L., & Cattell, R. B. (1966). Refinement and test of theory of fluid and crystallized intelligence. *Journal of Educational Psychology, 57,* 253–270.

Horowitz, J. L., & Garber, J. (2006). The prevention of depressive symptoms in children and adolescents: A meta-analytic review. *Journal of Consulting and Clinical Psychology, 74,* 401–415.

Horrell, S. C. V. (2008). Effectiveness of cognitive-behavioral therapy with adult ethnic minority clients: A review. *Professional Psychology: Research and Practice, 39,* 160–168.

Horvath, A. O., & Bedi, R. P. (2002). The alliance. In J. C. Norcross (Ed.), *Psychotherapy relationships that work: Therapist contributions and responsiveness to patients* (pp. 37–69). London: Oxford University Press.

Horvath, A. O., & Luborsky, L. (1993). The role of the therapeutic alliance in psychotherapy. *Journal of Consulting and Clinical Psychology, 61,* 561–573.

Horvath, L. S., Logan, T. K., & Walker, R. (2002) Child custody cases: A content analysis of evaluations in practice. *Professional Psychology: Research and Practice, 33,* 557–565.

Hoza, B., Kaiser, N.M., & Hurt, E. (2007). Multimodal treatments for childhood attention-deficit/ hyperactivity disorder: Interpreting outcomes in the context of study designs. *Clinical Child and Family Psychology Review, 10,* 318–334.

Hubble, M. A., Duncan, B. L., & Miller, S. (Eds.). (1999). *The heart and soul of change.* Washington, DC: American Psychological Association.

Huey, S. J., & Polo, A. J. (2008). Evidence-based psychosocial treatments for ethnic minority youth. *Journal of Clinical Child and Adolescent Psychology, 37,* 262–301.

Hughes, T. L., Gacono, C. B., & Owen, P. F. (2007). Current status of Rorschach assessment: Implications for the school psychologist. *Psychology in the Schools, 44,* 281–291.

Hunsley, J. (2003a). Cost-effectiveness and cost offset considerations in psychological service provision. *Canadian Psychology, 44,* 61–73.

Hunsley, J. (2003b). Introduction to the special section on incremental validity and utility in clinical assessment. *Psychological Assessment, 15,* 443–445.

Hunsley, J., Aubry, T. D., Vestervelt, C. M., & Vito, D. (1999). Clients' and therapists' perspectives on reasons for psychotherapy termination. *Psychotherapy, 36,* 380–388.

Hunsley, J., & Bailey, J. M. (1999). The clinical utility of the Rorschach: Unfulfilled promises and an uncertain future. *Psychological Assessment, 11,* 266–277.

Hunsley, J., & Bailey, J. M. (2001). Whither the Rorschach? An analysis of the evidence. *Psychological Assessment, 13,* 472–485.

Hunsley, J., Crabb, R., & Mash, E. J. (2004). Evidence-based clinical assessment. *The Clinical Psychologist, 57*(3), 25–32.

Hunsley, J., & Di Giulio, G. (2002). Dodo bird, phoenix, or urban legend? The question of psychotherapy equivalence. *Scientific Review of Mental Health Practice, 1,* 11–22.

Hunsley, J., & Lee, C. M. (2007). Research-informed benchmarks for psychological treatments: Efficacy studies, effectiveness studies, and beyond. *Professional Psychology: Research and Practice, 38,* 21–33.

Hunsley, J., Lee, C. M., & Aubry, T. (1999). Who uses psychological services in Canada? *Canadian Psychology, 40,* 232–240.

Hunsley, J., Lee, C. M., & Wood, J. (2003). Controversial and questionable assessment techniques (pp. 39–76). In S. O. Lilienfeld, S. J. Lynn, & J. Lohr (Eds.), *Science and pseudoscience in clinical psychology.* New York: Guilford.

Hunsley, J., & Mash, E. J. (2007). Evidence-based assessment. *Annual Review of Clinical Psychology, 3,* 29–51.

Hunsley, J., & Mash, E. J. (Eds.). (2008). *A guide to assessments that work.* New York: Oxford University Press.

Hunsley, J., & Meyer, G. J. (2003). The incremental validity of psychological testing and assessment: Conceptual, methodological, and statistical issues. *Psychological Assessment, 15,* 446–455.

Hussein, A. H., & Sa'Adoon, A. A. (2006). Prevalence of anxiety and depressive disorders among primary health care attendees in Al-Nasiriyah, Iraq. *Journal of Muslim Mental Health, 1,* 171–176.

Institute of Medicine. (2001). *Crossing the quality chasm: A new health system for the 21st century.* Washington, DC: National Academy Press.

Institute of Medicine. (2002). *Medical innovation in the changing healthcare marketplace: Conference summary.* Washington, DC: National Academy Press.

Institute of Medicine. (2008). *Knowing what works in health care: A road map for the nation*. Retrieved October 9, 2008, from http://www.iom.edu/Object.File/Master/50/721/Knowing%20What%20Works%20report%20brief%20FINAL%20for%20web.pdf.

International Testing Commission. (2001). International guidelines for test use. *International Journal of Testing, 1*, 93–114.

Ivanova, M. Y., Achenbach, T. M., Rescorla, L. A., Dumenci, L., Almqvist, F., Bilenberg, N., et al. (2007). The generalizability of the Youth Self-Report syndrome structure in 23 societies. *Journal of Consulting and Clinical Psychology, 75*, 729–738.

Jackson, J. L., Passamonti, M., & Kroenke, K. (2007). Outcome and impact of mental disorders in primary care at 5 years. *Psychosomatic Medicine, 69*, 270–276.

Jacobs, G. D., Pace-Shott, E. F., Stickgold, R., & Otto, M. W. (2004). Cognitive behavior therapy and pharmacotherapy for insomnia. *Archives of Internal Medicine, 164*, 1888–1896.

Jacobson, N. S., & Addis, M. E. (1993). Research on couples and couples therapy: What do we know? Where are we going? *Journal of Consulting and Clinical Psychology, 61*, 85–93.

Jacobson, N. S., Christensen, A., Prince, S. E., Cordova, J., & Elridge, K. (2000). Integrative behavioral couple therapy: An acceptance based, promising new treatment for couple discord. *Journal of Consulting and Clinical Psychology, 68*, 351–355.

Jacobson, N. S., & Truax, P. (1991). Clinical significance: A statistical approach to defining meaningful change in psychotherapy research. *Journal of Clinical and Consulting Psychology, 59*, 12–19.

Jensen-Doss, A., & Weisz, J. R. (2006). Syndrome co-occurrence and treatment outcomes in youth mental health clinics. *Journal of Consulting and Clinical Psychology, 74*, 416–425.

Jerome, L. W., & Zaylor, C. (2000). Cyberspace: Creating a therapeutic environment for telehealth applications. *Professional Psychology: Research and Practice, 31*, 478–483.

Johnson, S., & Greenberg, L. (1985). Emotionally focused couples therapy: An outcome study. *Journal of Marriage and the Family, 11*, 313–317.

Johnson, S. M. (2004). *The practice of emotionally focused marital therapy: Creating connection*. New York: Bruner Routledge.

Johnson, S. M., Hunsley, J., Greenberg, L., & Schindler, D. (1999). Emotionally focused couples therapy: Status and challenges. *Clinical Psychology: Science & Practice, 6*, 67–79.

Jones, E. E., & Pulos, S. M. (1993). Comparing the process in psychodynamic and cognitive-behavioral therapies. *Journal of Consulting and Clinical Psychology, 61*, 306–316.

Kahana, S., Drotar, D., & Frazier, T. (2008). Meta-analysis of psychological interventions to promote adherence to treatment in pediatric chronic health conditions. *Journal of Pediatric Psychology, 33*, 590–611.

Kallestad, J. H., & Olweus, D. (2003). Predicting teachers' and schools' implementation of the Olweus Bullying Prevention Program: A multilevel study. *Prevention and Treatment, 6, Article 21*. Retrieved October 21, 2004, from http://journals.apa.org/prevention/volume6/pre0060021a.html.

Kaltenthaler, E., Parry, G., Beverley, C., & Ferriter, M. (2008). Computerised cognitive-behavioural therapy for depression: Systematic review. *British Journal of Psychiatry, 193*, 181–184.

Kamieniecki, G. W., & Lynd-Stevenson, R. M. (2002). Is it appropriate to use United States norms to assess the "intelligence" of Australian children? *Australian Journal of Psychology, 54*, 67–78.

Kangas, M., Henry, J. L., & Bryant, R. A. (2005). The relationship between acute stress disorder and posttraumatic stress disorder following cancer.

Journal of Consulting and Clinical Psychology, 73, 360–364.

Kaplan, R. M. (2000). Two pathways to prevention. *American Psychologist, 55,* 382–396.

Kaplan, R. M., & Saccuzzo, D. P. (2001). *Psychological testing: Principles, applications, and issues* (5th ed.). Belmont, CA: Wadsworth/Thomson Learning.

Karney, B. R., Davila, J., Cohan, C. L., Sullivan, K. T., Johnson, M. D., & Bradbury, T. N. (1995). An empirical investigation of sampling strategies in marital research. *Journal of Marriage and the Family, 57,* 909–920.

Katz, L. E., & Gottman, J. M. (1993). Patterns of marital conflict predict children's internalizing and externalizing behaviors. *Developmental Psychology, 29,* 940–950.

Kaufman, A. S., & Kaufman, N. L. (1983). *Manuals for the Kaufman Assessment Battery for Children.* Circle Pines, MN: American Guidance Service.

Kaufman, A. S., & Kaufman, N. L. (1993). *Manual for the Kaufman Adolescent and Adult Intelligence Test.* Circle Pines, MN: American Guidance Service.

Kaufman, A. S., & Lichtenberger, E. O. (1999). *Essentials of WAIS-III assessment.* New York: John Wiley & Sons.

Kazantzis, N., Busch, R., Ronan, K. R., & Merrick, P. L. (2007). Using homework assignments in psychotherapy: Differences by theoretical orientation and professional training? *Behavioural and Cognitive Psychotherapy, 35,* 121–128.

Kazantzis, N., Deane, F. P., & Ronan, K. R. (2000). Homework assignments in cognitive and behavioral therapy: A meta-analysis. *Clinical Psychology: Science and Practice, 7,* 189–202.

Kazantzis, N., Lampropoulos, G. K., & Deane, F. P. (2005). A national survey of practicing psychologists' use and attitudes toward homework in psychotherapy. *Journal of Consulting and Clinical Psychology, 73,* 742–748.

Kazdin, A. E. (1981). Drawing valid inferences from case studies. *Journal of Clinical and Consulting Psychology, 49,* 183–192.

Kazdin, A. E. (1988). *Child psychotherapy: Developing and identifying effective treatments.* New York: Pergamon.

Kazdin, A. E. (1993). Evaluation in clinical practice: Clinically sensitive and systematic methods of treatment delivery. *Behavior Therapy, 24,* 11–45.

Kazdin, A. E. (1995). Scope of child and adolescent psychotherapy research: Limited sampling of dysfunctions, treatments, and client characteristics. *Journal of Clinical Child Psychology, 24,* 125–140.

Kazdin, A. E. (1999). Overview of research design issues in clinical psychology. In P. C. Kendall, J. N. Butcher, & G. N. Holmbeck (Eds.), *Handbook of research methods in clinical psychology* (2nd ed., pp. 3–30). New York: John Wiley & Sons, Inc.

Kazdin, A. E. (2003). Psychotherapy for children and adolescents. *Annual Review of Psychology, 54,* 253–276.

Kazdin, A. E. (2004). Psychotherapy for children and adolescents. In M. L. Lambert (Ed.), *Bergin and Garfield's Handbook of psychotherapy and behavior change* (5th ed., pp. 543–589). New York: John Wiley & Sons.

Kazdin, A. E. (2006). Arbitrary metrics: Implications for identifying evidence-based treatments. *American Psychologist, 61,* 42–49.

Kazdin, A. E. (2007). Mediators and moderators of change in psychotherapy research. *Annual Review of Clinical Psychology, 3,* 1–27.

Kazdin, A. E., & Bass, D. (1989). Power to detect differences between alternative treatments in comparative psychotherapy outcome research. *Journal of Consulting and Clinical Psychology, 57,* 138–147.

Kazdin, A. E., Bass, D., Ayers, W. A., & Rodgers, A. (1990). Empirical and clinical focus of child and adolescent psychotherapy research. *Journal of Consulting and Clinical Psychology, 58,* 729–740.

Kazdin, A. E., & Whitley, M. K. (2006). Comorbidity, case complexity, and effects of evidence-based treatments for children referred for disruptive behavior. *Journal of Consulting and Clinical Psychololology, 74,* 455–467.

Keefe, F., J., Abernethy, A. P., & Campbell, L. C. (2005). Psychological approaches to understanding and treating disease-related pain. *Annual Review of Psychology, 56,* 601–630.

Keiser, R. E., & Prather, E. N. (1990). What is the TAT? A review of ten years of research. *Journal of Personality Assessment, 55,* 800–803.

Keller, M. L., & Craske, M. G. (2008). Panic disorder and agoraphobia. In J. Hunsley & E. J. Mash (Eds.), *A guide to assessments that work* (pp. 229–253). New York: Oxford University Press.

Kelly, M. A. R., Cyranowski, J. M., & Frank, E. (2007). Sudden gains in interpersonal psychotherapy for depression. *Behaviour Research and Therapy, 45,* 2563–2572.

Kendell, R., & Jablensky, A. (2003). Distinguishing between the validity and utility of psychiatric diagnoses. *American Journal of Psychiatry, 160,* 4–12.

Kendjelic, E. M., & Eells, T. D. (2007). Generic psychotherapy case formulation training improves formulation quality. *Psychotherapy, 44,* 66–77.

Kendler, K. S. (2008). Explanatory models for psychiatric illness. *American Journal of Psychiatry, 165,* 695–702.

Kendler, K. S., Gardner, C.O., Annas, P., Neale, M. C., Eaves, L. J., & Lichtenstein, P. (2008). A longitudinal twin study of fears from middle childhood to early adulthood: Evidence for a developmentally dynamic genome. *Archives of General Psychiatry, 65,* 421–429.

Kennedy, M. L., Faust, D., Willis, W. G., & Piotrowski, C. (1994). Social-emotional assessment practices in school psychology. *Journal of Psychoeducational Assessment, 12,* 228–240.

Kennedy-Moore, E., & Watson, J. C. (2001). *Expressing emotions: Myths, realities, and therapeutic strategies.* New York: Guilford Press.

Kenwright, M., & Marks, I. M. (2004). Computer-aided self-help for phobia/panic via internet at home: A pilot study. *British Journal of Psychiatry, 184,* 448–449.

Kessler, R. C., Berglund, P. A., Demler, O., Jin, R., & Walters, E. E. (2005). Lifetime prevalence and age-of-onset distributions of DSM-IV disorders in the National Comorbidity Survey Replication (NCS-R). *Archives of General Psychiatry, 62,* 593–602.

Kessler, R. C., Chiu, W. T., Demler, O., & Walters, E. E. (2005). Prevalence, severity, and comorbidity of twelve-month DSM-IV disorders in the National Comorbidity Survey Replication (NCS-R). *Archives of General Psychiatry, 62,* 617–27.

Kessler, R. C., Heeringa, S., Lakoma, M. D., Petukhova, M., Rupp, A. E., Schoenbaum, M., Wang, P. S., & Zaslavsky, A. M. The individual-level and societal-level effects of mental disorders on earnings in the United States: Results from the National Comorbidity Survey Replication. *American Journal of Psychiatry,* published online ahead of print May 7, 2008.

Kessler, R. C., Merikangas, K. R., Berglund, P., Eaton, W. W., Koretz, D. S., & Walters, E. E. (2003). Mild disorders should not be eliminated from the DSM-V. *Archives of General Psychiatry, 60,* 1117–1122.

Kessler, R. C., Zhao, S., Katz, S. J., Kouzis, A. C., Frank, R. G., Edlund, M., et al. (1999). Past-year use of outpatient services for psychiatric problems in the National Comorbidity Survey. *American Journal of Psychiatry, 156,* 115–123.

Kettman, J. D. J., Schoen, E. G., Moel, J. E., Cochran, S. V., Greenberg, S. T., & Corkery, J. M. (2007). Increasing severity of psycopathology at counseling centers: A new look. *Professional Psychology: Research and Practice, 38,* 523–529.

Kim, N. S., & Ahn, W. (2002). Clinical psychologists' theory-based representations of mental disorders predict their diagnostic reasoning and memory. *Journal of Experimental Psychology: General, 131,* 451–476.

Kirk, S. A. (2004). Are children's DSM diagnoses accurate? *Brief Treatment and Crisis Intervention, 4,* 255–270.

Klerman, G. L., Weissman, M. M., Rounsaville, B. J., & Chevron, E. S. (1984). *Interpersonal psychotherapy for depression.* New York: Basic Books

Kobak, K. A., Greist, J. H., Jefferson, J. W., Katzelnick, D. J., & Henk, H. J. (2004). Behavioral versus pharmacological treatments of obsessive compulsive disorder: A meta-analysis. *Focus, 2,* 462–474.

Korotitsch, W. J., & Nelson-Gray, R. O. (1999). An overview of self-monitoring research in assessment and treatment. *Psychological Assessment, 11,* 415–425.

Kovacs, M. (1992). *Manual for the Children's Depression Inventory.* North Tonawanda, NJ: Multi-Health Systems.

Kraemer, H. C., Morgan, G. A., Leech, N. L., Gliner, J. A., Vaske, J. J., & Harmon, R. J. (2003). Measures of clinical significance. *Journal of the American Academy of Child & Adolescent Psychiatry, 42,* 1524–1529.

Kraemer, H. C., Wilson, G. T., Fairburn, C. G., & Agras, W. S. (2002). Mediators and moderators of treatment effects in randomized clinical trials. *Archives of General Psychiatry, 59,* 877–883.

Kratochwill, T. R. (2007). Preparing school psychologists for evidence-based school practice: Lessons learned and challenges ahead. *American Psychologist, 62,* 829–843.

Krause, M. S., Lutz, W., & Saunders, S. M. (2007). Empirically certified treatments or therapists: The issue of separability. *Psychotherapy, 44,* 347–353.

Krishnamurthy, R., Archer, R. P., & House, J. J. (1996). The MMPI-A and Rorschach: A failure to establish convergent validity. *Assessment, 3,* 179–191.

Krishnamurthy, R., VandeCreek, L., Kaslow, N. J., Tazeau, Y. N., Miville, M. L., Kerns, R., et al. (2004). Achieving competency in psychological assessment: Directions for education and training. *Journal of Clinical Psychology, 60,* 725–739.

Krueger, R. F., & Markon, K. E. (2006). Reinterpreting comorbidity: A model-based approach to understanding and classifying psychopathology. *Annual Review of Clinical Psychology, 2,* 111–133.

Krueger, R. F., Chentsova-Dutton, Y. E., Markon, K. E., Goldberg, D., & Ormel, J. (2003). A cross-cultural study of the structure of comorbidity among common psychopathological syndromes in the general health care setting. *Journal of Abnormal Psychology, 112,* 437–447.

Krueger, R. F., Watson, D., & Barlow, D. H. (2005). Introduction to the special section: Toward a dimensionally based taxonomy of psychopathology. *Journal of Abnormal Psychology, 114,* 491–493.

Kvaal, S., Choca, J., & Groth-Marnat, G. (2003). The integrated psychological report. In L. E. Beutler & G. Groth-Marnat (Eds.), *Integrative assessment of adult personality* (2nd ed., 398–433). New York: Guilford Press.

Laatsch, L., Harrington, D., Hotz, G., Marcantuono, J., Mozzoni, M. P., Walsh V., et al. (2007). An evidence-based review of cognitive and behavioral treatment studies in children with acquired brain injury. *Journal of Head Trauma Rehabilitation, 22,* 248–256.

Lafferty, P., Beutler, L. E., & Crago, M. (1989). Differences between more and less effective psychotherapists: A study of select therapist variables. *Journal of Consulting and Clinical Psychology, 57,* 76–70.

Lally, S. J. (2003). What tests are acceptable for use in forensic evaluations? *Professional Psychology: Research and Practice, 34,* 491–498.

Lambert, M. J. (Ed.). (2004). *Bergin and Garfield's handbook of psychotherapy and behavior change* (5th ed.). New York: John Wiley & Sons.

Lambert, M. J., Hansen, N. B., Umphress, V., Lunnen, K., Okiishi, J., Burlingame, G., et al. (1996). *Administration and scoring manual for the Outcome Questionnaire (OQ 45.2)*. Wilmington, DE: American Professional Credentialing Services.

Lambert, M. J., & Ogles, B. M. (2004). The efficacy and effectiveness of psychotherapy. In M. J. Lambert (Ed.), *Bergin and Garfield's handbook of psychotherapy and behavior change* (5th ed., pp. 139–193). New York: John Wiley & Sons.

Lambert, M. J., Whipple, J. L., Hawkins, E. J., Vermeersch, D. A., Nielsen, S. L., & Smart, D. W. (2003). Is it time for clinicians to routinely track patient outcome? A meta-analysis. *Clinical Psychology: Science and Practice, 10*, 288–301.

Lampropoulos, G. K. (2000). Evolving psychotherapy integration: Eclectic selection and prescriptive applications of common factors in therapy. *Psychotherapy, 37*, 285–297.

Landman, J. T., & Dawes, R. M. (1982). Psychotherapy outcome: Smith and Glass' conclusions stand up under scrutiny. *American Psychologist, 37*, 504–516.

Langan-Fox, J., & Grant, S. (2006). The Thematic Apperception Test: Toward a standard measure of the big three motives. *Journal of Personality Assessment, 87*, 277–291.

La Rue, A., & Watson, J. (1998). Psychological assessment of older adults. *Professional Psychology: Research and Practice, 29*, 5–14.

Le, H., Muñoz, R. F., Ippen, C. G., & Stoddard, J. L. (2003). Treatment is not enough: We must prevent major depression in women. *Prevention and Treatment, 6, Article 10*. Retrieved October 21, 2004.

Lee, C.M., & Asgary-Eden, V. (2009). Family-based approaches to the prevention of depression in at risk children and youth. In C. Essau (Ed.). *Treatment of adolescent depression* (pp. 177–214). Oxford: Oxford University Press.

Lee, W., Bindman, J., Ford, T., Glozier, N., Moran, P., Stewart, R., & Hotopf, M. (2007). Bias in psychiatric case-control studies. *British Journal of Psychiatry, 190*, 204–209.

Leichsenring, F., Rabung, S., & Lebing, E. (2004). The efficacy of short-term psychodynamic psychotherapy for specific psychiatric disorders. *Archives of General Psychiatry, 61*, 1208–1216.

Lemsky, C. M. (2000). Neuropsychological assessment and treatment planning. In G. Groth-Marnat (Ed.), *Neuropsychological assessment in clinical practice* (pp. 535–574). New York: John Wiley & Sons.

Leventhal, H., Weinman, J., Leventhal, E. A., & Phillips, L. A. (2008). Health psychology: The search for pathways between behaviour and health. *Annual Review of Clinical Psychology, 4*, 477–505.

Levitt, E. E. (1957). The effects of psychotherapy with children: An evaluation. *Journal of Consulting Psychology, 21*, 189–196.

Levitt, E. E. (1963). The results of psychotherapy with children: A further evaluation. *Behaviour Research and Therapy, 60*, 326–329.

Levitt, J. M., Saka, N., Romanelli, L. H., & Hoagwood, K. (2007). Early identification of mental health problems in schools: The status of instrumentation. *Journal of School Psychology, 45*, 163–191.

Lewak, R. W., & Hogan, R. S. (2003). Integrating and applying assessment information: Decision making, patient feedback, and consultation. In L. E. Beutler & G. Groth-Marnat (Eds.), *Integrative assessment of adult personality* (2nd ed., pp. 356–397). New York: Guilford Press.

Lewinsohn, P. M., Antonuccio, D. O., Steinmetz, J. L., & Teri, L. (1984). *The coping with depression course: A psychoeducational intervention for unipolar depression*. Eugene, OR: Castilia.

Lewinsohn, P. M., & Clarke, G. N. (1999). Psychosocial treatments for adolescent depression. *Clinical Psychology Review, 19*, 329–342.

Li, F., McAuley, E., Chaumeton, N. R., & Harmer, P. (2001). Enhancing the psychological wellbeing of elderly individuals through Tai Chi exercise: A latent growth curve analysis. *Structural Equation Modeling, 8*, 53–83.

Lichtenberg, P. A., Murman, D. L., & Mellow, A. M. (2003). Integrated case studies. In P. A. Lichtenberg, D. L. Murman, & A. M. Mellow (Eds.), *Handbook of dementia* (pp. 403–412). New York: John Wiley & Sons.

Lichtenberger, E. O., Broadbooks, D. Y., & Kaufman, A. S. (2000). *Essentials of cognitive assessment with KAIT and other Kaufman measures*. New York: John Wiley & Sons.

Lichtenberger, E. O., & Kaufman, A. S. (2004). *Essentials of WPPSI-III assessment*. New York: John Wiley & Sons.

Lichtenberger, E. O., Kaufman, A. S., & Lai, Z. C. (2002). *Essentials of WMS-III assessment*. New York: John Wiley & Sons.

Lilienfeld, S. O. (2007). Psychological treatments that cause harm. *Perspectives on Psychological Science, 2*, 53–70.

Lilienfeld, S. O., Lynn, S. J., & Lohr, J. M. (2003). Science and pseudoscience in clinical psychology: Initial thoughts, reflections, and considerations. In S. O. Lilienfeld, S. J. Lynn, & J. M. Lohr (Eds.), *Science and pseudo-science in clinical psychology* (pp. 1–14). New York: Guilford Press.

Lilienfeld, S. O., Wood, J. M., & Garb, H. N. (2000). The scientific status of projective techniques. *Psychological Science in the Public Interest, 1*, 27–66.

Lilienfeld, S. O., Wood, J. M., & Garb, H. N. (2006). Why questionable psychological tests remain popular. *The Scientific Review of Alternative Medicine, 10*, 6–15.

Lima, E. N., Stanley, S., Kaboski, B., Reitzel, L. R., Richey, J. A., Castro, Y., et al. (2005). The incremental validity of the MMPI-2: When does therapist access not enhance treatment outcome? *Psychological Assessment, 17*, 462–468.

Lin, K. K., Sandler, I. N., Ayers, T. S., Wolchik, S. A., & Luecken, L. J. (2004). Resilience in parentally bereaved children and adolescents seeking preventive services. *Journal of Clinical Child and Adolescent Psychology, 33*, 673–683.

Linehan, M. M., Comtois, K. A., Murray, A. M., Brown, M. Z., Gallop, R. J., Heard, H. L., et al. (2006). Two-year randomized controlled trial and follow-up of dialectical behavior therapy vs therapy by experts for suicidal behaviors and borderline personality disorder. *Archives of General Psychiatry, 63*, 757–766.

Litz, B. T., Engel, C. C., Bryant, R. A., & Papa, A. (2007). A randomized, controlled proof-of-concept trial of an internet-based, therapist-assisted self-management treatment for posttraumatic stress disorder. *American Journal of Psychiatry, 164*, 1676–1683.

Livingston, G., Johnston, K., Katona, C., Paton, J., Lyketsos, C.G., &Old Age Task Force of the World Federation of Biological Psychiatry. (2005). *American Journal of Psychiatry, 162*, 1996–2021.

Loe, S. A., Kadlubek, R. M., & Marks, W. J. (2007). Administration and scoring errors on the WISC-IV among graduate student examiners. *Journal of Psychoeducational Assessment, 25*, 237–247.

Lohr, J. M., Lilienfeld, S. O., Tolin, D. F., & Herbert, J. D. (1999). Eye movement desensitization and reprocessing (EMDR): An analysis of specific and non-specific treatment factors. *Journal of Anxiety Research, 13*, 185–207.

Lohr, J. M., Olatunji, B. O., Baumeister, R. F., & Bushman, B. J. (2007). The psychology of anger venting and empirically supported alternatives that do no harm. *Scientific Review of Mental Health Practice, 5*, 53–64.

London School of Economics Centre for Economic Performance's Mental Health Policy Group. (June 2006). *The Depression report: A new deal for depression and anxiety disorders.* Retrieved on June 3, 2008, from www.lse.ac.uk.

Longwell, B. T., & Truax, P. (2005). The differential effects of weekly, monthly, and bimonthly administration of the Beck Depression Inventory-II: Psychometric properties and clinical implications. *Behavior Therapy, 36,* 265–275.

Love, S. M., Koob, J. J., & Hill, L. E. (2007). Meeting the challenges of evidence-based practice: Can mental health therapists evaluate their practice? *Brief Treatment and Crisis Intervention, 7,* 184–193.

Lowry-Webster, H. M., & Barrett, P. M. (2001). A universal prevention trial of anxiety and depressive disorders in childhood: Preliminary data from an Australian study. *Behaviour Change, 18,* 36–50.

Luborsky, L. (1954). A note on Eysenck's article "The effects of psychotherapy: An evaluation." *British Journal of Psychology, 45,* 129–131.

Luborsky, L. (1984). *Principles of psychoanalytic psychotherapy: A manual for supportive expressive (SE) treatment.* New York: Basic Books

Luborsky, L., Diguer, L., Luborsky, E., Singer, B., Dickter, D., & Schmidt, K. A. (1993). The efficacy of dynamic psychotherapies: Is it true that "Everyone has won and all must have prizes"? In M. E. Miller, L. Luborsky, J. P. Barber, & J. P. Docherty (Eds.), *Psychodynamic treatment research: A handbook for clinical practice* (pp. 497–516). New York: Basic Books.

Luborsky, L., Diguer, L., Seligman, D. A., Rosenthal, R., Krause, E. D., Johnson, S., et al. (1999). The researcher's own therapy allegiance: A "wild card" in comparisons of treatment efficacy. *Clinical Psychology: Science and Practice, 6,* 95–106.

Luborsky, L., Rosenthal, R., Diguer, L., Andrusyna, T. P., Berman, J. S., Levitt, J. T., et al. (2002). The dodo bird verdict is alive and well—mostly. *Clinical Psychology: Science and Practice, 9,* 2–12.

Luborsky, L., Singer, B., & Luborsky, E. (1975). Comparative studies of psychotherapies: Is it true that "Everybody has won and all must have prizes"? *Archives of General Psychiatry, 32,* 995–1008.

Luby, J. L., Belden, A., Sullivan, J., & Spitznagel, E. (2007). Preschoolers' contribution to their diagnosis of depression and anxiety: Uses and limitations of young child self-report of symptoms. *Child Psychiatry and Human Development, 38,* 312–338.

Luebbe, A. M., Radcliffe, A. M., Callands, T. A., Green, D., & Thorn, B. E. (2007). Evidence-based practice in psychology: Perceptions of graduate students in scientist-practitioner programs. *Journal of Clinical Psychology, 63,* 643–655.

Lundahl, B. W., Nimer, J., & Parsons, B. (2006). Preventing child abuse: A meta-analysis of parent training programs. *Research on Social Work Practice, 16,* 251–262.

Lutz, W., Leon, S. C., Martinovich, Z., Lyons, J. S., & Stiles, W. B. (2007). Therapist effects in outpatient psychotherapy: A three-level growth curve approach. *Journal of Counseling Psychology, 54,* 32–39.

Luxembourg Income Study (2000). *Relative poverty rates for the total population, children and the elderly.* Retrieved on October 22, 2004, from http://www.lisproject.org/keyfigures/povertytable.htm.

Lyons, J. S., & Howard, K. I. (1991). Main effects analysis in clinical research: Statistical guidelines for disaggregating treatment groups. *Journal of Consulting and Clinical Psychology, 59,* 745–748.

MacCallum, R. C., & Austin, J. T. (2000). Applications of structural equation modeling in psychological research. *Annual Review of Psychology, 51,* 201–226.

MacCallum, R. C., Zhang, S., Preacher, K. J., & Rucker, D. D. (2002). On the practice of dichotomization of quantitative variables. *Psychological Methods, 7,* 19–40.

MacMillan, H. L., Wathen, C. N., Jamieson, E., Boyle, M., McNutt, L.-A., Worster, A., et al. (2006). Approaches to screening for intimate partner violence in health care settings. *Journal of the American Medical Association, 296,* 530–536.

Magaletta, P. R., & Verdeyen, V. (2005). Clinical practice in corrections: A conceptual framework. *Professional Psychology Research and Practice, 36,* 37–43.

Malgady, R. G. (1996). The question of cultural bias in assessment and diagnosis of ethnic minority clients: Let's reject the null hypothesis. *Professional Psychology: Research and Practice, 27,* 73–77.

Malouf, J. M., & Rooke, S. E. (2007). Empirically supported self-help books. *The Behavior Therapist, 30,* 129–131.

Mancini, A. D., & Bonanno, G. A. (2006). Resilience in the face of potential trauma: Clinical practices and illustrations. *Journal of Clinical Psychology, 62,* 971–985.

Mariush, M. E. (2002). *Essentials of treatment planning.* New York: John Wiley & Sons.

Marks, I. M., & Mathews, A. M. (1979). Brief standard self-rating for phobic patients. *Behaviour Research and Therapy, 17,* 263–267.

Marks, I., Shaw, S., & Parkin, R. (1998). Computer-aided treatments of mental health problems. *Clinical Psychology: Science and Practice, 5,* 151–170.

Marlatt, G. A., Larimer, M. E., Mail, P. D., Hawkins, E. H., Cummins, L. H., Blume, A. W., et al. (2003). Journeys of the circle: A culturally congruent life skills intervention for adolescent drinking. *Alcoholism: Clinical and Experimental Research, 27,* 1327–1329.

Martin, D. J., Garske, J. P., & Davis, M. K. (2000). Relation of the therapeutic alliance with outcome and other variables: A meta-analytic review. *Journal of Consulting and Clinical Psychology, 68,* 438–450.

Martin, L., Saperson, K., & Maddigan, B. (2003). Residency training: challenges and opportunities in preparing trainees for the 21st century. *Canadian Journal of Psychiatry, 48,* 225–231.

Mash, E. J. (1979). What is behavioral assessment? *Behavioral Assessment, 1,* 23–29.

Mash, E. J., & Sattler, J. M. (1998). Introduction to clinical assessment interviewing. In J. M. Sattler, *Clinical and forensic interviewing of children and families* (pp. 2–44). San Diego, CA: Jerome Sattler.

Mash, E. J., & Foster, S. L. (2001). Exporting analogue behavioral observation from research to clinical practice: Useful or cost-defective? *Psychological Assessment, 13,* 86–98.

Mash, E. J., & Hunsley, J. (1993). Assessment considerations in the assessment of failing psychotherapy: Bringing the negatives out of the darkroom. *Psychological Assessment: A Journal of Consulting and Clinical Psychology, 5,* 292–301.

Mash, E. J., & Hunsley, J. (2004). Behavioral assessment: Sometimes you get what you need. In S. N. Haynes & E. M. Heiby (Eds.), *The comprehensive handbook of psychological assessment, Volume 3: Behavioral assessment* (pp. 489–501). New York: John Wiley & Sons.

Mash, E. J., & Hunsley, J. (2005). Evidence-based assessment of child and adolescent disorders: Issues and challenges. *Journal of Clinical Child and Adolescent Psychology, 34,* 362–379.

Mash, E. J., & Hunsley, J. (2007). Assessment of child and family disturbance: A developmental-systems approach. In E. J. Mash & R. A. Barkley (Eds.), *Assessment of childhood disorders* (4th ed., pp. 3–50). New York: Guilford.

Masling, J. M. (1992). The influence of situation and interpersonal variables in projective testing. *Journal of Personality Assessment, 59,* 616–640.

May, R., Angel, E., & Ellenberger, H. (Eds). (1958). *Existence: A new dimension in psychiatry and psychology.* New York: Basic Books.

Mayer, J. D., Roberts, R. D., & Barsade, S. G. (2008). Human abilities: Emotional intelligence. *Annual Review of Psychology, 59,* 507–536.

Mayer, J. D., Salovey, P., & Caruso, D. R. (2008). Emotional intelligence: New ability or eclectic traits? *American Psychologist, 63,* 503–517.

Mayer, J. D., Salovey, P., Caruso, D. R., & Sitarenios, G. (2003). Measuring emotional intelligence with the MSCEIT V2.0. *Emotion, 3,* 97–105.

McCarthy, O., & Carr, A. (2002). Prevention of bullying. In A. Carr (Ed.), *Prevention: What works with children and adolescents? A critical review of psychological prevention programmes for children, adolescents and their families* (pp. 205–221). Hove, UK: Brunner-Routledge.

McCarty, C. A., & Weisz, J. R. (2007). Effects of psychotherapy for depression in children and adolescents: What we can (and can't) learn from meta-analysis and component profiling. *Journal of the American Academy of Child and Adolescent Psychiatry, 46,* 879–886.

McClelland, D. C., Koestner, R., & Weinberger, J. (1989). How do self-attributed and implicit motives differ? *Psychological Bulletin, 96,* 690–702.

McCrone, P., Knapp, M., Proudfoot, J., Ryden, C., Cavanagh, K., Shapiro, D. A., et al. (2004). Cost-effectiveness of computerised cognitive-behavioural therapy for anxiety and depression in primary care: Randomised controlled trial. *British Journal of Psychiatry, 185,* 55–62.

McFall, R. M. (1991). Manifesto for a science of clinical psychology. *The Clinical Psychologist, 44,* 75–88.

McFall, R.M. (2006). Doctoral training in clinical psychology. *Annual Review of Clinical Psychology, 2,* 21–49.

McGrath, P. J., & Finley, G. A. (Eds.). (2003). *Pediatric pain: Biological and social context.* Seattle, WA: IASP Press.

McGrath, P. J., Finley, G. A., Ritchie, J., & Dowden, S. J. (2003). *Pain, pain, go away: Helping children with pain.* Halifax, NS: Dalhousie University.

McGrath, P. J., & Unruh, A. (1999). The measurement and assessment of paediatric pain. In P. D. Wall & R. Melzack (Eds.), *Textbook of pain* (4th ed., pp. 371–384). London: Churchill Livingstone.

McLean, P. D., & Woody, S. R. (2001). *Anxiety disorders in adults: An evidence-based approach to psychological treatment.* New York: Oxford University Press.

McLellan, F. (2003). Research by U.S. psychiatrists in danger of extinction. Expert committee recommends steps to strengthen research training in psychiatry residency. *Lancet, 362,* 1732.

McLeod, B. D., & Weisz, J. R. (2004). Using dissertations to examine potential bias in child and adolescent clinical trials. *Journal of Consulting and Clinical Psychology, 72,* 235–251.

McNally, R. J., Bryant, R. A., & Ehlers, A. (2003). Does early psychological intervention promote recovery from posttraumatic stress? *Psychological Science in the Public Interest, 4,* 45–79.

Measelle, J. R., Ablow, J. C., Cowan, P. A. & Cowan, C. P. (1998). Assessing young children's views of their academic, social and emotional lives: An evaluation of the self-perception scales of the Berkeley Puppet Interview. *Child Development, 69,* 1556–1576.

Measelle, J. R., John, O. P., Ablow, J. C., Cowan, P. A., & Cowan, C. P. (2005). Can children provide coherent, stable, and valid self-reports on the Big Five dimensions? A longitudinal study from ages 5–7. *Journal of Personality and Social Psychology, 89,* 90–106.

Meehl, P. E. (1954). *Clinical versus statistical prediction: A theoretical analysis and a review of the evidence.* Minneapolis: University of Minnesota Press.

Megargee, E. I. (2002). *The California Psychological Inventory handbook* (2nd ed.). San Francisco: Jossey-Bass.

Meichenbaum, D. (1977). *Cognitive-behavior modification: An integrative approach.* New York: Plenum.

Meisner, S. (1988). Susceptibility of Rorschach distress correlates to malingering. *Journal of Personality Assessment, 52,* 564–571.

Mellers, J. D. C. (2004). Neurological investigations. In L. H. Goldstein & J. E. McNeil (Eds.), *Clinical neuropsychology: A practical guide to assessment and management for clinicians* (pp. 57–77). Chichester, UK: John Wiley & Sons.

Menchola, M., Arkowitz, H. S., & Burke, B. L. (2007). Efficacy of self-administered treatments for depression and anxiety. *Professional Psychology: Research and Practice, 38,* 421–429.

Merikangas, K. R., Ames, M., Cui, L., Stang, P. E., Ustun, T. B., von Korff, M., & Kessler, R. C. (2007). The impact of comorbidity of mental and physical conditions on role disability in the U. S. adult population. *Archives of General Psychiatry, 64,* 1180–1188.

Merrill, K. A., Tolbert, V. E., & Wade, W. A. (2003). Effectiveness of cognitive therapy for depression in a community mental health center: A benchmarking study. *Journal of Consulting and Clinical Psychology, 71,* 404–409.

Messer, S. B. (2000). What makes brief psychodynamic therapy time efficient? *Clinical Psychology: Science and Practice, 8,* 5–22.

Meyer, B., Pilkonis, P. A., Krupnick, J. L., Egan, M. K., Simmens, S. J., & Sotsky, S. M. (2002). Treatment expectancies, patient alliance, and outcome: Further analyses from the National Institute of Mental Health Treatment of Depression Collaborative Research Program. *Journal of Consulting and Clinical Psychology, 70,* 1051–1055.

Meyer, G.(Ed.). (1999). The utility of the Rorschach in clinical assessment [Special section: I]. *Psychological Assessment 11,* 235–302.

Meyer, G.(Ed.). (2001). The utility of the Rorschach in clinical assessment [Special section: II]. *Psychological Assessment 13,* 419–502.

Meyer, G. J., Erdberg, P., & Shaffer, T. W. (2007). Toward international normative reference data for the Comprehensive System. *Journal of Personality Assessment, 89,* S201–S216.

Meyer, G. J., Finn, S. E., Eyde, L., Kay, G. G., Moreland, K. L., Dies, R. R., et al. (2001). Psychological testing and psychological assessment: A review of evidence and issues. *American Psychologist, 56,* 128–165.

Meyer, T. J., Miller, M. L., Metzger, R. L., & Borkovec, T. D. (1990). Developmental validation of the Penn State Worry Questionnaire. *Behaviour Research and Therapy, 28,* 487–496.

Mezulis, A. H., Abramson, L. Y., Hyde, J. S., & Hankin, B. L. (2004). Is there a universal positivity bias in attributions? A meta-analytic review of individual, developmental, and cultural differences in the self-serving attributional bias. *Psychological Bulletin, 130,* 711–747.

Middleton, J. A. (2004). Clinical neuropsychological assessment of children. In L. H. Goldstein & J. E. McNeil (Eds.), *Clinical neuropsychology: A practical guide to assessment and management for clinicians* (pp. 275–300). Chichester, UK: John Wiley & Sons.

Miller, G. E., & Prinz, R. J. (2003). Engagement of families in treatment for childhood conduct problems. *Behavior Therapy, 34,* 517–534.

Millon, T. (1993). *Millon Adolescent Clinical Inventory manual.* Minneapolis, MN: National Computer Systems.

Millon, T. (1997). *Millon Clinical Multiaxial Inventory-III manual.* Minneapolis, MN: National Computer Systems.

Mingroni, M. A. (2007). Resolving the IQ paradox: Heterosis as a cause of the Flynn effect and other trends. *Psychological Review, 114,* 806–829.

Miranda, J., Bernal, G., Lau, A., Kohn, L., Hwang, W.-C., & LaFromboise, T. (2005). State of the science on psychosocial interventions for ethnic minorities. *Annual Review of Clinical Psychology, 1,* 113–142.

Mischel, W. (1968). *Personality and assessment*. New York: John Wiley & Sons.

Mischel, W. (2004). Toward an integrative science of the person. *Annual Review of Psychology, 55*, 1–22.

Mischel, W., Shoda, Y., & Smith, R. E. (2004). *Introduction to personality: Toward an integration*. New York: John Wiley & Sons.

Mohr, D. C., Hart, S. L., Julian, L., Catledge, C., Honos-Webb, L., Vella, L., et al. (2005). Telephone-administerd psychotherapy for depression. *Archives of General Psychiatry, 62*, 1007–1014.

Mojtabai, R., & Olfson, M. (2008). National trends in psychotherapy by office-based psychiatrists. *Archives of General Psychiatry, 65*, 962–970.

Mokdad, A. H., Marks, J. S., Stroup, D. F., & Gerberding, J. L. (2004). Actual causes of death in the United States,2000. *Journal of the American Medical Association, 291*, 1238–1245.

Monahan, J. (1981). *Predicting violent behavior: An assessment of clinical techniques*. Beverly Hills, CA: Sage.

Morasco, B. J., Gfeller, J. D., & Elder, K. A. (2007). The utility of the NEO-PI-R validity scales to detect response distortion: A comparison with the MMPI-2. *Journal of Personality Assessment, 88*, 276–283.

Morey, L. C. (1991). *The Personality Assessment Inventory professional manual*. Odessa, FL: Psychological Assessment Resources.

Morey, L. C. (2003). *Essentials of PAI assessment*. New York: John Wiley & Sons.

Morey, L. C. (2007). *Personality Assessment Inventory professional manual* (2nd ed.). Lutz, FL: Psychological Assessment Resources.

Morgan, D. L., & Morgan, R. K. (2001). Single-participant research design: Bringing science to managed care. *American Psychologist, 56*, 119–217.

Morin, C. M. (2004). Cognitive-behavioral approaches to the treatment of insomnia. *Journal of Clinical Psychiatry, 65*(Suppl. 16) 33–40.

Morin, C. M., Colecchi, C., Stone, J., Sood, R., & Brink, D. (1999). Behavioral and pharmacological therapies for late-life insomnia: A randomized controlled trial. *Journal of the American Medical Association, 281*, 991–999.

Morley, S., & Adams, M. (1989). Some simple statistical tests for exploring single-case time-series data. *British Journal of Clinical Psychology, 28*, 1–18.

Morris, R. G. (2004). Neuropsychology of older adults. In L. H. Goldstein & J. E. McNeil (Eds.), *Clinical neuropsychology: A practical guide to assessment and management for clinicians* (pp. 301–318). Chichester, UK: John Wiley & Sons.

Mrazek, P. J., & Haggerty, R. J. (1994). *Reducing risks for mental disorders: Frontiers for preventive research*. Washington, DC: National Academy Press.

Mufson, L., & Dorta, K. P. (2003). Interpersonal psychotherapy for depressed adolescents. In A. E. Kazdin & J. R. Weisz (Eds.), *Evidence-based psychotherapies for children and adolescents* (pp. 148–164). New York: Guilford.

Mufson, L., & Dorta, K. P. (2003). Interpersonal psychotherapy for depressed adolescents. In A. E. Kazdin & J. R. Weisz (Eds.), *Evidence-based psychotherapies for children and adolescents* (pp. 148–164). New York: Guilford.

Mufson, L., Dorta, K. P., Moreau, D., & Weissman, M. M. (2004). *Interpersonal psychotherapy for depressed adolescents* (2nd ed.). New York: Guilford.

Mufson, L., Weissman, M. M., Moreau, D., & Garfinkel, R. (1999). Efficacy of interpersonal psychotherapy for depressed adolescents. *Archives of General Psychiatry, 56*, 573–579.

Mullen, E. J., & Streiner, D. L. (2004). The evidence for and against evidence-based practice. *Brief Treatment and Crisis Intervention, 4*, 111–121.

Mumma, G. H. (1998). Improving cognitive case formulation and treatment planning in clinical practice and research. *Journal of Cognitive Psychotherapy, 12*, 251–274.

Mungas, D., Reed, B. R., Crane, P. K., Haan, M. N., & González, H. (2004). Spanish and English Neuropsychological Assessment scales (SENAS): Further development and psychometric characteristics. *Psychological Assessment*, *16*, 347–359.

Mungas, D., Reed, B. R., Haan, M. N., & Gonzalez, H. (2005). Spanish and English Neuropsychological Assessment Scales: Relationship to demographics, language, cognition, and independent function. *Neuropsychology*, *19*, 466–475.

Mungas, D., Reed, B. R., Marshall, S. C., & González, H. (2000). Development of psychometrically matched English and Spanish language neuropsychological tests for older persons. *Neuropsychology*, *14*, 209–223.

Munsey, C. (2008, February). Psychopharmacology: Prescriptive authority in the states. *Monitor on Psychology*. Retrieved from http://www.apa.org/monitor/feb08/prescriptive.html on July 11, 2008.

Murray, H. A. (1943). *Thematic Apperception Test manual*. Cambridge, MA: Harvard University Press.

Mussell, M. P., Crosby, R. D., Crow, S. J., Knopke, A. J., Peterson, C. B., Wonderlich, S. A., et al. (2000). Utilization of empirically supported psychotherapy treatments for individuals with Eating Disorders: A survey of psychologists. *International Journal of Eating Disorders*, *27*, 230–237.

Myers, L. L., & Thyer, B. A. (1997). Should social work clients have the right to effective treatment? *Social Work*, *42*, 288–297.

Nagin, D., & Tremblay, R. E. (1999). Trajectories of boys' physical aggression, opposition, and hyperactivity on the path to physically violent and nonviolent juvenile delinquency. *Child Development*, *70*, 1181–1196.

Naglieri, J. A., Drasgow, F., Schmit, M., Handler, L., Prifitera, A., Margolis, A. M., et al. (2004). Psychological testing on the Internet, *American Psychologist*, *59*, 150–162.

Nathan, P. E. (2004). When science only takes us so far. *Clinical Psychology: Science and Practice*, *11*, 216–218.

Nathan, P., & Gorman, J. M. (Eds.). (1998). *A guide to treatments that work*. New York: Oxford University Press.

Nathan, P., & Gorman, J. M. (Eds.). (2002). *A guide to treatments that work* (2nd ed.). New York: Oxford University Press.

Nathan, P. E., & Gorman, J. M. (Eds.). (2007). *A guide to treatments that work* (3rd ed.) New York: Oxford University Press.

Nation, M., Crusto, C., Wandersman, A., Kumpfer, K. L., Seybolt, D., Morrissey-Kane, E., et al. (2003). What works in prevention: Principles of effective prevention programs. *American Psychologist*, *58*, 449–456.

National Association of Social Workers. (2008). Social work profession. Retrieved on June 19, 2008 from www.socialworkers.org.

National Center for Children in Poverty. (2007). *Who are America's poor children? The official story*. Retrieved on September 4, 2008 from www.nccp.org/publications/pdf/text_787.pdf.

National Center for Health Statistics. (2006). *Health, United States, 2006, with chartbook on trends in the health of American with special feature on pain*. Retrieved on October 22, 2008 from http://www.cdc.gov/nchs/.

National Institute for Clinical Excellence. (2004a). Anxiety: management of anxiety (panic disorder, with or without agoraphobia, and generalized anxiety disorder) in adults in primary, secondary and community care. Retrieved December 8, 2004 from http://www.nice.org.uk/CG022quickrefguide.

National Institute for Clinical Excellence. (2004b). *Depression: management of depression in primary and secondary care*. Retrieved December 8, 2004, from http://www.nice.org.uk/CG023quickrefguide.

National Institute for Clinical Excellence. (2005). *Depression in children: identification and* management of depression in children and young people in primary, community and secondary care. Retrieved February 15, 2005, from http://www.nice.org.uk.

National Institute for Health and Clinical Excellence. (2007). *Depression: Management of depression in primary and secondary care. Quick reference guide (amended)*. Retrieved October 9, 2008, from http://www.nice.org.uk/nicemedia/pdf/CG23quic krefguideamended.pdf.

National Institute for Health and Clinical Excellence. (2008, September). *Attention deficit hyperactivity disorder: Diagnosis and management of ADHD in children, young people, and adults*. Retrieved on October 31, 2008, from www.nice.org.uk.

National Institutes of Health. (1998). *Diagnosis and treatment of Attention Deficit Hyperactivity Disorder (ADHD), NIH Consensus Statement 16*, 1–37. Kensington, MD: Author.

National Institute of Mental Health (nd). *The numbers count: Mental disorders in America*. Retrieved on June 19, 2008, from http://www.nimh.nih.gov/health/publications/the-numbers-count-mental-disorders-in-america.shtml.

National Opinion Research Center. (2007). Doctorate recipients from United States universities: Summary report 2006. Retrieved on May 27, 2008, from http://www.norc.org.

National Sleep Foundation. (2008). *2008 Sleep in America poll*. Retrieved on October 21, 2008, from www.sleepfoundation.org.

Naugle, A. E., & Maher, S. (2003). Modeling and behavioral rehearsal. In W. O'Donohue, J. E. Fisher, & S. C. Hayes (Eds.), *Cognitive behavior therapy: Applying empirically supported techniques in your practice* (pp. 238–246). New York: John Wiley & Sons.

Neisser, U. (Ed.). (1998). *The rising curve: Long-term gains in IQ and related measures*. Washington, DC: American Psychological Association.

Nelson, G., Westhues, A., & MacLeod, J. (2003, December 18). A meta-analysis of longitudinal research on preschool prevention programs for children. *Prevention and Treatment, 6, Article 31*. Retrieved October 21, 2004, from http://journals.apa.org/prevention/volume6/pre0060031a.html.

Nelson, T. D., & Steele, R. G. (2008). Influences on practitioner treatment selection: Best research evidence and other considerations. *Journal of Behavioral Health.Services & Research, 35*, 170–178.

Nelson-Gray, R. O. (2003). Treatment utility of psychological assessment. *Psychological Assessment, 15*, 521–531.

Neuner, F., Schauer, M., Klaschik, C., Karunakara, U., & Elbert, T. (2004). A comparison of narrative exposure therapy, supportive counseling, and psychoeducation for treating posttraumatic stress disorder in an African refugee settlement. *Journal of Consulting and Clinical Psychology, 72*, 579–587.

Newman, D. L., Moffitt, T. E., Caspi, A., & Silva, P. A. (1998). Comorbid mental disorders: Implications for treatment and sample selection. *Journal of Abnormal Psychology, 107*, 305–311.

Newman, M. G., Erickson, T., Przeworski, A., & Dzus, E. (2003). Self-help and minimal-contact therapies for anxiety disorders: Is human contact necessary for therapeutic efficacy? *Journal of Clinical Psychology, 59*, 251–274.

Newsom, C. R., Archer, R. P., Trumbetta, S., & Gottesman, I. I. (2003). Changes in adolescent response patterns on the MMPI/MMPI-A across four decades. *Journal of Personality Assessment, 81*, 74–84.

Nezu, A. M., & Nezu, C. M. (1993). Identifying and selecting target problems for clinical interventions: A problem-solving model. *Psychological Assessment, 5*, 254–263.

Nichols, D. S. (2001). *Essentials of MMPI-2 assessment*. New York: John Wiley & Sons.

Nichols, D. S. (2006). The trials of separating bath water from baby: A review and critique of the

MMPI-2 restructured clinical scales. *Journal of Personality Assessment, 87,* 121–138.

Norcross, J. C.(Ed.). (2001a). Empirically supported therapy relationships: Summary report of the Division 29 task force [Special issue]. *Psychotherapy 38*(4).

Norcross, J. C. (2001b). Purposes, processes, and products of the Task Force on Empirically Supported Therapy Relationships. *Psychotherapy, 38,* 345–356.

Norcross, J. C. (Ed). (2002). *Psychotherapy relationships that work: Therapist contributions and responsiveness to patients.* London: Oxford University Press.

Norcross, J. C., Castle, P. H., Sayette, M. A., & Mayne, T. J. (2004). The PsyD: Heterogenity in practitioner training. *Professional Psychology: Research and Practice, 35,* 412–419.

Norcross, J. C., & Goldfried, M. R. (1992). *Handbook of psychotherapy integration.* New York: Basic Books.

Norcross, J. C., Karg, R. S., & Prochaska, J. (1997). Clinical psychologists in the 1990s: Part I. *The Clinical Psychologist, 50*(2), 4–9.

Norcross, J. C. Karpiak, C. P., & Santoro, S. O. (2005). Clinical paychologists across the years: The Division of Clinical Psychology from 1960–2003. *Journal of Clinical Psychology, 61,* 1467–1483.

Norcross, J. C., Kohout, J. L., & Wicherski, M. (2005). Graduate study in psychology: 1971–2004. *American Psychologist, 60,* 959–975.

Norcross, J. C., Koocher, G. P., & Garofalo, A. (2006). Discredited psychological treatments and test: A Delphi poll. *Professional Psychology: Research and Practice, 37,* 515–522.

Norcross, J. C., Sayette, M. A., Mayne, T. J., Karg, R. S., & Turkson, M. A. (1998). Selecting a doctoral program in professional psychology: Some comparisons among Ph.D. counseling, Ph.D. clinical, and Psy.D. clinical psychology programs. *Professional Psychology: Research and Practice, 29,* 609–614.

Norton, J., De Roquefeuil, G., Boulenger, J.-P., Ritchie, K., Mann, A., & Tylee, A. (2007). Use of the PRIME-MD patient health questionnaire for estimating the prevalence of psychiatric disorders in French primary care: Comparison of family practitioner estimates and relationship to psychotropic medication use. *General Hospital Psychiatry, 29,* 285–293.

Nunnally, J. C., & Bernstein, I. H. (1994). *Psychometric theory* (3rd ed.). New York: McGraw-Hill.

O'Brien, W. H. (1995). Inaccuracies in the estimation of functional relationships using self-monitoring data. *Journal of Behavior Therapy and Experimental Psychiatry, 26,* 351–357.

Ogden, T., & Hagen, K. A. (2008). Treatment effectiveness of parent management training in Norway: A randomized controlled trial of children with conduct problems. *Journal of Consulting and Clinical Psychology, 76,* 607–621.

Ogles, B. M., Lambert, M. J., & Fields, S. A. (2002). *Essentials of outcome assessment.* New York: John Wiley & Sons.

Ohayon, M. M. (2005). Relationship between chronic painful physical conditions and insomnia. *Journal of Psychiatric Research, 39,* 151–159.

Olds, D. L. (2002). Prenatal and infancy home visiting by nurses: From randomized trials to community replication. *Prevention Science, 3,* 153–172.

Ollendick, T. H., & King, N. J. (2004). Empirically supported treatments for children and adolescents: Advances toward evidence-based practice. In P. M., Barrett & T. H. Ollendick (Eds.), *Interventions that work with children and adolescents: Prevention and treatment* (pp. 3–25). New York: John Wiley & Sons.

Olweus, D. (1993). *Bullying at school: What we know and what we can do.* Oxford: Blackwell.

O'Riordan, B., & Carr, A. (2002). Prevention of physical abuse. In A. Carr (Ed.), *Prevention: What works with children and adolescents? A critical review of psychological prevention programmes for children, adolescents and their families* (pp. 154–180). Hove, UK: Brunner-Routledge.

Orlinsky, D. E., Rønnestad, M. H., & Willutzki, U. (2004). Fifty years of psychotherapy process-outcome research: Continuity and change. In M. J. Lambert (Ed.), *Bergin and Garfield's handbook of psychotherapy and behavior change* (5th ed., pp. 307–389). New York: John Wiley & Sons.

Ormel, J., Petukhova, M., Chatterji, S., Aguilar-Gaxiola, S., Alonso, J., Angermeyer, M. C., et al. (2008). Disability and treatment of specific mental and physical disorders across the world. *British Journal of Psychiatry, 192,* 368–375.

O'Rourke, N. (2004). Reliability generalization of responses by care providers to the Center for Epidemiologic Studies-Depression (CES-D) Scale. *Educational and Psychological Measurement, 64,* 973–990.

Pachana, N. A., Helmes, E., & Koder, D. (2006). Guidelines for the provision of psychological services for older adults. *Australian Psychologist, 41,* 15–22.

Packer, I. K. (2008). Specialized practice in forensic psychology: Opportunities and obstacles. *Professional Psychology: Research and Practice, 39,* 245–249.

Palmiter, D. J. (2004). A survey of the assessment practices of child and adolescent clinicians. *American Journal of Orthopsychiatry, 74,* 122–128.

Parker, J. D. A., Saklofske, D. H., Wood, L. M., Eastabrook, J. M., & Taylor, R. N. (2005). Stability and change in emotional intelligence: Exploring the transition to young adulthood. *Journal of Individual Differences, 26,* 100–106.

Parker, K. C. H., Hanson, R. K., & Hunsley, J. (1988). MMPI, Rorschach, and WAIS: A meta-analytic comparison of reliability, stability, and validity. *Psychological Bulletin, 103,* 367–373.

Patsopoulos, N. A., Analatos, A. A., & Ioannidis, J. P. A. (2005). Relative citation impact of various study designs in the health sciences. *Journal of the American Medical Association, 293,* 2362–2366.

Patterson, G. R. (1982). *Coercive family process.* Eugene, OR: Castilia.

Patterson, G. R. (2005). The next generation of PMTO models. *The Behavior Therapist, 28,* 27–33.

Paykina, N. L., Greenhill, L., & Gorman, J. M. (2007). Pharmacological treatments for Attention-Deficit/Hyperactivity disorder. In P. E. Nathan, & J. M. Gorman (Eds.). *A guide to treatments that work* (3rd ed., pp. 29–70). New York: Oxford University Press.

Pelham, W. E., & Fabiano, G. A. (2008). Evidence-based psychosocial treatments for attention-deficit/hyperactivity disorder. *Journal of Clinical Child and Adolescent Psychology, 37,* 184–214.

Pelham, W. E., Fabiano, G. A., & Massetti, G. M. (2005). Evidence-based assessment of attention deficit hyperactivity disorder in children and adolescents. *Journal of Clinical Child and Adolescent Psychology, 34,* 449–476.

Pelham, W. E., Wheeler, T., & Chronis, A. (1998). Empirically supported psychosocial treatment for Attention-deficit/Hyperactivity disorder. *Journal of Clinical Child Psychology, 27,* 190–205.

Perls, F. S., Hefferline, R. F., & Goodman, P. (1951). *Gestalt therapy.* New York: Julian Press.

Persons, J. B. (1989). *Cognitive therapy in practice: A case formulation approach.* New York: Norton.

Persons, J. B., & Bertagnolli, A. (1999). Inter-rater reliability of cognitive-behavioral case formulations of depression: A replication. *Cognitive Therapy & Research, 23,* 271–283.

Persons, J. B., Bostrom, A., & Bertagnolli, A. (1999). Results of randomized controlled trials of cognitive therapy for depression generalize to private practice. *Cognitive Therapy and Research, 23,* 535–548.

Persons, J. B., Davidson, J., & Tompkins, M. A. (2001). *Essential components of cognitive-behavior therapy for depression*. Washington, DC: American Psychological Association.

Peterson, C. (2006). *A primer in positive psychology*. New York: Oxford University Press.

Peterson, D. R. (2004). Science, scientism, and professional responsibility. *Clinical Psychology: Science and Practice, 11*, 196–210.

Peterson, R., McHolland, J., Bent, R., David-Russell, E., Edwall, G., Polite, K., Singer, D., & Stricker, G. (1991). *The core curriculum in professional psychology*. Washington, DC: American Psychological Association.

Petrie, J., Bunn, F., & Byrne, G. (2007). Parenting programmes for preventing tobacco, alcohol, or drugs misuse in children under 18: A systematic review. *Health Education Research, 22*, 177–191.

Petry, N. M., Tennen, H., & Affleck, G. (2000). Stalking the elusive client variable in psychotherapy research. In C. R. Snyder & R. E. Ingram (Eds.), *Handbook of psychological change: Psychotherapy processes & practices for the 21st century* (pp. 88–108). New York: John Wiley & Sons.

Pew Internet. (2003). Internet activities. Retrieved September 21, 2004, from http://www.pewinternet.org/reports/chart/asp?img=Internet_A8.htm.

Phillips, E. E. (1991). George Washington University's international data on psychotherapy delivery systems: Modeling new approaches to the study of therapy. In L. E. Beutler & M. Crago (Eds.), *Psychotherapy research: An international review of programmatic studies* (pp. 263–273). Washington, DC: American Psychological Association.

Phillips, E. L. (1991). George Washington University's international data on psychotherapy delivery systems: Modeling new approaches to the study of therapy. In L. E. Beutler & M. Crago (Eds.), *Psychotherapy research: an international review of programmatic studies* (pp. 263–273). Washington, DC: American Psychological Association.

Piasecki, T. M., Hufford, M. R., Solhan, M., & Trull, T. J. (2007). Assessing clients in their natural environments with electronic diaries: Rationale, benefits, limitations, and barriers. *Psychological Assessment, 19*, 25–43.

Piotrowski, C., Belter, R. W., & Keller, J. W. (1998). The impact of "managed care" on the practice of psychological testing: Preliminary findings. *Journal of Personality Assessment, 70*, 441–447.

Plous, S., & Zimbardo, P. G. (1986). Attributional biases among clinicians: A comparison of psychoanalysts and behavior therapists. *Journal of Consulting and Clinical Psychology, 54*, 568–570.

Poole, G., Hunt Matheson, D., & Cox, D. N. (2005). *The psychology of health and health care: A Canadian Perspective* (2nd ed). Toronto, ON: Pearson, Prentice-Hall.

Pope, K. S. (2003). Logical fallacies in psychology: 18 types. Retrieved July 8, 2004, from: http://www.kspope.com/fallacies/fallacies.php.

Price, J. M., Chamberlain, P., Landsverk, J., Reid, J. B., Leve, L. D., & Laurent, H. (2008). Effects of foster parent training intervention on placement changes of children in foster care. *Child Maltreatment, 13*, 64–75.

Prinz, R. J., & Dumas, J. E. (2004). Prevention of oppositional defiant disorder and conduct disorder in children and adolescents. In P. M. Barrett & T. H. Ollendick (Eds.), *Interventions that work with children and adolescents: Prevention and treatment* (pp. 475–488). Chichester, UK: John Wiley & Sons.

Prinz, R. J., & Sanders, M. R. (2007). Adopting a population-level approach to parenting and family support interventions. *Clinical Psychology Review, 27*, 739–749.

Proudfoot, J., Ryden, C., Everitt, B., Shapiro, D. A., Goldberg, D., Mann, A., et al. (2004). Clinical efficacy of computerised cognitive-behavioural therapy for anxiety and depression in primary care: Randomised controlled trial. *British Journal of Psychiatry, 185*, 46–54.

Psychology Today and PacifiCare Behavioral Health. (2004). *Therapy in America 2004*. Retrieved May 19, 2004, at http://cms.psychologytoday.com/pto/topline_report_042904.pdf.

Rachman, S. (1971). *The effects of psychotherapy*. Oxford: Pergamon Press.

Rae, W. A., Jensen-Doss, A., Bowden, R., Mendoza, M., & Banda, T. (2008). Prescriptions privileges for psychologists: Opinions of pediatric psychologists and pediatricians. *Journal of Pediatric Psychology*, *33*, 176–184.

Rae, W. A., & Sullivan, J. R. (2003). Ethical considerations in clinical psychology research. In M. C. Roberts & S. S. Ilardi (Eds.), *Handbook of research methods in clinical psychology* (pp. 52–70). Oxford: Blackwell.

Raimy, V. C. (Ed.). (1950). *Training in clinical psychology*. New York: Prentice-Hall.

Rapaport, C., Gill, M., & Schafer, J. (1968). *Diagnostic psychological testing* (Rev. ed.). Chicago: Year Book.

Rees, L. M., Tombaugh, T. N., Gansler, D. A., & Moczynski, N. P. (1998). Five validation experiments of the Test of Memory Malingering (TOMM). *Psychological Assessment*, *10*, 10–20 .

Regier, D. A., Kaelber, C. T., Rae, D. S., Farmer, M. E., Knauper, B., Kessler, R. C., et al. (1998). Limitations of diagnostic criteria and assessment instruments for mental disorders: Implications for research and policy. *Archives of General Psychiatry*, *55*, 109–115.

Retzlaff, P. D., & Dunn, T. (2003). The Millon Clinical Multiaxial Inventory-III. In L. E. Beutler & G. Groth-Marnat (Eds.), *Integrative assessment of adult personality* (2nd ed., pp. 192–226). New York: Guilford Press.

Reyno, S. M., & McGrath, P. J. (2006). Predictors of parent training efficacy for child externalizing behaviour problems: A meta-analytic review. *Journal of Child Psychology and Psychiatry*, *47*, 99–111.

Riccio, C. A., & French, C. L. (2004). The status of empirical support for treatments of attention deficits. *The Clinical Neuropsychologist*, *18*, 528–558.

Richters, J. E., Arnold, L. E., Jensen, P. S., Abikoff, H., Conners, C. K., Greenhill, L. L., et al. (1995). The National Institute of Mental Health Collaborative Multisite Multimodal Treatment Study of Children with Attention-deficit Hyperactivity Disorder (MTA) I: Background and rationale. *Journal of the American Academy of Child and Adolescent Psychiatry*, *34*, 987–1000.

Ridley, C. R., & Kelly, S. M. (2006). Multicultural considerations in case formulation. In T. D. Eells (Ed.), Handbook of psychotherapy case formulation (2nd ed., pp. 33–64). New York: Guilford Press.

Roberts, C., Kane, R., Thomson, H., Hart, B., & Bishop, B. (2003). The prevention of depressive symptoms in rural school children: A randomized controlled trial. *Journal of Consulting and Clinical Psychology*, *71*, 622–628.

Roberts, M. C., Lazicki-Puddy, T. A., Puddy, R. W., & Johnson, R. J. (2003). The outcomes of psychotherapy with adolescents: A practitioner-friendly research review. *Journal of Clinical Psychology/In session*, *59*, 1177–1191.

Robiner, W. N. (2006). The mental health professions: Workforce supply and demand issues, and challenges. *Clinical Psychology Review*, *26*, 600–625.

Robinson, L. A., Berman, J. S., & Neimeyer, R. A. (1990). Psychotherapy for the treatment of depression: A comprehensive review of controlled outcome research. *Psychological Bulletin*, *108*, 30–49.

Rogers, C. R. (1951). *Client centered therapy*. Boston: Houghton Mifflin.

Rogers, R., Sewell, K. W., Harrison, K. S., & Jordan, M. J. (2006). The MMPI-2 restructured clinical scales: A paradigmatic shift in scale development. *Journal of Personality Assessment*, *87*, 139–147.

Rogers, S. J., & Vismara, L. A. (2008). Evidence-based comprehensive treatments for early autism. *Journal of Clinical Child and Adolescent Psychology*, *37*, 8–38.

Roid, G. (2003). *Stanford-Binet Intelligence Scales* (5th ed.). Itasca, IL: Riverside Publishing.

Rosenthal, R., & DiMatteo, M. R. (2001). Meta-analysis: Recent developments in quantitative methods for literature reviews. *Annual Review of Psychology*, *52*, 59–82.

Rosenzweig, S. (1936). Some implicit common factors in diverse methods of psychotherapy. *American Journal of Orthopsychiatry*, *6*, 412–415.

Rossini, E. D., & Moretti, R. J. (1997). Thematic Apperception Test (TAT) interpretation: Practice recommendations from a survey of clinical psychology doctoral programs accredited by the American Psychological Association. *Professional Psychology: Research and Practice*, *28*, 393–398.

Roth, A., & Fonagy, P. (1996). *What works for whom? A critical review of psychotherapy research*. New York: Guilford Press.

Roth, A., & Fonagy, P. (2005). *What works for whom? A critical review of psychotherapy research* (2nd ed.). New York: Guilford Press.

Rothbaum, B. O., & Schwartz, A. C. (2002). Exposure therapy for posttraumatic stress disorder. *American Journal of Psychotherapy*, *56*, 59–75.

Rumstein-McKean, O., & Hunsley, J. (2001). Interpersonal and family functioning of female survivors of childhood sexual abuse. *Clinical Psychology Review*, *21*, 471–490.

Rupert, P. A., & Kent, J. S. (2007). Gender and work setting differences in career-sustaining behaviors and burnout among professional psychologists. *Professional Psychology: Research and Practice*, *38*, 88–96.

Ruscio, J., & Ruscio, A. M. (2000). Informing the continuity controversy: A taxometric analysis of depression. *Journal of Abnormal Psychology*, *109*, 473–487.

Ryan, J. J., Glass, L. A., & Brown, C. N. (2007). Administration time estimates for Wechsler Intelligence Scale for Children-IV subtests, composites, and short forms. *Journal of Clinical Psychology*, *63*, 309–318.

Ryan, J. J., & Schnakenberg-Ott, S. D. (2003). Scoring reliability on the Wechsler Adult Intelligence Scale-Third Edition (WAIS-III). *Assessment*, *10*, 151–159.

Ryba, N. L., Cooper, V. G., & Zapf, P. A. (2003). Juvenile competence to stand trial evaluations: A survey of current practices and test usage among psychologists. *Professional Psychology: Research and Practice*, *34*, 499–507.

Sabin-Farrell, R., & Turpin, G. (2003). Vicarious traumatization: Implications for the mental health of health workers. *Clinical Psychology Review*, *23*, 449–480.

Sackett, D. L., Rosenberg, W. M., Gray, J. A., Haynes, R. B., & Richardson, W. S. (1996). Evidence-based medicine: What it is and what it isn't. *British Medical Journal*, *312*, 71–72.

Salmon, K. (2001). Remembering and reporting by children: The influence of cues and props. *Clinical Psychology Review*, *21*, 267–300.

Salovey, P., & Mayer, J. D., (1990). Emotional intelligence. *Imagination, Cognition and Personality*, *9*, 185–211.

Sanders, M. R. (1999). Triple-P Positive parenting program: Towards an empirically validated multi-level parenting and family support strategy for the prevention of behavior and emotional problems in children. *Clinical Child and Family Psychology Review*, *2*, 71–90.

Sanders, M.R. (2008). The Triple P-Positive Parenting Program as a public health approach to strengthening parenting. *Journal of Family Psychology*, *22* (4), 506–517.

Sanders, M. R., Cann, W., & Markie-Dadds, C. (2003). The Triple-P Positive Parenting Programme: A universal population-level approach to the prevention of child abuse. *Child Abuse Review*, *12*, 155–171.

Sanders, M. R., Markie-Dadds, C., Turner, K., & Ralph, A. (2004). Using the Triple-P system of intervention to prevent behavioural problems in children and adolescents. In P. M. Barrett & T. H. Ollendick (Eds.), *Interventions that work with children and adolescents: Prevention and treatment* (pp. 489–516). Chichester, UK: John Wiley & Sons.

Santor, D. A., & Coyne, J. C. (2001). Evaluating the continuity of symptomatology between depressed and nondepressed individuals. *Journal of Abnormal Psychology*, *110*, 216–225.

Sareen, J., Cox, B. J., Afifi, T. O., Stein, M. B., Belik, S.-L., Meadows, G., & Asmundson, G. J. G. (2007). Combat and peacekeeping operations in relation to prevalence of mental disorders and perceived need for care: Findings for a large representative sample of military personnel. *Archives of General Psychiatry*, *64*, 843–852.

Sattler, J. M. (1992). *Assessment of children* (3rd ed.). San Diego, CA: Jerome Sattler.

Sattler, J. M. (2001). *Assessment of children: Cognitive applications* (4th ed.). San Diego, CA: Author.

Sattler, J. M., & Mash, E. J. (1998). Introduction to clinical assessment interviewing. In J. M. Sattler, *Clinical and forensic interviewing of children and families* (pp. 2–44). San Diego, CA: Jerome Sattler.

Saunders, S. M. (1993). Applicants' experience of the process of seeking therapy. *Psychotherapy*, *30*, 554–564.

Saunders, S. M. (1996). Applicants' experience of social support in the process of seeking psychotherapy. *Psychotherapy*, *33*, 617–627.

Schachar, R., Jadad, A. R., Gauld, M., Boyle, M., Booker, L., Snider, A., et al. (2002). Attention-deficit hyperactivity disorder: Critical appraisal of extended treatment studies. *Canadian Journal of Psychiatry*, *47*, 337–348.

Schneiderman, N., Ironson, G., & Siegel, S. D. (2005). Stress and health: Psychological, behavioral and biological determinants. *Annual Review of Clinical Psychology*, *1*, 607–628.

Schoenberg, M. R., Lange, R. T., Saklofske, D. H. (2007). A proposed method to estimate premorbid Full Scale Intelligence Quotient (FSIA) for the Canadian Wechsler Intelligence Scale for Children-Fourth Edition (WISC-IV) using demographic and combined estimation procedures. *Journal of Clinical and Experimental Neuropsychology*, *29*, 867–878.

Schulte, D., & Hahlweg, K. (2000). A new law for governing psychotherapy for psychologists in Germany: Impact on training and mental health policy. *Clinical Psychology: Science and Practice*, *7*, 259–263.

Scogin, F. (2003). Introduction: The status of self-administered treatments. *Journal of Clinical Psychology*, *59*, 247–249.

Scogin, F. R., Hanson, A., & Welsh, D. (2003). Self-administered treatment in stepped-care models of depression treatment. *Journal of Clinical Psychology*, *59*, 341–349.

Scott, S., Spender, Q., Doolan, M., Jacobs, B., & Aspland, H. (2001). Multicentre controlled trial of parenting groups for childhood antisocial behaviour in clinical practice. *British Medical Journal*, *323*, 194–197.

Scotti, J. R., Morris, T. L., Ruggiero, K. J., & Wolfgang, J. (2002). Post-traumatic stress disorder. In M. Hersen (Ed.), *Clinical behavior therapy: Adults and children* (pp. 361–382). New York: John Wiley & Sons.

Scott, T. J. L., Short, E. J., Singer, L. T., Russ, S. W., & Minnes, S. (2006). Psychometric properties of the Dominic Interactive Assessment, a computerized self-report for children. *Assessment*, *13*, 16–26.

Sechrest, L. (1963). Incremental validity: A recommendation. *Educational and Psychological Measurement*, 23, 153–158.

Seligman, L. D., Goza, A. B., & Ollendick, T. H. (2004). Treatment of depression in children and adolescents. In P. M. Barrett & T. H. Ollendick (Eds.), *Interventions that work with children and adolescents: Prevention and treatment* (pp. 301–328). New York: John Wiley & Sons.

Selwood, A., Thorgrimsen, L., & Orrell, M. (2005). Quality of life in dementia—a one year follow-up study. *International Journal of Geriatric Psychiatry*, 20, 232–237.

Sexton, T. L., Alexander, J. F., & Mease, A. L. (2004). Levels of evidence for the models and mechanisms of therapeutic change in family and couple therapy. In M. L. Lambert (Ed.), *Bergin and Garfield's handbook of psychotherapy and behavior change* (5th ed., pp. 590–646). New York: John Wiley & Sons.

Shadish, W. R., Matt, G. E., Navarro, A. M., & Phillips, G. (2000). The effects of psychological therapies under clinically representative conditions: A meta-analysis. *Psychological Bulletin*, 126, 512–529.

Shaffer, T. W., Erdberg, P., & Meyer, G. J. (2007). Introduction to the *JPA* special supplement on the international reference samples for the Rorschach Comprehensive System. *Journal of Personality Assessment*, 89, S2–S6.

Shapiro, A., & Taylor, M. (2002). Effects of a community-based early intervention program on the subjective well-being, institutionalization, and mortality of low-income elders. *The Gerontologist*, 42, 334–341.

Shapiro, D. A., & Shapiro, D. (1982). Meta-analysis of comparative therapy outcome studies: A replication and refinement. *Psychological Bulletin*, 92, 581–604.

Shapiro, E. S., & Cole, C. L. (1999). Self-monitoring in assessing children's problems. *Psychological Assessment*, 11, 448–457.

Shapiro, F. (1989). Eye movement desensitization: A new treatment for post traumatic stress disorder. *Journal of Behavior Therapy and Experimental Psychiatry*, 20, 211–217.

Shapiro, F. (1995). *Eye movement desensitization and reprocessing: Basic principles, protocols, and procedures.* New York: Guilford Press.

Shea, S. (1991). Practical use of DSM-III-R. In M. Hersen & S. M. Turner (Eds.), *Adult psychopathology and diagnosis* (2nd ed., pp. 23–43). New York: John Wiley & Sons.

Sherman, M. D., & Thelen, M. H. (1998). Distress and professional impairment among psychologists in clinical practice. *Professional Psychology: Research & Practice*, 29, 79–85.

Shiffman, S., Hufford, M., Hickcox, M., Paty, J. A., Gnys, M., & Kassel, J. D. (1997). Remember that? A comparison of real-time versus retrospective recall of smoking lapses. *Journal of Consulting and Clinical Psychology*, 65, 292–300.

Shiffman, S., Stone, A. A., & Hufford, M. R. (2008). Ecological momentary assessment. *Annual Review of Clinical Psychology*, 4, 33–52.

Shirk, S. R., & Karver, M. (2003). Prediction of treatment outcome from relationship variables in child and adolescent therapy: A meta-analytic review. *Journal of Consulting and Clinical Psychology*, 71, 452–464.

Sholomskas, A. J., Chevron, E. S., Prusoff, B. A., & Berry, C. (1983). Short-term interpersonal therapy (IPT) with the depressed elderly: Case reports and discussion. *American Journal of Psychotherapy*, 37, 552–566.

Shore, J. H., Savin, D., Orton, H., Beals, J., & Manson, S. M. (2007). Diagnostic reliability of telepsychiatry in American Indian veterans. *American Journal of Psychiatry*, 164, 115–118.

Siev, J., & Chambless, D. L. (2007). Specificity of treatment effects: Cognitive therapy and relaxation for generalized anxiety and panic disorders.

Journal of Consulting and Clinical Psychology, 75, 513–522.

Silverman, D., & Marvasti, A. (2008). *Doing qualitative research: A comprehensive guide.* London: Sage Publications.

Silverman, W. H. (1996). Cookbooks, manuals, and paint-by-numbers: Psychotherapy in the 90s. *Psychotherapy, 33,* 207–215.

Silverman, W.K., & Hinshaw, S. P. (2008). The second special issue on evidence-based psychosocial treatments for children and adolescents: A 10-year update. *Journal of Clinical Child and Adolescent Psychology, 37,* 1–7.

Silverman, W. K., & Ollendick, T. H. (2008). Child and adolescent anxiety disorders. In J. Hunsley & E. J. Mash (Eds.), *A guide to assessments that work* (pp. 181–206). New York: Oxford University Press.

Silverman, W. K., Ortiz, C. D., Viswesvaran, C., Burns, B. J., Kolko, D. J., Putnam, F. W., & Amaya-Jackson, L. (2008). Evidence-based psychosocial treatments for children and adolescents exposed to traumatic events. *Journal of Clinical Child and Adolescent Psychology, 37,* 156–183.

Silverman, W. K., Pina, A. A., & Viswesvaran, C. (2008). Evidence-based psychosocial treatments for phobic and anxiety disorders in children and adolescents. *Journal of Clinical Child and Adolescent Psychology, 37,* 105–130.

Sinclair, C. (1993). Codes of ethics and standards of practice. In K. S. Dobson & D. G. Dobson (Eds.), *Professional psychology in Canada* (pp. 167–224). Toronto, ON: Hogrefe & Huber.

Sitarenios, G., & Kovacs, M. (1999). Use of the Children's Depression Inventory. In M. E. Maruish (Ed.), *The use of psychological testing for treatment planning and outcomes assessment* (2nd ed., pp. 267–298). Mahwah, NJ: Erlbaum.

Slate, J. R., Jones, C. R., Coulter, C., & Covert, T. L. (1992). Practitioners' administration and scoring of the WISC-R: Evidence that we do err. *Journal of School Psychology, 30,* 77–82.

Slate, J. R., Jones, C. R., Murray, R. A., & Coulter, C. (1993). Evidence that practitioners err in administering and scoring the WAIS-R. *Measurement and Evaluation in Counseling and Development, 25*(4), 156–161.

Smith, J. D., & Dumont, F. (2002). Confidence in psychodiagnosis: What makes us so sure? *Clinical Psychology and Psychotherapy, 9,* 292–298.

Smith, M. L., & Glass, G. V. (1977). Meta-analysis of psychotherapy outcome studies. *American Psychologist, 32,* 752–760.

Smith, M. L., Glass, G. V., & Miller, T. I. (1980). *The benefits of psychotherapy.* Baltimore: Johns Hopkins University Press.

Smith, M. T., Perlis, M. L., Park, A., Smith, M. S., Pennington, J., Giles, D. E., et al. (2002). Comparative meta-analysis of pharmacotherapy and behaviour therapy for persistent insomnia. *American Journal of Psychiatry, 159,* 5–11.

Smith, T. C., Ryan, M. A. K., Wingard, D. L., Slymen, D. J., Sallis, J. F., & Kritz-Silverstein, D. (2008). New onset and persistent symptoms of post-traumatic stress disorder self-reported after deployment and combat exposures: Prospective population based U.S. military cohort study. *British Medical Journal.* Retrieved on February 29, 2008, from www.bmj.com.

Smith, T. D., & Smith, B. L. (1998). Relationship between the Wide Range Achievement Test 3 and the Wechsler Individual Achievement Test. *Psychological Reports, 83,* 963–967.

Smith, T. W., Kendall, P. C., & Keefe, F. J. (2002). Behavioral medicine and clinical health psychology: Introduction to the special issue, a view from the Decade of Behavior. *Journal of Consulting and Clinical Psychology, 70,* 459–462.

Smith, T. W., Nealey, J. B., & Hamann, H. A. (2000). Health psychology. In C. R. Snyder & R. E. Ingram (Eds.), *Handbook of psychological change: Psychotherapy processes and practices for the 21st century* (pp. 562–590). New York: John Wiley & Sons.

Smith, S. R., Wiggins, C. M., & Gorske, T. T. (2007). A survey of psychological assessment feedback practices. *Assessment, 14*, 310–319.

Snyder, C. R., & Lopez, S. J. (Eds.). (2005). *Handbook of positive psychology.* New York: Oxford University Press.

Snyder, D. K., Heyman, R. E., & Haynes, S. N. (2008). Couple distress. In J. Hunsley & E. J. Mash (Eds.), *A guide to assessments that work* (pp. 437–463). New York: Oxford University Press.

Sommers-Flanagan, J., & Sommers-Flanagan, R. (2003). *Clinical interviewing* (3rd ed). New York: John Wiley & Sons.

Sonuga-Barke, E. J. S., Daley, D., & Thompson, M. (2002). Does maternal ADHD reduce the effectiveness of parent training for preschool children's ADHD? *Journal of the American Academy of Child and Adolescent Psychiatry, 41*, 696–702.

Sörensen, S., Pinquart, M., & Duberstein, P. (2002). How effective are interventions with caregivers? *The Gerontologist, 42*, 356–372.

Spangler, W. D. (1992). Validity of questionnaire and TAT measures of need for achievement: Two meta-analyses. *Psychological Bulletin, 112*, 140–154.

Spearman, C. (1927). *The abilities of man.* New York: Macmillan.

Spence, S. H., Sheffield, J. K., & Donovan, C. L. (2003). Preventing adolescent depression: An evaluation of the Problem-Solving for Life program. *Journal of Consulting and Clinical Psychology, 71*, 3–13.

Spence, S. H., Sheffield, J. K., & Donovan, C. L. (2005). Long-term outcome of a school-based universal approach to prevention of depression in adolescents. *Journal of Consulting and Clinical Psychology, 71*, 3–13.

Spinhoven, P., Giesen-Bloo, J., van Dyck, R., Kooiman, K., & Arntz, A. (2007). The therapeutic alliance in schema-focused therapy and transference-focused psychotherapy for border-line personality disorder. *Journal of Consulting and Clinical Psychology, 75*, 104–115.

Spitzer, R. L., Kroenke, K., Linzer, M., Hahn, S. R., Williams, J. B., deGruy, F. V., et al. (1995). Health-related quality of life in primary care patients with mental disorders: Results from the PRIME-MD 1000 study. *Journal of the American Medical Association, 282*, 1511–1517.

Staller, J. A. (2006). Diagnostic profiles in outpatient child psychiatry. *American Journal of Orthopsychiatry, 76*, 98–102.

Steenbarger, B. N. (1994) Duration and outcome in psychotherapy: An integrative review. *Professional Psychology: Research and Practice, 25*, 111–119.

Steering Committee of the Empirically Supported Therapy Relationship Task Force. (2001). Empirically supported therapy relationships: Conclusions and recommendations of the Division 29 Task Force. *Psychotherapy, 38*, 495–497.

Sternberg, R. (1985). *Beyond IQ: A triarchic theory of human intelligence.* New York: Cambridge University Press.

Sternberg, R. J., Nokes, K., Geissler, P. W., Prince, R., Okatcha, F., Bundy, D. A., et al. (2001). The relationship between academic and practical intelligence: A case study in Kenya. *Intelligence, 29*, 401–418.

Stiles, W. B. (1988). Psychotherapy process-outcome correlations may be misleading. *Psychotherapy, 25*, 27–35.

Stiles, W. B., & Shapiro, D. A. (1989). Abuse of the drug metaphor in psychotherapy process-outcome research. *Clinical Psychology Review, 9*, 521–543.

Stiles, W. B., Barkham, M., Connell, J., & Mellor-Clark, J. (2008). Responsive regulation of treatment duration in routine practice in United Kingdom primary care settings: Replication in a larger sample. *Journal of Consulting and Clinical Psychology, 76*, 298–305.

Stiles, W. B., Leach, C., Barkham, M., Lucock, M., Iveson, S., Shapiro, D. A., et al. (2003). Early sudden gains in psychotherapy under routine clinic conditions: Practice-based evidence. *Journal of Consulting and Clinical Psychology, 71,* 14–21.

Stirman, S. W., Crits-Christoph, P., & DeRubeis, R. J. (2004). Achieving successful dissemination of empirically supported psychotherapies: A synthesis of dissemination theory. *Clinical Psychology: Science and Practice, 11,* 343–359.

Stirman, S. W., DeRubeis, R. J., Crits-Christoph, P., & Brody, P. E. (2003). Are samples in randomized controlled trials of psychotherapy representative of community outpatients? A new methodology and initial findings. *Journal of Consulting and Clinical Psychology, 71,* 963–972.

Stirman, S. W., DeRubeis, R. J., Crits-Christoph, P., & Rothman, A. (2005). Can the randomized controlled trial literature generalize to nonrandomized patients? *Journal of Consulting and Clinical Psychology, 73,* 127–135.

Stone, A. A., Schwartz, J. E., Neale, J. M., Shiffman, S., Marco, C. A., Hickcox, M., et al. (1998). A comparison of coping assessed by ecological momentary assessment and retrospective recall. *Journal of Personality and Social Psychology, 74,* 1670–1680.

Stormshak, E. A., & Dishion, T. J. (2002). An ecological approach to child and family clinical and counseling psychology. *Clinical Child and Family Psychology Review, 5,* 197–215.

Stout, C. E., & Cook, L. P. (1999). New areas for psychological assessment in general health care settings: What to do today to prepare for tomorrow. *Journal of Clinical Psychology, 55,* 797–812.

Strack, S. (2002). *Essentials of Millon Inventories assessment* (2nd ed.). New York: John Wiley & Sons.

Strack, S., & Millon, T. (2007). Contributions to the dimensional assessment of personality disorders using Millon's model and the Millon Clinical Multiaxial Inventory (MCMI-III). *Journal of Personality Assessment, 89,* 56–69.

Streiner, D. L. (2002). Breaking up is hard to do: The heartbreak of dichotomizing continuous data. *Canadian Journal of Psychiatry, 47,* 262–266.

Streiner, D. L. (2003). Being inconsistent about consistency: When coefficient alpha does and doesn't matter. *Journal of Personality Assessment, 80,* 217–222.

Streisand, R., & Efron, L. A. (2003). Pediatric sleep disorders. In R. M. Roberts (Ed.), *Handbook of pediatric psychology* (3rd ed., pp. 578–598). New York: Guilford.

Stringer, A. Y. (2003). Cognitive rehabilitation practice patterns: A survey of American Hospital Association rehabilitation programs. *The Clinical Neuropsychologist, 17,* 34–44.

Strupp, H. H., & Binder, J. (1984). *Psychotherapy in a new key.* New York: Basic Books.

Stuart, R. B., & Heiby, E. M. (2007). To prescribe or not prescribe: Eleven exploratory questions. *Scientific Review of Mental Health Practice, 5,* 4–32.

Stuart, R. B., & Lilienfeld, D. O. (2007). The evidence missing from evidence-based practice. *American Psychologist, 62,* 613–614.

Stuebing, K. K., Fletcher, J. M., LeDoux, J. M., Lyon, G. R., Shaywitz, S. E., & Shaywitz, B. A. (2002). Validity of IQ-discrepancy classifications of reading disabilities: A meta-analysis. *American Educational Research Journal, 39,* 469–518.

Sue, D. W., & Sue, D. (2008). *Counseling the culturally different: Theory and practice* (5th ed.). New York: John Wiley & Sons.

Sullivan, H. S. (1953). *The interpersonal theory of psychiatry.* New York: Norton.

Summerfeldt, L. J., & Antony, M. M. (2002). Structured and semistructured diagnostic interviews. In M. M. Antony & D. H. Barlow (Eds). *Handbook of assessment and treatment planning for psychological disorders* (pp. 3–37). New York: Guilford.

Swanson, J. M., Arnold, L. E., Vitiello, B., Abikoff, H. B., Wells, K. C., Pelham, W. E., et al. (2002).

Response to commentary on the Multimodal Treatment Study of ADHD (MTA): Mining the meaning of the MTA. *Journal of Abnormal Child Psychology, 30*, 327–332.

Swanson, J. M., Kraemer, H. C., Hinshaw, S. P., Arnold, L. E., Conners, C. K., Abikoff, H. B., et al. (2001). Clinical relevance of the primary findings of the MTA: Success rates based on severity of ADHD and ODD symptoms at the end of treatment. *Journal of the American Academy of Child and Adolescent Psychiatry, 40*, 168–179.

Takushi, R., & Uomoto, J. M. (2001). The clinical interview from a multicultural perspective. In L. A. Suzuki, J. G. Ponterotto, & P. J. Meller (Eds). *Handbook of multicultural assessment: Clinical, psychological, and educational applications* (2nd ed. pp. 47–66) San Francisco: Jossey-Bass.

Tamaskar, P., & McGinnis, R. A. (2002). Declining student interest in psychiatry. *Journal of the American Medical Association, 287*, 1859.

Tang, T. Z., & DeRubeis, R. J. (1999). Sudden gains and critical sessions in cognitive-behavioral therapy for depression. *Journal of Consulting and Clinical Psychology, 67*, 894–904.

Tang, T. Z., DeRubeis, R. J., Beberman, R., & Pham, T. (2005). Cognitive changes, critical sessions, and sudden gains in cognitive-behavioral therapy for depression. *Journal of Consulting and Clinical Psychology, 73*, 168–172.

Tang, T. Z., DeRubeis, R. J., Hollon, S. D., Amsterdam, J., & Shelton, R. (2007). Sudden gains in cognitive therapy of depression and depression relapse/recurrence. *Journal of Consulting and Clinical Psychology, 75*, 404–408.

Tang, T. Z., Luborsky, L., & Andrusyna, T. (2002). Sudden gains in recovering from depression: Are they also found in psychotherapies other than cognitive-behavioral therapy? *Journal of Consulting and Clinical Psychology, 70*, 444–447.

Target, M., & Fonagy, P. (2005). The psychological treatment of child and adolescent disorders. In A. Roth & P. Fonagy (Eds.), *What works for whom? A critical review of psychotherapy research* (pp. 385–424). New York: Guilford.

Task Force on Promotion and Dissemination of Psychological Procedures. (1995). Training in and dissemination of empirically-validated psychological treatments: Report and recommendations. *The Clinical Psychologist, 48*, 3–23.

Taub, G. E., McGrew, K. S., & Witta, E. L. (2004). A confirmatory analysis of the factor structure and cross-age invariance of the Wechsler Adult Intelligence Scale–Third Edition. *Psychological Assessment, 16*, 85–89.

Taylor, S., Thordarson, D. S., & Söchting, I. (2002). Obsessive-Compulsive Disorder. In M. M. Antony & D. H. Barlow (Eds.), *Handbook of assessment and treatment planning for psychological disorders* (pp. 182–214). New York: Guilford.

Taylor, S. E., & Brown, J. D. (1988). Illusion and well being: A social-psychological perspective on mental health. *Psychological Bulletin, 103*, 193–210.

Taylor, T. K., & Biglan, A. (1998). Behavioral family interventions for improving child-rearing: A review of the literature for clinicians and policy makers. *Clinical Child and Family Psychology Review, 1*, 41–60.

Tellegen, A., Ben-Porath, Y. S., McNulty, J. L., Arbisi, P. A., Graham, J. R., & Kaemmer, B. (2003). *The MMPI-2 restructured clinical scales: Development, validation, and interpretation*. Minneapolis: University of Minnesota Press.

Tellegen, A., Ben-Porath, Y. S., Sellbom, M., Arbisi, P. A., McNulty, J. L., & Graham, J. R. (2006). Further evidence on the validity of the MMPI-2 restructured clinical scales: Addressing questions raised by Rogers, Sewell, Harrison, and Jordan and Nichols. *Journal of Personality Assessment, 87*, 148–171.

Teyber, E., & McClure, F. (2000). Therapist variables. In C. R. Snyder & R. E. Ingram (Eds.), *Handbook of psychological change: Psychotherapy processes and practices for the 21st century* (pp. 62–87). New York: John Wiley & Sons.

Tharyan, P., John, T., Tharyan, A., & Braganza, D. (2001). Attitudes of "tomorrow's doctors" towards psychiatry and mental illness. *National Medical Journal of India, 14,* 355–359.

The Psychological Corporation. (2002). *Wechsler individual achievement test* (2nd ed.). San Antonio, TX: Author.

Thomas, J. C., & Rosqvist, J. (2003). Introduction: Science in the service of practice. In J. C. Thomas & M. Hersen (Eds.), *Understanding research in clinical and counseling psychology* (pp. 3–26). Mahwah, NJ: Lawrence Erlbaum Associates.

Thomas, R., & Zimmer-Gembeck, M. J. (2007). Behavioral outcomes of parent-child interaction therapy and TripleP-Positive Parenting Program: A review and meta-analysis. *Journal of Abnormal Child Psychology, 35,* 475–495.

Thompson-Brenner, H., Glass, S., & Westen, D. (2003). A multidimensional meta-analysis of psychotherapy for Bulimia Nervosa. *Clinical Psychology: Science and Practice, 10,* 269–287.

Thurstone, L. L. (1938). *Primary mental abilities.* Chicago: University of Chicago Press.

Tobler, N. S., Roona, M. R., Ochsborn, P., Marshall, D. G., Streke, A. V., & Stackpole, M. (2000). School-based adolescent drug prevention programs: 1998 Meta-analysis. *Journal of Primary Prevention, 20,* 275–336.

Tombaugh, T. N. (1997). The Test of Memory Malingering (TOMM): Normative data from cognitively intact and cognitively impaired individuals. *Psychological Assessment, 9,* 260–268.

Tompkins, M. A. (1999). Using a case formulation to manage treatment nonresponse. *Journal of Cognitive Psychotherapy, 13,* 317–330.

Townsend, C. O., Bruce, B. K., Hooten, W. M., & Rome, J. D. (2006). The role of mental health professionals in multidisciplinary pain rehabilitation programs. *Journal of Clinical Psychology, 62,* 1433–1443.

Tremblay, R. E., Pagani-Kurtz, L., Mâsse, L. C., Vitaro, F., & Pihl, R. O. (1995). A bimodal preventive intervention for disruptive kindergarten boys: Its impact through mid-adolescence. *Journal of Consulting and Clinical Psychology, 63,* 560–568.

Truax, C. B. (1966). Reinforcement and non-reinforcement in Rogerian psychotherapy. *Journal of Abnormal Psychology, 71,* 1–9.

Tryon, G. S. (2000). Doctoral training issues in school and clinical child psychology. *Professional Psychology: Research and Practice, 31,* 85–87.

Turk, D. C., & Burwinkle, T. M. (2005). Clinical outcomes, cost-effectiveness and the role of psychology in treatment of chronic pain sufferers. *Professional Psychology: Research and Practice: 36,* 602–610.

Turk, D. C., & Okifuji, A. (2002). Psychological factors in chronic pain: Evolution and revolution. *Journal of Consulting and Clinical Psychology, 70,* 678–690.

Turner, R. J., & Lloyd, D. A. (2004). Stress burden and the lifetime incidence of psychiatric disorders in young adults. *Archives of General Psychiatry, 61,* 481–488.

Turner, R. S. (2003). Neurologic aspects of Alzheimer's disease. In P. A. Lichtenberg, D. Murman, & A. M. Mellow (Eds.), *Handbook of dementia* (pp. 1–24). New York: John Wiley & Sons.

Tuschen-Caffier, B., Pook, M., & Frank, M. (2001). Evaluation of manual-based cognitive-behavioral therapy for bulimia nervosa in a service setting. *Behaviour Research and Therapy, 39,* 299–308.

Tversky, A., & Kahneman, D. (1974). Judgments under uncertainty: Heuristics and biases. *Science, 185,* 1124–1131.

Twenge, J. M., & Nolen-Hoeksema, S. (2002). Age, gender, race, socioeconomic status, and birth cohort differences on the Children's Depression Inventory: A meta-analysis. *Journal of Abnormal Psychology*, *111*, 578–588.

Ullman, J. B. (2006). Structural equation modelling: Reviewing the basics and moving forward. *Journal of Personality Assessment*, 35–50.

Umphress, V. J., Lambert, M. J., Smart, D. W., Barlow, S. H., & Clouse, G. (1997). Concurrent and construct validity of the Outcome Questionnaire. *Journal of Psychoeducational Assessment*, *15*, 40–55.

Unicef (2003, October 21). *New study shows one billion children suffer effects of poverty.* Retrieved October 22, 2004, from http://www.unicef.org.media/mediaj5082.html

U. K. Department of Health. (2001). *Treatment choice in psychological therapies and counselling: Evidence based clinical practice guidelines.* London: Author.

U. S. Census Bureau. (2002). *Demographic trends in the 20th century: Census 2000 special reports.* Retrieved on July 15, 2008, from www.census.gov

U. S. Census Bureau. (2008). *US Hispanic population surpasses 45 million: Now 15 percent of total.* Retrieved on July 15, 2008, from www.census.gov

U. S. Department of Health and Human Services. (1999). *Mental health: A report of the Surgeon General.* Rockville, MD: Author.

Vakoch, D. A., & Strupp, H. H. (2000). Psychodynamic approaches to psychotherapy: Philosophical and theoretical foundations of effective practice. In C. R. Snyder & R. E. Ingram (Eds.), *Handbook of psychological changes: Psychotherapy processes and practices for the 21st century* (pp. 200–216). New York: John Wiley & Sons.

Valla, J-P., Bergeron, L., & Smolla, N. (2000). The Dominic-R: A pictorial interview for 6–11-year-old children. *Journal of the American Academy of Child and Adolescent Psychiatry*, *39*, 85–93.

van Widenfelt, B. M., Treffers, P. D. A., de Beurs, E., Siebelink, B. M., & Koudijs, E. (2005). Translation and cross-cultural adaptation of assessment instruments used in psychological research with children and families. *Clinical Child and Family Psychology Review*, *8*, 135–147.

Verkuil, B., Brosschot, J. F., & Thayer, J. F. (2007). Capturing worry in daily life: Are trait questionnaires sufficient? *Behaviour Research and Therapy*, *45*, 1835–1844.

Vermeersch, D. A., Lambert, M. J., & Burlingame, G. M. (2000). Outcome Questionnaire 45: Item sensitivity to change. *Journal of Personality Assessment*, *74*, 242–261.

Vernon, P. E. (1961). *The structure of human abilities* (2nd ed.). London: Methuen.

Vessey, J. T., & Howard, K. I. (1993). Who seeks psychotherapy? *Psychotherapy*, *30*, 546–553.

Vessey, J. T., Howard, K. I., Lueger, R. J., Kächele, H., & Mergenthaler, E. (1994). The clinician's illusion and the psychotherapy practice: An application of stochastic modeling. *Journal of Consulting and Clinical Psychology*, *62*, 679–685.

Vittengl, J. R., Clark, L. A., & Jarrett, R. B. (2005). Validity of sudden gains in acute phase treatment of depression. *Journal of Consulting and Clinical Psychology*, *73*, 173–182.

Voros, V., Osvath, P., Kovacs, L., Varga, J., Fekete, S., & Kovacs, A. (2006). Screening for suicidal behavior and mental disorders with Prime-MD questionnaire in general practice. *Primary Care & Community Psychiatry*, *11*, 193–196.

Wade, W. A., Treat, T. A., & Stuart, G. L. (1998). Transporting an empirically supported treatment for panic disorder to a service clinical setting: A benchmarking strategy. *Journal of Consulting and Clinical Psychology*, *66*, 231–239.

Waehler, C. A., Kalodner, C. R., Wampold, B. E., & Lichtenberg, J. W. (2000). Empirically supported treatments (ESTs) in perspective: Implications for counseling psychology training. *The Counseling Psychologist, 28,* 657–671.

Wakefield, J. C. (1992). The concept of mental disorder: On the boundary between biological facts and social values. *American Psychologist, 47,* 373–388.

Wakefield, J. C. (1997). Diagnosing DSM-IV—Part 1: DSM-IV and the concept of disorder. *Behaviour Research and Therapy, 35,* 633–649.

Wakefield, J. C., Schmitz, M. F., First, M. B., & Horwitz, A. V. (2007). Extending the bereavement exclusion for major depression to other losses: Evidence from the National Comorbidity Survey. *Archives of General Psychiatry, 64,* 433–440.

Waldron, H. B., & Turner, C. W. (2008). Evidence-based psychosocial treatments for adolescent substance abuse. *Journal of Clinical Child and Adolescent Psychology, 37,* 238–261.

Wampold, B. E. (1997). Methodological problems in identifying efficacious psychotherapies. *Psychotherapy Research, 7,* 21–43.

Wampold, B. E. (2007). Psychotherapy: *The* humanistic (and effective) treatment. *American Psychologist, 62,* 858–873.

Wampold, B. E., & Bhati, K. S. (2004). Attending to the omissions: A historical examination of evidence-based practice movements. *Professional Psychology: Research and Practice, 35,* 563–570.

Wampold, B. E., & Brown, G. S. (2005). Estimating variability in outcomes attributable to therapists: A naturalistic study of outcomes in managed care. *Journal of Consulting and Clinical Psychology, 73,* 914–923.

Wampold, B. E., Mondin, G. W., Moody, M., Stich, F., Benson, K., & Ahn, H. (1997). A meta-analysis of outcome studies comparing bona fide psychotherapies: Empirically, "All must have prizes." *Psychological Bulletin, 122,* 203–215.

Wang, P. S., Gruber, M. J., Powers, R. E., Schoenbaum, M., Speier, A. H., Wells, K. B., & Kessler, R. C. (2008). Disruption of existing mental health treatments and failure to initiate new treatment after Hurricane Katrina. *American Journal of Psychiatry, 165,* 34–41.

Warren, R., & Thomas, J. C. (2001). Cognitive-behavior therapy of obsessive-compulsive disorder in private practice: An effectiveness study. *Journal of Anxiety Disorders, 15,* 277–285.

Waschbusch, D. A., & Hill, G. P. (2003). Empirically supported, promising, and unsupported treatments for children with Attention-Deficit/Hyperactivity Disorder. In S. O. Lilienfeld, S. J. Lynn, & J. M. Lohr (Eds.), *Science and Pseudoscience in Clinical Psychology* (pp. 333–362). New York: Guilford.

Watanabe, N., Hunot, V., Omori, I.M., Churchill, R., & Furukawa, T. (2007). Psychotherapy for depression among children and adolescents: A systematic review. *Acta psychiatricia Scandanavica, 116,* 84–95.

Watkins, M. W. (2003). IQ subtest analysis: Clinical acumen or clinical illusion? *The Scientific Review of Mental Health Practice, 2,* 118–141.

Watkins, M. W., & Canivez, G. L. (2004). Temporal stability of the WISC-III subtest composite: Strengths and weaknesses. *Psychological Assessment, 16,* 133–138.

Webster, C. D., & Bailes, G. (2004). Assessing violence risk in mentally and personality disordered individuals. In C. R. Hollin (Ed.), *The essential handbook of offender assessment and treatment* (pp. 17–30). Chichester, UK: John Wiley & Sons.

Webster-Stratton, C. (2006). Quality training, supervision, ongoing monitoring, and agency support: Key ingredients to implementing The Incredible Years programs with fidelity. In T. K. Neill (Ed.), *Helping others help children: Clinical supervision of psychotherapy* (pp. 161–175). Washington, DC: American Psychological Association.

Webster-Stratton, C., & Reid, M. J. (2003). The Incredible Years parents, teachers, and children training series: A multifaceted treatment approach for young children with conduct problems. In A. E. Kazdin & J. R. Weisz (Eds.), *Evidence-based psychotherapies for children and adolescents* (pp. 224–240). New York: Guilford.

Webster-Stratton, C., & Reid, M. J. (2004). Strengthening social and emotional competence in young children—the foundation for early school readiness and success. Incredible Years classroom social skills and problem-solving curriculum. *Infants and Young Children, 17,* 96–113.

Webster-Stratton, C., Reid, M. J., & Hammond, M. (2001). Preventing conduct problems, promoting social competence: A parent and teacher training partnership in Head Start. *Journal of Clinical Child Psychology, 30,* 283–302.

Wechsler, D. (1939). *The measurement of adult intelligence.* Baltimore, MD: Williams and Wilkins.

Wechsler, D. (1997a). *Manual for the Wechsler memory scale* (3rd ed.) San Antonio, TX: The Psychological Corporation.

Wechsler, D. (1997b). *WAIS III Administration and scoring manual.* San Antonio, TX: Psychological Corporation.

Wechsler, D. (2002). Wechsler preschool and primary scale of intelligence (3rd ed.) San Antonio, TX: The Psychological Corporation.

Wechsler, D. (2002). *Wechsler individual achievement test* (2nd ed.). San Antonio, TX: The Psychological Corporation.

Wechsler, D. (2003). *Wechsler intelligence scale for children* (4th ed.). San Antonio, TX: The Psychological Corporation.

Wechsler, D. (2008). *Wechsler adult intelligence scale* (4th ed.). San Antonio, TX: Pearson Education, Inc.

Weersing, V. R., & Weisz, J. R. (2002). Community clinical treatment of depressed youth: Benchmarking usual care against CBT clinical trials. *Journal of Consulting and Clinical Psychology, 70,* 299–310.

Wegner, D. M. (1994). Ironic process of mental control. *Psychological Review, 101,* 34–52.

Weinberger, J. (1995). Common factors aren't so common: The common factors dilemma. *Clinical Psychology: Science and Practice, 2,* 45–69.

Weiner, I. B. (1999). What the Rorschach can do for you: Incremental validity in clinical applications. *Assessment, 6,* 327–338.

Weisberg, R. B., Dyck, I., Culpepper, L., & Keller, M. B. (2007). Psychiatric treatment in primary care patients with anxiety disorders: A comparison of care received from primary care providers and psychiatrists. *American Journal of Psychiatry, 164,* 276–282.

Weiss, B., Catron, T., & Harris, V. (2000). A 2-year follow-up of the effectiveness of traditional psychotherapy. *Journal of Consulting and Clinical Psychology, 68,* 1094–1101.

Weiss, B., Catron, T., Harris, V., & Phung, T. M. (1999). The effectiveness of traditional psychotherapy. *Journal of Consulting and Clinical Psychology, 67,* 82–94.

Weiss, B., & Weisz, J. R. (1995). Relative effectiveness of behavioral versus nonbehavioral child psychotherapy. *Journal of Clinical and Consulting Psychology, 63,* 317–320.

Weissberg, R. P., Kumpfer, K. L., & Seligman, M. E. P. (2003). Prevention that works for children and youth. *American Psychologist, 58,* 425–432.

Weissman, M. M., Markowitz, J. C., & Klerman, G. L. (2000). *Comprehensive guide to interpersonal psychotherapy.* New York: Basic Books.

Weissman, M. M., Verdeli, H., Gameroff, M. J., Bledsoe, S. E., Betts, K., Mufson, L., et al. (2006). National survey of psychotherapy training in psychiatry, psychology, and social work. *Archives of General Psychiatry, 63,* 925–934.

Weisz, J. R., Donnenberg, G. R., Han, S. S., & Weiss, B. (1995). Bridging the gap between laboratory and clinical in child and adolescent psychotherapy.

Journal of Consulting and Clinical Psychology, 63, 688–701.

Weisz, J. R., Doss, A. J., & Hawley, K. M. (2005). Youth psychotherapy outcome research: a review and critique of the evidence base. *Annual Review of Psychology, 56,* 337–363.

Weisz, J. R., Hawley, K. M., Pilkonis, P. A., Woody, S. R., & Follette, W. C. (2000). Stressing the (other) three Rs in the search for empirically supported treatments: Review procedures, research quality, relevance to practice and the public interest. *Clinical Psychology: Science and Practice, 7,* 243–258.

Weisz, J. R., Jensen-Doss, A., &. Hawley, K. M. (2006). Evidence-based youth psychotherapies versus usual clinical care. *American Psychologist, 61,* 671–689.

Weisz, J. R., McCarty, C. A., & Valeri, S. M. (2006). Effects of psychotherapy for depression in children and adolescents: A meta-analysis. *Psychological Bulletin, 132,* 132–149.

Weisz, J. R., Weiss, B., Alicke, M. D., & Klotz, M. L. (1987). Effectiveness of psychotherapy with children and adolescents: A meta-analysis for clinicians. *Journal of Consulting and Clinical Psychology, 55,* 542–549.

Weisz, J. R., Weiss, B., Han, S. S., Granger, D. A., & Morton, T. (1995). Effects of psychotherapy with children and adolescents revisited: A meta-analysis of treatment outcome studies. *Psychological Bulletin, 117,* 450–468.

Westen, D. (1991). Clinical assessment of object relations using the TAT. *Journal of Personality Assessment, 56,* 56–74.

Westen, D., & Morrison, K. (2001). A multidimensional meta-analysis of treatments for depression, panic, and Generalized Anxiety Disorder: An empirical examination of the status of empirically supported treatments. *Journal of Consulting and Clinical Psychology, 69,* 875–899.

Westen, D., & Weinberger, J. (2004). When clinical description becomes statistical prediction. *American Psychologist, 59,* 595–613.

Westen, D., Feit, A., & Zittel, C. (1999). Methodological issues in research using projective methods. In P.C. Kendall, J. N. Butcher, & G. N. Holmbeck (Eds.), *Handbook of research methods in clinical psychology* (2nd ed., pp. 224–240). New York: John Wiley & Sons.

Westmacott, R., & Hunsley, J. (2007). Weighing the evidence for psychotherapy equivalence: Implications for research and practice. *Behavior Analyst Today, 8,* 210–225.

Westra, H. A., Dozois, D. J. A., & Marcus, M. (2007). Expectancy, homework compliance, and initial change in cognitive-behavioral therapy for anxiety. *Journal of Consulting and Clinical Psychology, 75,* 363–373.

Wethington, H. R., Hahn, R. A., Fuqua-Whitely, D. S., Sipe, T. A., Crosby, A. E., Johnson, R. L., et al. (2008). The effectiveness of interventions to reduce psychological harm from traumatic events among children and adolescents: A systematic review. *American Journal of Preventive Medicine, 35,* 287–313.

Whaley, A. L., & Davis, K. E. (2007). Cultural competence and evidence-based practice in mental health services: A complementary perspective. *American Psychologist, 62,* 563–574.

Whitten, J., Slate, J. R., Jones, C. H., & Shine, A. E. (1994). Examiner errors in administering and scoring the WPPSI-R. *Journal of Psychoeducational Assessment, 12,* 49–54.

Wicherts, J. M., Borsboom, D., Kats, J., & Molenaar, D. (2006). The poor availability of psychological research data for reanalysis. *American Psychologist, 61,* 726–728.

Wickrama, K. A., & Kaspar, V. (2007). Family context of mental health risk in tsunami-exposed adolescents: Findings from a pilot study in Sri Lanka. *Social Science and Medicine, 64,* 713–723.

Widiger, T. A. (2004). Looking ahead to DSM-V. *The Clinical Psychologist, 57*(1/2), 18–24.

Widiger, T. A., & Sankis, L. M. (2000). Adult psychopathology: Issues and controversies. *Annual Review of Psychology, 51,* 377–404.

Widiger, T. A., & Trull, T. J. (2007). Plate tectonics in the classification of personality disorders: Shifting to a dimensional model. *American Psychologist, 62,* 71–83.

Wiggins, J. S., & Trapnell, P. D. (1997). Personality structure: The return of the big five. In R. Hogan, J. Johnson, & S. Briggs (Eds.), *Handbook of personality psychology* (pp. 737–766). San Diego, CA: Academic Press.

Wilkinson, L., & the Task Force on Statistical Inference. (1999). Statistical methods in psychology journals: Guidelines and explanations. *American Psychologist, 54,* 594–604.

Williams, C. (2001). You snooze, you lose? Sleep patterns in Canada. Canadian Social Trends, 10–14. Catalogue No. 11-008. Ottawa, ON: Minister of Industry.

Williams, J., Hadjistavropoulos, T., & Sharpe, D. (2006). A meta-analysis of psychological and pharmacological treatments for body dysmorphic disorder. *Behaviour Research and Therapy, 44,* 99–111.

Wilson, B. A. (2004). Theoretical approaches to cognitive rehabilitation. In L. H. Goldstein & J. E. McNeil (Eds.), *Clinical neuropsychology: A practical guide to assessment and management for clinicians* (pp. 345–366). Chichester, UK: John Wiley & Sons.

Wilson, D. B., Bouffard, L. A., & Mackenzie, D. L. (2005). A quantitative review of structured, group-oriented, cognitive-behavioral programs for offenders. *Criminal Justice and Behavior, 32,* 172–204.

Wilson, G. T., & Rachman, S. J. (1983). Meta-analysis and the evaluation of psychotherapy outcomes: Limitations and liabilities. *Journal of Consulting and Clinical Psychology, 56,* 54–64.

Wilson, T. D. (2002). *Strangers to ourselves: Discovering the adaptive unconscious.* Cambridge, MA: Harvard University Press.

Wilson, B. (2008). Neuropsychological rehabilitation. *Annual Review of Clinical Psychology, 4,* 141–162.

Wilson, T. D., & Dunn, E. W. (2004). Self-knowledge: Its limits, value, and potential for improvement. *Annual Review of Psychology, 55,* 493–518.

Wise, E. A. (2004). Methods for analyzing psychotherapy outcomes: A review of clinical significance, reliable change, and recommendations for future directions. *Journal of Personality Assessment, 82,* 50–59.

Wood, J. M., Garb, H. N., Lilienfeld, S. O., & Nezworski, M. T. (2002). Clinical assessment. *Annual Review of Psychology, 53,* 519–543.

Wood, J. M., Lilienfeld, S. O., Garb, H. N., & Nezworski, M. T. (2000). The Rorschach test in clinical diagnosis: A critical review, with a backward look at Garfield (1947). *Journal of Clinical Psychology, 56,* 395–430.

Wood, J. M., Nezworski, M. T., & Garb, H. N. (2003). What's right with the Rorschach? *The Scientific Review of Mental Health Practice, 2,* 142–146.

Wood, J. M., Nezworski, M. T., Garb, H. N., & Lilienfeld, S. O. (2001). The misperception of psychopathology: Problems with the norms of the Comprehensive System for the Rorschach. *Clinical Psychology: Science and Practice, 8,* 350–373.

World Health Organization. (1992). *International statistical classification of diseases and related health problems* (10th ed.). Geneva, Switzerland: Author.

World Health Organization. (2002). *Towards a common language for functioning, disability, and health.* Retrieved February 4, 2005, from http://www.who.int/classification/icf

World Health Organization. (2003). *The history of vaccination.* Retrieved October 22, 2004, from http://www.who.int/vaccinesdiseases/history/history.shtml

World Health Organization. (2004). *Prevention of mental disorders: Effective interventions and policy options*. Retrieved October 28, 2004, from www.who.int.

World Health Organization. (2004a). *Mental health: The bare facts*. Retrieved April 23, 2004, from http://www.who.int/mental_health/en/.

World Health Organization. (2004b). *Project Atlas*. Retrieved April 23, 2004 from http://www.who.int.

World Health Organization. (2007). *Mental health: Strengthening mental health promotion. Fact sheet No. 220*. Retrieved on March 4, 2008, from www.who.int/mediacentre/factsheets/.

World Health Organization World Mental Health Survey Consortium. (2004). Prevalence, severity, and unmet need for treatment of mental disorders in the World Health Organization World Mental Health Surveys. *Journal of the American Medical Association, 291*, 2581–2590.

Wormith, J. S. (2002). Offender treatment attrition and its relationship with risk, responsivity, and recidivism. *Criminal Justice and Behavior, 29*, 447–471.

Wormith, J. S., Althouse, R., Simpson, M., Reitzel, L. R., Fagan, T. J., & Morgan, R. D. (2007). The rehabilitation and reintegration of offenders. *Criminal Justice and Behavior, 34*, 879–892.

Yalom, I. D. (1995). *The theory and practice of group psychotherapy*. New York: Basic Books.

Youngstrom, E. A., Findling R. L., Calabrese, J. R., Gracious, B. L., Demeter, C., et al. (2004). Comparing the diagnostic accuracy of six potential screening instruments for bipolar disorder in youths aged 5 to 17 years. *Journal of the American Academy of Child and Adolescent Psychiatry, 43*, 847–858.

Zabinski, M. F., Wilfley, D. E., Winzelberg, A. J., Taylor, B., & Calfas, K. J. (2004). An interactive psychoeducational intervention for women at risk for developing an eating disorder. *Journal of Consulting and Clinical Psychology, 72*, 914–919.

Zucker, R. A. (2003). Causal structure of alcohol use and problems in early life. In A. Biglan, M. Wang, & H. J. Walberg (Eds.), *Preventing youth problems* (pp. 33–61). New York: Kluwer Academic.

Author Index

Subject Index